Digital Supply Chain, Disruptive Environments, and the Impact on Retailers

Ehap Sabri
University of Texas at Dallas, USA

IGI Global
PUBLISHER of TIMELY KNOWLEDGE

A volume in the Advances in Logistics, Operations, and Management Science (ALOMS) Book Series

Published in the United States of America by
IGI Global
Business Science Reference (an imprint of IGI Global)
701 E. Chocolate Avenue
Hershey PA, USA 17033
Tel: 717-533-8845
Fax: 717-533-8661
E-mail: cust@igi-global.com
Web site: http://www.igi-global.com

Library of Congress Cataloging-in-Publication Data

Names: Sabri, Ehap H., 1967- editor.
Title: Digital supply chain, disruptive environments, and the impact on retailers / edited by Ehap Sabri.
Description: Hershey, PA : Business Science Reference, [2023] | Includes bibliographical references and index. | Summary: "Digital Supply Chain, Disruptive Environments, and the Impact on Retailers brings together the field's latest best practices on digital supply chain enablement, giving business professionals a comprehensive framework to ensure successful supply chain business transformation programs. Covering topics such as business planning, digital transformation, and volatile demand, this premier reference source is an excellent resource for managers, directors, vice presidents, supply chain executives, IT directors, consultants, students and educators of higher education, librarians, researchers, and academicians"-- Provided by publisher.
Identifiers: LCCN 2022062313 (print) | LCCN 2022062314 (ebook) | ISBN 9781668472989 (hardcover) | ISBN 9781668472996 (paperback) | ISBN 9781668473009 (ebook)
Subjects: LCSH: Business logistics--Technological innovations. | Business planning.
Classification: LCC HD38.5 .D543 2023 (print) | LCC HD38.5 (ebook) | DDC 658.500285--dc23/eng/20230201
LC record available at https://lccn.loc.gov/2022062313
LC ebook record available at https://lccn.loc.gov/2022062314

This book is published in the IGI Global book series Advances in Logistics, Operations, and Management Science (ALOMS) (ISSN: 2327-350X; eISSN: 2327-3518)

British Cataloguing in Publication Data
A Cataloguing in Publication record for this book is available from the British Library.

Advances in Logistics, Operations, and Management Science (ALOMS) Book Series

John Wang
Montclair State University, USA

ISSN:2327-350X
EISSN:2327-3518

Mission

Operations research and management science continue to influence business processes, administration, and management information systems, particularly in covering the application methods for decision-making processes. New case studies and applications on management science, operations management, social sciences, and other behavioral sciences have been incorporated into business and organizations real-world objectives.

The **Advances in Logistics, Operations, and Management Science** (ALOMS) Book Series provides a collection of reference publications on the current trends, applications, theories, and practices in the management science field. Providing relevant and current research, this series and its individual publications would be useful for academics, researchers, scholars, and practitioners interested in improving decision making models and business functions.

Coverage

- Operations Management
- Decision analysis and decision support
- Organizational Behavior
- Information Management
- Services management
- Political Science
- Finance
- Marketing engineering
- Risk Management
- Networks

IGI Global is currently accepting manuscripts for publication within this series. To submit a proposal for a volume in this series, please contact our Acquisition Editors at Acquisitions@igi-global.com or visit: http://www.igi-global.com/publish/.

The Advances in Logistics, Operations, and Management Science (ALOMS) Book Series (ISSN 2327-350X) is published by IGI Global, 701 E. Chocolate Avenue, Hershey, PA 17033-1240, USA, www.igi-global.com. This series is composed of titles available for purchase individually; each title is edited to be contextually exclusive from any other title within the series. For pricing and ordering information please visit http://www.igi-global.com/book-series/advances-logistics-operations-management-science/37170. Postmaster: Send all address changes to above address.

Titles in this Series

For a list of additional titles in this series, please visit: www.igi-global.com/book-series

Change Management During Unprecedented Times
Kyla Latrice Tennin (College of Doctoral Studies, University of Phoenix, USA & Forbes School of Business, USA & World Business Angels Investment Forum (WBAF)-G20, USA & Lady Mirage Global, Inc., USA)
Business Science Reference • ©2023 • 413pp • H/C (ISBN: 9781668475096) • US $250.00

Multidisciplinary Approaches to Organizational Governance During Health Crises
Carla Sofia Vicente Negrão (CeBER, University of Coimbra, Portugal) Isabel Guerreiro Pimentel Maia (University of Coimbra, Portugal) and João António Furtado Brito (University of Cape Verde, Cape Verde)
Business Science Reference • ©2023 • 300pp • H/C (ISBN: 9781799892137) • US $250.00

Considerations and Characteristics of the Millennial Leader in Today's Global Society
Tymon M. Graham (TMGraham Consulting, LLC, USA)
Business Science Reference • ©2023 • 300pp • H/C (ISBN: 9781668447116) • US $240.00

Handbook of Research on Blockchain Technology and the Digitalization of the Supply Chain
Tharwa Najar (Gafsa University, Tunisia) Yousra Najar (Manar University, Tunisia) and Adel Aloui (EM Normandie Business School, France)
Business Science Reference • ©2023 • 520pp • H/C (ISBN: 9781668474556) • US $295.00

Perspectives on Women in Management and the Global Labor Market
Elisabete S. Vieira (GOVCOPP, University of Aveiro, Portugal) Mara Madaleno (GOVCOPP, University of Aveiro, Portugal) and João Teodósio (Polytechnic Institute of Santarém, Portugal)
Business Science Reference • ©2023 • 382pp • H/C (ISBN: 9781668459812) • US $240.00

Perspectives and Strategies of Family Business Resiliency in Unprecedented Times
Hotniar Siringoringo (Gunadarma University, Indonesia) and Ravindra Hewa Kuruppuge (University of Peradeniya, Sri Lanka)
Business Science Reference • ©2023 • 322pp • H/C (ISBN: 9781668473948) • US $240.00

Futuristic Technology Perspectives on Entrepreneurship and Sustainable Innovation
Sanjay Misra (Department of Applied Data Science, Institute of Energy Technology, Halden, Norway) Amit Jain (Amity University, India) Manju Kaushik (Amity University, India) and Chitreshh Banerjee (Amity University, India)
Business Science Reference • ©2023 • 300pp • H/C (ISBN: 9781668458716) • US $250.00

IGI Global
PUBLISHER of TIMELY KNOWLEDGE

701 East Chocolate Avenue, Hershey, PA 17033, USA
Tel: 717-533-8845 x100 • Fax: 717-533-8661
E-Mail: cust@igi-global.com • www.igi-global.com

Editorial Advisory Board

Table of Contents

Section 4
Key Enablers for Digital Transformations

Detailed Table of Contents

prescriptive analytics to manage the unpredictable through risk mitigation plans.

This chapter describes the challenges faced in achieving effective cross-functional decision making and quantifies the value of speed in supply chain decisions with a specific focus on determining the best supply plan in an outsourced manufacturing environment. The analysis presented uses a supply chain simulation model that helped achieve best-in-class supply chain results in the field. Practitioners can use this analysis to inform their supply chain transformation business cases and improve their probability of successful implementation by proactively addressing the transformation challenges described to accelerate cross-functional decision making.

This chapter highlights the need for capacity planning to meet the demand in the post-pandemic world and identifies key challenges that companies face. Following that, the chapter establishes five levels of capacity planning – Strategic Capacity Planning, Annual Budget Planning, Rough Cut Capacity Planning, Capacity Requirement Planning, and Detailed Production Planning. Each level of capacity planning is explained in detail with examples. Finally, the chapter defines a maturity model to understand gaps in the current process and concludes with an implementation roadmap.

Supply continuity is being challenged at every stage of the supply chain, with changing workforce dynamics, natural events, and consumer buying patterns. These changes in the operating environment are continuously introducing inefficiencies into the supply chains, and are putting pressure on costs to serve. Even during the pre-pandemic era, execution adherence to plans generated by advanced planning and scheduling systems (APS) was not more than 50%. Rapid evolution of emerging technologies accelerates digitization of supply chains and provides opportunities to enable paradigm shifts in supply chain planning. Integration of planning software with industrial internet of things (IIoT) platforms, which collect real-time data across the value chain, can drive the next level of supply chain optimization. In this chapter, the authors provide specific recommendations, to extracting maximum value from APS systems by addressing some limitations, e.g.: out-of-sync master data and lack of real-time transactional data, by using curated data feeds from the IIoT platforms to augments APS capabilities.

Traditional direct materials procurement systems have been designed for business processes with an introverted view of activities within the four walls of an enterprise. These assumptions were flawed all along and are now fast becoming outdated as digital ecosystems gradually take hold. Analysis is presented to show how these isolated enterprise centric processes have created complexity, latency and inefficiencies that inhibit alignment and agility across value networks. This chapter revisits the business objectives and challenges of direct materials procurement with an outside-in mindset and redesigns the overall processes end-to-end across the order lifecycle within digitally connected ecosystems.

The purpose of this book chapter is to explore different strategies that retail procurement managers can exploit when there are disruptions in their supply chains. The initial research of the chapter is based on a review of supply chain disruption literature and specific case studies of procurement strategies that factor into disruption events. With globalization and increasingly complex supply chains, disruptions can devastate a business as its entire supply stream can be cut off. This chapter summarizes key concepts and best practices from the literature and industry case studies to understand disruption-related supply chain issues and discusses strategies that can give a competitive advantage to retail procurement managers.

The chapter is focused on understanding the concepts of reverse logistics (RL) in the digital supply chain management era. In today's world, returned products and their recovery management has become very important for companies, thus, through this chapter the author summarizes the entire returns process from a buyer and seller point of view. What are the different factors involved in the decision making of returned products and how does it affect the entire supply chain? The chapter also aims to understand costs related to reverse logistics, optimization of the process, and lastly the significance of various reverse logistics strategies that can benefit organizations.

Section 4
Key Enablers for Digital Transformations

Achieving customer satisfaction requires seamless collaboration and coordination across the value chain of suppliers, manufacturers, regulators, logistics service providers, and retailers. At the same time, disruption in the supply chain causes increased costs, and, more importantly, lost revenue. Therefore, organizations are looking for transparency, flexibility, and agility in their supply chains. The internet of things and blockchain, as a part of efficient technologies in supply chains of organizations, build trust, transparency, and consensus among all stakeholders, creating benefits for every actor and ensuring flexible business outcomes .Due to the increasing importance of these technologies in today's world and the integration of these tools in all business processes, in this research, the dimensions, components, and vital indicators affecting the creation of a smart and efficient supply chain with high reliability and has been assessed as having strong resilience. Finally, the structure of a smart supply chain is shown by the interaction of these transformative technologies.

The COVID-19 pandemic has affected global supply chains at an unprecedented speed and scale. In response, these businesses are now transitioning toward data-driven decision making to anticipate future performance and improve operational efficiencies, which will require the gathering and analysis of a vast amount of data in real-time. This chapter explains how 5G, with its capabilities such as ultralow latency and high bandwidth, is shaping and transforming the global supply chain. The authors present how to prepare for and avoid future supply chain disruptions. Further, the authors have showcased some practical 5G use cases in the manufacturing and logistics industries.

This chapter discusses the role of supply chain analytics in managing digital supply chain, as well as the practical implementation approaches of supply chain analytics. The chapter first discusses a typical day in the life of supply chain analysts. It then discusses the categorization of supply chain analytics and some practical recommendations for the implementation of supply chain analytics. Finally, the chapter provides a case study illustrating some important considerations in supply chain design.

Preface

With the world having been plunged into uncertainty during the COVID-19 pandemic, it has become crucial for executives to stabilize their supply chain to a consistent flow of components and materials. Even before COVID-19, supply chain complexity had been an increasingly "hot" topic. When you consider additional recent issues, such as new tariff restrictions, port congestion, regional conflicts, and geopolitical events/disruptions due to the Ukraine war, you will know that securing access to materials and critical resources is not without difficulty and forecasting demand is even harder.

In response to the dramatic changes in the business landscape over the past few years beginning with COVID-19 and ending with the Ukraine war and inflation, many companies across different industries are launching technology-enabled (digital) business transformation programs to improve their strategic, tactical, and operational supply chain processes. The use of digital technology can not only help to stabilize supply chains—it can even be leveraged to thrive and succeed as these platforms improve efficiency and agility.

Supply chain management today, in most cases, is a series of largely discrete, siloed steps taken through marketing, product development, production, distribution, and fulfilling customers' needs. Digitization removes barriers across siloed processes and enables the supply chain to become a completely integrated ecosystem that is fully transparent to all stakeholders from the suppliers of raw materials, to the manufacturers of finished goods, to the customers.

The digital supply chain includes integrated planning and execution systems, intelligent logistics visibility, smart warehousing, digital procurement, and prescriptive advanced analytics. The result enables companies to anticipate and proactively address disruptions in the supply chain by fully modeling the end-to-end supply chain, creating 'what-if' scenarios, and adjusting the supply chain in real-time as conditions change. This offers a high degree of lean and agility, allowing companies to achieve a competitive advantage by providing customers with the most efficient and transparent service delivery. In a nutshell, digital supply chain can advance a business's performance by removing friction in processes and improving decision-making.

Digital supply chain will be based on full implementation of several digital technologies: the Cloud, Big Data, the Internet of Things (IoT), Machine Learning (ML), social networks, "what-if" scenario planning, "trace-and-track," and others. Together, they enable new business models and strategies, the digitization of products and services, and the digitization and integration of every link in a company's supply chain.

But if companies are to implement the digital supply chain ecosystem, they can't just gather technologies and build technical capabilities (i.e., technology is not the silver bullet). They must have the right digital strategy, proven implementation methodology, an effective performance measurement system, people with the right skills, and the management needed to shift to a culture that is willing to carry out the change. In other words, they must transform their entire business.

The digital strategy should include key characteristics to improve the execution: 1) Flexible strategy as changes occur in the global marketplace in addition to being prioritized and actionable, 2) A three-to-five year roadmap that guides the transformation of supply-and-demand capabilities and takes planning processes to the next level, 3) Clear linkage to one or more corporate goals such as growth or customer service levels, 4) Both large opportunities for improvement that deliver significant ROI over time and "quick win" operations improvements with a fast payback, and 5) The elimination of outdated roles and responsibilities, unnecessary activities, and performance metrics that no longer reflect current realities.

Once the digital strategy is determined, companies must drive changes and develop new capabilities in several areas including the following:

Processes. Establish the new end-to-end supply chain processes connecting suppliers and customers that digitization makes possible and eliminate non-value activities at the touch points of functions and processes.

Technology. Create a deployment roadmap for the technologies that will support the digital supply chain, including the information integration layer, database and analytics capabilities, security, and the cloud.

Governance. Establish a new governance for the new processes which enable the new business models. The new governance should include the following:

1. **Organization Structure and Culture.** Generate an end-to-end understanding of the mechanics of the supply chain followed by an organizational realignment. This means switching from a fire-fighter mentality (solving each problem as it pops up) to becoming proactive and acting as a supply chain "orchestrator" (sensing, predicting, and taking prescriptive decisions). The new organization structure and culture also requires a shift to an open, fast-learning digital culture that promotes communication across different media and stakeholders.
2. **Talent and Skills.** Develop the talent and acquire new expertise and skills needed to enable the new technology and carry out the new business models. Finding a company with the required in-house digital capability from the beginning is rare. Building strong expertise in an organization relies on the cultivation of long-term partnerships and ecosystems that can provide access to the required capabilities.
3. **Key Performance Indicators (KPIs).** Develop a set of KPIs to maintain the momentum and involvement of people and be able to measure progress. These KPIs should be comprehensive and drive the right behavior.
4. **Partnering Policies.** Establish new policies to partner closely with other companies. The fully integrated end-to-end supply chain cannot be built without collaborating with a wide variety of suppliers, distributors, and technology providers.

Supply chains are extremely complex networks, and no company has succeeded yet in building one that is truly digital across networks and functions. While it is true that several successful digital use cases have been witnessed, the industry is still waiting for a successful digital end-to-end supply chain transformation program. Also, several of the digital applications required are not yet widely used. However, this will change radically over the next five years, with different industries implementing digital supply chains at varying speeds.

To add to the above challenge, 70% of all technology-driven transformation initiatives fail. They fail firstly because of a lack of preparation and knowledge of the supply chain transformation life cycle, secondly because of a lack of a well-defined supply chain strategy, and thirdly because of poor addressing or altogether neglecting the "people-related" aspects in transformation (Sabri, 2019). Therefore, improvement initiatives have been short-lived or incomplete and expected business benefits are not achieved or materialized. It is important to note that these statistics are based on technology that is 5 to 10 years old and not digital technology that is less mature.

Although there is a lot of hype surrounding digital supply chain and multiple opportunities to apply it across an organization, the task of creating and implementing an effective digital strategy can seem overwhelming— especially when ROI is unproven. Several digital transformations were held back by ROI uncertainty. One thing is certain, if businesses look to the fanciest new tech to save the day but ignore their overall performance goal, then their strategies are already set to fail.

Many companies are trying to understand the best practices and master the recipe for success of transformation programs. They are connecting with universities, research centers, and consulting companies. Therefore, the editor decided to compile this book to help industry professionals improve their success rate in digital supply chain use cases and their transformation programs.

To address the above challenges in areas such as supply chain optimization, leveraging digital technologies, business transformation, performance measurement, and change management, there is a need for an edited collection of chapters. In addition, these chapters analyze cases from the retail industry and provide best practices for industry professionals.

This comprehensive and timely publication aims to be an essential reference source, synergizing with available literature in the supply chain and digital transformation field and providing proven tactics from the industry.

The target audience of this book includes professionals and researchers working in the field of supply chain optimization and business transformation. This book provides:

- Insight and support to executives concerned with achieving value as an output of supply chain digital transformation programs
- Supply chain and IT managers with suggested process, technology, and governance best practices
- Academicians, researchers, and advanced-level students with an excellent reference on supply chain, business challenges, change management, performance measurement, digital strategy development, case studies, and opportunities to extend the research in this field

The chapters stand alone in covering their individual topics, but also form a cohesive overview of library-related professional development as it stands now along with future trends in the field. The chapters in this book can be categorized into four broad sections: key considerations for successful digital transformations (Chapters 1-4); optimizing supply chain process leveraging digital technologies (Chapters 5-9); improving visibility, procurement, and logistics processes leveraging digital technologies (Chapters 10-14); and key enablers for digital transformations (Chapters 15-18).

The authors of each chapter followed the adage of "write what you know," having been personally involved in every topic they covered. After writing what they knew, the authors went beyond their experience to focus on future trends, assessments, and applicability to digital supply chain optimization and transformation. The result is a book that provides useful guidance to supply chain practitioners and researchers in the digital business world.

Thanks are given to the authors of these book chapters. Professionals from the industry and academia contributed excellent write-ups of their work in a timely and professional manner. In addition, many thanks are owed to the Editorial Advisory Board of this book. These experts reviewed proposals and peer-reviewed the finished chapters quickly and thoroughly. This book would not have been possible without the Board's assistance.

This book illustrates to the reader the best practices in optimizing and transforming supply chain management in contemporary organizations by leveraging digital technologies and presents several ideas for change that provide a roadmap for a smooth transformation journey with several case studies from the retail industry. Let this book help you deal with the changes and keep current with the profession.

Ehap Sabri
University of Texas at Dallas, USA

REFERENCES

Sabri, E. (2019). *Optimization of Supply Chain Management in Contemporary Organizations: Mastering Change Management for Successful Digital Supply Chain Transformation*. IGI Global.

Acknowledgment

The editor would like to acknowledge the help of all the people involved in this project and, more specifically, to the authors and reviewers that took part in the review process. Without their support, this book would not have become a reality.

Thank you to each of the authors who contributed their time and expertise to this book, and to the reviewers whose valuable contributions improved the quality, coherence, and content presentation of chapters. My sincere gratitude goes out to you all.

Section 1

Key Considerations for Successful Digital Transformations

Chapter 1
How to Master Change Management During the Supply Chain Digital Transformation Journey

Ehap Sabri
University of Texas at Dallas, USA & JDA Software, USA

ABSTRACT

In response to the dramatic changes in the business landscape over the last few years, more companies are launching business transformations leveraging digital technologies to drive sweeping changes in their supply chain processes. So, supply chain digital transformation is not a new buzz word anymore, it's the application of digital capabilities to processes, products, and assets to improve supply chain efficiency, enhance customer value, manage risk, and achieve competitive advantage. However, organizations are still facing numerous challenges to transform and perform. This chapter will dive deep into understanding major challenges to digital supply chain transformations, identify the key drivers and enablers of and provide a proven change management framework for a successful transformation journey.

INTRODUCTION

In today's complex and ever-changing business world, firms of all types are rethinking every aspect of their supply chain performance. Firms are exploring new enablers like digital technologies to optimize and manage their supply chains, beginning with demand planning and order management reviewing the entire supply chain up to procurement and transportation.

In today's globalized world, a firm's success is not just dependent on its own efforts. Rather, the success of an organization depends largely on how effectively it can orchestrate a vast, global network of supply chain partners to deliver goods and services that meet the needs of individual consumers. It's all about engaging with customers efficiently through new and improved customer experiences. Early adopters of digital disrupters such as Amazon, Uber, and Netflix have redefined traditional business models and

DOI: 10.4018/978-1-6684-7298-9.ch001

demonstrated how it's to be done. They focused on customers and not just provided exceptional, unique customer experience, but also engaged customers that keep coming back for more.

Digital Transformation is not restricted to supply chain; it's everywhere. It's in marketing, sales, products, Support, HR, Supply chain, etc. It opens new opportunities, challenges traditional methods, and changes the way we think and act. One of the key challenges faced around transforming a business is training the workforce to gain the new skills necessary to participate in the new way of doing business and to make the changes stick and last.

In all kinds of industries, from the relatively slow-moving ones such as Utilities and Cement to the rapidly changing businesses of the High-Tech and Retail industries, lean and agile supply chain processes have become critical in achieving competitive advantage. Companies can no longer view supply chain as a back office and a transactional-focused function. It is becoming extremely prevalent that companies are not simply looking to drive costs out of their businesses, but also striving to be more agile in securing a supply chain that can quickly adapt to a rapidly changing market.

Taking the initiative to transform supply chain by leveraging best practices and the latest digital technologies is no longer an option; it is a strategic mandate to stay relevant in the industry. Evidently, it is crucial to act rapidly and launch transformation activities. However, the industry's reality is that 70% of all transformation initiatives fail.

The low success rates of other transformation programs and the scary statistics make firms who are about to take the transformation journey reconsider moving forward. These firms typically have doubts and questions about the best practice in integrating new digital technologies into supply chain operations. At times they even postpone their efforts until an expert is able to address their concerns. Firms seek how to:

- Master change management and ensure users' adoption
- Address the need for new skills to support processes that span across suppliers and partners
- Ensure continuous senior management support
- Identify comprehensive metrics and ensure continuous monitoring
- Choose the right digital technology and the right software provider

Based on relevant research and the author's professional experience, the main cause for the low success rates of business transformation initiatives can be grouped into two categories:

1) The lack of preparation and familiarity with the transformation lifecycle
2) People-related aspects that are poorly managed or altogether neglected

This chapter provides the top 7 challenges under each respective category and explains how to address these challenges during supply chain digital transformation programs. This chapter also provides a practical change management framework to ensure smooth and successful digital supply chain transformation programs. This framework includes 8 steps (phases) needed to implement change in the culture of the organization, and 5 success factors for companies to maintain throughout the lifecycle of change. These five factors can be used as a checklist to evaluate the readiness of the organization to change and its chances of a successful digital transformation.

Historic background on change management in the context of supply chain digital transformations is provided in the next section.

BACKGROUND

Direct Correlation Between Change Management and Transformation

The complex, cross-functional nature of supply chains forces executives and managers to be more knowledgeable about successful implementation of change. Greer and Ford (2009) conducted an extensive study on this topic and highlighted the differences between implementing non-supply chain management (NSCM) changes and supply chain management (SCM) changes. Based on Greer and Ford's (2009) study, a lower level of success was shown to be realized when implementing SCM changes than when implementing NSCM changes due to complexity. Therefore, the majority of supply chain leaders are keen to transform their organizations, but they recognize that their organizations lack the knowledge and readiness to do so successfully.

Nadler and Tushman (1989) noted that because broader change programs are often more difficult to implement, the degree of success realized from implementing SCM changes might differ as well. Their article provides good insight into managing large-scale planned change.

Research shows the success rate of supply chain transformation has a direct correlation to the degree of mastering change management. Ford and Greer's (2005) research has indicated relationships between various change management activities and change success.

Effective Change Management Practices

Effective change management practices embrace both the inner shift in the individual's values, aspirations, and behaviors, as well as the outer shift in process, strategy, policies, and systems (Karp, 2005). Therefore, effective change management practices target the organizational culture, organizational structure and recruiting, performance measurements, incentive compensations, and alignment to corporate goals and strategies.

Carolyn Aiken and Scott Keller (2009) have identified insights into four conditions required for behavioral change:

1) Creating a Compelling Story

What motivates senior leaders may not motivate the employees. Therefore, change leaders must be able to tell a change story that motivates employees the most in their work. In doing so, they can unleash a tremendous amount of drive. Secondly, leaders should offer employees the opportunity to write their own story. It is detected in human nature that when we choose for ourselves, we are far more committed to the outcome. So, employees should be asked to suggest change rather than directly implementing change. This will help drive change that comes through a sense of ownership.

2) Role Modeling

It is a misconception that if we believe that if a leader is strong and influential then change will be successful irrespective of employees' views. Carolyn Aiken and Scott Keller (2009) have experienced that working with change programs suggests that success depends less on how persuasive a few selected leaders are and more on how receptive society is to the idea.

3) Reinforcing Mechanisms

Although it's difficult to establish a clear linkage between the successful change and monetary compensation, offering tokens of appreciation for the hard work of employees may boost their productivity.

4) Capacity Building

Often change management initiatives require employees to develop skills and talent needed for the desired change (new state of business). The important thing to understand here is that if employees are expected to play new roles with no proper training, they often feel neglected and lose belief. So, training is crucial and should include elements related to personality types, emotional intelligence and other new process specific training.

Transformation Programs' Common Mistakes

Ramanan and Anil (2011) from Wipro Consulting Services believe that most of supply chain transformation fails because most companies tend to make common mistakes such as falling into the "Leading Practices" trap, where companies fail to understand their own supply chain situation to make the right choices and try to follow leading practices in market. They believe that companies will be more successful if they rethink their supply chain in a way driven by how it supports their business strategy and meets customer requirements. They believe that if supply chain technology is deployed without incorporating critical business requirements and process redesign, it will simply be a collection of automated systems with routine supply chain issues.

The use of technology as an enabler is definitely important for effective supply chain, but one needs to understand that technology can't fix a flawed supply chain design. Whenever processes are refined and new technology is implemented, the organizational structure must be aligned to support these initiatives.

In the quest for growth, many companies implement change initiatives to create strong, differentiated, and better customer experiences. Leonard and Coltea (2013) believe that the majority of failed transformation change initiatives did not focus front-line managers on the exact actions they need to take to achieve the company's desired business outcomes.

Leonard and Coltea (2013) also highlighted that implementing a successful change management initiative isn't a one-time thing. Creating lasting change requires companies to evolve, and those that evolve successfully can achieve stronger financial performance.

Mastering Change Management Framework

Sabri (2019) provided a detailed analysis of the most common transformation failures. They also suggested a practical and comprehensive framework to master change management, addressing typical challenges and common mistakes in addition to leveraging best practices. This framework will be enriched in this book chapter to support supply chain digital transformation.

The next section will explain the top 7 challenges for supply chain transformations based on research and the author's experiences.

TRANSFORMATION LIFE CYCLE CHALLENGES

1) "Where" and "When" to Start

When making these kinds of drastic changes, the biggest challenges are often knowing when and where to begin in order to translate the vision into goals, goals into strategies, and strategies into process changes and projects. Very few companies have implemented a good supply chain digital strategy. There are a couple reasons for this, including: 1) The lack of resources and time, 2) The lack of familiarity with the strategy development process in general, 3) The lack of knowledge of the full opportunities that digital technologies can bring to supply chain processes, and 4) The difficulty of securing a consensus since supply chain digital strategy is an integrated cross functional strategy and requires investment from resources and money standpoints.

The author has observed companies trying to take the easy route and avoiding spending time on rethinking their supply chain in a way that is driven by how it supports their business strategy, meets customer needs, and deploys key enablers like digital technologies.

2) Environment is Not Ready

The culture of "playing it safe" is the second challenge. Firms get used to executing low-risk incremental improvements on the same business environment for an extended period of time, and they become resistant to big ideas of significant improvement because they do not know how to handle transformation programs and target big results.

A specific related challenge, which is relevant to supply chain digital transformation, is the need for intensive cooperation and cross-functional collaboration among executive peers. This challenge would force executives to get out of their comfort zones and their respective areas of responsibility and find time out of their busy daily operation schedule to envision an entirely new business. Also, when a company has a previous record of transformation failure, lack of strong vision, no visible commitment from above, and no clear articulation as to why this program is different, results are often upsetting.

3) Lack of Convincing "ROI"

Several companies struggled to find the best way to determine the business case including ROI (return on investment), identifying the right metrics that would capture the benefits, and defining "success" when it comes to business transformations. Therefore, they couldn't sustain the buy-in from executives.

Success and metric targets must be defined for the intermediate and end state phases of the transformation to sustain a high level of energy and focus. In an industry conference, the author asked an audience of more than 80 managers to raise their hands if they are "OK" with their own performance measurement governance (metrics identification, measuring, tracking, and controlling). Only 3 managers raised their hands! The widespread feeling among managers is that they are measuring too much or too little or are measuring the wrong metrics. The majority also feel that their performance measurement governance does not drive good behavior.

4) Inability to Select "the Right" Software Provider

Selecting a software provider is a hard undertaking and consumes time and internal resources. Companies are not just struggling to identify the right software provider (partner) for digital technology but are also struggling with choosing the right supply chain technology platform. In addition, executives frequently express their concern about their companies' ability to ensure that the technology is fully utilized once deployed. Supply chain digital applications—especially the planning ones— require a steep learning curve for most companies.

5) New Technology is the "Silver Bullet" Perception

Some executives perceived new technology to be the "silver bullet" to all their business problems and forgot that technology is just an enabler for best practice processes and requires effective change management to be adopted.

When the transformation program is driven by a date given by IT instead of a value-achieved milestone, it is a recipe for disaster. In an attempt to meet the often-unrealistic target date, training, documentation, and change management are often neglected, resulting in a transformation that has a short life span or does not deliver the full benefit. These transformation programs might be able to "go live" from an IT standpoint but will not be well accepted or embraced by end users.

For transformation programs to work, an amalgamation must happen between process changes, new technology capabilities, people readiness with the required new skills, and organization structure alignment changes.

6) No Clear Priorities for Day-to-Day Operations

Typically, the day-to-day operation of the company is already at full capacity when the executives call for a transformation program. Some companies try to add transformation activities to the preexisting calendar of "run the business" meetings, but it doesn't work because short term operational issues typically come first. People in most cases have occupied more than 100% of their capacity. This affects the productivity of transformation activities since people find it difficult to prioritize their work. Due to the unavailability of the right person for transformation activity because of preoccupancy with other day to day jobs, a substitute who may not be fully aware of the desired transformation activity is chosen, and hence overall productivity is affected.

When companies are in the process of implementing several incremental improvement projects like Six Sigma or Kaizen projects, it will be a challenge to add a transformation program targeting the same functions to the mix. Companies that try to stuff too much into the organization will clog it, causing employees and managers' capacity to execute to become a choke point unless the programs are prioritized and sequenced correctly.

7) Lack of Proven Transformation Methodology

Not having a proven, comprehensive, and practical methodology to show the way in the transformation journey makes it impossible to address any of the above challenges. To be successful, the transformation team requires not only knowledge and skills in organizational design and change management, but also a comprehensive methodology for planning, implementing, and sustaining the transformation changes (Sabri, 2019). There are at least three common methodology mistakes:

1. Some companies put more emphasis on IT activities compared to change management activities. They rush things and focus only on IT activities that they have to accomplish and cannot shorten.
2. The author has also witnessed another extreme, where companies spent a huge amount of time on the planning phase, little time on implementing the change, and no time on sustaining it.
3. Other companies put significant emphasis on the transformations' soft factors, such as culture, leadership, and motivation while missing out on the hard factors of change management like financial results, commitment levels of executives, the resources required to execute the program, and the program roadmap and duration.

The following real-life story will provide examples of some of the challenges mentioned in this section. A few years back, the author was asked to play the executive process advisory role for a global high-tech company. The company's largest end-to-end supply chain transformation program was underway. The program included process improvement and technology implementation to the following processes: Sales and Operation Planning (S&OP), Demand Management, Supply Planning, Order Planning, Inventory Planning, Order Fulfillment, Logistics, and Channel Management. The author joined 18 months after the program started. In the first phase of his engagement, he spent two weeks on site conducting his own assessment and came to a conclusion that the transformation was at risk and immediate corrective action was desperately needed. Here are a few of the findings:

First, the company was taking the transformation journey for defensive reasons; they were losing market share to competition, their margin was getting smaller and smaller, and they wanted to reverse the trend. Everyone in the company was fearful for his or her job.

Secondly, the author uncovered that the employees did not understand why the business must change and their own role in making it happen. So before providing any specific recommendations, the author wanted to investigate further to find out why there was a lack of communication and articulation to the employees regarding the need for change. He started by asking for the business case, and to his surprise, the sponsor did not have it handy. During the meeting with the finance representative on the program regarding the business case, the author discovered that the major cost saving element was "laying off" employees! This was the main reason why the company did not want to give clarity to employees about the program.

Thirdly, all program tracks were working in silos with little coordination. There was no master project plan covering the overall program progress and dependency. The author had to attend the project status meetings for all tracks to have a good picture of the status of the program. It was easy to notice the mistrust that every team had regarding the other teams' ability to deliver on time. In addition, around the same time, the blame game had just begun.

Fourthly, the author investigated the transformation program structure, and he found out that 7 different tracks were identified to execute the program: program management, process, technology, data, testing, suppliers, and change management track. The role of the author was under the process track. The shocker was that appropriate expertise was identified for all tracks except for the change management track, it was "TBD"! Basically, a major transformation program was underway for defensive reasons, layoff was one of the outputs of the program, the culture of the company to work in silos, the company had not done this type/scale of transformation before, and yet no one was assigned for change management!

Fifthly, there was no clear and structured transformation methodology. The transformation team took 18 months to identify the business requirements and socialize them with the IT organization. Since the duration of the first phase of the transformation program was two years; everyone was under pressure to implement, go-live, and transition in the remaining 6 months. Senior management from the business organization decided to take the IT date to "go-live" as the date they would communicate to their executives. They thought that IT would be the bottleneck and assumed that all other activities like designing the new (to-be) process, coming up with new policies, developing training manuals, conducting training sessions, defining roles and responsibilities for the new processes, defining new metrics and reports to support the new processes, and overcoming resistance issues would fall within the IT timeline!

Finally, there were no supply chain strategies defined. The transformation team came up with all the business requirements without considering the new strategies that they have to adopt to address their challenges and reverse the trend of losing market share.

It took this company several months and several drastic adjustments to clean up this mess and start moving in the right direction. Unfortunately, several senior managers and executives lost their jobs because they were slow to react.

The challenges of supply chain transformation related to people are explained in the next section.

PEOPLE CHANGE MANAGEMENT CHALLENGES

This section will cover the top 7 people change management challenges based on the authors' experience and relevant research.

1) Executives are Slow to Come Aboard

Not having all executives on the same page early on is one of the first challenges that the change agent must address. For this purpose, it is highly recommended to schedule a 15-minute one-on-one meeting with all executives in the first week of the engagement. This practice is used by the author, and it was very effective in highlighting any disconnect to address it and bringing all executives on board to support the transformation program.

Executives that are reluctant to support the transformation program visibly will disrupt the speed of the company's progress in planning effectively and undermine transformation significantly. Even the best-planned supply chain transformation initiative will fail if top management fails to demonstrate commitment to creating the sense of urgency necessary to overcome resistance to change. Executives' support is key to setting proper expectations for their employees.

2) Keeping Stakeholders Engaged and Motivated

Stakeholders are the employees and managers who will be impacted by the process changes or will play a role and have an impact on the success of the transformation program. In a nutshell, the stakeholders are the people who will make the transformation happen. Disengaged stakeholders can really slow down progress and can be a reason by itself for transformation failure.

Many firms underestimate this challenge which results in catastrophic implications. Because no matter how sophisticated and powerful the software applications or digital technologies are and how effective best practice processes may be, in the end, it is the stakeholders who play the most significant role in the success or failure of the program. Supply chain stakeholders represent different organizations and varying roles (operators, managers, planners, suppliers, customers, warehouse receivers, carriers, etc.) which adds another dimension to the challenge.

3) Lack of Organizational Structure Alignment

It is necessary to look at the structural support for the change transformation program. If the foundation structure is deemed to be inadequate, restructuring becomes critical. Restructuring changes range in degree from minor adjustments to large-scale organization-wide changes that affect virtually every member of the organization.

One of the author's organizational change management engagements was to help a tire manufacturing company become a global supply chain organization and to streamline and standardize their processes. One of the deliverables was to recommend a structure for the global supply chain organization and the related roles and responsibilities. Assigning an executive vice president reporting to the CEO to lead a centralized and global supply chain organization was one of the recommendations. Unfortunately, the sponsor did not have enough political clout with the CEO to make it happen before starting the design phase. This was one of main reasons that the transformation program ran into serious delays and severe change management and ownership issues.

4) Inability to Build the Right Transformation Team

Building the right transformation team is the most important change management activity in a business transformation program. In the process of building the team, senior management must be sensitive to the unique needs of the program environment.

Building the right effective team optimizes the efforts of the team and increases the chances of having a successful program. On the other hand, a weak team structure would undercut the efforts of hard-working team members, reduce morale, and impede project success.

5) Lack of an Effective Communication Plan

It is a common misconception that if people are talking to each other, it means they are communicating; communication needs to have a framework and format to be effective. Another common pitfall is the assumption that one communication plan template fits all programs or projects. While all programs or projects share the need for a communication plan, they differ in frequency, methods of communication, and the type of information needed (Sabri, Gupta, and Beitler, 2006).

Effective communication within the transformation team and between the team and other program stakeholders is essential for a smooth and successful journey.

6) Inability to Sustain On-Going Learning and Coaching

Supply Chain transformation programs require extensive and ongoing training, especially when it includes digital technologies and new skills and attitudes for the users of the new or improved processes. The proper allocation and commitment of resources (time, energy, and money) to conduct training and coaching to help employees in their skills acquisition is critical to the success of implementing and sustaining changes.

Although the "sustain" phase is the most difficult phase in any transformation program, there is relatively little attention paid by executives concerning sustaining change in organizations. While planning and implementing a change can happen relatively quickly, sustaining change occurs over a long period of time; this makes maintaining a sense of urgency and a significant level of interest difficult. The "sustain" phase can take months and sometime a few years. Therefore, the author typically suggests a separate budget for this phase to bring attention to it.

During this phase, the new process must be reinforced by the policies for recruiting, selecting, promoting, compensating, evaluating, and ongoing training of employees. Also, acknowledging and rewarding stakeholders for new behaviors is essential to stabilize the new process and anchor the new culture.

7) Lack of Comprehensive Incentive Program

While the Communication plan addresses the "why" question by providing the "awareness" about the importance of change and the risks of not changing for the company, the incentive plan addresses the "what's in it for me" question and creates the "desire" to change. Only when managers and employees have the "awareness" of the need to change and the "desire" to support the change, then learning "how" to change can start.

Unfortunately, the lack of comprehensive incentive programs is an issue in almost every transformation program that the author has audited. In some companies, senior executives make the incentive programs limited to managers and executives and do not include the employees. In other companies, incentive programs are in place, but not aligned to support the desired behavior and new process. Very few companies go the extra mile to come up with an incentive program for every member of the transformation team and the stakeholders who are responsible for planning and implementing change.

The rule of thumb is that every stakeholder whose processes will be impacted by the change or who will have an impact on the transformation should be part of the incentive program. Also, the objectives of the transformation should be reflected on the stakeholders' scorecards and aligned with their incentives. Therefore, the company's human resources (HR) department should be involved early on.

COMPREHENSIVE FRAMEWORK FOR MASTERING CHANGE MANAGEMENT

Figure 1 provides a comprehensive framework for mastering change management to ensure smooth and successful digital supply chain transformation programs and address the above challenges. This framework includes 8 steps (phases) needed to implement change in the culture of the organization, and 5 success factors for companies to maintain throughout the lifecycle of change.

What follows are the required steps to be taken during the life cycle of change transformation and the success factors for effective change management (as shown in Figure 1). By using these steps as a systematic and comprehensive framework, executives and managers can understand what to expect in their transportation journey and how to engage the entire organization in the process.

Figure 1. Digital supply chain change management framework

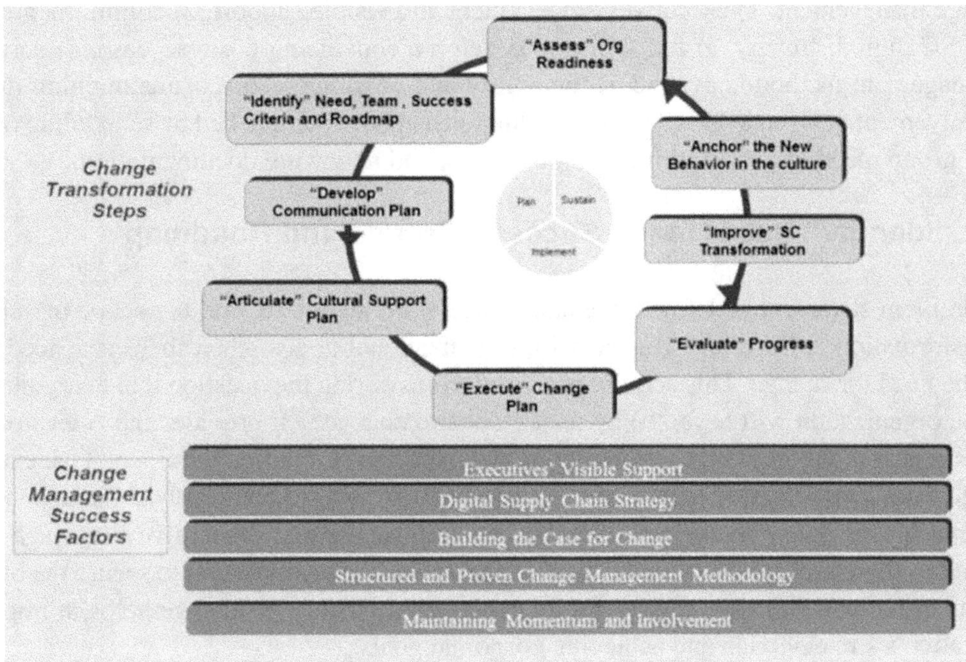

Eight Change Transformation Steps

The proposed framework suggests eight steps to go through the life cycle of change transformation effectively as shown in Figure 1 which are summarized as follows: 1) Assess, 2) Identify, 3) Develop, 4) Articulate, 5) Execute, 6) Evaluate, 7) Improve, and 8) Anchor. These steps can be also grouped under 3 phases:

- **Plan phase** which includes steps 1 to 4
- **Implement phase** which includes steps 5 & 6
- **Sustain phase** which includes steps 7 & 8

Let's understand every step in more detail:

Step # 1: "Assess" Organization Readiness

Organization Readiness for change gives insight into the current state of the organization with respect to desired position after change. The first activity in assessing organizational readiness is to identify the anticipated and desired change (end state). Then the next activity is to assess the alignment of the proposed change project with the organization's current vision, mission, and strategic plan.

A SWOT Analysis is a beneficial exercise in assessing organizational readiness for implementing a new program. SWOT identifies an organization's strengths and weaknesses and may identify areas that need change in order to move forward. SWOT identifies opportunities that can contribute towards success and also identifies threats which may be barriers in the process.

Another major activity for this step is evaluating the existence of the five success factors for mastering change management: 1) executives' engagement and visible support, 2) commitment to develop end-to-end SC digital strategy, 3) the ability to develop a convincing business case, 4) deciding on a change management methodology, and 5) the ability and previous record of maintaining the engagement & involvement of all stakeholders. This evaluation can be accomplished by scheduling one-on-one interviews, group meetings, distributing questionnaires, and reviewing documentation.

Step # 2: "Identify" Need, Team, Success Criteria and Roadmap

Once the problem statement is defined, the stakeholders are identified, and the scope of supply chain digital transformation is fixed and aligned with organizational goals—then there is a need to clearly articulate the need for change. This activity is crucial to answering the question that everyone across all levels in the organization will have: "Why do we need to change?" It provides the "elevator pitch" or the key message that will be communicated to provide awareness to all stakeholders. One example of a key message from a manufacturing company is "we need to transform our supply chain to penetrate new market channels while maintaining low inventory levels and gaining a competitive advantage in order to increase market share profitably" (Sabri, 2019). This activity is also important to secure the buy-in from the upper management who typically ask for an explanation of how the change helps in implementing the organization's strategic plan and achieving corporate goals.

Building the right (effective) team optimizes the efforts of the team and increases the chances of having a successful program. One of the biggest challenges of building and developing a transformation team for supply chain improvement programs in today's business is that every transformation program has its own nature and resource requirements. The senior management and sponsor must be sensitive to the unique needs of the program environment. The structure of the organization also plays a big role in selecting and building the transformation team. There is a need to document the required skills for every role (functional consultant, change agent, process consultant, developer, architect, program manager, project manager, etc...) based on the program charter document; this includes determining the number of resources needed for every role. In addition, establishing a process to evaluate the performance of resources and define an incentive plan to keep the team motivated is crucial (Sabri and Shaikh, 2010).

This step should consider the "why we are changing" key message to come up with the success criteria of the transformation program which typically provides some guidance on the expected benefits and how to measure success. A success criteria example for a company trying to improve market share by gaining a competitive advantage in customer service would be 1) improve customer service level by 10%, 2) improve market share by 2% next year, and 3) maintain inventory turnover rate.

This step is needed to identify the required process, technology and governance (KPIs, policies, roles and responsibilities. etc.) changes and finalize the implementation timeline to achieve the expected benefits (success criteria) of the transformation program. This step includes conducting an analysis for supply chain processes based on the transformation scope. Several industry-proven process analysis methodologies can help in this exercise such as six sigma, value stream mapping, benchmarking, etc.

Step # 3: "Develop" Communication Plan

Communications should have two major focus areas: Communications about the program (why and how we are changing), and communications about the end state and solution being delivered. This includes communication with stakeholders, team members, support team members, functional group members and front-end users (both inside and outside the company).

Communication about the project to stakeholders is very important to the success of supply chain transformation programs. Lack of information about the project's progress to stakeholders can be threatening to the program. Regular, targeted communication enables stakeholders to be educated, prepared and confident that the project is supporting their business needs. The mode and interval of communication should be clearly defined and shared with stakeholders. Program communication should be based on facts and figures. Showing progress helps to maintain confidence among stakeholders, instill pride in program members, and continue the program's energy. Program communication includes setting expectations, creating awareness of desired solutions, organizational changes, concerns, and successes. This communication should flow across all the stakeholders not only within the organization but also to vendors, suppliers and customers, etc. Many organizations underestimate the value of this part of communication but ensuring awareness of the solution to suppliers and customers helps them to prepare and understand their role, and if required, helps them plan their resources in advance.

Effective communication provides a clear understanding of what is taking place, motivates the team members, avoids any miscommunication between transformation team members, keeps senior executives committed, reduces the risk of conflicts, and most importantly, keeps everyone informed on the progress.

The communication plan should be comprehensive enough to satisfy the information needs of all of the stakeholders. It should provide a description of what piece of information is needed, who needs it, why it is needed, when it is needed, how it is communicated, and by whom. In addition, the communication plan should identify meetings, reporting, methods and format of communications that will occur with the transformation team, the program sponsor, stakeholders, partners, IT, and internal/external organizations.

Step # 4: "Articulate" Cultural Support Plan

Once the communication plan is established, it is necessary to articulate a culture support plan which includes the education plan and organization structure realignment activities. Any transformation program requires cultural support. Organizational culture by its very nature refuses to accept change, but over time and with education, organization structure realignment, and enforcement from executives—culture does change.

Leadership development is essential if some of the individuals who will be responsible for the program have little or no leadership experience. The education plan should be tailored to help the individuals acquire these skills. Conflict resolution is one example of the soft skills that leaders need to master if the transformation program is to be effectively implemented and sustained.

Training and skills acquisition for end users should be part of the education plan as well. Supply chain digital transformation programs require training, as well as new skills and attitudes for the end users of the new or improved processes. The proper allocation and commitment of resources (time, energy, and money) to conduct training and help employees in their skill acquisition is critical to the success of changes.

One major activity of this step is to plan for organizational realignment to support the end state. The Human Resources department might need to update job descriptions and bonus structure to reflect the changes. This might require a pipeline of candidates with a mix of demand, supply, and product expertise. Also, incentives for the company's talent should be aligned with the skill requirements for the end state.

Change leaders and agents (part of the transformation team) must anticipate resistance and be prepared to deal with various change adoption rates. It is important to focus on pioneers and early adopters first. These individuals who are a subset of the stakeholders' group are the most open to change; they are the first to embrace something new. Therefore, it is recommended to get these stakeholders on board as quickly as possible to help in changing the culture.

Step # 5: "Execute" Change Plan

Once the change plan (which includes change the implementation roadmap, communication plan, education plan, and organization structure alignment changes) is approved by senior management/executives, then the transformation team has the green light to go ahead and execute the plan.

Supply chain digital transformation programs typically take two to five years, with several intermediate projects (Go-Lives) that can pay for the rest of the program. Therefore, it is recommended to develop the change plan on the idea of incremental value delivery. It is crucial to have long-term (program) plan for success, but one should not ignore the importance of providing some quick-win projects). Organizational stakeholders look for short-term results, and the transformation team is under pressure to present short-term wins. Short-term wins should be woven into the timetable of the program. Each project delivers a set of capabilities that have a positive impact on process, metrics, and people, and addresses a distinct business need and contributes to the success criteria.

Step # 6: "Evaluate" Progress

In a transformation program, regular evaluation (health check) helps executives understand the current progress status and also helps anticipate the future progress trend. It is critical that the transformation team understands the current progress and takes key actions to avoid any unwanted delays. The prompt and proactive actions of the transformation team can save the transformation program from going off-track. If the program is delayed and the team is not able to bring it back on track, it will likely go off the radars of the executives' dashboard and eventually importance is lost, and the program fails. Progress evaluation should be done against the schedule and expected benefits (success criteria).

While tracking the transformation progress toward achieving the expected benefits and reaching the new targets of the KPIs, it is acceptable for the program manager and sponsor to rethink the goal and even adjust the targets either because of encountering roadblocks or because of some emerging opportunities that did not exist earlier.

This step requires the senior management's best efforts to stay engaged to build momentum for the change. Whenever executives or senior management let up before the job is done, critical momentum can be lost, and the change effort can stall.

Step # 7: "Improve" Supply Chain Transformation

Although the sustaining phase is the most difficult phase in any transformation, there is relatively little research concerning sustaining change in organizations. While planning and implementing a change can occur relatively quickly, sustaining change requires a substantial amount of time. Maintaining a sense of urgency and a significant level of interest is difficult over a long period of time. This phase can take months or years.

Once a successful project improvement (short-term win) is accomplished, management must work to make it part of the organizational culture. Step #7 helps in this aspect by encouraging a culture of continuous improvement and fine-tuning the new solution (combination of new process and technology). Improvement can also be achieved by enforcing the new process through drafting policies, providing additional coaching when needed, and recruiting people based on the new required skills. In addition, developing corrective actions for the root causes when performance measure targets are not achieved would achieve incremental improvement.

Step # 8: "Anchor" the New Behavior in the Culture

Acknowledging and rewarding stakeholders for new behaviors is essential to stabilize the new (improved) process and anchor the new culture. Because using new skills involves risk (the risk of failure) acknowledging and rewarding those who use the new skills encourages others to do the same.

This step also requires updating performance measures (metrics) to reflect the new performance baselines by coming up with new performance measures, modifying existing ones, modifying targets, or establishing owners to the performance measures.

Five Change Management Success Factors

Success Factor # 1: Executives' Visible Support

Since change is difficult and inherently unsettling, stakeholders will turn to the CEOs and executives for direction and answers. The leaders of the organization must embrace change first and then display their commitment and support. They must speak with one voice and model the desired behaviors, especially since supply chain transformations require intensive cooperation and cross-functional collaboration among executive peers. This visibility would force executives to get out of their comfort zones and their respective areas of responsibility and find time out of their busy daily operation schedule to envision an entirely new business.

While there are many reasons for the failure of the transformation initiatives, the lack of the executives' commitment is ahead of all the reasons. Interestingly enough, many executives do not know there is a direct correlation between leadership engagement levels and the success of a transformation initiative.

Having a broad picture of change in mind, executives would need dashboards and indicators to successfully pilot an organization to its desired destination. Active executives will build planned benefits/results into both the leadership team's and their own performance plans. Executives will initiate project-relevant communications in direct report meetings on a regular basis, visibly hold the organization's leaders accountable for the change, and if required will ask frequently for their direct participation. They also engage in communication events at all levels of the organization, try to resolve resource issues or constraints, understand the implications of the change across the organization's groups and demographic groups, and also monitor, identify, and address organizational resistance.

Another important aspect regarding the leadership of change is to understand the level of effort required for success. The executive's role and importance continue to increase over the life of the project. Towards the end of the change cycle, efforts from the transition team must be at maximum levels because of the sustain phase of the change cycle. Everything done up to the implementation phase can fall apart if the leader's proper attention and commitment is not there in the last phase of the change process.

Success Factor # 2: Digital Supply Chain Strategy

Very few companies have a good and documented supply chain strategy. Executives struggle with assessing the current state of the supply chain and envisioning the new state that is required to support the vision and address current challenges. This assessment ranges from digital technologies and processes to human resources and governance. They also struggle to decide when and where to begin and how to translate the vision into goals, goals into strategies, and strategies into process changes and projects. Serious attention consideration should be given to the following considerations while developing strategy.

Market changes – Strategies often fail because the market conditions which were intended to be exploited change before the strategy takes hold. Reasons may include a shorter product life-cycle, competition with new technology, unexpected change in financial market, etc.

Uniqueness of the strategy – Good strategy can distinguish the company from others in ways that make a difference to customers. Michael Porter (1996) has written extensively and persuasively on this topic. Leaders should take three simple steps in developing a distinctive strategy: 1) Understand the company's genuine strengths (particularly those that span multiple functions), 2) examine the marketplace to understand what market positions are unoccupied, and 3) focus the company's strategies on bringing its variable strengths to bear in capturing those unoccupied strategic positions. Executors of the strategy must also consider the potential reaction to the strategy by competitive companies. In order to effectively anticipate the reaction of competitors over strategy, a company should have competitive intelligence capability. This capability should involve understanding the competitor's market position, their competitive advantages and disadvantages, future planning, management decision trends, etc.

Alignment with business models – Sometimes companies fail to align their digital supply chain strategy with the organizational goal and business models. This is a critical step that is often overlooked. Lack of research on market trends, disconnecting with customers, gaps or misunderstandings of how demand would be met in the market can all lead to a poor business model. A basic assessment of organizational capabilities and the capability gaps created by a change in strategy is a very direct means of improving alignment.

Culture of "Playing it Safe" – Companies get used to executing low-risk incremental improvements on the same business environment for an extended period, and they become close-minded to drastic improvements because they do not know how to handle transformation programs and target big results; the scope can be overwhelming.

When companies are in the process of implementing several incremental improvement projects like Six Sigma or Kaizen, it will be a challenge to add a large transformation program to the mix especially when it includes new technology such as digital technologies. Companies that try to stuff too much into the organization will clog it, causing employees and managers' capacity to become a choke point unless the projects are prioritized and sequenced correctly.

Digital supply chain strategy ideally includes:

1) Flexible strategy as changes occurs in the global marketplace
2) Prioritized, actionable and practical improvement plans

3) A three-to-five-year roadmap that guides the transformation of supply-and-demand capabilities and take planning processes to the next level
4) Linkage to one or more corporate goals like growth or customer service levels
5) Both large opportunities for improvement that deliver significant ROI over time, as well as "quick win" operations improvements with a fast payback,
6) Elimination to outdated roles and responsibilities, unnecessary activities, and performance metrics that no longer reflect current realities
7) Metrics across the supply chain to reflect the overarching digital supply chain strategy.

Success Factor # 3: Building the Case for Change

The author strongly believes that in the coming years, no better core competency will help companies to compete in the market other than the ability to effectively implement transformation change. With increasing pressure both external and internal, organizations will tend to undertake more projects and initiatives to remain competitive in the market. So, the ability to achieve profit and benefits will be tied directly to how effectively we manage change by engaging employees. Building the business case for change is crucial to compel leadership to give the go-ahead for the transformation change program.

Developing a good business case for change is very important; every stakeholder's requirement must be taken into consideration. Three steps should be followed in developing the case: First, articulate a convincing need for change based on the company's current situation and market opportunities. Here, supporting details have to be strong enough to draw the attention of executives. The change case should be directly linked to the organizational goals, as this helps grab the attention of stakeholders.

Second, quantify the expected operational and financial benefits, estimate cost, and calculate the return on investment (ROI). This can be a challenging step sometimes because when the case is in the initial stage, one must come up with the expected financial benefit and return on investment close to actual. If the exercise is done with detailed consideration, the case becomes very convincing and can grab the attention of executives based on the extent of research that went through developing it.

Third, explain how to show progress and measure success. This includes which metrics will be improved to achieve the expected benefits, what will be the new performance targets and deadlines, and who will be accountable. If this step is not developed well then whole change process efforts can fail. As a part of developing the case, equal consideration should be given in developing performance measurement governance to track progress (Sabri, 2019).

During business case development, if consideration is given to identifying the key performance measures, these measures become more refined when executing the change program and can give accurate information on success.

Success Factor # 4: Structured and Proven Change Management Methodology

Ensuring a structured and proven methodology to show the way in the change transformation journey is a must. Any significant supply chain transformation program creates uncertainty and employee resistance. New leaders emerge, job descriptions are changed, and new skills and capabilities must be developed. Dealing with these change management issues on a reactive, case-by-case basis puts timeline, morale, and results all at risk.

A structured and formal plan for managing change—beginning with the transformation team and then engaging key stakeholders and leaders—should be developed early and executed effectively as changes move through the organization. The plan should be comprehensive to cover planning, implementing, and sustaining the transformation changes. It should also allow enough time for covering the soft factors of change management such as culture, leadership, and motivation because it takes time to change attitudes or relationships which are deeply ingrained in people as well as organizations. It requires time and effort to change the culture.

In addition, the structured change plan should not miss out on the hard factors of change management like financial results, the commitment level of executives, the number of resources and skills required to execute the program successfully, benchmarking and gap analysis, and the program roadmap and duration which are vital for the success of the transformation program.

Success Factor # 5: Maintaining Energy and Involvement

As transformation programs progress from defining strategy and setting targets to design and implementation, they affect different organizational levels and stakeholders. Setting the right KPIs & tracking, performance measurements, and awards & recognition have the most significant impact in maintaining energy and sustaining organizational improvement.

Right KPIs: To maintain the momentum and involvement of people in change programs, it is important to develop and measure the right KPIs. For example, as part of change initiatives a company adopts new pricing strategy to obtain high margins. Measuring the volume of sales was chosen to track the progress. But if were observe deeply, we find that measuring volume encourages discounts, rebates, and warranties, all of which erode margins. So, it becomes very important to measure the right things to create the right change (Sabri, 2019).

Performance measurement and support mechanism: When an organization is going through change, management's fostering of organizational trust, respect and caring pays off. Having a structured performance system also pays off. Communicate goals and performance targets to employees upfront. It is crucial to let employees know about the expected behavior and importance of the change with respect to what's in it for them and the organization.

It is important to provide resources, key materials, training, and enabled tools for employees to achieve target performance. This proactive activity helps build positive energy among employees which signifies the support of senior management in the change implementation phase. Evaluating the performance of employees based on their target—whether not achieved or exceeded—and providing feedback is a critical activity. The performance feedback activity should be motivating and encouraging, including performance compensation to maximize the target performance. If employees are in sync and excited about the change initiatives, they will make their maximum effort to achieve the target.

Awards & recognition: Positive attitude and work should get rewarded. It has been observed that rewards may not be exact compensation to the amount of effort put in by employees. However, even a small token of appreciation encourages employees to such an extent that they may boost their level of effort. Therefore, highly visible incentives, such as promotion, bonuses, and recognition should be provided as reinforcements to maintain energy and sustain change.

To summarize, stakeholders should understand why change is happening, how their work will change, what is expected of them during and after the transformation program, how they will be measured, and what benefits success will bring to them personally. Transformation team leaders should be addressing all of these questions explicitly and keep stakeholders involved and informed during the process to maintain momentum throughout the organization.

The key driver for this success factor is the transformation team. Building and empowering an effective transformation team is crucial to maintaining excitement and eventually embracing change. In building the transformation team, executives must be sensitive to the unique needs of the program environment and ensure that the team has the right skills like identifying resistance root causes and coming up with strategies to overcome resistance. The team should also try to avoid resistance in the first place by being proactive and mitigating the risk ahead of time (Sabri, 2019).

CONCLUSION

The success of supply chain digital transformation depends majorly on mastering the change management throughout the life cycle of the change program. Supply chain digital transformations are complex and multifunctional in nature. Therefore, the change leaders must be knowledgeable about the change life cycle in order to succeed in the transformation journey.

For effective change management, it is very important to have strong support from executives throughout the transformation cycle. Attacking change management with Digital Supply Chain Strategy and proven change management methodology makes transformation change cycle smooth. In order to sustain change management outcome it is necessary to maintain energy and assurance of everyone's involvement.

When firms make the decision to implement supply chain digital transformation programs which typically includes process improvement, software implementation, and organizational realignment across their global operations, there is a strong influence of cultural component to this program. The changes includes in the way work gets done every day, in individual roles and responsibilities, and in key performance indicators (KPIs).

A proven and well-defined change management framework for supply chain digital transformation can help companies overcome the culture of "this is the way we've always done it" and get employees at every level on board with the transformation plan — and achieve the expected benefits from improving supply chain performance. It will also help in accelerating the pace of change and achieve the success criteria quicker.

Every supply chain digital transformation program is unique because every firm has its own culture, industry challenges, organizational structure and skills, process maturity, and performance. However, proposed framework in this chapter is a comprehensive one that addresses all common challenges in implementing supply chain digital transformation programs and a practical one which provides executives and managers a good roadmap on what to expect and how to engage the entire organization in the process. This would ensure a successful and smooth supply chain digital transformation journey.

FUTURE TRENDS

Mastering change management is critical for the success of supply chain digital transformation. Importance of change management as separate department within an organization is increasing. Development of structured approach and formal process is concern for many industries as still failure rate of transformation programs is high. Several initiatives around the industry are under progress to develop the effective and efficient methodology on how to adopt change in organization. There is a demand to integrate change management throughout all levels of organizational system. Leaders have to link organizations goals to functional level department goals to personal level individual goals. With the advent of increase in transformation initiatives there is great demand for integration of project management methodology with change management cycle.

The author predicts more serious attention and enough allocated budget for change management track for transformation programs. This will be translated into higher industry success rate. This will have an impact on academia in two aspects: 1) more research and case studies will be available in this area, and 2) witnessing the introduction of change management as a separate MBA program in the universities.

REFERENCES

Cynthia, B., & Keith, L. S. (2011, January–March). Organizational Change Management: A Test of the Effectiveness of a Communication Plan. *Communication Research Reports*, *28*(1), 62–73. doi:10.1080/08824096.2011.541364

Ford, M. W., & Greer, B. M. (2005). The Relationship between Management Control System Usage and Planned Change Achievement: An Exploratory Study. *Journal of Change Management*, *5*(1), 29–46. doi:10.1080/14697010500036031

Karp, T. (2005). Unpacking the Mysteries of Change: Mental Modeling. *Journal of Change Management*, *5*(1), 87–97. doi:10.1080/14697010500057573

Kotter, J. P. (1996). *Leading Change*. Boston Harvard Business School Press.

Gallup. (2013). Most Change Initiatives Fail -- But They Don't Have To. *Business Journal.* http://businessjournal.gallup.com

Nadler, D. A., & Tushman, M. (1989). Organizational Frame Bending: Principles for Managing Reorientation. *The Academy of Management Executive*, *3*(3), 194–204.

Porter, M. (1996). What is Strategy. *Harvard Business Review*. PMID:10158475

Sabri, E. (2019). *Optimization of Supply Chain Management in Contemporary Organizations: Mastering Change Management for Successful Digital Supply Chain Transformation*, 85-106. IGI Global.

Sabri, E., Gupta, A., & Beitler, M. (2006). *Purchase Order Management in B2B Environment: Best Practice & Technologies J.* ROSS PUBLISHING.

Sabri, E. & Shaikh, S. (2010). *Lean & Agile Value Chain Management: A Guide to the Next Level of Improvement.* J. Ross Publishing.

Chapter 2

A Clustering Analysis to Identify the Performance of Food and Grocery Retail Companies Before and During the COVID-19 Pandemic

Mehmet Erdem
Ondokuz Mayıs University, Turkey

ABSTRACT

Food and grocery retail companies have a significant economic impact on local economies by creating jobs and providing daily needs of customers. The Covid-19 pandemic affects the food and grocery retail sector. Growing population, changing customer demands, and increasing competition are the main challenges in this sector. Hence, these problems have influenced the operational performance of the companies. Within the scope of the study, companies operating in Borsa Istanbul and having a widespread network in Turkiye were selected. In this study, the activities of the aforementioned companies for the years 2012-2020 were analyzed, and their performances before and during the pandemic were compared by means of the clustering method. Hence, a series of financial indicators such as liquidity ratios, efficiency ratios, solvency ratios, and profitability ratios were taken into account for this sector. The results also demonstrate that the companies with a high number of branches and good stock management continue their activities in the Covid-19.

1. INTRODUCTION

The retail sector is a crucial part of the country's economy and is the business that sells products to people through stores or alternative channels. This sector consists of an organized structure in relation to other industries as well as satisfying a significant need of the public. Nowadays, increasing competition experienced globally has also intensified in the retail sector (Goić et al., 2021).

DOI: 10.4018/978-1-6684-7298-9.ch002

The food and grocery retail sector has a crucial role in accessing the consumers to the products and services. This industry creates a place, time and means of ownership while providing customers access to the product and service at hand. It also helps to improve these facilitating activities and brand image. The retail industry supplies products and services just when the customer needs them (technofunc, 2021).

The global food and grocery retail market volume was calculated at $11,324 billion in 2021. This figure is expected to grow by 3% from 2022 to 2030 (GVR, 2020). Furthermore, according to a recent Mckinsey report based on the European region, in 2021, the Covid-19 pandemic has affected the grocery retail market in the region. Sales in 2021 were lower than in 2020; however, they were still significantly higher than in 2019 due to the partial shutdown of food services (Mckinsey, 2022). The Supermarkets and Grocery Stores industry size in the USA was $765.2 billion in 2022. This sector was ranked 2nd in terms of retail trade by its size (IBISWORLD, 2022). The primary negative factors affecting this industry are the urban population and high competition (IBISWORLD, 2022).

The retail sector in Turkiye, which grew behind the world economy average in the ten years after the 2009 crisis, achieved a 5% growth in 2019. It is estimated that the size, which reached 25 trillion dollars on a global scale last year, will exceed 30 trillion dollars in 2023. In Turkiye, the size of the sector is predicted to be 1.1 billion TL in 2019. Leading data signalled a recovery in 2020. Turkiye has excellent potential for retailers with its demographic advantage. Despite the positive signs and expectations for 2020, a slower period awaits the world economy in the coming years, according to experts. The regular increase in the number of households feeds not only retail but also many sectors such as housing, energy and automotive (KPMG, 2020).

The complexity of supply chain management has increased due to many factors such as system efficiency, delivery time, disruption rate and demand uncertainty, which must be considered for the success of supply chains in the delivery process to designated locations or markets. Real-life disruptions, often unknown and unpredictable series of events, are other critical circumstances that can occur at different stakeholders and parts of the supply chain and significantly affect the whole working process of a system (Yazdani et al., 2022).

With the emergence of the Covid-19 pandemic, governments worldwide have taken several precautions/measures to shut down restaurants, businesses, and schools. People could purchase food and various products from nearby stores and electronic commerce sites. From March to June 2020, a study conducted in the United Kingdom indicates that the pandemic increased grocery store sales by more than eleven per cent. During this period, it was also revealed that the retail sector players had difficulty satisfying consumer demands in the supply chain (GVR, 2020).

In addition to the changes on the supply side, many studies reveal that the pre-pandemic and post-pandemic periods are different on the demand side. In the United States, household online spending has increased to an unprecedented degree. Between 2020-2021, credit and debit card expenditures increased by 35 per cent in total (McKinsey, 2021). Because of this process, households prefer e-commerce and omnichannel services such as contactless payment, social commerce, virtual consultation and curb-side pickup (Accenture, 2020). This indicates the changes in brand loyalty. In the USA, people still do 80% of all their shopping in stores (NRF, 2022). Studies show that three-quarters of Americans have changed their shopping behaviour since the Covid-19 outbreak began. Similar research conducted in Europe shows similar results (McKinsey, 2021). Determining and predicting the direction of this rapid change is a complicated process (Tyagi and Pabalkar, 2021). Many factors globally affect consumer behaviour, such as gender, age, type of store, etc. (Timotius and Octavius, 2021).

In the food retail sector report published as of 2021, 30244 stores are currently operating in Turkey, while the sector is expected to grow by 45% by 2027 (Dünya, 2021). Migros Ticaret AŞ, Bim AŞ, Bizim Toptan Satış Mağazaları AŞ and CarrefourSA, which are traded in the Borsa Istanbul, constitute approximately 40% of the entire sector in terms of the number of branches as of 2019 (Gül and Erdem, 2022). In this study, the financial activities of the aforementioned companies from 2012-2020 were analyzed, and their performances before and during the pandemic were investigated.

In the first stage of the study, publicly available financial data of companies for the years 2012-2020 was collected from the publicly available reports. In the second stage, calculations were made using the obtained reports and financial tables. In addition to the ratios frequently used in the literature, non-financial indicators were also taken into account in this perspective. Finally, the financial activities of the aforementioned companies for the years 2012-2020 were analyzed, and their performances before and during the Covid-19 pandemic were compared through the clustering method.

This study aims to analyse the aforementioned companies in the food and grocery retail sector during the pre-pandemic and pandemic periods. In this way, the activities of the companies and the investments they make according to the changing customer expectations will be examined for the sector. Considering that some companies in the industry provide online home services in order to adapt to changing conditions, and some of them maintain the classical service approach. Hence, it is expected that the analysis results will reveal which companies are more successful in this highly competitive period. The difference between the study and the current literature studies is that the pre-pandemic and pandemic periods will be investigated with the clustering analysis. In this way, the financial performances of the companies will also be compared with her rivals. By using methodological analyses with the financial and non-financial indicators, the success of companies operating for many years will also provide several managerial insights into the sector.

Section 2 introduces the related studies and financial performance indicators in this field. Section 3 presents a K-means clustering algorithm used in the study. Section 4 presents the details about the case study and discusses an empirical experiment and its comparative result analysis. Finally, Section 5 concludes the study and proposes the limitation.

2. LITERATURE REVIEW

Supply chain management encompasses a variety of activities such as production, demand planning, distribution and marketing, etc.. With the help of these activities, product flow and its related information are provided from a supplier to a consumer. The supply chain network includes a significant portion of global trade operations. Hence, the performance of the network depends on the performance of the companies within it. Researchers have dealt with supply chain management to improve efficiency and solve overcoming problems.

Global trade faces high complexity and unpredictable disruptions. Hence, decision-makers try to deal with a variety of possible risk factors in the supply chain network. Yazdani et al. (2022) proposed (best worst method) BWM and fuzzy MARCOS methods to identify and evaluate the resilience faced by the food industry. The proposed multi criteria decision making (MCDM) method was used to analyse the food distribution operations in the agricultural sector in Andalucía in Southern Spain.

Giering (2008) analyzed retail sales to develop a recommendation system for a chain of retail stores. The authors regarded the daily sales information for 600 products in different stores and divided them into several non-overlapping customer types. The proposed system is based on an online Singular Value Decomposition method. The system has been tested for over one year, and the results show that sales and productivity have increased significantly.

Rodrigues and Ferreira (2016) proposed a hybrid algorithm to deal with a case study in the retail sector. The authors first calculate the RFM (recency, frequency, and monetary) model for the customers and then segment them with the K-means method. In addition, the results are analyzed by applying the association rule mining method. According to the results obtained, several numbers of products are recommended to customers that they have not purchased before.

Erdem and Erkan (2019) applied a hybrid approach that consists of the two-stage clustering and type-2 fuzzy TOPSIS method to evaluate the supply chain performance. The authors examined a performance evaluation for 133 companies in the service and production sector in Ankara. The comparative results indicate the companies with high and low success in the service and production sector.

Albors-Garrigos (2020) analyzed innovation barriers and drivers in the retail sector in Spain. The author concluded that a combination of customer focus culture, cooperation with suppliers, and brand development is vital for the successful performance of the sector. Furthermore, technology contributes to success as well as being a facilitator supporting communication with consumers.

Goić et al. (2021) dealt with an investigation of key drivers of the customer in the grocery retail sector. The authors used a dataset covering customer responses to the service quality questionnaire. Statistical analysis was performed using these answers, which included more than 25 thousand responses over a 5-year period. Results show that larger stores are associated with higher satisfaction levels. Furthermore, due to the poor performance affects more the satisfaction than the superior performance, the authors noticed a loss aversion on the shopping experience.

Zuokas et al. (2022) analyzed 150 market product categories using data from a large supermarket chain in the Netherlands during the pandemic. The sales of the determined product categories turned out to be different in terms of time and volume due to the pandemic. Hierarchical clustering was used and eight different classes were determined in the proposed study. The clusters are named as follows: Survival kit, Stay-at-home, Restaurant at home, A drink or two, Breakfast and lunch, In excess, School's out, and Solitary. The results predicted that the product categories used for cooking, baking or food preparation, in general, will be in high volumes after the pandemic.

When considering the financial performance analysis, several studies were used to evaluate the efficiency and competitiveness of companies in different sectors such as logistics (Lixin et al., 2008), banking, etc.. Kou et al. (2014) developed an MCDM-based method to evaluate the results of six popular clustering algorithms considering financial risk data sets. Takeda and Kanamori (2014) proposed a new unified machine learning model for regression, two-class classification and outlier detection. This study aims to minimize financial risks.

Erdoğan et al. (2016) applied TOPSIS, VIKOR and ELECTRE MCDM methods to evaluate a group of life food companies traded in the BIST for a four-year period (2011-2014) by using the eight financial ratios. Hou (2016) proposed a hybrid method combining K-means, genetic algorithms, and Rough Set Theory to predict financial risks. The author applied the developed model to a series of companies listed in the Shanghai and Shenzhen Stock Exchanges. Shen et al. (2017) considered several insurance companies in Taiwan and measured them by employing fuzzy-integral-based decision methods. The authors also used thirteen different financial ratios to compare five insurance companies.

Deste and Halifeoğlu (2019) compared their financial performance of 5 market chains (Migros Ticaret AŞ, Bim AŞ, Bizim Toptan Satış Mağazaları AŞ, CarrefourSA and ŞOK Marketler Ticaret AŞ) traded in the BIST retail sector. The authors used the 2018 financial and annual reports of these companies and applied the TOPSIS method. As a result of the analysis, Migros took first place, and it was concluded that it had a high asset volume. It is thought that the company's ranking in the first place is due to the high number of products and the low number of warehouses. It is understood that Bim, which was in second place, has good stock and distribution management, while ŞOK was in last place due to its high debt ratio and low equity. The proposed study differs from the study of (Deste and Halifeoğlu, 2019) in that it is not limited to two fiscal years but covers longer years and is analyzed according to the financial reports and activity results of 2020. Ülker and Arslan (2020) conducted a similar study to assess three market chains (Bim AŞ, Migros Ticaret AŞ and CarrefourSA) for the years 2015-2018 financial performance. The authors considered a series of economic indicators in their study. As a result of the analysis, Bim AŞ was determined as suitable for investment. In contrast, CarrefourSA was considered as unsuitable for investment according to financial structure, profitability, liquidity and activity ratios. Mazman İtik (2021) dealt with a financial performance evaluation covering the years 2015-2019 in a food company. The author compared the 2018 and 2019 fiscal years, concluding that less profit was obtained in 2019. The reason for this year is that the current ratio was not at the desired level, and the financial expenses were high.

Qian (2006) applied the K-means algorithm to 81 Securities Issuing in Zhejiang province that was listed in the Great Wall stock trading system. The authors selected nine financial ratios to assess these companies. The results indicate that while several clusters represent a low-risk profile, a series of companies that belong to generated clusters have a high-risk profile. Lee et al. (2010) developed a hybrid hierarchical agglomerative and recursive K-means clustering method to predict short-term prices in the S&P 500 index. Financial reports and Stock quotes are taken into account as input parameters. The authors also compared the results to the support vector machines regarding accuracy and profit. In order to evaluate the performance of the portfolio-building algorithm during the Covid-19 pandemic, Bin (2020) applied the K-means algorithm. Zhu and Liu (2021) used the K-means algorithm to develop a system for evaluating financial risks. The authors selected a series of multinational companies traded on a stock exchange. In order to define early warning of financial risks, five years of data from 2015 to 2019 are used in this system.

In this study, in contrast to the existing studies in the literature, the conducted analyses included longer fiscal periods. In this framework, the effects of changing consumer habits and the government's measures on the food retail sector before and during the Covid-19 pandemic were also investigated. In addition, the study was not limited to a few companies or ratios. This way, analyses will be more comprehensive in evaluating the financial performance of companies. It will also provide the opportunity to compare the companies within themselves and between their competitors. It is thought that the evaluation of critical financial ratios and non-financial indicators together in cluster analysis will have an important place both in making appropriate decisions and in filling the research gap in the literature.

3. METHOD-CLUSTER ANALYSIS

Cluster analysis is a method that helps to separate units, variables or units and variables in a given data matrix whose natural groups are not known precisely, into groups or classes that are similar to each other (Özdamar, 2004; Tan et al., 2018). Cluster analysis aims to create homogeneous groups by considering some metrics calculated based on the similarity or distance between the variables. Thus, as a result of the analysis, the elements that make up the clusters indicate similarity to each other in the cluster they belong to but differ from the elements of other clusters. As a result, when the result of the clustering process is expressed visually, the elements will be very close to each other in the cluster, while the other clusters created will be far from each other (Tan et al., 2018; Vatansever, 2008).

Although the general aim of cluster analysis is to classify data according to their similarity and aid the researcher in providing the necessary, relevant, and valuable information. Furthermore, it can also be used to clarify data structure, prediction for groups, facilitate model fitting, etc. (Martinez et al., 2017; Tan et al., 2018).

In line with the increasing dimension and capacity of databases, cluster analysis has recently become widely used, especially in data mining research. Cluster analysis has also found successfully used in many fields such as statistics, engineering, biology, psychology, medicine, sociology and machine learning (Tan et al., 2018).

3.1 K-Means Clustering Method

The K-means clustering method aims to divide the data sets with n variables obtained from a large number of units into k clusters to minimize the sum of squares within the group. Placing available units in a small number of clusters is carried out iteratively. These available units are assigned to different clusters in each iteration, and the most appropriate solution is determined by applying a permutational approach (Tan et al., 2018).

Since new cluster centres are determined by taking the average of the variables in the cluster formed in each iteration, it is recommended that the variables in the data set be at least in the interval scale in order to apply the k-means method (Martinez et al., 2017). The algorithm of the k-means clustering method is as follows:

Algorithm

K-Means algorithm

1 In the first step, the number of k clusters to be created is determined.
2 k units are randomly or specially selected as the initial cluster centre.
3 Afterwards, the distances of the non-cluster units to the cluster centres are calculated according to the distance measures determined.
4 Each unit is assigned to the cluster centre to which it is closest.
5 New cluster centres are created by taking the average of the variables in the k initial clusters.
6 Units are assigned to the new cluster centres they are closest to according to the selected distance measures.
7 At this stage, the distances of the units from the previous cluster centres to the newly created cluster centres are compared.
8 If the distance has decreased to a reasonable extent, return to step 6.
9 If there is no significant change, the iteration is terminated.

4. DATA-PERFORMANCE INDICATORS

Firstly, companies traded on the Istanbul Stock Exchange and operating in the food retail sector were selected for this study. In addition, the periodically published reports on their websites have been taken into account to track the financial performance. The balance sheet and income statements were examined by using these sources. As stated in the literature, a series of important financial indicators and ratios represent the company's financial performance. These ratios are quantitative measures that aid analysts, investors, and managers in assessing and evaluating the overall financial condition of businesses. Ratio analysis also makes it possible to compare two different companies that manage different operations and management styles (CFI, 2018). Therefore, the proposed study considers twenty financial indicators in this sector. A similar number of financial indicators and the years 2012-2020 are considered a reliable and fair comparison. In addition to the financial indicators, the proposed study considers several different non-financial indicators. Financial and non-financial indicators used in the study are grouped and represented as follows.

Figure 1. Performance indicators

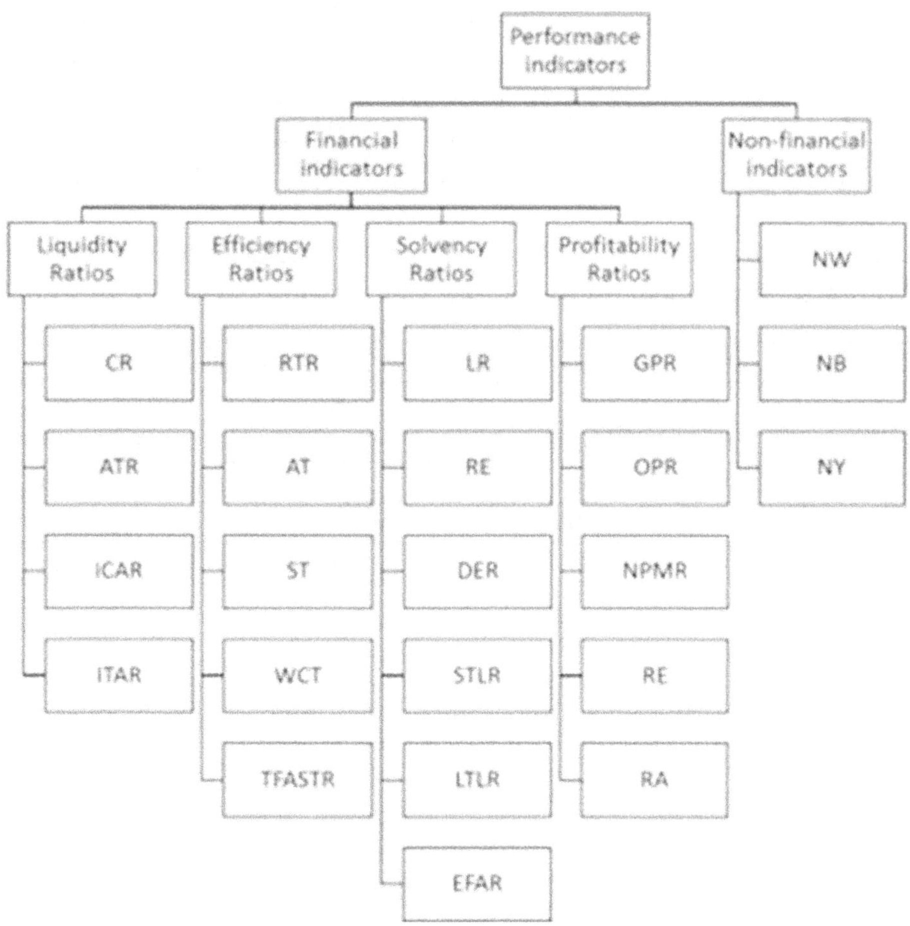

Within the scope of the study, four different supermarket chains that are traded in the stock market and that have a wide network throughout the country were selected. These companies are Bim A.Ş., Bizim Toptan Satış Mağazaları A.Ş., CarrefourSA, and Migros Ticaret A.Ş. (Bim A.Ş., 2021; Bizim Toptan Satış Mağazaları A.Ş., 2021; CarrefourSA, 2021; KAP, 2021; Migros Ticaret A.Ş., 2021).

4.1 Financial Indicators

Financial indicators are summarized in Table 1 with their formulas and abbreviations. The main ones of these indicators are liquidity ratios, efficiency ratios, solvency ratios and profitability ratios.

Table 1. Financial ratios

Selected Ratios	Abbreviation	Formula
Liquidity Ratios		
Current Ratio	CR	Current Assets/Current Liabilities
Acid-Test Ratio	ATR	Current Assets-Inventory/ Current Liabilities
Inventories /Current Assets Ratio	ICAR	Inventories/Current Assets Ratio
Inventories / Total Asset Ratio	ITAR	Inventories/ Total Asset Ratio
Efficiency Ratios		
Receivables Turnover Ratio	RTR	Net Sales/Trade Receivables
Asset Turnover Ratio	AT	Net Sales/Total Assets
Inventory Turnover Ratio	ST	Cost of Goods Sold / Inventory
Working Capital Turnover ratio	WCT	Net Sales / Working capital
Tangible fixed assets turnover ratio	TFASTR	Net Sales /Average Fixed Assets
Solvency Ratios		
Leverage ratio	LR	Total Liabilities/Total Assets
Equity Ratio	RE	Shareholder's Equity / Total Asset
Debt-to-Equity Ratio	DER	Total Liabilities / Total Shareholder's Equity
Short Term Liability Ratio	STLR	Short Term Liability / Total Liabilities
Long Term Liability Ratio	LTLR	Long Term Liability / Total Liabilities
Equity to Fixed Assets Ratio	EFAR	Equity / Total Fixed Assets
Profitability Ratios		
Gross Profit Ratio	GPR	Gross Profit / Net Sales
Operating Profit Ratio	OPR	Operating Profit / Net Sales
Net Profit Margin Ratio	NPMR	Net Profit / Net Sales
Return on Equity	RE	Net Profit / Equity
Return on Assets	RA	Net Profit / Total Assets

Source: Gül and Erdem, 2022; TCMB, 2021

Liquidity ratios indicate the soundness of a company. They are used to evaluate short- and long-term debt liabilities. Efficiency ratios measure how well a company uses its assets and resources. They are used to examine how many times a business can perform a performance indicator in a given period of time or how long it takes a business to accomplish its operations. Solvency ratios measure a company's capacity to meet its debt obligations and are often considered from the business lender's point of view. Profitability ratios are financial indicators used by analysts and investors to measure and assess a company's capacity to generate income relative to revenue, balance sheet assets, operating costs, and equity over a period of time. They indicate how well a business uses its assets to generate profit and value for its shareholders (CFI, 2018).

4.2 Non-Financial Indicators

The proposed study also takes into account several non-financial indicators. The number of operating year (NY), which provides essential information about the management policies of the firms and expresses its experience in the sector. In addition to this indicator, the number of branches (NB) was also taken into account in order to create excess stock and provide access to more customers. The successful service concept, which is frequently taken into account by the companies, the customer satisfaction consisting of fast service delivery and the number of employees (NS) that ensure the increasing company profitability are also taken into consideration. Hence, this study is different from the studies in the literature by including non-financial criteria.

5. RESULTS AND DISCUSSION

This section presents and examines the clustering results of the K-means clustering. In order to determine the number of cluster sizes in the K-means algorithm, the silhouette method is applied. It aids a user in the overall goodness of fit of partitioning (Bin, 2020). The average silhouette score is calculated according to the determined number of clusters. Hence, the average silhouette score refers to the lowest within cluster dissimilarity (Rousseeuw, 1987). Therefore, the number of clusters is chosen as a combination of both the high the average silhouette score and how realistic the retail industry dataset.

In order to determine the number of clusters for the K-means algorithm, clusters from two to eight are examined, and the average silhouette score is recorded. Hence, the results indicate that when k equals five, the average silhouette score has the maximum value of 0.625. Table 2 presents the number of created clusters. Furthermore, Figure 2 indicates the distribution of clusters. While clusters 2 and 4 have the highest number of companies, clusters 3 and 5 have the lowest number of entities.

Table 3 presents the Euclidean distances between final cluster centres, which are calculated using the centroid of each cluster centre. It is understood that the farthest distance is between clusters one and four, while the closest distance is between cluster two and cluster four.

Cluster 1 consists of the financial activities of Bim and Migros companies between the years 2012-2015, as represented in Table 2. When the cluster is considered on average, it is calculated that the current ratio is 0.85, the inventory turnover ratio is 10.4, and the gross profit ratio is 0.22. The average equity ratio is 0.25, and the average receivable turnover rate of Cluster 1 is 103.59. This figure has the receivable turnover rate within all clusters. It is understood that the number of employees in this cluster is around 23 thousand on average, and the average total number of branches is about 2700.

Table 2. Cluster membership

Cluster 1	Cluster 2	Cluster 3	Cluster 4	Cluster 5
Bim 2012	Carrefour 2012	Bim 2015	Bizim 2012	Bim 2020
Migros 2012	Carrefour 2013	Bim 2016	Bizim 2013	Bim 2018
Migros 2013	Carrefour 2014	Bim 2017	Bizim 2014	Migros 2019
Bim 2013	Carrefour 2015	Migros 2016	Bizim 2015	Bim 2019
Migros 2014	Carrefour 2016	Migros 2018	Bizim 2016	Migros 2020
Bim 2014	Carrefour 2017		Bizim 2017	
Migros 2015	Carrefour 2018		Bizim 2018	
Migros 2017	Carrefour 2019		Bizim 2019	
	Carrefour 2020		Bizim 2020	

Figure 2. Distribution of clusters

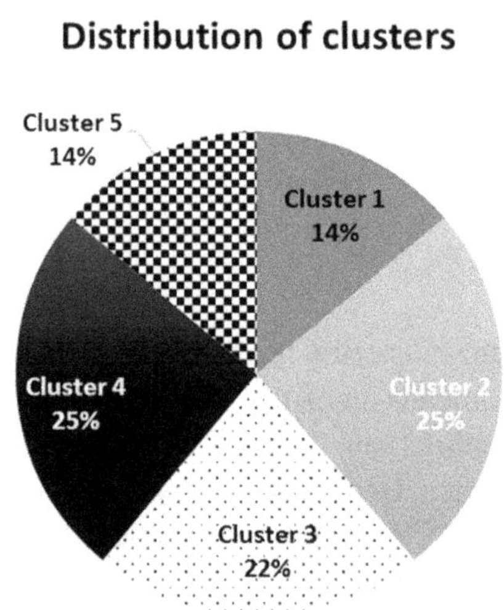

Table 3. Distances between final cluster centres

Cluster	1	2	3	4	5
1	-	41830,01	29002,10	49502,42	15572,76
2	41830,01	-	12830,44	7694,68	26269,70
3	29002,10	12830,44	-	20502,57	13439,56
4	49502,42	7694,68	20502,57	-	33934,33
5	15572,76	26269,70	13439,56	33934,33	-

Cluster 2 involves only Carrefoursa activities as a homogeneous cluster. The gross profit rate was 0.22, the tangible fixed asset turnover rate was 6.72, and the asset turnover rate was 1.62. The average of inventories/current assets ratio is calculated as 0.55. The average value of the equity to fixed assets ratio is calculated as 24.6. The receivable turnover rate is around 95.3. The short-term liabilities ratio was calculated as 0.66. The number of employees is about 9600, and the number of branches is about 530.

Cluster 3 consists of the activities of Bim and Migros between the years 2015-2018. The average current ratio, leverage ratio, gross profit ratio, and inventory turnover ratio of the cluster are calculated as 0.83, 0.74, 0.21, and 11.28, respectively. This cluster has the highest inventory turnover ratio. The cluster has the second largest number of employees and number of branches compared to other clusters. It can be said that the pre-pandemic financial activities of Bim and Migros companies are generally in this cluster.

Similar to cluster 2, Cluster 4 involves only the financial activities of Bizimaş. This cluster has the highest current ratio on average. The inventory/asset total ratio was calculated as 0.39 and the asset turnover ratio as 4.37. These values are higher than the averages of other clusters. It is calculated that the tangible fixed assets turnover ratio is 24.33, and the short-term liabilities ratio is 0.74. These ratios are the highest values considering the rest clusters. The number of employees of this cluster is lower than other clusters and is calculated at 1919. The number of branches is again less than the other clusters and is calculated as 162. In terms of liquidity ratios, Cluster 4 has the highest ratios. Hence, the members of this cluster have the highest short- and long-term repay ability.

The financial activities of BİM and Migros companies during the Covid-19 pandemic are included in Cluster 5. The average acid-test ratio is calculated as 0.48, and the working capital turnover ratio is 63.43. This cluster has the highest number of employees and number of branches. The gross profit ratio and asset turnover are calculated as 0.21 and 85.13 on average, respectively. In terms of solvency ratios, Cluster 5 has the highest debt ratios.

Considering the differences between Cluster 3 and Cluster 5 due to the Covid-19 pandemic are examined, return on equity decreased because of the Covid-19 pandemic. It is also thought that several members of Cluster 5 started investing to improve their alternative distribution channels before the pandemic. This investment may not be a highly profitable decision in a short time. Similarly, the asset turnover ratio has decreased; it is understood that it is due to the restrictions caused by the pandemic. It is observed that there has been an increase in working capital turnover ratio, leverage ratio, debt-to-equity ratio, long-term liability ratio, and equity to fixed assets ratio due to the pandemic. It can be said that debts have increased in this unexpected condition. Considering that long-term debts are financed from creditors, investors or partners, if the assets turn into cash in the short term, it can be stated that there is a situation in favour of the companies.

6. CONCLUSION

The food retail industry, which takes place in the supply chain and has an important place, is an essential part of meeting the most basic needs of people. Due to the Covid-19 pandemic, people's needs have changed, and the demand has increased rapidly in this sector. Hence, market players not only operate their activities in a highly competitive environment but also operate their activities in a highly competitive environment.

This study aims to evaluate companies' performances in the food retail sector traded in Borsa Istanbul by using cluster analysis. This study considers the selected companies' balance sheets and income statements covering the years 2012-2020 for the calculations. From these financial tables, a series of liquidity, efficiency, solvency, and profitability ratios are selected for the analysis. In addition to these financial indicators, several non-financial criteria are also included in the calculation to be used in the clustering method. Therefore, the K-means clustering method takes the determined financial and non-financial performance indicators as inputs. With the application of the clustering, a series of results have been reached for the companies' financial activities and sustainable growth based on their current situation. Unlike existing studies, this study considers a frequently preferred nationwide chain of food retail companies. In addition, this study compares the long-term financial performances and investigates the effects of pandemic conditions.

The results indicate that the companies with a high number of branches and good stock management continue their activities during the pandemic by maintaining their profitability. However, this process was observed that companies with poor stock management and high liabilities were adversely affected.

In order to achieve better performance in the food and grocery retail sectors, the companies may focus on the following financial recommendations. As a result of the global pandemic and war, there has been a decrease in the profitability rates of the companies. In addition, while short-term liability is high, long-term Liability Ratios rates are low during this time period. If this liability structure is changed, companies will face fewer financial costs or burdens. In terms of the efficiency of a company, they need to focus on so as to increase inventory turnover and receivables turnover ratios. For instance, in order to improve the stock turnover rate, it is recommended to create accurate and appropriate stock tracking, reduce costs, create a dynamic pricing policy, and increase the effectiveness of customer loyalty programs. For companies with low operating profitability ratios, it is recommended to deal with general administrative expenses, R&D expenses, etc., and to take managerial decisions to reduce expenses.

Since companies that have online sales channels achieve similar performance to companies that do not sell online, it can be said that a cluster of pandemic conditions is more dominant in creating a cluster. For this reason, different performance metrics from various sources may be included in the analysis for companies that have online sales channel in the future. In this way, sales follow-up and its effect on performance can be observed in more detail and from different dimensions.

In the future, data envelopment analysis can be performed for the effectiveness of companies or the effectiveness of branches within the company. In this way, it can be determined which branch is operating effectively or which branch should be closed. In addition, the success of effective branches can lead to the creation of new different strategies and take steps toward improvement.

REFERENCES

Accenture. (2020). *COVID-19: Consumers change how they shop, work and live*. Accenture. https://www.accenture.com/ie-en/insights/retail/coronavirus-consumer-behavior-research

Albors-Garrigos, J. (2020). Barriers and enablers for innovation in the retail sector: Co-innovating with the customer. A case study in grocery retailing. *Journal of Retailing and Consumer Services*, *55*, 102077. doi:10.1016/j.jretconser.2020.102077

Bim, A. Ş. Y. İ. (2021). *Finansal ve Faaliyet Tabloları*. BIM. https://www.bim.com.tr/categories/105/yatirimci-iliskileri.aspx

Bin, S. (2020). *K-Means Stock Clustering Analysis Based on Historical Price Movements and Financial Ratios*. [Theses, Claremont McKenna College] https://scholarship.claremont.edu/cmc_theses/2435

Bizim Toptan Satış Mağazaları, A. Ş. Y. İ. (2021). Bizim Toptan Satış Mağazaları A.Ş. Yatırımcı İlişkileri Finansal ve Faaliyet Raporları. https://www.biziminvestorrelations.com/default.aspx

Carrefour, S. A. Y. İ. (2021). CarrefourSA Yatırımcı İlişkileri Finansal ve Faaliyet Raporları. https://yatirimciiliskileri.carrefoursa.com/tr-tr

CFI. (2018). *Financial Ratios eBook*. CFI. corporatefinanceinstitute.com/resources/ebooks

Deste, M., & Halifeoğlu, M. (2019). Perakende Ticaret Sektöründeki İşletmelerin Tedarik Zinciri Yönetimi Açısından Finansal Performans Kriterlerinin Belirlenmesi: BIST'de Bir Uygulama Perakende Ticaret Sektöründeki İşletmelerin Tedarik Zinciri Yönetimi. *Journal of Social Sciences Institute/Sosyal Bilimler Enstitüsü Dergisi, 9*(18).

Dünya. (2021). 7 Yılda 15 Bin Yeni Market Açılması Bekleniyor. *Dünya*. https://www.dunya.com/ekonomi/7-yilda-15-bin-yeni-market-acilmasi-bekleniyor-haberi-612010

Erdem, M., & Erkan, T. E. (2019). Elvaluation Of Supply Chain Performance Using An Integrated Two-Step Clustering And Interval Type-2 Fuzzy TOPSIS Method: A Case Study. *Pamukkale Üniversitesi Sosyal Bilimler Enstitüsü Dergisi*, (37), 141–160.

Erdoğan, N. K., Altınırmak, S., & Karamaşa, Ç. (2016). Comparison of multi criteria decision making (MCDM) methods with respect to performance of food firms listed in BIST. *Copernican Journal of Finance & Accounting*, *5*(1), 67–90. doi:10.12775/CJFA.2016.004

Giering, M. (2008). Retail sales prediction and item recommendations using customer demographics at store level. *SIGKDD Explorations*, *10*(2), 84–89. doi:10.1145/1540276.1540301

Goić, M., Levenier, C., & Montoya, R. (2021). Drivers Of Customer Satisfaction In The Grocery Retail Industry: A Longitudinal Analysis Across Store Formats. *Journal of Retailing and Consumer Services*, *60*, 102505. doi:10.1016/j.jretconser.2021.102505

Gül, A., & Erdem, M. (2022). Gıda Perakende Firmalarının Finansal Performanslarının Entropi-TOPSIS Yöntemiyle Analizi. *European Journal of Science and Technology*. doi:10.31590/ejosat.1029907

GVR. (2020). *Food & Grocery Retail Market Size, Share & Trends Analysis Report By Product (Food Cupboard, Beverages), By Distribution Channel (Supermarkets & Hypermarkets, Online), By Region (APAC, Europe), And Segment Forecasts, 2022 - 2030*. Grand View Research. https://www.grandviewresearch.com/industry-analysis/food-grocery-retail-market

Hou, B. (2016). Financial Distress Prediction of K-means Clustering Based on Genetic Algorithm and Rough Set Theory. *Chemical Engineering Transactions*, *51*. Advance online publication. doi:10.3303/CET1651085

IBISWORLD. (2022). *Supermarkets & Grocery Stores in the US - Market Size 2002–2027.* Ibis World. https://www.ibisworld.com/industry-statistics/market-size/supermarkets-grocery-stores-united-states/

KAP. (2021). *KAP Finansal Tablolar.* KAP. https://www.kap.org.tr/

Kou, G., Peng, Y., & Wang, G. (2014). Evaluation of clustering algorithms for financial risk analysis using MCDM methods. *Information Sciences, 275*, 1–12. doi:10.1016/j.ins.2014.02.137

KPMG. (2020). *Sektörel Bakış 2020 - Perakende.* KPMG. https://home.kpmg/tr/tr/home/gorusler/2020/01/sektorel-bakis-2020-perakende.html

Lee, A. J. T., Lin, M.-C., Kao, R.-T., & Chen, K.-T. (2010). *An Effective Clustering Approach to Stock Market Prediction.* Paper presented at the PACIS.

Lixin, D., Ying, L., & Zhiguang, Z. (2008, 6-8 April 2008). *Selection of Logistics Service Provider Based on Analytic Network Process and VIKOR Algorithm.* Paper presented at the 2008 IEEE International Conference on Networking, Sensing and Control. IEEE. 10.1109/ICNSC.2008.4525400

Martinez, W. L., Martinez, A. R., & Solka, J. L. (2017). *Exploratory Data Analysis with MATLAB.* Chapman and Hall/CRC.

Mazman İtik, Ü. (2021). Mali Tablolar Analizi: Borsa İstanbul (BİST)'da Faaliyet Gösteren Bir Gıda İşletmesinde Uygulama (2015-2019). *Elektronik Sosyal Bilimler Dergisi, 20*(80), 1641–1661.

McKinsey. (2021). *Beyond COVID-19: The new consumer behavior is sticking in the tissue industry.* McKinsey. https://www.mckinsey.com/industries/paper-forest-products-and-packaging/our-insights/beyond-covid-19-the-new-consumer-behavior-is-sticking-in-the-tissue-industry

Mckinsey. (2022). *State of Grocery Europe 2022: Navigating the market headwinds.* McKinsey. https://www.mckinsey.com/industries/retail/our-insights/state-of-grocery-europe-2022-navigating-the-market-headwinds

Migros Ticaret, A. Ş. Y. İ. (2021). Migros Ticaret A.Ş. Yatırımcı İlişkileri Finansal ve Faaliyet Raporları. *Migros kurumsal.* https://www.migroskurumsal.com/yatirimci-iliskileri/kurumsal

NRF. (2022). State of Retail. *NRF.* https://nrf.com/topics/economy/state-retail#:~:text=Retail%20sales%20grew%20on%20average,than%20%244.9%20trillion%20in%202022

Özdamar, K. (2004). *Paket Programlar İle İstatistiksel Veri Analizi 2.* Kaan Kitabevi.

Qian, Y. (2006). K-means Algorithm And Its Application For Clustering Companies Listed. In *Zhejiang Province* (Vol. 37). WIT Transactions on Information and Communication Technologies.

Rodrigues, F., & Ferreira, B. (2016). Product Recommendation based on Shared Customer's Behaviour. *Procedia Computer Science, 100*, 136–146. doi:10.1016/j.procs.2016.09.133

Rousseeuw, P. J. (1987). Silhouettes: A graphical aid to the interpretation and validation of cluster analysis. *Journal of Computational and Applied Mathematics, 20*, 53–65. doi:10.1016/0377-0427(87)90125-7

Shen, K.-Y., Hu, S.-K., & Tzeng, G.-H. (2017). Financial modeling and improvement planning for the life insurance industry by using a rough knowledge based hybrid MCDM model. *Information Sciences*, *375*, 296–313. doi:10.1016/j.ins.2016.09.055

Takeda, A., & Kanamori, T. (2014). Using financial risk measures for analyzing generalization performance of machine learning models. *Neural Networks*, *57*, 29–38. doi:10.1016/j.neunet.2014.05.006 PMID:24914491

Tan, P.-N., Steinbach, M., & Kumar, V. (2018). *Introduction to Data Mining (2nd Edition)*: Pearson. technofunc. https://www.technofunc.com/index.php/domain-knowledge/retail-industry/item/importance-of-retail-industry#:~:text=the%20retail%20community.-,Consumers%20benefit%20from%20retailing%20as%20retailers%20perform%20marketing%20functions%20that,to%20enhance%20a%20product's%20image

Timotius, E., & Octavius, G. S. (2021). Global Changing of Consumer Behavior to Retail Distribution due to Pandemic of COVID-19: A Systematic Review. *Journal of Distribution Science*, *19*(11), 69–80. doi:10.15722/JDS.19.11.202111.69

Tyagi, P., & Pabalkar, D. V. (2021). Impact of covid-19 over purchasing behaviour of the consumers. *European Journal of Molecular and Clinical Medicine*, *8*(2), 561–571. https://ejmcm.com/article_7383_de7ea8fc87741a4ea22042820803b72d.pdf

Ülker, Y., & Arslan, Ö. (2020). Türkiye'de Gıda Perakendeciliği Sektöründe Finansal Analiz Ve Bir Uygulama. *MANAS Sosyal Araştırmalar Dergisi*, *9*(4), 2531–2546. doi:10.33206/mjss.704398

Vatansever, M. (2008). *Görsel Veri Madenciliği Tekniklerinin Kümeleme Analizlerinde Kullanımı Ve Uygulanması.* [Master thesis, Yıldız Teknik Üniversitesi].

Yazdani, M., Torkayesh, A. E., Chatterjee, P., Fallahpour, A., Montero-Simo, M. J., Araque-Padilla, R. A., & Wong, K. Y. (2022). A fuzzy group decision-making model to measure resiliency in a food supply chain: A case study in Spain. *Socio-Economic Planning Sciences*, *101257*, 101257. Advance online publication. doi:10.1016/j.seps.2022.101257

Zhu, Z., & Liu, N. (2021). Early Warning of Financial Risk Based on K-Means Clustering Algorithm. *Complexity*, *5571683*, 1–12. doi:10.1155/2021/5571683

Zuokas, D., Gul, E., & Lim, A. (2022). How did COVID-19 change what people buy: Evidence from a supermarket chain. *Journal of Retailing and Consumer Services*, *68*, 103010. doi:10.1016/j.jretconser.2022.103010

Chapter 3
Supply Chain Performance Measurement and Organizational Alignment in an Uncertain World

Rohan Vishwasrao
BlueYonder Inc., USA

ABSTRACT

In an extremely volatile environment, traditional performance measurement approaches have proven ineffective. To prepare for disruptions, companies historically have utilized scenario planning capabilities to build redundancy, flexibility, and develop early detection capabilities. In this chapter, the authors provide guidance on selecting the right 'causal linkages' between supply chain objectives and performance measures, relevant to the scenarios being evaluated. The authors describe how organizations can leverage the maturity model approach in conjunction with foundational concepts of perspective-based performance evaluation models, like the balanced scorecard (BSC), to define a comprehensive performance measurement framework. The authors propose using maturity models – which by design provide a roadmap to the next level of performance – as a structured way of identifying any supply chain's current capability or maturity level. A holistic framework for operational metric alignment and KPI governance, based on perspective-based modeling design principles is presented.

INTRODUCTION

Modern lean supply chains designed to minimize cost were fragile and over-stretched. COVID-19 is not the first epidemic to disrupt supply chains—SARS, measles, swine flu, Ebola, and avian flu all resulted in business interruptions—but none of these epidemics disrupted global trade and domestic supply chains as much as COVID-19. It has highlighted structural problems in global supply chains (Iakovou and White, 2020). Both public and private enterprises have recognized the need to design *dynamically resilient data-driven supply chain networks*, which will quickly detect, respond to, and recover from such

DOI: 10.4018/978-1-6684-7298-9.ch003

changes by making necessary adjustments. capacity as needed. To prepare for disruptions, companies historically have focused on building redundancy, flexibility, and developing early detection capabilities, using scenario planning techniques. The goal of simulation exercises in scenario planning is to get a deeper understanding of specific scenarios by studying the impact of potential choices. The effectiveness of these simulations depends on the fidelity of the underlying model, and measures used to evaluate the outcomes. In this chapter, the authors has tried answering two questions; (a) In steady state how do we align performance measurement with strategic objectives and (b) How to identify appropriate measures for evaluating strategic scenarios?

Financial metrics are useful lagging outcomes of the performance of an organization, but the operational metrics, in-turn are leading indicators of an organization's future performance. Operational metrics, when correctly defined, function as guiding posts to the desired performance end state. Thus, the key question which we attempt to answer is 'How to define metrics which are aligned to the strategic context, as well as deployable in operational reality?' There are two aspects to this question; alignment to the strategy and operational deploy–ability. 'Operating metrics are often poorly understood and guidelines for the use of metrics are often poorly articulated' (Melnyk et al., 2005). The primary challenge is to define metrics such that they are consistent with the strategic objective and the activities at the execution level. Whereas, the secondary challenge then becomes, maintaining this alignment, in the dynamic operational context.

Over the years, various performance measurement systems have been designed and studied by academics and consultants, but organizations struggle to leverage such systems effectively. Over a period of time, disconnect between strategy and metric deployment process are introduced due to changed operational realities. Sometime, minor changes to metric definitions – over-time – lead to incorrect understanding of the measures. To overcome these issues, we propose a comprehensive mechanism to maintain alignment between the operational metrics and organizational strategies, enabling organizations to – proactively evolve performance management systems as they grow, and refine operational processes. Subsequent sections of this chapter provide an overview of the fundamental building blocks of our proposed metrics alignment and governance framework. These building blocks are as follows: Balanced Scorecard, Supply Chain Maturity Models and Causal Loop Diagrams from System Dynamics for identifying 'causal linkages'.

Balanced Scorecard Fundamentals

The Balanced Scorecard (BSC) introduced by Kaplan and Norton in 1992, has been one of the most widely adopted management tools for describing, communicating, and implementing strategy. BSC retains financial metrics as the ultimate outcome measures for company success, but supplements these with metrics from three additional perspectives: customer, internal process, and learning and growth as the drivers for creating long-term shareholder value (Kaplan, 2010).

BSC has evolved from being a tool to translate and communicate strategy, into a strategy management framework. It helps define strategy as a collection of 'strategic objectives' and provides a comprehensive measurement framework, that links operational performance improvements to customer and financial performance. "Operational effectiveness and strategy are both essential to superior performance, which, [...], is the primary goal of any enterprise" (Porter, 1996).

When organizations change their strategies, though not a trivial or a frequent activity, the basic premise on which the BSC is designed for the organization, changes. A shift or change in strategy obviously calls for a re–design of the BSC for it to remain relevant in the changed context. But how does one go about accommodating the changing operational realities in the BSC system? As companies gain experience in execution, fine tune their processes and use better technologies, the premise on which operational effectiveness and corresponding measures are defined also change. These changes need to be accounted for in the BSC for it to remain relevant in the changed operational context. Changes in the operational contexts are more frequent but might not be incorporated in the BSC if a formal structure for defining the improved or changed measures does not exist. So how can organizations reflect changes to the operational context? Can a roadmap be created to deliberately move to a better operational state?

Maturity Models: Concepts and Relevance

The aim of supply chain management is to optimize supply chain and gain competitive advantage. So, instead of striving for the highest level of performance for all processes, organizations must aim for the most optimal level of performance (van Looy 2013b). This is where capability maturity models provide pragmatic guidance by prescribing a road map for advancing or improving business processes. Typically, maturity models have the following components: maturity levels, key process areas (level specific), key practices (level specific), specific goals and common features. The topmost maturity level always characterizes all process being managed in the state of "deliberate process optimization/ improvement".

A variety of business process maturity models (BPMM) have been developed; some have been specifically designed with a Supply Chain focus. von Looy (2014) has provided the most comprehensive review of BPMM to date. In this survey von Looy (2014) lists 24 maturity models, some of which have been developed in the academia, while the rest by supply chain consulting firms. This survey includes the SCOR model, which is one of the most well-known and widely adopted supply chain business process reference models. According to the Supply Chain Council (2014); SCOR model provides a unique framework for defining and linking performance metrics, processes, best practices, and people into a unified structure. By definition, a process reference model provides domain specific generic constructs, which can be used in different models. The author would like to highlight that, SCOR is a business process reference model and not a business process maturity model as classified by van Looy (2013a). The author recommends Fettke et al. (2005), for a detailed survey of business process reference model across various domains like; information technology, enterprise systems, supply chain and management organization to name a few. Nevertheless, van Looy (2013a) provides a comprehensive set of maturity models to choose from.

The purpose of a maturity model is to give guidance on levels of maturity and maturations path. Typically set of measures, corresponding to respective stages, help identify the current and desired levels of maturity. While most SC maturity models cover the entire supply chain, there are others which focus on specific areas like: Logistics, Sustainability, Efficient Consumer Response and so on. With so many models to choose from, it can be a daunting task to evaluate and select the models most relevant to an organization. The question then become how does one '*Choose*' the right measures in a given context, so that one can answer with *Certainty*: Am I measuring the right variable? Is the factor that I am measuring, relevant to the organization's strategic objective? How is the variable being measured affects the outcomes or performance of my supply chain?

One key choice the author will be making is that, irrespective of the maturity model being considered, the author will be leveraging the SCOR process reference model for the development of their operational metrics alignment and governance framework. The *Choose* the SCOR model for its depth of coverage and wide adoption, this model itself have hundreds of measures across the width of supply chain functional areas.

System Dynamics: Concepts and Relevance

System Dynamics is one of the six main disciplines (Operations Research/Information Technology, Logistics, Marketing, Organization and Strategy being the other five), that have contributed the most to the field of Supply Chain Management (Otto & Kotzab, 2003). It is a perspective-based methodology which uses information feedback and delays to understand the dynamic behavior of complex physical, biological, and social systems.

The causal loop diagrams (CLDs) which are used for system dynamics modeling are of particular interest to us. CLDs are used to create conceptual models, which represent the relationships between the variables in the system. They provide an understanding of the system structure as it identifies the important factors or variables influencing a system as well as the causal influence among these variables (Geethan et al., 2011).

From the point of view of evaluating performance of a supply chain, having a system dynamics perspective provides the proverbial 'most bang for the buck'. This is because causal loop diagrams can potentially provide answers to how certain variables influence the performance of a system, thereby providing insights on 'how' these 'key' variables influence the interconnected elements. A BSC on the other hand, in the context of a supply chain, simply provides information on how the performance measures roll-up or down the across the echelons of the organization. In the following section the author, leverage the power of CLDs and BSC, in conjunction with the maturity model approach and proposes a performance management framework which helps practitioners to deliberately manage the alignment of operational performance measures to the supply chain objectives in a dynamic operational context.

Proposal

Organizations employ strategies; define tactics and plans so that they know what choices to make in order to achieve their goals with some degree of certainty. BSC is a very effective tool to translate and communicate strategy, but it does not provide a mechanism for maintaining the relevance of defined measures. SCOR process model on the other hand adopts a building block approach and offers complete traceability (Thakkar et al., 2009). The SCOR–BSC framework developed by Thakkar et al. (2009) combines the salient features of performance management framework (BSC) and a supply chain specific process reference model (SCOR). The author builds upon the features of the SCOR–BSC framework by incorporating the salient features of capability maturity models, to enable organizations define operational tactics for processes at different levels of maturity and to provide guidance on improving supply chain processes, while maintaining alignment to corporate goals.

The proposed tiered framework, discussed in subsequent sections, for performance measurement and KPI governance is based on design principles rooted in perspective-based models like Balanced Scorecard and the SCOR model. It is structured in similar form to a capability maturity model, but the framework is agnostic to the maturity model selected. Additionally, the framework provides a toolkit which will enable practitioners to identify and define most relevant performance measures using the first principles of system dynamics, within the context of the supply chain objectives and key process area prescribed by the maturity model of their choice.

SURVEY, ANALYZE AND SYNTHESIZE

In this section we dive deeper into the three foundational themes of the proposed metrics alignment and governance framework; a) Supply Chain maturity models – selecting a relevant model, b) Performance measurement governance framework – combines features from Balanced Scorecard and Maturity models, and c) Identifying relevant performance measures – using Causal Loop Diagrams (CLDs). The objective of this section is to provide sufficient background on the framework's building blocks.

Survey of Supply Chain Maturity Models

Origins of Business Process Maturity Models (BPMM) can be traced to the discipline of Software Engineering in the early 1980s and were strongly influenced by quality management principles of the day (van Looy, 2014). 'The need for BPMMs increased due to a software crisis that started in the 1970 – 1980s. Many IT projects faced great difficulties in delivering on time, on budget and within scope. Consequently, the first maturity models for software development processes emerged' (van Looy, 2013a). The Capability Maturity Model (initially referred as Process Maturity Framework) developed by Software Engineering Institute is arguably the most well-known and widely adopted maturity model. The success of this software engineering-oriented process maturity model spawned a host of similar efforts for a variety of other business functions. The author restricts their enquiry to Supply Chain domain specific maturity models. Supply chain specific business process maturity models, adapted from van Looy (2013a), have been listed in *Table 1*.

Business processes reflect the way an organization operates, while maturity models, as mentioned earlier, are a reflection how organizations evolve. Reiterating a key concept, the basic purpose of the maturity model is to outline the stages of maturation path. This includes the characteristics of each stage and the logical relationship between them. This has in the pas led to criticism of being "step–by–step recipes" that oversimplify reality (Röglinger et al., 2012), however if utilized rationally they can function as valuable guidelines. The maturity models listed in *Table 1* are either collaboration focused (e.g.: SC Integration Model, Technology Maturity), or process focused (e.g.: Logistics, Customer Response, End 2 End Supply Chain). So, from a practitioner's perspective the question then arises, 'Which model is best suited for their enterprise and what should be the evaluation criteria for selecting a "relevant" model'?

Selecting Relevant Process Maturity Model

To answer these questions the authors, investigate two approaches; the first the one adopted by Röglinger et al., (2012); where they take the design approach to identify basic principles of a maturity model. These can be identified by answering the following three questions:

A. What are the improvement measures for each maturity level, and the level of granularity
B. What is the decision calculus for selecting improvement measures and
C. What is the adoption and/or assessment methodology (Röglinger et al., 2012)

The second approach proposed by van Looy (2014) is based on a Delphi study which resulted in 'criteria that must be strategically thought through' for selecting a business process maturity model. These questions are as follows:

Table 1. Supply chain maturity models

#	Model Name	Author / Institution
1	SC Integration Maturity Model	Aryee, Naim & Lalwani
2	SC Integration Evaluation Tool & Maturity Model	Böhme & Childerhouse
3	SC Integration Enhancement Framework (SCIEF)	Campbell & Sankaran
4	SC Management Maturity Model	McCormack et al.
5	Web-enabled SC Integration Measurement Model	McLaren
6	21st Century Logistics Framework	Michigan State University
7	SC Maturity Assessment Test (SCMAT)	Netland, Alfnes & Fauske
8	SC Management – Technology Maturity Model	Riverola
9	Logistics Scorecard (LSC)	Tokyo Institute of Technology
10	Global SC Maturity Framework	Aberdeen Group
11	SC Continuum	Accenture
12	Global Scorecard for efficient consumer response capability	CGF, Consumer Goods Forum
13	SC Management Maturity Model	CGR Management Consulting
14	SC Maturity Model	Chicago Consulting
15	SC Maturity Model	CSC, SC Management Review Magazine & Michigan State University
16	SC Maturity Monitor (SCM^2)	eKNOWtion
17	SC Maturity Model	IBM
18	SC Maturity Scan	Jeroen van den Bergh Consulting & VU University Amsterdam
19	GAIA SC sustainability Maturity Model	LMI Research Institute
20	SC Compass	JDA Software
21	SC Maturity Model	PMG & PRTM
22	SCORmark Survey	SCC, Supply Chain Council & APQC
23	SC Management Maturity Model	Schoenfeldt
24	SC Integration Model	Stevens
25	SCM-CMM	Sun, Ren & Yeo

+Adapted fromvan Looy (2014)

1. "Which capability areas must be assessed and improved according to the organization's specific needs?
2. Must the BPMM define a roadmap per capability area, a roadmap for overall maturity, or both?
3. How much guidance must the BPMM give on your journey towards higher maturity?
4. Must the BPMM be generic (i.e., for business processes in general) or domain–specific (e.g., for business processes in supply chains or collaboration situations)?
5. Which type of data must be collected during an assessment?
6. How must information be collected during an assessment?
7. For which purpose must the BPMM be used?
8. Must evidence be explicitly given that the BPMM is able to assess maturity and helps to enhance the efficiency and effectiveness of business processes?

9. How many business processes must be assessed and improved?
10. How long must a particular assessment maximally take?
11. Must the assessment questions and corresponding level calculation be publicly available (instead of only known to the assessors)?
12. Must the BPMM explicitly recognize to include people from outside the assessed organization as respondents in the assessment?
13. How many questions must be maximally answered during an assessment?
14. Must the BPMM be free to access and use?" (van Looy, 2014)

The authors are confident that these two approaches will provide sufficient guidance to practitioners on the approach to defining business specific selection criteria. As a closing remark to this subsection, the authors would like to specifically mention that the usefulness and elegance of the SCOR (Supply Chain Operation Reference), which lies in the form in which SCOR integrates Benchmarking, Performance measurement and Business process re–engineering across various entities in the Supply Chain. This process reference model provides over 140 measures across processes along pre–defined performance attributes. The question thus arises, 'How to identify and select the measure most relevant to a particular situation'? The authors attempt to answer this and related questions in the subsequent sections.

Performance Measurement Governance Framework

Metrics provide three basic functions; Control, Communication and Improvement (Melnyk, et al., 2004). It is important, however, to highlight the differences between a KPI, a metric, and a report — and to provide a collective understanding of these three terms. Key Performance Indicator (KPI) is a metric, but not all metrics are necessarily KPIs. For a metric to be considered as a KPI, it should support *specific organizational goals* and strategy, be *accepted by senior management* and displayed on executive dashboards, and still *convey meaningful information* at all lower organizational levels. On the other hand a metric is derived from a report or set of reports. So, a *Metric* must have 'a context and a target', is based on legitimate data, and should lead to tangible action or improvement. A perfect metric is characterized by; *being actionable*, having a *common interpretation*, being *transparent & simple to calculate*, and most importantly supported by *credible & accessible* data (Juice Analytics, 2009). Finally, *Reports* are defined as presentation of contextual data, either in aggregated or disaggregated form.

Some Challenges In Measuring Performance Effectively

'Effective performance measurement and governance are crucial, as many companies measure too much or too little—or are measuring the wrong things'. Supply chain performance measurement remains a challenge for most firms for the following reasons:

- Too many choices, which causes difficulty when identifying metrics that will yield the most information for the least investment of time and effort
- Isolated metrics are functional or departmentally oriented and not aligned to corporate strategy
- There is a need for new metrics in today's business to complement traditional metrics. Firms require metrics that can measure lean, agile environments.

- Professionals cannot understand the trade–off and interrelation between metrics when coming up with a comprehensive list; for example, an increase in fill rate can be at the expense of inventory levels and cash cycle time.
- There is lack of clear ownership for metrics and inability to drive good behavior.
- Consistently clean data are unavailable, which results in lack of confidence. (Sabri, 2012).

Sabri (2012) proposes the use of a performance management framework which addresses these challenges. Such a framework enables practitioners to effectively analyze the impact of improving individual processes on the overall performance of the value chain, propagates objectives and metrics down to the operational level, and determines the success of corporate strategies. He then outlines a governance framework which is effective in achieving four key objectives: 1) Identify the right KPIs, 2) Establish root–cause analysis and ownership, 3) Systematically track KPIs and metrics and 4) Establish governance for KPI and metrics reviews (Sabri, 2012).

In the remainder of this sub-section the authors delve into establishing metrics governance and discuss how KPIs could be tracked using the performance measurement governance framework. Whereas, in the next section, a toolkit is discussed that will help practitioners identifying the right KPIs and establish traceability between Tier I & II metrics for the purpose of root cause analysis.

Framework For Effective KPI Governance

The framework for KPI Governance is based on the four key objectives discussed earlier, and its elements are structured similarly. The primary objective is to 'Identify the right KPIs'. Sabri (2012) suggests that practitioners consider the following three aspects; 1) Avoid Hammer's Deadly Sins of Performance Measurement, 2) Focus on a handful of KPIs that are most critical to the business and align them to corporate

Figure 1. Aligning KPIs to corporate strategic goals

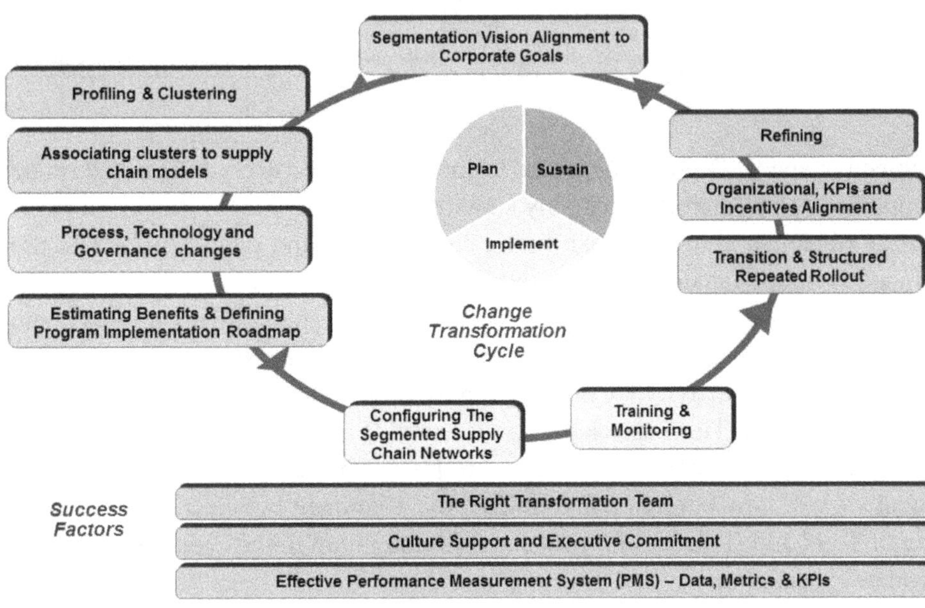

Table 2. Parameters for tracking metrics and KPI

Phase	Attribute	Description
Plan	Measure Name	A unique short name for the measure
	UoM	Unit of Measure
	Description	Brief description of usage and importance of the measure.
	Granularity	Identify dimensions: potential grouping
	Interpretation	Interpretation of value & its evolution; optimum & limiting values, expected (statistical) dispersion
	Example	Supply examples including units and format
	Baseline	Past or current level of performance
	Target	Derived from and aligned to corporate goals
	Metric Owner	Role accountable for achieving the target for the defined measure
Do	Computation	How are values obtained? Formula and algorithms used, data source.
	Data Source	Data repository which supplies the measure (or its components)
	Refresh Frequency	Frequency of data refresh
	Delivery Frequency	Frequency of re-calculation of the measure
	Delivery Mode	Means of consumption
	Calculation & Distribution Owner	Indicates team/ role responsible for generating and distributing the re-calculated measure.
Check	Venue	Indicates where the measure will be discussed and used for deciding on corrective action, if any.
	Audit Frequency	Scheduled frequency of review as the specified venue for oversight (?)
	Audience	Recipients and potential recipients of the measure.
	Inter-relationship	Indicate other measures which: are antagonistic to the measure, can be used to improve interpretation, are someway related to the measure.
Act	Corrective Action	Pointers to factors that may aid root cause analysis
	Timeline	Time window to act; begin at the point of problem identification
	Action Owner	Identify roles responsible & accountable for taking remedial actions, in case of deviations

strategy and objective and 3) Define a target performance level for every KPI based on benchmarking with other companies or based on the company's own goals.

The secondary objective is to 'establish root cause analysis and ownership'. 'The proposed KPIs need to be aligned to supply chain strategic goals and should be able to measure their successes. For example, forecast accuracy can assess the success of an effective sales and operations planning meeting mechanism. Inventory turns can measure the success of network and inventory strategy. Because it is impractical to measure every activity, identifying a reasonable number of metrics (Tier 2 metrics), that have a direct linkage to KPIs (Tier 1 metrics) is a necessity' (Sabri, 2012). With this level of granularity of investigation, ownership and corrective actions are just a consequence of the exercise. *Figure 1* provides a graphical view of how one can communicate the alignment between Strategic Goals and KPIs, and the pairing of Tier I and II metrics for root cause investigation in the event of deviation of KPI from the agreed upon or expected range.

For effective governance of performance measurement, the key to success lies in clarity of definition, interpretation and ownership of the metrics. 'A metric must be well defined so there is no dispute about it. Otherwise, managers tend to interpret it in ways that work well for them but that might lead to conflict. For example, if not clearly defined, the supplier can interpret an on-time delivery performance metric to be a shipping date, while the customer might assume the same metric represents a receiving date. A comprehensive set of metrics should be considered because improvement in one area is sometimes achieved at the expense of another. Also, metrics should stress results instead of activities' (Sabri, 2012).

'Identifying what needs to be measured is just the first step; finding the right way to measure and track is the next. Measuring at regular intervals is useful for base-lining the performance prior to a major transformation program and for getting a clear picture of the impact of the change on performance. Implementing a system which creates dashboards, on a periodic or as-needed basis, to sustain KPI tracking also is highly recommended' (Sabri, 2012). *Table 2* provides a comprehensive list of parameters for tracking the KPIs and Tier I & II metrics from a governance perspective.

Finally, to establish effective governance of performance measure reviews, establish a process to set targets, metrics without any target means no skin in the game. This can be achieved by defining the parameters in *Table 2* and establish a process that enables systematic review of the metric collection, communication and related corrective actions to enable (and or institute) continuous improvement. 'The highest level of maturity in establishing governance for measurement is to develop predefined corrective actions when targets are not achieved. This way firms can achieve sustainable gains and surpass the competition. Effective performance measurement and governance are at the heart of lasting success' (Sabri, 2012).

Identifying Relevant Performance Measure: Using CLDs

According to the discipline of System Dynamics, there are two structural methods for analyzing any dynamic system: Causal Loop Diagrams (CLDs) and Stock Flow Diagrams (SFDs). A CLD, also known as Influence Diagram, provides an understanding of the system structure as it identifies factors or variables influencing a system as well as the causal influence among these variables. It shows the governing inter–relations among a number of different variables using feedback mechanisms — the negative feedback loops (balancing) or the positive feedback (reinforcing) loops. Typically, a negative feedback loop indicates, goal–seeking behavior, i.e., the system or sub-system seeks equilibrium after a disturbance. Whereas, a positive feedback loop indicates an unstable system, i.e., initial disturbance leads to further changes to the state of the system.

According to Campuzano et al. (2008), CLDs play two important roles in System Dynamics; 'first, they serve as preliminary sketches of causal hypothesis during model development and second, they can simplify the representation of a model'. The authors recommend the use of group modelling approach to create CLDs in a collaborative manner. In the group modelling technique, the participants develop one or many models during structured sessions with the help of a facilitator, who must favor the elucidation of knowledge within the group. 'The highly interactive nature of the relationships both physical and interpersonal in supply chains makes the use of Group Modelling Techniques highly appropriate [...] The advantage of such a model is that it unearths the mental models of a range of decision makes, all whose decisions can influence the dynamics of the supply chain' (Bell et al., 2003).

Once a CLD or set of CLDs, has been developed by the group of stakeholders under the guidance of a facilitator, more often than not, the inter-dependencies and inter-relationship between various factors which previously were not obvious, will surface. This not only brings clarity to the group in terms of; insights into dynamics of the system as whole and but also reveals impact ones action can have on the supply chain objectives. This exercise if conducted properly will not only help define performance measures correctly, but will also be useful in eliminating potential issues arising out of selection of conflicting metrics.

Figure 2. Causal loop diagram

AREA	Profiling
Product Characteristics	❖Lifecycle Stage ❖Shelf Life ❖**Functional or innovative** ❖Handling characteristics ❖Product value density ❖Supply Lead Time ❖Product Variety
Customer Characteristics	❖**Demand volume** ❖**Margin** ❖**Demand variability** ❖Large vs. Small ❖buying behavior ❖Customer Lead Time ❖Strategic Importance ❖SLAs
Channels	❖Website ❖Retailers ❖Warehouses ❖**End Consumers (B2C)** ❖**Businesses (B2B)** ❖Geography
Customer Value Proposition	❖Brand ❖**Lead Time** ❖**Cost** ❖**Availability** ❖**Flexibility** ❖**Delivery Performance (DP)** ❖After-sales service

Figure 2a exhibits a simple causal loop diagram which maps factors influencing Current Inventory, which is a key performance indicator at many organizations. Typically organizations will have many KPIs and a large variety of overlapping factors influencing various measures; the *figure 2a* is just a rudimentary illustration of how CLDs are to be utilized for; identifying Tier I and Tier II metrics which have a bearing on the KPIs, and to provide guidance on factors to investigate if interested in conducting Root Cause Analysis.

The method to interpret the CLD in *Figure 2a* is as follows; ‘Current Inventory’ which is the key performance indicator under consideration is influenced by Demand and Production Rate. The direction of influence line, indicate the direction of effect. Whereas the polarity ‘+’ or ‘-’ indicate they type of effect, i.e., a ‘+’ indicates that both the variables change in the same direction, otherwise the change in opposite directions. For example, if ‘Demand’ is increases ‘Current Inventory’ decreases (assuming all other variables remain constant). Similarly, when ‘Production Rate’ increases, ‘Current Inventory’ will also increase, and the reverse will hold true. So, in this rudimentary example, we can quickly identify that the KPI is Current Inventory for which, one of the Tier I metric is ‘production rate’, and the related Tier II metric is ‘productivity’ of the workforce. It is understood that when CLDs are developed in a rigorous group modeling setting, will yield more detailed information, and generate valuable insights for the defining appropriate Tier I & II measures for all process areas and KPIs under consideration.

The next logical step, in the Systems Dynamics approach would be to create Stock Flow Diagrams (SFDs) based on the CLDs one develops, which help analyze systems in a more rigorous and quantitative fashion. One use of developing SFDs is to conduct simulation exercises to establish tolerance limits for

Figure 3. Stock flow diagram

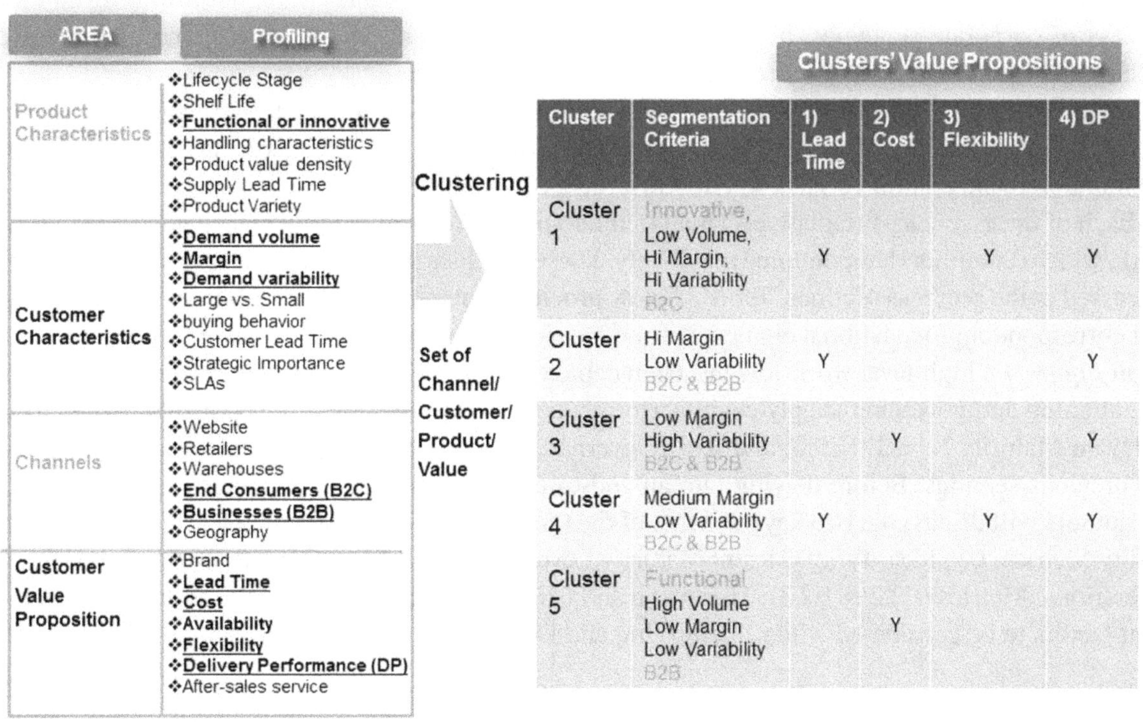

variables. Such an exercise will help define operating limits for related measure, such that when the process variables operate within these boundaries will not affect the KPI adversely. Another useful exercise is to potentially study the behavior of the system over time is to identify feedback loops. According to System Theory, all systems exhibit one or more of the three structures: Independent Growth, Reinforcing Growth and Balancing Goal Seeking. *Figure 2b* show the SFD for the CLD presented above, one will notice concepts like stock variables – Inventory & Workforce, flow rates – production rate, new hire rate and influencing factors – productivity, target production etc., need explicit mathematical relations between them. Defining SFD for simulation is a non-trivial, but nevertheless rewarding task, from the point of view of insights it generates.

OPERATIONAL METRIC ALIGMENT & GOVERNANCE FRAMEWORK

The three foundational themes of the framework: a) Supply Chain Maturity Models, b) Performance Measurement Governance and c) Identifying Performance Measures using Causal Loop Diagrams were discussed in the previous sections. With this background, the authors now outline the tiered framework for supply chain performance measurement and governance of key performance indicators. An example explaining the salient feature of the framework and how it is applied to achieve the four key objectives of 1) Identify the right KPIs, 2) Establish root-cause analysis and ownership, 3) Systematically track KPIs and metrics and 4) Establish governance for KPI and metrics reviews, is also discussed next.

The framework aims to provide executives with the means to propagate corporate objectives and define KPIs aligned to these objectives. The CLD technique when used in a group modelling setting provides managers with the means to effectively define non-conflicting measures, establish ownership, and tie operational metrics with the KPIs. Such a structured approach not only helps in analyzing the impact of individual processes on the overall performance of the value chain, but also determines the success of corporate strategies, by establishing accountability and by aligning operational measured with the KPIs and corporate goals.

Figure 3 illustrates in a pictorial fashion the four echelons of the framework; 1) Business KPIs, which drives 2) Accountability Metrics, which in-turn are reflected on 3) Dashboards and Scorecards; these are monitored and controlled via a 4) KPI Governance Model.

Each of these echelons (tentatively) map to the four objectives of a performance governance framework, which the authors have outlined previously. These echelons are anchored in the foundational blocks discussed in the previous sections. *Table 3* below provides a mapping of these echelons to the objectives and corresponding foundational elements of the metrics alignment and governance framework.

In *Figure 4* a high-level workflow has been depicted for implementing the framework; for identifying, aligning and governing supply chain performance measures. Some of the elements like 'Selecting Relevant Maturity Model' (E2.0) and 'KPI Governance Model' (E3.0) have been discussed briefly in the previous sections. Before delving into an end-to-end example about the usage of this framework, the authors will discuss the two key elements of the (arguably) most important echelon – Plan Accountability Metrics, i.e., Identifying Current Maturity Level (E2.1) and Identifying & Defining Level I & II Operational Metrics (E2.2 & E2.3). Then from an IT implementation perspective the authors will highlight factors to be considered while 'Identifying and Defining Reporting and Dashboard Needs' (E4.0)

Figure 4. Performance measurement, alignment & governance framework

			Supply Chain Processes' Key Strategies			
Cluster	**Supply Chain**	**Value Propositions**	**Supply Planning**	**Demand Planning**	**Procurement**	**Order Fulfillment**
Cluster 1	Supply Chain (SC) A	1, 3, 4	• Postponement • Six Sigma to control variability • Flexible Capacity	• Customer Collaboration	• Multi Source	• Air
Cluster 2	Supply Chain B	1, 4	• Build to Stock • Stored in Regional DC	• Demand Shaping	• Buffer stock • VMI	• Cross Docks
Cluster 3	Supply Chain C	2, 4	• Build to Order • Direct Ship	• What if Analysis	• Flexible Contracts	• FTL for B2B
Cluster 4	Supply Chain D	1, 3, 4	• Stored in Centralized Warehouse • Near shore capacity	• POS Forecasting	• Bulk buys • FTL for inbound material	• Expedites
Cluster 5	Supply Chain E	2	• Inventory stored closer to customers • Lean for streamlining • offshore capacity • Build to stock	• Statistical forecasting with exception driven adjustments	• Blanket PO with locked annual QTY	• Ocean & Rail with no expedites

SC A = Responsive & Flexible Supply Chain
SC B = Responsive Supply Chain
SC C = Efficient & Reliable Supply Chain
SC D = Efficient & Flexible Supply Chain
SC E = Efficient Supply Chain

Table 3. Mapping echelons, objectives & foundational elements

Echelon	Objectives	Foundational Elements
Business KPIs	Identify the right KPIs	Causal Loop Diagrams
Plan Accountability Metrics	Establish root cause analysis & ownership	Maturity Models, CLDs
Scorecard, Dashboard System	Systematically track KPIs & metrics	Business Intelligence Tools*
KPI Governance Model	Establish governance for KPI & metrics reviews	Sabri's (2012) KPI Governance Model

* Subsequently discussed as part of the section on Reporting & Dashboards – An IT Perspective

Figure 5. Framework implementation workflow

	Key Process, Technologies and Governance Changes for Supply Chain A			
	Supply Planning	**Demand Planning**	**Procurement**	**Order Fulfillment**
Process	• Profiling Customer Lead Time • Establish a sub-process for demand prioritization	• Modifying the forecasting process to include the customer input	• Establishing a process and criteria to split the sourcing demand by the vendors	• Establish a process for allocation
Technology	• Implementing Inventory Optimization Tool	• Enabling a collaboration workbench	• Enhancing the supplier portal to provide real time visibility for in-transit inbound material	• Supporting different modes of transportation • Enabling order promising based on allocation
Governance	• Establishing Center of excellence to supervise 6 Sigma initiatives	• Decentralized Demand Planning Group • Adding customer forecast accuracy to the set of existing metrics	• Adding supplier flexibility metric to the supplier scorecard	• Establishing a long term agreement with UPS and DHL

Identifying Current Maturity Level

The essence of any maturity assessment procedure is benchmarking, where the industry best practice and related goals form the highest level of maturity, while the current state of a process area indicates the level of maturity, as defined by the model selected. Let us first reiterate the key components of a maturity model; key process areas (level specific), key practices, specific goals and common features for a given maturity level. Qualitative or quantitative measure are necessary, for each process area and the corresponding highest level of maturity indicator, i.e., the industry best-practice. In addition to the best practices prescribed in the maturity model selected, Netland et al. (2007) provide three more sources of Best Practice repositories which one might want to consider. These are 1) SCOR Model's Best Practices Appendix, 2) Best Manufacturing Practices Center of Excellence (BMPCOE) and 3) European Foundation for Quality Management's (EFQM) Excellence Model.

We draw upon Netland et al. (2007) approach for assessing the maturity of a company's supply chain operations. Netland and Alfnes (2008) suggest that there are five types of test procedure for identifying the current state of an organizations supply chain: a) Standard maturity self-assessment, b) Gap–analysis {as–is and to–be}, c) Counterpart triangulation, d) Third-party triangulation and e) Maturity benchmark study. Though these procedures are mentioned in the light of the SCMAT Maturity Model (see *Table 1*, Row 7), they are generic in nature and can be used with any supply chain maturity model. Further they define these test procedures as follows:

- *Standard Maturity Self-assessment* – 'The test is carried out by a team of company representatives either alone or with the facilitation of researchers or consultants' (Netland and Alfnes, 2008).
- *Gap Analysis* – The evaluation team (of company representatives) attempt to answer two questions for each process area on a scale of 1 to 5 on the SCMAT Maturity Scale, to identify the largest improvement gaps. The first question (as–is) is phrased as: "To which extent does our supply chain use best practice stated?" (Netland and Alfnes, 2008), whereas the second question (to–be) is phrased as: "To which extent does our supply chain aim to use the best practice stated five years from now?" (Netland and Alfnes, 2008).
- *Counterpart Triangulation* – In this procedure the organizations upstream (vendors) and downstream (customers) supply chain partners are challenged to evaluate the organizations maturity across relevant process areas.
- *Third-party triangulation* – Similar to counterpart triangulation, third party consultants or researcher are challenged to evaluate the organizations maturity across key process areas.

We want to emphasize that selecting the right set performance measures are critical for making the correct assessment of the maturity of supply chain processes. Also, the fundamental reason for adopting maturity models is to "aid companies in benchmarking the maturity of their operations relative to industry best practice" (Netland et al., 2007). Akyuz and Erkan (2010) note that in recent years, the SCOR model has gained increased adoption and have contributed to the development of performance management systems and maturity models for the following reasons:

- 'Provides a standardized way of viewing the supply chain (cross-industry standard)
- Offers a consistent 'scorecard' framework for development of performance
- Emphasizes process orientation and de-emphasizes functional orientation
- Enables cross-industry benchmarks' (Akyuz & Erkan, 2010)

Next, we discuss the usage of metrics as defined by the SCOR Model, with respect to the proposed framework in greater details.

Plan Accountability Metrics Echelon

Akyuz and Erkan (2010) identified the need for 'developing measurement and performance systems in the form of new maturity models supported by SCOR, to enable benchmarking'. Najmi et al. (2013) provides a detailed survey of the adoption of the SCOR model by various researchers in performance measurement system of supply chains. Considering the needs identified in previous research, the authors decided on taking the current approach of incorporating the SCOR performance measure into the structure of a maturity model. 'Plan Accountability Metrics' echelon can be viewed as being at the crux of the metrics alignment exercise. Planning for 'accountability metrics' essentially has two–stages of selection; first stage is selecting the appropriate maturity model. All that a maturity model provides are the process areas of interest and the objectives or levels of performance expected at a particular stage of maturity. The second stage then entails selecting appropriate set of measures to ensure they provide 'coverage' for the process areas of interest.

Example: Echelon 2 – From Maturity Model to Level II Metrics Selection

Assume that a manufacturer of widgets, who also sell widgets through its own retail stores, wants to align its supply chain operational metrics to its corporate goals. Management's stated goal for the company is to; *increase market share by keeping its customers satisfied and expand customer, thereby increasing revenue and improve profitability*. An external consultant has been hired to achieve metrics alignment and she decides to use the proposed 'operational metrics alignment and governance framework'.

As the first step, the consultant identifies all key stakeholders and has set expectation with them regrading he outcomes, timelines, and the process to be followed (group modelling and workshops) for achieving the goal of aligning operational measures to the corporate objectives. Another decision the stakeholders made using guidelines provided earlier, is that the SCM–CMM model which considers 'Process, People and Technology triangle, across five levels of maturity,' is most relevant maturity model for 'evolving' the company's supply chain. Next the consultant facilitates a detailed assessment the supply chain processes, it is determined that *most* of the processes are at Maturity Level 3. The next critical task for the stakeholders is to prepare detailed design for developing 'accountability metrics' for all the key processes areas at SCM–CMM Maturity Level 3. Doing so will help them first define in detail the expectation for processes at Level 3 maturity and overtime validate, their hypothesis that their processes are indeed at Level 3 maturity.

In this subsection, the authors describe the outline of the process these stakeholders would have followed to prepare detailed design (stage 2 of echelon 2) for the 'Customer Service and Delivery' which is one of the process areas of SCM–CMM Level 3.

The procedure to prepare detailed design for all the key process areas at a maturity level is as follows:

0. Select the desired maturity level as defined by the maturity model
1. Identify the defining characteristics of the maturity level and related facets
2. Select a key process area
   i) Identify facet objectives vis-à-vis maturity level
   ii) Map facet objectives (at the maturity level) to the supply chain strategies
   iii) Identify KPIs relevant to both supply chain strategies and facet objectives
3. Identify key influencing factors and related SCOR measures
4. Determine parameter values for tracking metrics (refer to *Table 2*)
5. Repeat steps 2 to step 4, until all key process areas are covered
6. Begin at step 1, and repeat until all maturity level are covered

Note: In case of SCM–CMM, the facets are People, Process and Technology. And Maturity Levels are: Ad hoc, Initial, Defined, Extended and Networked.

As discussed previously, the authors strongly recommend taking a group modelling approach for creating the detailed design of accountability metric echelon. The idea is to enable participants develop the detailed design during structured sessions with the help of a facilitator. Such an approach will not just ensure collaboration, but at the same time will resolve potential conflicts by avoiding selection/definition of overlapping performance measures and generate insights into the dynamics of the supply chain system as whole. The core steps of the procedure are as follows:

Step 1: Identify Characteristics and Facet Objectives for a Given Maturity Level

According to Sun et al. (2005), Level 3 of the SCM–CMM "is the breakthrough level. Managers employ SCM with strategic intent and results. Cooperation between intra-company functions, vendors and customers takes form of teams that share common SCM measures and goals that reach horizontally across the supply chain [...] the SCM function becomes a serious part of the firm's strategic framework". The defining characteristic of an organization at this level of maturity is to '*Achieve logistics capability*'. The SCM–CMM Level 3 objectives for each of the process, people and technology facets can then be described as follows.

- Process – Well-defined demand/supply balancing process which combine forecasting and planning with sourcing and manufacturing are implemented.
- People – Become more responsive to customer requests and service level
- Technology – Software programs are applied to determine where the warehousing should be located, how much space should be involved, how much inventory is required to meet demand, how the goods should be stored and retrieved.

Once, the level objectives have been identified clearly, the next step is to quantify these in terms of metrics and targets.

Step 2: Align Facet and Organizational Objectives

Sub–Step 2a: Identify Facet Objectives vis-à-vis Maturity Level

SCM–CMM Level 3 has three key process areas: *Customer Service and Delivery*, *Advanced Planning & Scheduling (APS)* and *Network Planning*. In real life it is advisable to consider these three key areas together for the detailed design, for the purpose of illustration; we choose to focus on the '*Customer Service and Delivery*' process area. With respect to this particular process area, from the *People* facet perspective the objective is to "focus on customer satisfaction and service level", from the *Process* facet perspective the objectives would be: "Being Responsive To Customer Request", "Being Responsive To Service Levels", "Focus on Inventory needed for meeting demand" and finally "Supply & Demand Balancing". The *Technology* facet is primarily an enabler and is useful for identifying "decision support" requirements. Once the facet objectives have been listed, move to the next sub–step.

Sub–Step 2b: Map Level Objectives to Supply Chain Strategy

Before mapping the level objective identified in the previous step, one needs to know the specific supply chain strategies that help drive the corporate goals. This help align level objectives to the supply chain strategies, which is turn, are derived from the corporate goals themselves. The supply chain strategies relevant to the example have been briefly mentioned in *Figure 1*, but first let's review those in the context of the corporate goals. The company's stated goal can be translated into the following specific objectives: a) increasing market share, b) improve customer satisfaction, c) increase revenue and d) improve profitability. As noted in *Figure 1*, these goals can be achieved by employing these Supply Chain strategies: i) Align sales strategy with planning, purchasing and inventory strategies, ii) Improve delivery performance and iii) Create network & inventory strategy.

Sub–Step 2c: Identify Relevant KPIs

Next step then would be to identify the set of Key Performance Indicators (KPIs) which would accurately reflect the quantification of one or more goals. Typically, companywide KPIs would be derived from a BSC exercise, if the organization does not have a BSC or similar practice, then it is recommended that the KPI should be selected in such that they can be derived directly (as much as possible) from the measures which are relevant and acceptable to all the stakeholders. The corporate objectives, corresponding supply chain strategies have been mapped to some of the Level 3 objectives. Additionally, some KPIs relevant to these supply chain strategies and level objectives have been identified; some of these would be potentially used during detailed design.

Step 3: Identify Influencing Factors & Related Measures

The most important step is to identify all possible factors, which have influence on the process area under consideration. This is where authors make use of a powerful tool know as influence diagram (also called as causal loop diagrams), to map the causal influence among several factors and uncover the system structure. *Figure 5* indicates one feasible way to map the influence of the factors affecting the objectives under consideration which are represented by a measure or combination of measures. The authors would like to highlight a note of caution i.e., for the sake of illustration, they have taken a narrow view of the

Figure 6. Causal loop diagram for level 3 customer service and delivery process area

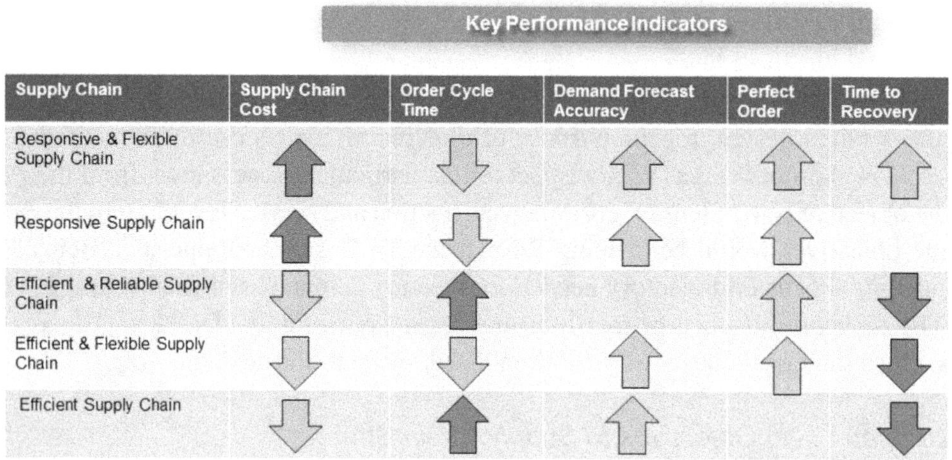

influencing factors and have limited the scope of investigation to just one of the three key processes areas at this level. In a practical setting it is advised that practitioner take a broader view for the sake of complete coverage and to avoid missing any important influencing factors.

In the causal loop diagram illustrated in *Figure 5*, the authors have identified the factors that influence three elements Revenue, Margin and Customer Satisfaction (which are corporate goals) from the 'Customer Service and Delivery' point of view (SCM–CMM Level 3 key process area). One will note that if the other two key process areas are considered, i.e., Network Planning and Advanced Planning & Scheduling, it will lead to additional factors being considered for mapping their influencing these three elements of the core corporate goals. Defining boundaries for identifying influencing factors is an important consideration and generating consensus on the same during group modeling workshops, will help avoid potential adoption issues in the future.

Step 4: Define Tier I & Tier II Metrics

One of the important outcomes of rigorous group modelling exercise for developing CLDs would be consensus on: a) the KPIs and 2) Related pairing of Tier I and Tier II measures. The author has provided a comprehensive list of parameters for tracking metrics as described in *Table 2* follow the PDCA format. The 'plan' parameters define how the metric is to be interpreted and identifies the owner. 'Do' parameters explicitly define the formula, frequency and role responsible for calculating and maintaining the metric definition. 'Check' parameters establish the governance details like venue, frequency, and audience responsible for review of the measure. And finally, the 'act' parameters define roles responsible for taking corrective action in case of deviations, the suggested corrective actions and the associated timeline. While the exact mechanism for establishing a governance structure has not been defined in this chapter, the author believes that the outcome of step 4 essentially prepares groundwork for establishing the foundation for governance as part of the metrics definition phase itself. To continue with the earlier example, from the CLD in *Figure 5*, consider the KPI 'Net Sales', the corresponding Tier I metrics in this case would be Customer Satisfaction and Forecast Accuracy, while the Tier II metric have be shown

Table 4. Accountability metrics design example

Stage I		Stage II		
Maturity Model	**Process Area**	**KPI**	**Tier I Metric**	**Tier II Metric**
SCM CMM	Level 3 Process Area: *Customer Service & Delivery*	Net Sales	Customer Satisfaction	• Delivery Performance • Product Quality • Customer Service
			Forecast Accuracy	• Demand Variability • Inventory Count Accuracy

Figure 7. Echelon 2 schematic

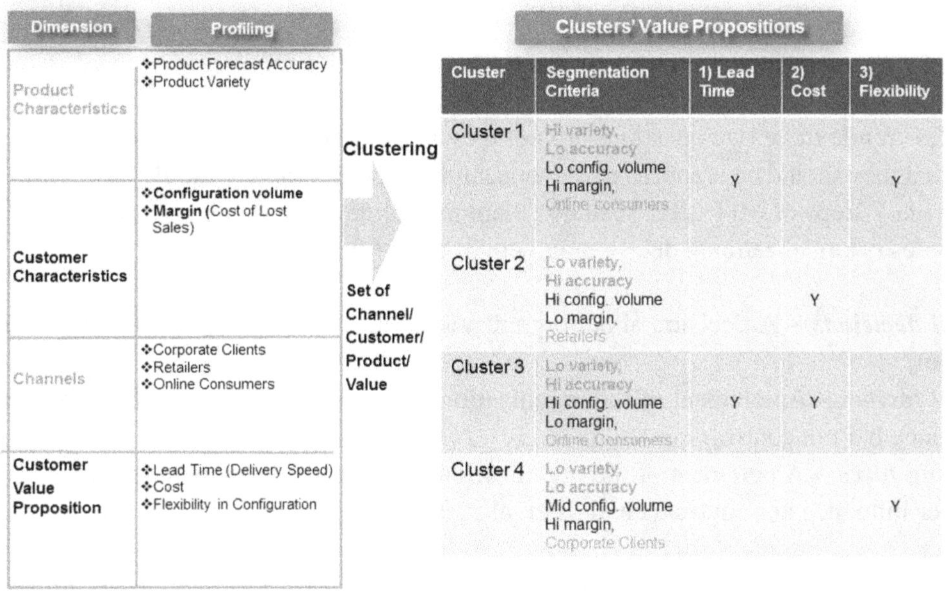

in *Table 4*. Those interested can work through the parameters from *Table 2* to continue working on the detailed design for these metrics.

Figure 6 is an attempt to show pictorially the composition of Echelon 2, vis-à-vis the maturity levels of a maturity model (in this case Level 3 to Level 5 of the SCM-CMM) and the linkages between corresponding KPIs and Tier I & Tier II metrics. In this figure only one KPI (Net Sales) has been shown and its corresponding Tier I and Tier II measures.

DESIGINING SCENARIOS FOR STARTEGIC ALIGNMENT

Supply chain systems and processes were designed for normal operations, and not for a once-in-a-lifetime disruption (Simchi-Levi, 2020). Given the hyper volatility of the business environment, as experienced in the past couple of year by events such as Suez Canal blockage, COVID pandemic, semi-conductor shortages followed by targeted restriction placed by countries like US and its allies; how can any organization craft a recovery plan? Simchi-Levi (2020) proposes that when designing scenarios, we consider three different realizations of the recovery length and magnitude – the pessimistic (worst-case scenario); the more optimistic (best-case scenario); and the most likely scenario. He further recommends that organizations prepare for each recovery scenario, based on the estimated Time-to-Recovery (TTR), and risk exposure associated with a disruption in each site of the network. Phadnis et. al. (2022), have provided a rigorous framework for Strategic Scenario Planning developed at the MIT Center for Transportation & Logistics (MIT CTL), which can be combine with Simchi-Levi's high-level approach. In this section we provide a summary of the process for developing and applying scenarios for strategic planning. And show how show the 'Performance Measurement, Alignment & Governance Framework' can be used to support the process developed by Phadnis et. al.

MIT CTL Scenario Creation Framework

Analyzing a company's business environment to create scenarios requires answering two questions: (a) which aspects of the business can the company influence? and (b) which aspects are predictable? (Phadnis et. al., 2022). While these two questions are not mutually exclusive, the first question helps distinguish between what they should be *prepared to respond*, and what the company should *aim to influence*. Before describing the 7-steps of MIT CTL Scenario Planning framework, we need to review the definition of three variables of organizational decision and environment for scenario creation:

- ***Focal decisions*** – A decision about organizational action or structure (within the organization's control)
- ***Local factors*** – An element of the organization's external environment that the organization can influence but not control.
- ***Driving force*** – An element of the organization's external environment that the organization can neither influence nor control (Phadnis et. al., 2022).

The 7-step scenario development process developed by MIT CTL, depicted in Figure 7 and summarized in Table 8 below, is based on a *set of axioms* about the knowledge of local factors and driving forces among individuals within and outside the organization, as well as other data sources that maybe the leveraged for developing scenarios.

These nine-axioms have been defined by Phadnis et. al. (2014) as follows:

Axiom 1: It is necessary that the organization's leader defines the scope of a scenario project responsible for the focal issue for the project to succeed.

Axiom 2: An individual member of an organization is knowledgeable about only a subset of the elements in organization's environment. Furthermore, different individuals in the same organization are knowledgeable about various parts of the environment.

Axiom 3: Compared to external experts, middle and senior managers in an organization are more knowledgeable about the local factors in their organization's environment.

Axiom 4: Neither a collection of external experts nor a diverse group of personnel from the organization can be guaranteed to know of all the driving forces the other group is aware of.

Axiom 5: It is easier for the member of an organization to understand how a local factor, as opposed to a driving force, affects the focal decision.

Figure 8. Generic scenario creation process

		Supply Chain Processes' Key Strategies			
Cluster	**Supply Chain Model**	**Supply Planning**	**Demand Planning (including Marketing & product Design)**	**Procurement**	**Order Fulfillment**
Cluster 1	Responsive & Flexible SC	• Pull Replenishment • No finished goods inventory	• Configuration is defined by Customers • Statistical Forecasting for components	• Outsourced Assembly • Collaborative relationship with suppliers • Production batch size is 1	• Air • Direct ship to consumer
Cluster 2	Efficient SC	• Push replenishment • Inventory kept at retailers	• Small # of configurations identified for market • Collaborating on the demand plan (forecast)	• Outsourced Assembly • Large production batch size • leveraging volume scale to reduce purchasing costs	• Ocean • Direct ship to Retailers
Cluster 3	Responsive & Efficient SC	• Push replenishment • Inventory including safety stocks stored in centralized locations	• Small # of configurations identified for market • Statistical Forecasting	• Outsourced Assembly • Large production batch	• Ocean
Cluster 4	Flexible SC	• Pull Replenishment • No inventory	• Small # of configurations defined by corporate client • Tight collaboration with sales	• Outsourced Assembly • Large production batch	• Ocean • Direct ship to clients

*Table 5. 'Essential steps and elements of the scenario creation process**

Process Step	Personnel/ Resources involved	Data collection and analysis method
1. Define the *scope of the scenario* planning project	• Identify and compile a list of driving forces • Representatives of relevant functions	• Consider functions involved in and affected by strategic decision
2. Identify & compile a list of *local factors*	• Experienced organization members • Project team	• Exploratory, open-ended data collection • Qualitative data analysis
3. Identify & compile a list of *driving forces*	• Experienced organization members • External domain experts • Industry trade publications, market research reports • Expert reports and weblogs	• Exploratory, open-ended data collection • Focused data collection (by driving force) • Qualitative data analysis
4. Estimate impact of driving forces on *focal decision*	• Experienced organization members • External domain experts, industry experts	• Assess the impact of local factors • Estimate association between driving forces and local factors • Analysis to map impact from local factors to driving forces
5. Analyze uncertainty of driving forces	External domain experts Industry trade publications, market research reports Expert reports and weblogs	• Gather projections from wide-ranging reputable sources (by driving force) • Comparison of different predictions
6. Choose *scenario logic*	• Project team	• Key driving forces based on impact and uncertainty evaluations • Scenario axes templates
7. Flesh out and name scenarios	• Project team • Professional writers • Video creators, artists, etc. (optional)	• Narrative: Scenario description • Narrative: Pathways to each scenario • Scenario name • Develop rich media collateral (optional)

*Adapted from Strategic Planning for Dynamic Supply Chains – Preparing for Uncertainty Using Scenarios, Phadnis et. al. (2022)

Axiom 6: Compared to an external expert, individual members of the organization have more accurate knowledge of the effect of a local factor on the focal decision.

Axiom 7: Individual middle and senior managers in an organization can correctly state whether a particular driving force influences the magnitude and/or direction of a particular local factor in the organization's environment.

Axiom 8: Scenarios should be described using driving forces only; they should not specify values for the local factors.

Axiom 9: For it to be judged plausible, a scenario should (a) be internally consistent and (b) describe how the world transitions from today to that scenario using the socioeconomic and technical artifacts present today, which are not disputed by the organization's members involved in creating and using the scenarios.

Influence Diagrams – For Step 4: Estimate impact of driving forces on focal decisions
Phadnis et al., suggest the following three step sub-process to estimate the impact of the driving forces:

a) Assess impact of local factors on the focal decision
b) Estimate how strongly each driving force influences each local factor
c) Estimate the degree of associate between the local factors and driving forces

Next step would be to solicit responses from sufficiently substantial number of people 'knowledgeable' about the organization and local environment. They suggest using a 9-point Likert scale to record and compile the effects for each of the three estimates to determine whether the effects are none, weak or strong for the combinations being evaluated. To identify the strong driving forces on the focal decisions. Note that the assessment of the effects of driving forces and local factors on each other and the focal decision are qualitative.

In previous section we have shown how Influence Diagrams can be used to map the causal influence among numerous factors and uncover the system structure. We propose that as the first step, influence diagrams should be developed to shows the influences between local factors, driving forces on focal decisions, to establish a consensus view of the association between these elements. To ensure that all respondents interpret the interactions between these elements consistently, prior to them scoring them based on their knowledge and judgement.

Stock Flow Diagrams – Step 7: Fleshing out Scenario – Define Operational Metrics & KPIs

The final step on the 7-step process involves writing narratives for each scenario based on the driving force(s) specified in the scenario logic. Including a pathway from today to the scenario's future. The author contends at this step, the Stock Flow Diagrams, discussed previously to establish tolerance limits for variables. Such an exercise will help define operating limits for related measures. Because unless the measures appropriate to the future scenarios are identified and defined, any scenario planning exercise will be incomplete. To fill this gap, the author proposes that Steps E1.0, E2.2 and E2.3 from the Framework Implementation Workflow (figure 4) should be executed, to validate relevance of the existing measures in use, and identify and define re-define measures that are appropriate for the future scenario. The above approach provides practitioners with a robust foundation for developing a pathway narrative from current state to the future state.

CONCLUSION AND FURTHER RESEARCH OPPORTUNITIES

In this chapter the author has presented a framework for the alignment and governance of supply chain operational metrics. Operational metrics are the leading indicators of an organizations future financial performance and are crucial from the standpoint of providing guidance on changing operational dynamics and identify opportunities for improving supply chain processes. The author has developed this comprehensive framework by incorporating the salient features of capability maturity models into the SCOR–BSC framework. The frameworks enable organizations define operational tactics for processes at different levels of maturity and also provides guidance on improving supply chain processes (depending on the maturity model selected), while maintaining alignment to corporate goals.

In addition to the proposed framework the author has presented a case for the use of 'system dynamic' tools like influence diagrams (or CLDs) using group modeling formats, which are very effective for developing conceptual models of an organizations' supply chain in a collaborative fashion. The author believes that such an approach will not only generate insights into the dynamics of the supply chain, but will also promote collaboration and avoid conflicting objectives and strategies across various functions. These techniques when used effectively will result in increased visibility, improved transparency and better governance of supply chain processes across levels of management.

The author, for the purpose of enabling the implementation of this framework, has provided guidance on; designing selection criteria of maturity models, a comprehensive list for detailed metric definition and governance and last but not the least factors to be considered for designing dashboard. They have also recognized the fact that in any scenario planning exercise, the step to identify measures relevant to the future state, is essential to develop an effective pathway narrative. Finally, the author then discusses the potential challenges in adoption and implementation of a business intelligence system.

Future Research Opportunities

Over the past decade researchers have approached supply chain performance measurement with a variety of methods; process based, six-sigma oriented, perspective based and even utility theory-oriented techniques (Najmi et al., 2013). But not enough research has been conducted on the application of system dynamic principles in supply chain performance management. Modeling supply chains and measuring their performance from a 'System Dynamics' perspective has the potential to add immense value. The following are the main guidelines identified for future research:

- Develop Stock Flow simulation models for supply chain what–if analysis
    - To examine the dynamics of the supply chain
    - To define operating tolerances for numerous factors influencing the performance of a supply chain
- Need for examining factors that influence various supply chain strategies
    - To establish 'metric pairs' for key influencing factors
    - Define 'metric pairs' either by key process areas and maturity levels or by industry characteristics

The author passionately believes that there is much value in investigating these areas from a practical standpoint, as they prompt researcher to look deeper into the dynamics of the supply chains and can potentially provide much needed guidance to practitioner, on industry or strategy specific situations, for implementing operational performance measurement in a rigorous fashion.

REFERENCES

Akyuz, G., & Erkan, T. (2010). Supply chain performance measurement: A literature review. *International Journal of Production Research*, *48*(17), 5137–5155. doi:10.1080/00207540903089536

Analytics, J. (2009). White Paper: A Guide To Creating Dashboards People Love to Use. https://goo.gl/QGGHty.

Bell, C., Higgs, R., Vickers, S., Toncinich, S., & Haslett, T. (2003). Using System modelling to understand the dynamics of supply chains. Monash University. *Working Paper*, *70*(03).

Bernard, M. (2012*). Key Performance Indicators (KPIs): The 75 Measures Every Manager Needs To Know*. FT Press. https://goo.gl/v7r4hZ,

Camerinelli, E., & Cantu, A. (2006). Measuring the Value of the Supply Chain: A Framework. *Supply Chain Practice*, *8*(2), 40–59.

Campuzano Bolarín, F., Lisec, A., & Esteban, F. (2008). Inventory cost consequences of variability demand process with a multi-echelon supply chain. *Logistics & Sustainable Transport.*, *1*(3), 1–12.

Davenport, T. (2006). Competing on Analytics. *Harvard Business Review*.

Dundas. (n.d.). *Dashboards Demystified*. Dundas. https://goo.gl/OriOSu.

Dykes, B. (2011). Web Analytics Action Hero: Using Analysis to Gain Insight and Optimize Your Business. *Adobe Press*. https://goo.gl/OWZSKn.

Eckerson, W. (2009). Performance Management Strategies: How to Create and Deploy Effective Metrics. *TDWI Best Practices Report Q1 2009*.

Enterprise Management Associates. (2012). White Paper: Business Intelligence Platforms for Mid-size Organizations: Comparing Birst, MicroStrategy, Oracle and SAP BusinessObjects. EMA. https://goo.gl/lm2XRC.

Fettke, P., Loos, P., & Zwicker, J. (2005). *Business Process Reference Models: Survey and Classification.* Third International Conference on Business Process Management (BPM), Nancy, France. https://goo.gl/TQILgk.

Geethan, K. A. V., Jose, S., Koshy, A., & Samuel, A. B. (2011). Methodology for Study of Characteristics and Time Reduction in Reverse Supply Chain Using System Dynamics. *International Conference on Sociality and Economics Development, IPEDR Vol.10*. IGI Global.

Iakovou, E., & White, C. (2020). *How to build more secure, resilient, next-gen U.S. supply chains*. Brookings. https://tiny.cc/hu13vz.

INFORMS. (n.d.). *What is Analytics?* Informs. https://goo.gl/odWhqS.

Kaplan, R. S. (2010). Conceptual Foundations of the Balanced Scorecard. Harvard Business School Accounting & Management Unit. *Working Paper No. 10-074.* https://ssrn.com/abstract=1562586

Melnyk, S., Stewart, D., & Swink, M. (2004). Metrics and performance measurement in operations management: Dealing with the metrics maze. *Journal of Operations Management, 22*(3), 209–217. doi:10.1016/j.jom.2004.01.004

Melnyk, S. A., Calantone, R. J., Luft, J., Stewart, D. M., Zsidisin, G. A., Hanson, J., & Burns, L. (2005). An empirical investigation of metrics alignment process. *International Journal of Productivity and Performance Management, 54*(5/6), 312–324. doi:10.1108/17410400510604494

Mulcahy, R. (2010). Business Intelligence Definitions and Solutions. *CIO Magazine*. https://goo.gl/VA8Wzx.

Najmi, A., Gholamian, M., & Makui, A. (2013). Supply chain performance models: A literature review on approaches, techniques, and criteria. *Journal of Operations and Supply Chain Management, 6*(2), 94–113. doi:10.12660/joscmv6n2p94-113

Netland, T., & Alfnes, E. (2008). *A practical tool for supply chain improvement – experiences with the supply chain maturity assessment test (SCMAT).* EurOMA/POMS/JOMSA Conference, Tokyo, Japan.

. Netland, T. H., Alfnes, E. & Fauske, H., (2007). *How mature is your supply chain? – A supply chain maturity assessment test.* EurOMA Conference, Ankara, Turkey.

Otto, A., & Kotzab, H. (2003). Does supply chain management really pay? Six perspectives to measure the performance of managing a supply chain. *European Journal of Operational Research, 144*(2), 306–320. doi:10.1016/S0377-2217(02)00396-X

Phadnis, Caplice, C., Singh, M., & Sheffi, Y. (2014). Axiomatic foundation and a structured process for developing firm-specific Intuitive Logics scenarios. *Technological Forecasting and Social Change, 88*(C), 122–139. doi:10.1016/j.techfore.2014.06.019

Phadnis, S., Sheffi, Y., and Caplice, C. (2022). *Strategic Planning for Dynamic Supply Chains.* Palgrave.

Porter, M. E. (1996, November – December). What Is Strategy? *Harvard Business Review*, 4. PMID:10158475

Pruyt, E. (2013). *Small System Dynamics Models for Big Issues: Triple Jump towards Real – World Complexity*. TU Delft Library. https://goo.gl/ge98Wt,

Röglinger, M., Pöppelbuß, J., & Becker, J. (2012). Maturity Models in Business Process Management. *Business Process Management Journal, 18*(2), 328–346. doi:10.1108/14637151211225225

Sabri, E. (2012). Enduring Transformation. *APICS Magazine.*

Simchi-Levi, D. (2003). Three Scenarios to Guide Your Global Supply Chain Recovery. *MIT Sloan Management Review.*

Sun, H., Ren, Y., & Yeo, K. (2005). Capability Maturity Model for Supply Chain Management. *International Conference on Management Science and Applications*, Chengdu, China.

Thakkar, J., Kanda, A., & Deshmukh, S. (2009). Supply chain performance measurement framework for small and medium scale enterprises. *Benchmarking*, *16*(5), 702–723. doi:10.1108/14635770910987878

van Looy, A. (2013a). *BPMM Sample (N=69).* Amy Van Looy. https://goo.gl/dbiVkQ, Accessed March 2014.

van Looy, A. (2013b). Which Business Process Maturity Model Best Fits Your Organization? *BPTrends*. https://goo.gl/1yCkEA.

van Looy, A. (2014). *Business Process Maturity: A Comparative Study on a Sample of Business Process Maturity Models*. Springer. doi:10.1007/978-3-319-04202-2

Wienberger, D. (2010). *The Problem with the Data–Information–Knowledge–Wisdom Hierarchy.* HBR Blog Network. https://goo.gl/tDtQQD.

Wilson, G. (2012). *Designing and Building Great Dashboards - 6 Golden Rules to Successful Dashboard Design.* Geckoboard Blog. https://goo.gl/cJLCLK

Chapter 4
How to Implement the Supply Chain Digital Segmentation Strategy Successfully

Ehap Sabri
University of Texas at Dallas, USA

ABSTRACT

Global supply chains, specificity, diversified product portfolios and different customers delivery requirements, COVID's lasting impact, disruptive environments, and digitization innovations are creating more and more complexity in supply chains. The purpose of this book chapter is to explore the factors that impact digital supply chain segmentation and provide a best practice transformation approach to ensure a successful implementation of the strategy. The chapter includes a literature review of supply chain segmentation and the application of relevant segmentation transformation steps to specific case studies. Supply chain digital segmentation strategy presents huge opportunities that are being tapped by very few companies who achieved significant benefits and gained competitive advantage. The chapter provides a practical and proven supply chain digital segmentation framework for companies who are about to take the segmentation transformation journey.

INTRODUCTION

In response to the dramatic changes in the business landscape over the past few years, companies are assessing whether they have the right supply chains to support their dynamic and digital business and exploring supply chain segmentation to reduce complexity and increase profit. Today's supply chains have become increasingly complex due to globalization, outsourcing, complicated networks, logistics capacity uncertainty and volatility, and the rapid proliferation of stocking keeping units (SKUs) and product configurations. However, many manufacturers and retailers continue to use an outdated approach to supply chain segmentation, hindering their attempts towards reducing complexity and improving margins.

DOI: 10.4018/978-1-6684-7298-9.ch004

It is also critical to deliver the right level of service for each product/customer/channel segment, especially as consumer behavior shifts towards more product customization and better service leading to a more compressed supply cycle.

Digital technology is transforming supply chain management and driving significant innovation. Machine learning as a concept has taken on a new meaning as the industry sees massive advancements in computing power and memory. Change is happening faster than ever as technology trends such as IoT, virtual reality, and big data are providing countless opportunities for manufacturers and retailers across the globe.

The tightening of budgetary constraints has driven more companies to explore ways to make the supply chain more agile, customer-focused, and profit-driven (i.e., to do more with less). This is another pressure driver for the increase in supply chain segmentation popularity.

Therefore, taking the journey of supply chain segmentation is no longer optional; it is a strategic mandate to stay relevant in the industry. The future belongs to the companies that can profitably match their supply chains to the specific needs of their customer segments.

This chapter explains the concept of segmentation, its historical background, its importance for today's business, and the challenges to its implementation. The chapter also provides an end-to-end supply chain practical segmentation framework. Companies can utilize this framework to ensure a smooth and successful implementation journey which leverages digital technologies. Several existing frameworks are relevant, but none are individually adequate or comprehensive. Several case studies will be discussed to illustrate the "fast track to success" framework.

BACKGROUND

Definition of Supply Chain Segmentation Concept

Sabri (2015) defined supply chain segmentation as managing profitably different virtual end-to-end supply chains defined by a combination of channel/customer requirements, product characteristics, business value considerations, and differentiated supply response strategies.

The Segmentation Concept is Not New

The concept of supply chain segmentation is not new in literature research. It emerged when Fisher (1997) mentioned that the root cause of the problems troubling many supply chains is a mismatch between the type of product and the type of supply chain response. For the past 20 years, supply chain literature has introduced several methods for segmentation using different criteria such as product demand volume, product demand variability, product handling, production variability, selling channel type, and end customer behavior. Authors agree that a 'one-size-fits-all' supply chain management approach is an outdated concept, yet, they use very different criteria (dimensions) and profiles for supply chain design selection.

Fisher (1997) used "Product characteristics," in particular the volume of product demand and the variability of that demand, as the criteria for supply chain segmentation and created two profiles to define the product dimension: "Functional" products and "innovative" products. "Functional" products, which have stable demand and long lifecycles, necessitate an efficient supply chain model, whilst 'innovative' products, with unpredictable demand and short lifecycles, necessitate a responsive supply chain model.

Fisher drew on examples from a diverse range of consumer products—including food, fashion apparel, and automobiles—to illustrate why different supply chain designs (models) were required depending upon whether products were "functional" or "innovative."

Naylor et al. (1999) compared the lean and agile manufacturing paradigms and argued that neither paradigm is better than the other. Rather, they complement one another. In addition, the authors developed a two-by-two matrix based on the product demand variability and production variability and assigned lean and agile supply chain models to them. For example, low variability for demand and production requires a lean supply chain model, while high variability requires an agile supply chain model. The authors also highlighted that an agile supply chain differentiates its products from the lean supply chain by concentrating on the service levels at the expense of reducing costs.

Similarly, Mason-Jones et al. (2000) suggested that the best approach is to design and implement a "Leagile Supply Chain." "Lean" can be achieved by eliminating waste (non-value-added time), while "agility" usually requires technology advances. The authors also demonstrated how the "Lean'' and "Agile'' paradigms may be combined. They introduced "order winners" as a segmentation criterion and developed a two-by-two matrix that uses "order winners" criteria to determine the appropriate supply chain model. For example, if "cost" is the order winner, then a "Lean" supply chain model should be selected. When service level is the order winner, then an "agile" solution should be recommended.

Lovell et al. (2005) also explored supply chain segmentation by examining product characteristics but used different criteria and profiles to define it. Two profiles (high value-density products such as microchips, and low value-density products such as packaging) were introduced and assigned to two different supply chain models. Products with high-value density should be manufactured in a few centralized, large-scale plants while low value-density items require production on a decentralized basis as close to the point of consumption as possible. The authors also mentioned that product handling characteristics should be considered in the supply chain model. Lovell et al. (2005) mentioned that perishable products are very different from fragile products, which are different from hazardous goods. The type of product will influence the type of packaging, the mode of transport, and the type of storage.

Christopher et al. (2006) argued the importance of considering "supply lead time" as another segmentation criterion. This is very relevant to the globalization trend that started in the Mid 2000s. The authors developed a two-by-two matrix where demand variability and supply lead time are the segmentation criteria. The authors came up with four different profiles and assigned four supply chain designs to them:

1. When the profile is unpredictable demand and short supply lead time, an agile supply chain model should be assigned to provide flexibility and responsiveness
2. When demand is predictable and supply lead time is long, a lean supply chain model should be used to reduce supply chain costs
3. When demand is predictable and supply lead time is short, a "continuous replenishment" model should be recommended
4. When demand is unpredictable and supply lead time is long, a "postponement" (leagility) model should be proposed

Christopher et al. (2006) highlighted that global sourcing and offshore manufacturing have dramatically altered the landscape of today's business and added to the importance of agility and responsiveness as competitive success factors. The challenge to today's global business is first to identify the appropriate supply chain models to meet the different needs of the different product/channel characteristics and then to manage multiple virtual supply chains.

Gattorna (2006) was the first to consider consumer behavior as a supply chain segmentation criterion and argued that segmentation criteria should go beyond just product characteristics, demand/supply attributes, and order winners. The author explained that companies should segment their customers along buying behavior lines sharing a specific value proposition and then assign the right supply chain design. The author identified four different profiles for buying behaviors segmentation criterion and recommended a specific supply chain design for each of them:

1. 'Understand Me' requires a "continuous replenishment" design that handles stable demand perfectly and allows a certain degree of collaboration
2. 'Be Consistent' requires a "lean" supply chain design to ensure an efficient response for fairly stable demand
3. 'Respond' is often associated with innovative or new products with a typical surge in demand and requires an "agile" supply chain design
4. 'Surprise' is associated with unpredictable products and a "fully flexible" supply chain design

Gattorna (2006) also introduced the "dynamic alignment' concepts, which allow the supplier to switch between the four supply chain models as the needs of the customer or consumer behavior change.

Christopher et al. (2009) explored more segmentation criteria and suggested five dimensions: stage of product lifecycle, delivery lead time window, volume based on Pareto classification, product form, and variability of demand.

Roscoe and Parker (2013) combined Fisher's (1997) product attributes, Mason-Jones et al.'s (2000) value proposition and order winning criteria, Christopher et al.'s (2006) demand predictability and lead times, and Gattorna's (2006) behavioral segmentation and concept of dynamic alignment. The authors came up with four supply chain models for the sporting goods industry based on the combined criteria tailored for a sporting goods manufacturer:

1. Agile – Customization
2. Agile Quick – Response
3. Lean
4. Continuous Replenishment

In summary, Table 1 shows the links between segmentation criteria (dimensions), profiles, and supply chain models for the previous work done in this area. The concept of segmentation is not new in academia (Sabri, 2019).

Table 1 demonstrates how several existing segmentation methods may be relevant to a specific company or industry, but none are adequate by themselves for every company or across industries. The literature conceptualizes the theory of supply chain segmentation but when it comes to reality, there are more factors in play. It is possible that pre-defined, scripted supply chain models based on certain segmentation profiles might not even be relevant to the company's customers or products (Sabri, 2019).

As previously stated, the concept of supply chain segmentation is not new. The author observed several manufacturing, fashion, and retail companies which have multiple supply chain models, but most of them were developed out of necessity (reactive mode) with manual and inconsistent business practices.

Table 1. Summary of segmentation dimensions, profiles, and related SC model

Author(s)	Segmentation Dimensions	Profiles	Supply Chain (SC) Models
Fisher (2007)	Product	Innovative Products Functional Products	Efficient SC process Responsive SC process
Naylor, Naim, and Berry (1999)	Product & Production	High variability of products and related production High variability of products and related production	Lean SC Agile SC
Mason-Jones, Naylor, and Towill (2000)	Order Winner	Cost Service Level	Lean SC Agile SC
Lovell, Saw, and Stimson (2005)	Product	High product-value density Low product-value density	Centralized large-scale plants Decentralized close to customer plants
Christopher, Peck, and Towill (2006)	Demand & Lead Time	Unpredictable demand and short lead time Unpredictable demand and long lead time Predictable demand and long lead times Predictable demand and short lead times	Agile SC Leagile (postponement) Lean SC Lean (continuous replenishment)
Gattorna (2006)	Buying behavior	'Understand Me' – collaborative approach 'Be Consistent' – efficient response 'Demanding' – respond approach 'Surprise Me' – innovative solutions	Continuous replenishment Lean SC Agile SC Fully flexible SC
Roscoe and Parker (2013) – Case Study for Sport Goods	Product Demand Channel & Order Winner/ Value Proposition	Innovative, unpredictable & Online Innovative, high quality, unstable demand & specialist stores Price sensitive, predictable & sports generalist Fit, brand, stable demand & lifestyle generalist	Agile – Customization Agile Quick –Response Lean Continuous Replenishment

Therefore, there is an urgent need for a comprehensive and practical framework for supply chain segmentation. This should not only provide best practices in profiling and identifying different supply chain models, but also provide an end-to-end approach for implementing and sustaining segmentation and successfully leveraging digital technologies.

The Benefits of Supply Chain Segmentation

Addressing Today's Business Challenges

Executives and supply chain leaders face many challenges today in every aspect of their operations and enterprise integration. The following are the top ten challenges:

- The disruption to the supply chain due to tactical risks such as demand variability and day-to-day supply fluctuations, or catastrophic events like COVID, the Ukraine war, Florida hurricanes, etc.
- Companies need to be more customer-oriented while managing the supply chain cost (bottom-line) more efficiently. Companies have long known the importance of designing offerings to serve the needs of different markets and consumers but accomplishing this can be difficult given how

quickly customers' behaviors and expectations change. Also, more business to business (B2B) customers are expecting a business to consumer (B2C) experience.

- Information delay or latency, which creates the need for companies to design business processes that realize the information flow between business partners.
- Globalization intensifies the competition and makes the competitive advantage crucial.
- The increased complexity of supply chains including the need for tighter control, the growing complexity of managing information flows, SKU proliferation, channel complexity, and the increasing trends of 3rd party logistics.
- Long and unpredictable product life cycles. Rapid product innovation forces the product introduction cycle to be faster to react to the market needs and gain a competitive advantage.
- The shift from vertical integration to horizontal supply chains calls for more efficient and effective collaboration with suppliers and customers. The new trend is for companies to buy out competitors in the same business or merge with them instead of buying their suppliers (i.e., to expand vertically instead of horizontally).
- Expensive operating cost structures, especially when companies are facing intensified competition. Related to that is the increase in transportation costs due to outsourcing.
- Supporting the redesigned processes with leading edge technology that is easy to integrate, cheap to maintain, and fast to achieve results.
- Outsourcing and having suppliers across the world. Companies continue to outsource assembly work, information systems management, call centers, and product engineering to contractors. The challenge is to decide what to outsource, and how to make sure that customer satisfaction, delivery service, and quality are not compromised.
- The need to explore insourcing for certain clusters to improve responsiveness rate. More than a decade ago, many companies started moving their production operations to lower-cost countries. The industry is again on the brink of a major global shift. Various offshore cost advantages that once existed are beginning to erode. Wage inflation, tariff taxes, rising oil prices — even natural disasters — are among the factors affecting outsourcing supply chain profitability, agility, and risk. Several companies underestimated the offshore impacts of long lead times and high inventory carrying costs. They are discovering that maintaining service levels, in addition to the inventory and logistics buffering costs necessary to support the long-distance supply chain, far outweigh any labor cost advantages. In addition, outsourcing production introduces a latency lag in bringing new products to market and responding to market trends (Johnston, 2012).

To address the challenges mentioned above, companies should look for certain key enablers to implement in their operations (Sabri, 2019). Supply chain segmentation is one of these key enablers. Other enablers can be grouped as follows:

1. **Cross organizational collaboration**: This can improve efficiency, reduce quality risk, and streamline processes
2. **Customer-centricity & Agility**: This includes building flexibility into product designs and manufacturing processes to become more "customer-oriented" to mitigate the challenge of supply and demand uncertainty by providing the ability to change plans quickly. Flexibility in manufacturing is measured based on the ability to shift production load, change production volumes and product

mix, and modify products to meet new market needs. It is important to note that cost reduction initiatives usually inversely impact flexibility.

3. **Visibility**: Real-time visibility reduces uncertainty and enables the reduction of safety stock. This in turn drives down operational costs. Visibility also improves customer satisfaction, which increases revenue by presenting the real picture and providing the ability to proactively address potential problems. Finally, visibility reduces the impact of disruption to the supply chain caused by demand and supply variability and uncertainty.
4. **Process innovation**: This addresses the following questions: How can companies reengineer their processes to increase the speed of delivery when introducing new products? What supply chain process improvements and digital technologies should companies invest in to gain a competitive advantage? How can companies restructure their supply chains to reduce costs and increase profitability across their total global network? How can companies reduce their supplier base? How can companies leverage best in class technology to enable best practice processes?
5. **Risk Management**: This addresses the risks related to product quality and service delivery that arise from a global supply chain and the rush of new product introductions in addition to catastrophic events like COVID, hurricanes, and wars.

Segmentation is Impacting the Company's Bottom Line

As any manufacturer or retailer knows, no two customers are the same. Each customer's perception of the value of a product or service and how much they are willing to pay for it is different. This is true for almost every product category available in the market from cars to snack bars.

That said, many retail and manufacturing companies are still using 'one size fits all' supply chain processes: Over-serving some channel/product combinations and under-serving others Through in-depth understanding of the profit profiles of their customers, channels, and/or products, companies can tailor a more profitable supply chain strategy to each of them and thus increase the overall margin of their portfolios. For example, an apparel retailer can satisfy the demand for their basic products through an efficient (less costly) supply chain model and deliver their fashion products through a highly responsive supply chain model. This approach creates one model for standard (predictable) products and another for fashion (unpredictable) products. Each model will have different demand planning, stocking, and fulfillment policies.

In addition, supply chain segmentation would improve customer service, which would improve sales by increasing the reliability of delivering on promises and improving forecast accuracy.

Companies that successfully deploy a segmentation strategy will improve the reliability of their customer service while increasing profitability across their product portfolio through better alignment of supply chain strategies/policies to customer/product value propositions. These companies will also increase inventory turnover through inventory positioning and aligning supply chain assets to customer value propositions and profitability (Thomas, 2012).

FRAMEWORK FOR SUPPLY CHAIN SEGMENTATION TRANSFORMATION

The recipe for success in managing the journey of supply chain (SC) digital segmentation transformation is mastering the change transformation cycle, leveraging digital technologies, and ensuring effective

Figure 1. Supply chain digital segmentation transformation framework

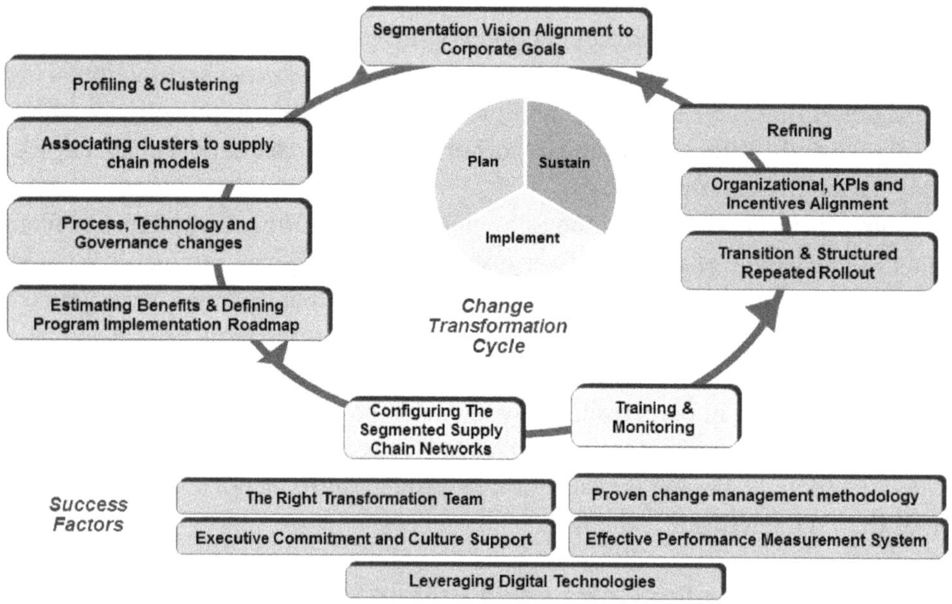

change management. Figure 1 introduces a practical and comprehensive SC segmentation transformation framework to help with implementation. This figure shows the 10-step transformation journey which typically lasts two to three years and consists of three phases: "plan" (five blue steps), "implement" (two yellow steps), and "sustain" (three green steps).

Planning starts by defining the vision and objectives and aligning them to corporate goals and needs. This is followed by profiling and clustering. Process analysis and associating clusters to supply chain models is next followed by identifying the changes in process, technology, and people required to support the new supply chain models and the new end state. The final step of the planning phase is building the business case (estimating benefits and costs) and defining the program implementation roadmap.

The "implement" phase starts by configuring the segmented supply chain networks and is followed by conducting training on the new processes and monitoring progress and adoption.

The "sustain" phase consists of three steps starting with transition and structured repeated rollout. This is followed by ensuring organizational, metrics, and incentives alignment and concluded by the "refining" step. The next planned transformation cycle can kick in after months of refining, corrective actions, and incremental improvement of the first cycle. Supply chain segmentation is not a one-time exercise or sprint; it is a journey. Five success factors are also emphasized in this framework to ensure the required support for the segmentation transformation program:

1. The right transformation teams
2. Culture support & executive commitment
3. Leveraging digital technologies
4. Proven change management methodology
5. An effective performance measurement system (PMS) which includes data availability, metrics, and KPIs

These success factors, in addition to the previously mentioned 10-steps, will be detailed in the coming section highlighting several best practices.

The 10-Step Supply Chain Digital Segmentation Framework

Step 1) Segmentation Vision Alignment to Corporate Goals

This step helps in clearly establishing how the supply chain segmentation transformation program is a crucial strategy to achieving corporate goals. This step includes developing the vision and objectives of the segmentation transformation initiative.

The key to supply chain segmentation is finding the right balance between agility and efficiency (lean) for each product/customer/channel combination. A one-size-fits-all strategy will not allow a company to compete on a global scale in today's business. Segmentation allows companies to get the right product/service with the right value to the right customer from the right distribution center while optimizing the supply chain.

Step 2) Profiling and Clustering

This step determines segmentation criteria, profiling, identifying customer value propositions, and clustering.

Segmentation Criteria

Companies need to determine the segmentation criteria that will fit their needs. The author would argue against a pre-defined segmentation criteria based on general literature or a specific case study. Existing literature and case studies are an excellent starting point, but they should not be the ultimate reference. Comprehensive segmentation criteria are presented in Figure 2 under each of the segmentation dimensions. Selected criteria are underlined to highlight examples that will be detailed later in this chapter.

- **Product Characteristics**
  - Product lifecycle stage
  - Shelf life
  - Functional or innovative
  - Handling characteristics
  - Product value density
  - Supply lead lime
  - Product variety
- **Customer Characteristics**
  - Demand volume
  - Margin
  - Demand variability
  - Large customers vs. small customers
  - Buying behavior (such as seasonal, planned, or spontaneous)
  - Customer lead time

- Strategic importance
- Service-level agreements (SLAs)

- **Channels**
    - Online (website)
    - Retailers
    - Warehouses
    - End consumers: business-to-consumers (B2C)
    - Business-to-business (B2B)
    - Geography

Figure 2. Segmentation criteria and related profiling list

AREA	Profiling
Product Characteristics	❖Lifecycle Stage ❖Shelf Life ❖**Functional or innovative** ❖Handling characteristics ❖Product value density ❖Supply Lead Time ❖Product Variety
Customer Characteristics	❖**Demand volume** ❖**Margin** ❖**Demand variability** ❖Large vs. Small ❖buying behavior ❖Customer Lead Time ❖Strategic Importance ❖SLAs
Channels	❖Website ❖Retailers ❖Warehouses ❖**End Consumers (B2C)** ❖**Businesses (B2B)** ❖Geography
Customer Value Proposition	❖Brand ❖**Lead Time** ❖**Cost** ❖**Availability** ❖**Flexibility** ❖**Delivery Performance (DP)** ❖After-sales service

Profiling

Once the segmentation criteria are determined, the company needs to document a portfolio of products, customers, channels, and related profiles based on detailed analysis. This analysis is typically more extensive than the analysis most companies would have carried out previously because in this step they are trying to predict the market conditions and customer (consumer or B2B customer) behavior that will prevail in the next three to five years, rather than examining how to best compete in the present time. Such forward-looking thinking requires extensive customer research and detailed marketing analysis. The aim is to understand the company's average customer and get a solid appreciation for each existing and potential customer type. It is not just customer profiling, it is product/customer/channel profiling.

Customer Value Proposition

Companies need to identify the customer value proposition by conducting customer satisfaction surveys and using business intelligence, market analysis reports, etc. This can also be accomplished by identifying the complexities that are present and identifying whether they are good complexities or bad complexities. Good complexities are those that improve the product or service and, most importantly, customers are willing to pay for. Bad complexities add no value and come at a price lie increased inventory or expediting.

Figure 2 provides a list of seven typical customer value propositions listed below:

1. Brand name
2. Lead time or speed
3. Cost (price)
4. Availability
5. Flexibility
6. Delivery performance (DP)
7. After-sales service

The company can select from the list based on the previously discussed analysis.

Clustering

The key for most companies who are interested in segmentation is to identify and better align to the natural tradeoffs that exist within their business. A simple but effective way to model this is by identifying the key customer value propositions that the customers apply to the company's business offering. These value propositions have natural trade-offs between them that allow the company to develop a differentiated supply chain response.

Segmentation allows companies to specialize and compete for all customers on their terms, rather than an average that appeases, but never delights (Mellins-Cohen, 2012).

In this activity, companies need to identify sets of clusters that best represent their business profiles and value propositions. Figure 3 provides a hypothetical example of profiling and clustering. In this example, a company selected 'Functional vs Innovative' as a profile parameter for the product characteristics segmentation dimension. 'Demand volume,' 'margin,' and 'demand variability' were selected under the customer characteristics dimension. In addition, B2B and B2C are the selected channels, and four customer value propositions (lead time, cost, flexibility, and delivery performance) are considered.

The next activity is to determine the clusters that best represent the selected profile parameters and value propositions. It is recommended to think big when creating this initial version and create clusters for as many profiles as possible that are relevant to the company. However, once the profile types are exhausted, it is critical to reduce them to the key few and bear in mind that each cluster probably represents a new supply chain design (model).

In the example in Figure 3, Cluster 1 represents innovative products and customers with low volume, high margin, and high demand variability (i.e., low forecast accuracy). Furthermore, this cluster represents B2C channel only. The value proposition for this cluster is reduced lead time (fast delivery), high degree of flexibility, and high delivery performance (on-time delivery). As shown in the figure, cost is not a decision-making factor.

Figure 3. Profiling and clustering approach with a retail example

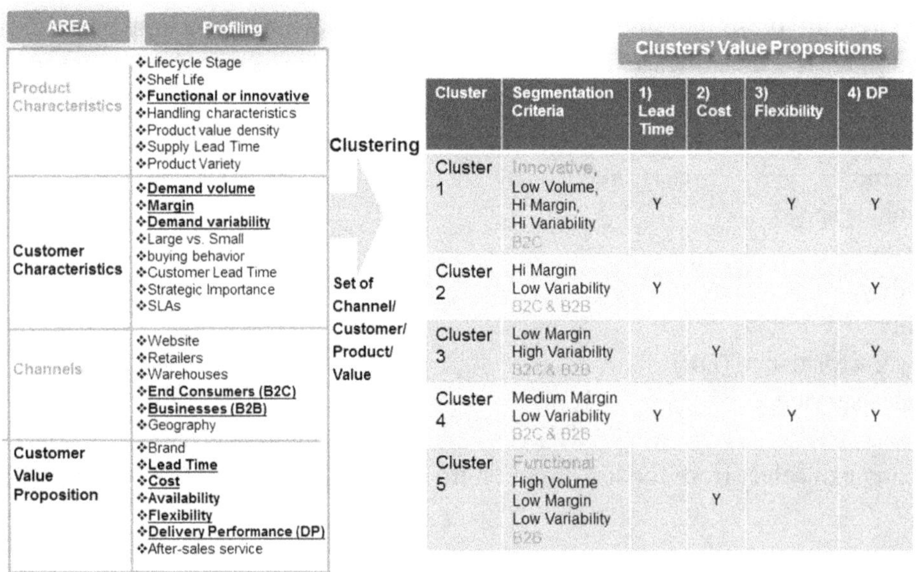

During this activity, it is often recommended to conduct a cost-to-serve analysis. The objective of this exercise is to understand which customer/product/channel combinations are winners and losers, and then to structure the clusters so that some or all the losers are turned into winners. For example, a large consumer goods company, with a significant portion of business coming from Wal-Mart, would likely have an assigned team and a set of strategies dedicated to that account. The high value of the Wal-Mart business warrants this level of premium service. However, the cost-benefit ratio (cost to serve) would not be positive if the same strategy is applied to every mom-and-pop store that also buys the same products. The company would need a different supply chain design for those customers.

In another example, the cost to serve a customer in the US for a US company will be different than the cost to serve a customer overseas. Estimating the cost to serve across extended supply chains requires visibility into many cost data elements. These can be enabled by digital technologies which are one of the key success factors for supply chain segmentation. This may require changing the replenishment model and service-level agreements for a specific customer/product combination. The author worked with a tire manufacturer to adjust its replenishment model to store products for customers (like Cluster 1) in the centralized and factory distribution centers (DCs) instead of storing them closer to customers in regional DCs. This moves the inventory buffer point upstream in the supply chain, reducing overall inventory. The upstream DCs hold a larger pool of inventory, increasing the odds that downstream demand will be filled with the required product.

Step 3) Associating Clusters With Supply Chain Models

When the clusters have been finalized, the next step is to decide what needs to be done to deliver each cluster's top value. It is time to design the supply chain models, and Step 3 is conducting process analysis and associating clusters to supply chain designs (models). The supply chain models will be driven by the unique value propositions of the clusters from the previous step. It is important to remember that the number of supply chain designs should be manageable. Most literature reviews suggest two or four models; the author typically recommends the number to be based on the business requirements and the company's capabilities in managing different supply chain models.

In Figure 4, five supply chain models are selected against five clusters. Column 3 covers the value propositions which put emphasis on lead time (responsiveness), cost, flexibility, and delivery performance (reliability). Let's assume that the key processes for supply chain management are supply planning, demand planning, procurement, and order fulfillment. For every key process, key strategies will be implemented to support certain value propositions.

For example, in Cluster 1 under supply planning, postponement (keeping inventory upstream in factories or central DCs) and flexible capacity strategies are selected since one emphasis (customer value proposition) of this cluster is flexibility. In this innovative, product-driven, and highly variable environment with a 'premium' type of customer, a 'postponement' manufacturing strategy is required. Under order fulfillment, air is selected as the main transportation mode since the other emphasis is on lead time reduction. The customer is given the benefit of choice, and a fast and flexible-focused supply chain is required to fulfill their requirements. In addition, working closely with customers when generating the forecast is a best practice strategy to control demand variability.

A multi-sourcing procurement strategy will be needed to provide flexibility in case of supply shortages for nonproprietary parts. Also, capacity contracts with key suppliers will need to have flexibility built in and delivery routes will need to be faster and more agile. As a result, the lower volumes of these innovative products will command increased prices due to higher cost and differentiated service. These additional costs should not be a customer barrier since this supply chain is designed around the customers who are willing to pay for it.

Cluster 5 targets purely cost-driven customers. The route to address 'lowest-cost' emphasis is often an efficient supply chain. This supply chain uses 'lean' concepts to streamline and eliminate waste from the process, implements a build-to-stock manufacturing supply strategy since demand variability is low for this cluster, and positions inventory closer to the customers due to high volume. In addition, advanced planning like forecasting enables high forecast accuracy, allowing things to be booked far in advance and for suppliers and logistics companies to plan for optimization. Offshore manufacturing capacity and

Figure 4. Associating clusters to supply chain models approach with an example

			Supply Chain Processes' Key Strategies			
Cluster	**Supply Chain**	**Value Propositions**	**Supply Planning**	**Demand Planning**	**Procurement**	**Order Fulfillment**
Cluster 1	Supply Chain (SC)A	1, 3, 4	• Postponement • Six Sigma to control variability • Flexible Capacity	• Customer Collaboration	• Multi Source	• Air
Cluster 2	Supply Chain B	1, 4	• Build to Stock • Stored in Regional DC	• Demand Shaping	• Buffer stock • VMI	• Cross Docks
Cluster 3	Supply Chain C	2, 4	• Build to Order • Direct Ship	• What if Analysis	• Flexible Contracts	• FTL for B2B
Cluster 4	Supply Chain D	1, 3, 4	• Stored in Centralized Warehouse • Near shore capacity	• POS Forecasting	• Bulk buys • FTL for inbound material	• Expedites
Cluster 5	Supply Chain E	2	• Inventory stored closer to customers • Lean for streamlining • offshore capacity • Build to stock	• Statistical forecasting with exception driven adjustments	• Blanket PO with locked annual QTY	• Ocean & Rail with no expedites

SC A = Responsive & Flexible Supply Chain; SC B = Responsive Supply Chain; SC C = Efficient & Reliable Supply Chain; SC D = Efficient & Flexible Supply Chain; SC E = Efficient Supply Chain

slower, cheaper routes — such as ocean — can also be used, allowing the company to reduce costs and provide the best price for the customer in this cluster.

By working with various clusters — combinations of customer types, channels, products, and value propositions — to identify their requirements and tailor their supply chain, companies can optimize their capabilities and improve the bottom line.

Step 4) Identifying Process, Technology, and Governance Changes

The segmented supply chain strategy requires process, technology, and governance changes to demand planning, supply planning, procurement, and order fulfillment processes. In doing so, even though physical supply chain resources could remain the same, the supply chain response operates differently from one supply chain model to another and from one cluster (segment) to another.

It is important to complete a detailed, future-state process map after supply chain models are approved by key stakeholders. A value stream mapping method can be leveraged to understand the cost drivers and come up with a more granular design of the future state. It is crucial to capture process, technology, and governance (organizational structure, metrics, and policies) changes and capabilities for every supply chain process that enables implementing the proposed strategies for every supply chain model in the previous step.

Companies have long struggled to deploy segmented supply chains because underlying decision support (planning) technologies have not been readily available for end-to-end supply chains. This has changed recently, with accessible technologies making it easier for companies to go through the segmentation journey.

To summarize, the segmented supply chain strategy requires process, technology, and governance changes to demand planning, supply planning, procurement, and order fulfillment processes. In doing so, even though physical supply chain resources could remain the same, the supply chain response operates differently from one supply chain model to another and from one cluster (segment) to another.

Figure 5 reflects an example from a real manufacturer. These are the changes that were required to support a supply chain design like Supply Chain A from Figure 4 (Responsive & Flexible Supply Chain).

Under demand planning, the manufacturer needed to implement a customer collaboration strategy which would require a process change of modifying the forecasting process to include the customer input, a technology change to enable a collaboration workbench leveraging digital technologies, and two people-related changes. The first people-related change was an organizational structure fine tuning which formed a decentralized Demand Planning Group to be closer to the customer and corresponding salesperson. The second people-related change was adding customer forecast accuracy to the set of existing metrics to establish accountability within the customer forecast.

The manufacturing company can no longer forecast demand based on past sales history alone. The segmented strategy will require market intelligence on similar products and markets along with close collaboration with marketing and sales personnel to get customer input. The cluster (product/customer/channel) under this supply chain design (model) would need to be tracked differently to monitor market acceptance and utilize more frequent feedback cycles relative to other clusters in the company's portfolio.

Figure 5. Example for identifying process, technology, and governance changes

Key Process, Technologies and Governance Changes for Supply Chain A

	Supply Planning	Demand Planning	Procurement	Order Fulfillment
Process	• Profiling Customer Lead Time • Establish a sub-process for demand prioritization	• Modifying the forecasting process to include the customer input	• Establishing a process and criteria to split the sourcing demand by the vendors	• Establish a process for allocation
Technology	• Implementing Inventory Optimization Tool	• Enabling a collaboration workbench	• Enhancing the supplier portal to provide real time visibility for in-transit inbound material	• Supporting different modes of transportation • Enabling order promising based on allocation
Governance	• Establishing Center of excellence to supervise 6 Sigma initiatives	• Decentralized Demand Planning Group • Adding customer forecast accuracy to the set of existing metrics	• Adding supplier flexibility metric to the supplier scorecard	• Establishing a long term agreement with UPS and DHL

Under the supply planning process, demand prioritization needed to be adjusted to increase the planning priority associated with this cluster since the margin was high and supply lead time was a competitive differentiator (customer value proposition). Profiling the expected lead time by customers is important in deciding if a replenishment postponement strategy (such as build-to-forecast to a semi-finished stage and assemble-to-order thereafter) could be enabled for this cluster.

Under order fulfillment, a substantial emphasis was put on allocation planning and order promising sub-processes. As the company strove for margin growth, the finished goods supply needed to be allocated more heavily toward this cluster. The company needed to adjust its allocation policies. Additionally, higher service levels for this supply chain model required faster replenishment. This often meant smaller, more frequent shipments which raised transportation costs. Careful planning of the shipments associated with this cluster, including load consolidation, mode selection, routing, and carrier selection, could significantly reduce transportation costs while ensuring high service levels. Establishing a long-term agreement with carriers was recommended to handle expedited high-value products effectively in this cluster.

Finally, under the procurement process, establishing a process and criteria to split the sourcing demand by vendors was necessary to provide flexibility and address the risk of shortage in raw material and components. Investment in technology to provide real time visibility for in-transit inbound material was required to reduce lead time variability and enable the company to react faster to delays.

Segmentation-based supply chain processes have helped this manufacturer balance value to the business against the service levels required to support corporate goals for their strategic products (Cluster 1).

Step 5) Estimating Benefits and Defining the Roadmap

Cost-to-Serve Analysis

The first activity of this step is to validate a "cost-to-serve" analysis against the new supply chain designs. "Cost to serve" analysis is very similar to Activity Based Costing (ABC). However, "cost-to-serve" must be much more granular because in virtual supply chain there will be shared assets that necessitate allocating costs differently since each virtual supply chain (supply chain design) must be managed differently. Various resources such as power, overheads, equipment, and technology costs must be allocated differently for each line according to usage. For example, premium freight service is used heavily for the Responsive & Flexible Supply Chain model which requires speed in delivery (short lead time) but is not used the Efficient Supply Chain. Therefore, no premium freight cost should be allocated to the Efficient Supply Chain. Currently, many companies assign all these resources to one area labeled as 'overheads,' but to execute the supply chain segmentation strategy effectively, they need to be separated. They also need to be analyzed more granularly to accurately estimate cost and price profitability. Based on the author's experience, getting finance involved early on during this step is crucial.

Capturing the Expected Benefits

The next activity is to estimate the benefits of every supply chain model and highlight the impact on key performance indicators' (KPIs) targets. During this phase, there is a need to: 1) identify the critical supply chain KPIs to grow the business and improve profitability, 2) capture an accurate baseline for each of these KPIs, and 3) explain how the new/updated supply chain models will impact the KPIs - positively (green color), negatively (red), or neutral (empty box) as shown in Figure 6. For example, supply chain A will get a hit from a supply chain cost perspective due to the use of Air as the main transportation mode, but this strategy will improve other KPIs like order cycle time.

It is important to mention that KPIs should be the same (applicable) for all supply chain designs; it is only the targets that change. Once these KPIs (such as SCM cost, cycle time, etc.) are established, average targets across all supply chain designs must also be agreed upon. These targets can be internal-based, industry–based, or competition-based. Then, KPIs targets are defined for each supply chain design based on the strategies that are being implemented with a goal of achieving the average targets across all of the supply chain designs. For example, the target for "Order Cycle Time" for an Efficient & Reliable Supply Chain will be lower than the average target. On the other hand, Responsive Supply

Figure 6. Different supply chain models impact KPI targets differently

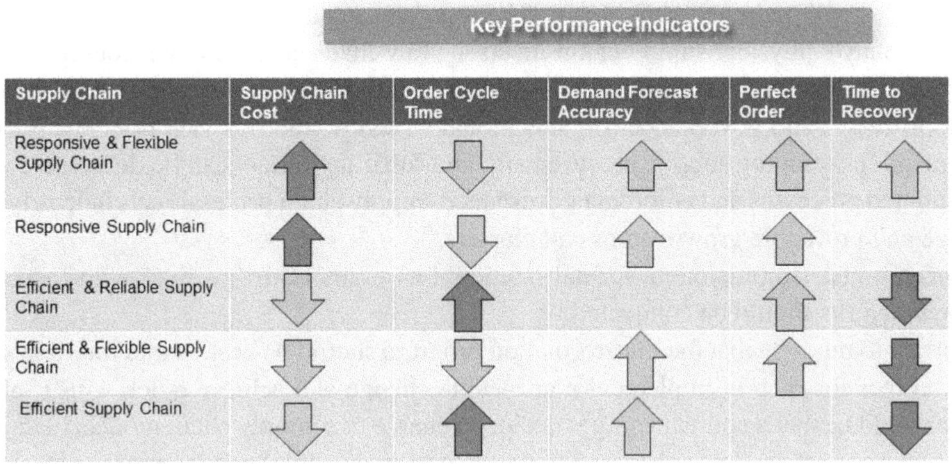

Chain is higher than the average target when it comes to supply chain cost KPI. To reiterate: Positively impacting one KPI might inversely affect others.

Building the Business Case

The next activity is to build the business case and significant ROI (benefits – costs) for executives to secure their buy-in on pursuing the supply chain segmentation journey.

To be able to conduct this activity successfully, the defined KPIs (as in Figure 6) should be aligned with corporate goals like increased margin, cost reduction, improvement in customer service, etc.

Building the Roadmap

The final phase of this step is to build the roadmap for the transformation program which should be broken into multiple phases (projects) with definitive outcomes for each to ensure manageable change. The idea here is to 'think big,' 'start small,' 'act quick,' and 'win fast.' No matter what your situation is, the journey to supply chain digital segmentation success is a radical ongoing overhaul of culture, process, organizational structures, technology, measurement framework, and operating models.

Senior management must approach supply chain digital segmentation as more than a single project. It must be approached as a transformation program and must become the new way of doing business.

Step 6) Configuring the Segmented Supply Chain Network

This step is the starting point for execution and implementing the supply chain digital segmentation strategy ('Implement Change' phase). It includes conducting detailed design and new process/technology deployment. As a best practice, it is recommended to use several pilots and implementation waves to "turn on" capabilities and strategies piece by piece to reduce risk and allow enough time for stakeholders to adopt the change. Advanced supply chain planning software applications should be in place as a prerequisite to support different virtual supply chains from a planning perspective. It is important to note that although a technology investment is not necessarily a requirement for supply chain segmentation, inadequate technology frequently surfaces as a concern in the segmentation process. Also, leveraging digital technologies will make segmentation much easier and scalable.

While a company's physical supply chain assets — raw materials, factory resources, warehouses, distribution centers, retail centers, and channels — are typically the same across all supply chain designs (models), its processes and governance (organizational structure, metrics, and policies) for predicting customer demand, positioning supply, procurement, and fulfilling orders can be different. In executing these differentiated processes and enforcing governance, supply chain professionals help drive competitive advantage and profitable growth across all clusters.

After configuration is complete, a formal readiness assessment to 'go live' with the new supply segmentation networks should be conducted.

It is important to reiterate that the transformation program should be broken into multiple stages with definitive outcomes for each to implement manageable change and achieve quick wins (Sabri, 2019). One example would be that a company might decide to enable two supply chain models in the first stage (which might take a year) and leave the last 3 to the second stage. Another example is to stack the stages based on the supply chain processes, like implementing the process, technology, and governances for the demand planning process in the first stage, followed by supply planning in the second stage, etc. This depends on the maturity of these processes and the size of changes. A third example would be to divide the process, technology, and governance changes into three groups: 1) 'crawl,' 2) 'walk,' and 3) 'run' and then stack the stages to implement "crawl" changes first, followed by 'walk,' and implement the remaining changes in the third stage. Some of the stages can overlap from a timing perspective and a coordinated timeline that highlights critical stop-gate dependencies can improve the efficiency of managing these initiatives (stages).

Step 7) Training and Monitoring

A structured and comprehensive education plan — starting with the transformation team and end users and ending with engaging key stakeholders and leaders — should be developed early and executed effectively as changes move through the organization. The plan should cover planning, implementing, and sustaining the segmentation transformation. This step is critical to ensure the effectiveness of the execution.

Additionally, the education plan for end users should be tailored based on which segment they work on. For example, enabling an "efficient supply chain" model requires strong knowledge of lean principles.

Monitoring is another phase of this step to ensure employee adoption of the new process of the segmented supply chain. It is important to proactively monitor the experience of the employees, suppliers, and customers to identify performance issues and provide additional training when needed. This will help sustain positive behavior by all stakeholders including supply chain leaders, managers, and planners.

Step 8) Transition and Structured Repeated Rollout

This step is the starting point for sustaining the new state of doing business ("Sustain Change" phase). During this step, the transformation team typically transitions to a different business team to take over the transformation initiative. The transformation team is responsible for planning and implementing the process, technology, and governance changes needed to support segmented supply chain strategy. The business teams (demand planning, supply planning, procurement, and order fulfillment teams), with the help of IT customer support, would take over to lead this step and the next two steps of making the changes part of the running of business environment.

During this step, a repeated rollout to other business units might occur based on the previously predefined roadmap for the segmentation transformation. Segmentation must be a living thing, with the ability to easily assign new products to existing clusters and eventually to existing supply chain designs (models).

Step 9) Organizational Structure, KPIs, and Incentives Alignments

Organizational Realignment

The first activity of this step is to ensure that organizational alignment (part of the governance changes defined earlier) is happening. The human resources department might need to update job descriptions and bonus structures to reflect the changes. This might require creating a pipeline of candidates for hiring with a mix of demand, supply, and product expertise. Also, incentives for the company's talent should be aligned with the skill requirements for the new process.

Incentive Alignment

The second activity is to ensure that the KPIs and incentives are aligned so each supply chain model can drive the right business decisions and behavior effectively. This requires a clear set of goals (targets for the KPIs) and incentives to be defined earlier during Step 5. Incentives, including bonuses, should always be based on the KPIs; getting the KPIs right allows the incentives to be altered to match, which will in turn stimulate behavioral change where it is required. For example, if salespeople are to provide input in the forecasting process, they will need an incentive (such as 20% percent of their bonus) to ensure that this is done in a way to which the supply chain organization can respond accordingly (i.e. no overestimating or underestimating). Equally, in terms of supply, the procurement team must be incentivized to work in line with the supply chain strategy — like total landed cost — rather than simply focusing on lowest-cost scenarios.

Cost and Benefits Data Gathering

During Step 2, cost allocation is determined for every supply chain model. This is needed to break down the shared overhead charges that have traditionally been spread equally across all products. This allocation is important to validate the cost-to-serve analysis and to estimate the cost and savings of a certain supply chain model. During this step (Step 9), the actual costs are captured and should be compared with the previous estimate. Also, the actual benefits would start to be realized and the expected business case (ROI) can be confirmed in this step.

Step 10) Refining

Fine-tuning profiles, clusters, and cost allocations are necessary as products move through their life cycles and demand shifts. Technology can be leveraged to move a product/customer/channel combination automatically from one cluster to another as the underlying attributes change. Revisiting and adjusting

KPIs targets are also needed to ensure a continuous improvement culture. A cross-functional governance monthly review cadence should exist, such as a monthly Sales and Operational Planning (S&OP) review. This will also allow the company to continually align with customer value.

The transformation journey is ongoing and not a one-time exercise; it is a multi-year journey which requires several cycles. Each cycle might take between two and five years. Refining is the last step in the cycle, during which incremental improvements and fine-tuning are done. Once the success criteria, expected benefits, and KPIs targets are achieved, a new transformation cycle should be considered. This is when the company goes from Step 10 back to Step 1 and repeats the cycle to achieve additional improvements and benefits. Changes to the business model and new opportunities such as an emerging market should also trigger another transformation cycle.

The 5 Success Factors for Supply Chain Segmentation

There are five key success factors required to ensure the successful implementation of supply chain segmentation as shown earlier in Figure 1.

Success Factor # 1: Having the Right Transformation Team

Having the right transformation team is crucial for the supply chain segmentation journey. Special skills should be considered when selecting the transformation team, such as process design and automation, lean principles knowledge, Six Sigma expertise, data analytics, systems optimization, program management, organizational influence, and communication skills.

Success Factor # 2: Executive Commitment and Culture Support

Supply Chain segmentation is not just a business initiative, it is a change to the culture. Executive commitment and visible support are key to success. For example, executives need to enforce the culture of customer-driven and differentiation, the culture of promising what you can deliver and delivering on every promise, the culture of commitment to continuous improvement as a way of life for the organization, and the culture of praising and promoting the managers who avoid fires (being proactive) versus promoting the fire fighters (being reactive).

Establishing a clear segmentation vision strategy enabled by digital technologies is so fundamental to a firm's future success that the CEO must inspire employees to pursue a vision of the company. However, many CEOs feel that segmentation is somewhat beyond their grasp. The CEO must step up and collaborate with the CMO, COO, and CIO to jointly create a vision that the CEO can sponsor.

Establishing "a differentiated supply chain response" culture, collaboration, agility, and digital innovation are second nature to employees in today's businesses. Therefore, its crucial fuel the differentiated response mindset by educating, training, and inspiring employees with roadshows and education programs.

Success Factor # 3: Leveraging Digital Technologies

Technology management teams must play a pivotal role in enabling digital transformation for supply chain segmentation. CIOs must champion a business technology agenda — investments in digital technologies to facilitate financial governance, capture KPIs, conduct cost-to-serve analysis, and collaborate with sales leveraging social media and research data to find out the value propositions for customers to win, serve, and retain them.

Let's give one use case as an example. Customers' perceptions of the value of a product or service and how much they are willing to pay for it is difficult to predict. On one end of the spectrum, you have value-conscious customers who are always looking for a deal. On the other end, you have customers that will only buy premium goods and services. The other issue is that customers' behaviors and expectations change. Therefore, many firms struggle to segment their customers and markets intelligently and provide tailored products and services to those segments on an ongoing basis. Using digital technologies like "machine learning" and predictive analytics can be leveraged to analyze customers by collecting data from thousands or even millions of customers. Mining the collected data and combining it with external data like social media will help keep pace with the analysis required to identify new correlations. This will help in identifying the segmentation criteria and making it dynamic.

Also, machine learning will enable firms to support different supply chain strategies/responses for each segment like higher visibility, simplifications, etc. Machine learning can support creating intelligent customer-product-channel segments and then developing supply chain strategies to deliver differentiated offerings to those segments—all while balancing the cost to serve each segment against the value that segment brings to the business.

Success Factor # 4: Proven Change Management Methodology

Having a structured and proven methodology to show the way in the change transformation journey is a must. Any supply chain transformation program creates uncertainty and resistance. New leaders emerge, job descriptions are changed, and new skills and capabilities need to be developed. Dealing with these change management issues on a reactive, case-by-case basis puts timeline, morale, and results all at risk. A structured plan for managing change—beginning with the transformation team and then engaging key stakeholders and leaders—should be developed early and executed effectively as changes move through the organization. The plan should be comprehensive to cover planning, implementing, and sustaining the transformation changes (Sabri, 2013).

For transformation programs to work, there must be convergence between the new process, new technology capabilities, people readiness with the required new skills, and organization structure alignment changes.

Success Factor # 5: Effective Performance Measurement System (PMS) – Data, Metrics, and KPIs

Comprehensive end-to-end measures of supply chain performance, such as total cost, inventory, forecast accuracy, and perfect order, must be established to show the trade-offs required. Supply chain performance results should be communicated to all layers. Operational and financial data will be needed at both aggregated and granular levels to analyze performance and conduct corrective actions.

The author has not come across many firms that could claim that they have mastered performance measurement across all their processes and levels. The widespread feeling among supply chain managers is that they measure too much, too little, or measure the wrong metrics. For the supply chain segmentation strategy to work, the culture of measurement should be anchored within the organization while leveraging some best practices such as: 1) focus on a handful of key KPIs and related metrics, 2) sustain KPI tracking, 3) conduct root cause analysis on a regular basis, and 4) align incentives to achieving KPIs targets. Finally, the list of the KPIs should be comprehensive enough to include related KPIs necessary to measure achieving the customer value propositions such as delivery performance and flexibility (Sabri, 2012).

In addition, data availability/accessibility is very important. It is considered a pre-requisite for supply chain segmentation because visibility to data such as customer requirements, demand, cost, materials, forecasts, product life cycle, revenue, and margin is required to drive the right decisions regarding segmentation during the planning and implementing phases.

Most supply chain leaders and executives understand the difference between "lean" and "agile" supply chain models. The first one seeks operational efficiency and cutting waste while the other focuses on responsiveness, flexibility, speed, and targeting higher service levels. The challenge for these leaders is knowing when to apply each supply chain model and how. Here is how Dell and Caterpillar addressed that challenge in the context of the above framework.

Case Study from Dell

Dell faced a challenge with its supply chain in 2008 when it realized that the highly responsive 'configure-to-order direct-to-consumer' supply chain that had made its online store the world's largest channel for personal computers sales no longer fit the needs of its new physical retail channel, its enterprise sales, or even its high-volume consumer products. Facing increasing pressure from emerging and revitalized competitors, Dell found its supply chain model was no longer the right fit for all aspects of its business, especially the emerging ones. For example, when Dell entered the retail channel, the company tried to use the same supply chain model as its online configure-to-order business. Because competition in conventional retail can be fiercer than its online channel and Dell's supply chain was not designed for lower cost, it was determined that Dell's 2008 supply chain model would not work well at the store level. Most retail orders are large and focused on fewer configurations compared to online orders.

Adding to this challenge, the company faced corporate and public sector customers who were looking for a complete and customized package for their IT needs. This required a different supply chain model than the one used for online customers (Simchi-Levi, Clayton, & Raven, 2012).

Dell had been in the top five of the Gartner Supply Chain Top 25 every year since it started in 2004, but demand for commoditized products, changes in customer channel preferences, emerging market growth, a more capable supply base, and globalization had challenged the one-size-fits-all supply chain model (Davis, 2010). Clearly, Dell needed to segment its supply chain and implement new supply chain models to serve new customers in new channels with new product types.

For the past several years, the company has been transforming its supply chain into a multichannel, segmented model, with different policies for serving consumers, corporate customers, distributors, and retailers. Through this transformation, Dell has moved up to the number two spot on Gartner's "Top 25 Supply Chains" list (Thomas, 2012). Dell's supply chain segmentation journey is summarized in the following section in the context of the segmentation framework explained in the previous section.

Segmentation Vision Alignment to Corporate Goals

Dell decided to create multiple supply chain models, each dedicated to a different segment of the PC industry and configured differently from a demand planning, inventory planning, production planning, and distribution planning perspective. But the models would be designed in such a way that the company could take advantage of synergies to reduce complexity and benefit from economies of scale (i.e. virtual supply chains with one physical supply chain).

Dell embarked on a three-year segmentation journey to achieve two of the corporate goals: improving margin and gaining market share in retail business.

Profiling and Segmentation

Dell started the profiling and segmentation step by determining how different groups of customers derive value from its products and services. The business-to-business (B2B) market demands predictability, speed, customization, services, and precision delivery. While the business-to-consumer (B2C) market wants multiple channel options, the ability to personalize niche products, low-price options, and devices that deliver content. Historically, Dell was organized by products and/or region (Davis, 2010). As part of globalization, Dell aligned organizations to customer value consistently across regions. Dell moved to the following segmentation dimensions to come up with the segmentation criteria: product characteristics, customer characteristics, and channel. Figure 7 shows the profiles that were selected to represent the majority of the business. During this step, customer value propositions were analyzed. Dell used historical customer data from contracts, survey results, and business intelligence (BI) data to begin

Figure 7. Selected profiles and clusters for Dell

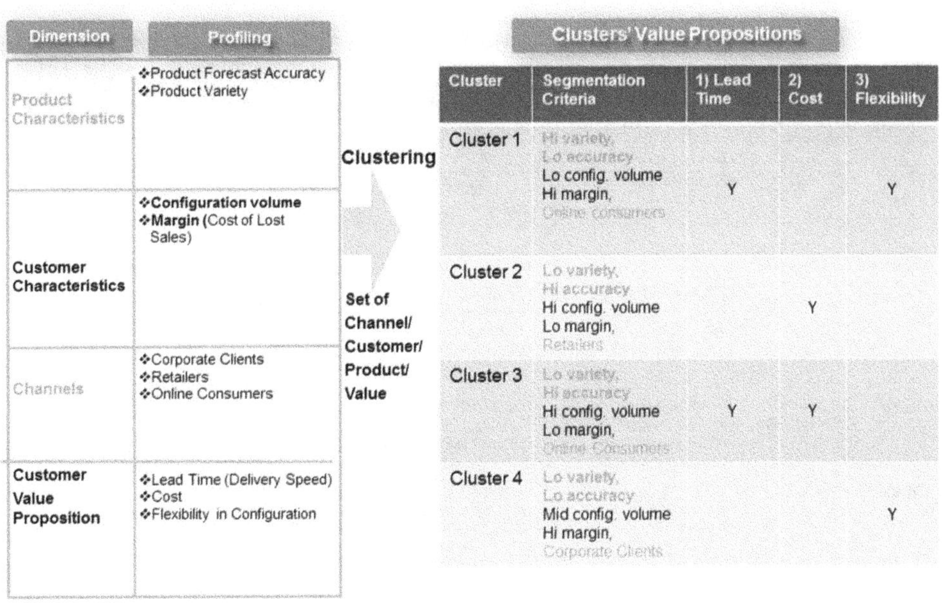

its exercise. To provide a robust, outside-in perspective, Dell invested in several resources to complete the detailed configuration profitability analysis, targeted surveys, and external marketing insights from multiple industries (Davis, 2010). Three customer value propositions were selected: 1) lead time, 2) cost, and 3) flexibility in configuration. Based on the segmentation criteria, four clusters were selected as shown in Figure 7.

Associating Clusters With Supply Chain Models

With a good understanding of selected clusters and the direction of the market, Dell began to design the new supply chain models by balancing the supply chain extremes of agility and efficiency. Dell used the 'voice of the customer' approach to identify the range of strategies it would require in different functions. The combination of these strategies created unique supply chain models. The company originally defined eighteen potential supply chain models simplified to six supply chain models. This resulted in models based on a mix of configurations predetermined by Dell and products configurable by customers (Davis, 2010). The six supply models were further consolidated into four supply chain models which have been referred to as Build-to-Order, Build-to-Plan, Build-to-Stock, and Build-to-Spec (Simchi-Levi et al., 2012). Since Dell is not using this exact naming convention for the supply chain models, the author refers to them as follows:

1. Responsive & Flexible Supply Chain
2. Efficient Supply Chain
3. Responsive & Efficient Supply Chain
4. Flexible Supply Chain

Figure 8. Selected supply chain models for Dell

		Supply Chain Processes' Key Strategies			
Cluster	Supply Chain Model	Supply Planning	Demand Planning (including Marketing & product Design)	Procurement	Order Fulfillment
Cluster 1	Responsive & Flexible SC	• Pull Replenishment • No finished goods inventory	• Configuration is defined by Customers • Statistical Forecasting for components	• Outsourced Assembly • Collaborative relationship with suppliers • Production batch size is 1	• Air • Direct ship to consumer
Cluster 2	Efficient SC	• Push replenishment • Inventory kept at retailers	• Small # of configurations identified for market • Collaborating on the demand plan (forecast)	• Outsourced Assembly • Large production batch size • leveraging volume scale to reduce purchasing costs	• Ocean • Direct ship to Retailers
Cluster 3	Responsive & Efficient SC	• Push replenishment • Inventory including safety stocks stored in centralized locations	• Small # of configurations identified for market • Statistical Forecasting	• Outsourced Assembly • Large production batch	• Ocean
Cluster 4	Flexible SC	• Pull Replenishment • No inventory	• Small # of configurations defined by corporate client • Tight collaboration with sales	• Outsourced Assembly • Large production batch	• Ocean • Direct ship to clients

In the first cluster shown in Figure 8, the interaction with online consumers and volume by configuration is low. As Dell offers to satisfy customers' value propositions of flexibility in defining the configuration and having short lead time for delivery, the focus of Dell is on higher margins and the cost of a lost sale is high. The supply planning strategy should be based on realized demand (sales order) or a pull strategy. This is the strategy that Dell uses in its traditional business. Dell employs a pull replenishment strategy where component inventory is managed based on forecast while sales order determines the final configuration. So, assembly is driven by the individual customer order and the production batch size is one. 'Direct ship' to the consumer and using 'air' as the main transportation mode are needed for fulfillment strategies to achieve a short lead time (high degree of responsiveness).

In 2008, as part of globalization, Dell began to heavily leverage its partner network of suppliers to perform assembly (outsourcing its assembly lines), which put more emphasis on strengthening relationships with suppliers to ensure a high level of quality and delivery performance with tracking capability. For this cluster, there is a need for assembly suppliers to master the production batch size of one.

The second cluster targets retailers and is associated with higher forecast accuracy, less product variability (configuration), and lower margin since retailers demand low prices to make money. This makes the traditional push-based replenishment strategy better because managing the supply chain based on long-term forecast lowers cost through economies of scale (high volume) and high forecast accuracy. In this supply chain model, procurement, assembly, and shipment decisions are all based on forecast. Extensive collaboration on the configuration and related forecast is expected between Dell and retailers. Ocean transportation mode is typically used to reduce cost.

Cluster 3 is defined for online end consumers who select popular configurations sold online. This cluster has limited configuration options (product variety) which increase forecast accuracy and call for a push-based replenishment strategy. In this supply chain model, popular product configurations are prepositioned in the supply chain network based on long-term forecasts, to provide a high response time (which is a customer value proposition). In this model, procurement, assembly, and ocean shipping to stocking points are all based on forecast, while shipment to consumers is based on sales orders using air for high response delivery.

Finally, a fourth cluster is defined for enterprise clients (corporates) where forecast accuracy is high and product variety is customized for individual corporations. The menu of available options offered to corporate clients has a longer product lifecycle with more overlap across generations of technology. This enables corporate clients to order the same configuration over a long period of time and lower their total cost of ownership. Because Dell has a close relationship with its corporate clients, forecast accuracy and volume are high (Simchi-Levi et al., 2012). Therefore, Dell uses the flexible supply chain model for this cluster. This model does not keep a finished goods inventory and products are assembled to sales order using components ordered well ahead of time, based on forecast.

In addition to adopting different strategies across different supply chain models, Dell adopted some best practice strategies to be the same across all supply chain models. The idea here is that one physical supply chain should be able to support several virtual supply chains. Some of the key common strategies are:

1. Procurement strategy to reduce purchasing cost by leveraging volume across the various supply chain models
2. Procurement/manufacturing strategy to outsource and consolidate manufacturing infrastructure
3. Product design strategy to standardize the components on the bill of material (BOM) across all supply chain models and reduce product portfolio

4. Order fulfillment strategy to use one physical infrastructure to support all supply chain models

Simchi-Levi et al. (2012) referenced an example where Dell took advantage of synergies in order fulfillment for the North American supply chain by using one infrastructure for all four supply chain models. Dell has U.S. fulfillment nodes in Atlanta, Chicago, Los Angeles, and New York and employs some of them in more than one supply chain model. In the online business where speed is critical, items are air shipped from manufacturing in Asia to the four locations in the U.S, and from there by parcel to customer locations. Retail is different. Because cost is the customer value proposition, products are shipped by ocean to Los Angeles and Chicago, and from there by truck to the retailers. However, for online consumers interested in popular products, items are shipped by ocean to North America and then trucked to two key locations (Los Angeles and Nashville) for shipping to individual consumers. This results in a simple logistics network that still meets the needs of a complex business.

Process, Technology, and Governance Changes for Dell

It is important to mention that one of the biggest challenges of segmentation is to coordinate the required changes across several supply chain processes to support different virtual supply chains.

Dell created a standard process to introduce new processes, technologies, and governance changes to enable the large range of supply chain strategies that were defined in the previous step. It has a dedicated center of excellence (COE) that collects requirements from sales, marketing, and operations, then evaluates the customer benefit and business strategy, and finally recommends the right changes within product development and supply chain design.

Critical factors to this effort were continuous improvement that utilizes lean methodologies to maintain a focus on customers' value and conducts benchmarking to provide an outside-in perspective (Davis, 2010).

Organizational realignment was a critical governance change to the new supply chain models. Dell went through this realignment in every aspect of their business, including product design, manufacturing, transportation, customer care, warranty, and technical support. Dell also simplified internal interactions by centralizing global operations and aligning to customer verticals.

Dell undertook a comprehensive transformation of the legacy technology that had only supported Dell's configure-to-order strategy. With the implementation of various supply chain models to support different customer segments, there was a need for technology to support large lot sizes and imply the existence of a finished goods inventory, something Dell had never considered before. As a result, the company needed to rethink its IT infrastructure so it could support multiple supply chain models.

Segmentation creates the need to develop a single process to allocate manufacturing capacity to different supply chain models and related clusters. This is sales and operations planning (S&OP) — one process applied across all supply chain clusters to align demand, supply, and inventory, and to allocate production capacity to the various supply chains based on actual and forecast demand.

Another process change benefiting mainly the "efficient & flexible" supply chain model was to simplify its product lines and market the most popular configurations. This simplification reduced costs and improved responsiveness through improved forecast accuracy. It also enabled the company to identify popular products which are good candidates to be produced in advance, prepositioned in the network, and offered online to consumers, thus enabling Dell to respond quickly to consumer demand (Simchi-Levi et al., 2012).

Implementation Roadmap for Dell Segmentation Transformation

Dell recognized that the scope of this transformation change would require a multiyear roadmap. The company set short-term project goals with specific benefits to show traction against the plan. Another key component of the implementation approach was to pilot segmentation capabilities manually, while designing the automated, scalable solution in parallel. Both strategies allowed quick wins to build momentum and mitigated risk during the transformation (Davis, 2010).

Refining and Evolving Journey

The result of Dell's supply chain segmentation was the creation of end-to-end supply chain models in which multiple capabilities can be arranged in unique designs to satisfy specific customer requirements. There was a need to sustain it and refine it to achieve the expected benefits. The key for Dell is that end-to-end supply chain segmentation is an ongoing, evolving journey. Improvement is never done, but rather continuously realigned to changing customer values.

Key Success Factors for Dell

Dell identified four critical success factors (Davis, 2010):

1. **The Right Transformation Team:** Dell identified 12 key work tracks (teams). Each had a VP sponsor, with small teams coordinating and program-managing the change. Specific skills for certain roles were required. For example, during the first part of the planning phase, the skills required were an outside-in perspective focused on customers, knowledge of market and other industries, end-to-end supply chain design. Then, for the second part of the planning phase, the skills required were process design, lean/Six Sigma expertise, data analytics, systems optimization, and process automation. Now, for the change management work stream, the following skills were required: Program management, organizational influence, and communication.
2. **Executive Sponsorship:** The supply chain segmentation strategy and potential benefits were shared with the entire executive leadership team to drive cross-functional buy-in. Dell's Vice Chairman was the sponsor of the effort throughout the transformation program.
3. **Unified, End-to-End Business Strategy for Culture Support:** The key to this strategy was the ability to clearly articulate and communicate the need for change, the vision, and the role of different organizations in the end state. To support this communication, several leaders started an internal blog to keep people up-to-date and engaged.
4. **Start with Customer Value:** Historically, customers were segmented by verticals (e.g., consumer, corporate, government, and small business) as well as regions. Dell had to look across an aggregated view of these existing groupings to identify shared values relating to product features and supply chain capabilities. A global view of customer value and KPIs was critical to this process. Dell wanted to balance customer metrics with operational metrics and achieve a Balanced Scorecard with clear accountability. In addition, data was essential. Visibility of customer requirements, demand, cost, materials, forecasts, product road maps, revenue mix, and multiple views to margin were required to drive the right decisions.

Achieved Benefits

Three years after starting the transformation program, Dell started to gain significant benefits. Product availability has improved 37%, and order-to-delivery times are 33% shorter. Dell now offers significantly fewer configurations resulting in a dramatic improvement in forecast accuracy by a factor of three. The tailored matching of transportation mode with the supply model led to a 30% reduction in freight cost for laptops and slashed manufacturing cost by 30% (Simchi-Levi et al., 2012). Dell also realized approximately $1.5 billion in operational cost reductions between 2008 and 2010. This transformation was a critical factor in that reduction (Davis, 2010). Key operational drives in this improvement were:

- Leveraging supplier capability and scale
- Addressing customers' value propositions,
- Simplified design and reductions in complexity
- Improved internal collaboration through collaboration across product design, supply chain, marketing, sales, and finance
- Improved forecast accuracy due to reduction in complexity and better connection to demand which resulted in a significant increase in forecast accuracy at the product, platform, and configuration levels

To summarize, Dell, which revolutionized both the computer industry and supply chain management with its direct-to-consumer business model in the 1990s, is one of several companies that are transforming their supply chains by leveraging supply chain segmentation and achieving significant benefits. Instead of using a one-size-fits-all approach to supply chain processes and policies, segmentation is helping these companies determine specific channels and customers that should be sourced from specific locations within their supply chains — and how these supply chains should be managed to profitably service all those clusters (Johnston, 2012).

Lessons Learned

Dell's situation is not unique. Many global companies underperform because of a mismatch between business needs and supply chain designs (models). Supply chain segmentation is increasingly necessary to compete in today's business and reverse poor/declining performance.

Supply chain segmentation strategies often result in manufacturers and retailers taking different value propositions to market to meet the needs of different customers while supporting corporate objectives. For instance, when pursuing market share growth for certain product-customer-channel combinations, manufacturers or retailers may need to adopt one supply chain model: Aggressive and dynamic pricing, high-product availability, and superior lead times. When looking to retain market share for other product-customer-channel combinations, the supply chain posture may be different: fixed pricing and competitive lead times.

FUTURE TRENDS

More companies are realizing that gaining a competitive advantage is no longer feasible when only optimizing their own resources without considering customers' needs and suppliers' capabilities. They need to get involved in managing all upstream organizations responsible for the supply, as well as the downstream network responsible for delivery and after-sales market. The challenge for companies is synchronizing supply chain processes (from product design and procurement to marketing and customer service management) to be more responsive to customer needs. The trend of mergers and acquisitions will continue to rise, and the complexity of supply chains will increase. This complexity will intensify the need for supply chain segmentation to streamline the process of collaboration between different entities and satisfy the value propositions for customers.

The author predicts the explosion of supply chain digital segmentation strategy implementation in the next few years. As companies redefine supply chain processes that span across suppliers and customers, there will be a need for segmentation that will significantly improve efficiency and help them achieve a competitive advantage. Companies that do not come on board will soon realize that they are losing ground and customers.

The widespread use of supply chain digital segmentation strategy will lead to new options for improving business-to-business and business-to-consumer collaborations, in addition to supply chain performance, monitoring, and controlling. Intelligent performance measurement systems that can capture negative performance trends and select the correct resolutions are expected to come into widespread use in the next few years. This will open new methods of integration between supply chain partners like system-to-system integration using web services (e.g. integrating one firm's inventory control system and another's logistics scheduling environment), the use of wireless devices, and the tight integration of front-end websites with the back-end systems of supply chain partners.

In the coming years, more and more companies will need to take the supply chain digital segmentation journey to deliver customer value propositions and gain competitive advantage and market share. Digital technologies will make the journey smoother and more effective. The future belongs to companies who can match their supply chains to the specific customers' needs, and therefore supply chain digital segmentation remains one of the key interests of supply chain leaders.

Segmentation criteria will be able to use structured and unstructured data (SNEW – social, news, events, and weather) and process large amounts of data. By leveraging ML / AI, it would be possible for ML to utilize self-clustering algorithms and create the segments dynamically in an automated fashion.

Whereas in the past, companies were limited to a few segments, supply chain designs would be increased beyond 2 or 4 segments. Digital technology would do the heavy lifting, ultimately leading to significant number of segments to satisfy customers' expectations and requirements.

CONCLUSION

Segmentation is gaining ground in manufacturing and retail, and the questions around it have evolved from "what is it?" to "how can we do it?," Supply chain digital segmentation is not a one-time exercise; it is a multi-quarter journey, but it does get easier after your first venture through the ten steps discussed as part of the proposed segmentation framework. Also, a structured assessment of the five success factors should be executed early on. Segmentation must be living and ongoing, with the ability to repeat the exercise. Segmentation is a continuous journey to keep your supply chain(s) relevant to your customer(s).

Supply chain digital segmentation is not just a business initiative; it's a change in the organization's culture. Therefore, executive commitment and visible support is mandatory to it's success.

Since segmentation often uncovers issues and gaps with current tools, technology is typically needed for the implementation. Leveraging digital technology makes the supply chain segmentation journey smoother and more effective. In absence of the right decision-support tools, segmentation strategies will not yield the expected benefits.

Supply chain digital segmentation strategy presents huge opportunities that are already being tapped by a few companies and supply chains who achieved significant benefits. Implementing supply chain digital segmentation strategy is key to gaining a competitive advantage, streamlining processes, reducing waste, and eventually achieving business agility which is significantly needed in the new age of globalization and intensive competition.

REFERENCES

Christopher, M., Peck, H., & Towill, D. (2006). A Taxonomy for Selecting Global Supply Chain Strategies. *International Journal of Logistics Management*, *17*(2), 277–287. doi:10.1108/09574090610689998

Christopher, M., Towill, D., Aitken, J., & Childerhouse, P. (2009). Value Chain Classification. *Journal of Manufacturing Technology Management*, *20*(4), 460–474. doi:10.1108/17410380910953720

Davis, M. (2010). *Case Study for Supply Chain Leaders: Dell's Transformative Journey Through Supply Chain Segmentation*. Gartner. https://www.gartner.com/doc/1468717/case-study-supply-chain-leaders

Fisher, M. L. (1997). What Is the Right Supply Chain for Your Product? *Harvard Business Review*, (March–April), 105–116.

Gattorna, J. (2006). *Living Supply Chains*. Pearson.

Johnston, D. (2012). The Shift to Reshoring. *Real Results Magazine*. http://www.jda.com/realresults-magazine/view-article.cfm?did=2867

Kartz, J. (2011). *Creating High-Value Supply Chains*. Industry Week. http://www.industryweek.com/companies-amp-executives/creating-high-value-supply-chains

Lovell, A., Saw, R., & Stimson, J. (2005). Product Value-Density: Managing Diversity Through Supply Chain Segmentation. *International Journal of Logistics Management*, *16*(1), 142–158. doi:10.1108/09574090510617394

Mason-Jones, R., Naylor, B., & Towill, D. (2000). Engineering the Leagile Supply Chain. *International Journal of Agile Management*, *2*(1), 54–61.

Naylor, J., Naim, M., & Berry, D. (1999). Leagility: Integrating the Lean and Agile Manufacturing Paradigms in the Total Supply Chain. *International Journal of Production Economics*, *62*(1–2), 107–118. doi:10.1016/S0925-5273(98)00223-0

Roscoe, S., & Baker, P. (2013). Supply chain segmentation in the sporting goods industry. *International Journal of Logistics*, *17*(2), 136–155. doi:10.1080/13675567.2013.837869

Sabri, E. (2012). Enduring Transformation: Performance measurement and governance make the difference. *APICS Magazine*. https://www.apics.org/apics-for-individuals/apics-magazine-home/magazine-detail-page/2012/10/04/enduring-transformation,

Sabri, E. (2013). Strategies for Supply Chain Transformation. *Supply & Demand Chain Executive Magazine*. http://www.sdcexec.com/article/11122122/companies-struggle-to-decide-when-and-where-to-begin-and-how-to-translate-their-vision-into-goals-goals-into-strategies-and-strategies-into-process-changes-and-projects

Sabri, E. (2019). Transformation Framework for Supply Chain Segmentation in Digital Business. In E. Sabri (Ed.), *Technology Optimization and Change Management for Successful Digital Supply Chains* (pp. 54–84). IGI Global. doi:10.4018/978-1-5225-7700-3.ch004

Simchi-Levi, D., Clayton, A., & Raven, B. (2012). When One Size Does Not Fit All. *Sloan Review*. https://sloanreview.mit.edu/article/when-one-size-does-not-fit-all/

Thomas, K. (2012). Supply chain segmentation: 10 steps to greater profits. *Supply Chain Quarterly*. https://www.supplychainquarterly.com/topics/Strategy/201201segmentation

KEY TERMS AND DEFINITIONS

Clustering: The process of associating and grouping very similar (but not identical) profiles that reveals patterns, trends, requirements, characteristics, relationships, and structures.

End-to-end Supply Chain: The philosophy of considering all value-added processes from supplier to customer and embracing the concept of eliminating middle steps and barriers to optimize the performance of supply chain.

Governance: Encompasses the establishment of organizational structure, metrics, & policies, and monitoring of their effectiveness.

Machine Learning: According to Wikipedia: Machine learning is a subset of artificial intelligence in the field of computer science that often uses statistical techniques to give computers the ability to "learn" (i.e., progressively improve performance on a specific task) with data, without being explicitly programmed.

Predictive Analytics: According to Wikipedia: Predictive analytics encompasses a variety of statistical techniques from predictive modelling, machine learning, and data mining that analyze current and historical facts to make predictions about future or otherwise unknown events.

Profiling: The process of learning information about behavior patterns, business characteristics, trends, requirements, relationships, and structures.

Supply Chain Digital Segmentation: Profitably managing different virtual end-to-end supply chains defined by a combination of channel/customer requirements, product characteristics, business value considerations, and differentiated supply response strategies leveraging digital technologies.

Transformation: The journey of taking an organization in a new direction and reaching an entirely different level of effectiveness. It is a change to processes, systems, structure, and culture.

Value Proposition: A concise statement to why a customer should buy a product of service or how it will add value. It should be appealing to the customers' decision makers.

Section 2

Optimizing Supply Chain Planning Processes Leveraging Digital Technologies

Chapter 5
Autonomous Integrated Business Planning

Salim Shaikh
Blue Yonder, USA

ABSTRACT

In the wake of the industrial revolution, the supply chain has been subjected to a linear evolution process over the course of the past four decades. However, companies today are operating in a new world, which presents new challenges. The digital revolution, which is characterized by innovations such social, news, events, and weather (SNEW) data, demand sensing, artificial intelligence (AI), machine learning (ML), amongst other things. Autonomous IBP involves a closed-loop continuous process, in which various internal and external stakeholders come together in a formal structured process to create an integrated company game plan. It has the ability to ingest real-time signals (from the digital edge via SNEW data and competitor promotions, as well as from physical assets like smartphones, sensors, radars, and satellites), provide predictive visibility to warn or sense a disruption before it happens, and then leverage prescriptive analytics to manage the unpredictable through risk mitigation plans.

INTRODUCTION

In the wake of the industrial revolution, the supply chain has been subjected to a linear evolution process over the course of the past four decades. This process has included material requirements planning (MRP), manufacturing resource planning (MRP II), distribution requirements planning (DRP), vendor managed inventory (VMI), collaborative planning, forecasting and replenishment (CPFR), sales and operations planning (S&OP) and integrated business planning (IBP). As supply chains evolved, these improvements were successful and appropriate. However, companies today are operating in a new world, which presents new challenges. The digital revolution, which is characterized by innovations such social, news, events, and weather (SNEW) data, demand sensing, artificial intelligence (AI), machine learning (ML), amongst other things, has shaken the very foundation upon which the supply chain is built.

Due to an increase in mergers and acquisitions, omni-channel conflict, direct-to-consumer channels, rapid proliferation of product configurations, shrinking product lifecycles, and market volatility, the supply

DOI: 10.4018/978-1-6684-7298-9.ch005

chains of the 21st century are becoming exponentially more complex. The globalization culture of "buy anywhere, make anywhere, and sell anywhere" has its advantages in terms of the ability to source the highest quality raw materials from all over the world, produce goods in the most cost-effective locations, and then sell those goods to customers in every corner of the globe. On the other hand, globalization is accompanied by a number of unfavorable effects, including an increased risk of natural disasters, labor unrest, tariffs, currency fluctuations, geopolitical situations, litigation, and trade sanctions. As a consequence of this, there is a tremendous amount of pressure to reduce the risks associated with the supply chain, and the possibility of business disruption or failure is becoming an increasing concern for global companies. The limitations of globalization have been brought to light as a result of recent political, environmental, and economic occurrences such as tariffs, the Brexit, trade wars, COVID-19, flooding in Thailand, and the geopolitical instability in the Middle East (Sabri and Shaikh, 2010). For many years, lean manufacturing has been an essential component in the ongoing effort to enhance the effectiveness of supply chain operations. Companies are able to improve their inventory levels and asset utilization as well as supply goods more quickly and at lower costs when they streamline their traditional supply chains to the greatest extent possible.

However, simply being lean is not sufficient anymore, and the global COVID-19 pandemic has shown that entirely lean networks have serious flaws that need to be addressed. The pandemic has recently revealed to a great number of companies that their supply chains are not only too fragile but also not robust enough to react to the extreme variations in demand and supply that have been caused by the pandemic.

The leaders of businesses in the supply chain need to reevaluate the cost of risk in light of the impending arrival of a second wave of coronavirus and make investments in operations that are nimble, efficient, and resistant. This means being able to meet the demand of customers with a supply chain that is intelligent enough to proactively identify problems, robust enough to withstand disruptions, agile enough to react swiftly to changes in the market, and efficient enough to improve the productivity and costs of planners.

In the aftermath of COVID-19, the companies and organizations that will emerge victorious are going to be the ones that have managed to strike a healthy balance between their supply chains' levels of efficiency and their capacity for resilience.

Additionally, customers of today are becoming more demanding of a personalized, consistent, and unified experience across all touchpoints, including retail, mobile, and online. Organizations need an autonomous integrated business planning (IBP) process that has the ability to act with speed, agility, responsiveness, and flexibility, leveraging machine learning and artificial intelligence for predictive and prescriptive analytics, and, as a result, enabling organizations to realign their plans quickly through a continuous closed-loop replanning process. This will allow organizations to serve a diverse spectrum of customers, products, markets, and channels while at the same time doing so in a win-win profitable manner. AI and ML help people understand the patterns behind the data, and they can leverage those insights to redefine and reimagine an organization's demand planning, master planning, inventory planning, and IBP processes for competitive advantage. This is because AI and ML now transcend human computational intelligence across many fields (Sabri and Shaikh, 2010). Prescriptive and predictive analytics allow for proactive automation and improvement of recommended actions for the future by storing the efficacy of planners' historical actions and using this data. In addition, businesses need to have capabilities for exception management, which will enable them to prioritize their responses to current and predicted disruptions based on the severity and impact of those disruptions, as well as run real-time what-if scenario analysis utilizing insights in order to gain a better understanding of the tradeoffs involved. Collaboration in real time with trading partners will be of great assistance to businesses in resolving exceptions and putting decisions into action across the supply chain and the extended network. Therefore, autonomous IBP is infused with AI, which enables it to analyze previously implemented supply chain strategies and data in order to identify the factors that contribute to failed supply chain operations. Using this information, one can forecast potential issues with the supply chain in the future and either proactively prescribe or independently carry out solutions. This will enable organizations to make decisions more quickly and more effectively, which will result in superior experiences for customers and a significant advantage in the marketplace.

BACKGROUND

What Exactly is Autonomous IBP, Though?

Autonomous IBP involves a closed-loop continuous process, in which various internal and external stakeholders, including sales, marketing, development, operations, sourcing, finance, and trading partners, come together in a formal structured process to create an integrated company game plan. This plan reconciles the views of all functional areas while at the same time making sure that this plan is in alignment with the strategic business plan. The IBP process needs to leverage SNEW data in order to get a real-time pulse of the market and connect with customers and clients in today's fast-paced, media-driven world (Sabri and Shaikh, 2010).The volume, velocity, and frequency of data have all seen significant increases as a result of the integration of IoT and big data into supply chains. It is becoming increasingly important for businesses to be able to see, analyze, and act on information across the supply chain in real time. Companies should also learn from their previous experiences to become better at sensing and responding to supply chain risks and opportunities. An autonomous IBP process has the ability to ingest real-time signals (from the digital edge via SNEW data and competitor promotions, as well as from physical assets like smartphones, sensors, radars, and satellites), provide predictive visibility to warn or sense a disruption before it happens, and then leverage prescriptive analytics to manage the unpredictable through risk mitigation plans (Sabri and Shaikh, 2010). These capabilities can be found in an autonomous IBP process. If a company is not agile and is unable to respond to disruptions in the supply chain or volatile market conditions, then demand will exceed supply, which will result in decreased customer service, increased expediting costs, and additional overtime. In a similar vein, if there is more supply than there is demand, this will result in surplus inventories, product obsolescence, decreased prices, and sales. Therefore, it is essential for the success of any company to exercise control over and effectively manage the impact of variability.

In the past, companies were able to solve problems caused by siloed planning by throwing inventory, capacity, and planners at them. However, in today's world of narrowing profit margins and cutthroat competition, where profitability is of the utmost importance, this strategy will no longer be sustainable. The following Lean and Agile Value Chain Chain Management (LAVCM) guiding principles were presented by Sabri and Shaikh (2010) in their book "Lean & Agile Value Chain Management (LAVCM): A Guide to the Next Level of Improvement." Autonomous IBP makes use of the same foundational principles and enhances them with the ingestion of real-time signals to provide predictive visibility using AI and ML to warn or sense a disruption before it occurs. After that, it makes use of prescriptive analytics to manage the unpredictable through risk mitigation plans (Sabri and Shaikh, 2010). As a result, Autonomous IBP is a game-changing differentiator that propels growth in both revenue and market share.

GUIDING PRINCIPLES OF AUTONOMOUS IBP

Principle 1: Focus on customer success. This principle places an emphasis on aligning and synchronizing the efforts of the entire organization to fulfill the requirements of the customers. This includes moving away from a focus on a product or channel and instead focusing on the most important reason for having supply chains, which is to satisfy customer demand; understanding the changing needs of customers across different markets and improving visibility into changing customer demand; and ingesting digital data signals into your Autonomous IBP process in order to be able to respond more effectively to the changing needs of customers (Sabri and Shaikh, 2010).

Principle 2: Create a win-win and trusted environment for all stakeholders. The second guiding principle is to establish a trustworthy environment that benefits all parties involved. According to the author's personal experience, in most cases, only a small percentage of the stakeholders are in agreement that their existing key performance indicators (KPIs) are driving the appropriate behaviors. This is due to the fact that many organizations make use of metrics that will invariably make the organization and its people appear positively. This is mainly due to the fact that the bonuses and promotions of various stakeholders are typically linked to the outcomes that are measured in terms of "feel good" performance metrics. For example, in the field of sales, it is quite common for a practice known as "sandbagging" to occur, in which a sales executive will have a lower forecast toward the end of the year when his quota for the following year is getting finalized, which is then immediately followed by an increase in his forecast at the beginning of the following year to make sure that he has enough supply to meet his quota. This principle encourages organizations to look beyond local, compartmentalized performance metrics and instead focus on an organizational performance measurement system that generates a win-win situation for all stakeholders while at the same time being in alignment with the business plan. Autonomous IBP is a cross-functional process, and this principle encourages organizations to look beyond local, compartmentalized performance metrics. This includes choosing the right things to measure, which are those aspects of organizational performance that are both controllable and important in achieving the success of the enterprise and developing an organizational culture and value system that encourages the use of metrics so that they become ingrained in the organization's very fabric (Sabri and Shaikh, 2010).

Principle 3: Eliminate waste and reduce non-value-added activities. This principle encourages businesses to become operationally efficient and lean by eliminating wasteful activities, which in turn frees up resources that can then be focused on value-added activities such as collaborating with one another and coming up with what-if scenarios for risk mitigation. For instance, by leveraging technology and standardizing processes, stakeholders can spend more time on solving real-world problems, thereby turning Autonomous IBP into an executive decision-making process rather than a wasteful activity consisting of simply collating data from multiple places and making it a reporting exercise. This is in contrast to the traditional method of IBP, which consists of simply collating data from multiple places and making it a reporting exercise (Sabri and Shaikh, 2010). The state of technology has advanced to the point where it is now possible to use ML to automate the storage of outcomes and the institutionalization of resolution workflows in order to solve pervasive and persistent problems.

Principle 4: Institutionalize continuous improvement. Institutionalizing a disciplined, structured, and repeatable Autonomous IBP process on a repeatable cadence that rewards continuous improvement and management by exception is something that should be done so that it can become ingrained in the organization's DNA..

Principle 5: Close the loop between planning and execution. Close the loop that connects planning and execution. That is the fifth principle. This principle places an emphasis on a "one-number" plan that the entirety of the organization strives to achieve through continuous closed-loop, vertical integration between strategic, tactical, and operational planning. This integration also links the Autonomous IBP process to annual budgets and daily execution. In the last few decades, markets have become more volatile, and supply chains have become more vulnerable to risk. The need for increased agility in business is a direct reaction to the instability of the global economy (Sabri and Shaikh, 2010).

The technologies of machine learning and artificial intelligence can be utilized to facilitate automation and agility, as well as to reduce risk by performing rapid prescriptive and predictive what-if scenario analysis. In addition, organizations are able to become more flexible, agile, and responsive when they position suitable capacity and inventory buffers and engage in multi-sourcing to protect themselves from the effects of uncertainty

Figure 1. Maturity levels

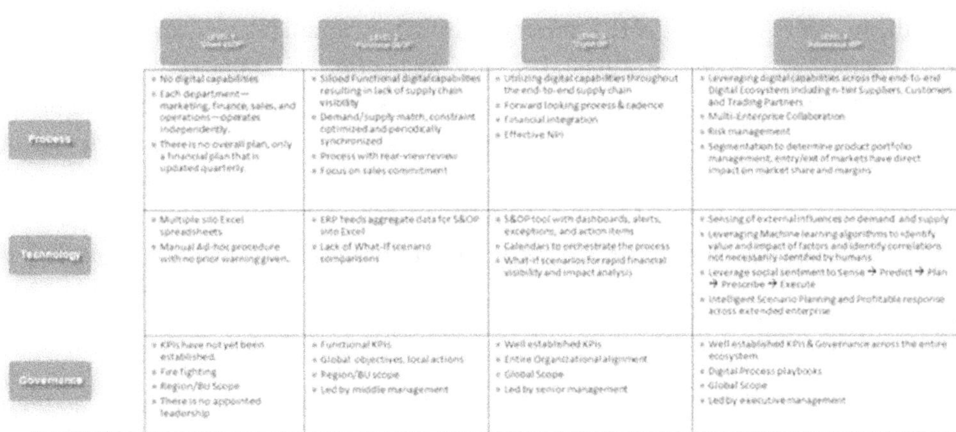

MATURITY LEVELS

A recent survey on IBP practices was carried out across a broad spectrum of industries, including discrete manufacturing (high-tech, semiconductor, auto, industrial, metals, diversified manufacturing, and aerospace and defense), as well as process manufacturing (chemical, consumer packaged goods, pharmaceuticals, and food and beverage). A number of the most important findings from the survey highlighted the fact that more than fifty percent of the companies were still utilizing technology based on spreadsheets to orchestrate their IBP procedures. Spreadsheets based on Excel are useful for displaying data, but they are incapable of providing the support required for what-if scenarios, data aggregation, and analysis across multiple plans. The respondents also highlighted that some of the key challenges in their current

IBP processes included a lack of suitable technology to provide end-to-end visibility and transparency, conduct what-if scenario analysis to explore trade-offs and formulate risk mitigation strategies, as well as an inability to link plans from different stakeholders and a lack of executive sponsorship. In addition, the respondents also highlighted that some of the key challenges in their current IBP processes included a lack of executive sponsorship (Sabri and Shaikh, 2010). Nearly ninety percent of respondents identified achieving effective cross-functional team alignment as one of the most significant challenges facing their organizations. Other important functional requirements that were brought to light include process orchestration through the use of calendars, plan visibility across a variety of stakeholders, and the capability to aggregate and disaggregate data across a variety of levels in the hierarchy.

Even though the majority of businesses are participating in IBP in some capacity, they are not realizing the full potential benefits because they are either operating at Level 1 (Pre-Digital S&OP) or, at the very most, at Level 2 in terms of the process maturity scale (Digital Functional S&OP). At the beginning of the year, these businesses typically create budgets for their expected levels of revenue and profit. However, at some point during the year, a disparity begins to appear between these budgets and actual levels of revenue and profit. The most frequently asked question is, "Will we be able to stay within budget? How will we make up the difference?" There is still the hope and the reassurance that the company will be able to get back on track and close the gap before that point. But sooner or later, both reality and panic set in, and then the question becomes, "How can we cut costs to meet our budget?"

Improving the already established IBP process and progressing to higher levels of maturity is not a one-time event; rather, it is a process that must be carried out over the course of a long period of time. In most cases, the maturity level of the IBP process within the organization is evaluated "as-is," and any existing gaps are uncovered. After careful analysis and inspection, an improvement plan is developed to lead the organization on a step-by-step journey to higher stages of "to-be" process maturity, ultimately culminating in Level 4 (Autonomous IBP), the highest level of IBP process maturity and excellence. This plan is designed to elevate the organization to Level 4 (Autonomous IBP), which is the pinnacle of IBP process maturity and excellence. Organizations that are looking to advance to higher levels of IBP maturity can make use of the maturity model as a guide to help them get there.

1. Level 1: Siloed S&OP

At the Siloed S&OP level, the supply chain does not have any digital capabilities, so there is no way to improve its end-to-end or functional performance. It is characterized by different stakeholders operating in silos, being entrenched in the process of resolving day-to-day priorities, constant firefighting, and knee-jerk responses to issues without any assigned leadership. Every department has its own ad hoc manual processes and its own version of the plan, and decisions are made as an independent functional group (Sabri and Shaikh, 2010). This results in a large number of activities that do not add value, which is contrary to Principle 3 of the organization (Eliminate waste and reduce non-value-added activities). The only plan that is in place is one that looks at the finances on a quarterly basis. There is a lack of visibility because signals of demand and supply are transmitted through nondigital mediums such as electronic data interchange (EDI), the telephone, or the fax machine. The S&OP process is fraught with difficulties because it requires using a "over the wall" approach to communicate between the various steps of the S&OP process. In addition, there is a lack of standardization of business processes throughout the organization, which means that each department has its own approach to completing tasks. This violates Principle 4 because it causes unnecessary duplication of effort and leads to redundant work

(Institutionalize continuous improvement). There are no KPIs established at any level, not even at the departmental level, and there is no ownership of the plan, which frequently leads to a game of blame and pointing fingers..

2. Level 2: Functional S&OP

Functional S&OP is characterized by siloed digital capabilities and the absence of a common end-to-end supply chain focus. Because each department focuses on its own operational efficiency, priorities, and goals, what ends up happening is that these things take precedence over what the customer wants, which is in direct opposition to Principle (Sabri and Shaikh, 2010). 1. (Focus on customer success). Even though demand signals may be collected digitally through customer portals or EDI, the organization of the supply chain is still siloed, which means that digital demand signals are not shared across the supply chain to produce an integrated supply response. This prevents an integrated supply response from being created. Similar to the previous point, supply signals are not fully shared consistently with the other functions of the supply chain, which results in a lack of end-to-end supply chain visibility. In many cases, businesses may be very effective at planning their sales, operations, and finances; however, the issue is that these planning processes are not connected. The end result is a plethora of plans that are compartmentalized into their own separate functional areas, each of which has its own myopic performance measurement. This results in gaming behavior and second-guessing, in which the winner is typically the person who yells the loudest. At this level, the focus is on the tactical short term rather than the organization's overall business strategy, and there is no connection between the two. In contrast to concentrating on making plans for the future and maintaining long-term visibility, the majority of time and effort is spent on conducting analyses of past performance. As a result of the data being distributed across a number of different systems, there are also significant gaps between the aggregate and the detailed plans. This violates Principle 3, as it causes a disproportionate amount of time to be spent, rather than analyzing the data, on collating data from multiple systems and creating meaningful reports (Eliminate waste and reduce non-value-added activities). Even if the organization puts in a lot of effort and is successful in achieving a demand supply balance, there is still a possibility that it will not be able to fulfill its obligations to the market in accordance with its business plan.

In addition, organizations operating at Level 2 utilize technology in a constrained manner. In most cases, technology is used to aggregate S&OP data from ERP feeds into Excel; however, it does not have the capability to compare different what-if scenarios.

3. Level 3; Digital IBP

The utilization of digital capabilities all the way through the supply chain is one of the defining characteristics of digital IBP. For instance, demand can be sensed by using demand signals from consumers' mobile devices, and then this data is shared throughout the supply chain. Additionally, in order to respond to or shape demand in a profitable manner, consideration must be given to cost-service trade-offs across the supply chain. It includes a structured Integrated Business Planning process that is led by senior management that cuts across departmental silos and leads to cross-functional synchronization in accordance with Principle 1 (Focus on customer success). At this level, there is a focus on the longer term as well as financial reconciliation across all of the demand and supply processes. In addition to this, there are well-established cross-functional KPIs that are aligned with the goals of the organization, which satisfies the requirements of Principle 2. (Create a win-win and trusted environment for all stakeholders). In order to orchestrate the IBP process, organizations that have reached Level 3 have mastered the use of technology to enable dashboards, alerts, exceptions, action items, calendars, and what-if scenarios for rapid financial impact analysis. Utilizing technology as a tool for the purpose of automating processes is consistent with Principle 3. (Eliminate waste and reduce non-value-added activities). When organizations are faced with increasingly volatile economic and market conditions, this IBP maturity level lacks the predicative visibility leveraging ML, AI, automation, flexibility, and responsiveness to recalibrate plans across the extended enterprise, including customers and suppliers, when inevitable surprises occur (related to personnel, materials, capacity, or demand), disrupting even the most efficient supply chains (Sabri and Shaikh, 2010). This is because this level of IBP maturity lacks the ability to leverage machine learning, artificial intelligence, automation, flexibility, and responsiveness.

A recent survey of supply chain executives revealed that over sixty percent of respondents indicated that sudden changes in market pattern caused key disruptions, and over seventy percent of respondents pointed to issues on the supply side as the primary cause of supply chain disruptions. Recently, I had the opportunity to interact with one of the original equipment manufacturers for automobiles. This particular OEM mentioned that it was required to expedite the shipment of two million pounds of steel from Germany due to a lack of visibility from its trading partners. Companies need to have the capability to capture and comprehend demand and supply variability as quickly as possible, and then they need to have the capability to rapidly assess the end-to-end impact of those changes throughout the entire end-to-end supply chain.

Level 4: Autonomous IBP

Autonomous IBP is the highest level of process maturity, and it leverages the five guiding principles in order to align and synchronize the entire organization in order to meet customer needs, which reinforces Principle 1. The supply chain collaborates with customers, suppliers, and trading partners to sense, shape, and respond to demand by relying on digital capabilities. At this highest level of maturity, the Autonomous IBP process is used as a lynchpin between strategic business planning, tactical planning, and execution, thereby emphasizing Principle 5 and creating a closed-loop continuous strategy deployment tool (Sabri and Shaikh, 2010). This is in contrast to the traditional method of simply balancing demand, supply, and inventory.

The process is led by executive management, which also defines the roles and responsibilities in a manner that is both clear and succinct. There are holistic cross-functional and cross-organizational KPIs that are geared toward internal and external collaboration. These KPIs are designed to motivate people to act in a certain direction that is aligned with the corporate goals, rather than acting in a direction that is aligned with myopic and conflicting departmental goals, and they align with Principle 2. There is an individual process owner who is accountable and responsible, and the metrics are ingrained in the very foundation of the organization. In addition, there is a target performance level established for each metric (Sabri and Shaikh, 2010). This individual keeps close tabs on performance in comparison to the goal, and as soon as a gap begins to appear between the two, this individual investigates the underlying cause of the deviation and proactively finds a solution to it in order to get things back on track. Instead of focusing solely on analyzing past deviations from the budget, the majority of the time and effort is put toward forecasting future product launches, trends in the market, competition, and new market opportunities. Senior management recognizes and commends those managers within the organization who make effective use of meaningful metrics, and they communicate this recognition to all levels of the organization and to all aspects of the business.

Utilizing segmentation, which is based on attributes such as risk, margins, criticality, revenue, volume, lead times, life cycle stage, and so on, helps the organization put more emphasis and resources on key customers and products as well as make decisions regarding product portfolio management as well as the entry and exit of markets (Sabri and Shaikh, 2010). A "peanut butter spread" approach is avoided in favor of segmentation, which is leveraged. Unsupervised machine learning has the potential to be utilized in the future to mine unstructured data and automatically create clusters that contain meaningful patterns in the data. The ability to automatically segment data based on dozens of features, rather than just one or two, is one of the most powerful aspects of machine learning.

This enables automation and eliminates a lot of the non-value-added activities (in alignment with Principle 3), which frees up stakeholders' time to spend on more value-added activities such as collaboration and what-if scenario analysis. Automating and eliminating repetitive tasks is made possible through the liberal use of cutting-edge technologies such as machine learning and artificial intelligence, which are leveraged to automate and eliminate these tasks. The autonomous IBP process is able to ingest real-time digital signals – from external sources such as SNEW data, competitor promotions, smartphones, sensors, radars, satellites, and more – to provide predictive visibility to sense a disruption before it occurs and then leverage prescriptive analytics to mitigate the risk (Sabri and Shaikh, 2010).

Machines will be able to analyze supply chain strategies to determine where supply chain failures have occurred in the past and what combination of external factors — such as customer loyalty, inventory levels, weather, competitor events, market performance, socio-economic events, and so on — contributed to those supply chain failures once AI and ML are embedded in a self-learning supply chain (Sabri and Shaikh, 2010). This will allow machines to become more proactive in preventing supply chain failures in the future. After that, machine learning algorithms will sift through this data to learn how the aforementioned factors interact with one another to produce a high likelihood of a supply chain failure. In the not too distant future, this type of self-learning supply chain will be able to inform a planner that the occurrence of a particular sequence of events at the same time is indicative of an impending failure in the supply chain. When this occurs, the machine will be able to prevent the failure by relocating the inventory to a new location, or it will alert the planner to take action in response to the problem.

Additionally, social sentiment data from Twitter feeds, Facebook and Instagram posts, as well as Google searches, are leveraged to incorporate unstructured data in ideation, new product introduction, demand sensing, marketing, and crowdsourcing (Sabri and Shaikh, 2010). This allows for improved customer insights, which can then be used to re-adjust plans and respond with agility in response to customer feedback. The patterns that lie behind the data can be easier to understand with the assistance of ML, as can the correlations that exist between the patterns. For example, if an event occurs today, then another event will occur in the future. In the not too distant future, supply chains will be driven by deep learning algorithms. They will be able to analyze all of these different combinations of factors, determine which of these factors are predictive of a service failure, and construct risk mitigation strategies to avoid service failures at the most cost-effective level possible. It is now possible to predict sales a considerable amount of time in advance thanks to the establishment of correlations between structured data, such as actual sales, and unstructured data, such as internet search queries.

Machine learning can also be used to automate the process of proactively resolving issues by storing the effectiveness of previous outcomes. The ability to calendarize and orchestrate the process ensures process compliance and the repeatability of the process steps, which helps bring structure and discipline to the process. In addition, technology is used to generate audit trails of the meetings that have been held, as well as the action items, action item assignments, and statuses. In order to ensure that there is transparency and accountability, each of the assumptions, risks, and opportunities associated with the various resolution options have been documented and tracked. This particular type of top-down, middle-out, and bottom-up reconciliation enables various stakeholders to enter inputs at different levels of the flexible hierarchy while simultaneously ensuring that everybody is working toward the same overarching corporate strategy. Autonomous IBP is an exception-driven S&OP process that increases stakeholder efficiency (Principle 3). It does this by allowing stakeholders to triage exceptions and proactively detect, analyze, and resolve gaps, with a focus on the plan-do-check-act framework for continuous improvement. In other words, Autonomous IBP is an exception-driven S&OP process (Sabri and Shaikh, 2010). Playbooks for digital processes, along with their associated lever libraries, are now structurally embedded into the organization's culture. For instance, if a gap has begun to appear between projected revenues and actual revenues, the digital process playbook would determine the underlying causes, which could be actions taken by competitors, a trend in the macroeconomy, or an incorrect product mix. Based on the identified root cause, the possible resolution levers could include launching a promotion, bringing in a new product launch, improving customer collaboration, increasing forecast accuracy to optimize product mix, or modifying pricing. It is possible to automate these pre-defined scenarios, which are based on playbooks, so that planners can spend more time analyzing the scenarios and choosing the one that best aligns with the corporate business goals of maximizing revenue, maximizing margin, reducing costs, or capturing market share.

An automotive company that operates in an industry that is known for its demand variability and long product lead times recently embarked on a journey to transform its end-to-end supply chain planning processes and tools in order to ensure that it could react more quickly to changes in the market. This was done in order to ensure that the company could meet the needs of its customers. The organization has been successful in moving from Level 1 (Pre-Digital S&OP) to Level 3 (Digital IBP), and it possesses the roadmap necessary to advance to Level 4. (Autonomous IBP). When the business first started down the path of digital transformation, it had homegrown S&OP tools, that severely limited its scalability and integration capabilities, which prevented it from successfully maintaining a dynamic business environment. In addition, it used a sequential planning process between sales, marketing, supply chain, and production, which led to a great deal of manual ad hoc firefighting and wasteful activities. This was in violation of Principle 3, which states that planning should not be done in sequential order (Eliminate waste and reduce non-value-added activities).

The business has been able to re-engineer its end-to-end planning processes and tools ever since it finished the transformation to Level 3 (Digital IBP), which has enabled it to react to shifts in the market in a more timely manner. The company has improved the accuracy of its forecasts, reduced the amount of time it takes to plan, and cut down on the amount of effort and errors associated with planning. In addition, it has cut down on the amount of time it takes to complete lead times. To synchronize supply, demand, and capacity across strategic, tactical, and execution levels and to orchestrate this best-practice continuous and collaborative process, technology is being leveraged as an enabler. Technology has also been used to facilitate rapid response demand realization simulations and capacity expansion simulations in order to see the impact on operational and financial plans. This ensures that the entire organization is able to respond nimbly to shifting market conditions and take appropriate actions when necessary, such as adding or offloading extra capacity (Sabri and Shaikh, 2010).

CONCLUSION

To summarize, businesses now operate with a mentality that was popularized by Amazon, in which customers anticipate receiving their orders in a matter of hours or days rather than weeks or months. Customers anticipate prompt and immediate responses to their inquiries. One of the most important differentiating factors for a company's ability to survive and achieve success is how well it can anticipate and intelligently respond to the needs of its customers. Customers nowadays have come to expect more selections, more available options, as well as simultaneous shipments, 100 percent product availability, and round-the-clock service. It is considered a performance failure if there is even one missed delivery. This shift in the expectations of customers is shaping what businesses now anticipate from the teams responsible for their supply chains. It is essential for businesses to continually improve their ability to recognize and react appropriately to both threats and opportunities. As a result, autonomous IBP has evolved into a requirement for achieving strategic objectives. Big data is experiencing an exponential growth in volume, variety, frequency, and velocity. As a result of this growth, businesses now have more opportunities than ever before to gain a deeper understanding of their customers. Companies are able to leverage real-time digital data signals in order to predict a disruption before it actually occurs, and then they can use prescriptive analytics in order to mitigate the risk of the disruption. This is made possible by the deployment of an autonomous IBP process. This continuous closed-loop process brings together various internal and external stakeholders in a formal and structured manner. These stakeholders include sales, marketing, development, operations, sourcing, finance, and trading partners. As a result, the company is able to create an integrated game plan that reconciles the views of all functional areas while simultaneously ensuring that the plan is in alignment with the overarching, strategic business plan.

The following five core principles are encompassed and enhanced by autonomous IBP: Put an emphasis on the fulfillment of the needs of the customer; establish a cooperative and trustworthy environment for all parties involved; cut down on activities that do not add value to the business; institutionalize a culture of continuous improvement; and complete the cycle of planning and carrying out the plan. An evaluation of business processes "as is" is the first step on the road to autonomous IBP. This evaluation should describe how the organization's processes and technology interact with one another and should also indicate where the company currently stands on the IBP maturity scale. Following this, the next step is to iteratively debate where improvements are needed (this is considered the to-be state), isolating a set of practical decisions to unify strategy across all levels of the business. Uncertainty and variability will persist, but they can be managed through responsiveness and agility by investigating various "what-if" scenarios (i.e., by making changes to key variables like volumes, capacity, mix and price, seeing its impact on bottom-line costs and top-line revenues, and developing contingency plans) (Sabri and Shaikh, 2010). With the help of process playbooks, a company can investigate and evaluate a number of potential courses of action, which paves the way for the establishment of an integrated game plan that takes into account the points of view of all of the functional areas of the business while simultaneously ensuring that the plan is in keeping with the overarching corporate strategy.

The development of artificial intelligence (AI) and machine learning (ML) has made it possible for businesses to predict events, identify trends and anomalies, analyze any correlations between patterns and variables, understand the ramifications of different response options, and provide recommendations. Companies are now in a position to have access to improved decision support as a result of the capability to analyze outcomes (including consumer insights and past behavior) and adjust supply parameter settings. Instead of being managed within individual business units, responses to internal and external disruptions are coordinated across the supply chain as part of the autonomous IBP process. This replaces the traditional management approach. In addition, the capability of sensing changes in demand and supply based on information or data analysis, and then incorporating that data into the planning processes of an organization, can make it simpler for an organization to connect with the specific requirements of its customer base. This not only helps an organization make decisions more quickly, effectively, and profitably, but it also cuts costs and waste across the supply chain. Companies now have the opportunity to leapfrog existing frameworks and move directly to predictive and cognitive models that reduce variability and mitigate risk when they have a supply chain that is enabled by digital technology.

Therefore, in order to compete in today's global marketplace, which is characterized by increased market volatility and uncertainty, shrinking product lifecycles, omni-channel fulfillment, direct-to-consumer channels, and same-day delivery, Autonomous IBP will emerge as perhaps the most compelling enabler for enterprise excellence. This is due to the fact that Autonomous IBP has the ability to not only reduce waste and increase efficiency, but it can also provide flexibility, responsiveness, and risk management in response to changing business conditions. Beginning a journey toward Autonomous IBP has the potential to have a positive impact on many different aspects of an organization, providing benefits such as improved forecast accuracy, improved asset utilization, increased supply chain visibility, higher on-time delivery performance, improved margins, reduced costs, improved profitability, quicker response time, faster time to market, and increased shareholder value (Sabri and Shaikh, 2010).

REFERENCES

Sabri, E., & Shaikh, S. (2010). *Lean & Agile Value Chain Management (LAVCM): A Guide to the Next Level of Improvement. J.* Ross Publishing.

ADDITIONAL READING

Sabri, E., & Shaikh, S. (2010). *Lean & Agile Value Chain Management (LAVCM): A Guide to the Next Level of Improvement. J.* Ross Publishing.

Shaikh, S., Sabri, E., & Esturi, S. (2017). Making the journey to a multimodal, segmented supply chain. *Supply Chain Quarterly*. http://www.supplychainquarterly.com/topics/Strategy/20170626-making-the-journey-to-a-multimodal-segmented-supply-chain/)

Thomas, H. (2018). *Davenport, Rajeev Ronanki*. Artificial Intelligence for the Real World.

KEY TERMS AND DEFINITIONS

Agile: Agile is the process of increasing flexibility and responsiveness

Autonomous Integrated Business Planning: Autonomous IBP involves a closed-loop continuous process, where different internal and external stakeholders from sales, marketing, development, operations, sourcing, finance and trading partners come together in a formal structured process to create an integrated company game plan that reconciles the views of all functional areas at the same time making sure that this plan is in alignment with the strategic business plan. An Autonomous IBP process has the ability to ingest real-time signals (from the digital edge via SNEW data and competitor promotions, as well as from physical assets like smartphones, sensors, radars and satellites), provide predictive visibility to warn or sense a disruption before it happens, and then leverage prescriptive analytics to manage the unpredictable through risk mitigation plans.

Change management: Managing people/teams/organization and transitioning them from the current AS-IS state to a future TO-BE state.

Lean: Lean is a process of waste elimination and increasing operational efficiency

Machine Learning: Machine learning is a field of artificial intelligence that uses statistical techniques to understand the patterns behind the data, establish co-relation between those patterns and "learn" from data, without being explicitly programmed

Risk management: Risk management is the process of doing what-if scenarios to enable risk mitigation strategies so as to minimize the impact of unfortunate events.

Segmentation: Segmentation is the process of stratifying the portfolio (product, market, channel etc.) into clusters based on attributes like risk, margins, criticality, revenue, volume, lead times, life cycle stage, etc., which helps the organization put more emphasis and resources on key customers and products and make decisions on product portfolio management, as well as entry/exit of markets to enable an organization to offer differentiated service treatment to certain groups.

SNEW: The ability to ingest real-time digital signals – from external sources such as SNEW (social, news, events, and weather data) can help provide predictive visibility to sense an event/disruption before it happens with the goal of making better and faster decisions.

Chapter 6
Value of Decision Speed in Delivering Supply Chain Benefits:
Benefits Require Rapid, Cross-Functional Decision Making

Mark T. Levy
KPMG, USA

ABSTRACT

This chapter describes the challenges faced in achieving effective cross-functional decision making and quantifies the value of speed in supply chain decisions with a specific focus on determining the best supply plan in an outsourced manufacturing environment. The analysis presented uses a supply chain simulation model that helped achieve best-in-class supply chain results in the field. Practitioners can use this analysis to inform their supply chain transformation business cases and improve their probability of successful implementation by proactively addressing the transformation challenges described to accelerate cross-functional decision making.

INTRODUCTION

Digital technology has great potential to enable better and faster decisions, but many companies have issues making decisions in the analog world, let alone an accelerating digital one. The most difficult decisions for companies are those that cut across functional silos, often as companies do not have the appropriate forums, organization, technical solutions, or collaborative 'way of working' in place. Establishing these collaborative processes (e.g., Sales & Operations Planning or its more advanced counterpart, Integrated Business Planning) and capabilities requires overcoming multiple challenges. Management focus and resources are critical requirements for a successful transformational change. This chapter aims to maximize the value of digital technology by addressing challenges and quantifying the

DOI: 10.4018/978-1-6684-7298-9.ch006

value of faster decision-making to help the reader support their business case for making the necessary investment to improve.

BACKGROUND

Processes and systems to improve decision making in end-to-end planning processes have been the subject of multiple articles in the business press, and to a lesser extent in academic circles. In industry, the process most associated with supply chain decision making is referred to as Sales & Operation Planning (S&OP), Sales, Inventory, and Operations Planning (SIOP), or Integrated Business Planning (IBP). While these processes are not identical, in each business segment, there will only be one of these operating – for brevity, the term **S&OP** will be used in this chapter to encompass these processes. This chapter is not focused on defining this process as further detail on S&OP and IBP may be found from multiple sources, including CSCMP, APICS, and their originator, Oliver Wight. Over the last decade, the importance of Sales & Operations Execution (S&OE) also has become more recognized as this shorter-term process enables S&OP to focus on making more critical supply chain decisions.

The S&OP process is one of only several formal cross-functional processes found at most companies and thus has a critical role in enabling faster decision making. Other cross-functional decision-making processes include strategic planning, annual business planning and budgeting, and the product development stage gate process.

Strategic Planning

The strategic planning process is conducted annually to produce a plan for the next 3 to 5 years. In mature companies, the strategic plan focuses not only on defining corporate objectives but also a meaningful focus on the programs and associated investments required for attainment.

Annual Business Planning and Budgeting

Business planning and budgeting is generally executed annually to create department financial budgets or annual operating plans (AOP) for the upcoming fiscal year. More mature companies derive portions of this plan from their 18 to 24-month horizon S&OP output to support a similar rolling horizon, in contrast to driving S&OP to meet the original AOP.

Product Development Stage Gate

The product development stage gate process is typically event-based for managing individual development projects with a monthly or quarterly cadence to manage the overall project pipeline and portfolio. The refreshed roadmap should feed product portfolio assumptions into the S&OP process; this could be through a shared assumptions package or a formal product review meeting, as described by Oliver Wight.

Two of these three processes are annual and instrumental to improving business performance, including establishing a more responsive supply chain. That said, annual processes are not as relevant for accelerating recurring cross-functional decisions. This leaves a large swath of decisions to be governed in other cross-functional forums, including the S&OP process.

Table 1. Sample decision matrix for a large consumer goods company

#	Category	Description	To-Be Forum	Illustrative decisions
1	Strategy: Demand	Long-term, proactive demand decisions	Strategic Planning	Enter a channel with new requirements, refine customer priorities, sever a relationship
2	Policies: Demand	Implementation of a strategic decision through policies	S&OP / ES&OP	Customer service policies & parameters (lead times) Modify demand consensus rules
3	Tactics: Demand	Short-term demand decisions	Demand Review	Quantify cannibalization, risks & opportunities in the base plan, consensus business rules exceptions
4	Strategy: Supply	Long-term, proactive supply decisions	E-Staff	Modify supply base, In vs Out, supply network changes, supply chain segmentation, postponement
5	Policies: Supply	Implementation of a strategic decision through policies	S&OP / ES&OP	Modify inventory target policy/parameters, payment terms
6	Tactics: Supply	Short-term supply decisions	Supply Review	Change components to mitigate availability issues, promote a shift in product mix, E&O write-offs, OT
7	Investment: Working Capital	Decision with direct working capital implication (over $X)	S&OP / ES&OP	Approve ship plan, purchase long-lead time materials, or produce finished goods for non-firm demand; last time buys
8	Investment: Capital	Decision with a direct capital investment implication	E-Staff	Modify distribution center or manufacturing capacity
9	Expense: Demand	Demand decision that will incur a clear expense (over $X)	Segment S&OP	Commit marketing programs, promos, price increases, FG liquidations
10	Expense: Supply	Supply decision that will incur a clear expense (over $X)	Segment S&OP	Expedite at a higher cost to meet demand; modify approved modes of transportation
11	Product	Product portfolio and roadmap decisions	Portfolio Mgmt.	Pull In/Delay SKU discontinuation, revise SKU rationalization targets, roadmap changes

(Data Source: Value of Speed, Mark Levy, KPMG, 2022)

In fact, many companies do not know where their supply chain-related decisions are made, yet this basic information is necessary to support effective cross-functional decision making, e.g., the S&OP process. Therefore, one of the first steps is to define which types of decisions will be made across existing forums and whether any new forums need to be established.

Clearly, S&OP can handle multiple key decisions. However, at a minimum, S&OP should enable cross-functional agreement on both unconstrained demand and associated supply plans to match supply to this demand statement. In manufacturing companies, this is the supply plan, or alternatively, the ship plan.

The following table is an example of a decision-making matrix created with a North American consumer goods company. Table 1 indicates which of the 11 decision categories are addressed in each forum, with a focus on better defining the S&OP process.

With strong governance in place, empowered employees at lower levels of the organization make decisions on less-critical demand/supply balancing matters. This process includes deploying available inventory across the network or estimating the impact of a planned promotion, often in the more tactical sales and operations execution (S&OE) process.

Existing technologies can help them make these decisions, and for advanced companies, machine learning and other innovations further support their decisions. However, technology can only go so far in helping individual employees or departments make supply chain decisions that have a wide-ranging impact across the company. There is a need for cross-functional perspectives for matters such as:

- Demand policies may include modifying customer priorities or updating demand consensus rules. For example, changes to customer prioritization rules used in allocation situations drive different satisfaction levels across customers or segments, making allocation a sensitive process in most companies. However, how these allocation decisions are made is not always clear. It is not unusual to find that the "squeaky wheel" or "loudest voice" was the greatest factor, instead of an informed analysis presented in a cross-functional forum.
- Modifications in supply/inventory policies and associated parameters impact service levels and financial performance. For example, modifying service level targets across inventory segments in an ABC/XYZ grid may reduce overall inventory but shift product mix, impacting margin. If a win-win solution is available, the decision may not be difficult. However, once the low-hanging fruit is harvested, decisions often result in tradeoffs that impact customer segments differently.
- Investments include financing incremental supply for uncertain demand that will affect results across financial statements and provide enhanced resilience. For example, inventory and long-lead time risk buys will increase working capital on the balance sheet but offer the opportunity to capture upside sales on the income statement.

With this understanding of cross-functional processes and illustrative decisions, we will discuss the obstacles to effective cross-functional decision making.

VALUE OF SPEED

Effective and rapid cross-functional decision making is not natural for most companies but a capability that must be nurtured and developed through significant effort and investment. There are at least five significant hurdles to overcome in building effective cross-functional decision-making capabilities per Figure 1:

Figure 1. Five hurdles to overcome
(Value of Speed, Mark Levy, KPMG, 2022)

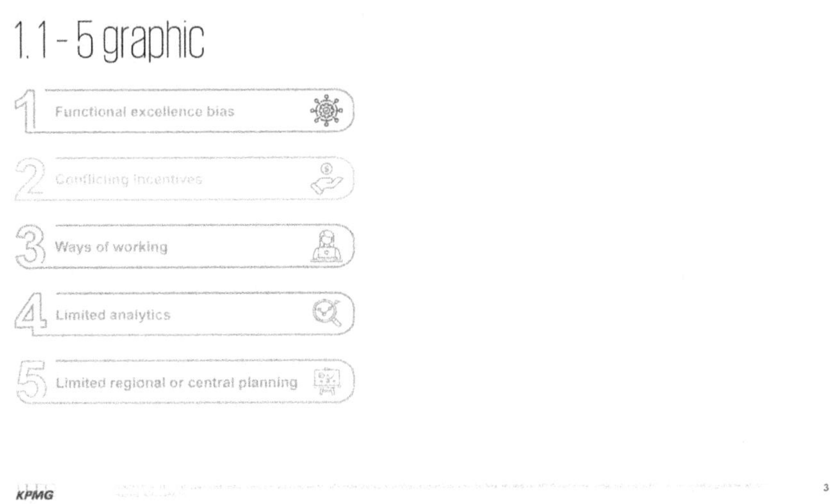

Functional Excellence Bias

The employees who rise through an organization tend to earn their positions by demonstrating strength in their specific domains. They may be highly competent in sales, marketing, finance, or another area of functional expertise. However, their ability to make good decisions may be limited to their function versus curating a wider perspective. While companies are getting better at recognizing that skills and capabilities should cross functional boundaries, legacy reward systems typically prioritize singular functional excellence - creating conflicting incentives.

Conflicting Incentives

"You get what you measure" is an old and powerful adage. Moreover, what companies measure most often are metrics that are easily quantified with direct traceability to the income statement. This environment is often rife with contradiction, slowing inventory decisions and risking execution.

Inventory policies offer rich examples of how conflicting incentives impact decision-making speed—especially as inventory ownership is fragmented and unclear at many companies.

Procurement

The procurement organization's most important metric is cost reduction. This metric is easy to quantify, and direct material cost savings improve the income statement. In contrast, the impact of supplier flexibility needs to be traced through a set of assumptions and, even then, may primarily affect inventory, a balance sheet asset without a direct income statement impact. This often leads procurement to favor the supplier that offers slightly better cost-reduction performance over another supplier that can operate with lower lead times and require less inventory.

Manufacturing

Most manufacturing plants are rewarded by producing the largest quantities of a given product possible, as this improves utilization and standard accounting cost measures through higher absorption. This behavior drives inventory up and is inconsistent with demand-driven approaches where customer demand is the driving force. To counter this tendency, mature companies with multiple plants employ central planning strategies to provide a balanced high-level plan for plants to meet.

Supply Chain

The supply chain function may have a balanced scorecard, but the function often focuses on maintaining internal service level measures and cost over assets. One tendency is to emphasize achieving transportation cost savings or limiting capital spending over flexibility.

Finance

Especially in public companies, finance is inherently calendar-oriented and focuses on meeting quarter-end inventory targets, therefore closely managing the cost accounting that promotes cost absorption and applies pressure to reduce quarter-end inventory. This can result in various unnatural short-term supply chain actions to ensure that average inventory is underrepresented in financial statements.

Sales

Sales is typically focused on revenue then on margin, which promotes an "inventory at any cost" approach and can lead to SKU complexity with an unnecessarily diverse portfolio. Salespeople may understand the negative impact, but their typical behavior is generally heavily rewarded.

Incentives that cross functions can facilitate balanced decision making, such as cash flow, e.g., EBITDA or return on invested capital (ROIC) goals that balance different functional perspectives. Some good news is that the effort of re-aligning incentives is less resource-intensive than developing and enabling core planning and analytics; however, implementing incentive changes requires significant change management and C-level attention.

Ways of Working

Executives may not be comfortable making decisions in more open forums outside of their "home" function. Implementing cross-functional decision-making forums might encourage new ways of working that support accountability up and down and help employees focus on supporting analysis without "CYA" behavior. Organizations can build or mature their existing S&OP process to serve this purpose when an appropriate forum to make cross-functional decisions does not exist.

However, companies need to watch for several common pitfalls. First, S&OP may be reporting-focused when it should be decision-making focused. Especially if no effective S&OE process exists, S&OP may focus on near-term concerns, whereas cross-functional supply chain decisions impact a longer time horizon. Finally, S&OP can lack appropriate heft in the organization, especially if leaders do not prioritize attendance.

Creating ways of working that encourage cross-functional collaboration is a cultural leadership role and responsibility. The S&OP process should focus on cross-functional decisions, preferably using scenario analysis to clarify the impacts of different decisions, to build an executive presence in the process.

Limited Analytics

Scenario management is a powerful and flexible technique for executives to consume data that provides insights into options and decision impacts. As we demonstrate in our subsequent supply plan decision example, scenario management projects impacts and tradeoffs across four key value dimensions:

1. Revenue, the top concern for many organizations
2. Cost, and hence margin
3. Assets, including working capital
4. Risk/Resilience/ESG, often overlooked, although less so post-COVID

However, scenario management is only as effective as data quality and technology tools that generate the analysis allow. A consistent approach, such as a uniform scenario format and option output that covers the four value dimensions, enables faster consumption and better decisions. This technique requires preparation and analytic capabilities but gets easier with experience and forces the team to think through options and impacts. Building these capabilities at a large company typically requires a technology-enabled transformation and associated investment.

Limited Regional or Central Planning

Many larger but less mature companies have limited central planning capability. Thus, manufacturing plants will make demand/supply decisions based on their limited visibility and siloed incentives. However, in most larger companies, plants have interdependencies from common products, suppliers, and/or customers that make a central planning capability essential to optimize demand/ supply decisions across the internal and external network.

Building a regional or central planning capability requires thoughtful design and implementation across six operating model layers (process, organization, service delivery model, technology, information, and governance). Implementing a meaningful capability often necessitates rebalancing decision rights across the company – as well as technical capabilities to manage across plants. These technical capabilities require aligned data and new technical capabilities that require investment.

Obtaining this investment typically requires developing a formal business case for review with the finance and leadership teams. In the next section, we cover the benefits of a planning transformation, including the business case and support from the value of speed.

SOLUTIONS AND RECOMMENDATIONS

For companies to maximize the value of their Digital investments, they must have a sound cross-functional decision-making model to exploit these new information streams. We just discussed five of the obstacles to overcome to implement and sustain decision-making, and the need to obtain the investment required to build the capabilities that speed critical decision-making.

Benefits of a planning transformation that improves decision making cut across three broad categories:

1. Financial predictability is the highest-level benefit that may be attractive to the C-level executive community. Per KPMG analysis of public companies, more predictable companies have 2 – 5% higher Return on Equity (ROE) than less predictable companies. Further details on this analysis follow in Figure 2.
2. Financial benefits serve as the foundation for business cases at most companies that gate the investment in new technology-enabled capabilities. Improvements reflected in the Income Statement and Balance Sheet are at the heart of the value of speed.
3. New capabilities benefit employees that will operate in a more mature and technology-enabled environment, including the ability to run scenarios that enhance decision-making quality and speed. The financial benefits category captures the 'hard' business benefits of these capabilities.

We will cover two of the three broad categories. First, financial predictability including a return on equity (ROE) analysis, and then financial benefits including a simulation analysis that reflects the value of speed in decision making.

Financial Predictability

Supply chain transformation leading to sustainable, long-term improvements can require significant investment and time. However, devoting company resources to improving supply-chain decision making can lead to more predictable financial results. One of the positive impacts is the company's ability to set and meet earnings targets which is highly valuable per KPMG analysis.

According to an analysis of publicly available financial data by KPMG, companies that are more "predictable" or very likely to meet earnings targets deliver a return on equity (ROE) 2 – 4 points higher than less predictable companies.

- "Predictable" companies are defined as those who reported annual earnings of 10% or more from expected earnings less than 20% of the time during the years studied, 2015–2020. Earnings from "less-predictable" companies were in line up to 80% of the time and not consistently negative in the same timeframe.
- The ROE advantage is the difference between the median ROE of predictable and less-predictable companies.
- The summary 2 – 4% comparison is from 2015 – 2020 by sector analysis; a previous analysis of 2009 – 2014 data produced the same relationship but higher ROE deltas.

Figure 2. Influence of earnings predictability on ROE by sector, 2015 – 2020
(Value of Speed, Mark Levy, KPMG, 2022)

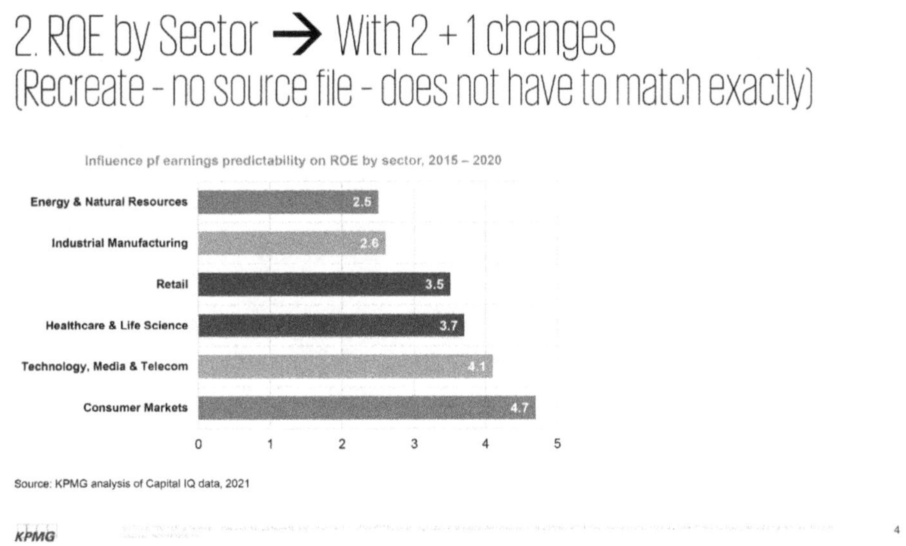

Financial Benefits

Expected income statement and balance sheet improvements are the primary elements used to create a corporate investment business case for a supply chain planning transformation. We typically group these into revenue, cost, and asset impacts – risk reduction is typically treated as a soft benefit and not quantified in the business case.

Some typical expectations are:

A. 1 – 4% Improved gross margin from higher sales driven by improved customer service level, higher launch margins, better product mix, improved promotions, and reduced contra revenue
B. 5 – 10% Reduced cost from reduced expediting, penalties, freight, E&O inventory write-offs, and improved productivity
C. 15 – 30% Cut working capital from lower inventory requirements

Typically, the business case will not quantify all three but focus on two of the categories and yield a gross margin improvement of 1 – 3%. Figure 3 is a benefits decomposition tying typical planning transformation benefits back to the financial statements.

Figure 3. Financial benefits decomposition with root causes
(Value of Speed, Mark Levy, KPMG, 2022)

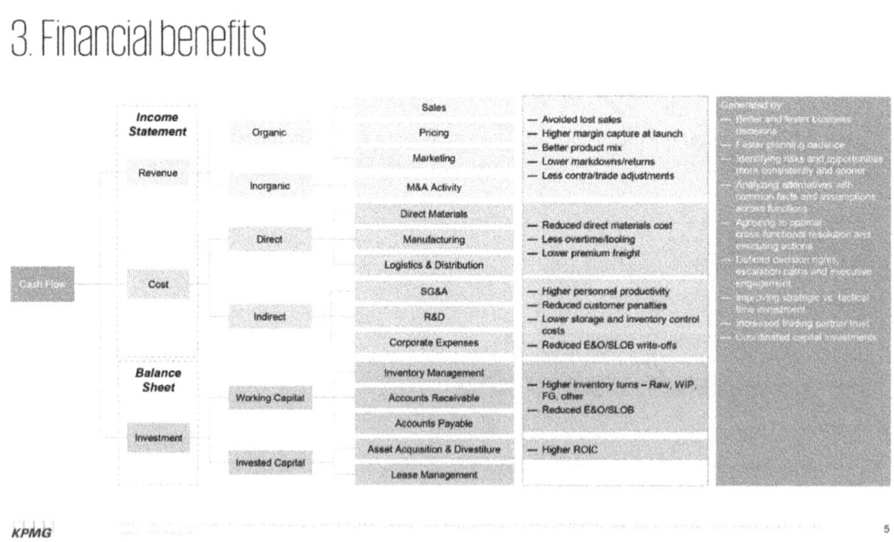

A critical root cause of these benefits is better and faster decisions – enabling faster decision making requires many elements but that is not the focus of this chapter. Here we explore the value of speed in decision making, starting with the meaning of decision speed in the supply chain. For example, an organization may make a difficult decision in just minutes, selecting one of three options to resolve a supply chain issue in a single meeting. However, if that issue arose six weeks ago, is that still a quick decision?

To explore this further, we break decision making into three primary elements:

1. ***When did you know a change would be meaningful?*** How fast does the company uncover a situation that requires action? For example, a core use case for digital technologies is detecting demand trends on social media, which may tee up the need to make an investment decision to support additional supply for a newly released product. The time it takes to detect a meaningful demand change and start the analysis is part of the simulation model.
2. ***How quickly can you analyze the data and decide?*** How long does it take to generate the scenarios required to make an informed decision? In all but the smallest companies, a solid S&OP process and scenario management technology is a requirement to deliver trusted analysis. Once the analysis is available, how fast does the decision get made? Is there a decision-making cadence that drove the analysis timing? If not, are the decision process and rights clear to maximize the benefit of the requisite scenario management capability?
3. ***How fast can you implement the decision?*** Finally, if teams do not execute decisions cleanly or if they second-guess, then the efforts to accelerate decision making will not deliver the impact organizations are working to achieve.

There are obstacles to implementing and sustaining sound cross-functional decision making. One hurdle is obtaining the investment required to build the capabilities to speed up quality decision-making. To help with this challenge, we present an analysis that demonstrates the value of speed in decision making.

Establishing the Value of Speed

Better allocation decisions can improve important customer relationships, thereby enhancing revenue and margin. Additionally, better inventory management can lower working capital for a given service level. It is also intuitive that making and implementing those quality decisions faster is beneficial. However, the value of that speed and agility is more difficult to quantify.

Standard enterprise planning solutions do not consider how long the organization takes to detect and decide that a given demand change is "real." Does the data indicate a trend, or is it just a result of a special event that is not yet understood? How many weeks need to go by before the demand changes are validated, and the implications are clear enough to define options? Similarly, these solutions do not consider that the scenario will be revisited in the next cycle and subsequent action may be taken.

However, practitioners can use the following analysis to inform their supply chain transformation business cases, ultimately helping multiple functions agree to invest in improvement and overcome the most difficult obstacle, inertia, or the status quo.

Simulation Analysis to Quantify the Value of Speed

Approving the supply plan is a foundational decision of S&OP - essentially, what will ship from third-party manufacturers and/or from internal plants. The value of speed analysis focuses on this core decision.

Figure 4 is a simplified summary of the simulation model results that reflects a 400-basis point service level and 5.5% gross margin improvement from deciding and acting quickly versus more slowly under a demand upside scenario.

Figure 4. Simplified scenario model summary output
(Value of Speed, Mark Levy, KPMG, 2022)

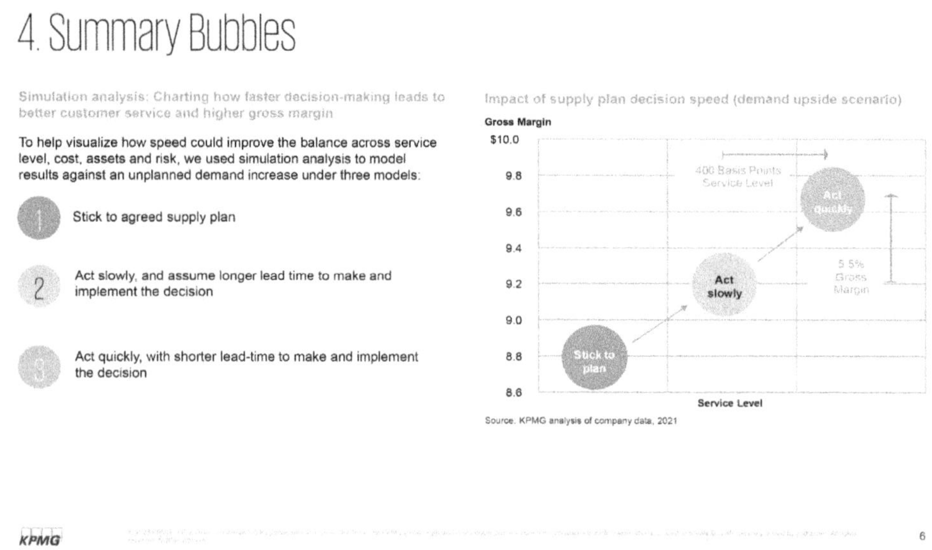

The simulation model that produced the summary result is described next, along with more complete results that provide further insight into how we created the summary view.

Simulation Model Description

The model objective is not to predict the future precisely but to provide clear implications of significantly different choices under different demand realization scenarios both to make better S&OP decisions (e.g., supply plan) and to help ensure the Executive Team aligns on trade-offs.

- Scenario output includes standard gross profit, service level, and end-to-end inventory implications, including estimated off-balance sheet liabilities.
- The model is typically run nine times with different sell-thru demand realization and ship plan decisions to generate a three-by-three matrix of demand realization (high – medium – low) vs. planned ship plan (aggressive – baseline – conservative).

The model is a multi-sheet Excel workbook configured to simulate the weekly movement of goods through a consumer supply chain with retail stores and external channels supplied by a single-level DC network and off-shore contract manufacturing.

The model consumes sell-through units by channel type per weekly demand, which then triggers replenishment from an in-country DC per channel inventory targets. In the same period, units are pushed based on the supply plan shared with third-party manufacturing. The push/pull boundary is the US-based DC, so the model determines what inventory to pull from the DC-based on target stock levels, while incoming inventory from the contract manufacturer is received per shipment mode mix indicated by the user.

From this core approach, the model generates multiple KPIs:

- Service level and financial results (revenue, gross margin)
- Inventory pipeline and performance
- Inventory liability for both channel FG and components

The model incorporates several complexities:

- Calculates revenue as net sell-thru revenue for OEM stores plus gross sell-in for other channels
- Offsets BOM cost changes for the delay in incorporating new components into product and sales timing through the inventory pipeline
- Recirculates select returns into the supply line
- Calculates component liability using reaction time, PO lead times & cancellation terms

The model features over twenty levers as depicted in figure 5 that the user can modify to create different scenarios. These include reaction times which are a unique feature of the model that recognizes two distinct, pragmatic factors:

1. In reality, sell-through demand changes are not instantly recognized and acted upon, so the model includes a number of weeks lever to reflect the time from a sell-through change to a reaction.
2. Typically models use supplier lead times to determine how fast the supply plan can be modified. This simulation enables the user to reflect that companies may outperform with special effort.

Figure 5. Simulation model levers
(Levy, 2022)

Category	Inputs
Scenario Definition	Sell-thru as %base plan by channel
	Ship plan as %base ship plan
	Ship plan pattern
	Ship plan changes per reaction
Reaction Time	Weeks to detect demand change
	Weeks for upside to be realized
Lifecycle Settings	Weeks in measurement horizon
	EOL week, if applicable
Liability	Weeks of demand used for liability
WOS Targets	WOS targets by Channel by week
	Lost sales estimate function parameters

Category	Inputs
Shipment Modes and Costs	Air shipment offset (MFG to DC)
	% by mode out of MFG by week
	Shipment cost ex-MFG by mode by week
	Shipment cost ex-DC by mode by week
Device Pricing	Weekly Retail price: permanent vs. pulse
	Margin to Channel partners by week
Return Rates	Return rate by Channel by week
	NTF1% (clean returns) by Channel
BOM	BOM cost by lead time category by week
MVA / WIP	Manufacturing Value Add (MVA) $ per unit
	Units in final assembly as %ship plan
	Units in sub-assembly and SMT as a %ship plan

Simulation Model Structure

The simulation model is a six-sheet Excel workbook as depicted in figure 6.

Figure 6. Simulation model high-level logical architecture
(Levy, 2022)

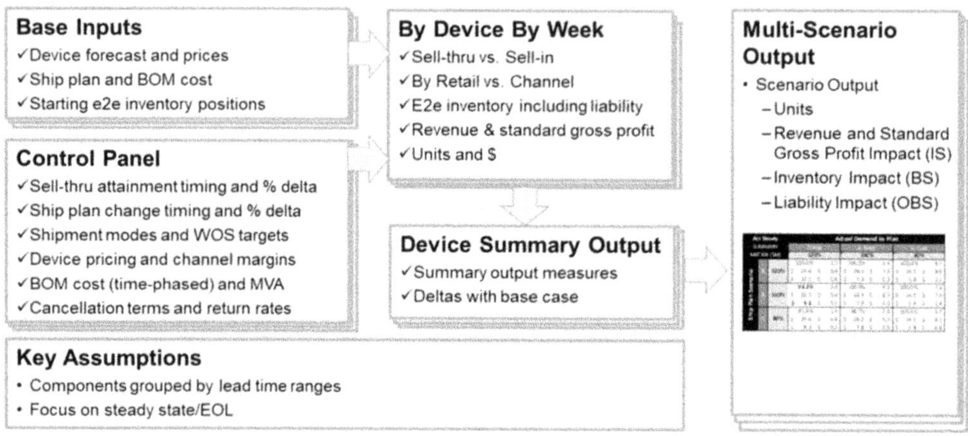

Simulation Model Output Details

Model outputs are organized into six categories as detailed in Table 2

Figure 7. Simulation model output detail by category
(Levy, 2022)

Category	Methodology
Financial	- Channel Partner (CP) Revenue: Gross sell-in units * (price – CP margin) - OEM Revenue: Net Sell thru units * current week price - 'COGS': units sold *(offset BOM + Offset MVA + Average freight per unit)
Service level	- Generates potential sell-thru for OEM vs. CP and tries to fulfill, if it cannot then service level will fall below 100%; demand expires weekly - If WOS is below 33% of the target, then the model loses 12% of sales which increases if WOS% falls further to a maximum of 50% lost sales at 1% WOS
Inventory Pipeline	- Channel Partner: Valued at price minus CP margin - OEM Store and DC: Uses COGS (as defined in financial category) - Components: Applies cost per BOM offset for PO lead-time
Partner liability	- Channel Partner: Price protects all channel inventory and estimates returns on weekly basis with no cap on returns - Component: Uses multiple logical functions to calculate weekly liability by projecting OH+OO and subtracting projected component demand
Inventory WOS	- Uses target WOS to generate a weekly replenishment request to DC - Fulfills OEM then channel partner request (channel has higher WOS target) - Recirculates NTF1 returns into the supply line
Effective Supply	- % of the actual supply delivered after the ship plan reaction implemented

Simulation Model Example

This section illustrates how the simulation model supports the simplified scenario summary.

The model is a weekly simulation of product movement, unconstrained by normal curve assumptions common in most stochastic models. It incorporates typical supply-side reactions to demand/supply imbalances to reflect that organizations are active supply chain managers.

To achieve valuable results, the model is run nine times with different demand and supply settings to create a 3 x 3 matrix per Figure 8, and each run is summarized with up to six outputs although fewer may be used for the executive review to help facilitate focus on critical factors.

In Figure 8, the middle scenario (Row B - Column 2) represents the default plan for demand and supply. The other eight results indicate the combination of demand that materializes largely outside of the company's control, and the supply plan decision to be made in the S&OP meeting. Essentially, the executive team decision is which supply/ship plan row (A, B or C) to select with the columns representing the performance the decision will generate under different demand realizations.

For example, if the decision team selects an aggressive supply plan (row A, 120% of base plan) and demand is lower than expected (column 3: Cold), then the inventory weeks of supply expands to 8.7 weeks – especially as this matrix represents a slow-reaction supply chain with 8-week decision time and 20-week supply plan response time.

Figure 8. Simulation model summary 9-scenario matrix output
(Levy, 2022)

Act Slowly SUMMARY MATRIX ($M)			Actual Demand to Plan: 1: Hot 120%		2: Base 100%		3: Cold 80%	
Ship Plan Scenario	A	120%	100.0%	1.3	100.0%	4.6	100.0%	8.7
			$ 24.6	$ 6.4	$ 19.4	$ 7.6	$ 14.5	$ 8.0
			$ 10.1	$ 0.0	$ 7.9	$ 0.3	$ 5.9	$ 2.1
	B	100%	93.3%	1.4	100.0%	4.2	100.0%	7.6
			$ 22.5	$ 5.4	$ 19.4	$ 6.7	$ 14.5	$ 7.0
			$ 9.2	$ 0.1	$ 7.9	$ 0.0	$ 5.9	$ 1.4
	C	80%	85.8%	1.4	98.7%	2.6	100.0%	6.7
			$ 20.4	$ 4.9	$ 19.2	$ 5.2	$ 14.5	$ 6.1
			$ 8.3	$ 0.3	$ 7.8	$ 0.0	$ 5.9	$ 0.8

Decision team picks a row (A, B or C)

Act Slowly

KEY	High best	Low best
	Service	WOS
	Revenue	Invy Pipe
	Margin	Liability

The summary simulation analysis is supported by three distinct nine-box summary matrices as shown in Figure 9:

Figure 9. Demand high – base supply plan (Row B – Col. 1) scenario summary with underlying grids
(Levy. 2022)

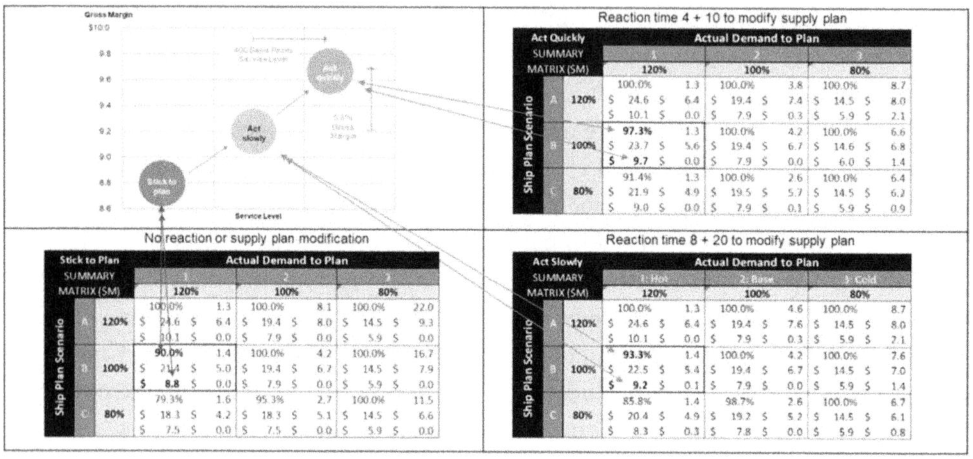

1. Lower left = "Stick to Plan" = No supply reaction
2. Lower right = "Act Slowly" = 8-week reaction time and 20 weeks to modify supply plan
3. Top right = "Act Quickly" = 4-week reaction time and 10 weeks to modify supply plan

Each bubble is drawn from Row B – Column 1 of its related matrix, which results when demand runs hot (120%) with the baseline supply plan (100%) and an appropriate reaction is taken by the team per the reaction time inputs. The following diagram links the scenario summary to the appropriate scenario on each of three matrices – Stick to Plan, Act Slowly and Act Quickly to help clarify the process used in creating the simplified summary scenario. Here the summary charts use only two of the six KPIs in each scenario run – gross margin and service level.

Figure 10. Demand high – base supply plan (Row B – Col. 1) with 4 models
(Levy, 2022)

Decision – 'Monte Carlo' Scenario Options – B1 Summary (120% Demand – 100% Ship Plan)

Table below summarizes the results across the different scenarios presented in Figure 9 and adds a new scenario
In this scenario, we switch 50% of volume to Air from Ocean in week 4

- Top 3 rows recap previous figure 9 scenarios
- Fourth row is performance if shifting to 50% Air in week 4 with rapid reaction capability

Scenario Summary	Eff Supply	Avg. CSL	Revenue	Gross Margin	OEM DC WOS	Avg. e2e Pipeline	OBS Liability	Note
Stick to Plan	100%	90.0%	$ 21.4	$ 8.8	1.4	$ 5.1	$ 0.0	No Reaction
React	109%	93.3%	$ 22.5	$ 9.2	1.4	$ 5.3	$ 0.1	Supply Plan up 20% - week 29
Rapid Reaction	115%	97.3%	$ 23.7	$ 9.7	1.3	$ 5.6	$ 0.0	Supply Plan up 20% - week 14
Rapid + Air	115%	100%	$ 24.7	$ 9.5	1.6	$ 6.6	$ 0.0	Switch 50% to Air - week 4

Result... A more difficult decision perhaps

- Service level and revenue up
- Margin down

The simplified summary simulation analysis did not incorporate switching from ocean to air, figure 10 summarizes the preceding matrices as three rows and adds a fourth row where the shipment mode is switched to air for 50% of the supply plan under the rapid reaction scenario. This results in a scenario where service level reaches 100%. However, the margin is reduced due to higher freight costs. The table also demonstrates the reaction modeled for each matrix as we assume that supply chain managers are active and will react to the demand surprise – whether high or low.

These scenarios are just a few of the possibilities created using a small portion of all the levers that can be adjusted to create an almost unlimited number of scenarios. The approach for executive decision making is to create scenarios that reflect the key decisions that the executive team needs to make at that time. Enabling many levers does help the planner adjust to changing circumstances without having to modify the core simulation logic.

FUTURE RESEARCH DIRECTIONS

As leading companies strive to achieve higher levels of integration across functions to support better cross-functional planning – including true Integrated Business Planning with Finance – the need for tech-enabled transformation is increasing. The Value of Speed simulation presented here illustrated just one of many use cases and scenarios that could be analyzed. In the future, the model can be used to demonstrate the value of speed for different levers, supply chains, and different scenarios.

CONCLUSION

Business value results from making better and faster decisions that benefit from rapid execution. Developing digital capabilities to support cross-functional decisions often requires a technology-enabled transformation – especially for more complex companies with multiple manufacturing and supplier sites that would benefit from central or regional planning approaches. For most organizations, an early step in this journey is creating a business case covering at least two of the four value categories - revenue, cost, assets, and risk improvements. The value of speed simulation described is a proof point for the value of enabling faster decision making.

ACKNOWLEDGMENT

This research received no specific grant from any funding agency in the public, commercial, or not-for-profit sectors. KPMG supported the return on equity analysis, the earlier publication of Value of Speed in a condensed form, and the opportunity to apply the simulation model to an additional consumer electronics company. The author also acknowledges that the perspectives reflected have been developed over many years from interactions with many skilled supply chain planning professionals, too numerous to name herein.

REFERENCES

Levy, M. (2022). *Value of Speed.* KPMG. https://advisory.kpmg.us/articles/2022/value-of-speed.html

KEY TERMS AND DEFINITIONS

Integrated Business Planning: True integration of mature S&OP and mature Financial Planning & Analysis (FP&A) processes so that duplicate forecasting, reporting, and decision making efforts are eliminated.

Sales & Operations Execution (S&OE): A tactical cross-functional process that drives alignment and decision-making inside the current quarter to maximize performance to the S&OP plan.

Sales & Operations Planning (S&OP): A key cross-functional process that drives alignment and decision-making over a time horizon of three to 24+ months on strategic demand and supply plans, related policies, and significant investments. Also referred to as Sales, Inventory, and Operations Planning (SIOP).

Chapter 7
Capacity Planning:
A Process to Prepare Companies to Fulfill Volatile Demand in the Digital World

Amit Gupta
KPMG, USA

ABSTRACT

This chapter highlights the need for capacity planning to meet the demand in the post-pandemic world and identifies key challenges that companies face. Following that, the chapter establishes five levels of capacity planning – Strategic Capacity Planning, Annual Budget Planning, Rough Cut Capacity Planning, Capacity Requirement Planning, and Detailed Production Planning. Each level of capacity planning is explained in detail with examples. Finally, the chapter defines a maturity model to understand gaps in the current process and concludes with an implementation roadmap.

INTRODUCTION

No large company can run the business without a capacity planning process; however, the process' effectiveness has also been a point of contention in the supply chain organization. The effectiveness of the process was evident in the recent supply chain disruptions caused by the pandemic and logistic disruptions in the Suez and Panama Canal. Companies were aware of the capacity planning process issue, but very few could clearly understand its impacts on customer service and cost of service. No company was immune to the supply chain disruption as cities were in lockdown. Still, companies that had investments in proper processes, tools, and skillsets could navigate some of the challenges.

In the past, capacity planning was time-consuming and performed either locally or at a strategic, high level; however, with today's digital capabilities, an organization can not only link its strategic plan to a detailed execution-level capacity plan but also gain visibility outside its four walls to ensure the complete network can support its strategic plan.

The capacity planning process has been broken into multiple levels to link the strategic plan to the operational plan and support specific decision needs. Each level has different granularity, frequency, and

DOI: 10.4018/978-1-6684-7298-9.ch007

distinct purpose. While APICS divides end-to-end capacity planning into four levels (resources requirement planning, rough-cut capacity planning, capacity requirement planning, and input/output control), this chapter divides end-to-end capacity planning into five levels with an added strategic capacity planning level designed to align corporate objectives with the execution plan. Variations in the number of levels have existed; for example, Bram Desmet of Solventure and Adrian Bentley of McBride divided the capacity planning process into five levels during a webinar[1]. The figure below shows the proposed

Figure 1. Capacity planning levels

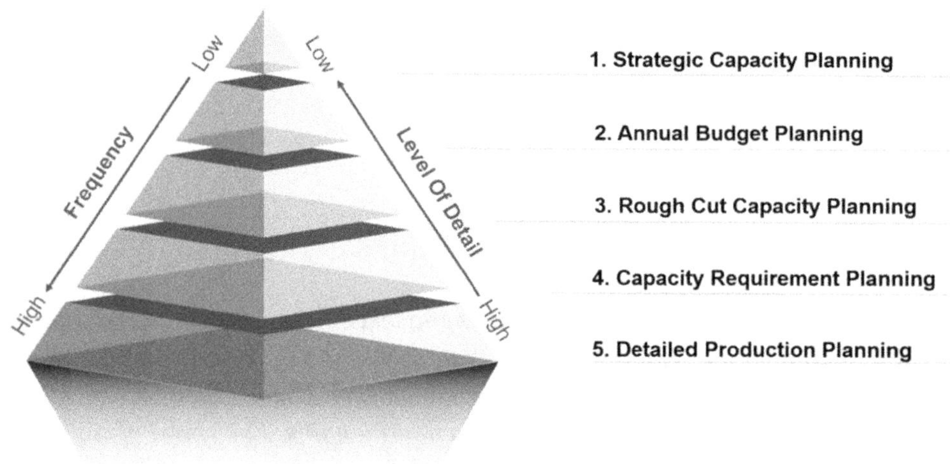

five levels of capacity planning.

The five levels in capacity planning provide a holistic, top-down view of the capacity—validating and verifying the process's end goal at each stage and disseminating the information to the next level to make execution-level decisions. For example, leadership defined a long-term goal in strategic capacity planning that is disaggregated into a yearly plan considering market conditions in the annual budget planning process. Following the budget, rough-cut capacity planning and capacity requirement planning generate and track a tactical strategy to achieve the annual plan. Finally, detailed production planning adds execution-level detail for day-to-day execution. The sophistication and need for supporting technology increase as the process moves from Level 1 to Level 5.

The subsequent sections will provide background information, expand on the five levels of the capacity planning process, and provide a maturity model for organizations to assess capabilities and define a roadmap to build capabilities.

BACKGROUND

Capacity Definition

Capacity is the output of a resource for a period (Nada R. Sanders & R. Dan Reid, 2012, para. 1). A resource can be a manufacturing plant, assembly line, warehouse space, truck, or any equipment that assists in producing a product or delivering a service. Resources can exist within an organization's four walls or outside, with suppliers supplying components, raw materials, or supporting select operations. For example, Samsung© builds components for its Galaxy© product line at its facilities in South Korea while it also uses Foxconn© for assembly operations in China; therefore, Samsung has internal assembly capacities in South Korea and external assembly capacities at Foxconn in China.

The following diagram shows a simple linear supply chain with five nodes—supplier, manufacturing, transportation, warehouse, and store. Each node in this supply chain has one or more capacities. For example, the raw material supplier, a mining company, has the capacity of labor and heavy machinery to extract ore; the earthmover's capacity can be defined as 1,000 tons of dirt per hour. The transportation company has trucking capacities to support the movement of the goods; truck capacity can be defined as space 1,000 cubic feet or weight 25-ton.

Figure 2. Different types of capacities in the supply chain

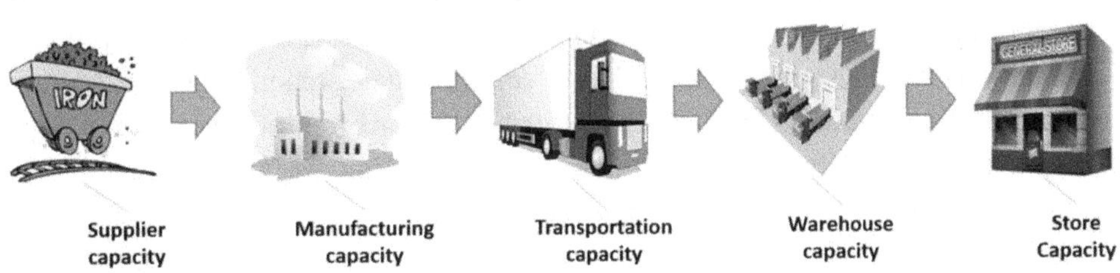

Capacity Planning

Capacity planning is a technique to plan optimum resource levels to meet future demand in all market conditions (Prachi Juneja, n.d.). The key to effective capacity planning is maintaining optimal resource capacity because excess capacity ties up working capital, while inadequate capacity causes lost sales leading to unhappy customers.

While organizations can make minor capacity adjustments through overtime/idle time, adding tools, or adjusting run rates to respond to short-term demand variations, large capacity additions/decommissions—such as inaugurating a distribution center to add storage space or shutting down a plant to eliminate excess capacity—are done only in large chunks with an associated long lead time (a few months to several years involving large capital outlay).

Most examples and concepts in this chapter are manufacturing-organization oriented; however, similar concepts can be applied to service organizations where manpower is the primary resource. Service organization challenges include assessing manpower capacity, which varies from person to person. Additionally, most of the concepts in this chapter are aligned with APICS[2] definitions with certain variations based on the author's 20 years of experience at various organizations in the field.

Now, with a fundamental understanding of capacity planning, we will move to understand the need for the capacity planning process and the implications when process gaps exist.

Need for Capacity Planning

If the demand for products was uniform or resources had no constraints, the capacity planning process would have been a trivial task; however—except for a few government agencies such as tax authorities—a product or service forecasts have low accuracy and high volatility with access to only finite resources to meet this demand. Coping with demand volatility and making long-term decisions with hundreds of unknowns while mitigating risks make the capacity planning process challenging. Some of the challenges of capacity decisions are as follows:

- **Volatile demand:** Organizations struggle with demand volatility (peaks and troughs), timing, and accuracy. Forecast accuracy and demand variability ranked second in Gartner and Supply Chain Digest 2016 supply chain barriers survey[5]. In current market conditions, where shorter product life cycles are becoming the norm and supply chain shortages due to disruptions lead to demand gaming and threaten previously optimized flows, achieving a comfortable demand accuracy for a sustained period is becoming more challenging. For example – during the pandemic, due to chip shortages, companies knew that their suppliers were allocating products; therefore, companies placed large orders in the hopes of getting some of those orders fulfilled. This disruption caused large backorders and distrust in customer signals. To manage these challenges, companies need to be agile and flexible on the supply side to absorb some of the demand challenges.
- **SKU proliferation:** Online sales channels offering customized products with unprecedented choices leave online and offline players with an extensive catalog to manage. On the supply side, additional product variations complicate capacity planning because factories need to run considerable product variations leveraging the same resources while minimizing changeovers (Bowman, 2013). With SKU proliferation, the lack of a defined capacity planning process and the absence of enabling technology to execute the strategy cause significant challenges in fulfilling the demand.
- **Shorter product life cycle:** It is not apparent, but a shorter product life cycle has significant implications for capacity planning because supply organizations constantly need to refresh capacities to phase out old products and launch new products (Pierce, 2012).
- **Need for visibility:** Digitization of the supply chain necessitates high visibility so that companies can commit to their customers confidently; however, with the absence of the right tools and SKU proliferation, providing true visibility to end nodes in the supply chain is challenging. Visibility is also needed to manage disruption. For example, when supply chain disruption strikes, companies find understanding the impact and defining the solution challenging without good visibility.
- **The influx of new digital capabilities:** Internet of Things (IoT) sensors in machines, radio-frequency identification (RFID), and collaboration technologies are enabling organizations to share and receive information to respond better to market needs; however, many organizations are not prepared to harness new information that may cause them to lose to a competitor who has built these capabilities.

Given the challenges outlined above and their implications for the organization's prospects, a better capacity planning process can boost revenue, lower capital requirements, and provide a true competitive advantage.

Challenges in Capacity Planning

Realizing the importance of capacity planning, many organizations have begun focusing on improving the capacity planning process but are facing several challenges. The list below highlights some of the key challenges.

1. **Defining the right level for planning:** Every organization performs capacity planning in some shape or form, but the ultimate objective of the process is to conduct at a level that puts forth the right detail to support leadership in making the right decisions. For example, capacity planning for high-level resources, such as total factory capacity to make shoes at a shoe manufacturer, can be used to determine the need to build a new factory or expand the factory; however, this high-level information cannot predict whether the company can deliver 10,000 shoes in three months. Many companies are performing capacity planning either at a very high level for long-range strategic planning or at a detailed factory planning level, which is a complex, resource-intensive process and challenging to respond rapidly to market fluctuations. Defining the right levels for capacity planning is vital to supporting the right decisions.
2. **Availability of the right data:** The capacity planning process relies heavily on the correct data with sufficient detail to support the process, such as time-phased capacity information for resources, products' capacity usage, etc. Without accurate data, the process generates inaccurate results leading to wrong decisions.
3. **Defining the proper hierarchy:** To perform capacity planning at different levels of aggregation to support different decisions, organizations need to have good, common hierarchies and the right levels in the product, location, geography, and time hierarchies. Right levels in the hierarchies enable aggregation and disaggregation for different functional groups to view the same information at different levels. For example, the finance team considers total revenue at the business unit level, while the S&OP team regards revenue by product lines. Hierarchies enable functional groups to collaborate on the process and extract relevant information without duplicating the efforts.
4. **Set up the right organization:** Many organizations lack a dedicated group to manage the capacity planning process. Several groups support part of the process, but a single group does not cover the holistic capacity picture, which cuts through cross-functional boundaries. The lack of the right organizational structure leaves the organization with localized suboptimal results.
5. **Executive support:** Capacity planning is performed at multiple levels and needs executive commitment to enlist support from stakeholders and commit the resources to execute the process.

Capacity Planning Levels, Maturity, and Implementation

Before discussing each level of capacity planning mentioned in Figure 1, it is essential to understand some of the concepts related to capacity planning.

Capacity Unit of Measure

Capacity is measured using various units of measure. The three commonly used measures are as follows:

1. **Run rate:** The run rate for a machine is defined as the total output produced in a specified time—for example, 200 units/minute for an injection-modeling machine or 40 tons of steel per hour. Run rate is mainly used to quote capacity for resources producing a single product line. For example, a simple one-liter water bottle-filling machine can fill 4,000 bottles in an hour.
2. **Total available time:** Some resources can produce various products, and each product can have a different run rate on the resource. For example, a lathe machine can produce 20 small gears per hour while producing only two pistons per hour. Depending on the product type, the resource's run rate can vary; therefore, instead of quoting the resource's capacity as multiple run rates, the resource's capacity can be quoted as total available hours, such as 18 available hours per day.
3. **Space:** The capacity of warehouses, retail stores, service organizations, etc., as defined in square feet.

Capacity Calendar

Due to maintenance activity, operator's availability, or various other reasons, a resource's capacity can vary each week. To apply variations, resource capacities are defined in a calendar format, which provides the flexibility to maintain different capacities for different periods. For example, a gear-cutting machine can be available 18 hours per day on most days, but for a few days, due to maintenance and operators' availability, it can be available only for 8 hours.

Additionally, resources have two types of capacities—design capacity and effective capacity. The design capacity is the maximum output of the resource, while effective capacity is the capacity that can be generated consistently over a long period. The reason for the two different types of capacities is that resources can run at maximum capacity only for a short time, as running at maximum capacity for a prolonged time may cause breakage, which results in downtime or reduced capacity. For resource load planning, effective capacity is used. The table below shows an example of an effective capacity calendar of a lathe machine.

Table 1. Capacity calendar

Lathe capacity	Week 1	Week 2	Week 3	Week 4	Week 5	Week 6	Week 7	Week 8
Hour per day	18	18	18	18	10	10	12	18
Number of days	5	5	5	4	4	4	5	5
Total weekly capacity (hours)	**90**	**90**	**90**	**72**	**40**	**40**	**60**	**90**

Product Routing

Routing defines the resources needed to build a product or deliver a service. For example, gear routing can include forging, cutting, and finishing operation.

Planning Horizon and Planning Buckets

The planning horizon is the period in the future that an organization plans capacity (Swamidass P.M, 2000). The planning horizon can be between 4 weeks to 5+ years, depending on the level of capacity planning. The planning horizon is divided into planning buckets. Planning buckets can be daily, weekly, monthly, quarterly, or yearly. Most often, daily and weekly planning buckets are used for short-term planning, such as detailed production at Level 5 in Figure 1, where detailed information is necessary to execute orders in a factory or place a raw material order to support production. Monthly and quarterly buckets are used primarily for a medium-term planning horizon, while yearly buckets are used for strategic planning. Based on the organization's structure and product type, organizations can define the length of the planning horizon and planning bucket for different planning levels.

The following picture shows the five-year planning horizon with weekly, monthly, and quarterly buckets. Different planning buckets in the same horizon are called mixed bucket horizons or telescoping buckets. Telescoping buckets provide more granular detail (weekly and monthly) in near-term horizon and time aggregation, such as quarterly buckets, which later reduces uncertainty.

Figure 3. Planning horizon and planning buckets

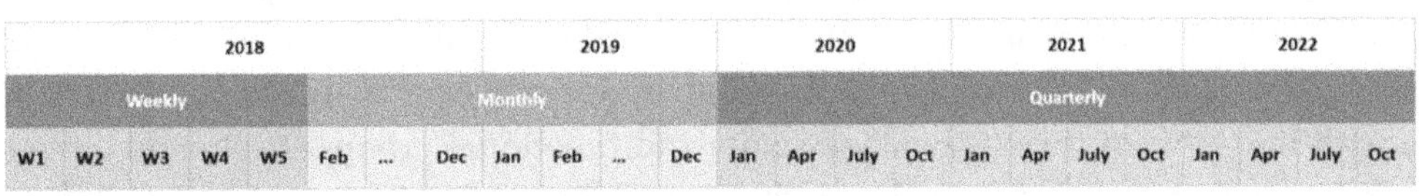

Top-Down Approach to Capacity Planning

At the beginning of the chapter, Figure 1 introduces five levels of capacity planning. Each level of capacity planning is done to meet a particular objective and to make specific decisions. The following section provides detail of each level.

Strategic capacity planning: Strategic capacity planning is tied to the organization's strategic planning process, which defines its strategic direction for the next 3 to 5+ years. As a part of the strategic planning process, strategic capacity planning helps leadership understand the total capacity required to achieve the organization's long-term growth plan. Strategic capacity planning is performed for overall capability considering plants', subcontractors', and suppliers' capacity to understand, at a high level, if the supply chain has the required throughput to support the growth plan. Strategic capacity planning is performed yearly for a 3 to 5-year planning horizon (in the case of auto OEM, 5 to 10 years) in quarterly or yearly planning buckets. Strategic capacity planning enables leadership to make significant capital investment decisions, such as opening a new factory or building new supplier capability.

For example, a shoe manufacturer has \$5 billion in annual revenue and has factories to fulfill \$5.5 billion in revenue to accommodate growth. A new CEO joins the company and sets up a new target for the next five years: Achieve 4 percent compounded growth year over year to achieve \$6 billion in revenue by the fifth year. To support this long-term growth plan, in the strategic capacity planning process, leadership validates the supply organization's capability to support the growth and makes capital investment decisions to fill the gap. Based on revenue projections year-over-year for five years (Table 2 below), the organization will face a $500 million revenue shortfall for the fifth year and a total of $870 million cumulative revenue gaps over five years due to capacity shortages. To fill these capacity shortages, leadership has multiple options: Expand capacity at the beginning of year 2, buy a supplier in year 3, open a new factory in year 3, improve the performance of existing capacity, and so on.

Table 2. Strategic capacity planning analysis example and resolution options

	Current year	Year 1	Year 2	Year 3	Year 4	Year 5
Revenue	$5.0B	$5.2B	$5.41B	$5.62B	$5.85B	$6.0B
Supply capacity	$5.5B	$5.5B	$5.50B	$5.50B	$5.50B	$5.5B
Shortfall				($120M)	($250M)	($500M)
Cumulative shortfall				($120M)	($370M)	($870M)
Plan to fill the shortfall		Initiate improvement	Expand the plant	Buy a supplier		

Annual budget planning: Annual budget planning or annual operating planning occurs yearly to define the goals and operating plan for the whole organization for the upcoming financial year. It is an organization-wide process with the supply chain group as one of the participants. Finance typically leads the process with inputs from various business units and functional groups. In this process, the leadership defines revenue targets, which translate into demand targets for different business units to achieve the collective annual plan (Martin, 2015, para. 5). Based on demand targets, the supply planning group identifies, in collaboration with procurement, an operating plan to fulfill the demand and gaps in current capacities. The supply planning group presents the operating plan and capacity gaps to the supply chain leadership to obtain the operating budget and investment to fill capacity gaps, such as acquiring a new machine, hiring additional labor, etc. Annual budget planning is performed in quarterly buckets and tracked to quarter-ends in a financial year.

For example, this year, the shoe manufacturer in the previous example aims to achieve $5.2 billion in revenue, 4 percent, or $200 million above the last year's plan. The organization plans to introduce a new product line to meet the additional revenue goal. The supply planning group, responsible for capacity, determines that the organization would need to expand the capacity of three assembly lines and buy three new machines to support the additional revenue. During the annual budget planning process, the supply planning group will produce the plan to expand capacity to the leadership. Based on the proposal, leadership may assign a capital budget to expand the capacity.

Rough-cut capacity planning: Rough-cut capacity planning (RCCP) is part of a mature monthly sales and operation (S&OP) process (Dr. Ken Fordyce, 2015). A key objective of S&OP is to get the product volume right considering consensus demand and available capacity (ORTEC, n.d.); therefore, RCCP, which assists the S&OP team in validating capacity, is done at an aggregated level, such as at the product family level. Since RCCP is performed at an aggregated level, resources in RCCP are also aggregated to enable the S&OP team to make tradeoffs among product families to maximize fill rate, increase margin, and fill any gaps between the annual operating plan and current operational plan. Here is a guideline for selecting resources for RCCP:

- Factory throughput can be one of the constraints.
- For select strategic products, the overall output can be a constraint.
- Overall product output can be a constraint when a product is sourced from multiple sources.
- An aggregated resource, which dictates a factory or product output, for example, Bliss press capacity in forging operation or molding capacity for a foundry or plastic part manufacturing

RCCP is performed in monthly buckets for the next 18- to 24-month planning horizon, and if the horizon is longer than 24 months, then in quarterly buckets. RCCP aims to highlight demand/supply gaps in the midterm (outside of the 3-month horizon) and assist in filling the gaps using different strategies, such as prebuilding to accommodate peak demand, offloading volume to suppliers, etc. The output of the RCCP is called production requirements.

RCCP is one of the parts of the larger monthly S&OP process, and S&OP is a more important topic in itself. Without going into detail about S&OP, the following depiction will briefly expand the shoe manufacturer example to demonstrate RCCP.

Sales, operations, marketing, and finance teams together finalize the annual plan and break it into a monthly or quarterly plan for execution and tracking. Additionally, to plan for the longer term, the planning horizon is extended to 2 years using projections considering the strategic plan, demand history, product roadmap, and market conductions.

Table 3. Annual plan example

In million $	M1	M2	M3	M4	M5	M6	..	M23	M24
Annual plan	$100	$100	$100	$110	$110	$110	..	..	..

In RCCP, demand planning and supply planning first bring their best plan along with several scenarios to fill revenue gaps or eliminate supply shortages. For the review meeting with leadership, the demand plan is aggregated to Business Units (BU) and families to assess the gap between the unconstrained demand plan and annual plan, and the supply plan is aggregated to view supply shortages for a BU and a family.

Table 4 shows demand, supply, and supply gaps for one product family, Sports Shoe, in both units and dollars. Showing the demand plan in both units and dollars is vital because different groups talk in different units of measure. For example, Finance cares about revenue while demand planning cares about units; therefore, aligning groups by showing the plan in their unit of measure helps make quick decisions.

In the leadership review meeting, apart from highlighting supply gaps, the supply planning group proposes various scenarios to fill those gaps, such as running plants overtime for three days in a month, or if plants are already running at the maximum capacity, shifting the load to a supplier, and so on.

After resolving supply gaps for individual families, leadership reviews revenue gaps between the demand plan and annual plan (an example in Table 5) and reviews proposed options to fill gaps, such as running a promotion to close revenue gaps or launching a product early, etc. After the assessment, leadership approves an execution plan.

Capacity requirement planning: Capacity requirement planning (CRP) is part of the master planning process. In master planning, the output of RCCP—production requirement at an aggregated volume

Table 4. Family level supply gaps example

Sports shoe	M1	M2	M3	M4	M5	M6	..	M23	M24
Demand plan ($)	$30M	$35M	$33M	$34M	$36M	$37M	…	…	…
Demand plan (units)	1.2M	1.4M	1.32M	1.36M	1.44M	1.48M	…	…	…
Supply plan unit ($)	$30M	$32.5M	$32.5M	$32.5M	$32.5M	$35M	…	…	…
Supply plan unit(s)	1.2M	1.3M	1.3M	1.3M	1.3M	1.4M	…	…	…
Supply gap ($)		($2.5M)	($0.5M)	($1.5M)	($3.5M)	($2M)	…	…	…
Supply gap (units)		(0.1M)	(0.02M)	(0.06M)	(0.14M)	(0.08M)	…	…	…

Table 5. Revenue gaps example

	M1	M2	M3	M4	M5	M6	..	M23	M24
Sport shoe	$30M	$32.5M	$32.5M	$32.5M	$32.5M	$35.0M	…	…	…
Formal shoe	$20M	$25.0M	$30.0M	$35.0M	$35.0M	$34.0M	…	…	…
Casual shoe	$52M	$40.0M	$39.0M	$39.0M	$38.0M	$38.0M	…	…	…
Total plan	$102M	$97.5M	$101.5M	$106.5M	$105.5M	$107M	…	…	…
Annual plan	$100	$100	$100	$110	$110	$110	…	…	…
Gap	$2M	($2.5M)	$1.5M	($3.5M)	($4.5M)	($3.0M)	…	…	…
Cumulative gap	$2M	($0.5M)	$1.0M	($2.5M)	($7.0M)	($10.0M)	…	…	…

level—is used to plan individual products to drive a master production schedule (MPS) at an item or SKU level. At an aggregate level, MPS should match the production requirement of the S&OP process (Martin Murray, 2018, para. 1). CRP considers only key bottleneck resources; therefore, it should not be confused with detailed production planning. The number of resources in CRP is generally more than in RCCP but fewer than in the detailed production planning process, which considers most resources. For example, RCCP may consider total molding capacity as a consolidated capacity constraint, while CRP may further divide molding into three constraints divided by tonnages, such as 1000-ton, 2000-ton, or 5000-ton. Unlike RCCP, CRP can plan some of the detailed capacities because the demand in CRP is at the item level; thus, the load on an individual machine can be determined to identify the load on the capacity.

CRP is performed in weekly buckets for the next 2- to 6-month planning horizon, and monthly buckets follow the weekly buckets. Since CRP input—production plan—is in monthly buckets, it needs to be broken into weekly buckets for the first few weeks. Monthly buckets to weekly buckets can be done differently, for example, equally to all weeks or a specific percentage for each week.

CRP aims to understand the short-term production plan for the next few months so that procurement can order materials and resources. The output of CRP—MPS—is used for alignment between sales and production—the customer representative team uses it to make customer promises, while plants and vendors use it as an expected production plan to prepare raw materials and resources.

A question often asked about CRP is, "which resources should be part of the CRP process?" A simple guideline is to include the constraints that can give sufficient confidence in committing the production plan to the sales team while avoiding getting into the complex details of production planning. Here are a few additional guidelines for selecting resources for CRP:

- Consider bottleneck resources that often hit their ceiling.
- Plan resources at an aggregated level, not at an individual tool level.
- Avoid labor as a constraint; however, if labor is a significant roadblock, consider leveraging it in other forms, such as a total number of hours.
- Consider selected long lead-time parts or raw materials that often pose scheduling challenges.

In CRP, as well as in RCCP and detailed production planning, resource constraints are applied in two ways: Soft constraints and hard constraints. The difference between the two types of constraints is overloading—hard constraints cannot be loaded more than 100 percent, while soft constraints can be loaded more than 100 percent. The reason for overloading soft constraints is to alert the planners to overloading and have the planner identify an alternate, which can expedite material by paying premium freight, using another supplier, etc. In the case of hard constraints, if the constraint hits 100 percent, the system seeks unused capacity in adjacent planning buckets, and if it cannot find available capacity, it alerts the planner to unresolved capacity gaps.

The output of the CRP process is MPS, which feeds the detailed production planning process. Additionally, MPS drives material requirement planning (MRP) to release purchase orders to suppliers or change an existing purchase order, for example – push out, pull in, or cancel a purchase order. The CRP process is demonstrated in Table 6 using the shoe manufacturing company.

In CRP, the production plan of families—sports shoes, formal shoes, and casual shoes—is disaggregated into the product-level production plan to model and validate selected critical bottleneck resources. The table below shows CRP analysis on sewing capacity. While weeks 2 and 3 have excess capacity, weeks 4, 5, 7, and 8 have a capacity shortage. To balance the capacity load, the capacity planner may pull forward some week four load to weeks two and three, week seven load to week six, and run overtime or extra shifts in week 8. While this example shows manual capacity balancing, modern capacity planning systems can perform this task automatically.

Table 6. Resource capacity example

Sewing capacity (hrs.)	Wk 1	Wk 2	Wk 3	Wk 4	Wk 5	Wk 6	Wk 7	Wk 8	..	M 23	M 24
Available capacity	20k	20k	20k	20k	20k	20k	20k	20k	…	…	…
Required load	20k	19k	19k	22k	21k	19k	21k	22k	…	…	…
Gap		1k	1k	(2k)	(1k)	1k	(1k)	(2k)	…	…	…
Cumulative gap		1k	2k	0	(1k)	0	(1k)	(3k)	…	…	…

Figure 4. Capacity balancing

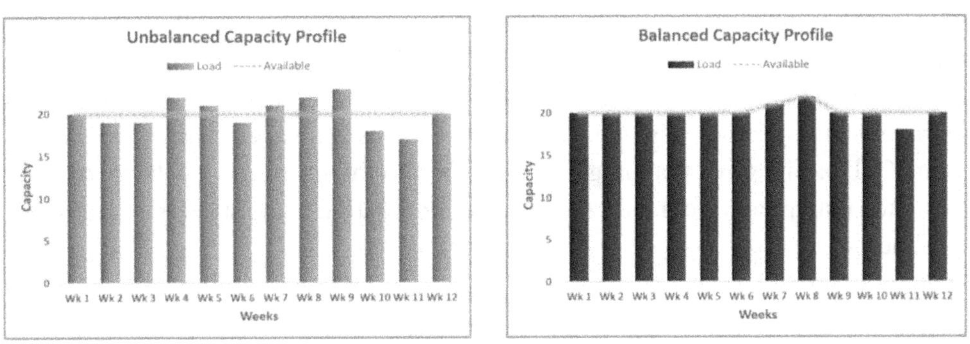

After balancing the critical bottleneck resources, the final master production schedule (MPS) is released for detailed production planning for execution.

Detailed production planning: Detailed production planning uses MPS as input and develops a production plan at a daily level of detail. All major resources are considered to plan a full production day in detailed production planning. Detailed production planning runs weekly (rerun daily for production misses and minor changes) to plan for the whole week in daily or weekly planning buckets. The output of detailed production planning is shared with the shop floor to schedule production, which drives material release orders to warehouses to draw the material. Detailed production planning is a time- and resource-intensive process; therefore, the focus on detailed production planning is only 2 to 5 weeks, with the planning horizon in daily buckets.

Some smaller companies or companies with simpler manufacturing skip detailed production planning and move to factory scheduling directly. If these companies have a sophisticated system incorporating detailed production planning in the CRP, they can execute the process; however, if they are planning manually, they will eventually spend more time in CRP to balance the plan, which makes the process rigid to respond to the market demand.

The following table illustrates the detailed production planning process using a shoe manufacturer example.

After receiving MPS for a specific shoe, the production planner creates a short-term production plan for 4 to 5 weeks in daily buckets. In detailed production planning, the production planner checks the capacities of major factory resources that may constrain the plan, including labor resources to run lines.

Table 7. Detailed capacity example

RS-001XBND	D1	D2	D3	D4	D5	D6	..	D27	D28
Production plan	1,000	1,000	1,000	1,000	1,000	1,000	...	...	...
Sewing requirement	83h	83h	83h	83h	83h	83h	...	...	...
Sewing available	200h	10h	100h	80h	100h	100h			
Assembly hours required	167h	167h	167h	167h	167h	167h	...	...	...
Assembly hours available	200h	100h	200h	200h	200h	200h			

In the above example, due to the sewing capacity shortage on D2, the production planner can move some of the units to D1 and D3.

Planning Zones and Controls

With the different planning levels, a discussion on planning zones cannot be omitted, as the zones drive change types in the capacity plan. The planning organization defines rules for making changes to the plan in a planning zone and establishes governance to manage the zones. A planning horizon can be divided into three planning zones—frozen, firm, and free—with a varying time horizon for each zone (APICS Forum, 2012). The three planning zones are tied to the last three levels of capacity planning: Detailed production planning to the frozen zone, master production planning to the firm zone, and RCCP with the free zone.

Figure 5. Planning zones

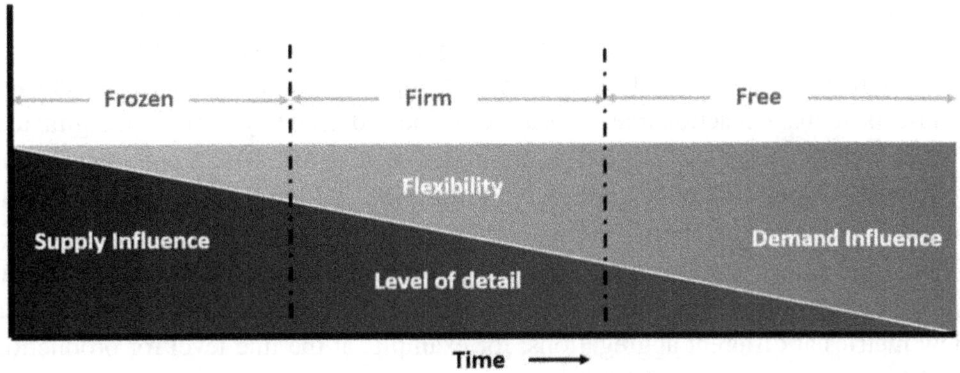

Frozen zone: Frozen zone, as the name suggests, does not allow many changes. Once committed, production planned in the frozen zone remains mostly unchanged, with some exceptions made for a valid reason with approvals. A frozen production plan in the short term provides the manufacturing stability to commit resources internally and externally. Production planners and production managers control the frozen zone. Any change in a quantity larger than a certain percentage in the frozen zone requires production manager approval.

Firm zone: Firm zone provides a little flexibility to accommodate a moderate number of changes because not all sources in the firm zone duration are committed to the production; however, long lead-time materials are already ordered for the production in the firm zone, which restricts significant changes without expediting material. Master planners, jointly with production managers and procurement managers, control the firm zone. Tactical demand and supply weekly/bi-weekly meetings with a sales and marketing perspective provide guidelines and ensure both manufacturing and customer priorities stay in equilibrium.

Free zone: Free zone is for long-term planning and visibility. No commitments are made in the free zone, and most of the changes within the overall capacity level can be accommodated. Supply chain leadership controls the free zone through the monthly S&OP process.

In frozen and firm zones, the available and committed supply influences the demand (what can be fulfilled based on available resources); in the free zone, demand influences supply (what supply should be arranged).

Capacity Utilization Tracking and Identifying Resources for Planning

Resources capacity is measured in utilization percentages; the higher the utilization, the better the cost efficiencies; however, utilization above 90 percent denotes close to full utilization and an inability to accommodate any maintenance downtime or short-term demand changes.

Resource utilization = (Used capacity/Available capacity) * 100

Resource utilization is the percentage of available capacity used.

In capacity planning, keeping a history of resource utilization month over month helps identify trends in resource loading, which can help identify resources for RCCP and CRP. Maintaining a history of both high and low utilization is also valuable for determining the list of resources for planning.

A challenge in tracking resource utilization is identifying the right level in the hierarchy and measuring in near real-time to make it actionable. This issue can be addressed by deploying digital technologies and business intelligence (BI) tools. Digital technologies such as IoT, RFID, and factory collaboration can provide constant availability of resources and throughput, which can be captured in BI tools and displayed in a dashboard for planners' actions. Additionally, these digital signals can be fed into the planning system to identify capacity issues' impact on fulfilled demands. To measure utilization at the right level, it is better to collect the data at the lowest level and leverage BI tools to give planners the ability to view metrics at different aggregations; for example, at the line level for production planners and plant level for plant managers or S&OP planners.

Implement the Capacity Planning Process

This section provides a high-level capacity planning maturity model for companies to assess their current maturity level and a brief implementation approach for them to move to a higher level. Since the maturity model in this chapter considered only high-level processes, companies will benefit from further assessing their maturity within each level on four dimensions—process, system, organization, and delivery model. The detailed maturity model and implementation approaches are out of the scope of this chapter.

Capacity Planning Process Maturity Model

Most companies, small or large, benefit from performing all five levels of planning as each level has a distinct objective and associated decisions. The following diagram shows the capacity planning maturity model.

Figure 6. Capacity planning maturity model

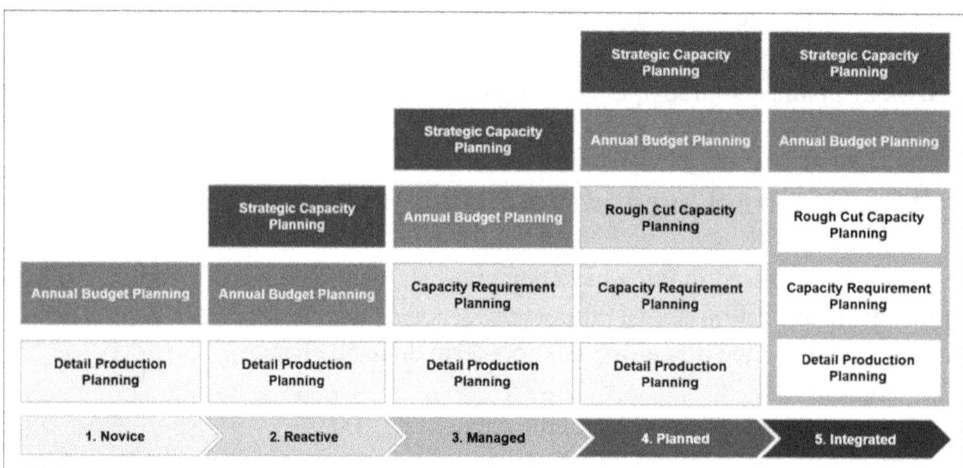

Many job shops or small companies perform only basic capacity planning that focuses on planning for a week's work or a single job. These companies performing only ad hoc capacity planning will fall at Level 1 or novice maturity on the diagram.

All medium and large companies are at least at the level-two maturity level, which includes strategic capacity planning, annual budget planning, and detailed production planning; however, the level of maturity and process efficiency among companies varies widely, which requires a separate discussion. Each subsequent maturity level adds an additional level of capacity planning. At maturity level five, boundaries among the last three levels start disappearing. Additionally, level five requires a sophisticated system that can run RCCP, CRP, and detailed planning in a single model with different aggregation and disaggregation logic catering to the needs of different levels.

Implementation

To implement an effective capacity planning process, organizations can start by understanding the planning organization's current process maturity level, solution capabilities, and nature of business. After that, evaluate the current capabilities with the desired capabilities to identify gaps. Following the gap identification, create a roadmap to bridge the gaps in phases—attain one maturity level and move to another.

As previously discussed, the capacity planning process relies heavily on data—the correct process with the incorrect data will lead to failure; a lack of trust in results will cause a relapse into silo processes and broken links in the top-down process. A data assessment before implementation will provide insight into data quality and gaps. For example, assessing product, customer, and location hierarchies to understand if hierarchies are consistently maintained across product lines and business units. Additionally, assess if the same hierarchies and hierarchy levels are used across functional areas, such as Finance, sales, marketing, demand planning, supply planning, etc. If differences exist, consider harmonizing hierarchies to bring all the groups under one hierarchy.

In large implementations, running a pilot program always pays off down the line. A pilot program allows the implementation team to establish and test the new processes with a business unit and a selected product type to identify the challenges at a smaller, more manageable level and resolve them before rolling out the process to the broader organization. After a successful pilot, the organization can begin adding products and regions to the program.

Since the capacity planning process is rarely performed to precision, start the process with what is readily available to build the team, process, capability, and cadence. Initially, apply the 80-20 principle to run the process for high-demand products and critical or high-shortage resources. Once the value is proven, add additional resources or detail to the process.

CONCLUSION

While most medium and large companies run some capacity planning process, companies need to give capacity planning processes a holistic view—implementing five levels in the capacity planning process—by looking from the strategic level at corporate headquarters to detailed daily-level scheduling at factories while integrating other groups in the levels in between. Additionally, digitalization of the supply chain has bestowed powerful capabilities, such as Artificial Intelligence and Machine Learning, in planning tools and control towers, enabling organizations to run self-healing processes with reduced human intervention.

Transforming an organization to build a robust capacity planning process is a long journey. Organizations can begin this journey by first enabling the fundamental processes to support higher maturity in the future. A five-level capacity planning maturity model assists organizations in setting up those basic processes and helps ensure a foundation is established before moving to the next level. A robust multilevel capacity planning process prepares the organization to control the supply chain and respond to uncertainty in the new digital age.

REFERENCES

APICS. (n.d.). *Rough-Cut capacity planning*. APICS. http://apicsforum.com/ebook/capacity_planning

Bowman, R. J. (2013). *SKU Proliferation: Is There a Cure for the Disease?* SupplyChainBrain. https://www.supplychainbrain.com/blogs/1-think-tank/post/17575-sku-proliferation-is-there-a-cure-for-the-disease

Farrell, L. (2020). 4 Capacity Planning Challenges in L&D (And How to Overcome Them). *Cognota.* https://cognota.com/blog/4-capacity-planning-challenges-in-ld-and-how-to-overcome-them/

FencesT. (n.d.). Retrieved from http://apicsforum.com/ebook/time_fences

Gademann, N., van Helden, F., & Kuijsten, W. (n.d.). *S&OP a threefold approach to strategic planning*. ORTEC Counsiling. https://www.ortec-consulting.com/market-views/s-and-op-a-threefold-approach-to-strategic-planning/

Gartner and Supply Chain Digest. (2016). Highlights of the Gartner-SCDigest Supply Chain Study 2016. SC Digest. http://www.scdigest.com/firstthoughts/16-07-21.php?cid=10995

Juneja, P. (n.d.). *Capacity Planning*. Management Study Guide. https://www.managementstudyguide.com/capacity-planning.htm

Murray, M. (2018). Master Scheduling Tracks Manufacturing Output. *The Balances MB.* https://www.thebalancesmb.com/master-scheduling-2221212

Pierce, F. (2012). The product life cycle is in decline. *Supply Chain Digital.* https://www.supplychain-digital.com/procurement/product-life-cycle-decline

Solventure, S. (n.d.). *Rough Cut Capacity Planning*. Solventure Group. https://www.solventuregroup.com/content/rough-cut-capacity-planning/

Time Buckets. (2000). In P. M. Swamidass (Ed.), *Encyclopedia of Production and Manufacturing Management.* Springer.

Chapter 8
Augmenting Capabilities of Advanced Planning and Scheduling Systems With Curated IIoT Data

Amol Mate
Altizon Inc., USA

Rohan Vishwasrao
BlueYonder, USA

ABSTRACT

Supply continuity is being challenged at every stage of the supply chain, with changing workforce dynamics, natural events, and consumer buying patterns. These changes in the operating environment are continuously introducing inefficiencies into the supply chains, and are putting pressure on costs to serve. Even during the pre-pandemic era, execution adherence to plans generated by advanced planning and scheduling systems (APS) was not more than 50%. Rapid evolution of emerging technologies accelerates digitization of supply chains and provides opportunities to enable paradigm shifts in supply chain planning. Integration of planning software with industrial internet of things (IIoT) platforms, which collect real-time data across the value chain, can drive the next level of supply chain optimization. In this chapter, the authors provide specific recommendations, to extracting maximum value from APS systems by addressing some limitations, for example, out-of-sync master data and lack of real-time transactional data, by using curated data feeds from the IIoT platforms to augments APS capabilities.

INTRODUCTION

Advanced planned and scheduling (APS) describes any computer program that uses advanced mathematical algorithms or logic to perform optimization (or simulation) on finite capacity scheduling, sourcing, capital planning, resource planning, forecasting, demand management, etc. The five main components

DOI: 10.4018/978-1-6684-7298-9.ch008

of APS systems are – (a) Demand Planning, (b) Production Planning, (c) Production Scheduling, (d) Distribution Planning, and (e) Transportation Planning (APICS Dictionary, 2022). These systems are relevant in environments where simpler planning methods like MRP II cannot address complex trade-offs between competing objectives. A best-in-class APS system supports the 'Plan' process associated with developing plans to operate the supply chain, i.e., all SCOR Level 1 processes – Order, Source, Transform, Fulfill and Return processes. These include determining requirements, gathering information about available resources, balancing requirements and resources to determine planned capabilities and gaps in demand or resources, and identifying actions to correct these gaps (SCOR Digital Standard 2022).

For an APS system to be effective, it needs data feeds from multiple systems of record like ERP, CRM, WMS, Order Management, MES systems, etc. With this data, APS systems generate feasible plans and efficient schedules, which in theory, enable fast and reliable customer response. Typically, data fed from multiple systems is transformed and refreshed at a set frequency. Herein lies a fundamental limitation of such a system – data latency, validity, and completeness. The second issue is the complexity of integration – cost overhead, additional points of failure, and limits on degrees of freedom. In the subsequent sections, we will address both these limitations in some detail and provide actional recommendations to address them.

Complex Systems

Complex systems have been studied across multiple scientific, engineering, and mathematical disciplines, and therefore no single definition has been developed to describe a complex system. For this chapter, we use the definition proposed by Magee and de Weck (2004), 'Complex system: a system with numerous components and interconnections, interactions or interdependence that are difficult to describe, understand, predict, manage, design, or change'.

A non-connected system is normally perceived to be simple and easy to measure and optimize, while a highly interconnected system is perceived to be very complex and difficult to measure and optimize. Complex systems are characterized by their; (a) parts, (b) interconnections between the parts, and (c) function or purpose. Interactions between parts produce behaviors that are driven by the function or purpose of the system. Thus, simple interactions between parts lead to the emergence of new order and coherence. This new order is not evident in the parts alone but only in the system as a whole.

To facilitate continuous measurement, command, and control, we can measure system complexity by

- Extent of connectedness
- Number of data exchanges between different entities in the system
- Degrees of freedom

The essence of most examples of Complex systems – a collection of interacting objects or agents – can be encapsulated in three aspects: (a) emergent phenomena arising out of the interactions and (b) objects competing for limited resources, and (c) influence of the environment on the system. We will discuss these in some detail in the subsequent sections (Johnson, Neil. 2009. Simply Complexity).

Figure 1. Siloed and connected systems

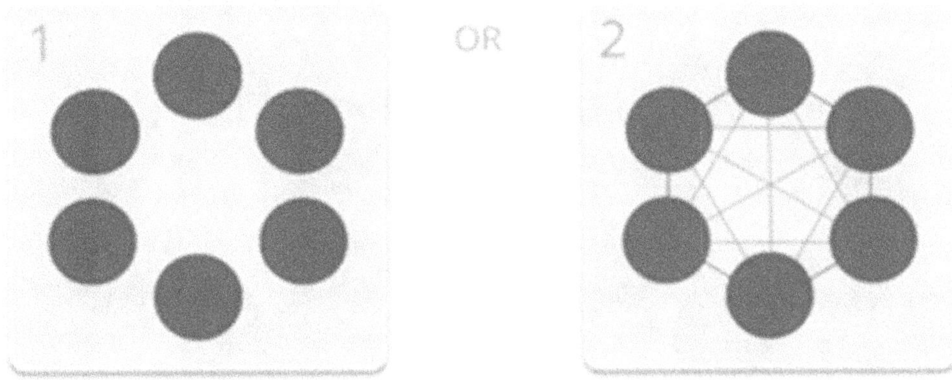

Directed System of Systems

A System of Systems (SoS) is a collection of independent systems integrated into a larger system that delivers unique capabilities. The independent constituent systems collaborate to produce global behavior that they cannot produce alone. The study of the emerging system-of-systems concept describes the large-scale integration of many independent, self-contained systems to satisfy a global set of objectives.

Systems are becoming increasingly complex and interdependent. The ability to assess and predict the effectiveness and the emergent behavior of these interconnected systems is essential for critical business decisions. This is why it is important for any organization to develop the ability to capture key system interdependencies and measure effectiveness at the SoS level.

A directed System of Systems is the kind of SoS that is created to fulfill specific purposes, and the constituent systems are subordinated to the SoS. The component systems maintain an ability to operate independently; however, their normal operational mode is subordinated to the centrally managed purpose.

Industrial System of Systems: Components and Characteristics

In the industrial setting, be it Manufacturing or Retail, independent systems like – ERP, CRM, Sales, Planning (APS), PLM, etc., are some of the core component systems of the over-arching Industrial System of Systems. In a non-connected environment, figure 2.1, component systems are typically measured, run, and controlled by different groups (siloed entities), each having its own rules to manage them. Whereas, in a highly connected environment, figure 2.2, component systems are typically measured, managed, and controlled by a central command center adopting various advanced tools for continuous learning and optimization at a system level Adoption of revolutionary technologies like the Internet of Things (IoT), Machine Learning (ML) and Artificial Intelligence (AI) can enable an industrial organization to centrally manage, learn and optimize this highly connected and interlinked SoS resulting into sustainable value creation.

Figure 2. Industrial siloed and connected systems

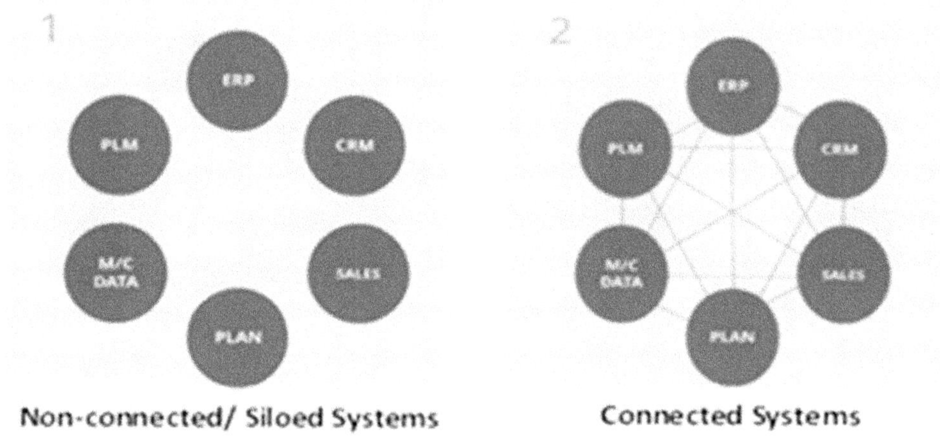

Table 1. Characteristics of non-connected and connected systems

Non-connected systems	Connected systems/ System of systems
• Lagged / Asynchronous & Inaccurate Data measurement • Siloed Decision Making with many degrees of freedom • Sub-Optimal Decisions • High Latency between a failure and corrective action • Unpredictable Responses to external stimuli	• Continuous Real-Time Accurate Data Stream • Centralized Decisions with limited degrees of freedom • Global Optima • Very low latency between a failure event and corrective action • Predictable Responses to external stimuli

Limitation of Advanced Planning and Scheduling Systems (APS)

Over the decades, APS systems have evolved into a decision support system that facilitates supply chain management and integration of supply chains. However, their effectiveness is restricted by the fidelity of the supply chain representation and by the availability and completeness of the data to support these models. The sub-optimal usage of APS features impacts the overall performance of the decision support these systems provide.

Some of the challenges of typical APS implementations today in an industrial environment are:

- Process Related
  - Fundamental process improvements normally don't happen before go-live
  - Absence of Business Process Re-Engineering (BPR) exercise before Greenfield APS Installation
  - Delayed Reactive Re-planning
  - Perception based Management Decisions
- Data Related
  - Incorrect Baseline data for process improvements
  - Difficult to associate Part to Process
  - Periodic Manual Data Entry
  - Absence of dynamic alert-based Master Data sync

- Integration Related
    - Out of sync Master Data (garbage in – garbage out)
    - Process level Traceability
    - Difficult to Map Issues and Vendors
    - Absence of Critical KPI Integration
    - No real-time inventory/operational KPI visibility

Next-generation technologies are unraveling new realities in operations and ensuring new corrected baseline data is made available for effective implementation and utilization of Advance Planning Systems. These technologies enable platforms to collect real-time data across multiple manufacturing and distribution dimensions (objects) like machines, manpower, material, utilities, tools, spares, products, processes, logistics, transportation, and consumption. Real-time raw data is then transformed into operations measures in each dimension. These measures are then exchanged at the optimal frequency with ERP and APS systems for optimal decision-making.

INDUSTRIAL INTERNET OF THINGS AND DIGITAL TWINS

The Internet of Things (IoT) is a system of interrelated computing devices, mechanical and digital machines, objects, animals, or people that are provided with unique identifiers and the ability to transfer data over a network without requiring human-to-human or human-to-computer interaction. Industrial Internet of Things (IIoT) refers to an Internet of Things systems deployed in a typical industrial environment, including operations, logistics, and retail. Any discussion regarding Industrial IoT is incomplete without reviewing the idea of Industry 4.0, which essentially aims to revolutionize how products are

Figure 3. Industry 4.0 in the context of next-generation technologies

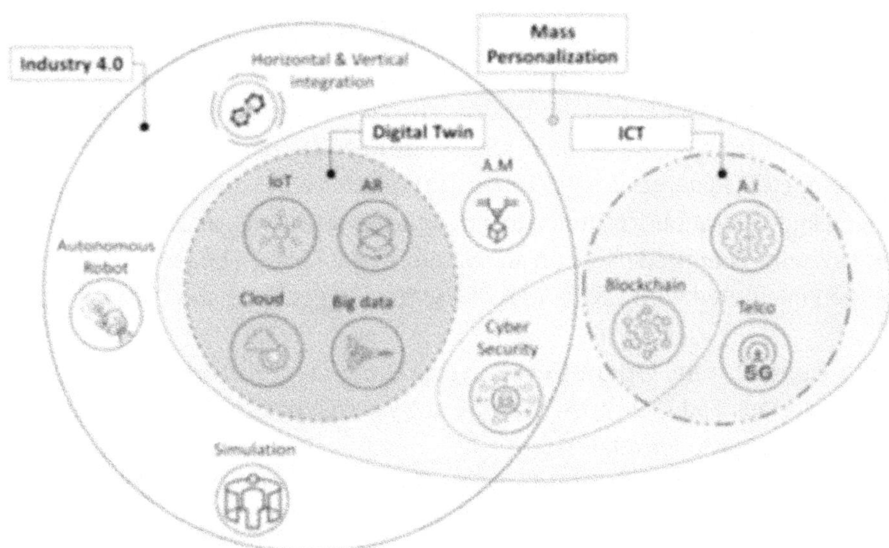

manufactured to form the smart factories of the future towards increased innovation, lower cost, and better responses to needs.

Industry 4.0 puts forward a value proposition where higher customer satisfaction can be achieved as manufacturing and supply chain systems have become smarter using IoT, cyber-physical systems (CPS), Cloud Computing, and Big Data (Aheleroff, et. al, 2021). It is a vision of smart factories built with intelligent objects to sense, act and behave within intelligent cyber-physical systems (CPS) (see figure 3 below). These digital representations or *Digital Twins* provide an important complementary capacity to physical assets.

Digital Twins

Digital twins capture past, present, and predicted behavior of physical assets. Bi-directional information flows from the real-world object to the digital representation and then back to the real-world object is the defining characteristic of any Digital Twin (Icaro et al., 2020). Digital Twins are updated periodically to represent the current state of physical assets. This distinguishes digital twins from conventional simulations because sensor data can continuously feed them.

Kritzinger et al. (2018) identify three types of digital representations based on the intensity of the integration of the information:

- **Digital Model** – all updates are made to the digital representation manually
- **Digital Shadow** – updates to the digital representation are made automatically. However, the information flow is bi-directional, i.e., physical objects are not updated automatically
- **Digital Twin** – the information flow is bi-directional. Both the digital representation and physical object influence each other

Virtual data management, automatic model generation, static and dynamic simulation, integration, and communication are paramount to realizing a digital twin. The type of curated information on the state of physical assets' history depends on how digital twins are used (Kenett and Bortman, 2020).

IIoT Platform: Basic Building Block for Digital Twins

To ensure that the necessary data to build the Digital Twin is available, it needs to be gathered from different sources, e.g., the current status of the machines from MES, details of released/ approved orders from the ERP system, etc. (Icaro et al., 2020). An IIoT platform acts as a convergence layer, with IT Systems on one side and Operations Systems, manufacturing resources, and sensors on the other. Information from these systems is unified to create an operations data lake. The raw and computed metrics in the data lake are then integrated with ERP and APS systems to generate significant value in operations.

- **Automation, Control, and Operations Layer:** These are software systems such as SCADA, DCS, MES, Historians and Quality Management Systems that are used for the day-to-day operations at a plant, warehouse, or retail store
- **IT and OT Convergence Layer:** Information Technology (IT) Systems are software systems used for managing business processes – these include PLM, ERP, APS, and Business Intelligence

Figure 4. Connected ecosystem capabilities

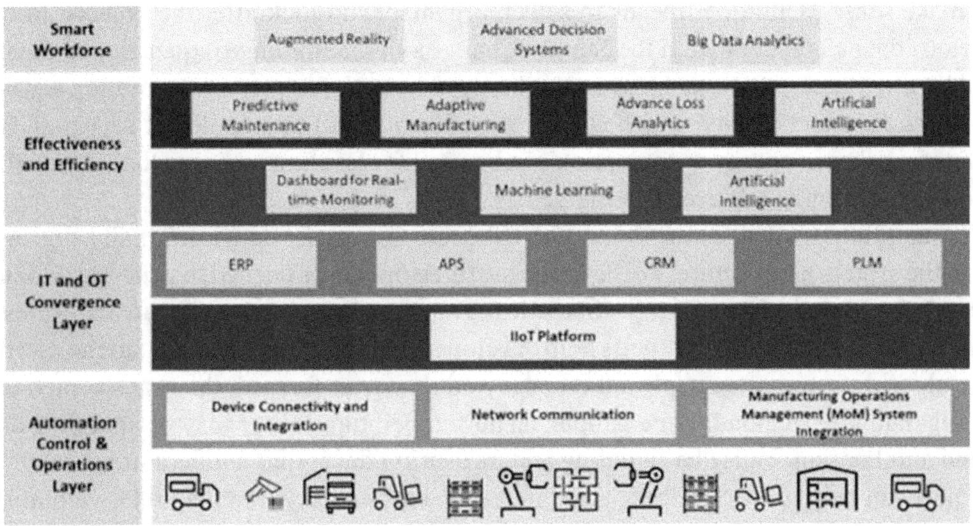

solutions. Whereas Operational Technology (OT) Systems are both the software and hardware that detects or causes a change through the direct monitoring and control of physical assets

- **Effectiveness and Efficiency**: Capabilities provided by this layer enable significant improvement in the efficiency and effectiveness of operations. Tools for advanced loss analytics and predictive maintenance enhance efficiency, while predictive quality analytics leads to further improvement in effectiveness.
- **Smart Workforce:** The toolset in this layer enables decision-makers across the enterprise to choose their limited bandwidth on real issues in the value chain. Management by exception is implemented in the true sense. The minimum time is spent on exploratory analysis and more on advanced analysis and taking actions wherever immediate interventions are required. A new generation of smart workforce carries the enterprise to newer heights of excellence.

British mathematician Clive Humby stated in 2006, *"Data is the new oil. Like oil, data is valuable, but if unrefined, it cannot really be used. It has to be changed into gas, plastic, chemicals, etc., to create a valuable entity that drives profitable activity. so, must data be broken down, analyzed for it to have value"*. 'Curated Data' is the refined gasoline that fuels the system of systems in any enterprise. In the next section, we will review the specific data elements in the context of the Supply Chain Operations Reference framework.

CURATED DATA: THE HOLY GRAIL

Need for Curated Data

Enormous amount of raw time series data is being generated across multiple echelons of the supply chain. Primary sources of this data are Sensors, Equipment Controllers, IT systems, RFID/Bar Code Systems, etc. Raw time series data by itself has limited end business value unless and until it is contextualized and curated to make sense. 'Curation' means to select, organize, and look after the objects. In our context it is the various data elements within the Supply Chain model. Sampling frequencies of data sources is determined by the use-case for which the data is being collected, for example, vibration sensor data can be used to predict product quality, which is critical, and hence will be sampled at very high frequencies (kHz). Whereas spikes in energy consumption can be used for leveling resource loading, so these would be sampled less frequently, say every 15 mins.

Once the sampling frequencies are determined, the raw time series data is normally aggregated on an edge layer in the system architecture. We describe the three operators needed to generate 'Contextualized Curated Data': (a) Domain Expertise, (b) Statistical Transformation and (c) Cleansing Rules.

Domain Expertise: Functional experts help develop algorithms to give context to the raw time-series data. These algorithms are often deployed on edge and then transformed, this transformed data is then sent to the big data lake in cloud. For example, an air temperature sensor may be sampling at say every 1 second and another sensor may be sampling and measuring dew point temperature at same frequency. Domain expert can help transform these two input variables and say establish relative humidity based on scientific logic. This new derived value of relative humidity can be associated the same time stamp as the input variables. Only the humidity value then can be sent to the big data cloud data lake.

Statistical Transformations: Converting high frequency data to more compressed representative sample is another way to curate the data. This achieved by applying appropriate statistical transformations on the raw time series data on edge, for example, typical vibration sensors sample may sample at very high frequency (KHz.). More often simple transformations like minute-level mean, peak values may be a good starting point. Sophisticated transformations like fast Fourier transforms can be applied and the transformed data can be pushed to cloud data lake.

Cleansing Rules: anomaly detection algorithms are deployed on raw data and can help identify outliers in the data. Rules can be setup to adjust/delete these outliers and then sent for further analysis. Many a times, cleansing rules are not mathematical algorithms but more process driven guidelines. For example, if a new product is setup to run on a line, then it may take say 20 mins after the part is loaded for it to stabilize. In this case, cleansing rules can be deployed to ignore or adjust this first 20 mins of data every time a new run is scheduled.

In majority of digitization and analytics projects, raw data is curated with a combination of all the above. It is highly recommended that further business analytics algorithms are run on this curated data for providing actionable insights to operations.

Curated Data and Supply Chain Model

The Supply Chain Operations Reference (SCOR) model describes the business processes required to satisfy a customer's demands. It also helps to explain the processes along the entire supply chain and provides a basis for how to improve those processes. SCOR model focuses on seven primary management processes: Orchestrate, Plan, Order, Source, Transform, Fulfill and Return. We will discuss the influence of IIoT on 'curating' some of the key data elements for specific process areas like *Transform* within the SCOR framework. The seven high-level processes are described in some detail below (SCOR DS, 2022):

- **Orchestrate** describes the activities associated with the integration and enablement of supply chain strategies.

- **Plan** describes the activities associated with developing road maps to operate the supply chain
- **Order** describes the activities associated with the customer purchase of products and services, including attributes such as locations, payment methods, pricing, fulfillment status, and any other order data.
- **Source** describes the activities associated with procuring, ordering, scheduling the ordering, delivery, receipt, and transfer of products and services.
- **Transform** describes the activities associated with scheduling and creating products, including production; assembly and disassembly; maintenance, repair and overhaul; and more.
- **Fulfill** describes the activities associated with the scheduling and creating products, including production, assembly, and disassembly; maintenance, repair, and overhaul; and more.
- **Return** describes the activities associated with the reverse flow of goods and services, as well as any service components from a customer through the network, in order to diagnose the condition, evaluate entitlement, disposition back into Transform or other circular activities.

The infinity loop diagram illustrates that supply chains are an ever-moving series of activities, with no artificial starts or stops from process to process. To illustrate the importance of OT and IT integration, a case study in the *Transform* management process of the SCOR model is discussed in a subsequent section.

Figure 5. SCOR digital standard

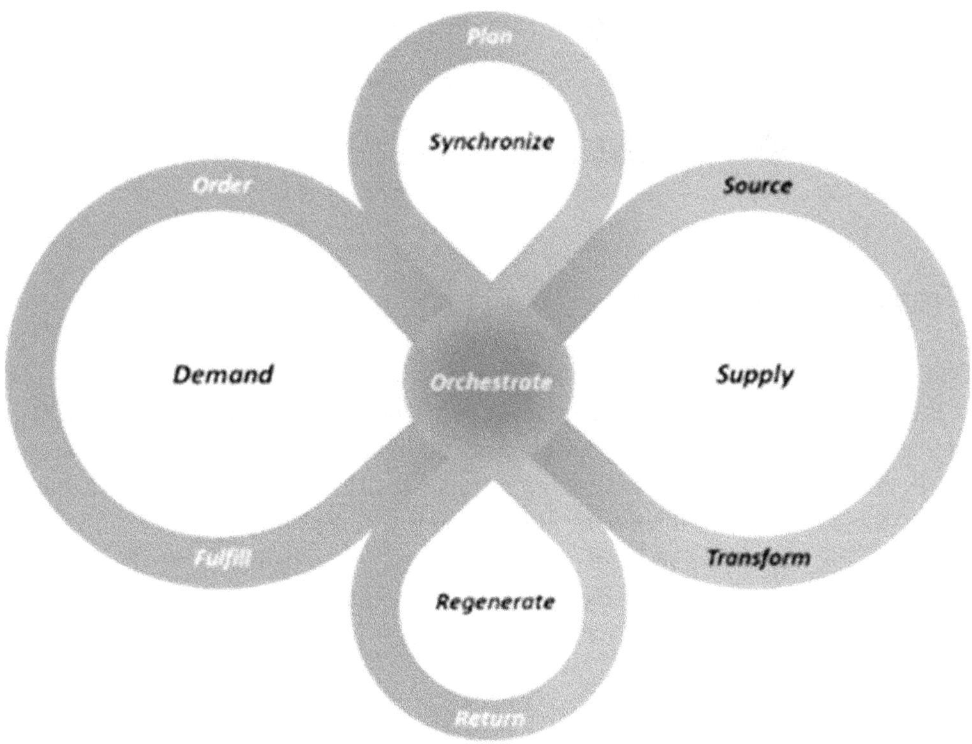

Logical Architecture – Augmenting APS with IIoT

Existing Transactional systems or Advanced Planning systems are not designed to handle the magnitude of data velocity and granularity that is available due to the deployment of IoT sensors and devices. In the past few years, the concept of Data Lake has gained traction because it allows you to manage unstructured and unrefined data. Additionally, massive volumes of structured and unstructured data can be stored cost-effectively and analyzed in new ways using the data lake approach. In figure 6, we describe the logical architecture that leverages a Data Lake based on a IIoT platform to manage data generated from both the Operational and Information Technology layers of applications.

Figure 6. Logical architecture and high-level data flow for augmenting APS with IIoT

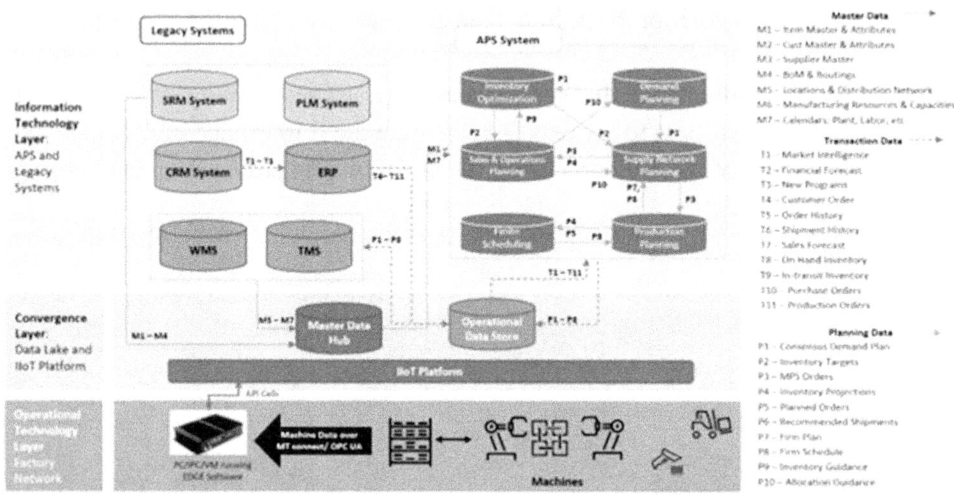

Planning Transformation Enablers

In this section, we deep dive into the limitations of specific data elements (referenced in Figure 6) and discuss how these data elements can be augmented or enriched by IIoT platforms. From the perspective of APS implementations, these data elements were selected based on their impact and the opportunities IIoT capabilities provide for improving the quality, velocity, and availability. We believe that the information provided in Table 2, will be valuable for identifying use cases within your organization to support the proposal of an IIoT initiative and further provide the basis for determining the criteria of success for such implementations. These data elements have been organized into the following six categories:

1. Part and Process
2. Machines
3. Materials
4. Manpower
5. Energy and Utilities
6. Orders

Table 2a. Post IIoT: potential improvements in data quality

Part & Process	Pre-IIoT Issues	Post-IIoT Improvement
Cycle Times Critical master data for any planning implementation	Data suggests that average cycle times are off by more than +/- 40% from standard cycle times maintained in the master data Most of the time, this variance is negative, which means that the actual cycle times are significantly shorter than the standard cycle times Artificially inflated capacity buffers are created in APS if these cycle times are not updated on a periodic basis	Actual cycle times at part-operation-machine in routing are monitored in real-time on an IIoT platform If there is a significant variance between standard and actual cycle times, then an automatic notification can be triggered for a master data custodian to update the masters
Production Booking Critical transactional data for re-planning and for monitoring planned versus actuals	Production confirmation books periodically or at the end of the shift. Any time lag potentially results in lost opportunities for recovering from deviations from planned activities.	IIoT platforms monitor the actual production quantity by part-operation-machine in real time. Production confirmation can be automatically booked against released orders, and inventory updates in ERP systems can be done in almost real-time. This enables dynamic updates to inventory and visibility to planners on value stream planned vs. actual
Process Adherence	Any time lag potentially results in lost opportunities for preventing additional deviations from the standard.	IIoT platforms monitor critical quality process parameters in real time as the parts move in the manufacturing value chain. Significant deviations in process parameters can be highlighted by order, and early warning notifications can be generated for proactive actions in operations. These orders can be flagged for re-work, re-process, or additional quality checks in real-time and re-planning in APS. Impact on due date adherence due to non-compliance can also be computed.
Changeover Times	Data suggest at least 20% variance in part changeover times from one instance to another, and hence it becomes even more important to capture this data in real time.	The from-to part changeover matrix, which becomes the basis for APS scheduling, can be maintained in real-time based on actual data from the floor. The IIoT platform data also become the baseline for operations excellence-led SMED (single-minute exchange of dies) kind of initiative on the floor.
BoM Consumption	Incorrect BOM consumption leads to sub-optimal procurement planning decisions. It has been observed that actual BOM consumption varies by at least +/- 15%, especially in process plants, where BOMs contain different ingredients.	IIoT platforms monitor the actual consumption of critical parts in the Bill of Materials (BOM). This consumption is compared with standard consumption in ERP BOM Masters. Master data custodians are alerted if significant variances are observed in actual vs. standard BOM consumption.

Table 2b. (continued).

Machines	Pre-IIoT Issues	Post-IIoT Improvement
Unplanned Downtimes	Unplanned downtimes are typically recorded at the end of the shift or day, and there is a significant delay in actual downtime, reporting, and corrective actions taken The unplanned downtime data itself is manually collected by operators and often inaccurately booked without system-level checks and balances	IIoT platforms monitor real-time machine status and report actual runtime and unplanned downtimes. If significant downtimes occur on the bottleneck machine, then the APS system can be notified for potential re-plan based on the actual situation on the floor. Re-planning in APS significantly improves overall planning performance. Historical data on machine availability on the IIoT platform is used in subsequent planning runs of APS.
Rates for RCCP	Production Rates used for Rough-cut capacity planning are typically refreshed annually, and depending on the function that drives these activities, these could be based on machine ratings – when driven by the engineering dept., or Costing based rates, if the activity is driven by finance and accounting teams Clearly, these approaches of using an ideal rate or using calculated rates are disconnected from reality, and so are plans based on these rates.	IIoT platforms monitor real-time machine status and report actual runtime and unplanned downtimes. Condition-based rates can be determined at a pre-defined frequency when master data refresh needs to be pushed to the APS system. However, the frequency of rate refresh must be determined judiciously, as frequent changes in planning rates will introduce nervousness in plans
Machine health – MTBF, MTTR	MTBF, MTTR is often calculated at periodic intervals (weekly/monthly) and not made available to planning and scheduling in weekly planning and scheduling decisions These metrics are also calculated based on manually collected data which is likely to be highly error-prone	Condition monitoring and predictive maintenance alerts on the IIoT platform can be integrated with APS systems for a more real-time view of resource availability in operations. Metrics like MTBF (mean time between failure) and MTTR (mean time to recover) are computed in real-time and fed to the APS system for re-establishing new machine availability constraints.

Table 2c. (continued)

Materials	Pre-IIoT Issues	Post-IIoT Improvement
Material Availability	Material in-transit visibility is missing and hence leading to a significant shortage, downtimes as well we as excess inventory	IIoT platforms monitor the real-time availability of critical materials and components in the supply chain. Location-wise real-time inventory levels are monitored along with visibility into inbound and outbound materials in transit. Significant deviations in actual stock quantities and arrival times can be flagged to APS, which in turn can trigger re-plans for material planning.
Material Yield	Material yields in master data in ERP / Planning systems are manually maintained and typically updated every 6 months or during the annual budgeting and costing cycle. These yields are inaccurate and lead to out-of-stock or over-stock scenarios As the process is manual, degradation in process quality parameters is realized late, and hence the significant cost of poor quality is incurred	IIoT platforms monitor rejection levels in real-time and estimate rolled throughput yield. If there are significant standard deviations, APS systems can automatically re-plan with new data.
Vendor Evaluation	With no real-time visibility, issues at vendor plants are often not highlighted to OEMs leading to significant downtimes of OEM lines because of shortages and part quality issues Vendor evaluation and rating are manual and biased, leading to long-term quality and supply chain problems	IIoT platforms are used to monitor end-of-line production and are critical to quality parameters at vendor plants. If there are significant unplanned downtimes or quality issues at the vendor, then APS systems can re-plan and re-schedule the OEM lines based on the actual status of operations at vendor plants. This is especially critical for automotive supply chains where material may be presented directly online. Real-time vendor rating and evaluation can be done on platforms for appropriate actions by supply chain organization.
Materials/ Spare Parts Inventory	Physical Kanban card-based systems have their own limitations of inaccurate stock, cards getting lost, delays in response times to replenish inventory, leading to line stoppages and quality issues on the floor Often redundant stock-keeping units, tools, and spares are maintained at multiple locations due to poor visibility into stock and consumption data from the floor	IIoT platforms and technologies like RFID are being used to establish a real-time inventory of materials, spares, and tools by different storage locations in industrial setups. This real-time inventory status can be published to APS systems at appropriate intervals for re-planning and prioritization.

Table 2d. (continued)

Manpower	Pre-IIoT Issue	Post-IIoT Improvement
Availability of Skilled Manpower & Absenteeism	Actual time-in at gates for operators and absenteeism is only known at the start of the shift. Supervisors manually take stock of the situation, re-plan and then deploy manpower present Significant shift start-up losses lead to a drop in throughput and employee morale. Also, there is significant uncertainty in the availability of skilled manpower, especially since Covid.	IIoT platforms track the actual status of skilled manpower likely to arrive at plants and can provide an early warning alert to planners in case of significant lateness and absenteeism. It has been found that almost 10% of plant capacity is lost in re-planning and re-deployment of manpower due to unplanned absenteeism in the plants. Most of the manufacturing operations plan around the availability of skilled manpower in the shift, and this is becoming a critical component that needs to be explored in APS along with real-time data from IIoT platforms.
Operator Skill Matrix	The operator skill-matrix is updated 6 monthly or annually based on manual data collection. The skill rating itself tends to be highly biased based on limited data The absence of real-time monitoring of critical skills leads to deterioration in safety, quality, and productivity at the workplace The skill matrix is rarely integrated with the APS system, and hence the planners are not able to derive an advantage from the improvement in skills over time	IIoT platforms monitor the real-time performance of operators on different machines and generate an automated real-time skill matrix. This matrix can be published to APS systems as soon as changes are observed for re-planning based on the updated matrix.

Table 2e. (continued)

Energy & Utilities	Pre-IIoT Issue	Post-IIoT Improvement
Specific Energy Consumption	The absence of real-time monitoring of specific energy consumption leads to sub-optimal planning decisions Sub-optimal planning leads to an increase in energy consumption and costs Incorrect baseline and target setting for energy KPIs in the sustainability journey of the plant	In process and energy-heavy plants, IIoT platforms help establish specific energy and utilities consumption by SKU/recipe/batch. Considering the focus on sustainability and implementation of standards like ISO 50001, specific energy consumption is becoming a critical pivot parameter for advance planning and scheduling. Loading of assets in APS can be first done on most energy efficient equipment / lowest specific energy consumption and then other assets in the same asset class.
Real-time Energy & Utilities	The absence of real-time utility consumption data leads to significant penalties by an electricity providers, local governments, and regulatory bodies Inefficient utilities and planning lead to an increase in energy consumption and costs	IIoT platform monitor energy and utilities consumption in real-time and forecast energy bill for the given plan. Energy or utilities-constrained energy planning is also a norm in certain industries. Ex. Certain industries, like food and beverages, have an upper limit on the total amount of water that can be drawn from the water table. Advance planning to optimize the use of flexible electricity plans in peak and non-peak hours of the day is also common.

Table 2f. (continued)

Orders	Pre-IIoT Issue	Post-IIoT Improvement
Order Status	Planners get post facto delayed information on the status of orders, and hence an early window to re-plan and optimize is missed leading to delayed orders and significant customer dissatisfaction	IIoT platforms provide the capability to monitor the real-time progress of released orders in operations as they move from the first to the last operation of the routing. If there are significant delays in actual end times vis-à-vis planned end times, then planners are automatically alerted to evaluate alternatives and re-plan.
Bottleneck Identification	Absence of real-time data results in inaccurate bottleneck identification leading to delay and shortages in orders, customer dissatisfaction Management is not able to focus their limited bandwidth on real issues in the value stream, especially in high product-mix and low batch size kind of an environment	Real-time moving average data of different KPIs, like OEE, capacity utilization, cycle times, etc., are fed into the APS system for bottleneck identification for the release and open orders in operations.

CASE STUDY: AUTOMOTIVE OEM

A leading global Auto OEM with facilities worldwide wanted to: (a) improve the OEE of critical production resources and assembly lines at their plant in Asia and (b) improve due date performance. In-house operations at this location include finish machining, paint shop, assembly, and testing operations. Vendors supplying critical parts were located within a 10-mile radius of the plant. These vendors would deliver parts and sub-assemblies directly to the lines.

The key objectives of this engagement were:

- Enable process traceability for each vehicle across the value chain for critical to the environment and quality parts and parameters
- Provide real-time visibility to planning systems to the availability of the material at the vendor end of line
- Provide near real-time visibility to the availability of skilled operators before the beginning of the shift to minimize loss of through-put

The following measures were considered as part of evaluating the success of this engagement:

- **Machines**: OEE, MTBF, MTTR, unplanned downtimes, production count, rejection count, spindle load, spindle rpm, etc.
- **Assembly Stations**: OLE, production count, rejection count, torque, angle of torque, leak test
- **Vendor Plants**: End-of-line production count, rejection count, uptime, plan vs. actual
- **Operators**: Number of check-ins, on-time arrival, unplanned absenteeism, etc.

Solution Approach

Critical workstations, end-of-assembly stations, critical-to-quality stations at OEM plants, and vendor plants were identified. Cloud-based architecture to converge data from connected assets into a central OEM instance with vendor child accounts.

Data from disparate control systems like Fanuc, Siemens, Mazak, and Allan Bradley converged onto a plant edge instance from where it was stored in a central operations data lake in the cloud. Digital Factory and Supply Chain visibility applications were deployed on the cloud and made available through mobile apps for different personas in the organization, from operators to corporate executives.

Traceability was enabled through integration with RFID and barcode-based tracking system on the floor and included engraving at certain stations. Master data exchange with a leading ERP system and integration with a leading provider of APS solutions.

Figure 7 shows the high-level architecture across the value chain. OEM plant provided transportation to operators, and real-time data of the operators traveling on the bus to the plants as per the shift schedule was available through a separate application. All the data exchange between various software solutions was enabled through APIs. The overall system architecture was identical to the one laid out in Figure 6.

Figure 7. High-level architecture

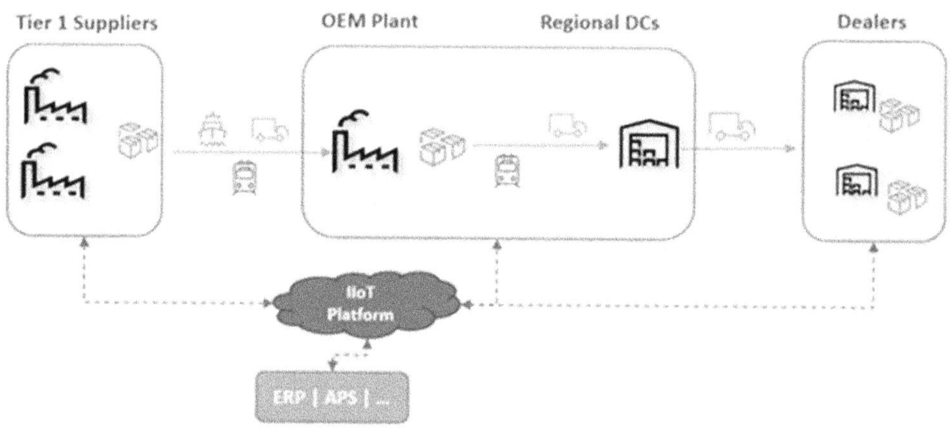

Recommendations

Operating Model

Technology can bring benefits if and only if it diminishes an existing limitation. Long before the availability of technology, plants develop modes of behavior, policies, measurements, and rules to help accommodate the current limitations. To get the benefits of the new technology, plants need to change the rules. New rules for the different personas using the overall system were laid out. Figures 8 shows some of the new rules/SOPs adopted by different user groups/ personas.

Figure 8. Operating Model

Technology

IIoT Platform Data Exchange with ERP and APS solutions in Real-time.

- **APS –** Planned Orders, Confirmed Orders, Line Performance KPIs, Vendor Production Count, Actual Cycle Times by SKU, Skilled Operator Availability, and Deployment.
- **ERP –** Part Master, Routing Master, BOM Master, Vendor Master, Operator Master, Asset Master, Tools Master, Quality Control Plans by SKU, Production Confirmations, etc.

Business Impact

Time to Deploy

The whole solution went live in phases. The first phase of machine and asset connectivity took almost 3 months. It was followed by IT (ERP and APS) integrations for another 2 months. UAT and Go-Live another month.

Results

The improvements in KPIs before and after one year of implementation are indicated in Table 3 below. The estimated payback period on the overall project investment was approximately 15 months.

Table 3. Measurable benefits

KPI	Baseline before implementation	1- year after implementation
Overall Equipment Effectiveness	73%	87%
Order Fulfillment Percentage	58%	75%
Cost of poor quality	14%	11%
Unplanned Absenteeism	15%	6%

In addition to the above business benefits, there were numerous in-direct benefits of integrating the IIoT platform with APS, as listed in Table 4.

Table 4. Indirect Benefits

KPI	Baseline before implementation	1-year after implementation
Incorrect Routings as a % of Total Routings	88%	12%
Range of Actual / Standard Cycle Time Ratio	60% to 150%	95% to 105%

CONCLUSION

Implementation after implementation, it has been proven that the return on investment in an APS solution accelerates if it is accompanied by an IIoT platform implementation. As a best business practice, the IIoT platform implementation should precede the APS implementation as very rich curated master and run-time data shall be made available to the APS solution for achieving very effective outcomes. The recommended approach for digital – APS implementation in a medium-scale industrial facility (less than 100 machines) is indicated in Figure 9 below. Adopting this approach will reap significant benefits for the organization.

Figure 9. IIoT platform implementation timeline for APS

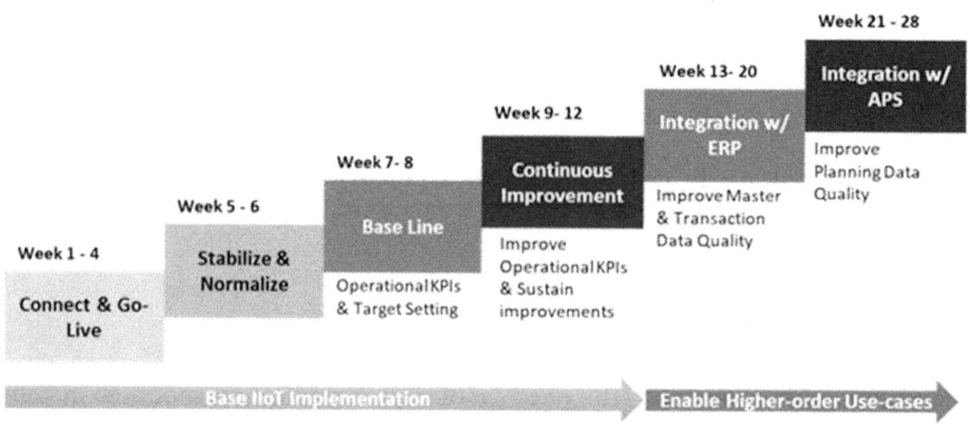

The benefits of the above approach are:

- Clean, normalized Master Data available for APS implementation
- Runtime operations data also normalizes before the APS deployment and go-live
- IIoT data lake becomes the single source of real-time truth from operations
- Accelerated return on investment on APS implementation

- With the deployment of IIoT platform, the garbage in-garbage out problem is solved to a significant extent; sophisticated APS algorithms allow for central control, system-level optimization, and faster end-user adoption
- Significant reduction in overall time to configure, test, and validate the outcomes of the APS implementation
- Ability to identify issues in real-time and re-plan with very low latency is enabled.

The benefits of IIoT platform-APS software integration outweigh the initial investment needed to digitally prepare operations before the APS implementation. Running sophisticated APS software on real-time accurate data is the future and will do real justice to the sophisticated APS heuristics and algorithms developed over time. Authors envisage a future where every APS implementation will be preceded by an IIoT platform implementation and integration, leading to a successful and effective planning implementation.

REFERENCES

ACSM. (2022). *SCOR Digital Standard 2022*. SCOR Model.

Aheleroff. (2020). *A Digital Twin Reference for Mass Personalization in Industry 4.0*. ScienceDirect.

Aheleroff. (2021). *Digital Twin as a Service (DTaaS) in Industry 4.0: An Architecture Reference Model.* ScienceDirect.

Bakken Center for Spirituality & Healing. (n.d.). *Understanding Complex Systems.*

Greig, S. (2018). *Measuring Integration Complexity. IT's Complicated!* Medium.

Icaro. (2020). Using a Digital Twin for Production Planning and Control in Industry 4.0. International Series in Operations Research & Management Science book series (Vol. 289). ISOR.

INCOSE. (n.d.). *Systems of Systems Primer*. INCOSE.

Johnson, N. (2009). *Simply Complexity: A Clear Guide to Complexity Theory*. Oneworld Publications.

Kenett, R. S. (2020). *The digital twin in Industry 4.0: A wide-angle perspective*. AEAI.

Sandia National Laboratories (n.d.). *System-of-Systems – Center for Systems Reliability.* SNL.

SEBoK, (2022). *Systems of Systems (SoS).* Sebokwiki.

Chapter 9
Digital Supply Chain:
A Proposed Solution to the Global Supply Chain Disruption Impact on Business Sustainability

Ahmed Sedky
https://orcid.org/0000-0002-8087-4175
Walden University, USA

ABSTRACT

Businesses have been exposed to the risk of closure because of the global supply chain disruption post the COVID-19 pandemic. Uncertainty and lack of products and services led firms to encounter losses ranging from decreased market shares to a total failure to sustain operations. Leaders invest in the digital supply chain to improve firms' performance and mitigate global business risks. Grounded in Duchek's organizational resilience theory, the purpose of this chapter is to explore the digital supply chain, a proposed solution to the global disruption impacting business sustainability. Data were collected from a review of previous literature and cases of digital supply chain successful implementation in the US retail industry. A key recommendation for firms is to invest in digital supply chain models that fit businesses' needs. Digital supply chain may allow supply chain members collaboration, reduce the closure risk, extend opportunities, and positively impact communities' stability and growth.

INTRODUCTION

As the world has become a global village, countries have developed many dependencies on each other. With the developed production capabilities within countries, governments and private entities rely on political, economic, cultural, and trade capabilities to respond to their communities' demands and needs (Davies & Wenham, 2020). For example, Mao and Gorg (2020) emphasized how the United States market relies on imports from China and Mexico to respond to the U.S. community's needs for the consumed products. Like the United States market, many GCC region countries import their communities' requirements from China (Almujeem, 2021), in addition to the United States and other relevant sources

DOI: 10.4018/978-1-6684-7298-9.ch009

based on the implemented relationship and other factors such as the costs and availability of products (Siderius et al., 2020). The geopolitical relationships between countries provide the decision-makers a comparative advantage in determining their communities' needs origins. Therefore, countries—besides the power of purchase—need robust supply chain implementations to respond to their communities' needs in a reasonable timeframe and at controlled costs.

A well-designed supply chain network enables business success and allows firms to respond to the targeted demand. Whether the supply chain owner is a governmental entity or a private firm, the ultimate goal is to respond to the needs within a reasonable timeframe and at the right cost to secure a high volume of market demand (Dadzie et al., 2022; Ivanov, 2020). There is always a need for a market-responsive supply chain network to enable success and ensure business sustainability. As a result, organizations need to build resilience in their supply chain components to ensure business sustainability through times of disruption and pandemics.

Many organizations have lost business opportunities since the COVID-19 pandemic. Losing those opportunities had a negative impact on business operations and, ultimately, the gross domestic product (GDP) and employment rates. Many firms, including small and medium-sized enterprises, failed to continue their operations as they lost control of the continuous supply of products and services, which led to losing their market shares (Turner & Endres, 2017). For example, firms operating in the retail industry faced the risk of operations disruptions and the loss of talented calibers. In analyzing the reasons behind such a negative impact on the retail industry, the global supply chain disruption is a critical aspect that impacts the existence of firms and the continuity of their operations (Singh et al., 2020). Lockdowns, closure of borders, securing approved quality products, and lack of containerized shipments represent critical challenges to operating firms. Firms could not secure supplies, hold market shares, achieve profit margins, and retain their talents. Retail organizations' managers need to find ways to mitigate global supply chain disruption risks. Many business managers may rely on local sources to secure products and services supply, develop business continuity plans, and invest in artificial intelligence to overcome the global supply chain disruption impact on their firms' operations. However, many managers also took a different approach by adopting a digital supply chain in their systems as a solution that may reduce the impact of global supply chain disruption on business sustainability.

In this chapter, the researcher explored digital supply chain as a proposed solution to the global supply chain disruption impact on business sustainability. The aim of this chapter was to enable business sustainability in the retail industry. The researcher relied on reviewing previous literature, including published case studies of digitization solutions based on their successful implementations highlighting the implementations' impact on organizations.

DUCHEK'S ORGANIZATIONAL RESILIENCE CONCEPTUAL FRAMEWORK

Stephanie Duchek (2019) introduced the organizational resilience conceptual framework through which she focused on firms' need to implement resilience within their organizational structure and DNA, enabling them to manage operations through unexcepted events. According to Chen et al. (2021), organizational resilience allows business leaders to predict business threats and prepare and respond properly to help their businesses survive those threats. Organizational resilience enables leaders to manage the needed change so that their businesses pass through the hard times and existing risks surrounding the business. In other words, the conceptual framework aims to provide insights into how organizational leaders are determined to anticipate crises before they occur to continue through those bottleneck times and achieve organizational goals by adapting and developing their firms to continue operations. According to Duchek et l. (2019), the organizational resilience model consists of three identified important stages: (a) the anticipation stage, (b) the coping stage, and (c) the adaptation stage (see Figure 1) which demonstrates the components of Duchek's organizational resilience model. The anticipation stage represents the period before the crisis. In contrast, the coping stage is the actual time of the crisis through which leaders should bring their plans into action to pass to the third stage, the adaptation stage, where the business recovery takes place.

Figure 1. Duchek's Organizational Resilience Model
(Duchek, 2019)

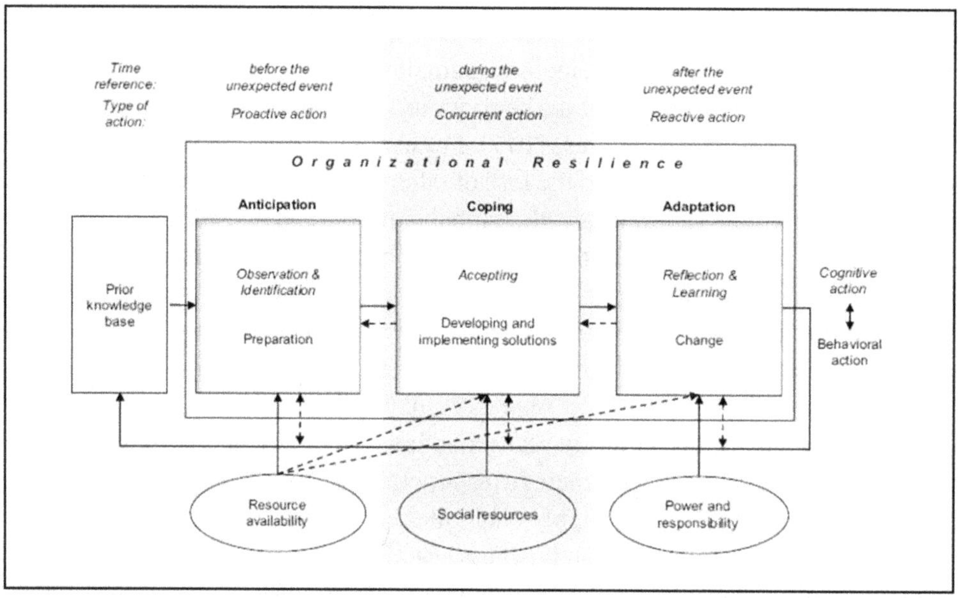

When organizations are able to anticipate the threats they might face, business leaders can plan and develop solutions to keep their firms operating when crises arrive. Duchek's model demonstrated three stages of organizational resilience. During the three stages of a crisis, business leaders need to adopt cognitive and behavioral actions. For example, in the anticipation stage, leaders need to investigate their operating environment for expected threats that may tackle the firms' operations. If a threat is detected, business leaders could build several actions to prepare for the threats when they exist (Rai et al., 2021). For example, when a firm anticipates scarcity of the materials needed for its production, it would build more inventory of the critical materials to keep the manufacturing units producing, unlike if the firm does not predict the crisis and the hard times start. Such firms would encounter massive losses without a proper action plan and crisis management. Firms without action plans will not cope with the crisis and may face the risk of closure (& Guenther, 2020). However, firms that pass to the post-crisis stage, known as the adaptation, may develop learning plans to ensure their readiness to face those risks if they occur again. Thus, researchers expect that organizational resilience may lead to business growth as a result of avoiding the increased risk of a crisis.

Researchers find the organizational resilience framework a valuable framework in organizational performance research. The framework allows researchers to understand the importance of preparing for crises before they may exist to implement action plans that benefit firms through the crises. As et al. (2020) and Xiao and Cao (2017) did, and Lawrence (2022) used Duchek's organizational resilience framework to understand the implementation of organizational resilience within firms' functional, operational, and strategic resilience. The framework provides researchers with the needed guidance to understand firms' readiness and strategies to face operational risks. From this perspective, the researcher relied on Duchek's organizational resilience conceptual framework to explore the digital supply chain as a proposed solution to the global supply chain disruption impact on business sustainability.

LITERATURE REVIEW

Digital Supply Chain

As international business relationships advanced, managing the relationships between international businesses became more sophisticated. Such complication in relationships is not only on the financial aspects and priorities; it has also extended to managing the supply from all points from origin to delivery to end users of products and services. There was an increasing need for a concept that sets definitions of such complicated relationships and translates this science into a group of actions to ensure proper implementation in real life. In the 1980s, the supply chain management concept was introduced as a reflex to this growing need and after many approaches to managing those international relationships (Nguyen et al. 2020). There are many definitions for the supply chain concept; however, Chopra (2021) defined the supply chain management concept as the involvement of all parties to fulfill a customer's request or need. Supply Chain Management (SCM) is about managing the flow of information, goods, and funds from the upstream origins to the downstream destinations reaching the final destination at a controlled cost to respond to a customer's need or demand. Thus, from such a time, the SCM started and continued to enable organizational leaders to manage their international relationships.

All involved parties in the international business relationships from the upstream origins to the downstream destination are members of the supply chain related to providing a product or a service requested by a customer. According to Zhang and Li (2020) and Vanyi (2012), members of a supply chain could be manufacturers, suppliers, distributors, retailers, and customers. In addition, logistics service providers connected the supply chain members' locations and the customer service teams involved in providing and receiving feedback from and to the customers (see Figure 2), demonstrating a simple example of the involved parties along a supply chain.

The international supply chain networks performed significantly until the COVID-19 pandemic, which led to massive losses along the supply chain nodes. With the increase in COVID-19 cases, countries worldwide had to apply strict rules to ensure public safety ranging from complete lockdowns to more eased procedures and testing phases (Buyukkececi, 2020). The impact of such procedures was disruptive and led to massive business losses that ranged between lost opportunities and revenues until severe cases ended with firm closures (Shafi et al., 2020). From such a perspective, the need for an enhanced supply chain model has increased to accomplish more controls and monitoring to anticipate and carefully plan

Figure 2. Members of an International Supply Chain

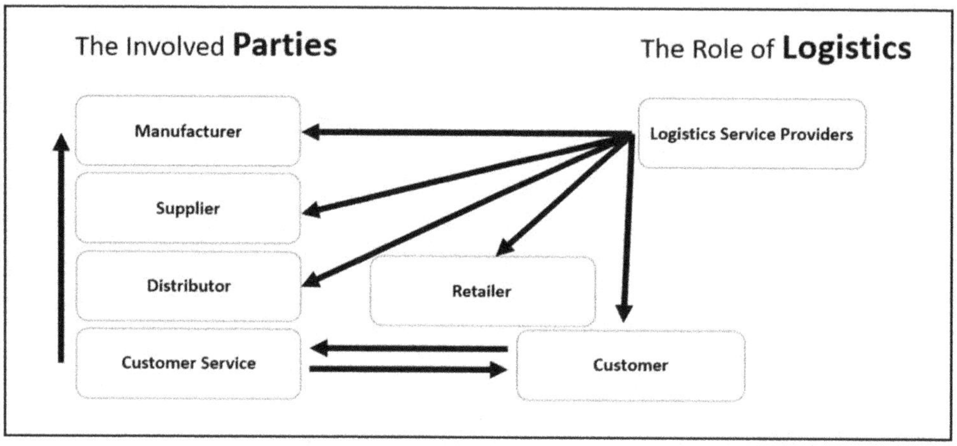

in order to minimize losses and generate revenues. Therefore, the traditional supply chain management concept could not stand the severe disruption caused by the pandemic.

Digital supply chain (DSC) became the replacement concept of the traditional supply chain with the latter's failures to respond to business needs. Many organizations entered the transformation path to develop their models to rescue their businesses from a total collapse (Choudhury et al., 2021). Business leaders aim to enhance their operating model to enable them to anticipate and plan better (Zekhnini et al., 2020). DSC enabled business leaders to find a way to revive their firms and plan on recovering their businesses through improved efficiencies, reduced wasted resources, and promoted higher profits across sectors. DSC relies on advanced technology to enhance visibility, communication, collaboration, and coordination between supply chain members. Therefore, DSC enables businesses to survive, retain their market, and continue to grow.

The benefits of DSC are numerous and can fill the gap that business leaders could not fill with the reliance on the traditional supply chain by enabling the use of data. SC enables business leaders to use technology for increased visibility of supply chain activities, such as real-time traceability and dynamic decision-making, which allows adaptation to change in situations. In addition, information results from the integration between the operational technology and systems, which allows for an equilibrium state between profit and service quality levels. Deepu and Ravi (2021) emphasized that organizations can share data for better coordination and collaboration for a successful business relationship under controlled and secured channels. The use of DSC enabled leaders to improve their decision-making processes by developing multiple scenarios to select what may provide a better advantage. In aggregate, DSC could enable business operations to succeed and increase profits (see Figure 3).

DSC, as a technology-based solution, enabled businesses to achieve a state of total transparency. According to Choi (2021), firms needed to optimize their processes post-pandemic to achieve safety stock levels and enhanced delivery time. Firms could also use the technology to perform tasks that individuals could not because of the pandemic, enabling operational activities to continue (Ivanov, 2020). Companies' performances shifted to higher levels when their leaders adopted DSC models in

Figure 3. Digital Supply Chain Benefits
(NetSuite.com, 2020)

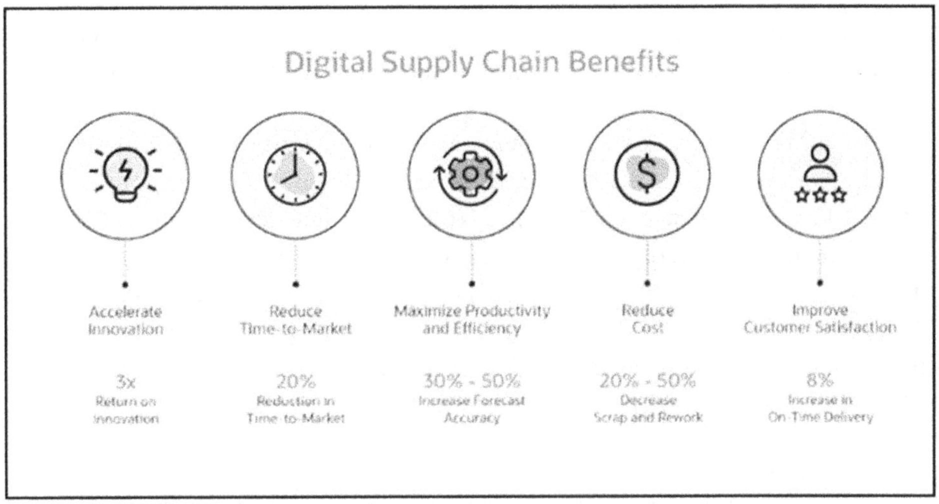

their operations to recover their business from the pandemic effect. Therefore, the use of DSC enabled firms to continue doing business.

DSC provided business leaders with the needed visibility and access to quality information. According to Ye et al. (2022), DSC's visibility allows for three important types of visibility: (a) supply visibility, (b) demand visibility, and (c) market visibility. Such visibility played a significant role in anticipating and seeing opportunities out of transactional uncertainty, which reflected in more flexibility and reduced costs through optimizing product stocks and avoiding out-of-stock and overstocking cases from occurring (Swift et al., 2019). Kochan et al. (2018) also confirmed that supply chain visibility enabled firms to avoid inventory costs while improving their responses to their customers. Further, the visibility resulting from implementing DSC in organizations was the main reason managers gained access to big data analytics and the Internet of Things (Wamba et al., 2019). DSC also enabled supply chain agility. Through this important characteristic of DSC, business leaders could accurately predict market demand shifts before they occur. Then, the business leaders' responses to such demand trends have improved to enable their firms to retain and gain market shares (Tarafdar & Qrunfleh, 2016; Wamba et al., 2019; Ye et al., 2022). DSC agility's impact was a significant reduction of risks and an improved business operating environment. Also, in investigating the importance of DSC agility, Kim and Chai (2017) surveyed firms. They found out that the information access shared across the supply chain model drastically influenced the success of those firms through speedy decisions. Managers made better decisions and responded to the changes in market demands over a period of time. The key aspect was the ability to be flexible in supply to the market based on the information across the DSC, starting from allowing flexible manufacturing to product stocking based on demand. In addition to the mentioned transparency, visibility, and agility, the supply chain's overall performance is one of the factors that impact the success of the firms, and performance is directly correlated to the other three factors. Thus, those firms were able to secure their market shares and overcome the dramatic impact of the international supply disruption.

Digital Supply Chain Technologies

Firms worked to accelerate the supply chain transformation as a response to the pandemic and the disruption in the global supply chain. With the use of technology, business leaders were able to connect, integrate, and improve their supply chain performance as a form of collaboration with other businesses, such as suppliers and customers, involved in the stages of the global supply chain (Agrawal and Narain, 2018; Rasool et al., 2021). Digital technology enabled simplifying the complexity of the global supply chain challenges, reducing costs, and improving service levels by promoting supply chain flexibility and business volumes. The key to such success comes from the technology solutions that link businesses' operating systems together, improving the levels of collaboration. Firms could estimate demand to take necessary actions that enabled quality responses to the supply chain needs responding to such a demand. Those capabilities of technology were the missing links in the traditional supply chain. Thus, technology allowed business leaders to close the traditional supply chain gaps. There are many technological examples of the digital supply chain, such as: (a) the Internet of Things, (b) digital twin, and (c) blockchain.

Internet of Things (IoT)

IoT represents connecting physical objects through embedded sensors and software that allow those objects to communicate to exchange data using the internet. Researchers expect that by 2025, firms will spend USD 25 billion to invest in a fully relying DSC on IoT automation (Men et al., 2022). For example, household appliances connected through applications to control them are a sort of IoT. The same concept applies to industrial equipment and extends to the entire supply chain operations. According to Boyson et al. (2021), a DSC model relying on IoT technology can integrate global operations starting from manufacturers, suppliers, distributors, and customers. A firm can track its overseas subsidiaries' operations and warehouses through IoT technology to monitor efficiencies to respond to market demand at controlled costs. In other firms operating in virtual trade, IoT made it easy to perform and generate significant revenues with speedy operations and live collaboration between machines and leaders who were able to make faster decisions than in the traditional operations model (Zouari et al., 2020). Using barcode scanners in global firms like DHL and FedEx to check shipments' status as they pass through those scanners is a simple form of IoT. Those scanners are a sort of advanced data tagging equipment. In the ocean freight industry, shipping lines such as Maersk use global positioning systems (GPSs) to track the movement of their vessels and containerized cargo along the logistics network. This tracking IoT system is a sort of advanced data capture equipment. In the automotive industry, reputed manufacturers such as Mercedes-Benz and BMW implemented sophisticated IoT technology in their vehicles. Vehicles could self-diagnose and communicate technical aspects along with the needed parts to replace the damaged ones calculating their related costs and time for delivery to fix at their local agencies based on the vehicles' GPS locate identified by communicating with satellites. Those are all examples of successful and beneficial IoT implementations that work to serve humankind and save a lot of money. So, instead of relying on humans' efforts to fill in the data of those shipments, the collaboration between scanners and humans supervising them enabled speedy tracking and data filling to control operations by communicating those data back and forward across the supply chain network through to the end user.

Digital Twin

Instead of optimizing a supply chain in the real world, digital twin technology enables firms to duplicate their supply chain to perform the optimization process in a virtual context. Many firms that belong to the manufacturing, construction, security, and pharmaceutical industries rely on digital twin technology in simulating their supply chain activities and using the related data to develop solutions. According to Gai et al. (2022), digital twin technology acts like an entity simulator on a digital platform that allows testing the supply chain management solutions without exposing the real supply chain to risks of trials. For example, when a firm looks to enhance its supply chain, the IT consultants would gather the organizational data and build the supply chain virtually to evaluate the optimization solutions before applying them in the real world. Digital twins allow the IT consultant to manage the costs and risks of new implementations (Abrazeh et al., 2023). In a traditional supply chain, firms implement solutions in the real world. If those solutions fail, the entire supply chain could be exposed to risks and financial losses caused by the wrong implementations. To avoid these, businesses operating in the global marketplace tend to use digital twin technology to operate their new means before a serious application in the global supply chain. Digital twins operated well in supply chain management when many countries applied lockdowns post the COVID-19 pandemic to enable firms to continue the supply of products to the markets in those countries. In simple words, firms simulated their existing supply chains and used their data to develop virtual scenarios before implementing them in the real world. Therefore, digital twins brought increased benefits to the supply chain management environments and systems by enabling optimization for more resilience and cost savings.

Blockchain

Blockchain is a revolution in technology dealing with data. The idea of blockchain is creating authorized channels of data sharing with the partnering firms across the supply chain without breaching data and transaction confidentiality (Yerpude et al., 2022). Since supply chains are considered the backbone of industries playing a significant role in determining the shelf life of organizations, there is always a growing need to create the right environment that enables operating firms to collaborate across the supply chain. With the failure of the traditional supply chain, DSC arrived and enabled firms' integrations and data sharing to ensure proper planning and execution exist for the sake of a successful business relationship and long-living business (Yang et al., 2021). However, one big challenge always stands against the success of such a relationship: cyber-attacks. Organizations needed to share their knowledge securely and confidentially to ensure that firms implement with resilience, minimized costs, and customer-centricity. Cyber-attacks or the absence of security over the internet threaten those firms' confidential systems data with the provided access between those firms. From this need, the growing role of blockchain arrived to ensure that those firms operate securely. Blockchain allows firms to encode and share information within an authorized network after stocking information in blocks related to the relevant transactions without exposing identities with the ability to track those transactional records. No one can imagine how threatening it is to insecurely share a customer's data in a network, which is why blockchain provides security coverage in digital transactions.

Blockchain has four traits that differentiate it from other technologies. The four traits are (a) decentralization, (b) encryption, (c) audibility, and (d) effective execution. A very obvious advantage of blockchain over IoT is that identities in blockchain are always covered, while in IoT-based systems, identities are always confirmed. RFID, barcodes, GPS tags, and other IoTs rely on confirming identities, a demand of the involved organizations in those transactions. The implemented and integrated sensors will always confirm identities related to those transactions with every exposure (Men et al., 2022). The cure to this breaching situation is to build IoT technologies on the blockchain infrastructure so the data can be aggregated and posted only to a post-encrypted network (Jayabalasamy & Koppu 2021). From this perspective, only the users of this network are authorized to receive updated, traceable, verified data and high-quality performance information, which promotes trust across the DSC between firms ranging from vendors to customers. Thus, all involved firms improve their decisions to serve customers' demands, the ultimate reason for the existence of DSC. In contrast, firms work hard to reduce operating costs and enhance lengthy processes to meet those demands.

Business Sustainability

The United Nations republished The Brundtland Report, which introduced to the world the sustainability term back in 1987. Sustainability is balancing relationships between development and distribution to protect the environment, business growth, and the community. From this perspective, business sustainability represents the continued growth of business profitability and employment opportunities offered to the community (Nitescu et al., 2019). Small businesses represent 96.5% of the existing US businesses and almost 99% of the European firms, employing almost 49% of the private sector's workforce in the United States and Europe (European Commission, 2019; Sedky, 2021). So, whether the business is a small, medium-sized, or large firm, business leaders need to find innovative solutions from time to time to keep their businesses ahead of the competition and sustain their operations.

With the increased importance of the private sector for economic growth and employment offering to the market, governments interfered with different means ranging from established laws to even offering training programs to ensure the positive functionality of such a sector. The idea is to protect the private sector business, mainly the small firms, from the risk of closure to avoid a negative impact on the economy and the community. For numerous governments worldwide, small business has the flexibility, agility, and quick response ability to their local demands (Ludmila & Renate, 2019). In addition, the private sector, in general, is deeply involved in the global supply chain through partnerships and business relationships that benefit the economy and respond to the local demand of the community. So, the pandemic's effect tested most of those firms, and some even closed, leaving behind a negative impact. In a reflex to the negative impact, many governments revisited the provided support to firms operating in the global market (Pu et al., 2021). Governments set rescue plans by easing the banking system regulations, strengthening the technological infrastructure, training, supporting transformation, and adapting to digital business environments. Of course, those steps were expected to promote business continuity and sustainability to the private sector, the economic and social partner of the governmental sector in responding to society's demand.

DIGITAL SUPPLY CHAIN AND BUSINESS SUSTAINABILITY

DSC came to fill the gap that the traditional supply chain could not fill, and the pandemic was the real test for firms' strength in hard times. Firms' responses to the pandemic could have been better if their structure had been designed properly and embedded the needed resilience (Choudhury et al., 2021; Yang et al., 2021). Relying significantly on human resources within organizations failed to keep those firms operating at higher performance levels when governments imposed lockdowns. As a result, the need to move away from the traditional supply chain is a necessary need that correlates to the firms' existence and sustainability.

Firms that took serious steps in implementing DSC technology enablers gained access to big data. Big data refers to the biggest portion of data, which exceeds that of traditional data within an organization (Men et al., 2022). Firms build solutions to existing problems by developing scenarios that require access to firms' big data to make decisions in disruption times (Yerpude et al., 2022). Instead of expanding resources, firms can implement a technologically designed solution that fits their operational model. Following this direction, firms gain better and faster access to the benefits of big data, while acquiring talents can be directed to areas that technology cannot fill, such as decision-making and risk management. Thus, firms' talents and technology work hand-in-hand to enable firms' sustainability.

IoT technology is a valid example among the DSC technologies, such as the digital twin and the blockchain, which promote business sustainability. Many firms and even researchers believe that if firms could predict and anticipate demand through data exchange applications that enable real-time data analysis, those firms can minimize risks and operate for longer periods. This business model development is a lesson learned from the pandemic impact when plenty of firms went out of operation for a long period generating massive losses. The idea behind using IoT technology is to remove the redundancy within operating processes and keep continuous operations without disruptions (Ben-Daya et al., 2017; Boyson et al., 2021). At the same time, firms can rely on the human factor to decide based on artificially articulated scenarios (Jones, 2018). The articulated scenarios are a development of artificial intelligence (AI) which uses algorithms, sensors, and data filters when dealing with firms' data to cleanse what is irrelevant to specific situations. The data will be narrowed down to similar cases with different approaches enabling multiple choices for the decision-makers within firms. The data analysis process complexity is given to the IoT technology that can access various firms' data to work on the data processing and transformation into treated information in no time. Thus, when managers within firms control data and gain visibility to risks, the decision-making process becomes reduced risk decisions based on well-articulated scenarios.

IoT enables firms to complete each other along established blockchain networks. When connected through IoT technology, firms can plan their operations together (Boyson et al., 2021). For example, a manufacturing facility will plan the procurement process of the needed raw materials tailored to respond to the demand from a buying firm. The buying firm from the manufacturer will place orders with no excess inventories to reduce its costs based on the demand from the product distributor. The distributor will manage its stock levels based on geographical selling potentials balancing between the inventory solidified costs and the risk of losing business opportunities to the competition. The retail firm will place orders based on its technological access to its stocks and the on-shelve products available in the distributor's warehouses. In such a pattern, every company along the supply chain is connected to maintain market existence and satisfy a demanding customer. Those firms could continue their operations and sustain their business in a decentralized and traceable model along the supply chain (Zouari et al., 2020). Therefore, IoT allows for better visibility, communication, and decision-making, which may enable business managers to connect through firms along the supply chain for sustained business relationships.

Cases From The United States Retail Industry

Walmart Inc.

Walmart Inc. is a well-known gigantic US multinational retail brand that owns more than 10,500 supercenters across the United States and globally. Walmart stores are of many forms, such as discount stores, grocery stores, and wholesale stores. Walmart established 210 distribution centers as logistics hubs that enable market access and continuous supply to its stores. Walmart owns a massive fleet of trailers reaching 80,000 vehicles to serve the movement of the products to their stores. Walmart relies on innovation to provide their customers with a special shopping experience through their existence physically and online (Walmart, 2019). Also, Walmart employs 2.3 million employees, including 1.6 million in the United States. Walmart's strategy relies on attracting its customers by offering products at decreased prices. Walmart's successful strategy enabled the business to be considered one of the most successful businesses leading the list of the largest companies by revenue (Fortune, 2022). Walmart implemented a business continuity plan that uses six disaster distribution centers at strategic locations that allow for a continuous supply of products to the targeted countries. To better serve its customers, Walmart took steps ahead into deploying technology into its operations by partnering with Symbotic to the operating model and the supply chain. The partnership with Symbotic aimed to transform how Walmart operates by automating the pre-shipping stage at its facilities. The system uses an algorithm that enables high-speed mobile bots to store cases in a way that helps the speedy handling of future orders. Thus, the technology takes care of storing and preparing the shipments to dispatch once an order is placed.

Like all firms around the world, Covid-19 had an impact on Walmart's business. Walmart lost business opportunities because of the disrupted supply chain. The firm, like others, worked on implementing a cross-organizational information system. The idea is to mitigate risks by gaining access to big data and understanding the changes in the marketplace environment. In other words, Walmart needed to move forward as a data-driven firm post-pandemic in a systemized, successful manner that the traditional supply chain could not secure for the business. Possessing the right data relevant to business cases at the right time is increasingly important for the firm. Data accuracy could enable businesses to find solutions to existing supply chain problems (Zhao & Li, 2021). Relying on blockchain technology, Walmart developed its system that provides access to data with the needed governance. The system, through numerous algorithms, relates the data and validates them before presenting them to the decision-makers. With the development of its system, Walmart's leaders were able to manage the flow of information across the supply chain in a way that served the firm's responses to the market demand. In addition, the system successfully provided the needed security to avoid data breaching and enabled customers to shop online securely. Walmart ensured through the implementation of its system that the system is smart enough to provide Walmart customers with multiple solutions to meet their demands. Online shopping is essential to customers, and it has increased compared to the past because of the pandemic impact on individuals' way of living.

In another problem related to the supply chain, Walmart Canada had a challenge with transportation. The firm possesses the data. However, the related invoices had discrepancies, which affected the payment process for the contracted freight carriers (Lacity & Van Hoek, 2021). The traditional means of handling such situations could not allow a proper solution, and a huge effort was required with an impact of more delay in settling the due payment. The business leaders identified the root cause of the problem: the use of multiple systems that did not allow the company to communicate properly with the shipping lines. The solution was to use blockchain technology to connect Walmart Canada with its freight carriers, which successfully improved communication between Walmart and the carriers. Thus, the disputed invoices dropped from 70% to less than 1%.

The Kroger Co.

The Kroger Co. is an American retail company with more than 2,720 grocery retail stores across the United States and global supply chain partners. The Kroger Co. is also considered the largest American supermarket operator from the revenue perspective and the second overall retailer, just behind Walmart. The Kroger Co. was founded in 1883 in Ohio, and over the years, the stores spread over the United States, employing the largest network of US private label manufacturing (The Kroger Co, 2017). Kroger operates to serve its customers by shaping the shopping experience supported by the loyalty application Kroger Pay, which provides customers with discounts and purchase points to retain their customers. Kroger also partnered with sources and manufacturers to prioritize supplies and used its data to understand and analyze the trends and changes in demand.

Like all the retail industry competition, Kroger faced the same pandemic challenge of lockdowns, making it challenging for customers to pick up their orders. In response, Kroger enhanced their online ordering platform. Kroger also moved faster to develop a well-distributed network of warehouses near every store it owned to ensure the flow of products to those stores and the readiness to respond to customers. Then the firm planned an enhanced delivery process to ensure delivering products to customers within a few hours.

Kroger is a firm driven by innovation in developing and improving how it works. The firm partnered with Nvidia to develop a digital twin of its processes that include international and national relationships to enhance and automate supply chain operations and logistics milestones. Another outcome was an enhanced distribution network model based on high-tech customer fulfillment centers (CFCs) operated by over 1000 robots to automate the stocking and order preparation processes. Further, Kroger also partnered with Nuro, an autonomous car company, to automate the last-mile delivery phase of the supply chain, relying on driverless cars (Chain Store Age, 2022). With all their efforts and investment in enhancing operations, Kroger delivered high results and increased revenues. Thus, using the digital twin improved Kroger's supply chain performance, embedded resilience, and enabled the business to sustain itself.

RECOMMENDATIONS

Reviewing the literature and cases in this chapter, the researcher recommends that retail firms transform their traditional supply chains into digital ones. The need for DSC is increasing daily because of the circumstances surrounding the business environment of the global supply chain post-pandemic and related disruption. Switching between the traditional and digital supply chain is no longer an option for firms but an essential matter for business survival. DSC could be the breakthrough to sustainable business with the possibility to anticipate, to properly plan for facing potential business risks. The competition is severe, resources are scarce, and supply chain disruptions may trigger a massive negative impact on firms' margins that could result in ending those firms' existence. Thus, there is a growing need to expedite the supply chain switch into a digital model that managers can rely on to strengthen their businesses to face global disruptions.

With the business leaders' decision to adopt DSC in their firms' global business relationships and before investing in DSC technologies, leaders need to identify their needs properly for selecting the relevant DSC technology. The right selection of the DSC technology will significantly enhance their supply chain performance and enable their firms to continue operations. The idea is not only about implementing DSC solutions but extends further to what the technology can provide business leaders, to ultimately allow firms to continue existing. Therefore, business leaders need to understand their organizational needs to implement the right technology to promote business sustainability.

The selection of the DSC technology to be implemented within a firm is a critical aspect that business leaders need to manage with care. After identifying firms' needs, business leaders and their teams need to understand the available DSC solutions and their differences to gain comprehensive knowledge for relevant technology implementation. Research proved that when individuals gain knowledge, they are more likely to implement constructive solutions relevant to their organizational needs. Many firms even prefer to invest in uplifting their leaders' knowledge to ensure they can select the best option to achieve the ultimate goal of business success. There is a real need to use DSC technology for enhanced business performance. The business leader's role is to implement the relevant solution to the firm's business to achieve business sustainability in the global market circumstances.

FUTURE RESEARCH DIRECTIONS

Through this chapter, the researcher emphasized the importance of transforming the traditional to a digital supply chain to support business sustainability. COVID-19 was one of the reasons, if not the main one, for so many firms to lose their existence, especially in the retail business where the transactional margins are competitive. Business leaders need to be ready to switch between various models of doing business for the sake of keeping their firms existing. The researcher relied on reviewing the existing literature and providing two US retailers' cases where DSC models supported those retail firms to gain a remarkable position in the marketplace and expand beyond that. The researcher suggests that future chapters may explore the topic through a qualitative approach, such as a multiple case study with leader interviews from retail firms to explore how their DSC models aid their business to sustain. The researcher also suggests that in future chapters, researchers could follow a quantitative approach to include an increased sample size and generalize the results. Also, for future chapters, researchers could explore other regions' retailers to compare their research results to this chapter's results. For future chapters, researchers may explore the impact of analyzing data generated from two different DSC models to investigate which model could support innovation to drive a longer impact on businesses. Finally, researchers may assess future investments in DSC and how this could reflect on enhancing the decision-making process in small and medium-sized businesses.

CONCLUSION

Firms' increased risks through their daily supply chain operations imply that businesses need more collaboration between all supply chain members. DSC's flexibility and increasing advantages could be reasons for a business to survive in the global disruption times, which enables decreased risks to those businesses operating in the global model. Strengthening relationships, exchanging data, and developing strategic partners' integrations enable firms to increase visibility along the supply chain activities and anticipation to plan together, adapt to global changes, and face potential risks resulting from global disruptions. Accordingly, firms need to move from traditional supply chain practices to the DSC, utilizing technology to enable their business sustainability. Implementing DSC technology allowed leaders to work in a more cooperative and decentralized model, moving out of their silos and enabling better decision-making based on analyzing big data. Data exchange enabled leaders to make high-quality decisions that benefitted all members of the DSC through a secured blockchain environment that protects from the data breach risk. DSC is no longer a choice for business leaders operating in the global model—it is a business sustainability need. The faster that firms adopt, the better it is for their business success and survival. Firms relying on DSC technology managed to improve their business and mitigate risks from global disruption circumstances that could have led to business closure. On the contrary, DSC enabled business success by creating a competitive advantage and better responding to the demanding markets for those firms. Therefore, DSC allows for business sustainability, a drastic decrease in business closure rates, continuous contribution to economies' GDP, and a stable employment market, which serves communities' stability and continuous growth.

ACKNOWLEDGMENT

This research received no specific grant from any funding agency in the public, commercial, or not-for-profit sectors.

REFERENCES

Walmart. (2019). *Homepage*. Corporate Walmart. https://corporate.walmart.com

Abrazeh, S., Mohseni, S.-R., Zeitouni, M. J., Parvaresh, A., Fathollahi, A., Gheisarnejad, M., & Khooban, M.-H. (2023). Virtual hardware-in-the-loop FMU co-simulation based digital twins for heating, ventilation, and air-conditioning (HVAC) systems. *IEEE Transactions on Emerging Topics in Computational Intelligence*, *7*(1), 65–75. doi:10.1109/TETCI.2022.3168507

Agrawal, P., & Narain, R. (2018). Digital supply chain management: An overview. *IOP Conference Series. Materials Science and Engineering*, *455*(1), 012074. doi:10.1088/1757-899X/455/1/012074

Almujeem, N. S. (2021). GCC countries' geoeconomic significance to China's geopolitical ends. *Review of Economics and Political Science*. https://doi.org/ doi:10.1108/REPS-11-2019-0152

Annarelli, B., Battistella, C., & Nonino, F. (2020). A framework to evaluate the effects of organizational resilience on service quality. *Sustainability (Basel)*, *12*(3), 958. doi:10.3390u12030958

Ben-Daya, M., Hassini, E., & Bahroun, Z. (2017). Internet of things and supply chain management: A literature review. *International Journal of Production Research*, *57*(15-16), 4719–4742. doi:10.1080/00207543.2017.1402140

Boyson, S., Corsi, T. M., & Paraskevas, J.-P. (2021). Defending digital supply chains: Evidence from a decade-long research program. *Technovation*, *102380*. doi:10.1016/j.technovation.2021.102380

Buyukkececi, Z. (2020). Cross-country differences in anxiety and behavioral response to the Covid-19 pandemic. *European Societies*, 1–31. doi:10.1080/14616696.2020.1828975

Chain Store Age. (2022). *Home Page*. Chain Store Age. https://chainstoreage.com/kroger-launches-ambitious-ai-trans formation-program

Chen, R., Xie, Y., & Liu, Y. (2021). Defining, conceptualizing, and measuring organizational resilience: A multiple case study. *Sustainability (Basel)*, *13*(5), 2517. doi:10.3390u13052517

Choi, T.-M. (2021). Fighting against COVID-19: What operations research can help and the sense-and-respond framework. *Annals of Operations Research*. doi:10.100710479-021-03973-w PMID:33688111

Chopra, S. (2021). *Supply chain management: Strategy, planning and operation* (7th ed.). Pearson Education.

Choudhury, A., Behl, A., Sheorey, P. A., & Pal, A. (2021). Digital supply chain to unlock new agility: A TISM approach. *Benchmarking*, *28*(6), 2075–2109. doi:10.1108/BIJ-08-2020-0461

Dadzie, K., Dadzie, C., Johnston, W. J., Winston, E., & Wang, H. (2022). The integration of logistics and marketing practice into baseline supply chain practices in the emerging markets. *Journal of Business and Industrial Marketing*, *38*(2), 367–383. doi:10.1108/JBIM-01-2022-0002

Davies, S. E., & Wenham, C. (2020). Why the COVID-19 response needs international relations. *International Affairs*, *96*(5), 1227–1251. doi:10.1093/ia/iiaa135 PMID:34191916

Deepu, T. S., & Ravi, V. (2021). Supply chain digitalization: An integrated MCDM approach for inter-organizational information systems selection in an electronic supply chain. *International Journal of Information Management Data Insights*, *1*(2), 100038. doi:10.1016/j.jjimei.2021.100038

Duchek, S. (2019). Organizational resilience: A capability-based conceptualization. *Business Research*, *13*(1), 215–246. doi:10.100740685-019-0085-7

Duchek, S., Raetze, S., & Scheuch, I. (2019). The role of diversity in organizational resilience: A theoretical framework. *Business Research*, *13*(2), 387–423. doi:10.100740685-019-0084-8

European Commission. (2019). *SME performance review*. EC. https://ec.europa.eu/growth/smes/business-friendly-environment/performance-review_en

Fortune. (2022). *Global 500*. Fortune. https://fortune.com/ranking/global500/

Gai, K., Zhang, Y., Qiu, M., & Thuraisingham, B. (2022). Blockchain-enabled service optimizations in supply chain digital twin. *IEEE Transactions on Services Computing*, 1–12. doi:10.1109/TSC.2022.3192166

Hepfer, M., & Lawrence, T. B. (2022). The heterogeneity of organizational resilience: Exploring functional, operational and strategic resilience. *Organization Theory*, *3*(1), 263178772210747. doi:10.1177/26317877221074701

Hillmann, J., & Guenther, E. (2020). Organizational resilience: A valuable construct for management research? *International Journal of Management Reviews, 23*(1). Wiley. https://doi.org/ doi:10.1111/ijmr.12239

Ivanov, D. (2020). Viable supply chain model: Integrating agility, resilience and sustainability perspectives—lessons from and thinking beyond the COVID-19 pandemic. *Annals of Operations Research.* Springer. https://doi.org/ doi:10.1007/s10479-020-03640-6

Jones, W. A. (2018). Artificial intelligence and leadership: A few thoughts, a few questions. *Journal of Leadership Studies*, *12*(3), 60–62. doi:10.1002/jls.21597

Kim, M., & Chai, S. (2017). The impact of supplier innovativeness, information sharing and strategic sourcing on improving supply chain agility: Global supply chain perspective. *International Journal of Production Economics*, *187*(1), 42–52. doi:10.1016/j.ijpe.2017.02.007

Kochan, C., Nowicki, D. R., Sauser, B., & Randall, W. S. (2018). Impact of cloud-based information sharing on hospital supply chain performance: A system dynamics framework. *International Journal of Production Economics*, *195*, 168–185. doi:10.1016/j.ijpe.2017.10.008

Lacity, M. C., & Van Hoek, R. (2021). How Walmart Canada used blockchain technology to reimagine freight invoice processing. *MIS Quarterly Executive*, 219–233. doi:10.17705/2msqe.00050

Ludmila, V., & Renate, Z. (2019). The role of small business in the economy and methods of its government support using the example of the Republic of Latvia. *Economics and Culture*, *16*(2), 72–81. doi:10.2478/jec-2019-0023

Mao, H., & Gorg, H. (2020). Friends like this: The impact of the US – China trade war on global value chains. *World Economy*, *43*(7), 1776–1791. doi:10.1111/twec.12967

Men, F., Yaqub, R. M. S., Yan, R., Irfan, M., & Fatima, M. e. (2022). Resource-based theory perspective in the textile industry: The impact of the digital supply chain on operational performance. *Frontiers in Environmental Science*, *10*, 1017297. doi:10.3389/fenvs.2022.1017297

NetSuite.com. (2020, November 26). *Decoding the digital supply chain*. Oracle NetSuite. https://www.netsuite.com/portal/resource/articles/erp/digital-supply-chain.shtml

Nguyen, H. A., Ha, H. H., & Doan, T. D. (2020). The impact of supply chain quality management on firm performance: Empirical evidence from Vietnam. *Uncertain Supply Chain Management*, 331–350. doi:10.5267/j.uscm.2019.11.005

Nitescu, D. C., Murgu, V., & Caprita, E. D. (2019). Impact of labor, FDI and R&D on business sustainability. *Amfiteatru Economic, 21*(Special Issue 13), 795-815. https://doi.org/ doi:10.24818/EA/2019/S13/795

Pu, G., Qamruzzaman, M., Mehta, A. M., Naqvi, F. N., & Karim, S. (2021). Innovative finance, technological adaptation and SMEs sustainability: The mediating role of government support during COVID-19 Pandemic. *Sustainability (Basel)*, *13*(16), 9218. doi:10.3390u13169218

Rai, S. S., Rai, S., & Singh, N. K. (2021). Organizational resilience and social-economic sustainability: COVID-19 perspective. *Environment, Development and Sustainability*, *23*(8), 12006–12023. doi:10.100710668-020-01154-6 PMID:33519297

Rasool, F., Greco, M., & Grimaldi, M. (2021). Digital supply chain performance metrics: A literature review. *Measuring Business Excellence*. doi:10.1108/MBE-11-2020-0147

Sedky, A. (2021). *The relationship between transformational, transactional, and passive-avoidant leadership styles and small business sustainability.* [Dissertation, Walden University]. https://scholarworks.waldenu.edu/dissertations/11331

Shafi, M., Liu, J., & Ren, W. (2020). Impact of COVID-19 pandemic on micro, small, and medium-sized enterprises operating in Pakistan. *Research in Globalization*, *2*(1), 100018. doi:10.1016/j.resglo.2020.100018

Siderius, C., Conway, D., Yassine, M., Murken, L., Lostis, P.-L., & Dalin, C. (2020). Multi-scale analysis of the water-energy-food nexus in the Gulf region. *Environmental Research Letters*, *15*(9), 094024. doi:10.1088/1748-9326/ab8a86

Singh, S., Kumar, R., Panchal, R., & Tiwari, M. K. (2020). Impact of COVID-19 on logistics systems and disruptions in food supply chain. *International Journal of Production Research*, *59*(7), 1–16. doi: 10.1080/00207543.2020.1792000

Swift, C., Guide, V. D. R. Jr, & Muthulingam, S. (2019). Does supply chain visibility affect operating performance? Evidence from conflict minerals disclosures. *Journal of Operations Management*, *65*(5), 406–429. doi:10.1002/joom.1021

Tarafdar, M., & Qrunfleh, S. (2016). Agile supply chain strategy and supply chain performance: Complementary roles of supply chain practices and information systems capability for agility. *International Journal of Production Research*, *55*(4), 925–938. doi:10.1080/00207543.2016.1203079

The Kroger Co. (2017). The Kroger Co. https://www.thekrogerco.com/

Turner, S., & Endres, A. (2017). Strategies for enhancing small-business owners' success rates. *International Journal of Applied Management and Technology*, *16*(1), 34–49. doi:10.5590/IJAMT.2017.16.1.03

Vanyi, N. (2012). Members of a supply chain and their relationships. *Apstract, Applied Studies in Agribusiness and Commerce*, *6*(5), 133–136. doi:10.19041/APSTRACT/2012/5/21

Wamba, S. F., Gunasekaran, A., Akter, S., & Dubey, R. (2019). The performance effects of big data analytics and supply chain ambidexterity: The moderating effect of environmental dynamism. *International Journal of Production Economics*, *222*, 107498. Advance online publication. doi:10.1016/j.ijpe.2019.09.019

Xiao, L., & Cao, H. (2017). Organizational resilience: The theoretical model and research implication. *ITM Web of Conferences, 12*, 04021. 10.1051/itmconf/20171204021

Yang, M., Fu, M., & Zhang, Z. (2021). The adoption of digital technologies in supply chains: Drivers, process and impact. *Technological Forecasting and Social Change*, *169*, 120795. doi:10.1016/j.techfore.2021.120795

Ye, F., Liu, K., Li, L., Lai, K.-H., Zhan, Y., & Kumar, A. (2022). Digital supply chain management in the COVID-19 crisis: An asset orchestration perspective. *International Journal of Production Economics*, *245*, 108396. doi:10.1016/j.ijpe.2021.108396 PMID:34931109

Yerpude, S., Sood, K., & Grima, S. (2022). Blockchain-augmented digital supply chain management: A way to sustainable business. *Journal of Risk and Financial Management*, *16*(1), 7. doi:10.3390/jrfm16010007

Zekhnini, K., Cherrafi, A., Bouhaddou, I., Benghabrit, Y., & Garza-Reyes, J. A. (2020). Supply chain management 4.0: A literature review and research framework. *Benchmarking*, *28*(2), 465–501. doi:10.1108/BIJ-04-2020-0156

Zhang, N., & Li, B. (2020). Pricing and coordination of green closed-loop supply chain with fairness concerns. *IEEE Access : Practical Innovations, Open Solutions*, *8*, 224178–224189. doi:10.1109/ACCESS.2020.3045152

Zhao, J., & Li, Y. (2021). Supply chain security evaluation model and index system based on a 5G information system. *Neural Computing & Applications*. doi:10.100700521-021-06584-5 PMID:34728901

Zouari, D., Ruel, S., & Viale, L. (2020). Does digitalising the supply chain contribute to its resilience? *International Journal of Physical Distribution & Logistics Management*, *51*(2), 149–180. doi:10.1108/IJPDLM-01-2020-0038

KEY TERMS AND DEFINITIONS

Advanced Data Capture Equipment: Include equipment that interacts with extensive data tagging, such as voice recognition and radio frequency identification systems.

Advanced Data Tagging Equipment: A category that includes two-dimensions bar codes, smart bar codes, and smart containers. Those communicate with the advanced data tagging equipment on packages within them and transmit status reports.

Artificial Intelligence: Intelligence by machines that take over humans in redundant tasks and use implemented algorithms to develop scenarios based on relevant organizational data analysis.

Blockchain: A digital supply chain technology where distributed ledger databases consisting of transactional records are stored as encrypted blocks.

Decision-Making: A process through which managers select actions based on developed scenarios from experience, knowledge, and gathered information.

Gross Domestic Product: A standard measure of the value added by a provided product or service within a country within a specific period, probably a year.

Retail Industry: An industry consisting of companies that interact with customers to sell a product or service.

Section 3

Improving Visibility, Procurement, and Logistics Processes Leveraging Digital Technologies

Chapter 10
Shifting Gears:
Redefining Supply Chain Visibility

Chris Hanebeck
Truckl, USA

ABSTRACT

The concept of visibility is often associated with seeing everything that is going on across an entire supply chain. The following chapter takes a close look at the current understanding and practice of supply chain visibility to establish what it means and how the concept is applied in organizations today. It investigates current problems and introduces an innovative approach to supply chain collaboration that allows all participants in a process to work together, eliminate manual communication and coordination, and achieve higher efficiencies than any one company could reach on their own. The chapter includes several practical examples and illustrates the benefits of collaboration through a real-life business case.

INTRODUCTION

In this chapter, we investigate several topics to ultimately address one question: How can companies dramatically increase the effectiveness and efficiency of transportation and supply chain processes? The past few decades have seen great increases in technological maturity. Today nearly all aspects of our lives have either been digitized and automated or are about to be. These capabilities range from controlling the air conditioning in our home to monitoring our well-being in real time. We have digital access to more knowledge than any previous generation in history, and yet, supply chain execution has not reaped many of the same benefits stemming from these technological advances.

In essence, we still ship things from one place to another as we have for millennia. The parties that have the most to lose—recipients, shippers, and 3PLs—are often least in control. Once freight leaves their dock, they become vulnerable to any disruption, error, or exception that may occur. Many are constrained and blinded by outdated systems, a lack of data sharing and control during the execution of supply chain processes, and a lack of accountability. Today, 95% of all transportation processes are still handled to a large degree through interpersonal calls, emails, and conversations, and are often accompanied by redundant data inputs. Many of the systems we use cannot connect different organizations

DOI: 10.4018/978-1-6684-7298-9.ch010

quickly or efficiently. When APIs are used, they are typically expensive and time-consuming to build and as such are only implemented for the largest payloads.

A solution that addresses these issues effectively must rely on supply chain collaboration. It allows for higher levels of process control and can instill trust through the use of new technologies such as blockchain. Other important aspects include the motivation of operators to actively share vital information that would otherwise be lost. Collaborative supply chain systems need to augment and enhance rather than replace existing ERP and TMS systems or GPS and ELD devices, or even iPaaS platforms. Any solution must fit perfectly in-between planning and execution feedback systems in order to dramatically improve performance as a whole. In the end, everybody engaged in the execution of a supply chain process needs to reduce risk and save time and money while providing higher levels of customer service to ultimately grow revenues. The objective is that everybody wins.

Why the Current Understanding of Visibility is Flawed

Throughout history, knowing one's location has always been of strategic importance. Military campaigns and commerce have always depended on it. Without knowledge of where you are, you are hardly in a position to reach your destination. In fact, it was important enough that in 1711 the British Parliament offered the then astronomical sum of £20,000 to the first person to invent a method of establishing one's position. The challenge was to find a practical solution for sailors who routinely got lost at sea. A gentleman by the name of John Harrison, who was a clockmaker rather than an astronomer, ultimately created a chronometer that won the prize.

Things have obviously progressed since the days of traditional seamanship. We have even come a long way from the early 1970s, when Navistar launched its first satellite for a global positioning system. We rely on location more than ever, be it on our phones, in autonomous vehicles, or on commercial trucks. Leveraging highly accurate latitudinal and longitudinal data is a requirement for many applications. GPS systems for example allow us to not only provide guidance to drivers but also establish the location of products being transported on trucks, railroads, ships, or planes. By knowing the location of a transportation asset, we can deduce when freight will arrive. This information is of vital importance in many subsequent processes ranging from manufacturing runs that depend on just-in-time materials to retailers who may need additional stock while running promotions or selling prized items such as iPhones or game consoles.

However, a long-standing issue has been falsely equating location with visibility. A whole industry has sprung up over the past 20 years that sells GPS receivers to solve problems such as knowing when a truck is stuck in traffic or how many hours a driver can spend on the road. Yet, these receivers do not address many other issues such as knowing the condition of freight, sharing of freight documents, or planning information. Nor do they eliminate the myriad of emails, conversations, calls and redundant data inputs that all occur when a shipper transports freight. In essence, the where and when of a thing only captures a fraction of the required data that is needed to attain efficiencies that are possible today.

Assessment of Supply Chain "Visibility" Today

The short answer is, it's not. For most, supply chain visibility is defined as "shedding light" on anything that happens during the physical movement and handling of parts, materials, and goods. Visibility in this sense is both a misnomer in that we actually don't need to watch everything all the time and precarious as we don't want to be blinded by an avalanche of data. Instead, it is important to know when something goes wrong, doesn't proceed according to plan, or breaks down. Visibility as in "shedding light" is simply a means to this end.

The difference between visibility and being able to react when problems arise is absolutely critical to everything under discussion. Even if you see that something goes wrong, you still need to be able to remedy the situation. After all, what good does it do to know there is a problem if you can't fix it? There is some value in understanding circumstances or the why of an issue, of course. In this regard, we often talk about actionable control in supply chain processes. To solve all of the issues that plague supply chains today you need both: visibility and control.

Control has as much to do with data collection as it does with communication: we cannot improve business process outcomes unless we are able to communicate and coordinate with all of the parties involved. This in turn necessitates data sharing as well as the ability to reach others at the right time. Many shippers, intermediaries, and carriers still handle this challenge manually. When a truck does not arrive at a dock, the recipient calls the manufacturer or seller, who is usually the shipper of the freight. The shipper calls their third-party logistics provider (3PL), broker, or carrier with which they have been working. In many cases, all of these organizations can be involved in every single transport.

Figure 1.

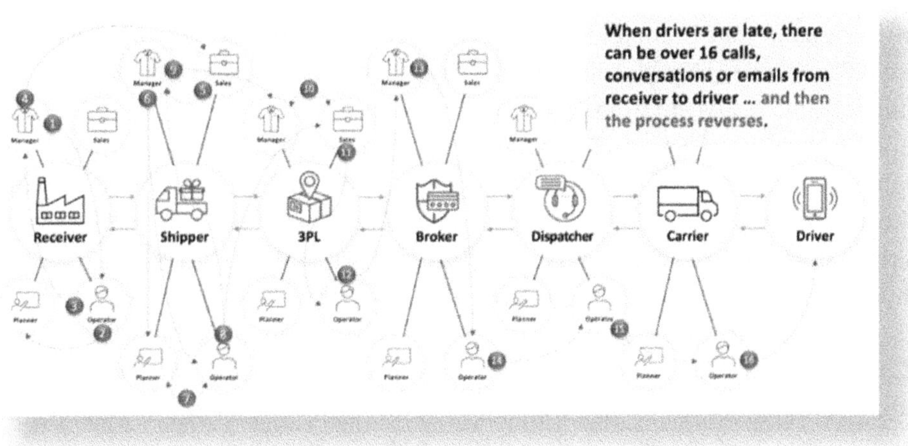

To make matters worse, it is usually not just one call or conversation, but many. Managers talk to operators, planners, and sales execs and they in turn to each other. Each has questions and they are all trying to understand what has actually happened. These calls, conversations, and emails jump from one organization to the next and the amount of time and money that is spent on communication and coordination quickly spirals out of control. All because a single driver is late. Imagine the expense incurred when a pallet of brand-new cell phones or sought-after sneakers is delivered to the wrong address or when raw materials that are required for a production run do not arrive on time?

To a large degree, this situation is caused by silos that exist in traditional supply chains. Each party ranging from recipients and manufacturers to brokers, dispatchers, and carriers has its own processes, systems, resources, culture, and objectives. Today these parties have no way to electronically communicate, which necessarily leads to manual tasks. For example, when two systems do not exchange information automatically, all new data is entered into a first system, then communicated verbally or through email only to be reentered into the second.

Traditional approaches to integrating supply chain systems involve interface mechanisms such as application programming interfaces (APIs) or outdated standards such as Electronic Data Interchange (EDI). These approaches are often not feasible and always very expensive. They only make sense when there is enough data to be exchanged to justify the effort. More important, there are several parties in typical supply chains that are hard or impossible to integrate such as brokers, dispatchers, or drivers.

Another part of the problem is that there is often not enough data captured during the execution of a transport. Think about it this way: the people on the ground know exactly what happened at any given point in time, but these insights are rarely shared throughout the supply chain. For example, when a forklift drives into a pallet and crushes one of the boxes on it, the forklift operator may not always see the benefit of reporting the incident nor is there an efficient, trustworthy method for tracking these events.

Obviously, there is no easy solution to such issues. We encounter situations where people are forthcoming and others where operators prefer to remain silent. The best way to deal with the problem is to collect as much data as possible, document as many process steps as feasible, and hold everyone accountable. The data needs to be collected in the field with mobile devices.

Data capture, communication, and data sharing alone aren't entirely the answer either. People need to work with one another. Specifically for supply chains and transportation you may need to motivate parties that are not under your immediate management control and who may only work for you occasionally. As any effective people manager will confirm, you achieve a lot more with carrots than with sticks. Unfortunately, the sticks are used vastly more often.

Take drivers for example. They often care the least about data integrity, yet they carry the biggest responsibility. In fact, drivers are often in a hockey goalie situation: you play a perfect game for 59 minutes, then make a tiny mistake and 20,000 people jump out of their seats to scream at you. Drivers are often the first to be criticized and they rarely get applauded when things go according to plan.

Equally important, the parties that have the most to lose are often least in control: recipients, shippers, and 3PLs. Once freight leaves the dock, these parties become vulnerable to any disruption, error, or exception that may occur. As we suggest above, today they react after the fact and are seldom in a position to correct exceptions before it is too late. Part of this problem is that there aren't unified controls in processes and we aren't getting enough data during process execution.

A Practical Solution to Supply Chain Visibility and Collaboration

It is easy to play the armchair quarterback, sitting back and pondering all of the things that aren't right. Yet, practitioners know they still have a job to do and supply chain operators are among the finest professionals in any field. The issue is that many of them simply do not have the proper tools to do their job.

Looking at communication, it is easy to see that if we were able to freely share data among all parties, we would not have to make as many calls, have as many conversations, and send as many emails. More importantly, other tasks such as sending and receiving planning information and freight documents would be eliminated altogether while redundant data inputs would be kept to a minimum. At the same time, if we could collect more data during process execution, we would spend less time communicating and could avoid some types of exceptions that occur in the field. Today's supply chain technology needs to address these issues effectively.

Figure 2.

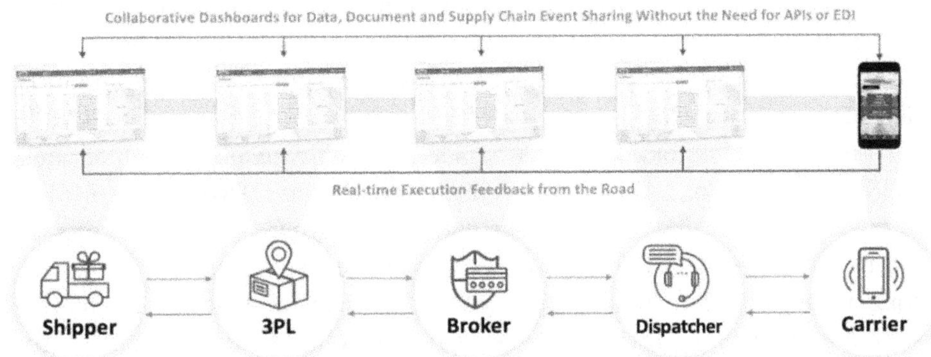

(1) Collaborative Dashboards for True Visibility and Control: Allow all parties to view a transportation process from beginning to end that does not require APIs or EDI to share data. This can be extremely fast to configure and easy to use. One party (such as a shipper) sets up a new transaction or imports it into the system and then invites the next responsible party in the supply chain, who becomes a part of the same transaction on the same dashboard. This latter party only sees transactions they have been invited to, of course. They in turn can invite the next link in the chain until someone invites a driver who receives and handles the transaction on a mobile device. The entire supply chain is now connected through a discrete, shared dashboard that captures and distributes relevant information in real-time.

When all of the dashboards are linked together, we have a platform on which everyone shares data, receives updates, and sees the latest status of a transportation load. The shipper can upload a bill of lading, manifest, or commercial invoice and it immediately becomes available to all parties. The 3PL creates a rate confirmation for the shipper that is kept confidential between them, the broker creates a rate confirmation for the 3PL that is kept confidential between these two parties, and so forth. When the driver collects data from the road, the entire chain sees it and customized milestones are updated.

(2) Mobile Applications for Comprehensive Data Capture: Through mobile applications—typically developed natively on iOS and Android—users have the ability to configure what data a driver needs to collect. Data inputs go far beyond just providing a dot on a map; they can include check-in and check-out times along with automatically establishing detention charges, taking photos of freight, vehicle conditions, sensors, or documents, as well as receiving signatures from managers at pickup and drop-off. They can also include more sophisticated capabilities such as capturing videos, going through checklists, integrating IoT devices and RFID, as well as barcode scanning into the process as needed.

The specific configuration of a mobile application depends on user requirements and thus may never be exactly the same. For example, in some industries it is important to document sustainable practices, while in others the constant monitoring of freight conditions is essential, and in yet others, it may be required to ensure the security of freight at all times. Only a flexible and configurable mobile application can accommodate this variety of crucial requirements.

(3) Active Motivation of Operators and Drivers: Another aspect that is necessary for workable solutions is to actively motivate operators—particularly drivers—independent of whether they are employed or work as outside contractors. For example, the deep integration of load factoring into the mobile application process achieves substantial operational efficiencies, especially when factoring banks use their

own dashboard to monitor factored loads and access documents that normally would have to be submitted by drivers. Once both the shipper and driver have been approved, the application can offer factoring as an option to the driver when they accept a new load. All documents are available to the factoring bank and users can provide this service at attractive interest rates far below the standard industry rate due to achieved efficiencies for all parties.

Users can also motivate operators through access to affordable healthcare or continuing education in the form of OSHA, Hazmat or DOT trainings, and certifications. Drivers access all of these perks directly on their own dashboards. Maybe even more enticing, users can "gamify" the application through raffles, contests, and gift exchanges. For example, drivers can receive a lottery ticket for every mile they drive and, as long as they maintain high compliance in their data collection, they enter a raffle to win a prize at the end of each quarter. Obviously, these and many other benefits can be custom-tailored to your specific requirements and objectives.

(4) Blockchain Technology for Every Transaction to Foster Trust: Another important differentiator for leading supply chain visibility systems can be blockchain technology. Blockchain is essentially an immutable ledger: what happens on the blockchain, stays on the blockchain. Systems can anchor each transaction to the public Ethereum chain once it is completed and thus establish an immutable audit trail. Users can prove that their documentation is beyond reproach and the applications help them to prove that all data was collected honestly as well.

In case there are differences in perception between two or more parties, an immutable audit trail greatly reduces the friction that occurs every time there is a dispute or insurance claim with the help of blockchain. This avoids weeks of forensics work and, equally as important, keeps everyone a bit more honest and committed in documenting their actions during the execution of a transport process. After all, these actions stay in the public record for a very long time.

Case Study: Advanced Route Optimization

Products move through supply chains from supplier or manufacturing sites to distribution centers and retail points and sometimes even directly to end-users or consumers. As end-users and consumers require more direct and free deliveries to their homes, offices, or nearby pickup locations with hourly time commitments; carriers and shippers have to commit to direct and faster deliveries without increasing cost while providing visibility on the whereabouts of their packages. These requirements are ubiquitous already.

Amazon and Walmart, arguably the technology leaders in the last mile today, are both continuously tightening delivery windows. Both companies understand that in order to own the customer, they must control the last mile. Amazon first started this battle for dominance when they offered free shipping, then further decreased delivery windows from several days to two, then to next day, to same day, and are now pushing for two-hour delivery in major metropolitan areas.

The next planned iterations in this cycle are 30-minute deliveries through drones and robotic delivery technologies combined with a tight network of local distribution centers. Amazon has grown its warehouse footprint from 200M to 360M square feet in 2020 through the addition of local delivery centers while Walmart has just begun to add dozens of fully robotic eCommerce delivery hubs to existing stores. Of course, consumer expectations keep evolving along the way, which is the strategic intent behind these developments and will eventually force everyone else into providing their shipments at higher speeds as well.

The problem is that as products are delivered directly to our homes, offices, or nearby smaller stores, companies need to serve many small-sized orders which requires increasing visits during the day in different parts of cities that necessitate more refined scheduling. Demand is more variable as well in terms of geography, timing, and order quantity; and the set of customer locations is growing and changing every day. Often shippers cannot repeat the same route plans that they have already optimized or rely on the experience of human planners due to the immense complexities of daily delivery networks.

Another industry issue is that fleet structures have changed as well. Today there are more types of vehicles in different sizes and with varying operating costs than ever before. The days of just same-sized trucks are behind us. In addition, instead of owning the whole fleet, companies often rent for short-term needs and use shared resources as well. Any optimization solution needs to take these changing requirements into consideration and compute far more than mere travel distance and time minimization. For example, the right selection and optimal mix of vehicles and drivers is crucial to meet new key delivery demands each day.

Instead of only focusing on daily service levels, companies need to commit to hourly timeslots and appointments for better customer service; they must be able to communicate expected travel times to their customers, which requires advanced intelligent planning that balances costs and service levels more fully. One example is that shippers cannot deliver to two neighbors on the same street in a single visit when one wants to receive a shipment in the morning and the other in the afternoon. The key to understanding this environment is not how shippers can accomplish these goals, but rather how they execute at minimal additional cost.

As mentioned, competitive pressures are added through increasing consumer expectations such as the "Amazon Effect," and cost pressures keep mounting as well. Shippers have witnessed a logistics spend increase from 3-5% to 12-20% on average as they transitioned from brick & mortar to online channels while carriers still face thin margins of around 3.6%. A 15% cost reduction could increase their profitability by a factor of five. These tangible savings are highly attractive and will drive investments in optimization and visibility based on integrated last-mile solutions for years to come.

An illustrative case of how supply chain collaboration enables all parties working on a process to achieve superior outcomes is the last-mile delivery of materials or goods to their point-of-sale or point-of-use. The application of collaborative dashboards solves a key problem for last-mile delivery: the deep integration of planning and execution processes. Route optimization, which is the algorithmic optimization of how to utilize vehicles and drivers on many consecutive stops, allows companies to manage their fleets more efficiently independent of whether they use employee drivers or work with contractors and partners. One of the biggest issues in route optimization is the lack of execution feedback, which is often an afterthought and, in many cases, never fully deployed.

By leveraging collaborative dashboards, last-mile shippers gain the ability to collaborate across their entire delivery chain without the need for APIs or EDI, receive more detailed execution feedback from the road than from any other application, and gain control over processes that have traditionally been out of their hands. The benefits are considerable and range from the automation of route scheduling across a diverse population of drivers, locations, and assets to feeding execution feedback from the road back into optimization algorithms.

The solution we propose here is an integrated system that continuously optimizes deliveries, routes, and destinations on the basis of a variety of different variables, which tracks the execution of each delivery and then uses the data to further improve planning algorithms. An AI-based route optimizer helps shippers dramatically improve logistics procurement while carriers can improve daily route operations on a continuous basis. The latter may elect to pass some of their cost savings on to shippers or may use them to invest in further efficiency gains as a means to enhance their competitive advantage. In this scenario, the AI-based route optimizer allocates orders across the fleet and sequences them to minimize fuel and fleet operational cost while satisfying time and operational constraints set by customers.

An AI-based route optimizer needs to be built on top of a comprehensive data model to capture the most realistic representation of operations. Beyond orders and available vehicles, additional variables related to fleet, orders, locations, and drivers can be integrated over time to create an increasingly realistic representation of operations. The AI-based route optimizer modular and tunable algorithm design can create custom-tailored solutions for various business environments both geographically and under varying priorities. The algorithm design itself needs to enable the creation of evolving planning algorithms that increasingly align with each business environment. Scenario planning, for example, can lead to additional and immensely valuable insights and allows all parties to benefit through the parallel optimization of shipper and carrier requirements.

One aspect that is highly important to the optimization of routes and deliveries is the integration of real-time supply chain execution feedback. This feedback serves as input for machine learning mechanisms such as the continuous fine-tuning of initial planning assumptions. In this way, the algorithms analyze and then learn from deviations between planning and execution data. The AI-based route optimizer algorithms can be fine-tuned based on data provided by collaborative supply chain visibility applications and improve continuously as a result. The more shippers and carriers use our joint solution, the better it performs and the more everyone ultimately saves.

However, any plan is only as good as the information that was used to define it. One often hears terms such as GIGO (garbage in, garbage out) to describe this insight, especially when things have not gone well. When plans are static, it is often easy to adjust underlying assumptions before plans are executed. However, in the dynamic environment of last mile deliveries, errors in planning assumptions can carry forward indefinitely. The only viable solution is the integration of route optimization and advanced supply chain execution feedback, often referred to as supply chain visibility.

Supply chain visibility is a bit of a misnomer in that "shedding light" doesn't address many problems, issues, and challenges that persist in today's logistics processes. Despite the availability of tracking technologies today, there is still a lack of data sharing, process control, and essentially trust. Too often, technology is used to float exceptions to the top so they can be addressed through manual reconciliation, which is costly and time-consuming. Yet, there is a better way: avoid them in the first place.

Data sharing can be enabled by the collaborative dashboards we describe in this chapter. Likewise, trust isn't built by people who talk about it. It comes naturally when everyone in the transportation process is motivated and when all parties utilize tools such as blockchain that foster it. The supply chain technologies we define here address these and other issues effectively. Their applications allow for higher levels of process control and instill trust through the use of blockchain technology while they motivate operators to actively share vital information that would otherwise be lost.

Collaborative dashboards augment and enhance rather than replace existing ERP and TMS systems as well as GPS and ELD devices. They dramatically improve performance as a whole. In the end, everybody engaged in the execution of a last-mile delivery process reduces risk and saves time and money while providing higher levels of customer service to ultimately grow revenues.

A collaborative supply chain solution leverages collaborative dashboards to enable real-time visibility while greatly enhancing the control that shippers have throughout the process. All parties engaged in the process view last-mile deliveries from beginning to end without the need for APIs or EDI. To engage in the collaborative dashboard, one party sets up a new delivery and then invites the next responsible party, who then become part of the same delivery on their dashboard. They in turn invite the next party in the chain until someone invites a driver who receives the delivery details and all other pertinent information on a mobile device. The entire supply chain is now connected through a discrete, shared dashboard that captures and distributes relevant information in real-time. Of course, this process can be automated so that all parties are invited as soon as a new delivery has been scheduled.

The driver uses a mobile application to input data such as check-in and check-out times, photos of freight, recording vehicle conditions, taking sensor inputs, sharing documents, and obtaining signatures from recipients at drop-off locations. They can further include video capture or operator checklists, leverage integrated IoT devices, image analysis, or RFID to name a few examples, into the process as needed.

Layering AI-based optimization capabilities on top of supply chain visibility enables many interesting possibilities that wouldn't be feasible otherwise. For example, when drivers make daily last-mile deliveries, algorithms can dynamically optimize routes based on traffic, weather, and road conditions while the driver mobile application provides real-time feedback about execution, which in turn helps to further optimize the next planning cycle.

Route optimization leads to higher discipline during execution as well. Operators who know that they need to follow a route for fuel or time savings, for example, are less likely to deviate from it. This instills a stronger culture of accountability in other areas as well. They are also more likely to comply with using a mobile application for their tasks, less likely to enter incorrect information, and more likely to report issues and problems.

Conversely, because operators use the mobile application, they are more likely to implement route recommendations on their daily drives and more likely to adhere to unfamiliar routes because they are being tracked so that route deviations can be reported. Additional capabilities such as in-vehicle inventory checks based on shipping documents or driver checklists for each route strongly augment optimization. After all, there is little benefit in getting to delivery locations on time when drivers do not bring the right products. In essence, all parties are more accountable and much more likely to execute flawlessly.

One area where supply chain collaboration, AI-based route optimization, and visibility work exceptionally well is in industrial or B2B last-mile delivery. Processes today are characterized by a high degree of manual data handling; shippers often use a diverse network of delivery partners that is focused on a specific geographical area and there is often no standardization of technology. Some business partners use sophisticated dispatch and routing systems while others rely on Google maps or Excel and yet others still use paper and pen. In this situation, it is near impossible for shippers to receive real-time feedback from the road, there is no way to proactively avoid exceptions and, worst of all, the recipients of freight, customers of the shipper, cannot be integrated into the process at all.

The described last-mile delivery solution differs from existing ones in several important ways. It enables dynamic route optimization through sophisticated algorithms for continuous efficiency gains, provides dashboard sharing and carrier integration, and offers a sophisticated mobile application. The solution is especially valuable when shippers use it with transportation partners who are often left to their own devices when it comes to technology integration. Blockchain for every transaction further provides an immutable audit trail and fosters trust. In addition, highly customizable mobile applications provide a much higher level of process control and allow shippers to brand the application as their own.

The graphic below illustrates this integrated solution architecture for the optimization and tracking of delivery routes and inner-city transport based on orders, vehicles, and routes to achieve higher fleet efficiency, reduced operating cost, and better customer satisfaction. This last-mile delivery solution can receive hundreds of daily last-mile deliveries for dozens of urban distribution centers from an ERP system through a standard API.

Figure 3.

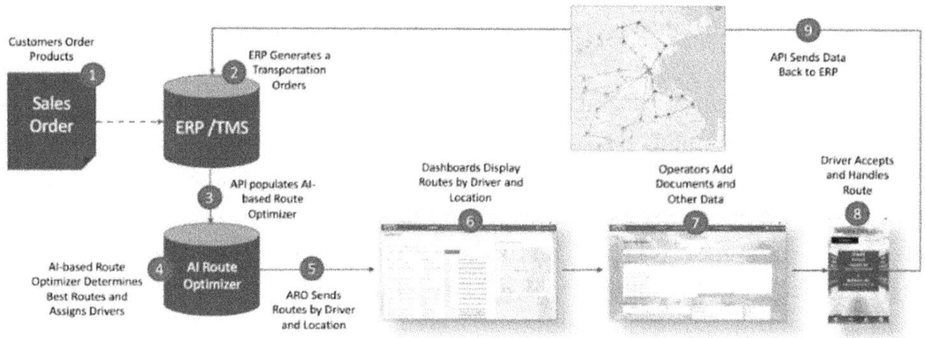

The AI-based route optimizer dynamically organizes the routes for each urban delivery center (UDC) based on customer preferences and availability, vehicle specifications, weight and size limits, fuel efficiency, or traffic and road conditions. Once the AI-based route optimizer has created routes for each UDC, it sends them to a central database underneath the collaborative dashboards where they are automatically assigned to drivers and displayed on dashboards for the shipper team and its transportation partners in each UDC. All data processing is fully automated and rule-based while there is room for adjustments when human operators—often relying on invaluable experience and knowledge—may require them.

Dispatchers, who are now connected to the shipper via collaborative dashboards, see driver, truck, and route assignments, and can add documents, delivery details, and operator instructions. This solution can automatically generate an inventory of parts and tools for each truck that UDCs use as a packing list and drivers leverage in the form of a checklist each morning before starting their routes. Using their handheld applications, drivers see their stops and collect data from the route for each delivery. The solution effectively provides the manufacturer with the ability to share a collaborative application with its supply chain partners while they have real-time visibility into everything that happens in each UDC and urban area.

The implementation of a highly sophisticated AI-based route optimization, collaboration, and visibility solution can seem daunting and complex. Yet, the reality is that we have evolved from the days when technology deployments required months of planning, programming, and other extensive preparations. Cloud-based applications can be delivered out of one hand through a collaborative dashboard and mobile applications.

The implementation of route optimization requires that users analyze historical data and look at current orders as well as delivery patterns to fine-tune the underlying algorithms early in a project and prior to going-live. AI-based route optimizers can run parallel to the initial phases in deployment so that the algorithms can be compared to UDC manager decisions in the field. The implementation team will typically interview managers about how routes are designed so they can understand where additional constraints or adjustments to the algorithm may be required.

In parallel, the implementation team prepares operators at the shipper site and in UDCs for the deployment of their collaborative dashboards and trains key users in the use of the system. The team also provides materials and hands-on support for drivers and UDC managers during the first stage of deployment. Initially, the solution can be implemented through manual data inputs while the team designs, implements, and tests an ERP or TMS interface. During this time, users can take on entering and managing route data up to the point where UDC managers or shipper operators take over to actively manage the respective routes.

The most important phase of the project is the training of users, which typically takes time. The implementation team talks to operators about the benefits that they gain by adopting the solution, trains them on the system, and often recruits thought leaders from among the operational staff who then train the next wave of users that will join after the initial deployment.

Once the solution is up and running, the ERP or TMS system interface has been configured and the AI-based route optimizer has been sufficiently refined, the team moves to deploy the solution across all geographic areas and UDCs. Every new load is now pushed from the ERP into the AI-based route optimizer and from there to collaborative dashboards where operators, UDC managers, and drivers receive automated data feeds for their daily routes. In the process the solution has eliminated manual communication and planning tasks as well as established effective data collection from the road; AI-based route optimization has eradicated inefficiencies in fleet management and the solution provides shippers with more control over the delivery process than they ever had before.

A key question that remains is how much better a fleet operates through AI-based route optimization and supply chain collaboration. Fleets may still be comprised of the same vehicles, except that companies might operate fewer trucks than before. Yet, the yield can be much higher to enable handling more deliveries or allow for reductions in deployed assets and resources. Tangible savings that stem from route optimization typically include a 15-20% reduction in miles driven, subsequent fuel and maintenance savings, a reduction in fleet size by 5-10%, and increases of OTIF (on-time, in-full) deliveries by 25-30%.

There is a saying that *ideas are cheap, but action is expensive*. While this is not entirely true, there is truth in the statement from the perspective that any technology is only as good as how an organization puts it to work. The best optimization and supply chain execution systems won't help, unless they are used effectively and have first been deployed with great care and in collaboration with those who operate them every day. This is certainly true in last-mile delivery as it is anywhere else.

How Users Capture Tangible Savings

At the end of the day, it does not matter how good technology is. What matters is that every time a user invests a dollar, they save more. Equally important, there are levels of benefits to consider. On one side of the coin are cost and time savings that enable operational gains and on the other are increases in delivered service quality and flexibility that foster market penetration and top-line growth. When both are combined, companies capture strategic value.

The manual handling of transactions in today's supply chains and the fact that many problems are not identified soon enough leads to a plethora of activity in the form of calls, conversations, and emails. Planning information is rarely shared throughout the supply chain. When it is, this often takes the form of calls, conversations, and emails as well. All of these tasks cost billions of dollars for the industry each year. Collaboration and dashboards help to eliminate or at least dramatically reduce all of these inefficiencies to unlock tangible savings.

Collaborative supply chain solutions allow for seamless data sharing between parties that cannot afford to have APIs or EDI. In addition, these platforms allow for the inclusion of parties such as the recipients of freight who aren't traditionally considered for data sharing yet can add valuable insights. 3PLs, brokers, or dispatchers, for example, can avoid the vast majority of check calls and do not need to

Figure 4.

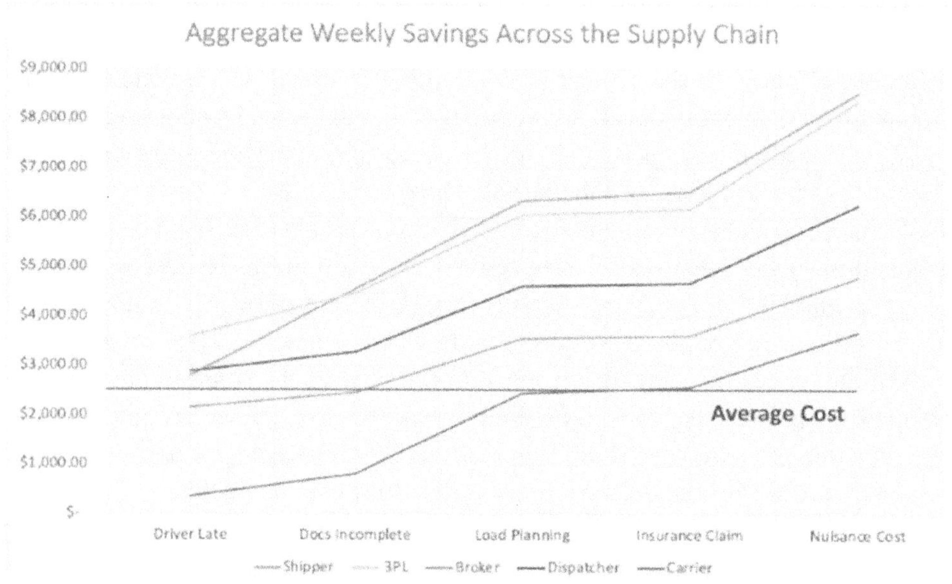

respond to cumbersome emails because the answers that customers seek are all available on the dashboard. The intermediaries each save between one to two hours per day, which is a productivity gain that translates directly into more business. Users of collaboration platforms have seen revenue increases of up to 20% at no additional effort.

For large supply chains, the same is true. Shippers, 3PLs, brokers, and transportation carriers save time and money when they work with collaboration platforms. The elimination of manual tasks more than pays for the cost of the solution while shippers, intermediaries, and carriers can now integrate their business processes as if they had APIs or EDI in place, yet with a more effective user interface and controls that allow the precise execution of each process.

Of course, the business case always depends on the customer. Savings are determined by where a company sits in the supply chain and also by how efficient they already are. In a recently completed business case for F1000 shipper, a large global manufacturer, was able to validate that all parties save time and money to a similar degree. To keep things simple, the company limited its business case to the most important benefits.

Equally important, their business case shows that beyond operational efficiency gains, all parties are able to provide substantially better customer service, which leads to deeper account penetration and top-line revenue growth.

Figure 5.

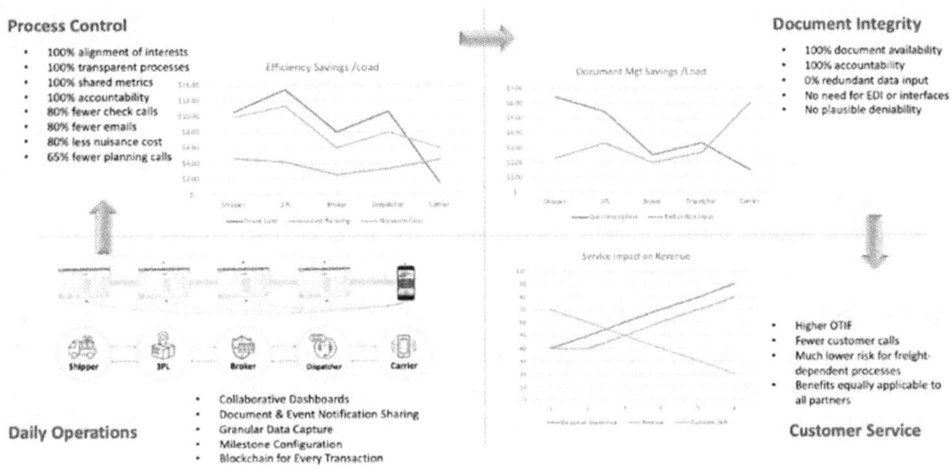

CONCLUSION

The Key to Success Lies in Change Management

Implementing any new technology requires change management and in every project of this nature, the human element is the most important factor of success. The people who use collaborative supply chain solutions need to understand why they do it and what's in it for them. This requires a 360-degree view of benefits and education about how business processes need to change. Using these platforms is highly intuitive, and the connected parties rarely encounter the need for extensive training. Users can literally sign up for such a solution in two minutes or less.

Change is always challenging and when you ask operators to perform tasks differently from how they have worked for years, it can feel threatening. Implementers typically work with end-users and engage them with direct support from management. Technology providers can offer detailed training, discussion guides, and hands-on materials that help users to talk to business partners. Often, users will bring

Figure 6.

important business partners such as 3PLs, brokers, or transportation providers to the table for a discussion of the process, benefits, and technology before they even engage in an implementation.

Of course, different users have different expectations that need to be met. The 360-degree benefit chart above illustrates that the motivation and perception of benefits depends on the context in which they work. This is normal and fosters a healthy diversity. There is something in it for everyone. The identification and communication of benefits is part of an alignment that is required when implementing any collaborative technology.

Equally important, collaborative supply chain applications positively affect the way in which every party works with its business partners. People and organizations move from finding fault to solving problems together. Something magical happens when everyone looks at the same screen during the execution of a process. It changes the way people act and think for the better. This is especially important for supply chains that may have developed patterns of contentious relationships where trust has eroded over years. Collaboration platforms enable a fresh start for all parties, although it takes a little bit of time before everyone is truly on the same page.

Collaboration platforms foster this trust in supply chains across all industries, enable everyone to become problem solvers together as opposed to apart, and increase the efficiency and profitability of operational processes. The use of such solutions certainly confirms that users can achieve all of these goals. The question is, are you ready to take the leap forward?

KEY TERMS AND DEFINITIONS

AI-based Route Optimization: The dynamic optimization of truck routes along multiple stops, often referred to as milk-runs, for several parallel vehicles based on a wide range of variables.

Blockchain: A technology that enables an immutable ledger for the documentation of supply chain data that is accessible to many different parties and provides a shared data store for all.

Collaborative Dashboards: A technology that allows more than one party involved in the execution of a supply chain process to share data on a dashboard. Each party has their own dashboard and the data that is shared is displayed to all parties in the same way.

Internet of Things: An approach to data collection that often leverages sensors wirelessly connected to backend systems to obtain information about the state of assets and objects.

Organizational Silos: The isolation of individual companies and organizations from others because they are not connected to one another. Each organization runs its own systems, has its processes, procedures and policies, and maintains its own resources, which leads to manual interfaces between different organizations.

Radio-frequency Identification: (RFID): Electronic identifiers that can be attached to assets and objects so that they can be uniquely identified when scanned by an antenna connected to a system that reports the scan to backend systems.

Supply Chain Collaboration: An approach for all parties involved in the execution of a supply chain process to work together, share data and updates without the need for application programming interfaces (APIs) or electronic data interchange (EDI).

Supply Chain Visibility: An approach to notify parties involved in the execution of a supply chain process to when exceptions occur, or corrective action needs to be taken.

Chapter 11
Supply Chain Visibility:
The Real-Time Necessity

Satyam Sinha
https://orcid.org/0000-0002-0682-652X
Diageo, India

ABSTRACT

This chapter will assist the stakeholders in their digital transformation journey for implementing a visibility solution. It will touch upon the broader need for Supply Chain Visibility in large organizations. A problem-solution approach will be followed. The problem of not having a single placeholder for visibility and tracking will be highlighted. A solution will be described in detail. A couple of solutions will be proposed. The process to implement a home-grown control tower solution will be explained. Another technology Driven SCV process with a focus on real-time data sharing will be proposed. This solution will be complemented with intelligent decision making using the latest technologies like IOT and AI. Use cases will be shared for both the approaches. A generic supply chain visibility framework with a high level of technical details will be shared. The Change Management process will be explained in detail and a process for efficient collaboration between various stakeholders will be shared.

INTRODUCTION

Supply chain visibility (SCV) is a critical component of any successful supply chain management strategy. It is the ability to track and monitor products, services, and information as they move from suppliers to manufacturers and ultimately to customers. It provides organizations with greater control over their supply chain operations, allowing them to identify potential issues and take corrective action before they become major problems.

Supply Chain Visibility solution has its roots in Supply Chain Performance metrics related to costs and on-time delivery. Several journals and textbook published in early 2000 started quoting SCV as a solution rather than a measurement of quality metric of Supply Chain (Thompson, Manrodt, Holcomb, Allen, and Hoffman, 2000; Joshi 2000; Reyes, Raisinghani, and Singh, 2002; Simchi-Levi, Kaminsky,

DOI: 10.4018/978-1-6684-7298-9.ch011

and Simchi-Levi, 2003). The industry started to realize the importance of the visibility solution, which was often ignored as a tracking metric.

SCV is important for a number of reasons. It helps organizations to better manage their supply chain operations. By tracking and monitoring the movement of goods and information throughout the supply chain. Organizations can identify potential issues and take corrective actions before they become major problems. SCV is also important for risk management. It allows organizations to identify potential risks and vulnerabilities in their supply chain operations and take steps to mitigate them. This is especially important in today's global economy, where supply chains are becoming increasingly complex and interconnected. Another important aspect of supply chain visibility is its impact on customer satisfaction. By providing customers with real-time information about the status of their orders, organizations can improve the overall customer experience and build stronger relationships with their customers.

This chapter will guide business owners in their Digital Transformation Journey to prepare a business case for implementing an SCV solution and evaluate the options available from a home-grown Control Tower Solution to a sophisticated AI/ML-based SCV solution. Technical details and a step-by-step guideline for implementing a generic SCV solution will be shared. Post Implementation, large enterprises fail to convince the ground staff in the logistics and inventory department to use the technology for the profitability of the company. There is always a resistance to change. With an efficient change management process and education, the stakeholders can steer a smooth transformation journey. The chapter will highlight the challenges faced in making an organization embrace a new solution. A large Alco-Bev company implemented the SCV solution during the Corona period and it helped the company to minimize its losses. This solution also helped the company to navigate through the crisis during the Suez Canal blockage in March 2021. A couple of use cases of SCV implementation will be shared.

The Problem

If you pop a question in a supply chain forum "Do you have problems in your Supply Chain?"

The answer will be a resounding "YES". Now ask a different question, "Do you have visibility to your problems in the Supply Chain?" You may hear a feeble "Yes" or even "No."

It is a common complaint among Supply Chain practitioners that they have implemented state-of-the-art supply chain solutions but a single placeholder is still missing when it comes to visibility and tracking. Disparate SCM systems can give visibility within its domain but integrated closed-loop visibility can only be provided by a Supply Chain Visibility Solution. Most of the time, the requirement is to have visibility across the following:

- Inventory
- Order
- Shipment

Since 2020, we have observed frequent large-scale disruptions in Supply Chain. There is no end in sight to the disruptions. Unanticipated problems pop up like the COVID-19 pandemic, the Ukraine war, or the Suez Canal Blockage—the list is endless. The supply chains have to be resilient to tackle such changes. To identify the root cause of the problem, one needs visibility in the Supply Chain Network.

Can you imagine a peak sales season in the retail industry where you do not have visibility into your order status? The supplier says that he has shipped the product and the logistic service provider has clubbed the shipment with another strategic partner. You have already booked several orders and you expect the right product at the right time at the right warehouse/retail outlet. This situation paints a grim picture if you need to find the status of your order. The missing link in the supply chain is 'visibility.'

When it comes to managing a global network of the supply chain, it becomes essential to have visibility of the inventory at various nodes like the DC, warehouse, docks, etc. The purchasing managers spend significant time finding out the status of their orders and dealing with exceptions. The logistics department have a tough time tracking the movement of goods and linking it to orders. They have to deal with dynamic changes like ETA updates or changes at trans-shipment ports. Additionally, customs clearance and other administrative tasks may add to the delay.

Apart from the problems related to inventory, order, and shipment mentioned above, disparate systems hold data. Data is lying in multiple systems and various departments do not have a standard way of sharing it. With some data still being managed in Excel and shared over emails, the organization does not have a snapshot of data in a centralized system. There is a lack of integration among the planning systems, operational systems, and execution systems. As the information is not available on hand, so business exceptions cannot be managed efficiently. Lack of visibility impacts pro-activeness and reactiveness.

Figure 1. SCV- the problem statement

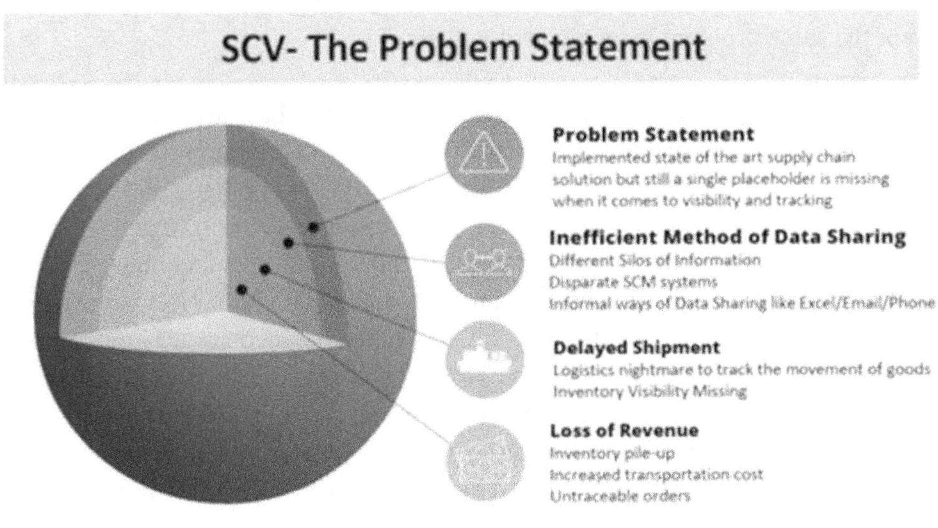

Lack of visibility in near real-time leads to inventory pile-up, increased transportation costs, and untraceable orders. This lack of visibility boils down to poor productivity of buyers, suppliers, logistics providers, and partners, resulting in customer service inefficiency which could negatively impact the business.

The Solution

The answer to the above problem lies in implementing the Supply Chain Visibility solution. It is indeed a real-time necessity. In the earlier days, Supply Chain Disruption alerts were sent by pager alerts or SMS.

Nowadays, graphs, interactive dashboards, and mobile apps are the basic requirement for an SCV solution. It is the need of the hour to build a technology-driven SCV process with a focus on real-time data sharing. It serves the Supply Chain Network by presenting a centralized dashboard of inventory, orders, and shipment status so that information flows among the partners and service providers in near real-time.

The SCV solution gives visibility to the supply chain problem and may suggest steps to solve it. Intelligent decision-making can be facilitated by new technologies like AI and ML. Earlier, visibility was provided by tracking RFID signals or capturing the actual movement of the shipments through the warehouse or in transit. The new solutions integrate GPS data to track the shipment and predict the arrival of the shipment by incorporating weather or traffic congestion data.

For over a decade, many companies have already embarked upon their visibility journey and are citing benefits after the implementation. The following are some of the old success stories:

- A large automobile manufacturer used visibility to track the vehicle right from production in the plant up to arrival at the destination port.
- A European aerospace company integrated an RFID solution to the Shipment document so that the movement can be tracked and documented.
- Using a visibility solution by i2 Technologies (Now Blue Yonder), Cooper Tire implemented a real-time, accurate view of actual as well as projected inventory. Increased visibility enabled the company to quickly determine the cause of the inventory problem and implement processes that can prevent the same problem from occurring again.

The above are success stories of the early 2000s. The demand and features of an SCV solution follow the human adaptation of technology. During the early evolution of Computer Science Technology, most of the word processing software followed a paradigm of WYSIWYG (What You See is What You Get). Now the trend has changed to What You See is What You Expect! If your pizza delivery is showing real-time status from baking to delivery, you would expect the same from other technology service providers.

The basic human expectation is to meet the standards set up by others. SCV solutions could not be left behind in this technology race. From the paper-based system of records, we graduated to emails and excels, and then moved to a web-based dashboard. Now, most of the services want to integrate real-time data on the app. As humans start adapting to new technology, they begin anticipating the same from other technology providers. There is a tectonic shift in the usage. Earlier we used to wait for our cab or our kid's school bus. Now we want to track the vehicle in real-time. Any tracking which falls short of real-time is not acceptable.

Now, Let's talk about the basic building blocks of a Visibility Framework.

Supply Chain Visibility Framework

A typical SCV solution must be able to track the path and status of finished goods or their components from source to destination within the supply chain network. Data is the basic building block of the SCV solution. With the help of technology, businesses can now leverage this data to have real-time visibility into their supply chain operations, enabling them to make informed decisions and improve their overall efficiency. One should consider the below points before designing the SCV framework:

Involvement of multi-party: Multiple parties are involved in collecting data to design a solution. For example, some established players in the market can fetch real-time data from ocean carriers across the globe. However, if you would like to integrate data related to air cargo, you may have to look at another service provider. There could be other players in the local market. For example, In India, all vehicles use "*FASTag*" to pay tolls across the road network. It is an RFID-enabled sticker that is fixed on the vehicle. It will be easier to track the milestones of Truck movement by integrating FASTag Data.

Varied requirements for Tracking: Some Manufacturing companies may want to track raw materials and key components for their plants. But other companies may be keen to just track the shipment of finished goods. The level of tracking also varies. One company may be keen to just track the container while others may want to have granular level visibility for tracking pallets. An Alco-Bev company had a business requirement to track empty bottles. During the COVID-19 crisis, the Alco-Bev industry faced challenges in procuring glass bottles as there are limited suppliers to provide the required quality of bottles. Reusing old bottles of the same brand came to the rescue. In this case, visibility into reverse logistics was a key input to the bottling process.

Additional requirement for Tracing: Some companies may have an additional requirement for tracing along with tracking. While tracking a shipment is mostly done downstream from the point of origin to the destination, the process for tracing would be quite different. For building a traceability solution, it would be required to identify the source of a particular item in the Supply Chain System of records. For example, in the pharmaceutical industry, a tracing solution would require looking up a particular batch of medicine to its factory where an API (Active Pharma Ingredient) would have been manufactured. Tracing solutions may play a key role during product recall in the pharma industry. While a tracing solution sounds similar to a tracking solution, it's implementation is vastly different.

Technologies that provide data to the SCV solution: Before designing the SCV solution, the organization should select the technology which will provide data for the solution. This is the list of key technologies used in SCV solutions:

- Radio Frequency Identification (RFID): In the earlier days, Barcode was the most common source of data for tracking products by scanning them. RFID took over the Barcodes. It is stuck to the package and the data is recorded each time it passes through the RFID reader. Although RFID was a bit more expensive than barcodes, they were chosen for their robustness and speed. The RFID tags could not be easily damaged and several tags could be read simultaneously. They contain a highly detailed level of data that could be captured by the backend system of the SCV solution.
- Global Positioning System (GPS): GPS technology can be used to track the movement of products through the supply chain, providing real-time data on location, speed, and other critical parameters. GPS technology can be attached to vehicles, equipment, and products, allowing businesses to monitor their entire supply chain in real-time.
- Internet of Things (IoT): IoT sensors can be used track the location as well as record critical parameters like temperature, humidity, of the product and it's storage environment. This data can be further leveraged to generate predictive capability in the SCV solution
- Blockchain: Blockchain technology can be used to trace the origin and movement of the product in the supply chain, providing system of records of the product and it's components. This technology can also be used to ensure the authenticity of products and prevent counterfeiting.
- Artificial Intelligence (AI): AI technology can be used to analyze data collected from IoT sensors, RFID tags, and GPS technology, providing insights into the performance of the supply chain. AI technology can also be used to predict potential delays and identify bottlenecks, allowing businesses to take proactive measures to improve their supply chain operations.

Data is available through different sources and in different formats. But first, the organization must evaluate whether they have a requirement to use this data or not. These 3 steps will help in the evaluation journey.

1) Evaluate the pros and cons of using one data system over another. For example, if your requirement is just to track your shipment, you can subscribe only to the events which will help you to calculate the ETA. If you can get the timing for planned load, pick up, customs clearance, etc. then your system can easily calculate the ETA. But if you want to shift your focus to a predictive time of arrival by using weather forecast data or real-time traffic data, then the requirement of data collection would be more elaborate. The weather-related data can be fetched by leveraging IoT technologies. Using this data, you can predict if your shipment could be delayed due to turbulent weather or not. If your visibility system shows the last mile tracking, then predicting peak traffic timings can help you predict the tentative time of arrival. For example, a particular area could be choked with traffic during peak office hours. During an extended holiday season, the exit out of the city could experience a heavy rush due to people traveling out of the town. Using historical data on previous traffic congestion would help you to predict the delivery time of your package.
2) Assess the reach of your requirement to track, whether it is global or local. For example, if you want to track various carriers in the global transportation environment, then FourKites would be a good choice. But if you just want to track Truck-related data in India, then SIM-based tracking or getting insights from FASTag API would be sufficient.
3) Evaluate the cost of subscriptions. In one of the implementations of Luminate Control Tower, the service provider, Blue Yonder had a contract with FourKites so there was not any additional cost for the client. If you want to leverage other data, then check the cost as well as the feasibility of using such data. For example, if you want to use FASTag data, there would be an upfront cost to use the API. The GPS service provider will charge you for tracking, so add these numbers to your cost sheet.

The suggestion is to subscribe to data events that are largely used in your network. Once you have decided on the data requirement, figure out the ways to upload data into your SCV system so that it can be processed to provide meaningful insights. Data can be uploaded by using an Extract-Transform-Load (ETL) tool or API integration. The next task will be to bring the data into action. Broadly, there are 2 options: Build a visibility platform from scratch or use a commercially available SCV system. These options are elaborated in detail supported by an industry use case.

Option 1: Build an in-house Control Tower System

To start with, finalize the set of KPIs to be displayed. Drill deep down into the KPI. For example, if the KPI is related to Timely pickup, find out what would go wrong if the order is not picked up on time. Can this be addressed by increasing labor? This thought process can help in defining actionable insights when a problem is discovered in the Control Tower Solution. In some implementations, it is seen that the company implements several dashboards but they do not have a process to take action on that. The Return on Investment (ROI) will be less if you do not define a process to implement the change.

The next step is to freeze the solution architecture. Choose the cloud platform, which could be Azure cloud or some other platform. Identify the source of data which could be the Data Lake or Data Warehouse. Configure it to check that data flows seamlessly to your Control Tower system.

Now finalize the visualization layer. You may evaluate between Tableau, Qlik Sense, and Power BI. In most of the Control Tower implementation, we have seen that the organization choose Power BI. Apart from Dashboard features, it has core analytical capabilities as well. It has compatibility with R and Python. Also, Power Apps integrate with Power BI, so this would be the platform of choice if you are planning for mobile app development as well. Another key input for decision-making would be the existing licensing agreement with the vendor. For example, your organization may have purchased Qlik or Power BI licenses. This information should also go as your input for the Visualisation Dashboard selection. Look out for additional requirements. Should the data be displayed on mobile apps, smartphones, or some kiosks? Define batch jobs for data refresh and archival strategies. Data archiving is also an important part of the reporting process otherwise it will slow down the report rendering time.

See if there are any requirements for a performance dashboard like a carrier performance report or the SLA report. Check if there is any requirement for Push Notifications or email alerts. They might want to schedule a report with an email attachment. Note that email attachments may have a certain size limit like 5 MB or 10MB. For specialized technical assistance, contact the domain experts within your organization. For example, an automation team may help you to automate several repetitive tasks like uploading data and running some jobs. They would be the best person to suggest whether to use UI path or some other tool for automation. Similarly, if you have a separate testing team, involve them from the very beginning, so that they can help you to design the test cases.

It is recommended to finalize the functional design as well as the technical design before initiating the development. As the development is done within the organization, so the internal stakeholder may ask for last minutes changes. Try to avoid such scenarios by getting a sign-off on the final design.

The use case shared below showcases Control Tower System implementation

Case Study: Logistics Control Tower

Company Profile: A large Global Brewery with a presence across the globe. This company experienced huge expansion through the acquisition of local breweries. It had acquired a stake in a major Australian brewery too. This Control Tower implementation was done only for the Australian region.

Problem Summary: The company had a decentralized approach to Transport planning and visibility. The company had poor visibility and control of the logistics cost, which led to poor customer service. Alert and Exception framework was missing so the Supply Chain Disruptions could not be resolved promptly. The European Counterpart had implemented a separate visibility platform but it could not be used by the Australian counterpart. The Enterprise system (SAP) of the Australian entity was different from the rest of the world.

Solution: It was decided by the steering committee to develop an in-house solution using Power BI.

This was done by utilizing the in-house technical team. The report was broadcasted to an external monitor.

Technology used:

- Microsoft Power BI (To Display the reports)
- SAP BODS (Data service for integration from SAP system)

- Azure Data Lake

Approach:

- Key Success Factors and KPIs were defined to track Logistics and Inventory KPIs
- Identified and analysed the master and transaction data source in the Logistics and Inventory planning system.
- The solution was set up on Azure Cloud with SQL and Azure Services.
- Validated the integration mapping to ensure that data is available at the required granular level. It was integrated with Transportation Management System (TMS) and Warehouse Management System (WMS)
- Defined the process to ensure data correctness. Defined the data entry point and timings.
- Decisions were taken in the control tower room wherever alerts were highlighted.

Challenges faced: The snapshot of data was not real-time as SAP had the latest data but it took time to refresh and render it in Power BI

Results Delivered:

- Improved Customer service and delivery optimization.
- Working capital reduction.

Option 2: Implementing an SCV System

Instead of building a Control Tower Solution, you may opt for implementing an SCV solution. Most of the SCV solutions are hosted on a cloud platform, so the key task will be to configure the system for your organization and build the integration layer. Before implementing an SCV system, it would be a worthwhile decision to take the following survey

- Look at some survey reports to see what others in a similar industry as yours are implementing in SCV. Check how the vendor is performing in Gartner's magic quadrant for visibility.
- See the credentials of the SCV service provider and organize a reference call. This will give you confidence before spending money on the vendor.
- Conduct internal surveys to see whether your logistics employees are happy with the current SCV solutions or not. What are the pain points? If these pain points can be addressed by the vendor, then it would be a good option to implement these.

Note that SCV solution has many features which have different levels of importance to various departments like the logistics and inventory. Each feature of the solution may benefit one or more departments. The department which is funding the implementation may prioritize the features suitable for solving its business problem. Due diligence should be done while preparing the business case.

Ensure that the benefits included in the business cases are tracked for accuracy and course corrections. For example, if you have listed the visibility benefits like Carrier performance or SLA improvement, then these should be tracked during the pilot implementation. Once you have identified a tool for visibility, set up a task force for your SCV implementation. Involve technical as well as functional experts. The activities should be governed by the Project Manager. The PM should be responsible for timely action to various activities.

- The initial task will be to set up the master data in the system. Mapping data from SAP or the Transportation Management system is a key task.
- Check the Basic Data requirement of your SCV system. Identify and Capture Data as Raw data are the building blocks of your SCV system. You must ensure that you have the required data for your SCV system.
- Understanding the security landscape is important. For example, your organization may have mandated a 2-factor authentication for login, but your SCV provider may not be having it in their product. It would be good to share the feedback with the product team so that they can develop such features at a later stage.
- If mobile app development is within scope, then there could be another requirement to check the version of the mobile operating system and the authentication requirement in the app. As mobile apps are governed by the corporate security framework, they may ask for additional authentication through OKTA.

The use case listed below exhibits the implementation of an SCV solution

Case Study: Luminate Control Tower Implementation (Vendor: Blue Yonder)

Company Profile: A large Alco-Bev company that is a global producer of spirits and beer products. It has company-owned and leased manufacturing facilities and a wide distribution network. The products are available in retail stores as well. Most of the shipments are done through trade partners. Most of the sale is done through designated trade partners.

Problem Summary:

The alcohol industry faced a worldwide disruption during the COVID-19 phase. The manufacturing facilities were not able to produce up to their planned capacity due to Covid restrictions and a shortage of labor and raw materials. The company has a huge export portfolio. It ships more than tens of thousands of product containers to over a hundred countries. With this level of complexity, visibility became imperative for managing an efficient supply chain. Tracking shipments became challenging as the company had to rely on third-party carriers and the process was manual.

Solution:

Various visibility platforms were evaluated and the leadership team selected Luminate Control Tower (LCT) solution by Blue Yonder. TMS solution by Blue Yonder was also rolled out to certain geographies before implementing LCT.

Tools/Technology Used:

- LCT Visibility platform by Blue Yonder
- FourKites – Partner in sharing Carrier Data
- Integration of LCT with FourKites
- Integration between Blue Yonder TMS and LCT platform using MuleSoft-based Integration

Challenges Faced:

- Integration issues due to the high volume of data.
- Freshness of Data- During the initial pilot phase, the LCT platform was not having real data due to integration delays. This was fixed before go-live

Results Delivered:

The LCT covers more than 90 percent of the company's ocean carrier network. The LCT solution proved its mettle during the Suez Canal obstruction in 2021, which was a global nightmare. The company could now respond to logistics challenges proactively and take corrective action. The below benefits were observed:

- Improved efficiency in the team as they can plan the warehouse capacity several months in advance and they have more time to manage other challenges.
- Before the LCT implementation, the delay in shipment was compensated by sending the freight by air. This cost drastically came down by 90%
- Better User experience. The tool has a modern UI with drill-down features from the alerts.

Whether you select option 1 or option 2, the basic premises of the SCV solution remains the same to use the available data to provide meaningful insights. The section below shows a generic technical framework of an SCV implementation. The actual design may differ from vendor to vendor.

Technical Framework

Designing a supply chain visibility solution is a complex task as it needs data from various enterprise systems. However, the benefits cannot be ignored when you find a solution reducing the complexity of the supply chain. As shown in Image 2, the Supply Chain Visibility and Events/Alerts framework sits in a middle covered by a web-based UI service. This layer exposes the information to the users. To display real-time correct data, the SCV system needs to synchronize with other systems. This can be done in two ways:

1) An integration service pulls in data from disparate systems and feeds it to the SCV system in near real-time. This data includes data from various customers, suppliers, partners, etc. An RFID service or GPS signals can also be integrated to pull in shipment data
2) Different systems in the enterprise can coherently share information using Enterprise Application Integration. Information and data can be shared with the SCV system using EAI.

The SCV system then processes this data and converts it into meaningful information like Inventory Min/Max violation and ETA update exceptions. It also suggests a method to resolve the exception like reallocation of inventory. The event detection framework and resolution will be defined in the next section.

Events/Alert Framework:

The key functionality of a Supply Chain Visibility solution is to manage and resolve business alerts or events. An event is described as a notification that a threshold has been reached or an incident has been

Figure 2. SCV- technical framework

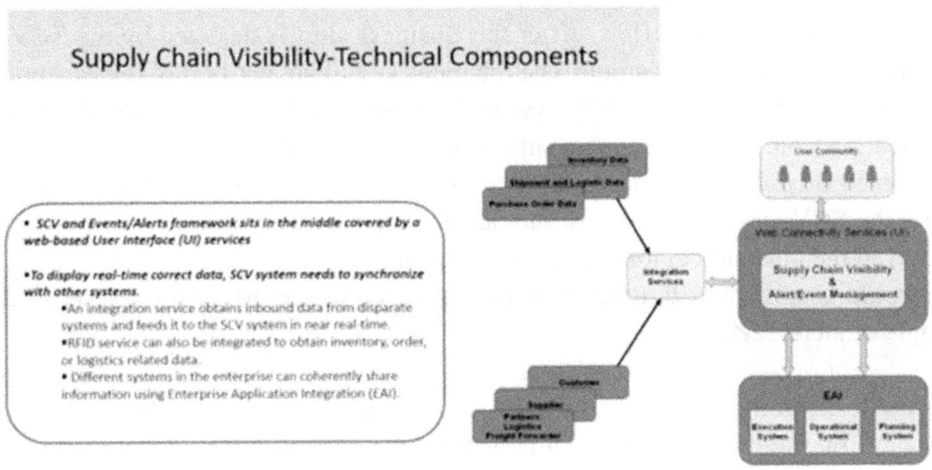

reached which requires attention. An SCV solution should have a dashboard facility that notifies a user about a threshold and time to resolve

A visibility solution needs to have an alert detection mechanism and a well-defined process to resolve it. Image 3 explains the framework in more detail.

Figure 3. SCV - events/alerts framework

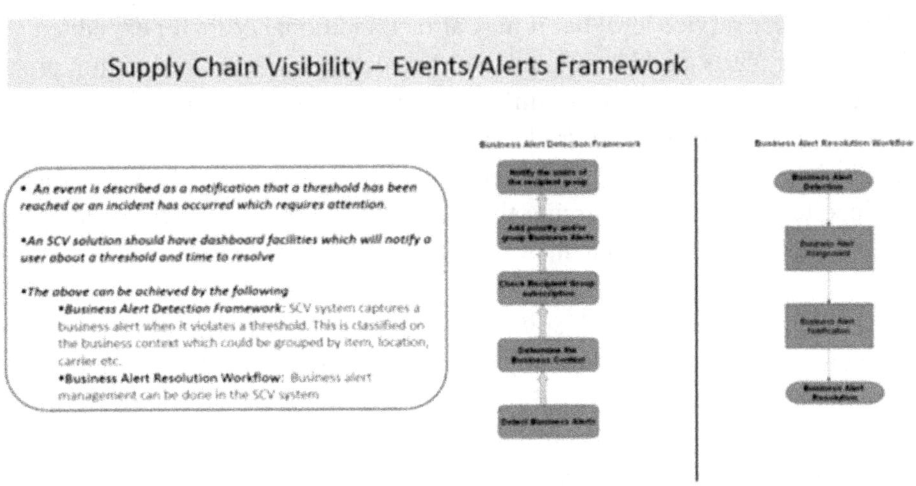

Business Alert Detection framework: The SCV system captures a business alert when it violates a threshold. It then broadly categorizes the information based on the business context which could be grouped by item, location, carrier, and so on. Now, it checks for the recipient group who has subscribed to this alert. A recipient group is a group of business users who are the key stakeholders in owning and resolving a particular type of business exception. The SCV system groups the alerts and adds priorities to them. It is then routed to the intended recipient for resolution.

Business Alert Resolution Workflow: After the Business alert is detected by the SCV system it is then assigned to a particular user or group. The recipient(s) will get notified of the exception. Business alert management can be done in the SCV system. The notification is usually displayed on the home page as a notification icon. The user can also subscribe to email/SMS notifications. The person to whom the alert is assigned should take the necessary action to resolve the alert. The resolution option can be triggered from the SCV system or the user should take the necessary decision in some other system. Once it is resolved then the alert automatically gets closed.

The user should be able to drill down from various alerts to see the granular level of details. Let's take an example of alerts related to

- Shipment Alerts: In the detailed screen, the user should be able to see the total number of shipments delayed per region and the main reason behind the delay. The delay could be due to late billing or custom clearance. The system should be able to calculate the ETA or PTA (Predictive Time of Arrival). If the delay is due to the ocean carrier, then the detail of the carrier and the receiving country should be displayed. The users can enter a virtual situation room and decide how to mitigate the risk. For example, even if the carrier is delayed, it may find some space in the next leg of transport by road. An efficient cross-docking strategy with minimum wait time can reduce the delay.
- Inventory Alerts: The inventory alerts should give more details about the stock positions across the futuristic time horizon at a plant. It should show the net demand and the confirmed orders so that the inventory analyst can take the necessary action. For example, the analyst may decide to create a rush order from a nearby distribution center if the order is of high priority. This would improve the customer service level but it may attract additional costs for expedited shipment.
- Order Alerts: Order alerts could be related to orders delayed, not booked, or not processed. There could also be a capacity constraint to fulfill that order. In this case, the SCV system should show the daily throughput of a plant. The Production Planning analyst can decide whether to fulfill this order from an alternate plant or not. If the order alert is due to a shortage of raw material, then the team can expedite that order by sourcing that raw material from an alternate supplier or create a stock transfer order from another plant.

The whole idea of implementing an SCV solution is to see a snapshot of the problems on the dashboard and then facilitate the issue resolution. It would be nice to have some reporting capabilities as well. For example, a common report is to check the delay by a carrier which can be used to evaluate a carrier's performance. Some software also allows configuring custom reports as they have Cognos or Power BI plug-ins. An SCV solution with an inbuilt event/alert framework along with reporting facilities should solve your problem. In the above sections, we talked about the SCV framework. Now, let's talk about the approach to implementing an SCV solution.

Analyze: Prepare a business case on why a visibility solution is required. Normally people confuse visibility solutions with only shipment tracking and tracing. However, this is not the case. Tracking shipment is just a part of this. Tracking your inventory in transit and stock levels at the warehouse or plant could be another use case. Using a dashboard, you can view Dynamic stock status and manage exceptions. A dashboard is a basic requirement of the SCV solution. Advanced solutions have a situation room simulator where you can take corrective action to mitigate risk. For example, you might choose to move an inventory from another location to a high-demand region or you can choose another logistic service provider. The latest solutions have historical data related to traffic or port congestion. Using this data, you can take an informed decision. For example, you might want to choose an expensive channel of transport if you want to avoid stock-out scenarios.

Identify the departments in your organization that would use this solution. If you are a large retailer and work on just finished goods, you might be keen to track only the shipments and ensure that the finished goods reach on time. If you manufacture finished goods then you would need to track your inward logistics of raw materials. Integrating reverse logistics or inbound logistics into your SCV solution will add to the complexity of the implementation.

Key Inputs to the business case

- One-time implementation and consulting costs by the vendor
- Cost of internal resources like SAP, Automation, Cyber Security
- PMO and Governance cost
- Incremental licensing cost on usage.

Key output KPIs of the business case

- Out-of-stock reduced by X %
- On-Time Shipment is close to 100%
- Total Dollar Saved in the first year and Year on Year considering a three-year plan

The above are just examples. You would have to prepare your business case to see how the above KPIs will get you ROI.

Choose

You may choose between a home-grown solution or a professional solution provided by SCM majors. If you have an in-house development team, you may plan to build a homegrown solution on Power BI or another visualization tool. There could be a one-time consulting exercise to define the KPI and the underlying data. Once it is done, you would need to schedule the jobs so that data flows between the legacy system to the dashboard. Utilizing your in-house analytics team is a cost-effective and quick solution if your visibility goals can be achieved by the solutions.

However, you may evaluate a solution from the market. The latest products have enhanced capabilities like syncing with real-time data and new service providers. Some products also integrate weather forecasts and traffic/port congestion data.

See the list of a few SCV solution providers (Names listed in Alphabetical order)

- Blue Yonder
- FourKites
- Infor
- Project44
- SAP IBP

A couple of new vendors have come up with their visibility solution. They come with their unique proposition and success stories.

- Intugine
- SmartLinks

While exploring SCV solution for an India-based Alco-Bev industry, the company evaluated the solution by SmartLinks. They had SIM-based tracking and they had partnerships with major telecom service providers in India. They aggregated GPS data from multiple data sources into their platform. They also had a mobile app for real-time tracking. The geo-fencing solution was an out-of-the-box feature on their mobile app. This feature addressed a major problem of the Alco-Bev company as Alcohol is a controlled commodity in India and some brands are stored in a custom bonded warehouse. The company wanted to track the movement of alcohol through the bonded warehouse so a geofencing solution was required. This became a win-win situation for both parties as the anticipated solution was already available.

It is advisable to evaluate the established vendors as well as the new entrant. The established players would have solved the common problems of visibility and they would be happy to share relevant references but they are slow to respond to changes or accept new suggestions in their product design. In contrast, the new entrants are quick to respond to your requirements which could be unique. They also have a knack to get the job done by using new technology or tools. It's worth exploring them too.

Let's assume that you have finalized your requirement and tool to shape your SCV solution. The next important phase in your digital transformation journey is to manage the change management in your organization for implementing this new solution.

Change Management

Define every process in detail, whether it is the user onboarding process or making Standard Operating Plan.

Initiating the Change

Planning is the key to defining a detailed change management plan. It is advisable to involve the stakeholders from the very beginning to prevent resistance from them saying that they were not consulted. Define the RACI matrix and assign ownership to various leaders or their representatives. Various departments of your organization may work in silos and the supply chain visibility framework touches many departments. A visibility solution may be owned by the logistics department but it would have a dependency in terms of data and action from another department like the Inventory and Planning department. Identify the Champions from various regions.

IT department will be at the heart of execution as it will be responsible for maintaining the systems and running the IT general controls. If your company takes IT audit seriously, then you may need to engage one of the Big 4 consulting firms to design your IT General controls. You would need to involve these folks in planning for the change

- Champions from your company – Various Department, Regions

- Third Party Visibility Solution provider- Include Product Development and Consulting team so that they understand your problem and see if they can achieve your visibility goals by doing minor tweaks to the product.
- Data Aggregator: If you have a direct contract with the Data aggregator, then involve them too. Correctness and Timeliness of your data will define your success.

Mitigating Resistance to Change

You are about to launch a Visibility solution but the effort will be futile if one department or region cannot be onboarded due to resource constraints. You may expect resistance from a particular department as they would see this implementation as additional work. They may not be able to take up this task due to resource availability. They are used to old ways of working. These 2 approaches will make the transition easier

- Explain the vision of your Digital Transformation Strategy so that they appreciate the reason why the organization is embracing a new solution.
- Clearly explain the new ways of working and the roles and responsibilities
- Try Automation for mundane tasks. If you ask someone to extract some data from SAP and upload it in the visibility framework, it will not be the best approach. So, leverage the automation tools.

Sustaining the Change

Now that you have invested in a Visibility Solution and the solution is Live. It is important to sustain the change otherwise the users will not get full value from the solution. A way to approach this is to define and publish a Change Management Process. You may classify the changes into a Simple and Complex change

- Simple Change: It could be updating master data which will have minimal impact on the existing process and it could be done by an admin of your organization. An example of such a change would be updating the threshold for an alert or a change in reporting requirements. Due diligence must be done to ensure that other users are not impacted. For example, an alert of delayed shipment by 2 days could be very high for the logistics department but it may be an amber alert for the inventory department which has enough buffer for that item. So, a preferred change in alert settings for one group should not impact the other. Approval from relevant stakeholders before implementing this change would be sufficient.
- Complex change: If there is a change in the product functionalities or a new bug fix is pushed then rigorous testing has to be done. Most of the failures occur at the integration touchpoints. A complex change should be approved by all the major stakeholders. Complete regression testing should be done before pushing the solution to the Production System. Using Automation testing for regression tests should help to identify the bugs earlier in the system.

These 2 steps will keep you ahead in sustaining the change.

- Define the SOP and what happens in your visibility when a change happens in the upstream Transportation Management System. For example, when a new plant is created, will that master data flow into your visibility system? Would you have the real-time transportation data for the new plant?
- Make an effective communication plan to avoid scenarios like "Oh, I was not aware" or "I did not approve." Everyone who needs to know should be on the list. The following high-level meeting should be organized and calendars should be booked.
    1) Steering Committee meeting: Involve the vendor, third party, and project stakeholders. Key decisions related to budget and high-level scope can be discussed in this forum.
    2) Global Operating Forum: Involve internal technical stakeholders like your Enterprise Architect. Most organizations have a Change Advisory Board (CAB). Involve them too as they will be aware of the changes across various systems. The organization may have a release calendar for pushing major changes and it may have a freeze calendar during peak sales season. Only emergency change could be pushed into a freeze calendar if a fix is required for some critical failure. The CAB team will be well-placed to take such a decision.

You may proceed with the implementation once the SCV tool is finalized, the budget is approved and the Change Management process is defined.

To summarize, we would suggest selecting and implementing a solution that meets your visibility goals. You can build the solution or go for a cloud-based solution that is laced with the latest technology like AI/ML. This new-age technology uses weather and events data along with carrier movement data to give predictive visibility into your supply chain network. Blockchain can be used to trace the origin of your manufactured good or component.

We can still think of futuristic innovation like implementing an AR/VR solution so that all participants enter a virtual situation room for solving a major disruption. Having visibility into sustainability goals can also be implemented. The plant's emission can be tracked and a red alert can be issued before it becomes a red alert for the environment.

We are living in the age of Uber where people would expect to track last-mile delivery the same way they track their pizza. The company may plan to give a delivery option that has the lowest carbon footprint. This could be called a Green Delivery option. The last-mile delivery solution should enable the customer to choose a green delivery option which may not be the fastest but it may club the customer's delivery through a delivery vehicle that has a planned delivery in that area at a later point in time. Of course, the customer may not be willing to pay an extra dollar for the green delivery but they may be willing to wait for a day if they are told that they are contributing to the environment. If the visibility solution can track the last mile delivery and showcase its benefit to the users, then it can become a game changer.

There are several benefits to implementing an SCV solution. You may plan to implement a basic solution and then follow a continuous improvement strategy.

CONCLUSION

Supply chain visibility is critical to the success of any supply chain management strategy. It provides organizations with greater control over their supply chain operations, allowing them to identify potential issues and take corrective action before they become major problems. Achieving supply chain visibility requires a comprehensive strategy that addresses all aspects of the supply chain, including technology, data selection, process standardization, and change management. By implementing these strategies, organizations can improve their operational efficiency, increase their agility, enhance their risk management, improve customer satisfaction, and increase their competitiveness

REFERENCES

Blokdyk, G. (2020). *Supply Chain Visibility Initiatives A Complete Guide.* IBM.

Blue Yonder. (2020). *Supply Chain Visibility in a Time of Crisis: What the 2020 Visibility Report Tells Us.* Blue Yonder. https://blog.blueyonder.com/2020-visibility-report/

Chu, S., Leung, J., & Cheung, W. (2015). *On IoT Impact Of Supply Chain Visibility.* ICEB 2015 Proceedings, Hong Kong, SAR China.

Diageo. (2022). *Supporting supply chain visibility in volatile times.* Diageo. https://www.diageo.com/en/news-and-media/stories/2022/supporting-supply-chain-visibility-in-volatile-times

i2 Technologies. (2007). *Supply Chain Leader Magazine.* i2 Technologies.

Khan, N., Silva S., & Kandl, T. (2012). *A software based solution to facilitate end to end information supply chain visibility.* ICSSSM12, Shanghai, China. . doi:10.1109/ICSSSM.2012.6252359

Lee, H.L. & Tang, C.S. (2000). *A review of recent developments in supply chain management.* NIH.

McIntire, J. (2016). Supply Chain Visibility – From. *Theory into Practice.*

Youngsu, L. & Rim, S. (2016). Quantitative Model for Supply Chain Visibility: Process Capability Perspective. *Mathematical Problems in Engineering.* Hindawi. doi:10.1155/2016/4049174

Chapter 12
Rethinking Direct Materials Procurement Within Digital Ecosystems

Adeel Najmi
University of Texas at Dallas, USA

ABSTRACT

Traditional direct materials procurement systems have been designed for business processes with an introverted view of activities within the four walls of an enterprise. These assumptions were flawed all along and are now fast becoming outdated as digital ecosystems gradually take hold. Analysis is presented to show how these isolated enterprise centric processes have created complexity, latency and inefficiencies that inhibit alignment and agility across value networks. This chapter revisits the business objectives and challenges of direct materials procurement with an outside-in mindset and redesigns the overall processes end-to-end across the order lifecycle within digitally connected ecosystems.

INTRODUCTION

Today's direct materials procurement business processes and systems have evolved from origins deep within the enterprise dating back to the middle of the 20th century. In 1990 Gartner coined the term "Enterprise Resource Planning" (ERP) systems. A decade later, Gartner introduced the term "ERP II" to add the concept of ERP systems interacting with other systems outside the enterprise. A patchwork of transactions was created to enable flow of information between enterprises—this idea was an afterthought. It may digitize the legacy paper processes at best but does not actually tackle the fundamental flaws in the inside-out view of business. To this day, business systems are designed with a single company as their target and paper processes at their origins.

We live in a highly interconnected, interdependent, and dynamic world. All supply chains start from the consumer. Today's consumer is fickle and less loyal to traditional brands. She is always connected and always informed through a wide array of social and business platforms. How she buys has changed. How manufacturers, distributors, and retailers deliver in such a dynamic and volatile world has changed.

DOI: 10.4018/978-1-6684-7298-9.ch012

Digital ecosystems are now the norm. It is time for us to rethink business processes and systems with an outside-in mindset to match with today's reality.

In this paper, we first explain why the existing procurement paradigm is not only irrelevant but also how it is destroying business performance. Then, we map out the framework for a new paradigm that is designed to be outside-in from the ground up, leverages digital technologies at its core, and eliminates the flaws of the legacy approaches to deliver unprecedented business advantage.

THE CASE FOR A NEW APPROACH

Supply chain procurement processes and practices have origins in the post-industrial age, but they have not caught up with the digitally connected world of today. This section describes fundamental flaws in the existing paradigm and makes a case for why a new approach is needed.

TRADITIONAL ISOLATED PROCESSES

Isolated Inside-Out View

Business information systems such as ERPs are designed to run the business by taking an inside-out view of a company. On the one hand, we have an Accounts Receivable module (Figure 1) for selling, processing orders, fulfilling orders, invoicing, collecting payments and reconciling payments.

Figure 1. The typical accounts receivable process as represented in the ERP

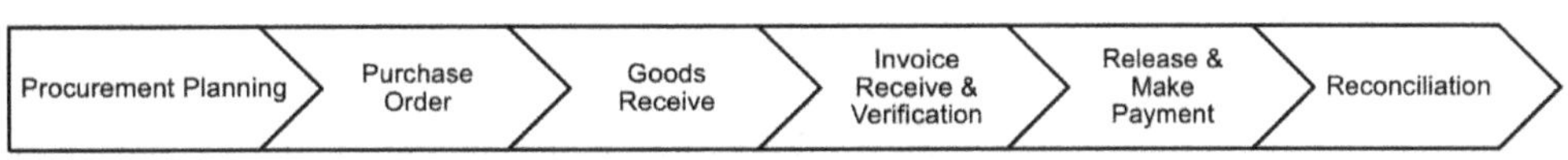

On the other hand, we have an Accounts Payable module for ordering purchases, receiving goods, verifying invoices, making payments, and reconciling payments (Figure 2).

Figure 2. The typical accounts payable process as represented in the ERP

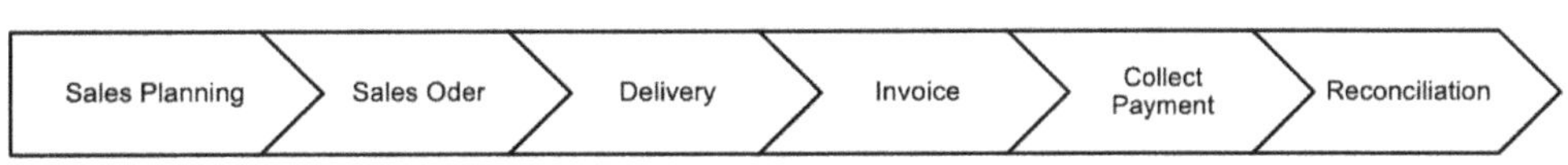

Figure 3. The traditional SCOR model
[Diagram available via license: Creative Commons Attribution-NonCommercial-NoDerivatives 4.0 International. *]*

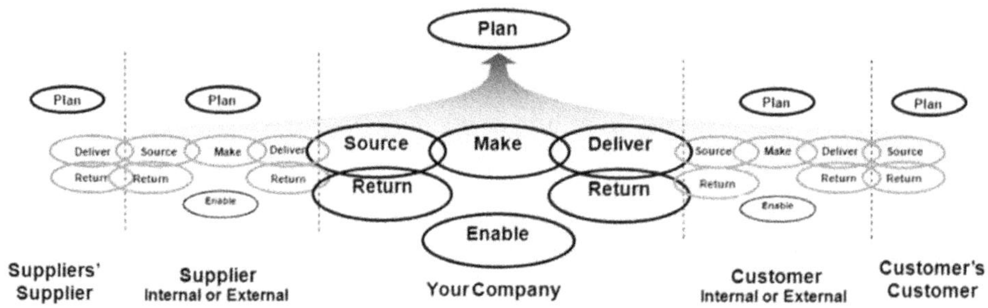

When there is a purchase transaction, we have a Purchase Order in the buyer's Accounts Payable module and a Sales Order in the seller's Accounts Receivable module. Since both systems are internally focused, we must try to keep synchronizing and reconciling the two systems as the order is fulfilled.

The supply chain operations processes within companies suffer from the same flaw as well. The original versions of the Supply Chain Operations Reference Model were decidedly of a view from a given company looking out (as shown in the familiar diagram in Figure 3). It consisted of processes for plan, source, make, deliver, and return within "your company" that intersected with similar processes at your upstream and downstream supply chain partners.

Figure 4. The most recent version of the SCOR model

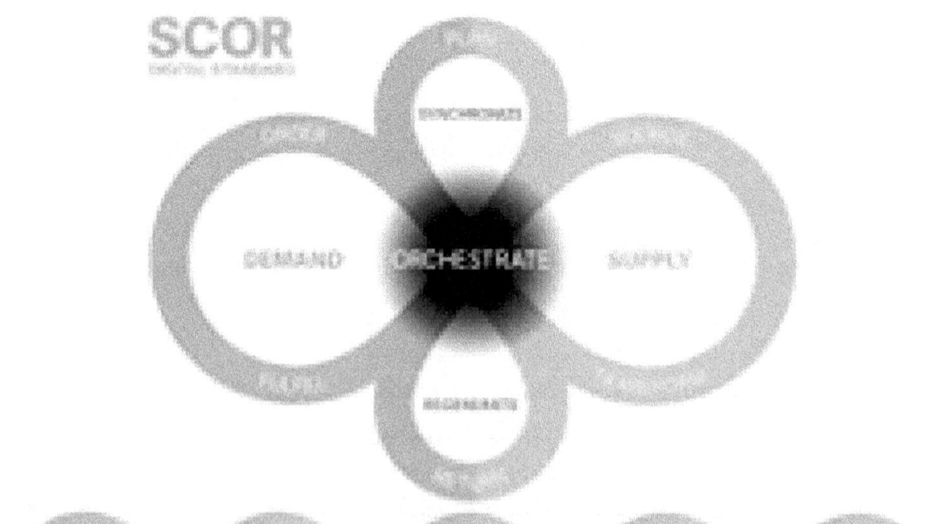

The latest version[1] (Figure 4) shows more concurrent processes for order, plan, source, transform, fulfill, and return with orchestration at the center. Yet, the inside-out view lingers at its core since the orchestration is still limited to be across functions *within* the enterprise. Also, the sequential chain view prevails and is shown at the bottom with the "Your Organization" or the enterprise at the center.

The focus of the orchestration is across functions within a single business. The problem of corralling value chain partners to execute in lock step is not addressed.

In contrast, let us look at the Collaborative Planning Forecasting and Replenishment (CPFR) process from the retail industry's Voluntary Industry Standards Committee (VICS). CPFR is defined as a business practice that combines the collaborative intelligence of multiple trading partners in the planning and fulfillment of customer demand. VICS takes an outside-in view by putting the consumer at the center (Figure 5) and all processes are designed on the premise of shared visibility and collaboration across all trading partners in the value network. Note how each of the business process stages shown in the middle ring begins with the consumer and spans across both the retailer and the manufacturer.

Figure 5. The VICS collaborative forecasting and replenishment model

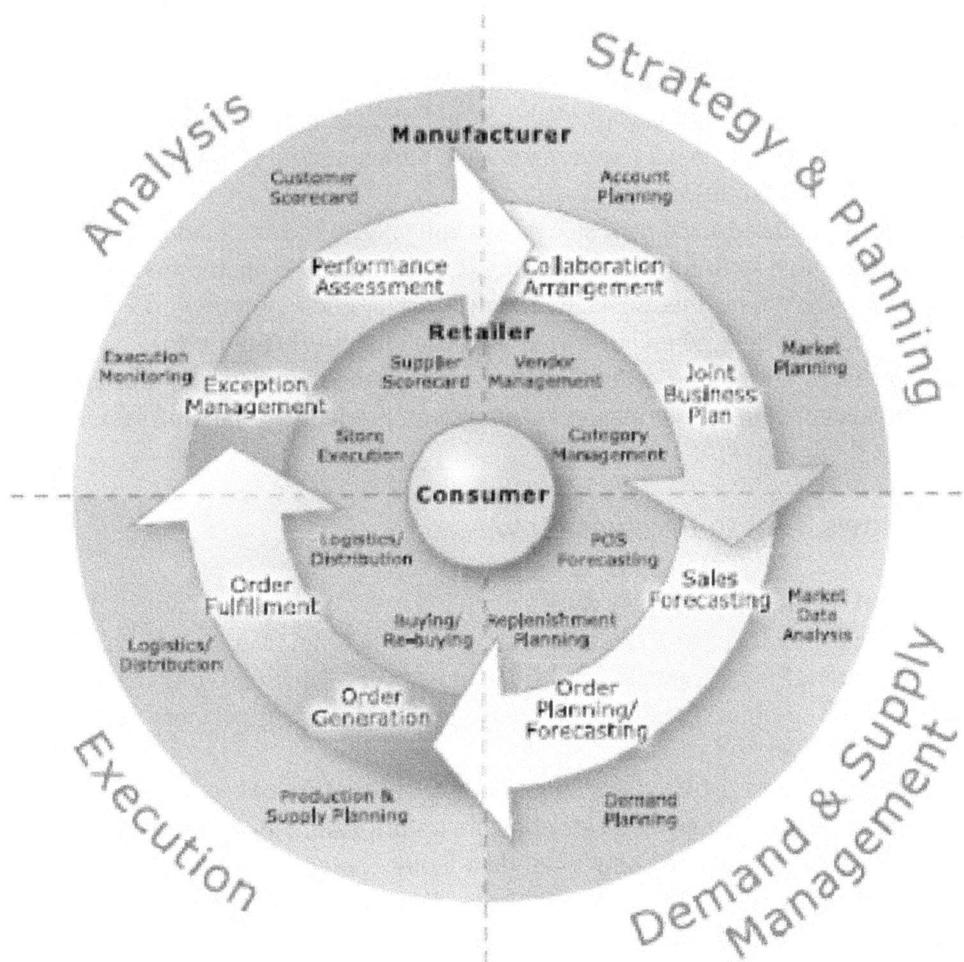

Figure 6. Disintegrated systems across the supply chain

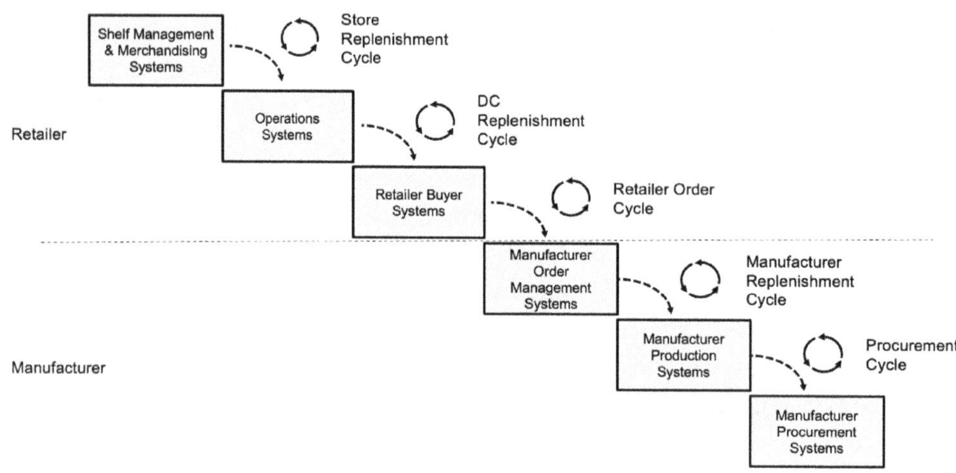

The overarching objective is to synchronize business processes across all participants with consumer demand. Every CPFR participant from suppliers and manufacturers to distributors and retailers can view the forecast, propose changes, and share plans, assumptions, and constraints.

But, as explained by Richard Sherman,[2] CPFR initiatives failed to scale due in large part to dis-integrated systems across the supply chain and lack of visibility and insight into channel behavior. The inside-out viewpoint with no visibility to channel requirements and the sequential chain view with cascading local data and processing has killed this noble idea.

Consumer demand is sensed as point of sale data is collected at the retail store. This data is leveraged by the shelf management system for merchandising, but it is the DC operations systems that manage inventory and the buyer systems that manage replenishments. Each system works on its own cadence and the demand signal gets delayed and distorted with each hand-off (Figure 6).

The same happens as the retailer orders are projected on the manufacturer and the demand signal propagates via the manufacturer order management system, production planning systems, and procurement systems.

Information Flows Tied to Product Flow

The batch sequential cascade of business cycles shown in Figure 6 have a fundamental drawback: information only flows sequentially upstream with the flow of the product from link to link and a cadence of periodic batch processes. Every company, and frequently, every function within each company stands as an island with point-to-point "pipes" between systems and trading partners where information is periodically pushed through.

The consequences of these isolated systems are disconnected processes both within the company and across the supply chain. Planning and execution are traditionally viewed sequentially and supported through different systems, with huge volumes of data being copied from silo to silo. This takes hours and means that execution systems are running on stale data (Figure 7). The world has moved on since the original snapshot, yet that outdated data snapshot still drives the supply chain.

Figure 7. Latency across the supply chain

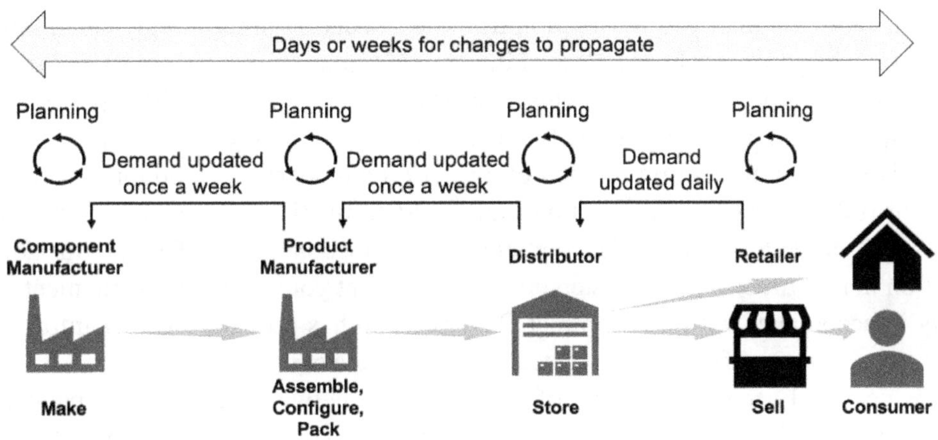

These unnecessary delays and the compounding of bad data with bad decisions results in supply-demand mismatch, shortages, overstocks, and poor customer service. In addition, data needs to be matched, reconciled, cleansed, and synchronized across all these copies creating unnecessary effort, wasting resources, and causing further delays.

The supply chain is not a chain but a network (Najmi , 2022) of business partners working together to serve the end customer. This has very different implications for how information can flow across these business partners. With the widespread acceptance of SaaS cloud networks today, there is no reason to settle for any information latency at all.

Figure 8. The physical and financial supply chain

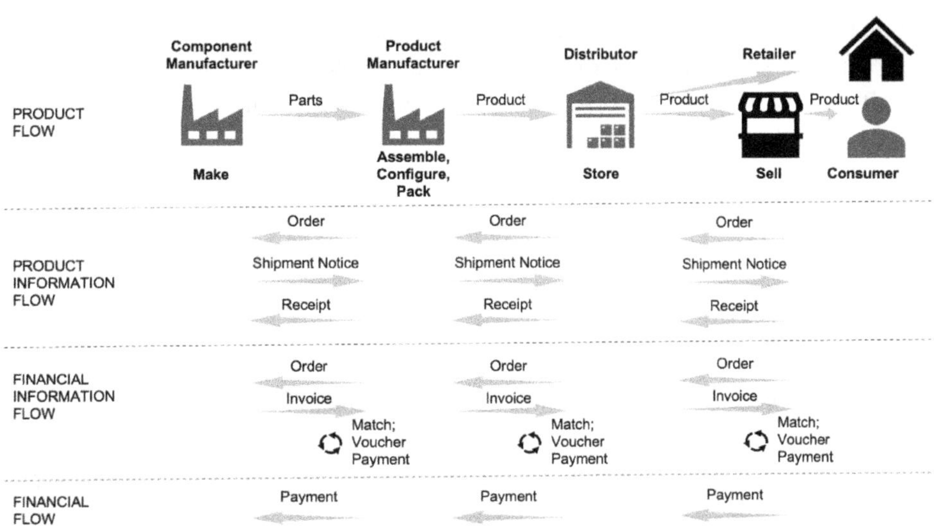

Financial Transactions and Flows Separated From Execution Decisions

Today, financial flows are managed in isolation from the execution in the supply chain. So, in parallel to the physical flow of goods, we have a flow of information transactions via orders and invoices which when matched and reconciled, trigger payments. It is the invoice, a remnant of the paper-based processes, that links the supply chain operations to the financials and payment process (Figure 8).

Compare this with the modern transaction of a rider on a modern ride app for instance. When you tap on the "Confirm" button with your pickup location and destination, you enter a smart contract with a commitment to pay either for the ride when completed or a cancellation fee. The app tracks your and the driver's location in real-time. When you step out of your ride at your destination, payment is transacted automatically in accordance with this contract. The ride app has brought together information flows, physical flows, and financial flows to reengineer the entire ride service solution.

With the widespread access to internet of things, digital networks, and digital payment services, there is no reason why financial transactions cannot be triggered directly from execution actions and information flows.

Fixed Planning Assumptions

The years 2020 through 2022 of Covid disruptions followed by the Ukraine war have exposed underlying weaknesses and structural flaws in the way supply chains have been managed for decades. We have landed into the "new abnormal." Volatility in demand, supply, lead times, and prices across supply chains is here to stay.

The chart in Figure 9 shows lead time trends during 2021 for semiconductors:

The lead times for semiconductors – a category of components that feed almost every modern supply chain – changed drastically from month to month. In recent years, we have seen drastic variations in lead times across almost every category. Yet almost all materials planning systems and fancy supply chain planning and optimization algorithms use a static lead time assumption to decide when and how much to order from upstream suppliers. To make matters worse, the lead time parameters driving these plans are almost always maintained manually.

Use of fixed lead times to plan orders between businesses is foolhardy. If lead times are stale, which they usually are, our plans will be in error. If lead times are increasing, then the order will already be late by the time it is triggered. If lead times are decreasing, there will be excess inventory and orders will be frequently pushed out or canceled in subsequent planning cycles.

If your navigation system can predict your estimated time of arrival at your destination using real time traffic data along your route rather than using fixed drive time assumptions, there is no reason we cannot expect to do the same for planning supply chain activities – say by leveraging modern machine learning approaches.

PLAN CHANGES TREATED AS AN AFTERTHOUGHT

Given the sustained volatility, order changes have been consistently increasing over recent years (Figure 10).

The premise that lead times will be stable is flawed. Changes become necessary and are proposed by either the buyer or the supplier on an ongoing basis. Since both buyer and supplier processes and systems

Figure 9. Electronics components' lead times from September 2020 through November 2022[3]

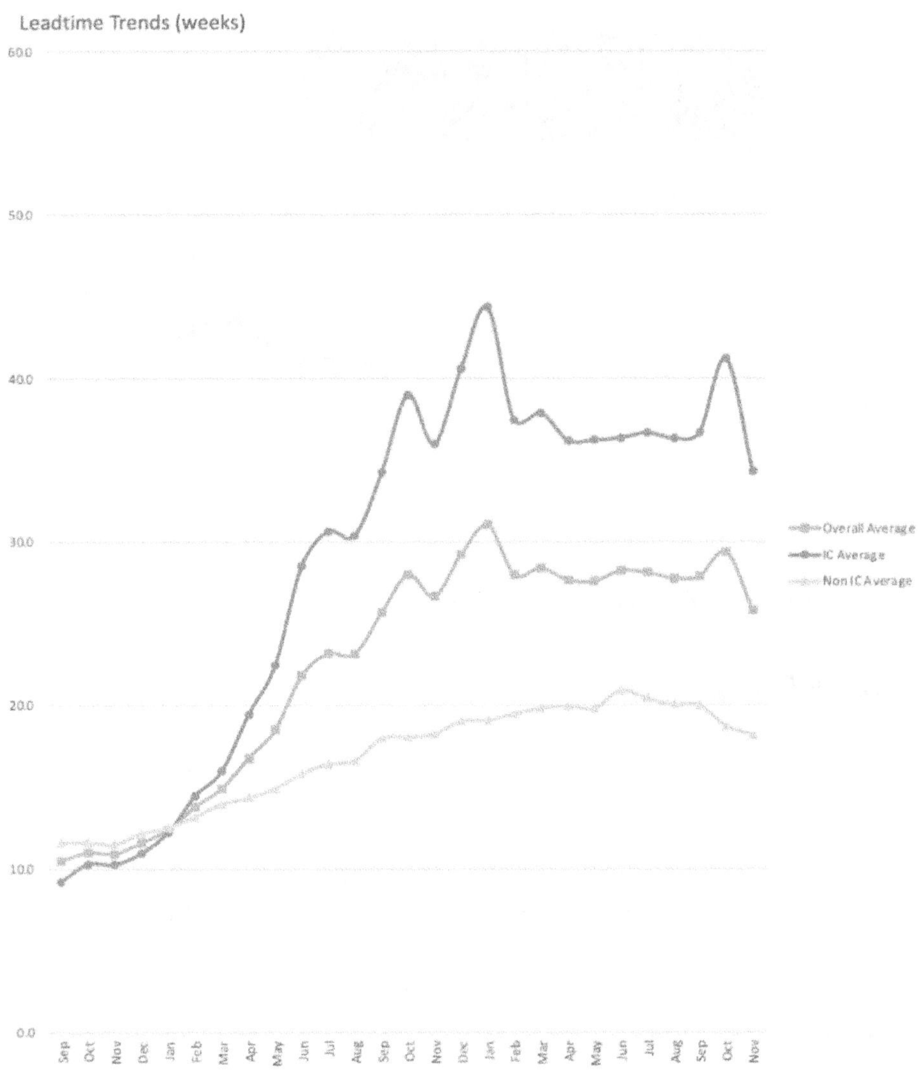

are based on an isolated inside-out view of the world, these plan changes are treated as an afterthought and implemented as even more transactions between the trading partners that must be transmitted, acknowledged, aligned, and persisted.

ASSUMPTIONS OF PERFECT DATA

Data in enterprise systems is never clean. With the rise in volume, variability, and velocity of big data, we have also seen a compounding deterioration in data veracity. Yet most business systems today do not yet directly address data verification as part of the data pipeline.

Figure 10. Trend in order line changes (initiated by either buyer or supplier) after being placed (SourceDay, 2023)

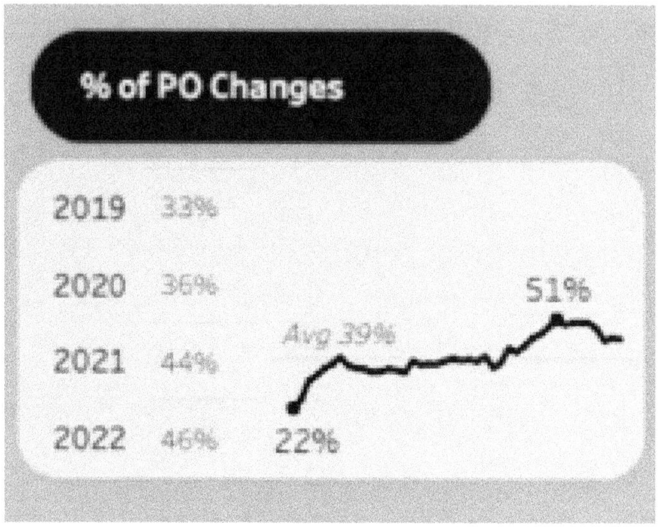

HOW ISOLATION IS IMPACTING BUSINESS

Isolation Creates Complexity

We are managing highly interconnected, interdependent, and dynamic business ecosystems with processes and systems designed with the premise of isolated enterprises, each working with its own business systems. But business transactions are between companies, not within them. To complete a single simple business-to-business transaction today, these isolated systems must talk to each other, move data, reconcile data, and then deal with mutual changes as afterthoughts (Figure 11). This has created unnecessary complexity.

Figure 11. A single transaction in the current paradigm with isolated enterprise centric systems

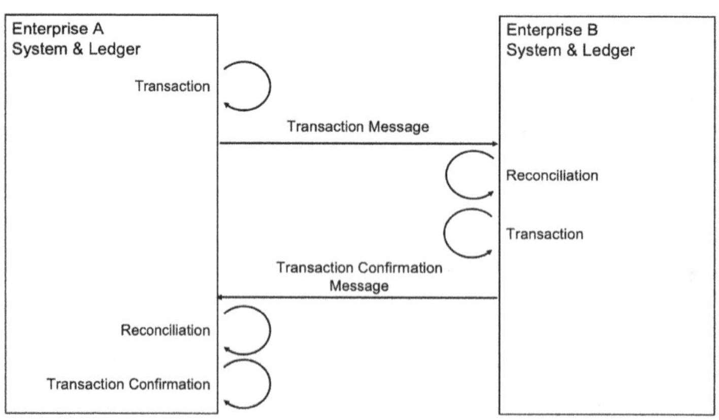

Redundant Data Constructs in Multiple Systems

When a buyer orders an item from a seller, they record a purchase order in their Accounts Payable System. On the other hand, the seller records a sales order in their Accounts Payable system upon receiving this order (Figure 12).

Figure 12. A simplified view of the order lifecycle across two ERPs

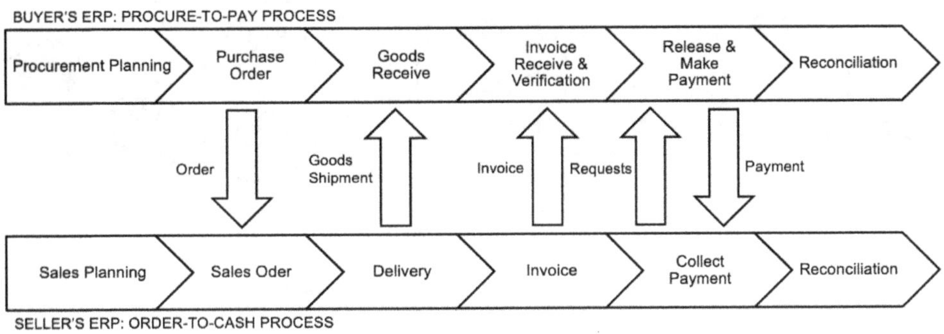

Then, once the supplier ships the goods, an advance ship notice is sent. The seller sends an invoice separately to request payment. The buyer must confirm that invoices are legitimate and accurate by matching them with purchase orders and reconciling receipts of goods. Once matched payment vouchers are issued, the payments are made. All these need to be reconciled with accounting ledgers. On the other hand, the seller must collect payments against invoices and reconcile that all open invoices are paid.

What is lost in all this is that there is just one "order" between the buyer and seller that is simply going through a lifecycle of being created, confirmed, shipped, received, and settled.

Redundant and Conflicting Taxonomies

Things are further complicated by the fact that there are redundant and conflicting taxonomies on both sides of the buyer-seller transaction. Item identities and classifications are different in each company. The same part will have a manufacturer part number, a distributor part number and a buyer's own company part number. Duplicated data in different systems with different taxonomies can also easily become inconsistent. The disconnects in these taxonomies must be resolved when matching invoices with purchase orders, shipments, and receipts for instance. At a deeper level, market trends on lead times, prices, demand, and supply cannot be evaluated unless these data from disparate systems are collected, cleansed, harmonized, and reconciled.

Isolation Creates Latency

Unnecessary handoffs and transactions between the isolated systems require unnecessary movement of data that need to be subsequently matched and reconciled with other data at every stage of the supply chain. The handoffs, transactions, movement of data, matching, and reconciliation are all activities that

Figure 13. Isolation of partners in the supply chain creates latency

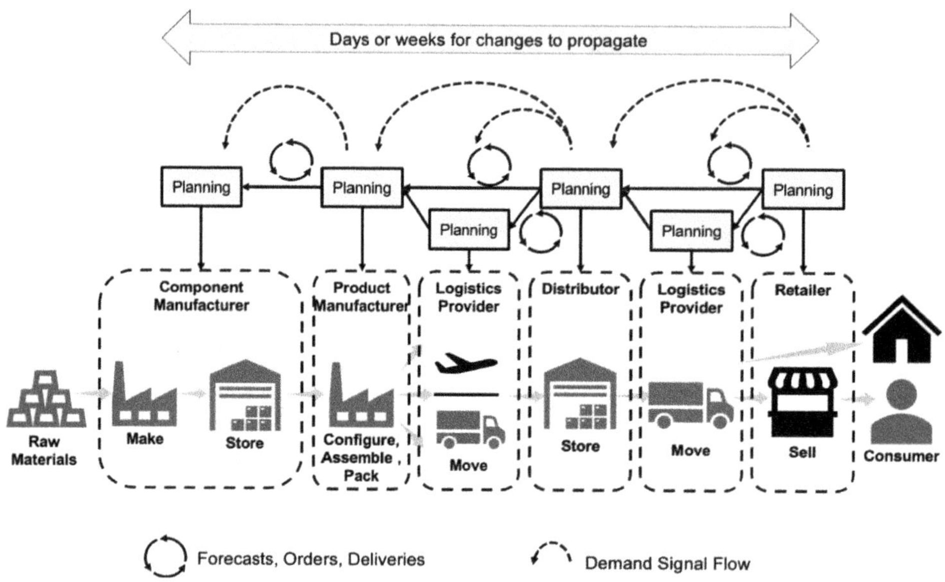

themselves take time and require waiting times in between due to system cadences and availability of human actors (Figure 13).

Latency Makes Alignment Impossible

For the supply chain to operate smoothly, trading partners need to coordinate their execution. However, even if you take a single buyer-seller pair at any stage of the value chain, there are ongoing changes initiated by both parties (Figure 14).

Figure 14. There are ongoing changes initiated by both sides[4]

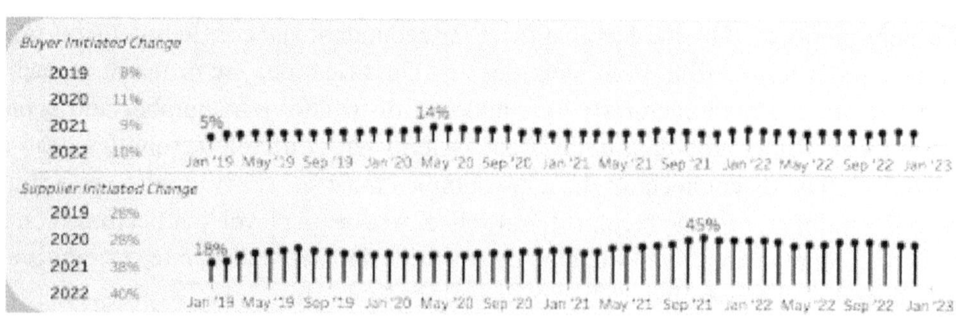

As recorded by SourceDay, (2023) changes may impact 40% to 50% of the order lines, and the total number of changes typically exceed the total number of order lines. It is humanly impossible to keep up with such a volume of changes with manual iterations. Thus, supply chain partners never have accurate visibility. To get around system latency, people turn to emails and spreadsheets and circumvent their systems – making matters even worse.

Misalignment Destroys Business Performance

Supply chain plans based on noisy data drive a domino effect. Orders are late or missed. Revenue is lost. Expedite fees are paid to rush materials. Factories oscillate between downtime and overtime to cope. Excess inventories are created. Buyers and sellers are caught by surprise. There is chaos and eroded trust across the supply chain.

THE PROCUREMENT PROCESS MUST CHANGE

Everything about the supply chain has changed since the times when the current supply chain processes and systems were developed. The way consumers buy, and businesses deliver has changed. Supply chain problems have changed. Computing power has changed. Information technologies have changed. Against this backdrop, incremental improvements within the existing paradigms will not be enough.

Faster Iterations are not Enough

Software tools have delivered significant increases in speed and performance with better algorithms and access to increased and more economical computing power. But, maintaining isolated systems and simply trying to speed up planning and iterate faster will not solve the problem. The cascading flow of information and iterations can never result in alignment across multiple partners.

Interfaced Tools are not Enough

Connecting the islands of information in point-to-point integrations will not solve the problem either. We will still need to move data, cleanse it, translate it, harmonize taxonomies, and reconcile inconsistencies between them.

EDI Signals are not Enough

For the same reasons as above, Electronic Data Interchange (EDI) signals are helpful but not enough by themselves either. Moving data electronically and faster will not tackle the underlying alignment challenges.

It is time to ditch flawed assumptions, ineffective processes, and outdated technologies and change the procurement processes.

COLLABORATIVE PROCUREMENT

Outside-In Planning

The shift to an outside-in paradigm is fundamental to Collaborative Procurement. Procurement Plans are no longer created in isolation with your trading partners. All trading partners such as materials buyers, materials suppliers, and logistics service suppliers must concurrently evolve their plans and collaborate to maintain alignment with each other.

Planning and execution are ongoing and interdependent activities. Planning is not the process of creating the optimal plan. Rather, it is an ongoing process of coordinating activities across functions and trading partners to achieve desired objectives. The plan is a vehicle for alignment and coordinated execution.

A collaboration is a process where two or more participants work together to *complete a task or achieve a shared goal.* In our context here, the task is to maintain and execute a procurement plan that is aligned across all trading partners.

A Network is Necessary for Collaboration

To collaborate, trading partners must be able to interact. A **supply chain collaboration network** platform (SCCN) is essential to supply chain collaboration. It provides the infrastructure and governance for a marketplace where trading partners can securely interact with one another exchanging data and value.

The SCCN as an Ecosystem Commerce Platform

The set of **member enterprises** forms the **Community**. Every member enterprise must have one or more people serving as member agents (or simply **members**) representing them on the network platform serving in roles such as Buyers, Sellers, Planners, AP Clerks, and Customer Service Representatives.

Value chains are heterogeneous and there is no single network that manages all aspects for all member companies. Just as airline reservation systems connect multiple airlines' reservations systems to multiple travel agencies into an interoperable network leveraging Global Distribution Systems, the SCCNs can form a network of networks to orchestrate commerce across multiple manufacturers, distributors, buyers, sellers, and logistic providers.

The SCCN can not only help each member enterprise plan operations outside-in, it can also orchestrate commerce at an overall ecosystem level across the community. Traditionally, companies have built control towers to better manage their own supply chains. In contrast, Richard Sherman has pointed out that an airport has a control tower, but it is used to help manage all the flights from all the airlines coming into an airport. "The emerging issue is that while internal control towers have visibility and control over their loads, they don't have visibility to all of the loads in the market ecosystem in which they operate," (Banker, 2022).

Content on the Network

The SCCN also manages **Content,** which is data residing on the platform about the community. Content can consist of enterprise first party and second party data, 3rd party data, interaction data, or derived data. **Enterprise data** is provided by and specific to one company. **First party data** of member enterprises is provided by the members directly. **Second party data** is data about supply chain partners that are provided by the members. These can include part information, pricing, and lead times for instance. **Third party data** is data acquired by the platform from parties outside the network and made available to one or more members. These can include financial ratings, environment, social and governance (ESG) ratings, weather, natural events, geopolitical events, labor rates, and other economic data. **Interaction data** is produced directly from interactions between members on the platform. These can include responsiveness metrics, mutual ratings, and negotiation outcome metrics. There may also be **derived data** on the platform that are typically aggregated, anonymized, and/or derived metrics and trends combining one or more the categories of data.

Content can either be private or shared. **Private data** is owned and visible only to a single member enterprise. **Shared data** is data that a given member explicitly shares with one or more trading partners. Shared data can include public catalogs available to all members or collaboration data available only to partners engaged in a specific collaboration.

Any member can be a producer or a consumer of content depending on their role in each interaction.

The Network Eliminates Latency

A community of trading partners connected to a SCCN can share information instantly. Awareness of demand and supply changes can now propagate immediately across the SCCN (Figure 15). There is zero latency.

Figure 15. The SCCN eliminates information latency

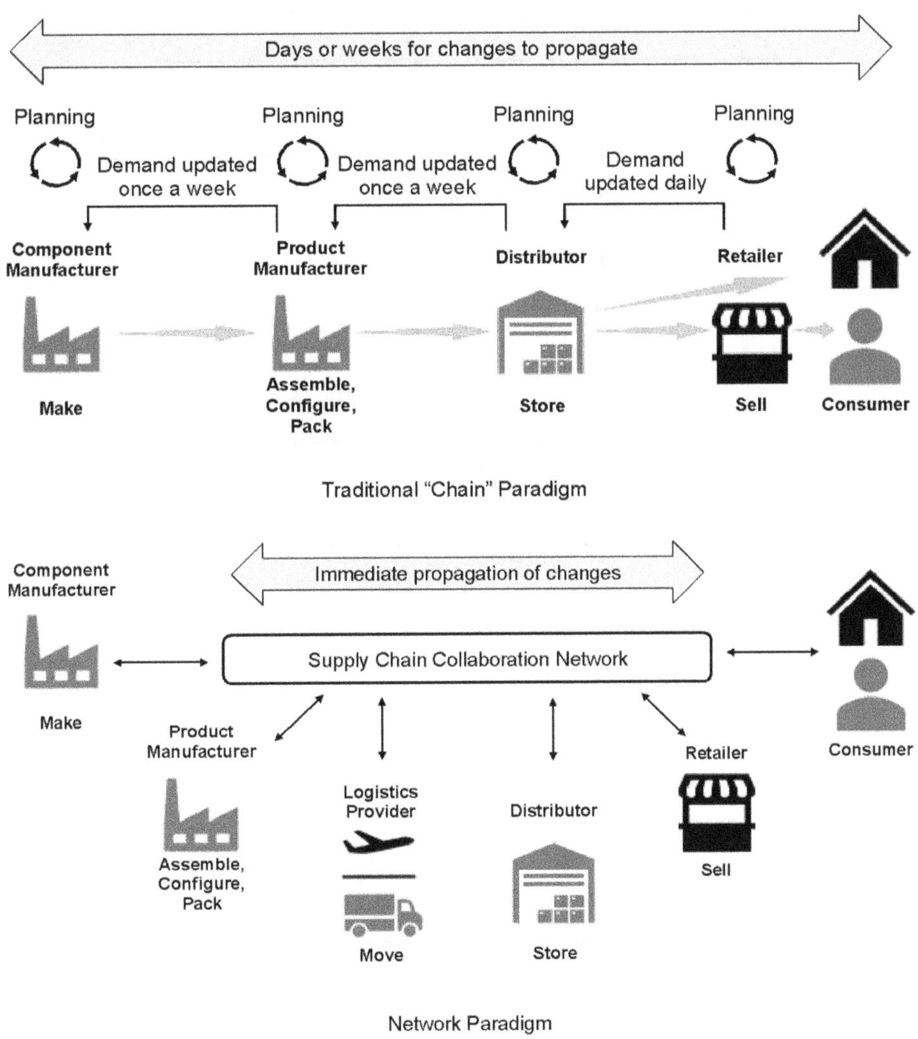

The Three Levels of Supply Chain Collaboration

Collaboration between trading partners can happen at three levels: Operational, Tactical, and Strategic. If we visualize each partner's business processes as a pyramid, we can then illustrate these levels as varying degrees of overlap (Figure 16) between these pyramids to bring outside-in information and considerations from the partner into the internal processes.

Figure 16. A conceptual view of the three levels of supply chain collaboration

This is of course a simplification. Buyers and Sellers are rarely equal partners in the relationship. Yet, in a direct materials context, there are inevitably touchpoints on both sides when one partner sees the other as strategic to their supply chain.

POWER DYNAMICS IN A PROCUREMENT RELATIONSHIP

A.T. Kearney has developed the Purchasing Chessboard[5] framework, which is largely inspired by the logic of demand power and supply power to help procurement executives reduce costs and increase value with their suppliers.

High Demand Power

When the demand is concentrated in the Buyer and supply is diversified across many competing suppliers, the Buyer is in a position of overwhelming power. Such a Buyer can exploit the supplier to its own advantage and will have a strong upper hand in the Buyer-Supplier relationship. In such situations, the partners must collaborate at the operational level at a minimum and the Buyer dictates business processes, information technology, and compliance requirements as conditions of doing business.

High Supply Power

This is the case where the supply is concentrated in a limited number of market players. This is true for supply of specialized semiconductor manufacturing capabilities as well as in the case of commodities being sold through a limited number of exchanges that can dictate the pricing and availability. In such situations the partners must again collaborate at the tactical level, but the supplier may end up dictating the business process, information technology, and rules of engagement.

High Supply and Demand Power

This is the situation where the demand may be concentrated on the one hand to a few Buyers and the supply is also concentrated on the other hand within a few suppliers. In such situations the partners must collaborate beyond the operational level to include tactical and strategic levels as they are equally dependent on each other for their long-term success.

Low Supply and Demand Power

When both demand and supply are diversified we have more balanced market dynamics. The rise of e-commerce served to balance the power dynamics between the retail sellers and the buying consumers but ended up shifting power into the hands of the large online marketplaces such as Amazon that dominate the sales channels. However, the manufacturers and the distributors or retailers in these situations still need operational collaboration excellence to deliver products to the consumer when and where demanded.

Since operational collaboration is essential to supply chain performance, the remainder of this chapter covers operational collaboration in detail while covering tactical and strategic collaboration at only a very high level.

OPERATIONAL COLLABORATION

Direct materials procurement relationships have higher stakes than typical indirect purchase relationships. The items being purchased, and their quality or delivery performance will become part of the buyer's own product. They will shape their customer's experience and influence brand perceptions. Therefore, supply chain partners must go beyond mere completion of purchase order transactions to collaborate for superior supply chain performance. Operational collaboration represents the minimum hygiene bar of collaboration needed between supply chain partners. Operational Collaboration also serves as a foundation for higher levels of collaboration. Sadly, this is usually neglected, and its absence inhibits the effectiveness of supply chain processes at all levels.

Promising is Planning

At the operational level, the assignment of a due date to an order is the most pivotal planning activity as it commits both the buyer and seller and links them into an interdependent supply chain execution plan. Any disruptions on either side can now have a material impact on the other partner's business operations and outcomes.

To enable operational collaboration, the buyers' Procurement Systems (PS) and the sellers' Order Systems are connected to the SCCN (Figure 17).

Figure 17. The SCCN connects many buyers' procurement systems to many suppliers' order systems across the community to form a marketplace

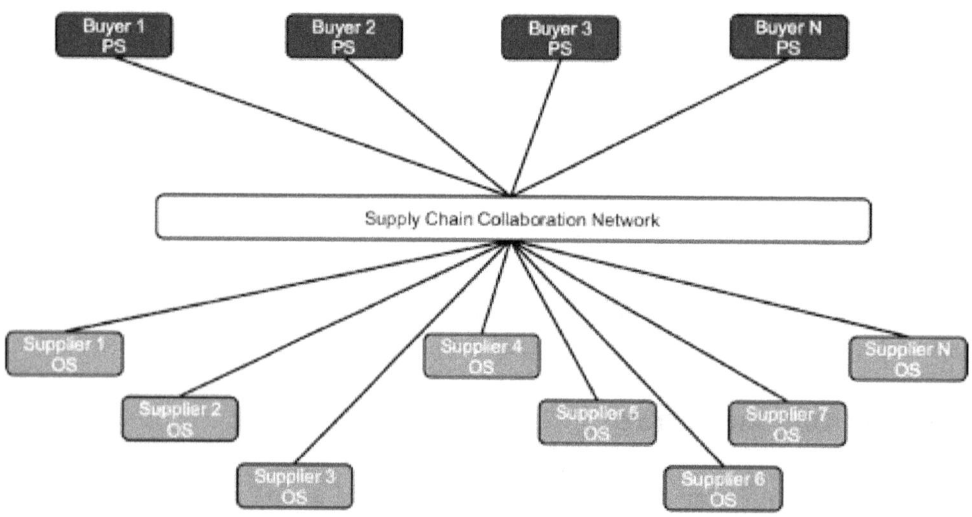

Mutually Aligned Orders

Once onboarded to the SCCN, Buyers and Sellers can collaborate in real-time to maintain a mutually aligned supply plan. Every new order request is acknowledged and confirmed until both parties are aligned (Figure 18). If either party proposes a change, then the other party can review and accept the change or counter with their own proposed changes until both parties come to an agreement.

Figure 18. The SCCN enables collaboration, so every new order request is confirmed till both parties are aligned

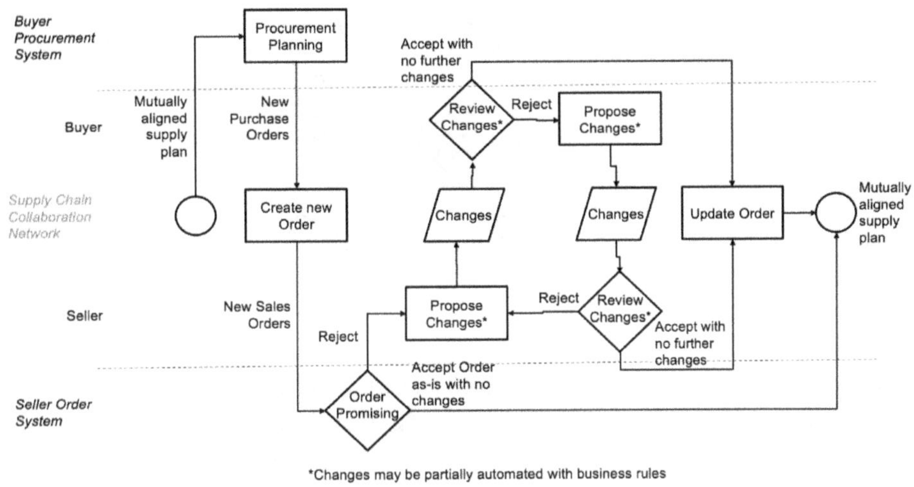

The Human Element in the Collaboration

Note that the SCCN does not simply move data, it also facilitates human to human messages and conversations in context of the orders, their relative priority, and additional special considerations – unlike traditional EDI solutions.

Using configurable business rules, change proposals and change reviews may be partially automated. Gradually, as business processes and relationships mature, the percent of exceptions that require manual review reduces significantly.

Mutually Aligned Changes

Data shows that between 40 to 60% of order line items change during the lifecycle of a direct materials purchase order (SourceDay, 2022). The SCCN also facilitates efficient collaboration so that plans for both partners stay aligned on an ongoing basis.

Every time the Buyer's procurement plan is updated, it can require changes to existing orders. Orders may be moved in, moved out or out canceled if the updated demand supply picture no longer requires them. The extent of changes that are allowed for consideration are governed by business rules that are mutually agreed up-front when the buyer – supplier relationship is established. Figure 19 shows how Buyer initiated changes are resolved through mutual collaboration.

Figure 19. How the SCCN facilitates alignment for buyer initiated changes

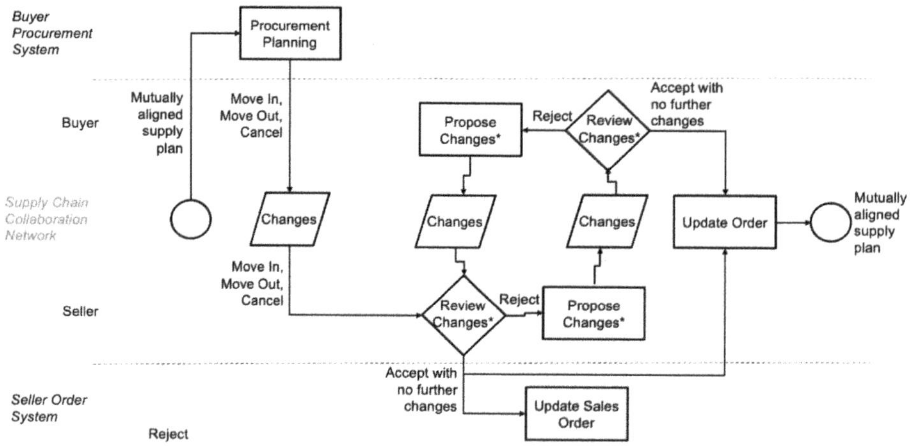

If a Seller initiates a change, the SCCN facilitates a similar collaboration process to bring both parties into alignment (Figure 20). Seller-initiated Move Ins, Move Outs, or Splits are reviewed mutually until both parties agree on the changes. Again, the extent of allowed changes is governed by business rules that have been mutually agreed up front by both parties. Also, the percent of changes that must be reviewed manually can be reduced over time through automated business rules that are learned and persisted over time.

Figure 20. How the SCCN facilitates alignment for seller initiated changes

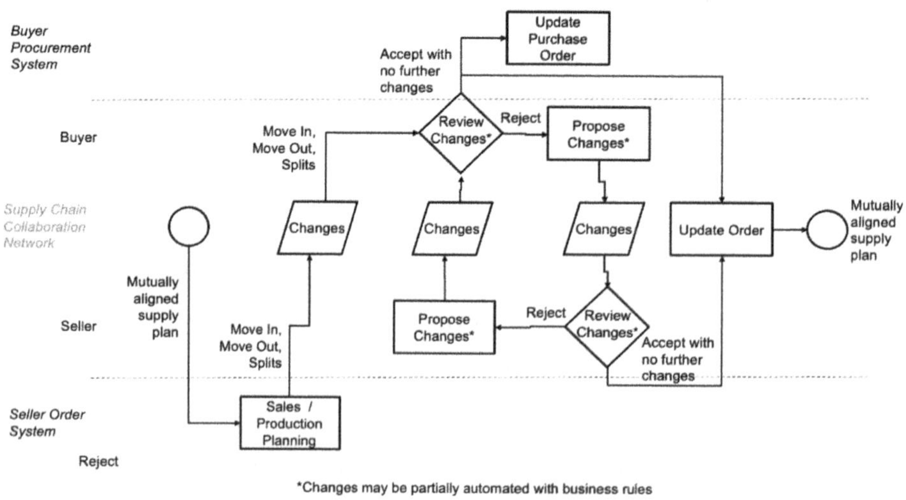

Integrated View Across Procurement, Sales, and Logistics

Shippers, Carriers, and 3rd party logistics providers can also connect to the same SCCN (Figure 21). Now, regardless of whether the freight responsibility is with the buyer or the seller, the logistics partners can also work directly with the mutually aligned supply plan. As orders are promised and aligned, the logistics forecast is updated. As shipments are planned, the SCCN maintains a cross-reference between orders and shipments that is visible to all participating partners.

Figure 21. SCCN Enables an end-to-end order lifecycle integrated across buyer procurement, seller sales, and logistics

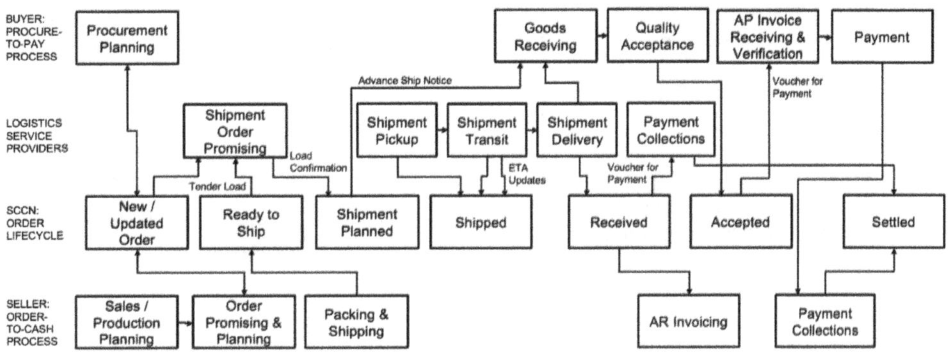

Ongoing Updates to all Parties

Once the Buyers, Sellers, and logistics partners are all boarded onto the network, all partners have full ongoing visibility of the order across the full order lifecycle. As product is prepared and ready to ship, the logistics partner is advised of the available loads. As shipments get planned by the logistics partner, the SCCN sends an Advanced Ship Notice to the Buyer. As product is in-transit, the logistics partner provides real-time Estimated Time for Arrival (ETA) updates to the SCCN that are then visible to the Buyer and the Seller. As goods are received, inspected, and accepted, the sellers can have visibility of the status.

A More Reliable View of Inventory Position

The traditional view of inventory position for inbound supply lines is simply the awareness of what is On Order in addition to what one has On Hand. All planning systems assume that what is "On Order" will be delivered as expected until the actual delivery is recorded and the inventory and on hand are updated in subsequent plans. Now, we have a granular view where "On Order" quantities can be further broken out into states such as "Waiting acknowledgement," "Acknowledged," "Ready to Ship," and "In Transit," along with an up-to-date view of ETA. There are varying levels of supply disruption risks depending on which of these states a particular order is in.

Single View of the Order: No Matching Needed

The SCCN maintains a single primary order record across the entire lifecycle. This order record creates the cross reference between the Purchase Orders in the Buyer's procurement system and the sales orders in the Seller's order system. As the order updates are received from either party, the single order is updated. There is no need for matching and reconciliation (Figure 22).

Figure 22. The SCCN eliminates the need for matching and reconciliation

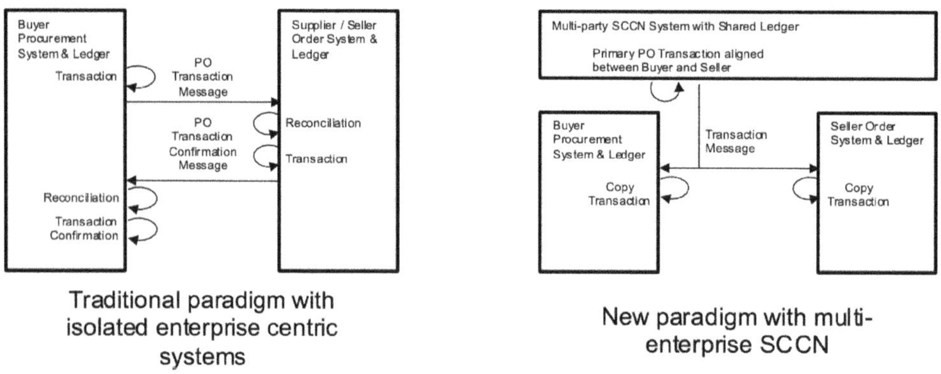

Smart Contracts Govern Order Payments and Settlement

The SCCN also establishes and enforces **smart contracts** for agreed payment terms and conditions between the seller and the buyer. Smart contracts are simply digital programs on the SCCN that run when the predetermined conditions representing the agreements between the buyer and the seller are met. They automate the execution of the payment agreements so that all participants can be immediately certain of the outcome without any intermediary's involvement, manual reconciliation, or time loss.

The SCCN orchestrates information flows, product flows, and financial flows between the value chain partners. There is zero latency in the information flows and resulting execution signals. The SCCN has full visibility to the status of the order in terms of purchase orders, delivery, receipt-in-full, and quality acceptance. When required terms are met, the SCCN automatically generates payment vouchers and triggers the payment process in the Buyer's accounts payable systems. There is no need for the Seller to send an invoice and the Buyer to have to match it to Purchase Orders. To enable compatibility with legacy systems, the SCCN can generate an invoice on behalf of the seller and send it alongside the payment voucher to the Buyer's Accounts Payable system and send a copy to the Seller's Accounts Receivables system.

Dynamic Planning Assumptions

In Collaborative Procurement, key planning assumptions such as lead times and pricing are also managed within an outside-in collaborative paradigm. Rather than assuming a fixed lead time for delivery, lead times are seen as an outcome of a collaboratively aligned delivery plan for individual orders. From the

Seller's vantage point, there may be agreed pricing, availability, and service level tradeoffs offered with different lead time windows. From the Buyer's vantage point, the lead times are seen as time fences for how far in advance orders with specific quantities, dates, and prices will be released and committed. If additional orders, changes, or cancellations are needed inside of those time fences, there may be financial and operational consequences.

The SCCN plays an important role here and continuously monitors how lead times are behaving.

Observed lead times are visible to both parties. The SCCN can also flag exceptions relative to assumptions and contractual terms. It can leverage statistical methods to recalculate and suggest revised planning assumptions such as relevant time fences to both parties. Thus, the Collaborative Procurement practice is to neither run blind with stale assumptions nor to blindly update lead times with rolling statistics. Instead, SCCN can facilitate a collaborative conversation between the Buyer and Seller when actual metrics start drifting away from planning assumptions. Both partners may agree to revise to mutually re-align assumptions. The Buyer is accountable for changes inside of the agreed lead times and the Seller is accountable for delivery performance if their offered lead times are respected.

Transparency and Mutual Accountability

Network platforms enable transparency between trading partners and visibility of benchmarks and trends to the community. The SCCN tracks mutual metrics such as buyer and seller responsiveness, seller on-time-in-full delivery, and buyer payment timeliness. It not only enables mutual scorecards between trading partners but can also provide anonymized and aggregated performance metrics of buyers and sellers to the community. Just as it is hard for drivers and riders to game their ratings across thousands of rides on a ride-hailing app, it is also hard for sellers and buyers to game their metrics on the SCCN.

TACTICAL COLLABORATION

Collaboration at this level is at the Sales and Operations Planning level between the partners with mutual collaboration on forecasts and inventory policies. Buyers and suppliers share planned demand forecasts and capacity; and align on replenishment strategies to support those volumes. In addition, the SCCN can deliver 3rd party content and aggregated metrics across the community to give line of sight to buyers and sellers of channel inventory and market data such as point of sales data in the case of retail. The incorporation of market and channel data to drive demand signals is key to transforming the traditional S&OP processes to outside-in activities (Cecere, 2022).

There can be two flavors here: Customer Managed Inventory or Vendor Managed Inventory.

Customer Managed Inventory

In customer managed inventory (CMI) the Buyer initiates the purchase orders, and the Seller delivers to an agreed stocking location such as the supply line stores of the desired manufacturing facility.

Vendor Managed Inventory

In the Vendor Managed Inventory (VMI) arrangement, the seller owns and manages the stock inventory and is responsible for initiating replenishment orders to assure continuity of supply at contractually agreed service levels.

In both CMI and VMI cases, the SCCN enables shared visibility, collaborative workflows to drive mutual alignment, smart contracts to orchestrate execution, and transparent accountability to trading partners.

The Collaborative Procurement Funnel

For supply chain partners to execute in lock step, both partners' plans must gradually align as they evolve from far-term forecasts to medium-term plans and near-term execution actions. In Collaborative Procurement, the trading partners have shared visibility, and the alignment is treated as an ongoing process.

In the far-term, both parties forecast their business independently, leveraging market and channel data, and – depending on the level of collaboration between them – they may share these forecasts for visibility only. As time passes and forecasts move into the medium-term, they are formalized into Planned Orders. Planned orders are proposed commitments and trigger a process of alignment between the buyer and seller before firm commitments are made. If the seller is unable to support proposed quantities in proposed timeframes, then the buyer can adjust planned order volumes and dates, or switch to alternate sources amongst other options. By the time the medium-term moves into the near-term, order release lead time fences are crossed, and planned orders are finalized and converted to firm order commitments aligned by the buyer and the respective sellers.

The SCCN can enforce mutually agreed smart contracts to drive convergence between trading partners. For instance, the SCCN enables automation that if a seller has acknowledged a planned order in the medium-term and the order release lead time fence is crossed, then a firm order of a quantity within a specified tolerance will be automatically mutually accepted. Similarly, the SCCN can expire proposed changes if agreed change proposal response times are not met within the near-term (Figure 23).

Figure 23. The collaborative procurement funnel

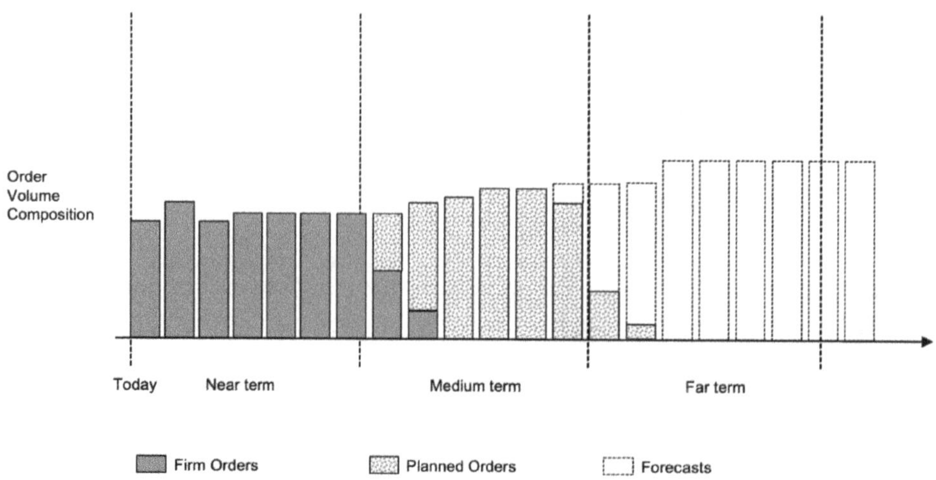

Strategic Collaboration

As mentioned earlier, strategic collaboration usually occurs in situations where both demand and supply power exist, and trading partners are mutually dependent on each other for success at a high degree. Strategic Collaboration spans collaboration on new product plans and supply chain network designs.

New Product Design Collaboration

New product design collaboration requires strong interaction between product and application engineering teams at both the Buyer and the Suppliers. During the Covid and post-Covid years of supply shortages, Sourcing teams, Product Design teams, and New Product Introduction Programs, Managers collaborated extensively to tackle supply shortages with design changes as well as alternate source qualifications to minimize product delays and launch disruptions.

Supply Network Design Collaboration

Supply chain considerations are also being brought up increasingly earlier in the product design lifecycle to reduce risk and lower the product cost at launch and later. This means that supply chain design teams, finance teams, and product teams must work together extensively not only prior to launch but throughout the product lifecycle.

THE PROCESS TRANSFORMATION JOURNEY TO COLLABORATIVE PROCUREMENT

To achieve excellence in Collaborative Procurement, companies and their trading partners such as suppliers and logistics providers can use the following five-stage maturity model as a guide to navigate their transformation journey.

The Collaborative Procurement Maturity Model

The Collaborative Procurement Maturity Model[6] maps stages in progression along two dimensions: the pivot from inside-out paradigm to an outside-in paradigm, and the transition from isolated functions to internal cross functional alignment across the enterprise, and eventually to cross enterprise alignment across the value network.

Each of the five stages of maturity are defined next (Figure 24). Companies can assess their current process capability level, identify gaps relative to the next maturity level, and take actions to improve people skills, processes, and enabling technologies to move up to the next level.

Figure 24. The five levels of process maturity in the journey to collaborative procurement

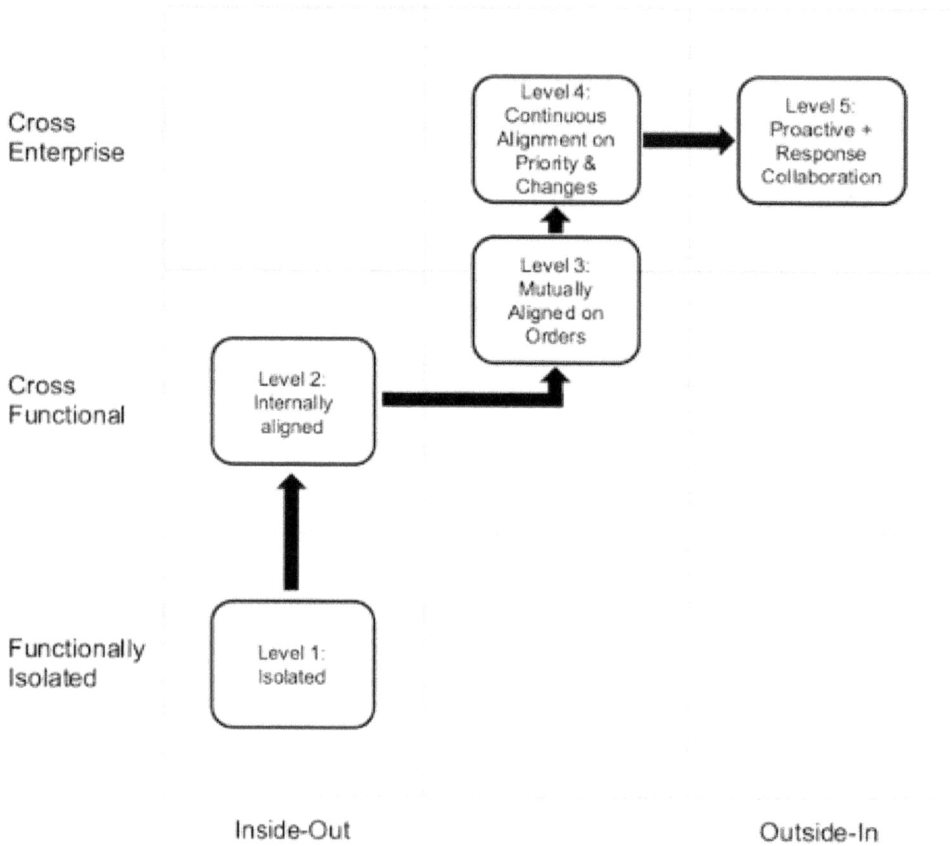

Level 1: Procurement as an Isolated Function

At the lowest level of maturity, procurement is a service to other functions within a company with little emphasis on its strategic value. A tell-tale sign of this level of maturity is that the procurement team is asked to execute strategic decisions but is not included in the decision-making itself. Procurement processes and systems are isolated and designed primarily for transaction efficiency and visibility.

Level 2: Cross Functional Alignment

The next level of process maturity is where the procurement team is an active participant in supply chain and operations decision-making. Typically, this is facilitated via an Enterprise Resource Planning (ERP) system and shared internal visibility across functions.

Level 3: Mutual Handshake and Shared Visibility

The hallmark of this stage of maturity is that alignment on supply plans extends to suppliers via virtual handshakes. Purchase orders are sent to suppliers and suppliers acknowledge or confirm each order line.

Most business relationships are virtual. In the realm of direct materials, this increases the need for up-front confirmation of commitment from suppliers. A virtual handshake gives you confidence that your supply is shipped on time and builds trust and accountability into your supplier relationships.

Level 4: Continuous Alignment on Priority and Changes

This level furthers the shift to the outside-in paradigm by adding processes for communicating priorities and continuously collaborating on order changes as well as supply changes.

Some order lines are routine re-stocking orders while others may be urgently needed for a product launch or to avoid an imminent stockout. In this level, Buyer companies establish clear signals and governance to define order priorities and bubble up specific order lines that are the most critical at any time. Additionally, processes are put in place to flag and act on changes. Procurement processes now operate at two levels: a foundation of automated processes and data exchanges between business partners that enable ongoing orchestration of routine transactions, and an overlay of manage-by-exception collaborative processes that ensure timely actions and coordinated responses to exceptions.

Level 5: Proactive and Response Collaboration

As supply chain collaboration processes and discipline mature, trading partners can go beyond response collaboration to collaborating proactively on anticipated market opportunities and risks.

CONCLUSION

Case Studies

Clothing Retailer

Sustainable clothing retailer Marine Layer was previously only focused on ecommerce and retail. In 2019, the company added wholesale as a third channel to their business, along with several new warehouse locations. These changes saw their purchase order volume increase from 1,500 orders annually to 4,500. Their buying team was looking at triple the work with the same antiquated processes in place.

Frankly, managing suppliers was a time-consuming, error-prone mess for Marine Layer. The company sent every PO back and forth via email, and all PO updates were entered manually into their ERP, NetSuite. Their approach has been called "laborious" and "error prone" by their higher-ups, and the entire sourcing chain was affected. It required more work than necessary and ultimately, their on-time delivery suffered. They needed a way to work smarter.

The company transformed their processes enabled by SourceDay's supply chain colloaboration network. Each of their 4,500 POs must be turned into a shipment and then received at one of the company's distribution centers. With SourceDay, the vendors update quantities across all clothing styles before those goods become an outbound shipment. This has greatly improved their accuracy on the receiving end, which can become a bottleneck if the DC receives goods that aren't expected. Marine Layer no longer has to manually check and count shipments, and the downstream effect is better accuracy before a shipment leaves the port.

The sourcing side of the business has seen drastic improvement. In the past, the team emailed 1,200 times (literally 1,200) to vendors about 10-unit PO changes. They committed two people to multiple days of gathering PO info, uploading it to Netsuite manually, downloading them as PDFs, attaching them to emails, waiting for every PO's terms and cost to be accepted and approved, then following up each one via email.

With the SourceDay's digital collaboration platform, they are now freed up from long, manual processes and can work strategically on value-add work. What previously required multiple days now only takes about 20 minutes. The team can focus on optimizing vendor flows and most importantly, effectively managing shipment tracking times.

Airport Gate and Equipment Manufacturer

JBT Aerotech makes airport gate and ground equipment. The company experienced a boom in business in 2018. They relied on their Syteline ERP to help with demand planning, but they quickly recognized a problem. Despite strong demand planning tools, they often found themselves without vital parts on the day production was scheduled to begin for a product. In fact, they found that critical parts were late nearly 1/3rd of the time. JBT AeroTech had also gotten into a pattern of ordering extra inventory – just in case. Like many organizations, the negative impact of slowing down production vastly outweighed the cost of buffer stock.

Then, under a process transformation initiative, JBT vowed to do away with the complicated spreadsheets and decided to communicate changes through a supply chain collaboration network from SourceDay instead, while asking their suppliers to do the same. They also required that suppliers acknowledge all POs through within 72 hours.

According to Terry Decker, Supply Chain Performance Manager at JBT AeroTech, these process changes allowed both JBT and their suppliers to have frank conversations around supplier performance for the first time, aided by supplier scorecards. She observed that if an order line was not acknowledged by the supplier, then the part would be late 100% of the time. "Once we got beyond the initial finger pointing, then the suppliers started seeing what their performance looked like and they wanted to get better," Decker said.

JBT AeroTech was able to move from the inside-out orientation of Level 1 and 2 process maturity to an outside-in orientation achieving mutual alignment on orders at Level 3. As a result of changing behaviors and leaning into technology, JBT found they could count on the parts they needed to arrive when they needed them. They also found that they could eliminate large swaths of buffer stock as a result as well.

By the end of 2020, fewer than 10% of parts arrived after the start of production (down from 32%) and 86% of POs were acknowledged by suppliers within 72 hours. Most important of all, JBT delivered to their own customers on time nearly 90% of the time, up from only 69% in previous years.

Medical Device Manufacturer

Another company, a manufacturer of medical and industrial devices, has almost all their suppliers in China. Given the nature of their technology, it is not easy for the company to qualify new substitutes quickly. Even before the pandemic, they were struggling to keep a handle on their inbound supply. All supplier communication was done via emails and phone calls. Every piece of data on every line of every PO was manually entered into their ERP every day. To make matters worse, there were daily changes from their MRP as well as changes from their suppliers across thousands of orders and tens of thousands of order lines. While their existing processes and systems worked well inside their four walls, they left them disconnected from their suppliers. They had a team of people trying to chorale supply to keep the manufacturing lines running. The complexity of their business was too much for the manual approach. So, the company adopted a supply chain collaboration network solution from SourceDay that integrated into their ERP and connected them to their suppliers in real time.

As an immediate benefit, they eliminated hundreds of hours of error-prone manual data entry. More importantly, they were able to institute a new communication process between the procurement team in North America and the suppliers in China. They used a capability called "radar" to proactively flag orders that were coming due soon. In the past, Buyers and Suppliers had to spend a couple of hours or more in each of their morning times just to catch up on emails, assess status, and identify the priority actions needed. Now, both parties were able to see the latest status, communicate issues, flag actions, and specify priorities systematically through the collaboration network. They used "hot-lists" to orchestrate buyer and supplier actions to mitigate anticipated supply issues. The company was able to progress from Level 1 and 2 of process maturity to Level 3 and 4. The company and their suppliers were able to execute in lock step despite time zone differences and continuous changes. As a result, they were able to cope with the unprecedented challenges of the Covid crises. Unlike their peers, the company managed to have zero factory downtime during the pandemic.

REFERENCES

Ascm. (2022, September 19). *ASCM releases new SCOR Digital Standard.* PR Newswire. https://www.prnewswire.com/news-releases/ascm-releases-new-scor-digital-standard-301626710.html

Automate Po Changes & enable supplier collaboration. (2022, April 14). SourceDay. https://sourceday.com/

Banker, S. (2022). Supply Chain Management is Broken. Can a Radical New Way Of Thinking Be The Solution? *Forbes.*

Cecere, L. (2022). Insights from a Two-Year Journey to Define Outside-In Supply Chain Planning Processes. *Forbes.*

Najmi, A. (2022, December 16). *What supply chains really are and why it matters.* The Network Effect. https://supplychainbeyond.com/what-is-a-supply-chain-and-why-it-matters/

Schuh, C. (2017). *The purchasing chessboard* (3rd ed.). Springer. doi:10.1007/978-1-4939-6764-3

Sherman, R. J. (2020, May 4). Why has CPFR failed to scale? *CSCMPs Supply Chain Quarterly RSS.* https://www.supplychainquarterly.com/articles/57-why-has-cpfr-failed-to-scale

Transform your direct materials sourcing. (n.d.). LevaData. https://www.levadata.com/

Chapter 13
Retail Procurement Strategies in Disruptive Environments: Concepts and Best Practices

Varun Gupta
University of North Georgia, USA

ABSTRACT

The purpose of this book chapter is to explore different strategies that retail procurement managers can exploit when there are disruptions in their supply chains. The initial research of the chapter is based on a review of supply chain disruption literature and specific case studies of procurement strategies that factor into disruption events. With globalization and increasingly complex supply chains, disruptions can devastate a business as its entire supply stream can be cut off. This chapter summarizes key concepts and best practices from the literature and industry case studies to understand disruption-related supply chain issues and discusses strategies that can give a competitive advantage to retail procurement managers.

INTRODUCTION

Retail procurement entails sourcing and purchasing: a) the products that are sold *directly* to the consumers, b) the input products that are required to make and sell the products, and c) the *supporting* products (e.g., cleaning supplies) for retail operations. Purchasing/ procurement managers working in retail are responsible for procuring a fraction or all of these products. Over the years, they have embraced digitalization (Gupta, 2019) for greater efficiency and transparency of their supply chains (SCs). The author considers retail procurement a more comprehensive term than *purchasing* in the context of SCs, as purchasing focuses more on the tactical aspects of acquiring goods, services, or work from an external source. In contrast, retail procurement encompasses the development of business strategies that align with the retailer's mission and goals. Managers can use widely adopted procurement strategies (cost-based, value-based, supplier-centric) and best practices (Sabri, 2019). These best practices can make the procurement process very efficient, resulting in cost savings, improved delivery lead times, and reduced

DOI: 10.4018/978-1-6684-7298-9.ch013

overordering or underordering. However, they do not account for external or internal disruptions that can destabilize either supply or demand.

The COVID-19 pandemic, which occurred due to the spread of a novel coronavirus in late 2019 (World Health Organization, 2020), resulted in widespread and devastating supply chain disruptions for almost all types of goods across the industry. Due to the unpredictable nature of the pandemic as well as its massive scale and global reach, the resulting supply chain was disrupted substantially across all its nodes (supply chain members) and edges (ties) (Chowdhury et al., 2021). Many companies that traditionally relied on procurement techniques based on stable supply chains, such as single sourcing, off-shoring, outsourcing, just-in-time, lean, etc., made the supply chains even more vulnerable to disruptions and less resilient. In the early stages of the pandemic, public health experts advocated for physical distancing and crowd management measures to contain and subdue the spread of the disease. These social distancing measures had negatively impacted the demand at retailers with a brick-and-mortar presence and necessitated the creation of a digital marketplace or participate in an existing digital marketplace. At the same time, many companies that had invested in digitalizing and diversifying their supply chains fared better than their competitors in meeting customer demand and securing supplies. Many companies made immediate investment decisions for digitalization to operate in the *new normal* with social distancing and take procurement decisions remotely by building or participating in digital procurement platforms.

The COVID-19 pandemic has accelerated the trend toward Digitalization within the industry and the importance of engaging customers through multiple platforms, including e-business. – Andre Simha, Chief Digital and Information Officer, MSC. (Leonard, 2020).

Modern-day procurement processes have become increasingly complex due to globalization, volatile and uncertain global tariffs, complex supply chain networks (*VUCA* world: Volatility, Uncertainty, Complexity, and Ambiguity), digitalization including online shopping and e-commerce, changes in customer demands, shorter product life cycles, and a rapid increase in the number of stock keeping units (SKUs). Budgetary constraints on businesses and hyper-personalization of the content for customers, which further aggravates this complexity. This requires firms to use procurement processes as a key strategic tool to deliver profits at the tiniest operational and sourcing costs. Consequently, it is increasingly crucial for retail procurement managers to be able to preferably mitigate or otherwise resolve supply issues due to disruptions in such complex supply chains.

The chapter discusses the concept of procurement for retailers by presenting the background that includes a detailed description of the terms associated with retail procurement, followed by state-of-the-art literature in the area, its importance, and the key theories. Next, a discussion on the difference between traditional procurement and procurement with disruptive environments is conducted via specific case studies. Next, there is a discussion of the best practices in retail procurement strategies comprising different retailers. Next is a discussion of the practical and proven managerial procurement strategies for retailers facing disruptions. This is followed by a brief discussion on future developments and other developing areas in retail procurement.

BACKGROUND

Definition for Retail Procurement

Retail procurement is the business process of managing purchases of different goods from wholesalers or suppliers for sale to the public (consumers) in small quantities for their use or consumption. Therefore, a retailer would typically purchase goods in large quantities directly from the manufacturer(s) or through a wholesaler and then sell the product to consumers for a profit margin. This is also referred to as direct procurement. Besides procurement of goods that are sold to the public, retailers need to source products to support their other business activities, which are supporting in nature – maintenance, repair, and operations (MRO). Given the difference in the nature of the MRO products, their procurement is *indirect*, volume is typically low, and they are ordered more frequently. Even though MRO products are indirect, if their procurement is disrupted due to an unpredictable event, the retailer's business operations can be impacted, resulting in losses. The key differences between the procurement for direct and indirect are summarized below in *Table 1.*

Table 1. Retail procurement for direct and indirect products

	Direct products	Indirect products
Examples	• Perishable fresh produce. • Durable goods. • Fashion goods. • Electronics and appliances.	• Mechanical equipment for repairs. • Fuel, tires, etc., for supporting logistics. • Stationery goods and janitor supplies for operations.
Purpose	• Sold directly to the consumer.	• Assist in business maintenance, repair, and operations (MRO).
Procurement strategies	• Purchased in large quantities. • Purchased at a lower frequency. • Purchased at the lowest cost as it directly affects profitability. • Purchased at customer-driven quality metrics with cost constraints to maximize profits.	• Purchased in smaller quantities. • Purchased at a higher frequency. • Purchased at low cost as it directly affects profitability. • Purchased at internally-driven quality metrics with cost and operational constraints.

From the above definition of retail procurement, it is easy to note the importance of procurement strategies that ensure a steady supply stream for both direct and indirect products to keep the business flowing. More importantly, the definition highlights the placement of retailers in the supply chain and their dependence on manufacturers and wholesalers to procure the products at the right cost, time, and quality. Over the years, supply chain experts have optimized the costs and timing of product delivery by off-shoring, reducing inventory and lead-times (Just-in-Time), and working with specialized manufacturers that ensure the consistent quality of their products. These supply chain efficiencies have been significant drivers in improving the profitability of retailers where customers were always able to find products at a low cost, with a huge selection, and always in stock at the retailer's brick-and-mortar store. To some extent, the customers got spoiled by these efficiencies, and when the retailers faced stockouts due to widespread supply chain disruptions in early 2020, it surprised everyone.

Supply Chain Disruptions are not a new Phenomenon

Supply chain disruptions became part of the mainstream discussion during the COVID-19 pandemic when the general public began to experience a scarcity of products. The shortage in products included routine products, such as meat, eggs, bread, toilet paper, and personal protective equipment (PPE), such as hand sanitizers, face shields, and face masks. According to Accenture (2020), about 94 percent, of Fortune 1000 companies reported supply chain disruptions due to COVID-19, and about 75 percent suffered negative impacts on their businesses in the short term. Accenture also reported that 55 percent of companies planned to downgrade their growth outlooks as a result of supply chain disruptions. However, supply chain disruptions at more minor scales were omnipresent even before the pandemic. For instance, retail supply chains for eggs, lettuce, peppers, and meat were disrupted as a result of the discovery of salmonella (USDA, 2022), automotive supply disruptions due to an earthquake in Japan (CNN, 2011), and compromise of the oil and gas pipeline computer systems and network (Bloomberg, 2021). The primary difference between earlier/other supply chain disruptions vis-à-vis the supply chain disruptions due to COVID-19 was the global, worldwide impact of different containment policies by different nations, the differences in the level of spread then, and the availability of containment resources such as medications, vaccines, and other PPE. Many business strategies that mitigate or address such minor scale disruptions could be tailored to apply in widespread supply chain disruptions.

Pandemic and Demand Disruptions: Bullwhip Effect for Supply Chains

When the shutdown occurred due to the global pandemic, there was *panic buying* among consumers, resulting in a sudden spike in demand for products with otherwise stable demand (Yuen et al., 2020). Such demand spikes are often associated with other disasters (earthquakes and hurricanes) or health crises (plague, Ebola, etc.). This demand spike phenomenon is socially undesirable, herd behavior when there is a stockout of daily necessities and medical supplies are purchased from markets. In other words, retail managers need help to meet the sudden increase in the demand for the products with their existing supply stream resulting in empty shelves or stockouts. Panic buying often results in overordering from the retail managers, which exacerbates across the upstream supply chain resulting in the *bullwhip effect* (Ivanov & Dolgui, 2020). This results in a short-term mismatch between the product demand and the available production and/or supply capacity.

Zero-Covid Policy and its Impact on Retail Procurement

In the initial stages of the pandemic, almost all economies shut down to control and minimize the spread of the novel coronavirus. Over time, with the development and immunization of the general population via readily available vaccines, most economies opened up, resuming their supply chain activities and letting go of social distancing requirements. However, certain economies, particularly in Asia – including China, Hongkong, Japan, etc. continued to enforce strict Zero-Covid policies (Higgins-Dunn, 2022; Time, 2022). China has a large presence of manufacturing firms in, that are suppliers for leading retailers in the United States and other economies. The strict Zero-Covid requirements created uncertainty in supply chains due to sudden shutdowns including manufacturing firm located in cities with any reported Covid-19 cases. As a result, there was a shortage of products and ripple effects across the supply chain due to a lack of predictability regarding production volume and delivery times.

Zero-Covid has become one of the select drivers of the global recession - Steve Morrison, senior vice president at the Center for Strategic and International Studies (Higgins-Dunn, 2022). In conclusion, while the demand for certain products spiked due to the pandemic, the supply chain disruptions and Zero-Covid policies reduced the production and supply capacity exacerbating the impact of supply chain disruptions.

The pressure on supply chains is presented in *Figure 1,* captured through the Global Supply Chain Pressure Index (GSCPI), a measurement of supply chain conditions created by the Federal Reserve Bank of New York from 2010 until 2022 (*Federal Reserve Bank of New York*, 2023). GSCPI combines variables from several indices in transportation and manufacturing, such as those related to delivery times, prices, and inventory. This creation of a supply chain index is part of the government initiatives to monitor supply chains and be able to proactively review supply chain trends and guide strategies that ease supply chain pressures. The figure demonstrates that the variability in supply chain pressures increased significantly during the pandemic and has recently started to improve as the pandemic and the supply chains stabilized.

Figure 1. Global supply chain pressure index (GSCPI) spiked during the pandemic (2020-2022)
(Federal Reserve Bank of New York, 2023)

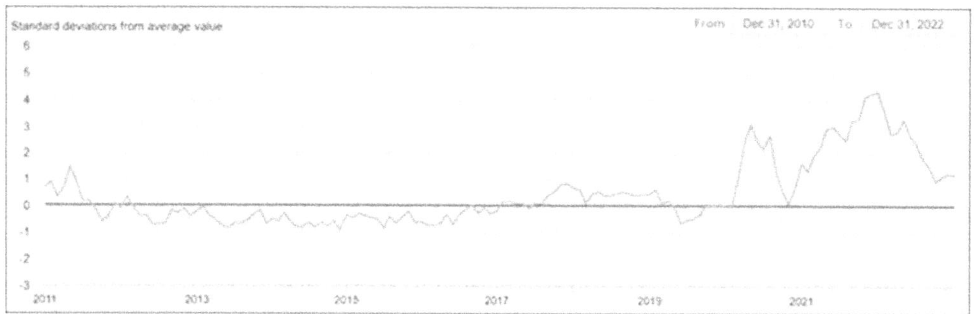

MAIN FOCUS OF THE CHAPTER

Traditionally, the retail procurement process (as shown in *Figure 2*) begins with a retailer listing their requirements based on the product requirements and delivery time. In the next stage, the retailer invites requests for proposals (RFPs) from different suppliers (or manufacturers and wholesalers) that may meet the requirements and then designs the contracts with a selected supplier. This stage is followed by placing an order and receiving the order with the supplier, including payments (remittance). Finally, the buyer rates and reevaluates the supplier's performance for future procurements. In a traditional setting, the product specifications and supplier proposals directly affect the procurement price of the product. The contract lays out the terms for the contracted quantity and delivery lead times for procurement from the supplier to the retailer.

The traditional aspects of the retail procurement process assume that the supplier can always meet the delivery quantity and timelines as there are no supply chain disruptions. In the presence of disruptive events, the procurement process must factor any changes in the product demand (such as demand spikes due to *panic buying*) and suppliers' inability to meet the new demand (supply disruption). Due to supply and demand imbalances, the retailer may source substitute products to increase the supply.

Figure 2. Traditional retail procurement process with stable demand and supply (Gupta, 2019)

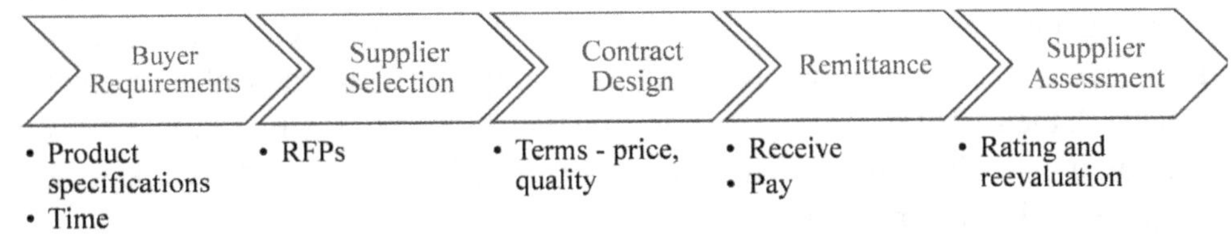

Depending on the product type, the procurement managers should recast their procurement strategy with the additional supply and demand caused by the disruptive environment. This is proposed as a new procurement process due to disruptions and is summarized in *Figure 3*. Next, a case study on Amazon is discussed, where the company was able to respond to the demand-side and supply-side changes swiftly and delivered more than 100 million PPE in a short period of time to hospitals and public health agencies in the United States.

Figure 3. Revised inputs for procurement process in disruptive environments

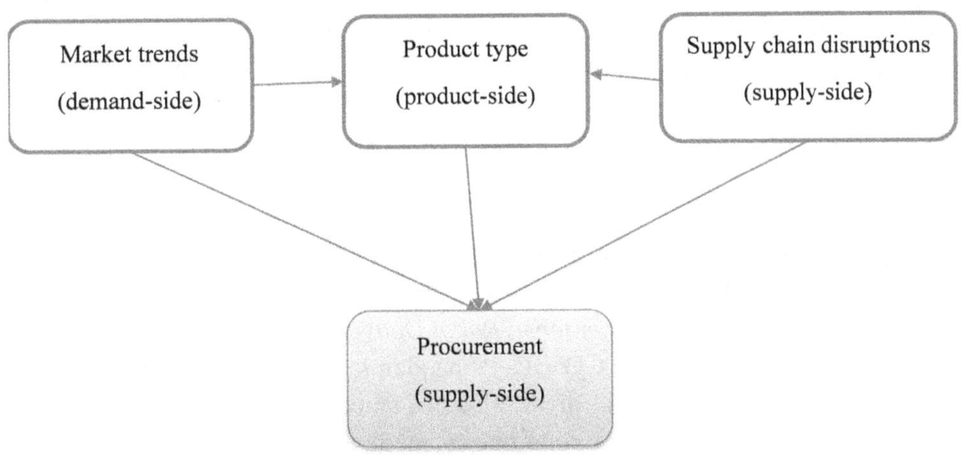

Case Study of Amazon: PPE and Critical Supplies

During the initial stages of the COVID-19 disruption, there was a sharp increase in the demand for PPE to mitigate the spread of the disease. More than 13,000 healthcare and 7,000 government organizations purchased PPE and other critical supplies (About Amazon, 2020) from the *COVID-19 Supplies* program created by Amazon Business. This resulted in a mismatch between the available PPE and critical goods and their demand. Amazon shipped the health and safety products such as facial shields, surgical masks, ventilators, digital thermometers, exam gloves, medical gowns, sanitizers, and wipes go directly to entities with the most urgent need with *Free and Priority Deliveries*. The program later expanded to other countries such as Canada, the United Kingdom, France, Germany, Italy, Spain, Japan and India. Amazon leveraged their supply chain expertise and existing resources to vet, certify, distribute, and deliver vital products to organizations delivering medical care and public health services. This was possible only because Amazon could identify customer demand, track suppliers using their platform and procure and deliver products with their existing and agile supply chain and logistics network. In other words, with a minimal reconfiguration of their supply chains (due to their agility), Amazon was able to deliver critical supplies to hospitals and government health agencies.

Omnichannel Retailing and Delivery Strategies due to Disruption

Many large retailers across the globe built or participated in online sales channels to reach out to their customers when physical stores were required to be shut down due to governmental policies in the early stages of the pandemic. For instance, Target and Wal-Mart adopted online delivery and/or pick-up options for their customers. Similarly, many retailers started contactless delivery using human labor and in some instances robots to avoid human-to-human interactions resulting in a transmission of the coronavirus. The following sections begin with a case study of JD.com, discussing how the company used robots for deliveries in areas that were quarantined with COVID-19 patients. Next, another case study of Target is discussed regarding their newly adopted "order online and pickup *contactless* in the store or do a curbside pick-up" policy resulting in omnichannel retail sales and its impact on their procurement policies. This helps the retailer learn the customer demand and allocate the available inventory to match the customer demand making it a pull inventory management system instead of the traditional push inventory management system with the presence of a brick-and-mortar store.

Case Study of JD.com: Robot Delivery for Social Distancing

JD.com is a large e-commerce company in China (comparable to Amazon.com in the United States). During the pandemic in 2020, when human-to-human contact was discouraged in observance of social distancing practices to control the spread of the coronavirus, JD.com launched their robot delivery fleet program in Wuhan (*JD.Com to Launch Unmanned Robot Delivery Fleet in Quarantined Wuhan*, 2020). Wuhan is considered the epicenter of the COVID-19 pandemic, and the robots would avoid any virus transmissions. For the virus-affected rural areas, JD.com launched a drone-delivery program where drones can deliver prevention supplies, including masks, medical gloves, goggles, disinfectants, etc., to major hospitals in those regions. With the adoption of novel contactless delivery strategies, the retailer was able to meet the demand for critical supplies with their existing product supply.

Case Study of Target: Buy Online With In-Store Pickup or Drive-Up

Target partnered with Shipt delivery for same day delivery services to its online customers and offered drive-up (contactless) pickup for customers on the same day. Adopting these two sales and product delivery programs resulted in an increase of about 10.8% in quarterly sales for Target in the second quarter of 2020.

Throughout the first quarter, our team and guests faced unprecedented challenges arising from the spread of COVID-19. In the face of those challenges, our team showed extraordinary resilience as guests relied on Target as a trusted resource for their families.- Brian Cornell, CEO, Target (USA TODAY, 2020).

In response to their increased online sales, Target's procurement team increased their online inventory instead of their in-store inventory. In particular, they launched one of their designer clothes product lines (Designer Dress Collection with partners LoveShackFancy, Cushnie, and Lisa Marie Fernandez) exclusively online because of the COVID-19 disruption (USA TODAY, 2020). This is an interesting case study for procurement managers as Target increased their sales effectively during the pandemic despite the disruptions. Target's ability to quickly adopt the online sales platform Shipt and reconfigure their drive-up program to meet the new normal were creative ways to match the increased demand with the reconfiguration of their online inventory and omnichannel sales platforms. Other retailers, such as Walmart, Walgreens, etc., also successfully adopted an omnichannel strategy to match customer demand with their supply.

Mitigation and Responsive Strategies to Supply Disruptions

Mitigation Strategies: In an ideal scenario, retailers must select procurement strategies (supply-side) that can *mitigate* or avoid the impact of a supply disruption. Operational mitigation strategies are typically divided into three categories: inventory, sourcing, and manufacturing (Gupta et al., 2015; Tomlin, 2006, 2009). Their purpose, advantages and limitations are discussed below:

1. **Safety stock inventory:** An extra quantity of a product stored in the warehouse to prevent out-of-stock scenarios and meet the increased demand or match demand in the event of supply disruptions. Adequate safety stock results in higher inventory costs but prevents the cost of losing customer demand due to stockouts.
2. **Multi sourcing:** A procurement strategy that involves working with multiple suppliers who may also be competitors. The suppliers can sell either the same product or substitute products with differences in quality and price. The primary advantage of working with multiple suppliers is managing the risk of supply disruption in the event a supplier is unable to meet the contracted supply quantity. However, working with multiple suppliers can result in issues such as higher product cost, lower product quality, differential lead times, etc.
3. **Rerouting:** An operational strategy where the retailer invests in excess manufacturing capacity before the supply disruption to be able to ramp up the production at a different manufacturing facility with sufficient production capacity that is not affected by supply disruption. The advantage of this strategy is that it allows for the same quality and consistency of the product allowing for a quick recovery from the disruption. However, this operational strategy relies on heavy financial investments in building production capacity that may be redundant when the product demand and supply chain are stable.

As discussed above, all the strategies lead to higher operating costs for the retailer. This will affect the company's bottom line, specifically when the risk of supply disruption is uncertain and the investments in mitigation are never realized. However, as retailers continue to digitalize their supply chains increasing visibility, tracking, and transparency, the risk can be calculated better. As a result, the companies can conduct a **cost-benefit analysis** to choose one or some of the mitigation strategies to avoid the negative impacts of disruption. There are other non-traditional mitigation strategies:

- information sharing between the supply chain partners,
- designing wholesale price contracts that are also risk-sharing contracts (Wakolbinger & Cruz, 2011), and
- financial investing in increasing the capacity of a supplier (Gupta & Chutani, 2020) to respond to supply disruptions.

Readers are recommended to review this literature to learn more about these additional mitigation strategies.

Responsive Strategies: In real life, the time of onset of a disruption in an environment is unpredictable, as is its impact on the different nodes in the supply chain. Therefore, most retailers would first assess the impact of a supply chain disruption on their supply stream and then select a strategy to respond. For instance, if a supply disruption occurs due port's shutdown, they can reroute the goods through a different logistics route. In another case, if the supply disruption occurred due to malfunctioning at a particular manufacturing plant, then the retailer may respond by sourcing from a different manufacturer or a supplier to meet the demand. In instances where the supply shortages are evaluated to be temporary, the retailer may also respond with strategies that manage or control the customer demand. For example, in the early stages of the pandemic, there was a sudden spike in demand for critical sanitizing supplies, such as hand sanitizers and disinfectant wipes. The retailers responded to this disruption by limiting (rationing) the units of hand sanitizer or wipes customers can purchase at a time. On the other hand, some retailers decided to increase the price of goods with limited supply, reducing the demand for the products or offering substitute products to help meet the demand.

Operational responsive strategies during disruption can be divided into three categories: inventory management, sourcing, and demand management (Gupta et al., 2015; Tomlin, 2006, 2009). Their purpose, advantages, and limitations are discussed below:

1. **Rationing:** A strategy to manage demand by limiting the number of units a customer or a household can buy. This is a useful strategy to ensure that most customers can buy essential products, such as healthcare and food products. For example, Target, Walmart, etc., restricted shoppers on how many COVID-19-related products they could buy (Tyko, 2020).
2. **Pricing:** Pricing is an effective tool to manage the spike in demand due to supply disruptions, especially for non-essential products with elastic demand (Gupta et al., 2021). Retailers can temporarily increase the product's price to reduce the demand to match the limited supply.
3. **Sourcing:** Contingent sourcing in the presence of disruptions is a procurement strategy where an *emergency* or *expedited* order is placed with a backup or undisrupted supplier to fulfill the demand (Gupta et al., 2021). The advantage of the strategy is that the retailer can still meet any excess demand. However, the cost of procurement is likely to increase due to the emergency order. The emergency product can be identical or a close substitute for the product.

All these strategies are responsive and do not need any investments to manage the supply chain risk before the disruption event. However, with these strategies, the retailer is likely to experience stockouts for a short time, and the recovery from the disruption event will be slower compared to the mitigation strategies. Most retailers had just-in-time procurement strategies and were responsive in their procurement strategies resulting in stocked out shelves during the pandemic. As the retailers digitalize their supply chains, the true risk of disruption can be calculated better. Companies can conduct a cost-benefit analysis and a scenario simulation to choose between different responsive or mitigation strategies.

Improving Supply Chain Visibility to Avoid Supply Disruptions

Supply chain visibility is the ability to track the product, its components, sub-components, and the raw materials in transit and at different supply chain nodes, giving managers a clear picture of the pipeline inventory and supply chain activities (transportation, production, customs, warehousing) (Svoboda, 2020). The visibility across the supply chain helps proactively resolve and reduce the impact of supply disruptions. When it is impossible to mitigate the disruption, transparency in supply chains can help retail procurement managers respond to a future disruption sooner than the scenario with limited or no visibility in the supply chains. Some of the benefits of supply chain visibility to retail procurement include:

1. **Risk management:** Procurement managers can mitigate any supply risks with easier and real-time tracking and traceability of the products.
2. **Reduction in costs:** Due to fewer disruption costs, procurement can save on the costs related to service and delivery disruptions.
3. **Better data access:** Supply chain visibility is implemented by digitalizing the supply chains via RFID (radio frequency identification) tags, blockchain, and software (IBM, 2023). Procurement managers can strategize their procurement decisions (contracts, service levels, etc.) with more data across the supply chain. This can even drive retail sales up to 5.5% (GS1, 2018).

Case Study of Nordstrom: Centralized Sourcing With Visibility and Automation

Nordstrom, a leading fashion retailer in the United States, began their supply chain transformation journey in 2019 when they hired Karoline Dygas as Chief Procurement Officer (Trebilcock, 2021). Before the transformation, Nordstrom had a decentralized approach to procurement where every business unit within the company could source products from any supplier they wanted. Nordstrom transformed that procurement model to a centralized sourcing model, where they had one master contract with a supplier with consistent pricing streamlining their supplier base. Another advantage of centralization is risk management. Centralization improves supply chain visibility, resulting in reduced risk.

Besides centralizing the procurement and visibility on its upstream supply chain, Nordstrom invested in their downstream supply chain for improved inventory, fulfillment visibility, and predictability. They implemented a combined solution of Attabotics and Tompkins Robotics to modernize the storage and sortation of these products, which uses up to an estimated 90% less footprint within their distribution facility. Attabotics enables Nordstrom to house aisles worth of products in a compact space and is highly flexible, so it can fit into a variety of spaces and adapt to changes in customer demand. Tompkins Robotics utilizes small autonomous robotics to sort the products by orders, shipping destination, and shipping timing, improving the fulfillment process.

In conclusion, besides traditional supply disruption mitigation strategies, many leading retailers are investing in digitalizing their supply chains to improve visibility. This makes the supply chains more resilient to disruptions. With better supply chain visibility, the procurement managers for retailers can respond proactively to any unpredictable, disruptive events and secure supplies for products using the traditional responsive strategies highlighted earlier.

Issues, Controversies, Problems

The solutions discussed in this book chapter are agnostic to the size and resources of a retailer. During prolonged and widespread disruptive environments, many small and medium-sized enterprises (SMEs) lacked the capital resources toimplement costly but effective procurement strategies to sustain their operations (McKinsey, 2020).

More recently, most retail procurement managers are facing the challenge of including the retailer's ESG goals via a sustainable procurement strategy (NRF, 2021; Thomson Reuters, 2022). Sustainable procurement can potentially result in sourcing practices where there are only a limited number of suppliers, substitute products, or production capacity. This may amplify the impact of any supply chain disruption on the retailer. Another challenge with the current solutions is that they are primarily focused on the recovery of the supply stream in the most efficient way. The strategies discussed do not factor in any issues with increased carbon footprint, the wastefulness of resources, the impact on climate, and the impact on other industries and labor. For instance, having redundancy in the supply chain is good. However, once that redundancy needs to be eliminated when supply chains become stable, there will be a loss of business that can potentially lead to a loss of jobs for labor at the supplier. However, with digitalization and improved supply chain transparency, retailers and suppliers must better align their objectives so that these issues can be resolved at an earlier stage without leading to environmental, labor, or other issues.

SOLUTIONS AND RECOMMENDATIONS

Procurement managers can respond to supply disruptions after the fact or devise strategies that reduce the risk of unpredictable disruptions. The primary goal of retail procurement is to establish a steady supply stream to match the consumer demand for their products and services. These strategies rely on efficiently managing their supply stream and are summarized in *Table 2.*

Table 2. Strategies for managing supply chain disruptions for retail procurement

	Responsive (short-term)	**Mitigation (Long-term)**
Purpose	Responsive strategies are employed when supply disruption has occurred.	Mitigation strategies are employed to prevent supply disruptions.
Examples		
Inventory Management	• Rationing. • Limit the number of units purchased by a customer.	• Maintaining safety stock inventory. • Prevents stockouts.
Sourcing	• Contingent sourcing with emergency or expedited orders from suppliers. • Source substitute products.	• Broaden the supplier base with multi-sourcing strategy. • Invest in supplier to reduce their supply disruption risk.
Other methods	• Change the product prices temporarily to better manage the increased demand. • Utilize supply chain visibility data to predict and respond to disruption sooner.	• Build excess manufacturing capacity so that there is quick recovery from the supply disruption. • Improve supply chain transparency and visibility to reduce the risk of supply chain disruptions.

Besides the long-term mitigation strategies presented above, it is always necessary for the procurement team to work in tandem with other functional units in retail, including warehousing, stores, finance, etc., to devise a strategic plan that relies on improving inventory visibility among all the entities. Most mitigation strategies require capital investments and may not be a good return on investments in the short term resulting in fewer buyouts from the senior management in the company. However, if there is a high level of supply chain visibility, the risk of disruptive environments can be estimated more accurately and understood better by the stakeholders. Therefore, procurement managers must evaluate their specific supply chain risks to adopt a responsive or mitigating strategy.

FUTURE RESEARCH DIRECTIONS

This book chapter explores different challenges that retail managers experience when supply disruptions occur. It provides strategies and insights into different strategies with several case studies and tips for academics and practitioners. The contents of the book chapter are written with an organization and managerial view where procurement is an integral part of a retailer's operations and is not outsourced to a third party. Procurement processes, in practice, are also affected by the size of the retailer and its supply chain partners, country, legal regulations, etc., which are not discussed in the current book chapter. In addition, as indicated in the section on future trends in retail strategies, the procurement processes are undergoing radical changes. In the near future, some of the steps and processes which are highlighted in the book chapter may not be relevant anymore. Detailed future research must be carried out to observe and predict the changes in retail procurement strategies due to the implementation of smart contracts, blockchains, digital supply chains, and ESG (environmental, social, and governance) concerns (NRF, 2021). It will also be interesting to see the detailed impact of the use of social media and social networks on the retailer's procurement decisions. In conclusion, the area of best practices for retail managers is evolving rapidly. In conclusion, the area of best practices for retail managers is evolving rapidly. More research is required to assess the overall impact of the process changes and to build helpful case studies for academics and practitioners.

CONCLUSION

Disruptive environments, including the global pandemic, hurricanes, earthquakes, cyber-attacks, or strict government policies, such as the Zero-Covid policy in China, resulting in distinct supply chain disruptions. Additionally, customer demand for certain retail goods may spike during such disruptions challenging the strategies for procurement developed by retailers for supply chains with stable and predictable demand and steady sources of supply. Therefore, retail managers must adopt procurement plans that are resilient to disruptions and agile enough by adopting strategies such as near-shoring, dual- or multi-sourcing, inventory pooling, etc., to meet the short-term demand and recover smoothly from such disruptions. Most retailers admit that supply chain disruptions impact their business negatively. However, not many procurement managers planned to overcome the impact before the COVID-19 pandemic.

Procurement managers must review their existing supply chains and examine the weaknesses that can result in supply bottlenecks due to disruptive events. Additionally, retailers must proactively mitigate the spiked customer demand and alleviate the *panic buying* phenomenon by limiting purchases, rationing, pricing, etc. In conclusion, supply chain transparency measures, such as digitalization coupled with existing procurement strategies to reduce supply disruption risk and demand management strategies, can be effective response tools during disruptive environments.

REFERENCES

Amazon. (2020). *More than 100 million items delivered to healthcare and government organizations*. Amazon. https://www.aboutamazon.com/news/company-news/over-100-million-items-delivered-to-healthcare-and-government-organizations

Accenture. (2020). *Supply Chain Disruption & How to Respond.* Accenture. https://www.accenture.com/us-en/insights/consulting/coronavirus-supply-chain-disruption

Bloomberg. (2021). *Colonial Pipeline Cyber Attack: Hackers Used Compromised Password*. Bloomberg. https://www.bloomberg.com/news/articles/2021-06-04/hackers-breached-colonial-pipeline-using-compromised-password

Chowdhury, P., Paul, S. K., Kaisar, S., & Moktadir, M. (2021). COVID-19 pandemic related supply chain studies: A systematic review. *Transportation Research Part E, Logistics and Transportation Review*, *148*, 102271. doi:10.1016/j.tre.2021.102271 PMID:33613082

CNN. (2011). *Toyota making drastic production cuts after Japan quake, tsunami*. CNN. http://www.cnn.com/2011/WORLD/asiapcf/04/20/japan.toyota/index.html

Federal Reserve Bank of New York. (2023). *Global Supply Chain Pressure Index*. New Yotrk Fed. https://newyorkfed.org/research/policy/gscpi

GS1. (2018). *New report shows RFID delivers retail sales increase by up to 5.5%*. GS1. https://www.gs1.org/articles/new-report-shows-rfid-delivers-retail-sales-increase-by-55

Gupta, V. (2019). Procurement Strategies for Digital Supply Chains: Concepts and Best Practices [Chapter]. *Technology Optimization and Change Management for Successful Digital Supply Chains,* IGI Global. doi:10.4018/978-1-5225-7700-3.ch002

Gupta, V., & Chutani, A. (2020). Supply chain financing with advance selling under disruption. *International Transactions in Operational Research*, *27*(5), 2449–2468. doi:10.1111/itor.12663

Gupta, V., He, B., & Sethi, S. P. (2015). Contingent sourcing under supply disruption and competition. *International Journal of Production Research*, *53*(10), 3006–3027. doi:10.1080/00207543.2014.965351

Gupta, V., Ivanov, D., & Choi, T.-M. (2021). Competitive pricing of substitute products under supply disruption. *Omega*, *101*, 102279. doi:10.1016/j.omega.2020.102279 PMID:32836689

Higgins-Dunn, N. (2022). *How China's strict Covid policies led to supply chain bottlenecks*. CNBC. https://www.cnbc.com/2022/08/19/how-chinas-covid-policies-lead-to-hampered-supply-chains-higher-inflation.html

IBM. (2023). *Supply Chain Visibility Software and Solutions.* IBM. https://www.ibm.com/supply-chain/visibility

Ivanov, D., & Dolgui, A. (2020). Viability of intertwined supply networks: Extending the supply chain resilience angles towards survivability. A position paper motivated by COVID-19 outbreak. *International Journal of Production Research, 58*(10), 2904–2915. doi:10.1080/00207543.2020.1750727

JD.com to launch unmanned robot delivery fleet in quarantined Wuhan. (2020, February 5). KrASIA. https://kr-asia.com/jd-com-to-launch-unmanned-robot-delivery-fleet-in-quarantined-wuhan

Leonard, M. (2020). *MSC adds instant quotes to website.* Supply Chain Dive. https://www.supplychaindive.com/news/msc-instant-booking-quotes/580869/

McKinsey. (2020). *Tracking the impact of coronavirus on US small businesses.* McKinsey. https://www.mckinsey.com/industries/financial-services/our-insights/tracking-us-small-and-medium-sized-business-sentiment-during-covid-19

NRF. (2021). *Retail Supply Chains and ESG.* NRF. https://nrf.com/topics/sustainability/esg-tool-kit/retail-supply-chains-and-esg

Sabri, E. (2019). *Technology Optimization and Change Management for Successful Digital Supply Chains.* IGI Global. https://www.igi-global.com/gateway/book/209464

Svoboda, S. (2020, August 17). *Ways Supply Chain Visibility Can Help Mitigate Risk.* Hitachi Solutions. https://global.hitachi-solutions.com/blog/supply-chain-visibility/

Thomson Reuters. (2022, January 31). *How procurement and supply chains drive corporate ESG objectives.* Thomson Reuters. https://tax.thomsonreuters.com/blog/procurement-supply-chain-environmental-social-governance-objectives/

Time. (2022). *China's Zero-Covid Is Here To Stay, Experts Say.* Time. https://time.com/6233563/china-zero-covid-end/

Tomlin, B. (2006). On the Value of Mitigation and Contingency Strategies for Managing Supply Chain Disruption Risks. *Management Science, 52*(5), 639–657. doi:10.1287/mnsc.1060.0515

Tomlin, B. (2009). Disruption-management strategies for short life-cycle products. [NRL]. *Naval Research Logistics, 56*(4), 318–347. doi:10.1002/nav.20344

Trebilcock, B. (2021). *Transforming procurement at Nordstrom.* Supply Chain 24/7. https://www.supplychain247.com/article/transforming_procurement_at_nordstrom/Procurement

Tyko, C. M. (2020). *Coronavirus rationing: Target, Walmart limit purchases of hand sanitizer, disinfecting wipes, toilet paper.* USA TODAY. https://www.usatoday.com/story/money/2020/03/11/coronavirus-preparation-walmart-target-ration-limiting-hand-sanitizer-di
sinfecting-wipes/5020751002/

USA Today. (2020). Target same-day services like Drive Up and Shipt delivery grew by 278% fueled by COVID-19. *USA Today.* https://www.usatoday.com/story/money/2020/05/20/target-earnings-2020-digital-sales-grow-coronavirus/5226791002/

USDA. (2022). New USDA Policy on Salmonella in Poultry Offers Hope for Progress on Foodborne Illness · Consumer Federation of America. *Consumer Federation of America*. https://consumerfed.org/press_release/new-usda-policy-on-salmonella-in-poultry-offers-hope-for-progress-on-foodborne-illness/

Wakolbinger, T., & Cruz, J. M. (2011). Supply chain disruption risk management through strategic information acquisition and sharing and risk-sharing contracts. *International Journal of Production Research*, *49*(13), 4063–4084. doi:10.1080/00207543.2010.501550

World Health Organization. (2020). *Pneumonia of unknown cause – China*. WHO. https://www.who.int/emergencies/disease-outbreak-news/item/2020-DON229

Yuen, K. F., Wang, X., Ma, F., & Li, K. X. (2020). The Psychological Causes of Panic Buying Following a Health Crisis. *International Journal of Environmental Research and Public Health*, *17*(10), 10. doi:10.3390/ijerph17103513 PMID:32443427

KEY TERMS AND DEFINITIONS

Blockchain: A digital ledger that is decentralized, distributed, and public. Blockchains are deployed to record transactions across many computers so that the original assets can be tracked and traced for any changes.

Bullwhip Effect: A supply chain phenomenon describing how small fluctuations in the retail demand results in progressively larger fluctuations in the upstream supply chain demand at the wholesale, distributor, manufacturer, and raw material supplier levels.

Cost-Benefit Analysis: A way to compare the costs and benefits of a strategy, where both the costs and the benefits of implementing a strategy are expressed in monetary units. A strategy will be implemented when the benefits outweigh the costs and not otherwise.

Cyber Security: The protection of computer systems and networks from attack by malicious agents that may result in unwanted or unauthorized information disclosure, theft of, or damage to the hardware, software, or data, as well as from the disruption or misdirection of the services provided by the computer systems.

Digitalization: The process of converting information into a digital (bits – 0,1) format, i.e., readable by computers. This allows any information to be stored, processed, and transmitted easily by using a network of computers.

Disruption: An event or occurrence that results in the interruption of an activity or a process. The global spread of COVID-19 led to a complete stop and often interrupted supply chain flows.

End-to-End Supply Chain: Refers to the philosophy of considering the entire supply chain from the customer to the end supplier, eliminating any wasteful processes or middle steps, and optimizing the entire supply chain.

e-Procurement: The process of using an electronic or online (web-based) network to buy and sell products in a B2B (Business-to-business) setting or a B2C (Business-to-consumer) setting. Government organizations also use it for procurement. RFQ, RFP, etc., are conducted online in an e-Procurement setting.

Machine Learning/AI: The statistical process allowing machines to learn and act intelligently (make decisions using information) using historical data.

Omnichannel: A multichannel approach to sales that seeks to provide customers with a seamless shopping experience across different channels, including online, in-store, third-party platforms, mobile, etc.

Panic Buying: A socially undesirable herd behavior when a demand spike of daily necessities and medical supplies are purchased from markets, often resulting in stockout situations at the retailers.

Chapter 14
Reverse Logistics in the Digital Supply Chain Era

Laxita Sabadra
University of Texas at Dallas, USA

ABSTRACT

The chapter is focused on understanding the concepts of reverse logistics (RL) in the digital supply chain management era. In today's world, returned products and their recovery management has become very important for companies, thus, through this chapter the author summarizes the entire returns process from a buyer and seller point of view. What are the different factors involved in the decision making of returned products and how does it affect the entire supply chain? The chapter also aims to understand costs related to reverse logistics, optimization of the process, and lastly the significance of various reverse logistics strategies that can benefit organizations.

INTRODUCTION

As the world is growing into digitalization and e-business models, reverse logistics is getting more and more crucial to companies. Today with online businesses, we just think of a product and get it ordered knowing that if we don't like it, we can return it without any explanation and get a full refund with a single click.

It seems really tempting as a customer, but is it as simple as it looks for the companies? Being a supply chain professional, what are the things that come to mind? Is reversing the flow of product that easy? In the current era of highly volatile geo-political situations and other uncontrollable external factors like pandemics and natural disasters, when even the forward supply chain is greatly disrupted, how are companies dealing with reverse supply chain? Why should one learn the reverse logistics principles and research optimization techniques? To get the answers to these questions, it is important to understand the concepts around logistics and reverse flow. The chapter discusses about supply chain, digitalization, reverse logistics and related concepts.

DOI: 10.4018/978-1-6684-7298-9.ch014

LITERATURE REVIEW

Reverse logistics is the process of planning, implementing, and controlling the efficient and cost-effective flow of raw materials, finished goods, and related information from the point of consumption to the point of origin for the purpose of recapturing value or proper disposal. In the digital era, with the increasing use of technology and e-commerce, reverse logistics has become more complex and critical for businesses. This literature review explores the latest trends, challenges, and opportunities in reverse logistics in the digital era.

1. Trends:

The emergence of e-commerce has significantly impacted reverse logistics, resulting in a surge of returned products. As per the national retail federation and digital commerce surveys, return rates in e-commerce industry are 16.5 compared to 9.7% in physical stores (Conley, 2023 and Inman n.d., 2022). Returns rate in e-commerce industry is 40% more than physical stores. In addition, customers' expectations have changed, with more emphasis on easy returns, faster processing, and transparent tracking of the return status. The integration of technology, such as artificial intelligence, blockchain, and the internet of things, has enabled the automation of many reverse logistics processes, resulting in reduced costs and improved efficiency (Eljelly, 2019).

2. Challenges:

Despite the benefits of technology, there are still challenges that businesses face in managing reverse logistics in the digital era. One significant challenge is the complexity of reverse logistics operations, which require coordination between different departments, partners, and systems. The lack of standardized processes and metrics further complicates the management of reverse logistics (Kiesmüller et al., 2017). In addition, the increasing volume of returned products puts pressure on companies to find sustainable and cost-effective ways to dispose of or recycle them, which is becoming more difficult due to stricter regulations and limited recycling options (Singh & Gupta, 2021).

3. Opportunities:

Reverse logistics in the digital era presents several opportunities for businesses to improve their sustainability, customer satisfaction, and profitability. One opportunity is the use of data analytics to gain insights into the reasons for returns and to identify patterns and trends that can help prevent future returns (Barnett & Clark, 2019). Another opportunity is the collaboration with third-party logistics providers and recyclers, which can help companies to optimize their reverse logistics processes and reduce costs (Ganesan et al., 2019). Finally, the adoption of circular economy principles, such as designing products for reuse and recycling, can create new revenue streams and reduce waste (Linton et al., 2016).

4. Conclusion:

Reverse logistics is a critical component of supply chain management, and in the digital era, it has become even more complex and important. The integration of technology, such as AI and blockchain, has enabled businesses to automate many reverse logistics processes, resulting in cost savings and improved efficiency. However, there are still challenges that need to be addressed, such as the lack of standardized processes and sustainable disposal options. Businesses can leverage the opportunities presented by the digital era, such as data analytics and circular economy principles, to improve their reverse logistics operations and achieve their sustainability and profitability goals.

Introduction to Reverse Logistics

Logistics is the organized management of material from point of origin to point of consumption. It is a crucial part of supply chain management without which the supply chain is incomplete. There are two major types of logistics: forward logistics and reverse logistics. Reverse logistics is exactly the opposite of natural forward supply chain logistics; It is the movement of the product from buyer to seller. The foremost objective of reverse logistics is to reduce cost by minimizing expenses and creating maximum value out of the returned products to recover most of the cost. The basic common flow of reverse logistics can be seen in the below diagram. Eventually, reverse logistics merges back to the natural chain of buying/selling operations. Hence, this principle is called as circular economy principle where products are repurposed in various ways like resell, recycling or scrapping.

Figure 1. Reverse logistics process

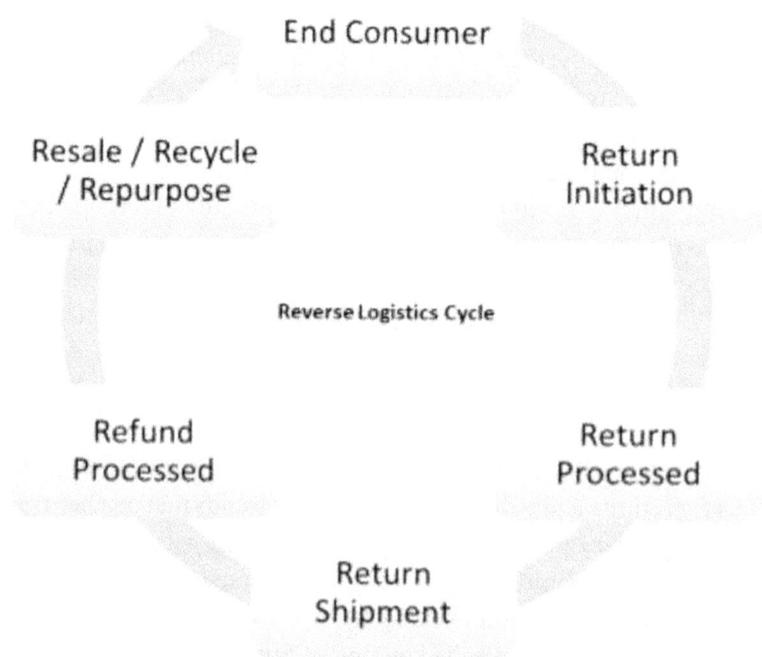

History of Reverse Logistics

Though the Reverse Logistics term officially entered the supply chain industry in the late 90s, the concept is similar to the practice of the historical barter system in some form. The differences between now and then are returns were not a part of the business, the burden of the cost of return operations was on the consumer, and there was no guarantee of a refund. It is human nature to check for the good quality of a purchased item and get it returned or exchanged if the quality is not satisfactory.

In the recent history, the roots of reverse logistics can be seen and traced during civil wars in 18th century and world wars in 19th century. Most of those operations were relating to military as the wars were at the end and every country was trying to get back their resources. All the resources such as equipment, vehicles which were damaged from wars and cannot be repaired were resold, remanufactured and reused. Another story to trace back the reverse logistics is of an American furniture store founded in 1872. A consumer could return any furniture purchased from Montgomery Ward, for a full refund if they were not completely satisfied (Mzugovic, 2022).

And later reverse logistics came into high attention when environmental awareness was raised. Many recycling and reusing programs were initiated by different countries, environmental activists. And recently offering returns services has been one of the top selling features for companies especially with the growing competition all around the world.

Why Study Reverse Logistics?

Though reverse logistics has been practiced for a long time, it needs to be studied and optimized properly in today's globalized market. It is a highly competitive era which is becoming increasingly complex for several reasons.

In the current market, according to Gautam (2022), "44% of retailers say their margins are negatively affected by handling returns, and 37% of companies cited software as the main impediment in handling Reverse Logistics". This signifies deeply that reverse logistics is needed to be studied and hence improved.

One of the major reasons for studying reverse logistics is rising customer expectations. The more the competition increases, the more companies will try to offer exceptional services like free returns. With the current market situation, the competition is not just limited to city, state, or country—it is global. And even local companies and small businesses must acquire the new practices with a change in customer expectations to help businesses remain relevant in such global competitive environment.

Another reason to study and optimize reverse supply chain is to recover the maximum salvage value from the returned item before the end of its useful life. With time, the percentage of returns have begun to rise and soon will become a significant part of total sells. According to Lazar (2022), "new studies finds that 15% to 40% of purchases are returned, with returns doubling over the past 3 years alone".

It is going to be difficult to fully eliminate returns, but the related costs can certainly be optimized and reduced. For that, it is important to understand which factors are making customers initiate the returns and come up with business strategies to deal with it.

Reverse Logistics in Retail Industry

The retail industry is an integral part of the economy, and the success of this industry relies heavily on its supply chain management. Reverse logistics, the process of handling returned goods and their associated information, is becoming increasingly important in the retail industry. The reverse logistics process includes the collection, transportation, processing, and repurposing or disposal of products, as well as the information management involved in these activities. There are several vital reasons which explains why reverse logistics is critical to the retail industry:

1. Reduced Costs: One of the main reasons why reverse logistics is critical to the retail industry is that it helps to reduce costs. When customers return products, it can result in additional expenses for the retailer, including transportation costs, processing fees, and disposal costs. By implementing effective reverse logistics processes, retailers can minimize these costs and increase profitability. For example, they can use consolidated returns programs to minimize transportation costs, and they can implement recycling programs to reduce disposal costs.
2. Improved Customer Satisfaction: Another reason why reverse logistics is critical to the retail industry is that it can improve customer satisfaction. When customers can return products easily and efficiently, they are more likely to have a positive perception of the retailer. In the world of e-commerce, the ability to easily return items has become a key factor in customer satisfaction. By implementing effective reverse logistics processes, retailers can ensure that customers receive prompt refunds or exchanges, and that their needs are met in a timely and efficient manner. This can help to build customer loyalty and improve the overall customer experience.
3. Inventory Management: Reverse logistics plays a crucial role in managing inventory levels for retailers. Effective management of returned products enables retailers to minimize inventory holding costs, optimize inventory levels, and improve stock availability.
4. Environmental Sustainability: Reverse logistics is also critical to the retail industry because it promotes environmental sustainability. By implementing recycling programs and other sustainable practices, retailers can reduce their environmental impact and help to protect the planet. This can also help to improve the retailer's image and reputation, as more and more consumers are becoming aware of the importance of sustainability.

As the retail industry continues to evolve, reverse logistics will become even more important in helping retailers to stay competitive and successful.

Strategizing the Reasons for Returns

The reasons behind returning items may vary from product to product. For example, the most common reason for returning clothing items is wrong size or poor fit, while electronic items are often returned for being defective. Though it is impossible to get inside the mind of every customer, the most common reasons for returns are as follows:

1. Wrong product: This reason contains two sides: Either the customer has ordered the wrong product, or the seller shipped the wrong one. Incorrect product selection on the customer's end can be reduced by improving visibility of the key features and articulating the item's concerns/compatibility. Wrong product shipment on the seller's end can be reduced by improving the order management and logistics processes.
2. Poor fit: This reason for return is prominent with fashion accessories, footwear, and clothing companies. A poor fit product has zero use to the customer. To curb this down companies can make

sure the product has Q&A answered, real customer reviews, and photos/videos of customers. This will help the potential customer order precisely.

3. Defective product: This reason is found in most household, decorative, and electronic item companies. It is very difficult to conduct the root cause analysis for this reason, as the product can be damaged at any step in the supply chain. To reduce this type of defect, one can set quality control checks at the various steps in the supply chain process.
4. Product no longer needed: Sometimes we see random and irrational purchasing behavior among the customers. These types of purchases result in the returns or product in this category. One can only eliminate these types of returns by providing the maximum number of benefits in the item description to let customer understand the usability of the product.
5. Found better pricing elsewhere: This type of reason is found during the holiday seasons when offers and discounts flood the market. It is natural consumer behavior to get the item at the lowest cost. To eliminate these types of returns, many companies do price matching. Another thing companies can do is set competitive prices in the first place.
6. Fraudulent returns: This return is a type of fraud that could be done on digital platforms. Customers intentionally claim several reasons such as the item being defective, the package never arriving, or even that the return package was shipped but they never received the refund. At times, the customer just uses the product for some occasion and returns it once event is over, i.e., a Halloween costume. You may also see that your product was swapped with a low-quality item and then returned. To lessen these types of returns one can take several actions, such as preferring credit cards for refunds as they protect transactions from theft, request signatures on return documents, or reduce the number of days in the return window.

Basically, improving customer satisfaction by all means is the only solution to reduce the initiation of returns on the customer's end. Scrutinizing the refunds, their respective reasons, related information, and solving them strategically can help the company substantially reduce the returns and related costs.

Returns Total Cost

The above-mentioned reasons can help companies understand and strategize the number of returns initiated. But returns are from now onwards an integral part of the business—even though they cost companies. One cannot improve what they cannot measure. Hence it is important to know what falls under the umbrella of total return cost.

Total returns can be impacted by external or internal factors. External factors can include but are not limited to: Oil prices, geo-political situations, tariffs and taxes, international regulations, the labor market, and supply-demand balance. Internal factors can include return processing, packaging, return logistics, warehousing and storage, digital software usage, digital storage, information handling, inventory handling, labor, refund processing, repairs, and reselling. It is difficult to consider all the different costs related to return logistics when the customer is expecting a return and free shipping. There is only one solution, and that is to optimize the return cost. There is no one-notch solution that fits all the industries, businesses, or product categories. But one can use a combination of all the different strategies.

Returns Optimization

Returns are an inevitable division of businesses and corporate strategies. Returns cost businesses heavily, so why are companies still doing it and branding it as customer service? Since the customer can return items that are not useful, they feel liberated during the shopping experience which increases their probability of purchasing that product. Also, a strong return policy increases brand loyalty with a rich and heartwarming post-purchase experience. Here, human psychology also plays an important role. Once there is money-back guarantee, customers feel safe about the product quality and usefulness. Upon understanding the several benefits and seeing the competitive market, it seems impossible to fully eliminate returns. In the future, it won't be non-normal to claim that returning the purchased item is a basic customer right. If this is the case, it is important to find ways to optimize the return product's logistics and supply chain.

Return Cost Optimization Strategies

The application of any optimization strategy won't eliminate the cost completely. Also, one cannot eliminate or reduce all the costs. For example, in the e-commerce industry, software usage or digital storage for the returns operation cannot be eliminated, and even refund processing or labor cost cannot be made zero. One should start with understanding the whole returns operations neatly; find the pain points of the process, scope of improvement, steps and solutions to overcome the shortcomings, pilot run the new potential solutions, monitor the results and then completely implement the strategy. Monitoring the results of the final implementation is of utmost importance. Here are a few key strategies to reduce the cost:

1. Transportation mode: Finding the best and most economical way of transportation. In most cases of B2C operations, road transportation is the most economical way. However, if the operations are between B2B, then many times rail and water transportation are better choices.
2. Outsourcing return logistics: It is difficult to find economy of scale in returns operations as they are random and rare in nature. In such cases, opting for third-party logistics is the best solution as you don't have to waste your resources on one unique operation.
3. Shipment closeness: It is always beneficial to get the returned item shipped to the closest location to the customer which would reduce the current and future costs of shipments during reselling. Shipment closeness can also help reduce the product damage that occurs during shipping.
4. Standardization: If the company is big with good resources, then one can develop an in-house standard process for return shipments. The best example for this is Amazon's e-commerce business. Return shipment standardization eventually keeps all the business and customer information safe. Also, standardization of reverse logistics can be helpful to gain the shipment and logistics data to find the pain points and emerging trends of these processes.
5. Keep it as a gift: If the product value is way less than the return operations cost, one can tell the customer to keep the product as a present. Many big e-commerce companies use this strategy, such as Amazon and IKEA. Offering the return product as a gift enhances both customer satisfaction and the desire to buy from the company next time.
6. Gift cards: Companies can offer a gift card to the customer who has initiated a return for the product. In this strategy, the company can ask the customer to keep the current product and offer a gift card of 50% or the best value of the cost of the return-initiated product for their next purchase. This

strategy is best suited for delicate and fragile items. It helps to retain the customer and reduce the potential damage of the product during shipping and handling.

7. Automate the process: Automating the process helps eliminate labor and other operational costs. This type of strategy is best suited for businesses that have e-products, subscription products, or financial services. This strategy can also be used for products and services that required a deposit which is supposed to be returned. For example, housing, rentals, etc.
8. Packaging: One can re-use the packaging material received from returns to ship the same product or new product (considering the packaging is in good condition). For example, using the shipping packages and envelopes by just swapping the inside of the packages or envelopes out. Re-using the dunnage bags, bubble wrap, or even the polystyrene packaging is a good option not just from a cost point of view but also from a sustainability perspective.
9. Collaborate with retailers: Collaborating with big retailers or local shops to sell and manage returns reduces the last-mile delivery cost and increases customer satisfaction.
10. Secret sauce: Use personalized improvement ideas. Customer feedback, out of the box thinking, and market awareness are all key to getting your company to move forward with developing a new operations strategy.

Remodeling Solution

Apart from gaining value from customer satisfaction and loyalty, companies can obtain value by processing returned items in various ways. Here are a few plans of action to increase profitability by remodeling the returned product:

1. Resell: Many companies resell the returned product if it is in completely new condition. This way the company can gain the maximum or whole amount from the returned product.
2. Refurbish and sell: This plan of action is often implemented with e-products such as earphones, laptops, tablets, etc. Refurbishing involves resetting all the settings to factory setup and making the product as good as new in order to resell it.
3. Remanufacturing: In this strategy, one can disassemble the product and reuse sub-parts for manufacturing that are serviceable or functional. For example, batteries or mechanical components.
4. Recycle: Recycling is the best option when products cannot be reused. It can be done for metallic, paper, glass, cardboard, food, or even some types of plastic materials. Recycling helps reduce pollution, cost, and waste, as well as conserve energy.
5. Harvest: It is best option when the final product is not working properly but the sub parts of the products are in completely good condition and can be reused easily and as it is.
6. Compost: Composting is a process of decomposition of organic matter. It is best suited for agriculture and perishable food-related products. Composting helps improve soil health and reduces soil erosion. It is the foremost example of getting the best out of waste projects.
7. Donate: Often, the returned items are not in bulk amounts but cannot be resold because of brand values. Donating such products after proper rework to charities or to non-profit organizations is a good option. These donations increase the company's brand value in society and help achieve the Corporate Social Responsibility goals as well.
8. Scrap: The products that do not fit into any of the above categories need to be scrapped. The best example of this are plastic bags or polystyrene packaging. Sometimes, products also contain

hazardous or poisonous materials which need to be disposed of properly without impacting the environment.

KPIs for Reverse Logistics

Data driven strategies and decisions are always backed up by evidence. Also, management is more confident about those approaches. If one can implement the solution based on historical trends and data analytics, the chances of success are higher. Following are some KPIs that can be used to measure before and after conditions and effectiveness of strategy implementation.

1. Rate of return: Rate of return signifies the volume of returns. Rate of returns and resold per product category or per specific reason can help in strategizing the business solution and examining its results afterwards.
2. Rebound rate: Rebound rate is number of times any particular product has been returned. It is an important factor when incidence of return is more than one. If this situation is occurring many times, there are high chances that the product quality is not as expected, and company must take immediate actions.
3. Defect rate: It is the number of items getting returned because of it is being defective. If this rate is high, it shows an urgent need of improvements in packaging-handling and logistics processes.
4. Operations cost: Each operation in supply chain and logistics process incurs cost. In case of the returns, the incurred cost is always extra and hence it is important to keep a check on it during each step.
5. Rate of resalable returns: These are the items which are absolutely in perfect condition and can be returned to the shelf for reselling. It helps to understand how much cost can be recovered by reselling the product.
6. Processing Times: As the reverse logistics processes get mature, tracking the processing times for refunds and returns with an increase in volume would help to understand the efficiency of the systems.

Additional metrics such as customer retention and satisfaction rate could help to determine whether the reverse logistics processes are leading to success in the businesses. Every industry will have their own benchmarks for the above KPIs and metrics as products will vary with volume, financial values, and processing times.

Reverse Logistics Across Various Industries

1. Retail Industry: The retail industry is a major user of reverse logistics, particularly in the area of product returns. Retailers must manage the process of accepting returned products, inspecting them, determining their disposition (i.e., restocking, refurbishing, harvesting parts from them or disposing of them completely), and returning them to their proper destination.
2. Healthcare Industry: The healthcare industry also uses reverse logistics to manage the return and disposal of medical supplies, equipment, and medication. This may include the return of expired or unused medication to the manufacturer, the collection and disposal of medical waste, and the return and refurbishment of medical equipment. The reverse logistics in health care is not as criti-

cal compared to other industries as majority of the medical products are one time use and throw types and hence need to be disposed of completely.

3. Electronics: The electronics industry deals with a lot of returned, obsolete, or damaged products that require reverse logistics for refurbishment, repair, or disposal. This process involves the transportation of the products, disassembly, inspection, and the separation of reusable and recyclable materials. Another way to save some cost is by harvesting working good sub parts of non-working final product and reusing them.
4. Automotive Industry: The automotive industry uses reverse logistics to manage the return and disposal of used or damaged parts and equipment. This may include the collection and disposal of hazardous materials, the refurbishment and resale of used parts, and the management of end-of-life vehicles.
5. Food Industry: The food industry uses reverse logistics to manage the return and disposal of expired or damaged products, as well as the collection and recycling of packaging materials. This may also include the donation of excess food to food banks and charities. The major challenge here is about managing reverse logistics of perishable items and hence lot of companies, especially retailers do not process returns for perishable items.
6. Clothing Industry: The clothing industry uses reverse logistics to manage the return and disposal of unsold or returned clothing, as well as the donation of excess inventory to charitable organizations. The reverse logistics of these items is simple, but the returns could be trickier sometimes when they are fraudulent.
7. Construction: The construction industry deals with a lot of waste and excess materials that require reverse logistics for proper disposal or recycling. This process involves transportation, sorting, inspection, and the proper handling of hazardous materials.

These are just a few examples of the many industries that utilize reverse logistics. The specific processes and challenges involved in reverse logistics can vary greatly depending on the industry and the types of products involved.

Digitalization of Reverse Logistics

All throughout the world, digital technology is changing how business is done. Innovative hardware and software are enhancing corporate operations and improving customer service in a variety of industries, including retail and restaurants. Brands can almost always find a way to improve how they conduct their business because of the many shapes that digital technology can take. When it comes to digital transformation, there are plenty of options available, including automation, augmented reality, and virtual reality.

Reverse logistics, on the other hand, is one sector that has lagged behind in hopping on the pleasant ride of digital transformation. This is beginning to change, and businesses are looking for new methods to employ cutting-edge technology to streamline customer returns. The reverse logistics adoption became popular mostly after the e-commerce industry boomed. Reverse logistics got attention only after businesses succeed into the e-commerce industry. Because this digital transformation of businesses usually needs a lot of capital investments and in such cases the secondary services like reverse logistics are usually ignored at the first glace.

But with increasing number of both sells and returns, companies are looking towards reverse logistics as an opportunity to save massive amount of money. Thus, increasing the speed of innovation and digital transformation in reverse logistics.

With high amount of transportation involved and no economies of scales, reverse logistics leaves a large amount of carbon footprint behind. Which raises another issue related to sustainability of operation and social responsibility of the company to look over it. Hence, the digital transformation of reverse logistics is playing a vital role in overall development of the businesses.

Digital Technologies in Reverse Logistics

With increasing competition in the market more and more businesses are using digitalization to transform from traditional approach of managing operations to completely new digital approach, ultimately resulting in increased speed, efficiency and value of the business. After the pandemic hit, companies are looking to the digital technologies as a big hope to transform their business not only financially but also physically to make it more touchless. According to Butcher (2021), "McKinsey survey of global executives, companies digitized many activities 20-25 times faster as a result of COVID-1". One can choose one or more technologies in combination depending upon the size and type of business one is in. Here are the few technologies which are transforming today's supply chain and forward-reverse logistics.

1. Internet of Things (IoT): It is one the most trending technologies in the market. A technology which can be utilized in both commercial and also non-commercial aspects. Another important point behind the success of this technology is its easiness of use that even small kids can use it easily. These products are affordable as well. The IoT has potential to connect everything and anything over network, share live data while providing remote access and transparency. This wireless technology boosts the speed of data sharing, quick updates and real time solutions for issues which is key for managing supply chain and logistics operations. Businesses get chance to monitor, track and record operations in depth and mitigate risks before they grow any further. One of the simple examples of IoT is getting system updates for the equipment over the air like mobile phones or vehicle. These updates can be for new system features, changing the equipment settings or even connecting it to other devices on the same network.
2. Automation: Automation is the type of technology which reduces the human intervention in operations. This makes difficult jobs easier, simple and effortless. Automations ranges from high-tech humanoids to as simple as auto-saving option in excel. This field is highly innovative and important as it directly impacts on quality, quantity, time, and cost of the operation. In supply chain, automation helps to keep the product and processes moving and helps to deal with uncertainty. It can be used in different sectors of supply chain like manufacturing, transportation, forward/reverse logistics, inventory management and demand management. Many companies use automatic robot system for warehouse and inventory management.
3. Management tools: These are the software tools used by businesses to improve co-ordination between the operations and keep everything centralized. These tools are usually the heavy investments at first but help a lot to deal with management problems which ultimately increase the speed and efficiency of supply chain projects and operations. The different types of software serve different part of the supply chain. For example, WMS (Warehouse Management System) helps in managing warehouse operations, while ERP (Enterprise Resource Planning) helps in order management,

resource management. Supply chains can function more effectively as a unit due to digital collaboration capabilities these tools provide. This timely and accurate information will be more and more important when disruptions persist since it will let businesses respond more rapidly and efficiently.

4. AI and Machine learning: Artificial intelligence is a problem-solving capability of a computer and machine learning is a branch of artificial intelligence. Processes in the supply chain could be changed significantly by artificial intelligence (AI) and machine learning technologies. These technologies learn and get better over time as they get exposed to more and more data. They give businesses the ability to gather data from various sources and put in self-analyzing and improving models. Across the supply chain, AI can be used to identify trends, predict possible outcomes, spot flaws in data, underline risks and hazards, elevate IoT insights, and enhance material-demand planning, order management, and transportation-logistics.
5. Blockchain: A blockchain is a digitally distributed, decentralized, public ledger that exists across a network. This digital ledger contains blocks, and each block records a large number of transactions. Once a block is attached to a chain then it cannot be changed or updated. This helps create a secured network with transactions that are distributed and has no single point of central authority. Blockchain Technology can be applied to reverse logistics to create records of transactions that are involved in the returns process from start to end point. Once this is done, any historical record can be retrieved anytime which can help with better tracking, monitoring, controlling the process flow, and making informed decisions. Thus, this leads to more efficiency and transparency in the reverse logistics process. Although to implement Block chain technology there are certain requirements such integration with the current system, pre-requisites, and training to use the technology, data privacy and security, and lastly the cost associated to adopt the technology.
6. Advanced analytics: Advanced analytics has become very important in the recent years due to the volume of data being collected by companies about their daily transactions. Analytics can help leverage the big data collected to identify trends, derive patterns, and gather business insights. In the context of reverse logistics, data can be used to analyze which can help minimize the number of returns, maximize utilizations, prevent fraud, reduce costs. Identifying frequently returned items and common reasons for returns can shape the business tactics as well as improve product quality. Detecting trends in fraudulent returns will not only identify offenders but also save significant losses. Advanced analytics can be easily integrated with the current supply chain system due to high compatibility and easy to use tools and software available in the industry. It does come with additional costs such as data storage, maintenance and security.

When right strategies are matched with right tools and integrated with new digital technologies, it revamps the businesses. Above mentioned are just few examples of digital tools. As the companies are comprehending the potential of digitalization, there is a lot more innovation to come up with and overhaul the world.

Challenges in Digitalization of Reverse Logistics

Changes in any system or in any form are difficult to manage because of various reasons. Hence, whenever the changes are planned, it is always preferred to study the challenges faced during implementation phase and ways to overcome these challenges prior to the implementation. Digitalization is one such change which needs upper management's attention when it's implemented in highly volatile and primarily service oriented reverse logistics field.

1. Principal Investment: Budget is one the most important aspect of digitalization. It is one of the costliest investments for the company which repays its fruit over the time. Currently, reverse logistics is more of customer service strategy than money making strategy for the businesses. Hence putting another big part of budget into digitalization of the reverse logistics gets trickier. The companies are supposed to analyze all the aspects of this investment very critically. Getting the right kind of technology for company's type of business depending upon company's size, customer's market segment and the industry it is in.
2. Resistance to Change (Push back): People enjoy routines by nature because they make them feel secured, it is a part of human psychology to be in their comfort zone. This psychological trait in humans, make them pessimistic when they are faced by change. When human's habits are disrupted and uncertainty enters in their lives, things can quickly begin to appear gloomy. As the height of discomfort, going through a digital change may make employees feel intimidated which creates the push back challenge for the digital transformation. To keep up with the times, change is necessary because staying the same is much riskier. Digital transformation is one such crucial change. It can be more challenging when it comes to reverse logistics because it is the tail of the businesses which get least attention from strategical perspective. Upper management being aware and prepared for such cases can reduce the employee push back and alleviate their motivation towards adopting new digital tools and processes.
3. Security of data: Breaches of company data is unfortunately increasing day by day with the surge in usage of the technology. Companies have tons of data related to their products, business, processes or even customers, which is highly confidential. Hence securing the data from breaching, corrupting or cybercrimes has become significant importance given the trends of last few years. Many times, such issues lead to stealing of sensitive data and invading company's privacy policy. Reverse logistics in that case can be more vulnerable as it is more customer facing and related to product repurposing practices. Companies should proactively try to prevent these issues even before they happen by having cyber security policies in place.
4. Maintenance: Maintenance is a constant effort taken by an entity to make sure that their systems are running and up to date. Technology maintenance is one such effort which needs continuous attention and improvement. If the technology is not maintained, it may create gaps into the system, which would make it more of a bane rather than making it a boon for the company. The companies should have a dedicated IT team which would help to implement and maintain the technology from time to time. Technological maintenance can be related to the strategy development, IT, cybersecurity, data migrations, system architecture and software integrations.
5. Obsoletion: This is one of the threat which by default comes with any technology. Companies must make deliberate efforts in making sure that it is equipped with modern cotemporary technology in its operation, processes or even product it is selling. Otherwise, the obsolete technology would outdate the business. This is one of the challenges which companies turn blind eye to and become the biggest fiasco in the industry. Few popular examples for this in history are Blackberry, Kodak or even Skype.

Simple tip to successfully transform the business is to choose a technology that offers the highest return on investment and is in line with the business objectives of the organization. Continuous evolution of digital transformation according to the internal or external customer need is another key point to consider.

Sustainability, Digitalization, and Reverse Logistics

Sustainability is prevention of the loss of natural resources in order to preserve ecological balance around the globe. As the world is getting more and more revolutionized, it needs the sustainability practices in place to retain the natural balance. And digitalization and reverse logistics will both play a vital role in order to maintain the sustainability practices in the corporations.

There are sustainable digitalization practices which helps to increase the efficiency of resource management ultimately impacting the financial goals of the company and sustainability goals of the company. For example, with the reach of digitalization, lot of operations in big corporations like banks have gone paperless or another example is getting the remote access to the work sites, impacting the fuel costs and other related costs for travelling to the site. But the dark side of the digitalization is about creating the e-waste at the end of the e-product life cycle.

Reverse logistics on other hand itself is practice of sustainability. It helps companies to repurpose their products in different way. Either by reselling them if the product is working or otherwise refurbish, remanufacture, recycle or scrap them. There are other ways as well for repurposing like keeping the product in spare and then utilizing it for verification or testing purposes and other way is to harvest the specific part of the product which is in good working condition.

In short, sustainability, digitalization and reverse logistics go hand in hand if implemented correctly. It improves company's brand name, customer satisfaction, competitiveness and operational efficiency. It also helps companies to work towards their corporate social responsibility goals.

Role of Government in Reverse Logistics

Government policies and regulations play a crucial role in shaping the reverse logistics practices of companies, and their impact on sustainability and social responsibility. Government policies and regulations can influence the reverse logistics practices of companies in several ways. For example:

1. Mandatory recycling and disposal regulations: Governments may enforce laws that require companies to recycle or dispose of certain products in a specific way, such as hazardous waste or electronic waste. These regulations can impact the reverse logistics practices of companies by dictating the way they handle and dispose of such materials.
2. Extended Producer Responsibility (EPR): This is a policy framework that shifts responsibility for managing a product's end-of-life from the consumer to the producer. Governments may require producers to take back and recycle their products or pay a fee to support the collection and recycling of their products. EPR policies can influence the design and production processes of companies to ensure that products are easily recyclable and can be recovered after use.
3. Green procurement policies: Governments may encourage or require companies to procure environmentally friendly products and materials, such as those made from recycled materials. This can incentivize companies to incorporate sustainable and circular practices in their supply chain and reverse logistics processes.

4. Tax incentives: Governments may offer tax incentives to companies that adopt sustainable and circular practices, such as recycling or refurbishing products. This can encourage companies to invest in more sustainable practices, which can have positive impacts on their reverse logistics processes.
5. Beverage packaging fee: It is a policy related to the reverse logistics of the beverage packaging. It makes consumers pay certain amount of fee while purchasing the beverages and the money is returned to the consumers when they recycle beverage containers at certified recycling centers.

The impact of government policies and regulations on the reverse logistics practices of companies can be significant. For example, regulations that mandate the recycling or disposal of certain products can reduce the amount of waste going to landfills and encourage companies to find more sustainable ways to handle their products. EPR policies can incentivize companies to design products with the end-of-life in mind, which can improve their reverse logistics processes and reduce environmental impacts. Green procurement policies can create a market for sustainable products and materials, which can drive innovation and reduce the environmental impact of production processes.

By creating incentives for companies to adopt more sustainable practices, governments can help reduce the environmental impact of businesses and create a more circular and sustainable economy.

Future of Reverse Logistics

The reverse logistics trends are expected to be rising every year. Companies are trying to maximize the recovery rate from returns, and with the growing volume in returns there will be an economy of scale that can be leveraged along with digitalized, matured and optimized solutions. New technologies like blockchain, machine learning and artificial intelligence would join the world of return supply chain making it smoother, easier, and efficient. There will be boom for companies solely focused on providing reverse logistics services to small and medium sized businesses. Data will play a crucial role in steering the direction of logistics and returns processing. Dedicated software will be available to provide insights and valuable reports. To curb fraudulent returns and reduce transactional costs, companies will tighten the rules for consumer returns to find an optimal balance for reverse logistics.

In the end, studying the principles of reverse logistics plus supply chain management, applying them to real-life problems will teach why it is important to optimize reverse logistics, what is the role of digital technology and how it can transform business models. Starting with understanding the problem in current reverse logistics processes, performing root cause analysis, finding out potential solutions and finally implementing them is what it needs to resolve the issues. This will ultimately lead to improve the processes and optimize the operation plus reduce the costs.

Though reverse logistics is a new member of the supply chain family it is going to be with us forever. This is the era where industries are getting distinguished based on their services provided and returns is one of the top criteria within it.

REFERENCES

Barnett, J., & Clark, T. (2019). Reducing e-commerce returns through product presentation. *International Journal of Retail & Distribution Management, 47*(9), 1008–1020.

Butcher, D. (2021, October 27). 5 ways digital technology will transform the supply chain. *MasterControl.* https://www.mastercontrol.com/gxp-lifeline/5-ways-digital-technology-will-transform-the-supply-chain/

Conley, P. (2023, February 24). Online return rates dropped in 2022, according to NRF study. *Digital Commerce 360.* https://www.digitalcommerce360.com/2022/12/15/online-return-rates-dropped-in-2022-according-to-nrf-study/

Eljelly, A. M. (2019). Reverse logistics in the era of e-commerce: A review. *International Journal of Supply Chain Management, 8*(1), 292–303.

Ganesan, S., Venkatesan, S., & Karthikeyan, K. (2019). An empirical analysis of reverse logistics practices in e-commerce. *Journal of Cleaner Production, 209*, 1539–1550.

Gautam, A. (2022, August 31). Transforming Reverse Logistics through the Digital Route. *Innoverdigital.* https://innoverdigital.com/transforming-reverse-logistics-through-the-digital-route/

Inman, D. (n.d.). *2022 Retail Returns Rate Remains Flat at $816 Billion.* NRF. https://nrf.com/media-center/press-releases/2022-retail-returns-rate-remains-flat-816-billion#:~:text=As%20retail%20sales%20continue%20to,returned%20to%20retailers%20this%20year.%22

Kiesmüller, G. P., Inderfurth, K., & Zsifkovits, H. (2017). Reverse logistics network design in the era of the internet of things. *International Journal of Production Economics, 183*, 487–501.

Lazar, M.-J. (2022, March 30). 20 statistics on ecommerce returns you need to know in 2021. *ReadyCloud.* https://www.readycloud.com/info/20-statistics-on-ecommerce-returns

Linton, J. D., Klassen, R., & Jayaraman, V. (2016). Sustainable supply chains: An introduction. *Journal of Operations Management, 41*, 1–8.

Mzugovic. (2022, June 30). History of reverse logistics is at the core of the stories of war, Retail, eCommerce, and automotive aftermarket. *GlobalTranz.* https://www.globaltranz.com/resource-hub/history-of-reverse-logistics/

Rogers, D. S., & Tibben-Lembke, R. S. (2001). Going backwards: reverse logistics trends and practices. *Reverse logistics: Quantitative models for closed-loop supply chains*, 1-27

Singh, A., & Gupta, H. (2021). Reverse logistics: Issues and challenges in the era of e-commerce. *International Journal of Logistics Management, 32*(2), 300–319.

Section 4

Key Enablers for Digital Transformations

Chapter 15
The Role of Internet of Things and Blockchain in the Development of Agile and Sustainable Supply Chains

Hamed Nozari
Faculty of Industrial Engineering, Iran University of Science and Technology, Iran

Javid Ghahremani-Nahr
Academic Center for Education, Culture, and Research (ACECR), Iran

Esmaeil Najafi
Islamic Azad University, Tehran, Iran

ABSTRACT

Achieving customer satisfaction requires seamless collaboration and coordination across the value chain of suppliers, manufacturers, regulators, logistics service providers, and retailers. At the same time, disruption in the supply chain causes increased costs, and, more importantly, lost revenue. Therefore, organizations are looking for transparency, flexibility, and agility in their supply chains. The internet of things and blockchain, as a part of efficient technologies in supply chains of organizations, build trust, transparency, and consensus among all stakeholders, creating benefits for every actor and ensuring flexible business outcomes .Due to the increasing importance of these technologies in today's world and the integration of these tools in all business processes, in this research, the dimensions, components, and vital indicators affecting the creation of a smart and efficient supply chain with high reliability and has been assessed as having strong resilience. Finally, the structure of a smart supply chain is shown by the interaction of these transformative technologies.

DOI: 10.4018/978-1-6684-7298-9.ch015

1. INTRODUCTION

Supply chains are at the heart of the process of delivering products to customers at the right time and at the right cost. Regardless of what type of product an organization produces or sells, keeping customers satisfied and achieving financial goals depends on building an efficient and reliable supply chain network. The global supply chain is worth more than $40 trillion annually. Logistics requires complex international regulations to oversee the movement of goods around the world. Due to the existence of information asymmetry in the large volume of information flows, such a system is prone to error or corruption among the intermediaries involved (Najafi et al., 2022).

Shipment tracking is a manual process that is limited to only a few specific points in the supply chain. While with smart logistics that support IoT, users can track the desired shipment in every part of the supply chain (start to finish). This kind of real-time tracking is not possible without the ability to receive fast data from IoT devices connected to the shipment. The Internet of Things can be very efficient in the fast and safe transportation of cargo by informing all stakeholders about the status of the goods. The integration of supply chain management systems based on the Internet of Things is one of the most important technological trends in the warehouse. Its benefits range from increasing the efficiency of warehouse processes to better inventory management and employee safety (Aliahmadi et al. (a), 2022). In addition to the previously mentioned items, the Internet of Things and data analysis using smart technologies—along with the presence of technologies such as blockchain—help supply chain managers take into account traffic and weather for possible accidents or other events, such as plan routes causing delays. The Internet of Things controls all the data needed to prepare flexible contingency plans and find the cause of existing delays. This technology provides immediate alerts to supply chain managers (Aliahmadi et al. (b), 2022).

Achieving customer satisfaction requires seamless collaboration and coordination across the value chain of suppliers, manufacturers, banks, regulators, logistics service providers, and retailers. At the same time, disruption in the supply chain causes increased costs and more importantly, lost revenue. Worse, these disruptions are exacerbated by inefficient processes designed on ineffective data. Organizations are looking for transparency, flexibility, and agility in their supply chains to control these disruptions. The ability to establish instant trust in recorded transactions can lead to improved efficiency in many functions related to supply chain operations, including monetary exchanges, operational transactions, contracting, sourcing, etc., without the exclusive need for a centralized system. Blockchain technology along with Internet of Things technology provides the possibility of documenting and presenting all documents and as a result facilities such as full tracking and tracking of the location of goods, how to procure, purchase, allocate and use them (Tavakkoli-Moghaddam et al., 2021).

It is obvious that the use of this technology improves transparency and accountability and facilitates the authentication process of the goods and materials received. In addition to this acceleration of the flow of goods, timely delivery of products and greater transparency in logistics activities are the benefits that will accrue to all stakeholders of the supply chain through the adoption of this technology. In such a situation, the vertical integration of industries is given more attention because, with the increase in transparency, the costs related to the movement of products between intermediaries are reduced. In a traditional hierarchical supply chain network, the flow of data across the network often mimics the flow of goods. In a distributed ledger environment using blockchain, data and information can be shared in a decentralized manner so that all parties can view the same data. In such a situation and when sharing information, there is no need for each supply chain actor to act as an intermediary between nearby partners. More precisely, each node must be able to view transactions in order to approve or reject them, but this approval or rejection depends on the nature of the supply chain program (Aliahmadi et al. (c), 2022).

Also, connected systems collect the data needed for predictive analysis at different stages of the supply chain (equipment failure detection, maintenance forecast, etc.). The analytical and predictive power of the Internet of Things is widely used to improve resource management in many industries. Just by being able to predict system downtime, supply chain and warehouse managers can significantly reduce downtime, hence saving a lot of money. Therefore, it can be observed that the simultaneous use of these technologies can increase the capabilities and efficiency of the supply chain and increase its agility. In the platform of blockchain, supply chain managers can get a detailed picture of how to use resources such as electricity and water and implement green strategies and environmental initiatives, which is a valuable solution for the sustainability of supply chains.

In the following, the role of each of these transformative technologies in the development of smart supply chains will be examined.

2. IOT BASED SUPPLY CHAIN

The Internet of Things means a global network of related and connected objects, each of which has its own address and communicates with each other based on standardized contracts. This concept may have originated in the industry a long time ago, but today it refers to small computing devices. Objects and things that we don't even think about such as food, clothing and medicine are connected using this technology. With the development of the application of Internet of Things, a lot of data is generated, which increases the need for exploration and analysis. Objects communicate with each other through sensors and networks and receive data and information to store and process them (Nozari et la., 2022).

Today, more and more companies and startups are building the foundation of their business based on the Internet of Things. The range of applications of Internet of Things in daily life is expanding every day, and various services are trying to improve the quality of their services by using it.

Supply chain management, which in its new form is looking for ways to reduce as much as possible the production cycle of desired products and services, and in this way uses one of the latest developments in management science and technology (including the Internet, the World Wide Web and technology Information, Internet of Things, etc.). Today, the guarantee of sustainable development depends on the preservation and optimal use of limited and irreplaceable resources. Due to the pressure of government regulations to obtain environmental standards for the supply of natural (green) products, a new concept of green supply chain management has emerged, which includes the stages of the product life cycle from design to recycling in a way that is compatible with the environment (Nozari & Jarosz, & Nahr, 2022).

The Internet of Things can be used in the supply chain to improve the effectiveness of information transfer between parts of the supply chain. Unnecessary transaction cost is eliminated due to the effectiveness of information exchange because companies will be more closely related to each other. On the other hand, the amount of inventory is also reduced because the supply and demand information is transferred in time, improving the use of the stored information and reducing the cost of storage and labor in the logistics center. Compared to the traditional supply chain, the information sharing mechanism is used in the supply chain based on the Internet of Things. Product information on the supply chain is sent to the management base through information readers in different parts of the network, and this base sends the necessary feedback through information analysis. This makes price corrections get completed in a timely and correct manner. The information sharing mechanism can make manufacturers, distributors, and retailers respond to market supply and demand information in a timely manner and finally balance supply and demand and prevent product price fluctuations (Corazza et al., 2023).

The application of Internet of Things in the product supply chain not only improves the information level of the supply chain, but also reduces the risk of product security problems, especially food products, through the control of the supply chain. Also, when a product security problem occurs, companies can help solve these problems through IoT and product tracking. Consumers can also access product information through electronic product labels and reduce their purchase costs by reducing the time to access products. Traditional productions are often small-scale, products and goods often go through a long cycle from production to consumption, and information is exchanged slowly during this cycle, the supply chain is inefficient, and products often reach the market with many issues and problems (Nozari et al., 2018).

The Internet of Things connects every part of the supply chain, helping transfer information at the right time, correctly, and efficiently. Manufacturers, transport operators, wholesalers, and retailers in the supply chain can receive market information and analyze it correctly to finally make accurate and appropriate decisions. When supply and demand information is shared in the market, everyone from the manufacturer to the retailers will benefit from it—the logistics institutions can integrate the resources, the operational cost will decrease, and the scale of the business will increase. In the long run, this will help to create well-known brand names and industrial development.

IOT can provide several benefits in retail and supply chain management. For example, by equipping product shelves with equipment such as RFIDs, a retailer can properly manage their product requirements. For example, if the major manufacturers know about the retailers' needs, they can better manage their production and control the market situation. Therefore, by collecting information sent from retailers' requirements, they can optimize their production. IOT can create a huge potential for product warehousing in retail stores (Nozari et al, 2021). According to annual statistics, about 0.4% of retailers' sales are lost due to lack of goods. Therefore, this technology is able to play a big role in the production and supply chain of goods by showing the inventory and sales of each product at a moment's notice. Figure 1 shows the connection between the smart supply chain and the Internet of Things.

Figure 1. Supply chain based on the internet of things

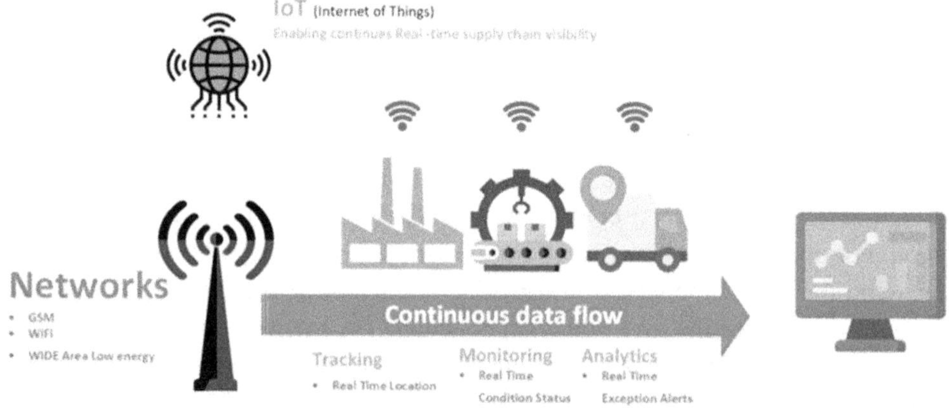

There are many applications of IoT in supply chain management that help in the automation of warehouse operations, warehouse condition monitoring, and remote control. Supply chain automation helps warehouse managers increase productivity, reduce costs, and increase flexibility, sustainability, and agility. Connected systems collect data needed for predictive analytics at different stages of the supply chain (equipment failure detection, maintenance forecasting, etc.). The analytical and predictive power of the Internet of Things is widely used to improve resource management in many industries. Just by being able to predict system downtime, supply chain and warehouse managers can significantly reduce downtime, hence saving a lot of money (Nozar et al., 2021).

In a smart supply chain, the Internet of Things is one of the technologies that help managers comply with environmental laws and emission limits. By using various IoT sensors for supply chain management and asset tracking, supply chain managers can now gain an accurate picture of how resources such as electricity and water are being used to then implement green strategies and environmental initiatives.

Some other advantages of the Internet of Things in the supply chain are:

- Intelligent route planning tools and IoT tracking technologies are exponentially increasing the overall speed of the supply chain.
- All parties involved in the supply chain cycle have access to relevant data and can resolve issues quickly and accurately.
- The Internet of Things provides managers with detailed insight into the flow of goods.
- Combining IoT and supply chain management is a good way for retailers to learn more about their products, customers, and demand, and to build strategies accordingly.
- The Internet of Things in the supply chain creates greater awareness of resource and labor management.

Therefore, as stated, Internet of Things tools play a fundamental role in changing supply chain management. Smart sensors and Internet of Things tools make it possible to identify products along the chain and thus help to reduce bottlenecks, increase efficiency and, as a result, reduce production costs. In this way and by using environmental information, the basic processes of the supply chain are facilitated, resulting in supply chains becoming more agile and stable in line with social needs.

3. BLOCKCHAIN-BASED SUPPLY CHAIN MANAGEMENT

The global supply chain has become a vast and complex system that businesses use to manufacture and distribute their products globally. Its complexity has led to many technological innovations in the past few years, including the adoption of blockchain technology. Sustainable supply chain management deals with the provision of economic, social, and environmental needs that arise in the flow of materials and services between suppliers, manufacturers, and customers. Blockchain technology has the potential to design, organize, operate, and manage the supply chain and guide organizations in achieving the strategic goals of a sustainable supply chain (Ghahremani-Nahr et al., 2022).

The application of blockchain in the logistics industry is like a public ledger that permanently records all the changes that have happened. Every product has a long journey from the moment of registration and leaving the warehouse to delivery to the customer. At each step of this path, information about the changes that have occurred can be recorded without the possibility of changing them. For example, the date of registration in the warehouse, the date of departure, and the appearance condition such as color, registration number, delivery date, etc. are among the information that is recorded in different parts of the transportation process such as the warehouse, the main agency, and the local agency, and the customer can use various methods such as Scan the QR code to get this information. With blockchain technology, customers can ensure that information is correctly recorded and not tampered with.

Blockchain technology allows companies to track all types of transactions with greater security and transparency. The potential impact on supply chain performance is enormous. The most important use of blockchain in the supply chain is that companies can trace the history of a product exactly from the point of origin to where it is now. With the help of this technology, parties collaborating on a common platform can dramatically reduce the time delays, overhead, and human error often associated with transactions. Reducing intermediaries in the supply chain also reduces the risks of fraud. Finally, where fraud occurs, comprehensive records enable organizations to pinpoint its source. A shared blockchain ledger provides a reliable, tamper-free audit trail of the flow of information, inventory, and finances in a supply chain. Using a shared blockchain, companies can synchronize logistics data, track shipments, and automate payments. Moreover, they can do this without significantly changing their legacy systems by sharing only relevant data. At the core of the blockchain is the decentralized ledger, which consists of encrypted blocks or nodes of stored, chained data that form a real-time source of truth that can be shared between multiple parties. The blockchain ledger is transparent and secure, making it a core technology for every sector, including supply chain and logistics (Nahr et al., 2021).

By implementing a blockchain along with the Internet of Things, devices such as smart sensors and RFID tags record the movement time of products in different stages of the supply chain and their status (temperature, vibration, humidity, etc.) more effectively. This data is then stored on a blockchain and smart contracts are applied to ensure real-time visibility. This means more accurate visibility and accurate information in the tracking process, which can help companies identify and address issues faster. It also means cost savings. A distributed network that digitally shares resources and data can reduce inventory loss and waste and eliminate the need for paper-based workflows. This means any additional storage and labor costs required to process and manage physical documents are eliminated.

The following are examples that demonstrate the potential of blockchain in reducing supply chain costs and improving service levels.

- **Finding resources**

Sourcing is considered one of the most important application areas of blockchain. Buying companies can assess the supplier's value and risk based on detailed information about how they are procured, produced, and transported. Because transactions between a vendor and its partners can be visible to others in the chain, buying companies can monitor a supplier's performance and gain the knowledge needed to negotiate better prices. Such information can also represent how the cost is distributed throughout the supply chain. Providing economic visibility enables better participation of smaller companies in the supply chain value network. In addition, information may be shared with insurers to negotiate transportation coverage with logistics providers and manufacturers (Nahr et al., 2021).

- **Tracking and interception**

Information asymmetries and inconsistencies among supply chain participants are always present, creating barriers to tracking specific transactions and commodities. Downstream participants in the supply chain often need information about a product, including the assembly process, material lists, and cautionary warnings. The integrity of a product's transaction records requires extensive processes and controls that are not easily achieved. Using a distributed ledger, the transfer of goods between two parties identified as two addresses on the blockchain can be recorded.

- **Payment process**

Blockchain can also be used to improve payment processing in the supply chain, especially where buyers use a supply chain finance platform (SCF) to pay their suppliers' invoices.

- **Logistics and transportation**

The ability to track the shipment of a container along its journey from origin to destination has historically been a major supply chain challenge and has not changed much in the past 50 years. By encoding insurance policies, customs clearance, and information related to a shipment, blockchain can be used to simplify shipping processes and reduce the processing time of a shipment.

- **Insurance**

Figure 2. Coordination between roles in the blockchain platform for the sustainable supply chain

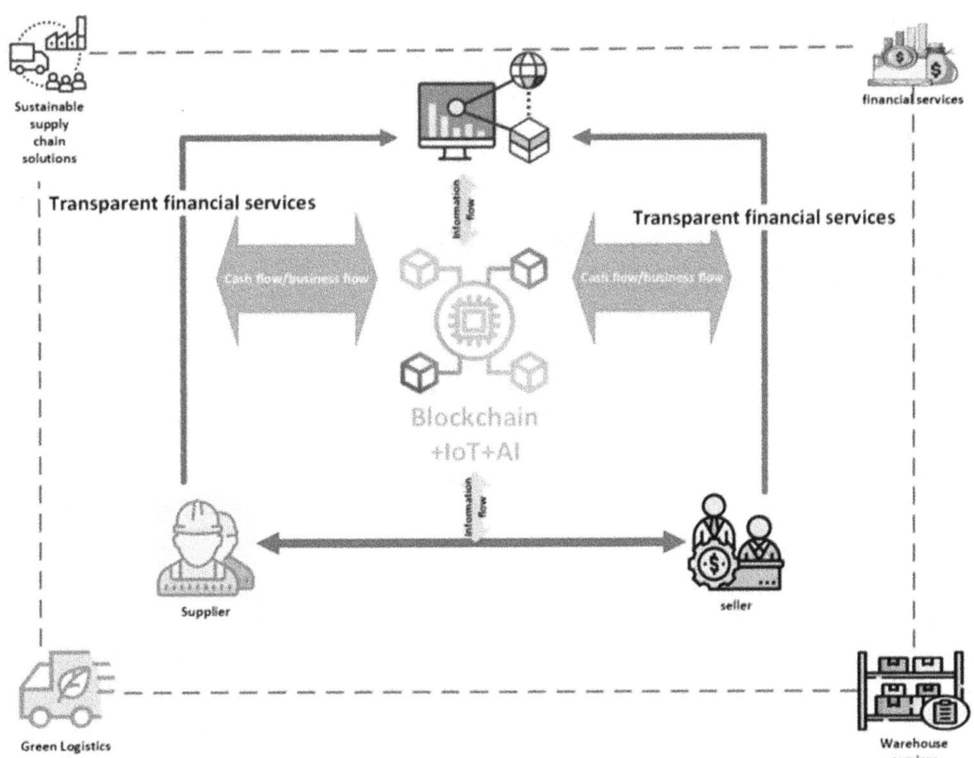

Blockchain features can be combined with Internet of Things (IoT), sensors, and data analytics. The combination of these technologies leads to the detection of information related to the journey of a cargo and makes it possible to predict the amount of delay, damage, and arrival time. The joint ledger can record information related to such risks and assist carriers in complying with insurance regulations.

Blockchain technology has the potential to contribute to the social sustainability of the supply chain by creating stable and immutable information. Given that information cannot be changed without the consent of authorized actors, chain organizations can prevent people's assets from being unfairly seized by individuals, governments, or corrupt organizations. Blockchain traceability helps to better ensure human rights and sustainable, fair, and safe work practices. For example, a clear history of the product's history assures the buyer that the goods purchased are from genuine and ethical sources. The transparency of the supply chain causes the adoption of practices based on the social responsibility of suppliers in the purchase of customers and makes all competitors have to behave responsibly (Oudani et al., 2023).

Blockchain technology also contributes to the environmental sustainability of the supply chain, which is applicable from important perspectives. First, accurate tracking of normal products and identification of more product transactions can help reduce rework. This helps to reduce resource consumption and reduce greenhouse gas emissions. There are several powerful platforms based on blockchain technology to reduce supply chain waste, such as electricity chain and solar contract. Second, blockchain can be used to ensure that green products are environmentally friendly. Green product processing information is often unavailable and difficult to verify. If a product's manufacturing process is certified as green, environmentally conscious customers may be more inclined to purchase green products (Karumanchi et al., 2023).

At the same time, the transparency of information will play a role in improving the performance of the supply chain and ultimately lead to the dynamism, agility, and integrity of the mentioned system. Therefore, the use of blockchain technology as a supply chain management mechanism and information management along with infrastructures such as smart contracts and the Internet of Things in a stable network will be of great importance because it increases the transparency of the data from the supply chain and It adds to data security.

4. BLOCKCHAIN AND INTERNET OF THINGS APPLICATIONS IN SUPPLY CHAINS

Internet of Things technology connects people, places, and products and creates opportunities to provide value; Chips and sensors embedded in products transmit data to the IoT network. Of course, there are still many technical and security concerns regarding this technology; In this regard, blockchain technology can help the Internet of Things and be useful in solving many of its problems. The application of blockchain in the Internet of Things will transform the processes in various industries, including production, trade, transportation, financial sector, and health. Despite these developments, security is still a very important issue for the IoT ecosystem. Because this technology involves multiple devices, a large amount of information, supply chain partners, and society, it is not easy to keep it secure.

The blockchain-based supply chain management system runs on a shared distributed ledger and records irrefutable records of all data related to the status of shipments, the status of cargo vehicles, the environmental conditions of warehouses, etc. Blockchain in the Internet of Things is defining the future of supply chains based on the initial success of proof-of-concept (PoC) programs. These programs also focus on procurement, warehousing, and supply chain tracking and tracing areas in factory construction. Supply chain driven testing programs are very popular today and business organizations want to know how the IoT can achieve more for them using blockchain architecture (Kaur et al., 2022).

Incorporating blockchain into the Internet of Things provides real-time monitoring and traceability that will redefine supply chains. Blockchain has shown its potential to increase the speed, size, and visibility of supply chains. While improving sorting, routing, and inventory control, blockchain also eliminates transactions related to counterfeit goods. Blockchain's distributed ledger structure is becoming a catalyst for IoT adoption and business application in organizations. Combining the real-time monitoring support feature of the Internet of Things with the distributed database feature of the blockchain will enhance the accuracy and volume of tracking and tracing and lead to improvements across supply chains. Improved tracking eliminates the need for additional storage by providing visibility into inventory levels and shipments. Essential orders can be expedited and re-routed, minimizing disruption to production schedules and customer shipments. The combination of blockchain and IoT sensors has the potential to revolutionize food supply chains. In this case, sensors are used to track the freshness, quality, and safety of perishable foods. Improving inventory management and reducing bank fees for letters of credit with the integration of blockchain and the Internet of Things demonstrates the potential of this integration to save costs. Blockchain and the Internet of Things work together to ensure the safety of cargo transportation even in cross-border transactions. This system regulates the communication of all parties present in the transaction. In this way, the terms and conditions of the contract are written in the form of computer codes and the financial transactions between all unknown parties are easily done without disputes. This makes the financial performance transparent and as a result the stability and agility of the supply chain system (Chen et al., 2023).

Figure 3. IoT and Blockchain based supply chain
(Awan et al., 2021)

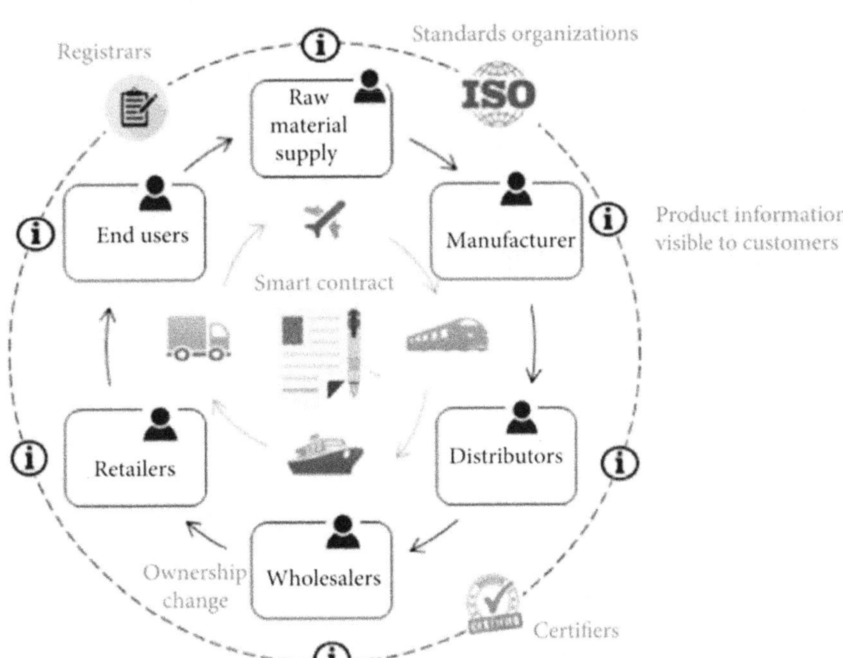

One of the other benefits of blockchain and Internet of Things technologies is the minimization of paperwork and administrative work. Currently, there are many intermediaries in the process of moving a container from one place to another. Because most companies still use traditional methods of doing business, the need for paperwork is still there. Blockchain and the Internet of Things allow companies to save money and time by eliminating red tape and paperwork, and in addition to growing supply chain agility, ensure better data protection across the ecosystem. Figure 3 shows the components of a supply chain based on the Internet of Things and Blockchain.

According to the mentioned cases, it can be seen that both companies and consumers can track the entire product life cycle in the supply chain using blockchain and Internet of Things technologies. This shows the power of the simultaneous use of these technologies. Of course, it should be taken into account that the use of these technologies always has challenges to minimize.

5. CONCLUSION

The global supply chain has become a vast and complex system that businesses use to manufacture and distribute their products globally. Its complexity has led to many technological innovations in the past few years, including the adoption of IoT and blockchain technologies. IoT is a modern technology that has security problems if used alone; Therefore, this research examines the dimensions and components of the impact of the Internet of Things on smart supply chains to show the use of impact technologies such as blockchain in the Internet of Things to make IoT technology much more powerful. The simultaneous combination of these technologies can increase power and safety and reduce costs in supply chain systems. Blockchain technology is a decentralized network and distribution system that creates high security through encryption and also enables the exchange of information in a completely secure environment. Unlike the blockchain system, IOT object systems are a traditional centralized system in such a way that the information from your smart device is sent to the cloud server, and after the information is processed, it is returned to the device. This system is fully scalable and the security in this system is weak. The use of blockchain in the Internet of Things provides security for this technology. Also, by automating the process of validation and transaction processing in the blockchain, the entire ecosystem can be activated at a lower cost. Therefore, it can be seen that the simultaneous use of these technologies, in addition to creating transparency—which itself is one of the parameters of social sustainability—can speed up activities. Simultaneous use of blockchain and Internet of Things technologies is also effective and increases the performance of supply chain processes. All these things mean that these technologies are valuable tools for sustainable industrial and organizational development.

REFERENCES

Aliahmadi, A., & Nozari, H. (2022, July). Evaluation of security metrics in AIoT and blockchain-based supply chain by Neutrosophic decision-making method. In *Supply Chain Forum: An International Journal* (pp. 1-12). Taylor & Francis.

Aliahmadi, A., Nozari, H., & Ghahremani-Nahr, J. (2022). Big Data IoT-based agile-lean logistic in pharmaceutical industries. *International Journal of Innovation in Management. Economics and Social Sciences, 2*(3), 70–81.

Aliahmadi, A., Nozari, H., Ghahremani-Nahr, J., & Szmelter-Jarosz, A. (2022). *Evaluation of key impression of resilient supply chain based on artificial intelligence of things (AIoT).* arXiv:2207.13174.

Awan, S., Ahmed, S., Ullah, F., Nawaz, A., Khan, A., Uddin, M. I., Alharbi, A., Alosaimi, W., & Alyami, H. (2021). IoT with blockchain: A futuristic approach in agriculture and food supply chain. *Wireless Communications and Mobile Computing, 2021*, 2021. doi:10.1155/2021/5580179

Chen, K., Golhar, D. Y., & Banerjee, S. (2023). Blockchain applications and challenges for supply chain and Industry 4.0: A literature review. *International Journal of Applied Decision Sciences, 16*(1), 1–41. doi:10.1504/IJADS.2023.127957

Corazza, L., Zhang, J., Arachchilage, D. K., & Scagnelli, S. D. (2023). Blockchain and Sustainability Disclosure: A Scenario-Based Application for Supply Chains. *Sustainability (Basel), 15*(1), 571. doi:10.3390u15010571

Ghahremani-Nahr, J., Aliahmadi, A., & Nozari, H. (2022). An IoT-based sustainable supply chain framework and blockchain. *International Journal of Innovation in Engineering, 2*(1), 12–21.

Karumanchi, M. D., Sheeba, J. I., & Devaneyan, S. P. (2023). Nonlinear integrity algorithm for blockchain based supply chain databases. In *Pervasive Computing and Social Networking* (pp. 169–181). Springer. doi:10.1007/978-981-19-2840-6_13

Kaur, A., Singh, G., Kukreja, V., Sharma, S., Singh, S., & Yoon, B. (2022). Adaptation of IoT with Blockchain in Food Supply Chain Management: An Analysis-Based Review in Development, Benefits and Potential Applications. *Sensors (Basel), 22*(21), 8174. doi:10.339022218174 PMID:36365871

Nahr, J. G., Nozari, H., & Sadeghi, M. E. (2021). Green supply chain based on artificial intelligence of things (AIoT). *International Journal of Innovation in Management. Economics and Social Sciences, 1*(2), 56–63.

Najafi, S. E., Nozari, H., & Edalatpanah, S. A. (2022). Artificial Intelligence of Things (AIoT) and Industry 4.0–Based Supply Chain (FMCG Industry). *A Roadmap for Enabling Industry 4.0 by Artificial Intelligence*, 31-41.

Nozari, H., & Aliahmadi, A. (2022). Lean supply chain based on IoT and blockchain: Quantitative analysis of critical success factors (CSF). *Journal of Industrial and Systems Engineering, 14*(3), 149–167.

Nozari, H., Fallah, M., Kazemipoor, H., & Najafi, S. E. (2021). Big data analysis of IoT-based supply chain management considering FMCG industries. *Бизнес-информатика, 15*(1, 1 (eng)), 78–96. doi:10.17323/2587-814X.2021.1.78.96

Nozari, H., Fallah, M., & Szmelter-Jarosz, A. (2021). A conceptual framework of green smart IoT-based supply chain management. *International journal of research in industrial engineering, 10*(1), 22-34.

Nozari, H., & Szmelter, A. (Eds.). (2018). *Global supply chains in the pharmaceutical industry.* IGI Global.

Nozari, H., Szmelter-Jarosz, A., & Ghahremani-Nahr, J. (2022). Analysis of the Challenges of Artificial Intelligence of Things (AIoT) for the Smart Supply Chain (Case Study: FMCG Industries). *Sensors (Basel)*, *22*(8), 2931. doi:10.339022082931 PMID:35458916

Oudani, M., Sebbar, A., Zkik, K., El Harraki, I., & Belhadi, A. (2023). Green Blockchain based IoT for secured supply chain of hazardous materials. *Computers & Industrial Engineering*, *175*, 108814. doi:10.1016/j.cie.2022.108814

Tavakkoli-Moghaddam, R., Ghahremani-Nahr, J., Samadi, P., Nozari, H., & Najafi, E. (2021). Applications of Internet of Things in the Food Supply Chain: A Literature Review. *J. Appl. Res. Ind. Eng*, *1*, 34–55.

Chapter 16
How the Use of 5G in Supply Chain Operations Can Prevent Future Disruptions

Likhit Verma
Ericsson, USA

ABSTRACT

The COVID-19 pandemic has affected global supply chains at an unprecedented speed and scale. In response, these businesses are now transitioning toward data-driven decision making to anticipate future performance and improve operational efficiencies, which will require the gathering and analysis of a vast amount of data in real-time. This chapter explains how 5G, with its capabilities such as ultralow latency and high bandwidth, is shaping and transforming the global supply chain. The authors present how to prepare for and avoid future supply chain disruptions. Further, the authors have showcased some practical 5G use cases in the manufacturing and logistics industries.

INTRODUCTION

We are living in an era where consumers demand personalized products and services delivered on the same day or within a minimal lead time at the lowest possible cost. "The Amazon Effect" (Lin G 2018) and customer behavior are fueling the growth of e-commerce. Shopping has seen a remarkable transformation over the years. From being a monthly or weekly ritual, shopping habits have transformed into a just-in-time activity for both individual and business customers. The volume of shipments has increased manifold while the size of the individual cart has reduced. Pitney Bowes estimates that global parcel volume surpassed 100 billion in 2019 and is forecast to reach more than 220 billion parcels by 2026 (Pitney B, 2020). Meanwhile, the COVID-19 pandemic has exposed the vulnerabilities and deficiencies of the lean, just-in-time global supply chain model, and companies must now decide how to move forward (Eric K., 2022). Pandemic-related shutdowns, geopolitics, labor shortages, and even weather have had a big impact on supply chains everywhere on the globe, resulting in supply chain bottlenecks, increased costs, and disruptions.

DOI: 10.4018/978-1-6684-7298-9.ch016

In response to the dramatic changes within the business landscape over the past few years, starting with COVID-19 and finishing with inflation, many companies across different industries are launching technology-enabled (digital) business transformation programs to improve their strategic, tactical, and operational supply chain processes. According to McKinsey's survey, 93% of supply-chain executives said that they intended to make their supply chains far more flexible, agile, and resilient (Knut and Ed 2021). According to the latest prediction by Gartner (Sarah H, 2022), by 2026, more than 75% of commercial supply chain management application vendors will deliver embedded advanced analytics (AA), artificial intelligence (AI), and data science. Now, improved decision-making using advanced analytics and AI is a high priority for supply chain users in all markets and industries. Gartner (Sarah H., 2022) also predicted that by 2025, 25% of supply chain decisions are expected to be made across intelligent edge ecosystems. Edges are physical locations where things, people, and data connect, such as operators, machines, sensors, and devices that are located across the supply chain network. Edge ecosystems allow complex processing and storage closer to where data is collected. 5G (wireless technology) will further support edge ecosystems and complement traditional centralized supply chain solutions. Edge computing decision-making is already occurring; however, the focus over the next three years will be to identify further use cases where connected, automated, and autonomous networks of edge computing can be enabled.

Supply chain technology is progressing from current less collaborative/ fragmented applications to highly integrated /collaborative architecture. Fragmented application means where many stand-alone applications run on different technology and from multiple vendors. However, as per the recent survey conducted by Gartner, only 22 percent of supply chain professionals described their organization's use of technology as highly integrated or collaborative, where their organizations have implemented multi-enterprise process orchestration to enable collaborative network-wide value creation. A highly integrated process and tools enable supply chain operators to reduce delivery time and cost. At the same time, it gives customers transparency in the supply chain, allows them to adapt to changing levels of demand and supply, and ultimately allows them to get customized solutions and higher-quality service. Achieving these goals depends on how efficiently we implement digitization and automation, also known as supply chain 4.0. The new telecom networks and the Internet of Things (IoT) will play a major role in enabling supply chain 4.0, where sensors can be connected to almost anything. For example, all goods are connected, machines are controlled remotely or autonomously, and big data analytics creates self-optimizing networks fueled by artificial intelligence. Things that were done manually, such as packing and moving goods, can now be completely automated, and with the help of augmented reality, even operators can be removed from the immediate vicinity.

This chapter will cover how 5G is shaping the future of the supply chain. How leveraging existing and upcoming technologies can prevent future supply chain disruptions. It will give business professionals 5G use cases showing how transformation is happening in the logistics and supply chain industries and discuss the following:

- What is the digital supply chain?
- What are the top supply chain technology trends?
- How to prevent future supply chain disruptions
- How a new telecom network and edge computing are enabling supply chain 4.0

Supply Chain Technologies That are Shaping the Future

Supply chain technology offers great opportunities to streamline the supply chain process. The traditional supply chain model is ineffective in the uncertain times we are currently experiencing. The traditional supply chain is a more linear model as compared to the new supply chain model, which allows organizations to be more responsive and agile to survive and lead the market (see Figure 1 and 2). Innovative technologies reorganize the traditional model, changes how information flows within the chain, and help to achieve greater business success through automation and digitalization.

Figure 1. Traditional supply chain

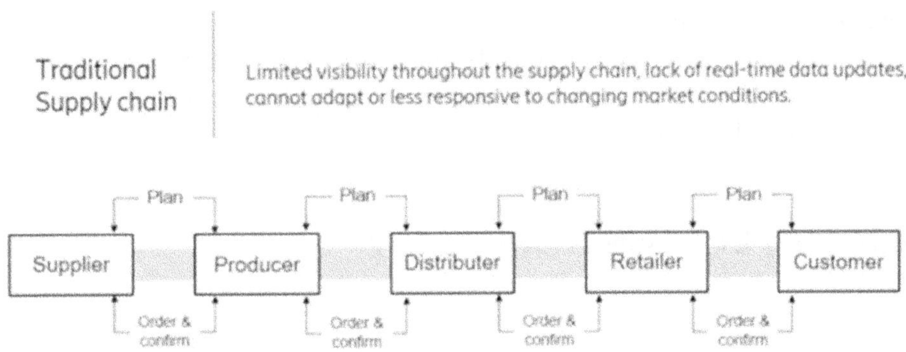

Figure 2. Digital supply chain ecosystem (supplychainbbeyond.com, 2019)

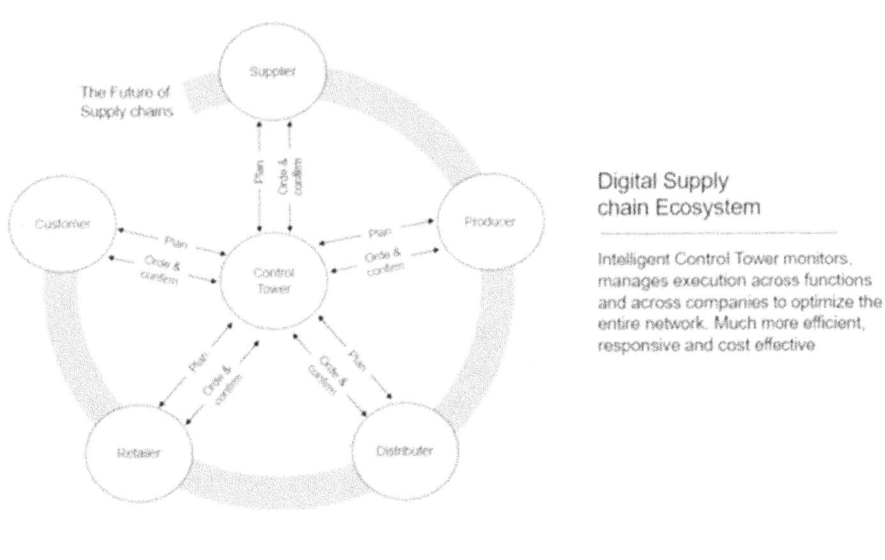

In today's globalized world, organizational success is not just dependent on its own internal efforts; it also largely depends on how effectively the organization can orchestrate a vast, global network of supply chains to deliver goods and services to its consumers. With the growing complexity of supply chains and the number of stakeholders involved, it is even more important to be able to track products in real time by accessing data and making quick decisions within the supply chain. This requires a massive transformation of the supply-chain network.

Digital twin technology (Geoff 2019) is one such emerging technology with the potential to provide substantial value. "Digital twins" are merely digital representations of actual items or systems, including parts, engines, cars, containers, and even businesses. This notion has been extended to supply chains by Gartner. The "digital supply chain twin," which Gartner defines as "a digital representation of the relationships between all the relevant entities in an end-to-end supply chain, such as products, customers, markets, distribution centers and warehouses, plants, finance, attributes, and weather," is one of the top supply chain technology trends (Geoff 2019).

Behind the scenes, advancements in machine learning, artificial intelligence, supply chain visibility platforms, big data analytics, the Internet of Things, cloud technologies, and 5G are paving the way for more efficient and profitable supply chains across the world.

BENEFITS OF SUPPLY CHAIN TECHNOLOGY

Improved Overall Efficiency

Supply chain technology can increase productivity by giving a more straightforward view of complicated data structure. Artificial intelligence, for instance, can track several supply chain routes and let us know exactly how each one is doing. It can also blend historical and real-time data to provide you with a precise prediction of future performance indicators.

Root cause analysis is one example of a technology that makes use of AI to assist IT and maintenance teams in quickly determining the root of an issue. For instance, root cause analysis can prevent hours of downtime for an IT team by rapidly identifying the location of a configuration error and coupling it with a recommended patch based on closed tickets.

Better Decision-Making

Tons of data points are produced by supply chains, but few companies can turn those data points into useful information. Companies may now collect all their data through streamlined interfaces and automated data processing, then design procedures to extract useful KPIs.

Supply chains, for instance, can keep an eye on all their sales channels and distribution locations to get a real-time snapshot of sales and inventory patterns. Such measurements can be analyzed in real-time with the help of predictive monitoring via low-latency wireless communications offered by private 5G, which can also send alarms or even create an order to refill centers that are running low on supplies.

Predictive analytics can be used with this same technology to identify trends. For instance, based on prior sales information, one can determine how much merchandise each location will require. With the capacity to foresee demand, one can plan their supply chain's flow and anticipate operational costs during periods of peak output.

Reduction in Supply Chain Expenditure

Large supply chains can be extremely complicated, with duplicate data and unused links connected by a patchwork of technology. Managers may visualize their supply networks with the help of supply chain technology software and use artificial intelligence to cut out redundant links and improve routes.

Automation has a significant impact on lowering supply chain expenses. For example, the development of private 5G recently made it possible for logistic enterprises to create their own private network to support their fleet of robotics and autonomous cars. Despite the higher CAPEX that robotics normally entails, they typically pay for themselves within a few years and give supply chains dependable, continuous labor.

In many cases of new supply chain model (Andrew 2022), 5G acts as the communication backbone for data collection and transmission across the supply chain. Up until now, even if the connected device was in a private location inside a factory, shipping yard, or warehouse, companies had to rely on commercial carriers, who had complete control over their network resources and cellular budget.

By owning their own network, private 5G enables supply chains to minimize operational costs by eliminating the need to rely on a public cellular network for use cases that are present within such facilities. Additionally, it guarantees low latency and the level of security that many supply chain businesses correctly require for communication in important applications.

Private cellular offers up to 10 times the physical coverage of Wi-Fi per access point, enables performance and latency assurances for mission-critical applications, and speeds up network setup.

How Does Supply Chain Technology Really Work?

A simple explanation would be Data is collected, processed, and transformed into insights by modern supply chain technology so that both human and automated platforms can benefit from them (table 1).

Data Collection	From product location to inventory levels, supply chains can create hundreds of data points. These metrics can be tracked and analyzed to reveal untapped opportunities and efficiencies. In terms of software, APIs are used to transfer data across systems. For instance, a customer portal and fleet monitoring system API link can let customers know exactly when their orders will arrive. IoT technology is used by many supply chains to gather data from their internal operations. IoT sensors can keep an eye on things like product locations, inventory levels, and environmental conditions. This information is frequently forwarded to a server for processing over wireless or cellular networks
Data Processing	A server receives the collected data so it may be processed and evaluated. Typically, during this stage, insights and performance measures can be extracted using artificial intelligence and data processing technologies. The server frequently includes an interface for managers and data analysts. Artificial intelligence is crucial during the processing stage because it automatically applies various formulae and algorithms to draw conclusions from the data you have gathered.
Data Transformations	Finally, data transformation turns straightforward observations into business intelligence, enabling supply chain managers to make wiser choices. Simple data points can be converted into corporate intelligence using techniques like predictive analytics, future forecasting, and risk analysis models.

A dependable, adaptable, and predictable network is needed to collect data when approaching supply chain technology from a data-driven perspective. To provide comprehensive coverage across their warehouses and tailored coverage for mission-critical devices, several logistics organizations and corporations are turning to private 5G (Joe 2021). Businesses may benefit from 5G's coverage, performance, and dependability with private 5G without having to sign constrictive contracts or give up control over their network. Administrators can gather and handle supply chain data on their own cellular networks by integrating it into their IT infrastructure. This ensures improved data privacy and seamless interaction with their current systems.

How to Prevent Future Supply Chain Disruptions

As supply chains become more global and complicated, any problems have a bigger effect. Changes in the environment or in the way people act can cause problems in the supply chain. The COVID-19 pandemic is a big example of a disruption in the supply chain. In the second quarter of 2020, McKinsey & Company [Knut et al., 2020] polled 60 senior supply-chain executives from different industries and parts of the world. "The vast majority of respondents said that the crisis had shown weaknesses in their supply chains that they are now working to fix," says the report.

- 73% of their supplier base had problems.
- 75% had problems making and selling their products.
- 85% of those who answered had trouble with digital technologies that weren't working well in their supply chains.

Because supply chains are becoming more global, it's important for aspiring and current supply chain managers to know how to understand supply chains and make plans for business continuity. Future emergency plans that include IT infrastructure, total quality management, strong business partnerships, government support, inventory visibility, the use of data analytics, and alternatives to raw material production will keep the supply chain from breaking down.

Based on industry experience, the author suggests nine ways to minimize supply chain disruptions.

1. Audit your supply chain's vulnerabilities.

Conduct a risk assessment to identify potential points of failure in your supply networks. In doing so, you may zero in on the areas where you need to start looking for solutions. Consider the environmental, social, and political factors that might influence your supply routes (Grace 2022).

Evaluate the risks to your supply chain with the help of technology. Try out some of the artificial intelligence-enhanced mapping and environmental analysis tools, aggregating applications that give global overviews, and systems that can assess cyber risks. If you want to anticipate shortages or interruptions, you may even utilize social media platforms as a predictive tool.

2. Upgrade your IT infrastructure.

Investing in IT infrastructure makes it easier to see what's going on in the supply chain, builds trust and cooperation among business partners, and makes the supply chain stronger (NewStream 2022). The following are important parts of IT infrastructure: Hardware, Software. network components, and data storage. When a company buys supply chain software, it improves its IT infrastructure and makes the supply chain more reliable. IT infrastructure is becoming more important for managing supply chains because it helps your company simplify its supply chain, get rid of links that aren't needed, increase productivity, and cut costs.

In short, you need an inventory management system that connects you to your suppliers, production facilities, warehouses, and sales organization. These systems will help you integrate data from customers, sales, suppliers, and producers into your secure and up-to-date digital network.

3. Incorporate agility into your supply network design.

Companies sometimes spend months on the network design process, trying to integrate information from a wide variety of sources, only to end up with an inflexible structure that makes it difficult to respond to unexpected events. The ability to think quickly and adapt is a cornerstone of resilience (Josh et al 2019). Companies in the fast fashion industry, for example, cannot afford to wait 18 months while they put together the correct model in order to satisfy rising consumer demands for more social responsibility in their sourcing methods. They need to source new suppliers rapidly so that they may begin constructing numerous regional supply chains. Likewise, businesses need to be nimble enough to adapt to new tax and tariff regulations, as well as trade laws like embargoes.

Most businesses now recognize that they can't just source whatever is cheapest. Environmental, social, and governance (ESG) concerns may be on the periphery now, but they will quickly become central to the missions of most companies. Improving your network's flexibility will let you strike a better cost-benefit balance between various priorities. Companies that invest a lot of time in supplier sourcing and onboarding will fail in the future. Instead, we'll have a network architecture that's flexible enough to accommodate any changes in demand and comes equipped with a reliable group of providers that have already been vetted and approved for onboarding.

4. Set up a "procure-to-pay" system for purchasing

Many parts of a business don't work well together. In many middle-market businesses, people still use Excel spreadsheets and do things by hand. Procure-to-pay is a business process cycle that starts with getting the goods and services you need, moves on to receiving them (including checking them), and ends with accounts payable and accounting. Payable duties include matching vendor invoices to purchase orders, receiving reports, getting invoice approvals, paying approved invoices, recording transactions, and making reports. In short, instead of buying things manually and on paper, switch to cheaper, easier-to-control automated buying that links all the relevant parts of your business.

5. Leveraging Supply Chain Data

Changes in the way businesses use data analytics are caused by the exponential growth of data. Data analytics can be used by all businesses, no matter how big or small, to improve performance, drive business strategy, and boost the bottom line. The process of analyzing raw data is called "data analytics." One of the most important ways to use data analytics is to spot and plan for problems in the supply chain. Most supply chains create a huge amount of data. If your employees know how to look at this data, you'll be able to predict future demand better. This helps a business decide which products to cut back on when they aren't making as much money or figure out what a customer will want after they place an order.

6. Make your business more resilient by preparing ahead of time for possible disruptions.

The best way to deal with problems in the supply chain is to be ready and plan. So, if you know what kinds of problems could happen and how they might affect your supply chain, you will be better prepared to handle a crisis (Brad 2022).

For example, proactive risk management should consider global events and risks that have a direct effect on your company's operations and those of your suppliers.

Building a strong supply chain is an ongoing process that requires people to work together, be flexible, and be proactive. Even though global supply chains are complicated, there are many tools and resources that can help build detailed visibility, find risks, and help plan for future disruptions. Use the data and technology of today to your advantage to gain insights and run your business in a more sustainable way.

7. Identify backup suppliers and diversify your supply base.

In an economy that has been affected by a pandemic, manufacturers and retailers are thinking about changing their suppliers. Those who had stock in warehouses and supply chains in other countries realized that relying on a single supplier made it harder for them to change direction (NewStream 2022). People didn't expect the delay caused by the pandemic to last as long as it did, and many businesses had to rush to find a solution. Having options for suppliers could help prevent problems in the future.

Diversifying your supply base means making sure you have the right people in the right place to fix problems if they happen in a certain place. The effects of supply chain disruptions will be lessened by finding suppliers that have supplies or manufacturers in more than one place and have a diverse supply base.

When you have relationships with more than one supplier, you can still ship orders even if one supplier is limited or temporarily unable to do so. If you research and plan for alternative suppliers ahead of time, you can keep your profit margins instead of using a supplier in a pinch, which could increase operational costs.

8. Invest in IoT platforms to improve the transparency of the Supply Chain

Supply chain visibility, or supply chain transparency, is a challenging goal to reach yet essential for managing disruptions in the supply chain (Agustin 2021). Supply chain transparency refers to the ease with which participants in the chain may see and evaluate its operations and the businesses involved. While you may be familiar with your suppliers, how well do you know their distributors and suppliers? If you answered "nothing," then there is a lack of transparency in your supply chain. Learn as much as you can about the procedures and potential problems at each stage of your supply chain. Businesses can now see more of their supply networks thanks to technology.

Tools and software for managing stock and tracking shipments fall under this category. To track things like traffic patterns, temperature, and moisture levels at each stage of the supply chain, and real-time updates on production, shipping, and stock levels, some companies are investing in Internet of Things (IoT) technology and platforms (see Figure 3).

Figure 3. IoT platform

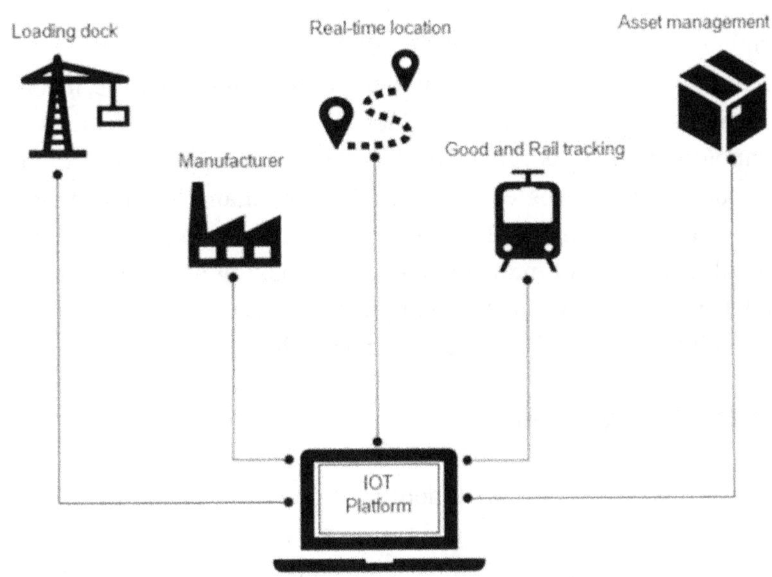

9. **Leverage emerging technology to reduce dependence on low-cost labor locations.** Global supply chains are largely based on where cheap labor can be found. But in the last five years, a lot has changed. Human labor can finally be replaced by technology in a wide range of supply chain tasks. This will give companies more freedom to operate wherever they want and make them less dependent on Asia. Here are a few things that are happening and that are starting to make a difference (Suketu HBR 2022).

    ◦ AI is getting better, and people are getting better at using it. This gives us new ways to get out of the cost trap. Major advances in cobots, which are robots that work directly with people in factories, combine AI and human intelligence to lower labor costs while keeping the value of human oversight.
    ◦ Additive manufacturing (3D printing) is getting better, which makes it easier for companies to make a wide range of parts and products at a low cost. They help them shorten the time it takes to make things in factories closer to home, so they don't have to rely on as many suppliers from far away.
    ◦ Advancements in three-dimensional simulations—metaverse applications such as Nvidia's Omniverse They let manufacturers make digital copies of their processes and simulate factory layout, workstation design, and assembly design.
    ◦ Recognition Technology: In manual manufacturing processes, like putting together an engine for an automobile, AI-driven action recognition technology uses live video and ana-

lytics to make sure that workers are following complicated steps correctly and not making mistakes. As a result, quality control is better, productivity is higher, and data can be used to make processes better.

How 5G is transforming the supply chain operations

The new wireless technology, 5G, goes beyond just a standard system upgrade; it goes beyond speed. It involves device latency and density, and this will revolutionize industries all over the world. For instance, a square mile of 4G technology may support over 10,000 devices. However, more than a million devices can be handled by 5G technology in a single space. This is more than 250 times what 4G can handle.

Additionally, 4G covers its area to enable all devices, which consumes a significant amount of energy that might not be essential. 5G employs multi-targeted user tracking applied via robust MIMO (many inputs/multiple outputs) technologies, which result in greater capacity, speed, and coverage. With more than five times the bandwidth of 4G, 5G is over eight times quicker.

Streamlined Logistics Operations

In the current market, most businesses still track and trace products manually. With 5G, supply chain firms will be able to automatically label, track, and trace every shipment, which will reduce problems like lost cargo, missing containers, smuggling, counterfeiting, and generally ineffective manual processes.

While widespread adoption of 5G technology is yet to come, some businesses have already implemented private networks with great success.

For example, as per the Pallet Market Report (Wendy, 2021), the Port of Livorno, Italy, deployed a private 5G network to simplify the byzantine turnaround system, manage increasingly high volumes of cargo, and integrate employees across multiple locations. This innovation reduced vessel mooring time, optimized productivity, and saved around \$2.95 million in annual savings. Additionally, the port increased port security, increased worker safety, and improved commercial results. It also reduced its carbon emissions by around 8% annually.

Smart Inventory and Warehouse Management

5G will enhance warehouse and inventory management techniques (Roberto 2021). The collection, delivery, and storage of commodities and products will be more transparent and effective because of the 5G high-speed network. There are three essential areas of warehouse and inventory management that will be enhanced by 5G: remote maintenance and control, increased process efficiency, and the deployment of autonomous vehicles for cargo transportation.

Organizations may, for instance, have “grid” or “hive” warehouse systems that handle important items every day. Many supply chain businesses aim to use existing network solutions to enhance order processing, packaging, and delivery, reduce downtime, and increase overall system efficiency.

This requires a wireless communication infrastructure with more speed, latency, and capacity capabilities than most wireless can provide. Achieving large gains becomes possible with 5G networking.

Indoor Asset "Track and Trace"

5G promises numerous advantages over indoor location technologies available today (Eva 2023). In addition, supply chains will require a higher degree of synchronization to realize these benefits. Track and trace is one such area that will contribute to the bottom line. Throughout the inbound-to-manufacturing process, for example, the automotive sector primarily employs manual controls. 5G will automate the sequence of parts leading to the assembly line.

Visibility for tracking and tracing will be a huge boost for supply chain logistics. Increased visibility along transportation routes leading to warehouses is one of the benefits. Once components have arrived, the assembly process continues with track and trace. Costs will reduce because better devices will be utilized along the routes, which will also increase cargo and shipment visibility. If there is a faulty component, then the whole batch can be traced in the manufacturing facility to avoid faulty production. Just-in-time (JIT) manufacturing will track components destined for the assembly line in real-time, as opposed to relying solely on the anticipated delivery date.

Smart Fleet Management Operations

Successful fleet management in the supply chain is a big advantage of 5G. Information on how to prevent accidents and the overall condition of a fleet's vehicles will be sent automatically and in real time to the managers in charge. Autonomous vehicles will use advanced sensors and collision avoidance technology to keep them safely inside their lanes, alert the recipient of the delivery immediately, and contact the authorities in the event of an accident or emergency. For this to be secure and reliable, low-latency networking is essential.

The automated features of these vehicles are enhanced by the increased simplicity with which this network infrastructure can be deployed, made possible by the advent of 5G. In fact, 5G prototype technology has made test vehicles safer and better able to brake abruptly at high speeds. Thanks to their cutting-edge sensors and lightning-fast networking, they can react far faster than humans can.

These features can also be used by businesses to enhance communication between robotic fleets and automated trucks. This paves the way for more efficient supply chain management, a more streamlined human workforce, and fully autonomous fleet logistics. In the long run, this might result in savings of several billion dollars.

There are many reasons (5G Americas, 2018) for the automotive industry's shift toward connected and autonomous vehicles, including increased security, reduced congestion, reduced pollution, and reduced costs. Vehicle-to-everything (V2X) communication is a critical component of this development because it facilitates two-way dialogue between moving vehicles, pedestrians, roadside infrastructure, and the Internet. By enabling vital data exchange between vehicles, V2X helps increase situational awareness and decrease the likelihood of collisions. More than that, though, V2X gives you dependable access to all the cloud's vast information. For instance, real-time traffic, sensor, and high-definition mapping data can be made available, which is helpful for drivers now and will be crucial for autonomous vehicles in the future.

How 5G is Transforming Manufacturing Applications

A lot of the time, manufacturing is a linear process with long lead times and a high risk of breakdowns and waste. Manufacturers use sophisticated ways to monitor and improve their operations because they have to deal with growing global demand and more aggressive competition. One of the most important parts of what is often called Manufacturing 4.0 or Industry 4.0 is the ability to change i.e. flexibility. Some of these factors are the availability of production, which can be hurt by unplanned downtime, the performance of the equipment compared to its best capacity and production rate, and the quality of the output.

As the global pandemic made clear, factories need to be more flexible and able to change their layouts and production lines quickly to meet sudden changes in demand. 5G can help make the dream of a factory with modular machines that can be quickly rearranged to improve production a reality. It could not only make it easier for staff to talk to each other but also keep them safer by making it possible to collect data from a large number of sensors on a scale that was not possible before. And it will be able to prevent problems by letting systems automatically schedule maintenance or order replacements for consumables, so that there is as little downtime as possible. It makes it possible for manufacturing lines to set themselves up and for equipment maintenance to be planned ahead of time based on data from sensors.

Wireless technologies have been a priority for manufacturers in recent years, but various barriers have limited how much wireless solutions may boost production and operations. According to survey conducted by Manufacturing institute (Shawn & MI 2021) about half 51% of manufacturers questioned said cost is the biggest hurdle in using wireless technologies (see table 2).

Manufacturers also struggle with wireless reliability. As per survey conducted Manufacturing institute 40% of firms say guaranteeing wireless dependability is a top issue. This is especially true in radio-interference-prone interior areas. The criteria for Ultra Reliable Low Latency Communication services are one of the key performance indicators (KPI) outlined by 5G. This equates to 99.999% availability and dependability. 5G should assist manufacturers overcome this difficulty and allow them to use wireless technologies they had previously avoided due to unreliable network connectivity.

Existing equipment and infrastructure impede the adoption of wireless technology. Many manufacturers have legacy buildings, equipment, and procedures, and some have had trouble integrating wireless technology. Manufacturers cite interference from facility components (38%), facility obstacles (35%), facility environment (33%), and integration with old systems, processes, and equipment (31%).

5G can reduce many of these problems. Wi-Fi networks can face interference in packed environments, and cable connections can be challenging to handle in huge industrial buildings. 5G will accommodate 1 million devices per kilometer, compared to a few thousand with 4G. This allows manufacturers to implement wireless solutions in densely linked areas.

Challenges Related to Implementation of Wireless Technologies

Table 2. Challenges related to implementation of wireless technologies

Cost	51%
Ensuring reliability	40%
Interference from facility elements (i.e., vehicle cages, ductwork, machines with electrostatic discharge, etc.)	38%
Facility barriers (i.e., walls, glass, radio frequency interference, etc.	35%
Facility environments (i.e., temperature, humidity, moisture, shock, vibration, etc.)	33%
Legacy systems/processes/equipment	31%
Device density	23%

Challenges Related to Manufacturing Facility Analytics

Table 3. Challenges related to manufacturing facility analytics

Ease of integrating data from multiple sources	44%
Volume of data	40%
Cost	39%
Speed of system response	37%
Integration with legacy systems/processes/equipment	37%
Security challenges/concerns	33%

Challenges Related to Real-time Asset/Resource Tracking

Table 4. Challenges related to real-time asset/resource tracking

Unexpected breakdowns	33%
Identifying process inefficiencies	33%
Cost	33%
Human error	30%
Wrong/maintaining inventory estimations	28%
Eliminating redundant assets	26%
Identifying asset location	25%
Resource wastage	20%
Maintenance issues	20%
Theft occurrences	18%
Underutilization of the workforce	14%

Source: Manufacturing Institute. Connecting Manufacturers with the Future: How 5G Is Transforming the Manufacturing Landscape" [2021]

While connection is crucial to smart industries, data will drive the future. Manufacturers confront similar issues here. Manufacturers' top hurdles with facility analytics are data integration (44%), data volume (40%) and cost (39%) [Shawn & MI 2021]. These are followed by system response time (37%), legacy system integration (37%), and security issues (33%) (see table 3). 5G is designed to overcome several of these analytical obstacles. Machines generate monitoring, maintenance, and production management data. Much of this material went unrecorded until recently. Historically, employees on the shop floor did much of the monitoring. Machines that needed maintenance were put offline. Management may search for methods to enhance production results, but they often use old data or, in the lack of data, instinct. In recent years, manufacturers have equipped equipment with sensors that capture information digitally and continually. Much of the factory's data is still siloed. Manufacturers struggle to transform data into real-time insights that predict shop floor demands. 33% of manufacturers say unexpected failures are their main real-time resource tracking pain point. Identifying process inefficiencies (33%), cost (33%), human error (30%), inventory estimates (28%), eliminating redundant assets (26%) and locating assets (25%) (see table 4). 5G will assist factory and plant owners reduce some of these pain points. This will bring in a new era of AI and machine learning approaches that may assist firms get real-time operational expertise. 5G is geared to gather real-time data to automate manufacturing operations. In all circumstances, the appropriate data must come at the right time and location to impact the right process. 5G will provide increased computational capabilities within the network, closer to the end user, machine, and process.

5G allows manufacturers to apply AI to data quicker by supporting a large number of endpoints in a compact region. This allows for precise analytics and production in control applications. Better analytics in 5G will help producers to do granular and accurate work. Enabling machines to communicate information and insights in real time would help manufacturers automate certain operations and free up humans for higher-value duties.

Benefits of 5G Connectivity in Manufacturing Industry

Manufacturers anticipate several benefits to 5G connectivity. Nearly half of the surveyed participants (Shawn & MI 2021) say 5G will help their manufacturing operations by increasing data consumption (48%) and dependability (46%) (Table 5). Two-fifths of respondents say their processes can be enhanced by connecting additional devices (41%), reducing downtime (40%), increasing security (40%), and increasing safety (39%).

Ways in Which 5G Will Aid Manufacturing Processes

Manufacturers are mostly in agreement that 5G will improve existing business processes and procedures. Nine out of ten manufacturers feel that the implementation of 5G in their facilities would enhance existing business practices (92%) and procedures (88%).

Nine in ten manufacturers expect 5G to create new processes (88%) and businesses (86%). 5G deployment's introduction of new processes and business procedures offers second-order benefits for manufacturers. When asked about innovative goods and processes, manufacturers cite numerous categories. They featured augmented reality customer help, staff training tools, and remote maintenance. Some manufacturers anticipate 5G would improve first-time fix rates and remote access to their services. Manufacturers anticipate 5G to change factory automation and control systems.

Table 5. Ways in which 5G will aid manufacturing processes

Increased data usage	48%
Increased reliability	46%
Ability to connect more devices	41%
Reduced downtime	40%
Increased security	40%
Increased safety	39%
Increased machine productivity	39%
Ability to capture more data	36%
Reduced overall costs	35%
Reduced defects	32%
Reduced machine replacement rate	27%
Increased video usage	25%
Reduced spend on Maintenance and repair	22%

Source: Manufacturing Institute. Connecting Manufacturers with the Future: How 5G Is Transforming the Manufacturing Landscape" [2021]

5G will affect many production procedures, say manufacturers. Four-fifths of manufacturers say 5G will be vital for inventory tracking (83%) and facility security (81%). With 5G, manufacturers and logistic service providers may inform downstream consumers and upstream suppliers in real time. This will help manufacturers optimize incoming and outbound logistics and ensure goods are received and delivered. They can speed up shipping and receiving and synchronize information across the supply chain. Manufacturers can also communicate prospective delivery delays to supply chain partners and modify as needed. AI will help optimize fleet routes, logistics services, and warehouse management.

Three-quarters of firms say 5G will be vital for inspection (76%), assembly (76%), packaging (72%), and staff training (71%). Many of these benefits will reduce operating costs and boost manufacturing efficiency. Manufacturers say equipment monitoring and control (89%), real-time sensor data analysis (87%) and personnel safety (86%) will gain most from 5G connection. The great majority of manufacturers say 5G will offer remote analytics for real-time decision making (84%), condition-based remote monitoring for predictive maintenance (84%), asset tracking (83%) and preventative maintenance (82%). 5G improves data-driven decisions.

Nearly all manufacturers predict cost savings (93%) and better machine and labor productivity (93%) by connecting their machines and equipment wirelessly with 5G. Manufacturers predict 5G may reduce costs by 38% while improving machine and labor productivity by 42%. 5G will affect industry-wide profit and productivity.

How 5G is Transforming Transport and Logistics Industry

Below table 6 depicts some of the most important use cases analyzed and compiled by STL Partners (Miran and Chris 2020) that 5G will allow. Although some of these use cases currently exist, 5G will enhance them and boost their value. Existing logistics routing and scheduling systems, for instance, may compute the ideal path for a truck to take; but the inclusion of 5G will enable more dynamic solutions that can adapt in real-time to the fluctuating status and demands of the ecosystem.

Table 6. How 5G is transforming transport and logistics industry

Use case		Benefits	Why 5G?
Connected traffic infrastructure	Smart sensors or cameras are integrated into traffic infrastructure to collect data about oncoming traffic and trigger real-time actions	• Reduce congestion • Reduce accidents • Increase efficiency	• Device density • Low latency
Real-time routing and optimization	Sensors collect data throughput the supply chain to improve visibility and optimize processes through real-time dynamic routing and scheduling	• Increase supply chain visibility • Increase efficiency • Increase throughput	• Device density • Low latency
Automated last 100 yards delivery	Using drones or automated delivery vehicles for the last 'hundred yards' of delivery, where the delivery van acts as a mobile final distribution point	• Reduce time for delivery • Reduce distance driven by van	• Low latency • Reliability • Location-awareness
Predictive maintenance of fleets	Using dozens of sensors to give an accurate, real-time representation of the status of a vehicle to perform predictive and preventative maintenance	• Reduce downtime • Reduce spend on maintenance • Reduce vehicle replacement rate	• Device density • Reliability • Device costs
Advanced driver assistance	Using cameras to monitor behavior of the driver and the external surroundings to detect and alert driver to any potential risks	• Reduce accidents • Reduce damage to vehicle • Lower insurance costs	• Bandwidth (video data) • Low latency
Infotainment for public transport	Better connectivity on public transport to deliver information and entertainment services to travelers e.g. HD video streaming, gaming, video calls	• Improve passenger experience • Stimulate use of public transport	• Bandwidth (video or AR/VR applications)
Automatic vehicle software updates	Vehicles with embedded 5G modules receive over the-air updates to applications and software systems	• Increase efficiency • Enable more frequent updates	• Bandwidth

Source: STL Partners

In this section, we will take deep dive at three of these use cases, how they could help the industry (as described by STL Partners).

1. Real-time routing and optimization

Like many others, the road freight business has to deal with inefficient practices (such as with routing, loading, and unloading) and lengthy wait periods. As per Supply chain worldwide survey (GEODIS 2017), only 6% of organizations have full visibility of their end-to-end supply networks, making poor supply chain visibility another important concern.

Enhancing end-to-end visibility is crucial for businesses looking to boost supply chain efficiency and reliability. Several sensors placed strategically along the supply chain can help achieve this goal. All the way from warehouses (point of collection) to customer (point of delivery) including vehicle and their load information.

The data may be transmitted to an analytics platform, where an AI engine extracts insights and patterns and gives real-time automated supply chain suggestions. Long-term data analysis helps find improvement opportunities and develop better shipping routes. Enhanced route planning and dynamic scheduling help optimize the supply chain.

- Improved route planning — Algorithms can analyze past data to find the most effective path. With real-time data, the route may be continuously optimized to account for issues like traffic or weather. These algorithms differ from generic route planning apps like Google Maps because they must address fleet-specific criteria like avoiding low bridges or ensuring driver breaks are taken at appropriate intervals without diverting off course.
- Dynamic scheduling — Most logistics businesses provide each driver a predefined delivery and pickup schedule, which can't be changed automatically after they leave the central distribution center (though their progress may be monitored). If logistics timetables are centralized, 5G may update them in real-time to guarantee each driver uses the most efficient schedule. Changes to the timetable will take into consideration changes in warehouse stock levels, anticipated transit delays due to traffic or driver break needs, the need to pick up fresh products, and the status of other deliveries. If a high-priority order arrives and a driver is nearby, it can be added to their route. If a driver is late, another driver might take up their load to avoid missing a deadline. 5G's speed and latency are critical to enable this use case at scale, maybe in combination with edge computing to cut data transmission costs by conducting analytics closer to the drivers.

2. Automated last 100 yards delivery

Last mile deliveries are the final stage of delivery, from the final distribution point to the ultimate customer. Despite being a short part of the voyage, it accounts for 53% (Shelagh 2022) of the entire shipping cost. More shipments are being delivered due to e-commerce, and buyers want next-day or on-demand delivery and free shipping.

Last-mile delivery expenses are being slashed by automation. Companies are testing AGVs (Automated guided vehicles) and UAVs (Unmanned aerial vehicles), such as UPS's Flight Forward. Initial adoption of autonomous vehicles in the last mile of delivery will focus on high-value items like medical supplies, organs, and cash. Automation of normal B2C parcel delivery will roll out slowly because of limits.

Automating the last 100 yards of delivery solves this difficulty. STL Partners (Miran and Chris 2020) illustrate with drones. Instead of drones delivering goods all the way from the warehouse to the customers' doorsteps, the delivery van carries the parcels and drones, then stops 100 yards from the drop-off site and the drone flies out and carries the parcel. While the drone is engaged, the driver can hand-deliver a parcel or drive to the next location, where the drone can return and redock. The intricacy and automation of this approach might vary. The driver gets out of the vehicle at each stop, picks the next product to be delivered, loads the drone, and sets its next destination. After delivery, the drone docks, and recharges. Multiple drones may be employed in an advanced form, and they work totally independently without external input to load, reload, or set each destination. For example, Workhorse Group (Workhorse 2021) has built high-efficiency delivery UAV that is fully integrated with their line of electric delivery trucks. Their technology, Horsefly system is designed to conform to the FAA guidelines for UAV operation in the U.S. Most notably, being fully integrated with delivery trucks, the system is designed such that a driver or driver's assistant can maintain line-of-sight operation of the UAV delivery process.

The flexibility to deploy UAVs or AGVs to automate the final leg of delivery is significant. Drones can transport items quickly in rural and suburban areas, but their requirement to navigate through the skies might be troublesome in cities. AGVs are efficient in cities but less so across long distances.

4G can provide automated UAV/AGV routes. If UAVs were widely adopted and the number of drones in the sky reached the hundreds, they would need to communicate to avoid crashing. Real-time inter-drone communication requires 5G.

Real-time video streaming from several cameras is necessary for more autonomous UAV/AGV movement (when the path is not pre-planned). Real-time navigation commands are required. 5G's low latency and high bandwidth will enable this transmission.

3. Connected traffic infrastructure

Today there are 1.2 billion automobiles, and that number will double by 2050 as per global mobility report 2017. Even with additional roads, traffic will strain current road networks. Connected transportation infrastructure might ease this load.

Connected IoT devices such as sensors or video cameras are installed in roadways and traffic signals. These devices broadcast traffic and environmental data to a single analytics platform. Future linked automobiles will receive and exchange this data. Comparing aggregated data points to historical data can trigger real-time actions or help enhance traffic networks. This data collecting and analysis method may be used to:

- For smart traffic lights — Smart control of traffic lights may optimize traffic flow and minimize waiting times for cars by altering their timing according to real-time conditions and by advising drivers on the appropriate speed to maintain to avoid a red signal. Prioritize sustainable transit choices including buses, bikers, and ambulances. Traffic lights may slow down fast motorists by turning red and requiring them to stop.
- For smart road signs, speed limit signs can be changed dynamically to reduce traffic build-up (by lowering the limit at busier times); hard shoulders can be opened on highways to accommodate increased demand; and road signs can encourage drivers to take alternative routes when the regular route is overwhelmed, e.g. to reroute traffic in the event of a crash.

Data can help public transport run on schedule. Weather, accidents, or traffic can be considered, and actions made to guarantee public transport timetables are followed (e.g., holding buses to spread them out or rerouting services). This data helps anticipate arrival timings.

This is a massive IoT application case with many sensors streaming data. 4G provides acceptable latency and bandwidth when using a small number of sensors, but performance decreases as the number of devices rises. This is problematic since road network efficiency are most critical when traffic is ramping up, yet when places are crowded and numerous cars or phones are connecting to the local network, 4G struggles to send data in real time. 5G is needed because it can handle more sensors and provide a stable connection. High bandwidth allows HD video streaming. This is vital for multi-modal travel, as radar or inductive loops can detect a vehicle's existence, but video can determine the kind (e.g. bike versus car versus truck).

Fiber might also match the performance requirements for this use case, but laying fiber is costly and disruptive, requiring roads to be torn up. 5G sensors are predicted to be relatively simple and – once they reach scale – low-cost to deploy, making them a more feasible alternative for non-fiber rich places.

FUTURE STUDY / CONCLUSION

In the next few years, 5G is anticipated to transform global supply chains as it becomes more widely available. More firms are transitioning toward data-driven decision making to anticipate future performance and improve operational efficiencies, which will require the gathering and analysis of a vast amount of data, some in real-time.

Exponentially higher data rates and lower latency will create a more responsive network to facilitate this change and enable more Internet-enabled smart devices in the logistics supply chain. This will speed up, make safer, and improve the reliability of logistics processes.

5G will make the future of connected manufacturing possible. It will be the basis for a network of smart sensors that are all connected to each other. This will give manufacturers access to data and a source of new insights on a scale that has never been seen before. 5G will open up new uses for AI applications, predictive maintenance, and intelligent, autonomous, and semi-autonomous robots. Also, 5G will change the way factories work by letting people move around on their own. 5G is a must if these improvements are to be used across entire production sites and enterprise-wide systems.

REFERENCES

5G Americas. (2018). Ceullular V2X Communica*tions To*wards 5G. 5G Americas. https://www.5gamericas.org/wp-content/uploads/2019/07/201*8_5G_Americas_White_Paper_Cellular_V2X_Co*mmunications_Towards_5G__Final_for_Distribution.pdf

Cheng, E. (2023). 5G Indoor Positioning. Pointr Tech. https://www.pointr.tech/blog/5g-indoor-positioning

Dolan, S. (2022). Last Mile Shipping Delivery Explained. Business Insider. https://www.*businessinsider.com/last-mil*e-delivery-shipping-explained?r=US&IR=T

DuBravac, S. (2021). Connecting manufacturors with the future of how 5G is transforming the landscape. Manufacturing Institute. https://www.th*emanufacturing*institute.org/research/connectin g-manufacturers-with-the-future-how-5g-is-transforming-the-manufacturing-landscape/

Dyton, J. (2021*). 5G can be*tter communications. Connected Remag. https://connectedremag.com/das-in-*building-wireless/5g/can-bett*er-communications-and-5g-solve-some-of-the-supply-chain-problems/

GEODIS. (2017). Supply chain worl*dwide survey. GEODIS. h*ttps://geodis.com/sites/default/files/2019-03/170509_GEODIS_WHITE-PAPER.PDF

John, B. (2022). Reducing Supply Chain Disruptions in Life Science. The *Hartford. htt*ps://www.the-hartford.com/insights/covid-19/reduce-life-science-supply-chain-disruptions

Knut. (2020). Resettin*g Supple Chains* for the Next Normal. McKinsey. https://www.mckinsey.com/capabilities/operations/our-insights/resetting-supply-chains-for-the-next-normal

Lau, G. (202*2). Mitigate Supply Chain Disruptions. Shift 4 Shop.* https://blog.shi*f*t4shop.com/mitigate-supply-chain-disruption

Michael, R. (2021). How 5G connectivity can help your warehouse oper*ations. MMH. https://www.mmh.com/article/how_5g_connectivity_can_hel*p_your_warehouse_operation

*Miran, C. (2020). 5G's impact on transport a*nd logistics: $280bn of benefits in 2030. STL.

Morawski, A. (2022). Manufacturing 4.0: How 5G could revolutioniz*e the supply chain. Oracle Communications B*log. https://blogs.oracle.com/oracle-communications/post/manufacturing-40-how-5g-could-revolutionize-the-supply-chain

Nelson, J. (2019). *Understanding the benefits of supply chain agility. Th*e Hackett Group. https://www.thehackettgroup.com/insights/understanding-the-benefits-of-supply-chain-agility/

*NewStream. (2022). Five ways to minimize supply chain disruptions. NewStream Ente*rprises. https://www.newstreaming.com/5-ways-to-minimize-supply-chain-disruptions/

Pelaez, A. (2021). Supply Chain Management. Ubidots. https://ubidots.com/blog/iot-supply-chain-management/

Suketu, H. B. R. (2022). Leveragin*g New Tech to Boo*st Supple Chain Resilience. HBR. https://hbr.org/2022/10/leveraging-new-tech-to-boost-supply-chain-resilience

*UN. (2017). Global Mobility Report. UN. https://su*stainabledevelopment.un.org/content/documents/2643Global_Mobility_Report_2017.pdf

Chapter 17
Day in the Life of Supply Chain Analysts in a Digital World

Shiva R. Esturi
Micron Technology Inc., USA

Bo Liao
Micron Technology Inc., USA

Neale R. Smith
Tecnologico de Monterrey, Mexico

ABSTRACT

This chapter discusses the role of supply chain analytics in managing digital supply chain, as well as the practical implementation approaches of supply chain analytics. The chapter first discusses a typical day in the life of supply chain analysts. It then discusses the categorization of supply chain analytics and some practical recommendations for the implementation of supply chain analytics. Finally, the chapter provides a case study illustrating some important considerations in supply chain design.

INTRODUCTION

Digital technology continues to enable supply chains as a competitive advantage. A decade ago, technologies enabled supply chains to be Aligned between customers, organization, and suppliers; Adaptable for geo-political-pandemic disruptions; and Agile for speed for material, cash and information flow included material requirements planning (MRP), enterprise resource planning (ERP), and in-memory computing for advanced planning and optimization systems. In the current era, technologies that are emerging include big data, machine learning techniques, social media, robotics, blockchain, augmented and virtual reality, internet of things and many more. Unlike before, there is an increased pace at which innovative technologies are being introduced. It is more important than ever to identify specific technologies that provide a competitive advantage.

DOI: 10.4018/978-1-6684-7298-9.ch017

Under the backdrop of fast-paced technological advances, the role of supply chain analysts is also evolving. A decade ago, supply chain analysts were primarily responsible for creating supply chain plans from scratch on paper or in Excel. In the past decade, along with the maturity of enterprise resource planning and advanced planning systems, their primary responsibility changed from creating the plan into analyzing the plan output from the advanced planning systems. In the future, most likely, the task of plan analysis will be replaced by Artificial Intelligence. Once we are there, the role of supply chain analysts will further shift into taking actions to tackle unexpected circumstances. One could imagine that a Supply Chain analyst will receive alerts from Mobile Apps detailing actions required to address certain urgent upstream supply issues.

Supply chain analytics in a digital world is more important than ever because of the volume and availability of data. In the past, supply chain analytics enabled efficient supply chain management by validating or replacing conventional wisdom, but the value added to the business was limited by the availability of data and computer power. In the digital world, a vast amount of supply chain data is produced and recorded daily, thanks to big data infrastructure and cloud storage technologies. It is up to the capability of each company to either make efficient use of them or leave them untouched.

This chapter focuses on the consumer electronics value chain also referred to as the hitech or chips or semiconductor value chain, where the end customer buys electronic products from retailers through retail stores or online through e-tailers, consumer electronics manufacturer, or chip manufacturer website. Figure 1 illustrates a simplified end to end consumer electronics value chain that will be referenced in later parts of this chapter.

Figure 1. Consumer electronics value chain

In this Chapter, we first discuss the four categories of supply chain analytics and their respective impact on the business. We then describe a typical day for supply chain analysts and discuss how they may employ the concepts of supply chain analytics and optimization in daily life. Next, we discuss some critical factors regarding the development of successful supply chain analytics teams. Specifically, we discuss the impact of decentralization for various supply chain analytics categories, and the implementation model of supply chain analytics teams. In the last section, we discuss a few practical considerations of enabling supply chain analytics and optimization in a medium-size or large-size company, using the semi-conductor value chain as a case study.

Literature Review

There is a vast literature discussing and evaluating the application of analytics in supply chains. We first review literature discussing the applications and performance of supply chain analytics, which are not necessarily placed in the context of digital technologies. Then we review literature that specifically discusses the application of data science and big data in supply chain design and management.

We first review the research focused on evaluating applications of supply chain analytics. Trkman et al. (2010) conducted a systematic and structured analysis of the impact of business analytics on supply chain performance. Their research results show that the use of business analytics in critical process areas can affect a supply chain's performance. Specifically, they show that the analytical capabilities indicators alone could explain 66.7% of the variability in the performance of the companies in the sample studied. Chae et al. (2014) developed a theoretical framework for supply chain analytics and its impact on the performance of supply chain management. According to the paper, anecdotal evidence holds that the use of business analytics is positively associated with organizational performance, and the important question is whether the use of analytics for supply chain management is just hype, or if it has a real effect in enabling performance improvement. The finding from Chae et al. (2014) indicates that the positive impact of analytics on supply chain performance could be real. They also identified relevant latent variables and indicators for empirical research on this topic. Sahey and Ranjan (2008) discussed the traditional and real-time business intelligence and the advantages of implementing real time business intelligence in supply chain solutions to support supply chain analytics. O'Dwyer and Renner (2011) discussed the promises of advanced analytics on supply chain management and presented several case studies. They stated that the focus of advanced analytics on supply chain will shift from the internal cross-functional sharing of data to greater coordination and shared understanding of the data flows across value chain partners. With this, individual silos within the supply chain will be torn down and instead, a single, broader supply chain will emerge.

There is also emerging literature studying the impact of big data analytics and data science in supply chains. Waller and Fawcett (2013) proposed the definition of data science in supply chain management as "the application of quantitative and qualitative methods from a variety of disciplines in combination with supply chain management theory to solve relevant supply chain management problems and predict outcomes, taking into account data quality and availability issues". The paper examined possible applications of data science, predictive analytics, and big data in practice, and provided examples of research questions from these applications. Gunasekaran et al. (2017) studied the impact of big data and predictive analytics assimilation on supply chain and organizational performance. The paper conceptualized the assimilation of big data and predictive analytics as a three-stage process: acceptance, routinization, and assimilation. Their findings suggested that connectivity and information sharing under the mediation effect of top management commitment are positively related to the acceptance of big data and predictive analytics. Tan et al. (2015) proposed an analytic infrastructure for firms to assist firms to capture the potential of innovation afforded by data and to gain a competitive advantage. They showed from case studies that the proposed data analytic approach enabled firms to utilize big data to gain a competitive advantage by enhancing their supply chain innovation capabilities.

The Four Categories of Supply Chain Analytics

Supply chain analytics can be categorized as descriptive, predictive, prescriptive, and cognitive, based on the complexity of the analytics and the business value it may provide.

To explain each of the categories, "descriptive analytics" is the type of analytics that provides answers to the simple question of "what has happened?". For example, crunching historical demand data to arrive at an average monthly demand quantity for a product is descriptive analytics. It is the type of analytics that is relatively less complex and provides less value to the business, compared to the other three types of analytics. Rather than simply summarizing historical data, "predictive analytics" utilizes historical data to predict the future. In other words, it answers the question of "what will happen?". The third category of analytics, "prescriptive analytics", goes beyond summarizing historical data and making future predictions. It optimizes for the solutions to tackle business problems. It answers the question of "what should we do about it?". The final category of analytics, "cognitive analytics", is the category with highest complexity but also the potential to bring the highest value to the business. "Cognitive analytics" is the type of analytics that learns from historical data and human decisions, to train the computer to mimic and replace human decisions and naturally interact with people. Machine learning and artificial intelligence fall into this category of analytics. It answers the question of "what will the human decision be?". Figure 2 maps these four categories of supply chain analytics into various levels of analytics complexity and value to the business.

As an example, consider the newsboy in the newsvendor problem. The newsboy´s gathering of historical demand quantities and calculating the demand standard deviation is descriptive analytics. His predicting forward-looking demand is predictive analytics. Knowing that the demand would be uncertain but may follow a distribution, then utilizing the newsvendor model to calculate how many newspapers to procure to maximize his expected profit, is prescriptive analytics. Alternatively, if he records his decision and outcome every day and trains a computer to learn from the data and make decisions for the future, then he is implementing cognitive analytics.

Figure 2. Business value vs. analytics complexity

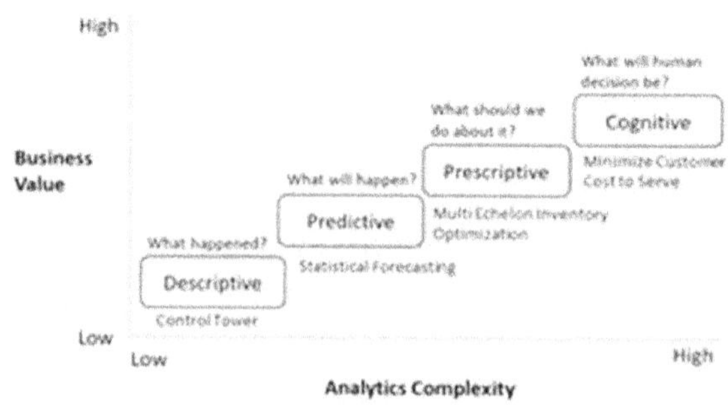

Below, we discuss the application and use cases for each of the analytics categories. Most mid-to-large sized companies are very sophisticated in utilizing the results from descriptive analytics as a control tower to orchestrate business activities. To enhance visualization power, business stakeholders commonly use charts, tables, and dashboards to present data from different angles, as well as visually track the progress of key performance indicators for the business such as forecast accuracy, shipments trend, point of sale at retailer, out of stock, number of product hits at e-tailer, on time delivery performance and so on. To facilitate this, Tableau or PowerBI is a commonly used software that provides sophisticated descriptive analytics power. There are also several other business intelligence systems, reporting systems, and cloud technologies that the companies may employ to extract, transform, load, and describe the company's data.

A common use case of predictive analytics is statistical demand forecasting. For example, a retailer may implement statistical forecasting models to predict customer orders based on point of sale historical order data and its correlation with events such as stock outs and promotions. While it is sometimes possible to achieve acceptable forecasting accuracy by implementing simple out-of-box statistical forecasting models, the accuracy can usually be improved by incorporating some of the additional data that may have explained the demand pattern, such as product life cycle, product seasonality, promotions, price changes,, competitors' promotions, inventory in the distribution network, etc. Furthermore, the outcome of the statistical forecasting models can be fine-tuned or adjusted by consensus and collaborative forecasting techniques. Companies are advised to establish a process that ensures that both statistical predictions and human collaborations are incorporated into the final numbers. For example, the initial demand forecast can be recommended by the statistical model, whereas the final numbers are enhanced through consensus among multiple departments such as marketing, sales, operations and other business units. Finally, these forecasting numbers can be shared with key suppliers through a collaborative planning forecasting and replenishment (CPFR) process. Of course, the extent of statistical forecasting versus consensus and collaborative forecasting should vary by customers, products, and markets. For example, niche products sold to a few customers may be more collaboratively driven, whereas commodity products that are established and have ample historical demand data may rely more on statistical predictions. Alternatively, eighty percent of value being due to twenty percent of products or customers can be predicted based on human decisions, while the long tail of eighty percent of products or customers contributing to twenty percent of value can be predicted based on the analytics.

There are ample use cases of prescriptive analytics. Consider a consumer electronics value chain. Below are examples of the problems that may be solved through prescriptive analytics and potentially save millions of dollars annually.

- What should be the inventory week-of-stock targets at each inventory stage in the supply chain?
- What is the optimal in-house versus outsourced manufacturing split?
- What is the optimal capacity buffer level to keep for each of the manufacturing equipment?
- Which product should be qualified to be built at which factory?

Most of the prescriptive analytics involves tradeoffs between multiple effects, and it is through optimization that the best solution can be found. Taking the problems above, solving for the optimal inventory week-of-stock across supply network can be viewed as a tradeoff between the customer service level versus the cost of holding inventory (Manary and Willems 2008). Solving for the optimal in-house versus outsourced manufacturing split for a semiconductor manufacturer is a tradeoff between the cost premium of outsourced manufacturing versus the cost of idle in-house facilities. Solving for the optimal capacity buffer level for manufacturing resources involves weighing the depreciation cost of the equipment against the missed demand opportunities due to capacity shortages. Solving for the best qualification structure between products and manufacturing sites is a tradeoff between manufacturing flexibility versus product qualification cost (Liao et al. 2017).

Cognitive analytics enables the computer to learn based on historical data and business actions, with the purpose to compliment or minimize the need for human decision interventions for business processes in the future. Cognitive analytics, if leveraged efficiently, can enable a company's supply chain to position products when and where its customers need them, even before they are requested by the customer. As a use case, one may analyze real-time point-of-sales information at a retailer and identify multi stage inventories across the supply chain and trigger replenishment based on prescriptive analytics. Often, human review results in overrides in consideration of other undefined factors such as new product release expectation, shortage indicated by supplier, excess inventory in the different distribution center or bull whip effects in the chain, competitors pricing changes and more that are not defined at this time. Cognitive analytics learn human overrides by co-relating human inputs with big data triggers and effectively recommend or replace human decisions. Cognitive analytics can learn for a subset of products from human decisions and then can easily scale up to millions of products. This could potentially speed up the decision-making process in an end to end supply chain from weeks to minutes.

Cognitive analytics often leverages structured and unstructured data which are provided by the big data architecture. Big data architecture can also be leveraged to construct a data lake for each functional area of the supply chain, such as customer, supplier, inventory, manufacturing, fulfillment, quality, etc. Efficient usage of the data lake and big data architecture will provide the required information for cognitive analytics and will help achieve quick wins in the respective functions. Furthermore, building bridges between these data lakes will enlarge the benefits by enabling cross-functional analytics and cross-functional learning and decision making. Cognitive analytics use case can be to minimize customer cost to serve by co-relating customer requirements, escalations or complaints with available big data and identify if customer care more about lower price or shorter delivery lead time or higher service level and segment supply change to cater to unique customer needs while minimizing cost to serve to respective customer.

Day in the Life of Supply Chain Analytics and Optimization

Figure 3 shows a typical day of a supply chain analyst. He or she starts the day by reading a newspaper. Then, he or she stands in line at Starbucks and grabs a morning coffee. He or she then carpools with his or her friends to go hiking. When it gets close to the lunch time, he or she orders sushi in a Japanese restaurant for lunch. After lunch, he or she goes horseback riding and then does household chores afterwards. At dinner time, he or she enjoys a pizza dinner party with his or her friends. Then he or she goes to sleep and turns the lights off.

Figure 3. Typical day of supply chain analyst

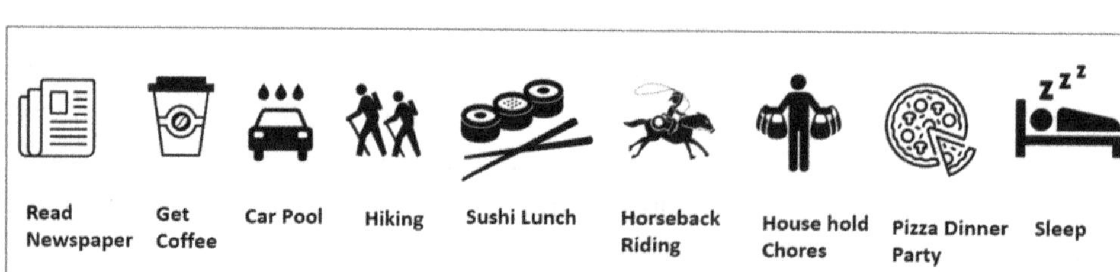

One may wonder how this can possibly be a typical day of a supply chain analyst. How can a person do this every day, and still get well-paid? Of course not. This is just a cartoon. However, taking a closer look at each of the activities described above, one could find the elements of supply chain analytics and optimization in each of them. Figure 4 shows the connections between these daily activities and the theories of supply chain analytics.

Reading newspaper

Starting the day reading newspaper is related to the classic "newsvendor problem" in supply chain analytics. In this problem, the newsboy faces uncertain demand and a fixed unit price per newspaper, which is a perishable product. The newsboy needs to decide how much inventory to stock before the demand quantity is realized, knowing that unsold copies will be almost worthless at the end of the day. The optimal solution for the newsvendor problem is to trade-off between the underage cost of stocking too few (in which case he would have unfulfilled demand) versus the overage cost of buying too many (in which case he will lose money on excess inventory) (see, for example, Cachon and Christian 2008 and Nahmias and Cheng 2009). See Porteus (1990) and Petruzzi and Dada (1999) for reviews of more applications and extensions of the newsvendor problems.

The same tradeoff needs to be weighed when a capacity planning team decides on how much equipment to procure for each manufacturing step in a supply chain. Taking semiconductor manufacturing companies as an example, if the capacity is kept too high, the factory is going to incur idleness on equipment; on the other hand, if the capacity is kept too low, the factory will not have the capacity to handle demand upsides. The optimal level of capacity to keep balances the incremental cost and benefit of having one additional equipment. Of course, the equipment buying decision is much more complicated than solving the newsvendor equation from traditional Operations Management textbooks. The newsvendor formula indicates that the optimal solution is to stock a quantity such that the probability of satisfying demand is equal to the underage cost over the sum of the underage and overage cost per unit. This is a simple equation that can be directly applied when there is only one type of unit to order in a single period. However, a capacity planning team in a medium to large-sized manufacturing company needs to decide on the number of machines to procure for hundreds of resources. Each of the resources are interconnected with each other through complicated manufacturing stages. The resources are shared to manufacture hundreds to thousands of products. In these cases, insufficient equipment investment can lead to a painful allocation of capacities on the production floor, resulting in a shortage of demand, while an excess amount of equipment in one manufacturing stage can be a waste if the other manufacturing stages are not equipped with sufficient capacity. This is a classic multi-product, multi-resource capacity investment problem, with newsvendor-type tradeoff, but a closed-form expression of the well-known "critical fractile" solution is impossible (see, for example, Lau and Lau 1995, and Harrison and van Mieghem 1999). In such environments, advanced analytical models such as stochastic programming are particularly useful to optimize for equipment-buying decision over hundreds of manufacturing steps. One may generate a large set of demand scenarios, simulate the work in progress flow across manufacturing stages, calculate demand satisfaction and cost, and optimize for the equipment capacity over the expectation of these demand scenarios.

Although the approach of stochastic programming is well-known in the literature, sometimes it is wiser to implement a simpler approach in the complex environments described above as an approximation. For example, partition the manufacturing line into a few key "segments" and model each segment as if it is a single resource required in manufacturing, and then apply the traditional one-product one-equipment newsvendor solution, which is closed-form. Although this approach is an approximation, there is vast benefit from implementing it, due to its simplicity, interpretability, tractability, and ease of implementation in practice. Often, the solutions are close enough to the "exact" optimal solution, which would be unknown anyway due to practical complications such as data imperfections.

The news vendor model can also be applied to define optimal inventory position at retail stores, and across retailer distribution center networks. Another application can be to optimize fulfillment center capacity of e-tailer.

Getting coffee at Starbucks

Standing in a line to get coffee at Starbucks, one would estimate how long it will take to be served. Subconsciously, one could be applying Little's Law. Little's Law is a theorem by John Little that states the long-term average number L of customers in a stationary system is equal to the long-term average effective arrival rate λ multiplied by the average time W that a customer spends in the system (Little and Graves 2008). Expressed algebraically, the law is $L = \lambda W$. In a stable system, the rate at which people enter Starbucks queue (called the arrival rate) is equal to the rate at which they exit it (called the exit rate). The estimation of the wait time at Starbucks may go like this: suppose there are 20 people in the queue and one person is entering the queue every minute, then the average wait time a customer spends at Starbucks is 20 people divided by one person per minute, which is 20 minutes. Similarly, in a semiconductor supply chain, one can apply Little's Law to estimate the overall manufacturing cycle time and find opportunities to improve it. As an example, suppose the wafer start rate in a semiconductor fab (which is assumed to be a stationary system) is λ= 1000 wafers/day, and suppose the average work-in-progress (WIP) in the fab is L = 45,000 wafers. Then one can estimate the average time a wafer spends in the fab is W = 45,000 wafers /(1000 wafers/day) = 45 days.

By understanding and applying Little's Law, one can find opportunities to improve the manufacturing cycle time. Applying conventional wisdom solely, a supply chain analyst may tend to break the supply chain activities into smaller tasks, and then measure and continuously improve the process time of each task. While this approach will contribute to the reduction of manufacturing cycle time due to a reduction of the example could be explained a little more in depth about what a wafer is, so that the reader can get connected more quickly. time lies in the reduction of queue time. It is clear from Little's Law that the wait time is longer at steps in which the average WIP is larger. By observing the manufacturing stages where WIP is most likely to accumulate, a supply chain analyst can focus on reducing the WIP at these stages, which will then reduce the overall cycle time. As another example, still taking a wafer fab to illustrate, the steps in a semiconductor assembly and test process could be 1) memory assembly → 2) transfer to a tray → 3) memory test → 4) transfer to a different packaging tray → 5) testing for customer applications → 6) shipping finished product to the customer. Applying the concept from Little's Law to reduce the overall cycle time, one can eliminate some of the steps by simplifying the manufacturing steps. For example, steps 3)-5) may be combined into a single step. In this way, the WIP accumulation between steps 3) through 5) is eliminated, which may reduce cycle time considerably, compared to simply reducing the process time of a step specifically.

Carpool to work

Carpool to work draws parallels with risk pooling. Cachon and Terwiesch (2008) thoroughly discussed several types of risk pooling strategies in Supply Chain management, namely, location pooling, product pooling, lead time pooling, and capacity pooling with flexible manufacturing.

Location pooling refers to the practice of having an aggregated distribution center which serves multiple locations, rather than segregated distribution centers that serve demand from different locations separately. Because the coefficient of variation (CV) of the combined demand seen by the aggregated distribution center is lower than the CV of individual demands, at the same stock level, the combined distribution will reduce stock outs compared to individually located distribution centers. Alternatively, to meet the same customer service level, the stock level at a pooled distribution center will be lower than if the distribution centers are segregated. Semiconductorvalue chains often adopt "virtual customer hubs" or regional distribution centers that achieve location pooling.

Product pooling refers to the practice of serving customers with fewer products to reduce demand uncertainty. Cachon and Terwiesch (2008) cited an example of combining two demands with the same mean μ and standard deviation σ. The CV of pooled demand will be $\sqrt{\frac{1}{2}(1+correlation)}*\frac{\sigma}{\mu}$. If the two demands are independent, then the CV of the pooled demand is reduced by the square root of two. If there are n independent demands, then the CV of pooled demand will be reduced by the square root of n. As such, the inventory requirement is reduced significantly to achieve the same service level when products are shored by more customers. Retail stores can achieve inventory and service level benefits by pooling single, dual, quad units in a package to one single pack size.

In the semiconductor manufacturing context, despite the benefits of product pooling, companies may want to preserve the variety of products to provide customers a more complete portfolio. Product variety itself is also a competitive advantage. Thus, "Delayed Differentiation" may be implemented in the manufacturing supply chain to hedge the uncertainty associated with product variety without taking options away from the customers. Achieving Delayed Differentiation in practice usually requires collaborative effort between multiple departments, including Product Engineering (PE), Product and Operations Management (POM), Business Units (BU), and Supply Chain (SC) to design the supply chain considering engineering feasibilities and the latest product technologies. It often entails a case-by-case study and the formation of core project teams. Despite the efforts, the outcome would be massively rewarding, in that it enables better customer service with significantly less supply chain complexities. Retailers can benefit from delay differentiation by bundling products at point of sale as opposed to pre-packaging all permutations of product combinations.

Hiking with friends

From hiking with friends can be drawn parallels to the theory of constraints (Goldratt and Cox 2016). The objective of hiking with friends is for everyone to reach the mountain peak together in the shortest time possible. The hiking group would easily identify the slowest person in the group, which is the "constraint", and have him lead the line while everyone follows. Moreover, to move faster, the group may have the fastest person carry the backpack of the slowest person. By shuffling the burdens, someone else may eventually become the slowest person. The group can repeat the same exercise throughout the hiking journey to reach the peak in the shortest time possible.

The same concept as in hiking can be applied to a supply chain to achieve profitability and efficiency. The group of supply chain analysts needs to analyze the market and business scenarios to understand whether the demand or the supply is constraining. Under the scenarios in which the demand is constraining, the supply chain analysts need to ensure that supply is sub-ordinated to demand and it does not exceed demand significantly, as the extra supply will be salvaged. In a manufacturing company, supply chain analysts may move the supply downstream and offer short lead time for customers to create an additional market. On the other hand, under scenarios in which the supply is constraining, supply chain analysts need to ensure to maximize dollar per unit constraint, the most profitable demand is satisfied out of the constrained capacity. This can be achieved by applying brakes to supply replenishment, once a target work-in-progress inventory level is reached, the supply chain will stop replenishment until the product is pulled by the customers. If the supply is more constrained, the inventory brakes will be held at more upstream stages of the supply chain and build upon demand certainty to maximize demand satisfaction. See Noreen et al. (1995) for more applications and implications of the theory of constraints. In case of retailer, when supply is excess than demand, then retailer can run promotions or provide bundle deals, when supply is shorter than demand, then retailer may charge premium or limit supply per customer as in the case of toilet paper phenomenon during COVID-19.

Having Sushi for lunch

Imagine that someone visits a nice Japanese restaurant for sushi, and the owner of the restaurant tells him “Sorry, we ran out of rice and we will not be able to serve you sushi today”. What would be the customer’s reaction? It is quite a waste for the restaurant to lose demand and customer goodwill by not carrying enough rice, which is a much lower cost item compared to fish. Even worse, the fish could go stale, and the restaurant would lose the cost incurred stocking fish. It is unfortunate for the sushi restaurant to be in a situation like this.

Similarly, supply chain analysts need to plan the supply chain by anchoring around expensive items. This requires placing sufficient stock of components with lower costs and ensure the demand opportunities are not lost due to unavailability of the low-cost items. Taking the silicon memory business as an example, companies manufacturing silicon memory should avoid shorting demand due to under-stocking end-product packing materials. Similarly, retailers and e-tailers should ensure they sufficiently stock must-have low cost accessories that are typically bought along with expensive consumer electronic devices. In summary, supply chain analysts need to consider all components of cost to serve demand, and accordingly define heterogeneous service level targets for diverse types of material in the supply chain.

Doing horseback riding

Doing horseback riding can remind us of the “bullwhip effect” in the supply chain. The whip in horseback riding oscillates stronger towards the tip than the portion closer to the handle. The similar behavior commonly seen in the supply chain and is well-known as the “bullwhip effect” (Lee et al. 1997). Even small volatilities in the end-customer demand (i.e., point-of-sale) will amplify to the distribution center, compound to the manufacturer, and further amplify towards the upstream suppliers. The bullwhip effect exists in value chains due to order batching, supply reliability, price fluctuations, demand signal frequency, and errors. Supply chain analysts are advised to understand various factors contributing to the supply chain bullwhip effect and tackle it effectively by leveraging statistical techniques and employing supply chain strategies such as implementing push-pull systems.

Running household chores

A big part of running household chores is to replenish assorted items for the house. These include groceries, maintenance items, replacement items, etc. One would usually employ different replenishment strategies for different segments of items to decide what and how many to buy. Aspects to consider when designing the replenishment strategy include:

- Perishables versus non-perishables
- High-cost versus low-cost
- Pictorial memory of current inventory levels
- Projected minimum or maximum inventory levels
- Family consumption patterns
- Expected events such as house parties

The same aspects are considered when a supply chain planner replenishes material and capacity for the supply chain. A supply chain planner in a medium-size to large-size company may handle up to hundreds of products. It is advised for supply chain planners to apply predictive and prescriptive analytics to predict future demand, to segment products and customers to replenish the material and capacity in a way that maximizes the profit for the company. There is a vast amount of operations literature on inventory control models that can be applied in this context. See, for example, Nahmias and Cheng (2009) and Simchi-levi et al. (2008) for overviews of inventory control models.

Within the class of inventory control models, Multi-Echelon Inventory Optimization (MEIO) models have received wide implementation and application in manufacturing companies. With single-stage replenishment inventory models there is typically only one stocking point between supplier and customer. A multi-echelon environment includes several stocking points between supplier and customer and differentiates the replenishment strategy by the customer and product types. Anecdotal evidence has shown that businesses deploying MEIO can significantly improve the probability of properly balancing cost versus service levels across their networks compared to companies not using MEIO and can see an increase in inventory turns while improving customer service levels.

Take a medium to large sized semiconductor manufacturing as an example. The company may have several stocking points in its supply chain, such as wafer bank, component bank, and finished good inventory. Accordingly, the company may implement a "push-pull" supply system, under which it builds inventory to these inventory stocking points and then apply a brake. The inventory will proceed to the rest of the manufacturing process when triggered by signals of customer orders. Along with this set up, the company may design several replenishment strategies depending on the product segments and customer requirements, such as "Build to Forecast" (BTF), "Build to Order" (BTO), and "Build to Target" (BTT). Retailers and eTailers can move away from a one size fits all products and customers approach to a segmented supply chain replenishment strategy to meet unique product and customer needs. Custom products can be built to order with a longer lead time whereas commodity products can be managed using a reorder replenishment model.

Having a Pizza Party

When organizing a pizza party and deciding on how many pizzas of each kind to order, one is essentially solving a mathematical programming problem, which is, how many pizzas of each kind to order to provide maximum possible satisfaction for the whole group with minimum waste, while adhering to the dietary restrictions of each guest (such as vegetarian restrictions). It is a kind of mathematical programming problem with hierarchical objective layers. Similarly, when supply chain analysts decide on the quantity of each product to build in the supply chain, they are also solving a mathematical programming problem with hierarchical objective layers. With the primary objective of maximizing demand fulfillment, one should also consider the secondary objective of balancing the inventory with the capacity, and the third objective layer of minimizing the cost to the supply chain, while satisfying a series of constraints related to capacity and demand, customer lead time requirements, etc.

Some companies have taken this hierarchical mathematical programming problem to the next level, by implementing scaled end-to-end enterprise supply chain optimization solution tools provided by commercial software companies. The enterprise tool can be designed to meet a sequence of business objectives through hundreds of hierarchical objective layers via linear programming. For example, a company may optimize its revenue target as the top objective layer, followed by maximizing service to customers, minimizing inventory, and finally minimizing manufacturing cost.

Within the umbrella of each of the above objective layers, there might be multiple sub-level objectives. For example, when optimizing for service to customers, the company may prioritize meeting certain critical demands over others, and prioritize meeting confirmed customer orders with committed delivery dates over unconfirmed orders or demands pegged to forecast only.

Companies may also run a few different linear programming engines which are configured differently, to answer different planning questions. For example, it may run the same linear programming engine with equipment capacities being hard constraints or soft constraints. The solution from a constrained run will be directly executable, whereas the soft-constrained engine run would provide the business a view of potential opportunities, and therefore guide the capacity planning team to drive the right actions. In the retailer context, linear programing optimization can be used for shelf space optimization, product assortment optimization. E-tailers can apply linear programming optimization for logistics route optimization.

Going to sleep

Going to sleep is the time for "lights-off". In the field of supply chain analytics, "lights-off" refers to the automation of predictive, prescriptive, and cognitive analytics, and planning and fulfillment activities . In the era of digital supply chain, a growing number of companies are employing automated guided vehicles (AGVs) with sophisticated routing algorithms on the manufacturing, in fulfillment centers and distribution centers of manufacturers, retailers, and e-tailers.

Critical Success Factors for Supply Chain Analytics Teams

Supply chain analytics teams may be centralized or decentralized. It is advised to weigh the advantages and disadvantages of both when deciding on the structure of the team. Centralized analytics teams are more scalable, and create more synergy across cross functional applications compared to the de-centralized analytics teams. However, decentralized analytics team could provide more agility and speed to

Figure 4. Enhanced typical day of supply chain analyst

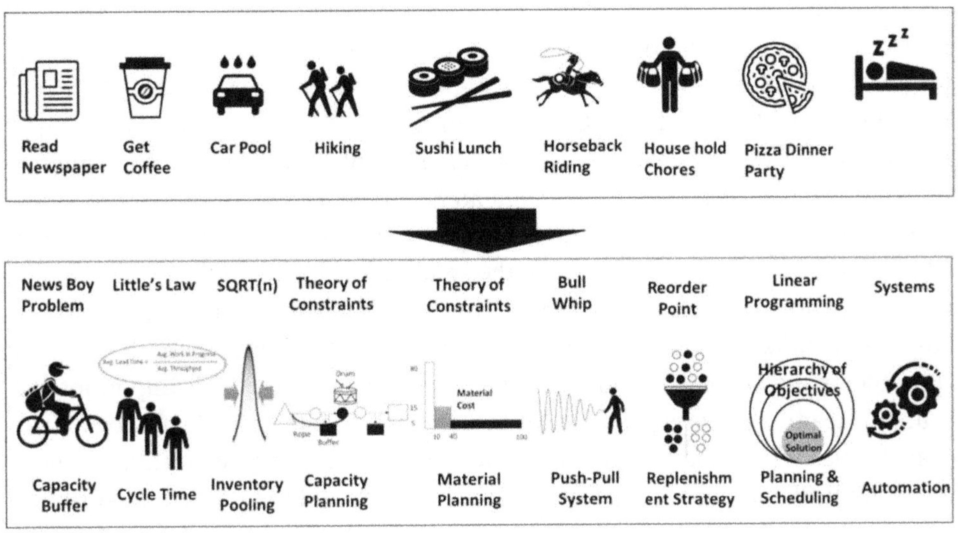

react within each of the individual functions. In most cases, we would recommend creating centralized teams for descriptive analytics while keeping predictive and prescriptive analytics teams decentralized. This is because descriptive analytics teams are often required to have considerable team sizes with data architecture, data engineering, and the skillsets of interacting with supply chain planning systems. Keeping the descriptive analytics centralized helps maintain a sustainable and scalable team catering to the needs of each function's teams. On the other hand, predictive and prescriptive analytics teams are sometimes small teams with advanced analytics skillsets and advanced degrees. They usually have the domain knowledge. Their expertise may play a dominant role in defining the right objectives for each of the analytics problems. Therefore, it is recommended to decentralize these analytics teams. However, even with the decentralized analytics teams, it is recommended to always have central governance of data architecture, analytical tool sets, and systems.

For all kinds of analytics teams, it is important to understand and align the overall business objective cross-functionally while solving each of the analytics problems. Analytics carried out in silos with only local objectives can be counter-impactful to the overall business. For example, if the analytics team under manufacturing optimizes solely on operating cost, whereas the analytics team under supply planning optimizes solely on service level, the decisions of both teams would be contradictory to each other and may counter the overall benefits of analytics. It is important to have an overall alignment on global business objectives while solving each of the analytical problems.

The implementation of supply chain analytics project usually requires collaboration across multiple teams. It is advised that, for each analytical project, after the problem statement is defined and the global objective is aligned, the analytical project team be formed with an analytical expert, a functional expert, and a system expert. The functional expert provides the business requirements and drives the data preparation and the final user acceptance test. The analytics expert is responsible for developing the model, whereas the system expert is responsible for implementing the solution. See Figure 5 for a conceptual representation of the coordination relationship among the three experts. Throughout the project, all three experts need to collaborate closely to define the problem and design the solutions.

As an example, consider an analytical project of implementing statistical forecasting models in a manufacturing company. The analytics expert would be someone from the analytical team who will test multiple forecasting models and optimize the parameters. The functional expert should provide the business requirement to the analytics expert—for example, what forecast granularity is required, or, is it weekly-level forecast at SKU level, monthly-level forecast at product-family level, or quarterly-level forecast at product-line level. The system expert needs to be able to either directly implement the solution inside the advanced planning system or design an infrastructure to feed the forecast results into it.

The companies should also avoid the pitfalls of poorly constructed supply chain analytics teams. One pitfall is having the infrastructure to develop the solution but having no infrastructure to sustain the solution. Even if the entire team is highly skilled in developing advanced analytics solutions, the efforts and time required to maintain the solution will accumulate, to the point where the team is stuck with handling past problems and not able to add additional value. To avoid this, it is important to either create a functional support team who is responsible for maintaining the analytical solutions, or develop data engineering capabilities within the team to automate the analytical solutions. Either way, the end goal is to embed the analytical solution into the supply chain system and the process footprint itself instead.

Figure 5. Venn diagram

Supply Chain Design: A Case Study

In this section, we discuss some practical considerations for enabling supply chain analytics and optimization in a medium-size to large-size semiconductor company. Specifically, we discuss the centralization of supply chain analytics and the design of supply chain analytics objectives.

Supply chain optimization activities and projects may lead to sub-optimization if managed locally. In the example of the sushi restaurant that we discussed in the "day in the life of supply chain analytics and optimization" section, it would harmfully impact the profitability of the restaurant if the supply of rice has been optimized in a silo to minimize the cost of the rice, without considering the overall objective of the restaurant. The consequence of it could be loss of sales for the restaurant due to the lack of rice, while the stock of fish perishes.

We advise that global supply chain optimization activities be carried out through a hierarchy of objective layers. To illustrate, in the above example in the sushi restaurant, it might be important for the restaurant to minimize the wastage of rice. Nevertheless, minimizing the excess of rice should not be the top priority of the restaurant. Instead, it could be an objective subordinate to the higher objective of serving customer demand in time. Towards the goal of achieving global optimization, it is critical for the business to define a hierarchy of objective layers. Once it is defined, the business needs to set guidelines or policies for each objective that is subordinate to the higher objectives. For example, in the sushi restaurant example, the service level target for the inventory positioning of rice may need to be set higher than the service level target for the inventory positioning of fish. These hierarchies of objective layers and corresponding supply chain guidelines and policies need to be established centrally through supply analytics and complemented by industry expertise, whenever applicable.

Next, we discuss the use case of centralized supply chain analytics and hierarchical objective design taking a typical vertically integrated semiconductor manufacturing company as an example. Consider a typical vertically integrated semiconductor manufacturing company that owns fabrication plants and back-end manufacturing operations in-house. The fabrication plants, commonly called fabs, manufacture silicon wafers from raw wafers. The back-end manufacturing operations then convert the silicon wafers into semiconductor chips. The semiconductor chips can then be used directly by end consumers or used by other original equipment manufacturers (OEMs). Silicon fab operation is usually the most expensive operation in semi-conductor industries. It has long manufacturing lead times, typically in months, while the types of silicon wafers manufactured are under a hundred at any given time. In contrast, the back-end manufacturing operations are relatively inexpensive. It has much shorter manufacturing lead times, typically on the order of weeks, but may produce thousands of different stock keeping units (SKUs).

Given the different attributes of cost, manufacturing lead time and product mix between fab operations and back-end manufacturing, the semiconductor manufacturing company needs to design different hierarchies of objectives when conducting supply chain optimization. The back-end manufacturing may be minimized for production cycle time, followed by the objective of maximizing agility, minimizing risk, and finally, minimizing the cost of production. On the other hand, the fab operations may be optimized for minimizing cost as the primary objective, and then optimized for maximum manufacturing throughput, followed by the objective of minimizing cycle time. The above objective layers, however, may vary by products and business scenarios. For example, at the times of new product introduction, the time to market is critical for the business. Therefore, the optimization priority for both backend manufacturing and fab operations might be designed to minimize manufacturing cycle time, followed by the objectives of minimizing cost and maximizing agility.

Because the hierarchy of objectives for fab operations and backend manufacturing is different, the corresponding replenishment guidelines set for them also need to differ accordingly. For example, the business may deploy a "push" replenishment strategy in fab operations to maximize for manufacturing

Table 1. Example objectives hierarchy of backend manufacturing in a semiconductor company - Summary

Priority	Objective	Focus	Key Performances Indices
1	Max Speed	Cycle time	Effective balance of Service Level and Inventory Turns • On time delivery to customer request date and to promise date • Supply chain inventory week of stock High service level for demand constraint scenario High inventory turns for supply constraint scenario
2	Max Agility	Risk Mitigation	Risk Index
3	Min Cost	Total cost	Total manufacturing and distribution cost

Table 2. Example objectives hierarchy of backend manufacturing in a semiconductor company: Details

Priority	Cycle time components	Cycle time break down	Improvement drivers	Analytics
1.1	Overall Inventory week of stock	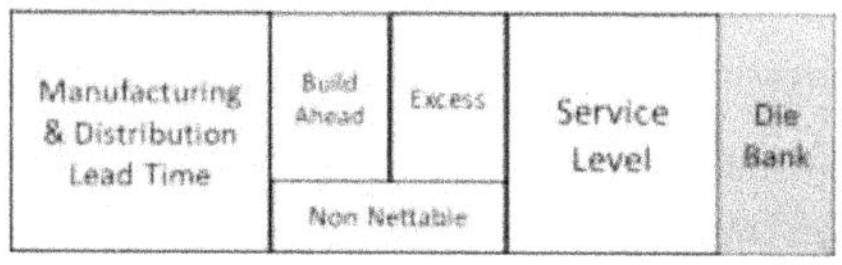	• Design for product commonality (delay differentiation) • Inventory buffer • Capacity Buffer • Low value material inventory buffer • Replenishment Strategy (Push-Pull)	• Little's Law • Multistage inventory & service level optimization • Newsvendor simulation • Safety Stock • Bull whip
1.2	Manufacturing Distribution Lead Time	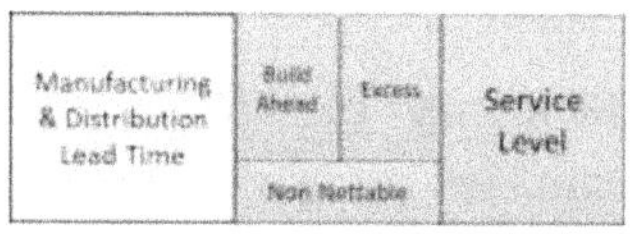	• Reduce process variability, then reduce process time • Simplify routings (eliminate steps) • Scheduling • Yield improvements	• Theory of constraints • Little's Law • Linear Programming • Statistical tool kits
1.3	Work order performance	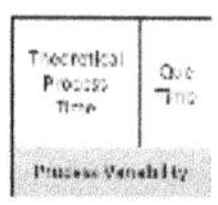	• Minimize queue • Minimize lot size	• Theory of constraints
1.4	Theoretical process time		• Simplify manufacturing process	• Factory Physics

Priority	**Key drivers**	**Description**	**Analytics**
2.1	Dual sourcing	Alternate suppliers and second tier suppliers at different geography for key components to mitigate risk of supply disruption	Simulation
2.2	Dual manufacturing sites	Alternate manufacturing sites at different geography to mitigate geo-political risks	Simulation

Priority	**Key drivers**	**Description**	**Analytics**
3.1	Inhouse vs outsource manufacturing split	Trade-off of un-used inhouse manufacturing cost and cost premium per unit for outsource manufacturing	Simulation
3.2	Capacity Buffer	Trade-off of the incremental cost of each additional unit of capacity and margin potential of this additional unit of capacity	Newsvendor simulation
3.3	Utilization vs inventory build ahead	Trade-off of cost of carrying inventory and cost of unused capacity	Simulation
3.4	Product and site qualification	Trade-off of cost of production qualification in additional site and upside flexibility to satisfy demand	Simulation Linear Programming
3.5	Minimize total manufacturing and distribution cost	Supply and Demand matching towards maximizing demand satisfaction, minimizing inventory and minimizing total manufacturing and distribution cost	Linear Programming

throughput, whereas it makes more sense to deploy a "push-pull" replenishment strategy (that is, deploying either push or pull strategy based on different business scenarios) in backend operations.

Table 1 and Table 2 show an example of hierarchy of objectives for backend manufacturing in a typical semi-conductor company. Table 1 includes a summary of three key objectives, ordered with descending priority. Table 2 includes more details for each of the objectives, including the drivers for improvement and the key theories and concepts that may be applied when conducting corresponding analytics.

CONCLUSION

Supply chain analytics has become indispensable for supply chain management in a modern company. Through discussions of the life of supply chain analysts, we aim to provide supply chain professionals with an understanding of the interrelationship between analytics and supply chain management. Further, this chapter discusses some practical considerations in carrying out supply chain analytics successfully. More specifically, we discuss the four categories of supply chain analytics. It is vital for a supply chain practitioner to choose the right category of supply chain analytics based on the maturity and requirements of the company. We then discuss a few critical factors of the supply chain analytics teams, focusing on the centralization and decentralization of supply chain analytics and the implementation approach of supply chain analytics teams. Finally, we describe the design of hierarchical objectives, taking a use case from semiconductor company. The future research directions on this topic include empirical studies of the savings achieved by digital supply chain analytics, empirical studies of the correlation between the maturity of the supply chain analytics team versus the success achieved, and more in-depth case studies of supply chain analytics in a digital world.

REFERENCES

Cachon, G., & Terwiesch, C. (2008). *Matching supply with demand*. McGraw-Hill Publishing.

Chae, B., Olson, D., & Sheu, C. (2014). The impact of supply chain analytics on operational performance: A resource-based view. *International Journal of Production Research*, *52*(16), 4695–4710. doi:10.1080/00207543.2013.861616

Goldratt, E. M., & Cox, J. (2016). *The goal: a process of ongoing improvement*. Routledge. doi:10.4324/9781315270456

Gunasekaran, A., Papadopoulos, T., Dubey, R., Wamba, S. F., Childe, S. J., Hazen, B., & Akter, S. (2017). Big data and predictive analytics for supply chain and organizational performance. *Journal of Business Research*, *70*, 308–317. doi:10.1016/j.jbusres.2016.08.004

Harrison, J. M., & Van Mieghem, J. A. (1999). Multi-resource investment strategies: Operational hedging under demand uncertainty. *European Journal of Operational Research*, *113*(1), 17–29. doi:10.1016/S0377-2217(97)00425-6

Lau, H. S., & Hing-Ling Lau, A. (1995). The multi-product multi-constraint newsboy problem: Applications, formulation and solution. *Journal of Operations Management, 13*(2), 153–162. doi:10.1016/0272-6963(95)00019-O

Lee, H. L., Padmanabhan, V., & Whang, S. (1997). Information distortion in a supply chain: The bullwhip effect. *Management Science, 43*(4), 546–558. doi:10.1287/mnsc.43.4.546

Liao, B., Yano, C. A., & Esturi, S. (2017). Optimizing Site Qualification Across the Supply Network at Western Digital. *Interfaces, 47*(4), 305–319. doi:10.1287/inte.2017.0898

Little, J. D., & Graves, S. C. (2008). Little's law. In *Building intuition* (pp. 81–100). Springer. doi:10.1007/978-0-387-73699-0_5

Manary, M. P., & Willems, S. P. (2008). Setting safety-stock targets at Intel in the presence of forecast bias. *Interfaces, 38*(2), 112–122. doi:10.1287/inte.1070.0339

Nahmias, S., & Cheng, Y. (2009). *Production and operations analysis* (Vol. 6). McGraw-hill.

Noreen, E., Smith, D., & Mackey, J. T. (1995). *Theory of Constraints and Its Implications for Management Accounting: A Report on the Actual Implementation of The Theory of Constraints*. North River Press, Incorporated.

O'Dwyer, J., & Renner, R. (2011). The promise of advanced supply chain analytics. *Supply Chain Management Review, 15*(1).

Petruzzi, N. C., & Dada, M. (1999). Pricing and the newsvendor problem: A review with extensions. *Operations Research, 47*(2), 183–194. doi:10.1287/opre.47.2.183

Porteus, E. L. (1990). Stochastic inventory theory. DP Heyman, MJ Sobel, eds. Handbooks in operations research and management science, 2, 605-652.

Sahay, B. S., & Ranjan, J. (2008). Real time business intelligence in supply chain analytics. *Information Management & Computer Security, 16*(1), 28–48. doi:10.1108/09685220810862733

Simchi-Levi, D., Kaminsky, P., Simchi-Levi, E., & Shankar, R. (2008). *Designing and managing the supply chain: concepts, strategies and case studies*. Tata McGraw-Hill Education.

Tan, K. H., Zhan, Y., Ji, G., Ye, F., & Chang, C. (2015). Harvesting big data to enhance supply chain innovation capabilities: An analytic infrastructure based on deduction graph. *International Journal of Production Economics, 165*, 223–233. doi:10.1016/j.ijpe.2014.12.034

Trkman, P., McCormack, K., De Oliveira, M. P. V., & Ladeira, M. B. (2010). The impact of business analytics on supply chain performance. *Decision Support Systems, 49*(3), 318–327. doi:10.1016/j.dss.2010.03.007

Chapter 18
Impact of the Coronavirus Pandemic on the Retail Industry and Its IoT Applications' Security Vulnerabilities

Kamalendu Pal
https://orcid.org/0000-0001-7158-6481
University of London, UK

ABSTRACT

The global retail industry changed drastically over the recent years as online shopping, led by gigantic Amazon, harvests an ever-increasing large share of the total retail market with the coronavirus pandemic making the future uncertain for traditional brick-and-mortar retailers. Today's customers are increasingly expecting a tailored, personalized shopping experience. They expect to be able to shop anywhere, at any time, and from any location. In this context, information and communication technology (ICT) is ushering in a new dawn for retail customers. The internet of things (IoT) is the new generation of internet-connected ICT systems in a digital environment that plays an essential role in retail business process automation. However, security issues in IoT-based retail applications have caught significant attention in academia and industry. Therefore, there is a need to educate retail business operation managers about the potential security risks of IoT-based business information systems.

INTRODUCTION

The coronavirus pandemic has disrupted global retail industries and supply chains, revealing dreadful gaps and vulnerabilities. Retailers face challenges in managing risks and organizing themselves to accommodate the '*new daily situation scenario*' (Pal, 2023). The coronavirus outbreak has established a fragile operating environment for retail supply chains. It has put forward the question of survival for regular business operations, forcing organizations to rethink resilient strategies to mitigate the long-

DOI: 10.4018/978-1-6684-7298-9.ch018

term effects of this virus on retail industries. At the same time, customers are increasingly looking for a tailored, personal shopping experience.

As a requirement, the personal shopping experience includes shopping anywhere, at any time, and from any location, such as in an office environment or on a bus journey. The perceptive customers thoroughly search for the right price and expect multiple purchase options and flexible delivery times. In addition, customers demand that the desired product is available, in the right size and colour, at the time of the purchase. Retail businesses are expected to meet these demands, regardless of the channel the customer is using. Leading retailers are also expected to be able to offer comprehensive product information, product reviews, and inventory visibility and availability information to the stakeholders. In other words, if the retailers are not meeting these expectations, business operations redevelopment should be the company's top priority and not lose market share.

In addition, the rapid changes in sales and distribution channels in recent years due to the coronavirus pandemic, with a central focus on human-centered shopping experience to the growing importance of more customized products and faster and safer delivery, has led to the recent trend of the Omni-channel sales and marketing objectives. The higher expectation for personalized products, services, disruptive production, information technology (IT), and information and data communication techniques are driving the improvement of production and service delivery activities. Asides from conventional software system technologies (SSTs) (e.g., enterprise resource planning (ERP)) help monitor supply chain functions such as purchasing, transportation, storage, distribution, sales, and return (Pal, 2018). Many intelligent devices recently joined the list under the coined technical term, IoT umbrella of technologies, and it has an essential means to address information capture and exchange it in real-time with neighboring devices/applications. In addition, the advances in IoT applications in the sensor technologies (i.e., metallic, liquid, and novel materials) are expected to revolutionize retail business (Kahlert et al., 2017); and its acceptance and potential to integrate retail supply chain processes are largely underdeveloped for theoretical and practical implications.

There have been many research studies that have investigated the IoT-based logistics services for Omni-channel in the literature, and the proposed information system's architecture does not only involve the new logistics distribution approach quick generative delivery with the latest IoT technology but also realizes the need for dynamic order fulfillment in the new paradigm shift of manufacturing or production, and transport systems. The proposed IoT-based logistics system has the potential to be a disruptive and novel logistics system by providing an integrated, seamless Omni-channel journey for modern customers.

Aside from conventional ICT technologies help monitor supply chain functions such as purchasing, transportation, storage, distribution, sales, and return (Pal, 2018). With many other intelligent devices recently joining the list under the newly coined IoT umbrella of technologies, the potential to address information capture and exchange in real time has multiplied (Atzori, 2018). Although the advances in IoT applications in the sensor are expected to revolutionize retail business (Kahlert et al., 2017), its acceptance and potential to integrate supply chain processes are largely underdeveloped for theoretical and practical implications.

Although there have been several research studies that have investigated the ICT-enabled supply chain processes integration in improving performance (Li et al., 2009) (Qrunfleh & Tarafdar, 2014) (Vanpoucke et al., 20017), no study is documented assessing the use of emerging IoT adoption on supply chain integration, supply chain integration includes both inter- and intra-organizational integration across the entire supply chain through a collaborative sensing mechanism (Pal & Yasar, 2023) (Alfalla-Luque et al., 2013), that can generate more excellent customer value by offering superior services (Christopher

& Towill, 2001). In a network-based competition scenario, a supply chain's strength is determined by how adequate the flow of goods and services is, information exchange, and find flows (Rai et al., 2006). IoT is perceived to strengthen supply chain integration by connecting objects through the Internet (Ping et al., 2011) (Tu, 2018). The adoption and use of IoT help organizations build their capability. From an organizational capability theory perspective, IoT will likely enhance the capability to integrate the suppliers, customers, and intra-organizational logistics processes.

IoT bridges the gap between the physical and digital worlds by synchronizing the information flow with the physical flow for greater supply chain integration (Ping et al., 2011). IoT capability is defined as additional capabilities gained by supply chains with everyday objects embedded with technology that provides identifying, sensing, networking, and processing capabilities to communicate with other devices and services over the Internet (Whitmore et al., 2014).

Since retail supply chains are demand-driven, intense digital connectivity and coordination within the supply chain via adopting new technology can be considered an intervention in service improvement (Fleisch & Tellkamp, 2005). The emerging IoT paradigm, therefore, plays a significant role in the retail industry in managing supply networks in response to customer demands (Yu et al., 2015). At the same time, the pervasive interconnection of smart IoT things which are physically distributed extends the computation and communication to IoT things' various specifications. The sensing capability of these devices helps collect real-time data from the physical world directly or remotely. Finally, analyzing the collected data provides IoT-based supply chain applications with the ability to build an intelligent world and make better decisions to manage it.

IoT devices are becoming pervasive, extending the Cyber world to the physical world and creating new types of more complex security issues and concerns. If those security concerns cannot be adequately understood and addressed, wider adoption of IoT applications will be greatly hindered. Serious consequences can be expected from security breaches in IoT application systems. The contributions of this chapter include an analysis of IoT security challenges, proposals for security function deployment, and identification of open issues in supply chain-related IoT-based applications security designs. The organization of the chapter is as follows. The next section presents an Overview of supply chain management and its business process automation. The following section includes IoT-based information systems architectural issues and different categories of security risks and their remedies. Finally, the chapter concludes with concluding remarks.

OVERVIEW OF SUPPLY CHAIN AND RELEVANT IoT APPLICATIONS

Today's retail business is changing the shopping scene that the retail industry is accustomed to; suppliers, transport companies, customers, and retailers are all playing their part in the move towards Omni-channel retail operations. For example, mobile shoppers are not excluding the in-store experience, nor are brick-and-mortar customers neglecting to use their tablet or mobile device to compare prices, product offerings, and purchasing terms. If customers are moving around and across various channels, so should retailers – a single-channel world is no longer sufficient. Instead, retailers should review their Omni-channel strategies to stay ahead.

Technological advancements are critical to winning new customers, so retailers should use prudent decisions to automate business processes (Pal, 2019). The recent pandemic has also taught the world some important lessons. First, retailers must create coherent, integrated organizations, front-end solutions, and

Figure 1. A diagrammatic representation of supply chain business processes

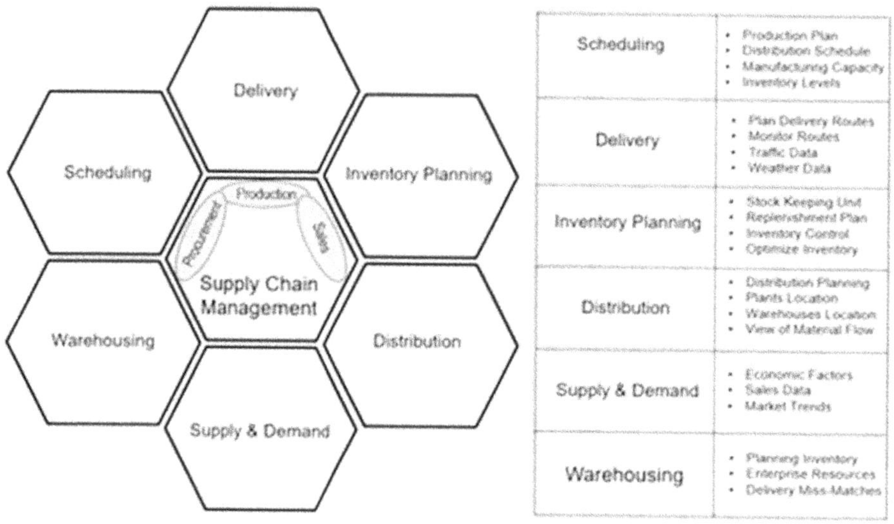

delivery models around their various product segments and channels. Second, customers are shopping across different product segments and demand a consistent shopping experience with one consolidated delivery, regardless of the channel through which the order is placed to the retailer. Third, retailers that do not adapt to the changing customers' shopping experiences risk falling behind.

Consequently, all retail businesses today appreciate the value and importance of building an effective and risk-free supply chain for organizational growth and profitability (Pal, 2019). A supply chain is a network of business facilities and distribution options performing vital functions, for example, raw material procurement, the transformation of these materials into intermediate and finished final products, distribution of these finished products to warehouses, and finally, moving these products to the distribution centers, from where the products will ultimately reach the final customers (Pal, 2017). In this way, supply chain management (SCM) uses various approaches to integrate suppliers, manufacturers, and distributors in doing their business operations and providing the appropriate strategy to deliver products and services to customers in the right quantities, to the suitable locations, and at the right time to meet the required service level with optimal cost. Finally, through collaboration and information sharing, the SCM system can produce efficient value-added services to its customers and create a competitive advantage in the marketplace.

This way, supply chain business partners need to create an agile network of business information that can respond rapidly to unpredictable changes in demand, and it needs close cooperation among business partners (Pal, 2017). In order to manage supply chain operations, business managers go through decision-making processes which consist of (i) market-specific supply and demand analysis, (ii) material procurement strategy, (iii) selection of production plant's locations and layout, (iv) warehousing and distribution related planning, (v) delivery of semi-finished and finished products, and (vi) finally scheduling and monitoring of all business operations. Figure 1 presents an integrated diagrammatic representation of a supply chain operational activity.

Information creation, communication, and decision-making (or actions) are inherent within supply chain operations. While its output is physical object identification, the business process inevitably begins with information. For example, a design is created via a drawing, design software, or scanning a physical object, creating data. This data is then communicated to machines that execute the identification, bringing it from the digital to the physical realm. Ideally, data from the creation process (and subsequent use) is further captured, sparking ongoing cycles between the digital and physical realms. Information and communication technology (ICT) is crucial in capturing, storing, and processing stored data.

In this way, supply chain operations are becoming complex due to a growing need for inter-organizational and intra-organizational connectedness, which make sure by advances in new information technologies (e.g., RFID, sensor, IoT technology, big data analytics, service-oriented computing) (Okorie et al., 2017) and tightly coupled business activities. Also, the supply chain business operations use information systems to monitor the operational activities in a nearly real-time situation. As a result, IoT technology is revolutionizing the retail business sector and will be the next giant leap of technology following the introduction of the Internet for industrial business operations management.

The vision behind IoT is to let people and intelligent things be connected at any time, in any place, to anything and anyone, via any network and services (Pal, 2021). So, by following this vision, retail business application areas of IoT will increase continuously and dramatically for every aspect of daily operations. For example, nowadays, with the diverse installation of IoT devices, operation managers can remotely sense and act upon situations relating to warehouse, factory, office, and retail outlets operations. In the event of intrusion into the premises, an alter can reach relevant managers asking for immediate attention or trigger an automatic response by the security forces. The pictures and videos being taken can be sent directly to the security forces so that they may approach the crime scene better prepared with the intelligence they gathered in advance.

Security in IoT-based wireless sensor networks (WSNs) and devices is an important issue, especially if they are commissioned for retail industry business-critical tasks, for example, in tactical business applications where a security gap in the network could cause casualties for the corporate profit in a retail business. No business managers would be happy if their confidential business data were exposed through leakages from misbehaving nodes of IoT networks or due to system failures. This way, algorithms and methodologies designed for securing WSNs will be relevant to any IoT system comprising one or more sensor networks. In addition, WSNs and IoT applications are integrated into many industrial applications in a retail business. Therefore, all cyber-security-related issues, especially attacks, their prevention, and mitigation, are significant for establishing secure and reliable IoT applications for the retail business.

WSNs are vulnerable to a wide range of attack types which might put critical threats to the security of those networks. Therefore, these attack types need to be investigated thoroughly. Security-related attacks against WSNs can be branched into two main categories: *active attacks* and *passive attacks*. In the passive attacks category, attackers are generally hidden (camouflaged) and either damage the functional components of the network or tap the communications link to collect helpful business information. Passive attacks can also be categorized into eavesdropping, node destruction, node malfunctioning, node outage, and traffic analysis types. Whereas in the active attacks category, an attacker affects the functions and operations of the targeted network. The result of this ill effect can be the fundamental objective of the attacker and can also be detected by security mechanisms (instruction detection). For example, network services might be degraded due to this attack. Active attacks can also be categorized into jamming, flooding, Denial-of-Service (DoS), blackhole, wormholes, sinkholes, and sybil types. Moreover, in information security engineering, solutions to defend against security attacks on networks comprise three essential components: *prevention, detection*, and *mitigation.*

- **Prevention:** This component aims at preventing attacks before they happen. In this case, any proposed method needs to be able to devise measures to defend against the specific type of attack (s). For example, intrusion prevention mechanisms can resist external attackers towards WSNs and IoT but are not explicitly designed to resist internal attackers.
- **Detection:** In the event of an attack, if an adversary manages to advance the measures taken by the prevention component, the define against the attack has failed. At the moment, security solutions devised for the detection component of the related attack would take in-charge and work in identifying compromised nodes. The only way to react against ongoing attacks, especially internal ones, is by using Intrusion Detection Systems (IDSs). After an intrusion is detected, a mitigation mechanism would be issued to minimize the adverse effects of the ongoing attack.
- **Mitigation:** Final component aims at mitigating attacks after they happen; for example, to secure a network, a security measure should be taken, such as – "dismissing the affected nodes in a network" or "disabling the ports of a computer which were used during the attack".

These three components constitute a whole security structure and cannot be considered separately in defending WSNs and IoT against diverse attacks. In the literature, various reviews are provided to present security issues in WSNs: Butun and other researchers (Butun et al., 2014) provided a survey of intrusion detection systems, Zhu and colleagues (Zhu et al., 2012) provided a survey of detecting node replication attacks, Chen and Chao (Chen & Chao, 2014) provided a survey of required distribution, A group of researchers (Han et al., 2014) provided a survey of trust management. In addition, researchers (Finogeev et al. 2017) surveyed attacks and security in WSNs of industrial Supervisory Control and Data Acquisition Software (SCADA) systems. This chapter presents a brief overview of different types of attacks and their associated defense mechanisms, and it will help pave a secure path toward the protection and managerial acceptance of IoT technology. In this way, privacy and security in IoT are the most critical concerns of the future business, and measures are required to make the system confidential and available in all operational situations. Moreover, some security protocols for IoT must be used, and innovations in the IoT protocols should also be considered. Finally, this chapter will try to analyze the various threats and issues in IoT systems with the primary aim of guiding future research and conclude with concluding remarks.

IoT APPLICATIONS AND EXTENDED SUPPLY CHAIN NETWORK

The vision behind the IoT is to create real-time connection and data communication with people or any business process along supply chain operation, anytime, anywhere, using any network. It facilitates overcoming the limitations of legacy systems and ways of data communication and processing. In this way, IoT systems embedded with industrial operations often consist of software, electronic components, actuators, sensors, detectors, and wireless connectivity that enable them to collect data from these objects can be defined as the "IoT". An IoT system has the following essential characteristics:

- IoT is a ubiquitous technological advancement that enables supply chain business-related objects to be connected to the Internet via wired or wireless networks to communicate.
- Several wireless sensor networks are available for IoT devices, including near-field communication (NFC), Zigbee, radio frequency identification (RFID), Bluetooth, and Wi-Fi.
- The sensors can be connected to various technologies, including long-term evolution (LTE), general packet radio service (GPRS), and global system for mobile communication (GSMC).
- The efficiency of an IoT system is largely determined by three main components, each of which is vital to its day-to-day operation: (i) perception layer, (ii) network and middleware (Edge, Fog, and Cloud) layer, and (iii) application layer.

Nevertheless, cloud computing offers virtually unlimited storage and system capabilities to address many IoT-related challenges. Consequently, the phrase "cloud of things" (CoT) is used to allude to the fusion of IoT and cloud computing. The CoT is a paradigm for increasing productivity and improving system performance that is widely used by most industries and manufacturers. Several researchers discussed in their research (Pal, 2023) the use of the cloud to analyze vast amounts of data (i.e., Big Data) when data storage and processing are required.

With the advent of the IoT, vast amounts of data are generated in real-time, which poses a significant concern for traditional cloud computing network topologies (Decker et al., 2008). A traditional cloud infrastructure condenses all processing, storage, and networking into a limited set of data centers, and the distance between remote devices and remote data centers is relatively wide (Wang et al., 2016). Edge computing could address this challenge since it provides access to computing resources closer to IoT edge devices and may lead to a new ecosystem for IoT innovation (Veza et al., 2015). In this way, architectural issues on IoT systems in automating supply chain operations play a significant role, and there are different types of layered architecture for supply chain industrial applications (Pal, 2022).

IoT Systems Architecture

The layered architecture is designed to meet the requirements of various industries (e.g., manufacturing, retail), enterprises, societies, institutions, and governments. The functionalities of the various layer are (Pal, 2023): (i) edge layer: This is the hardware layer and consists of sensor networks, embedded systems, RFID tags, and readers or various types of sensors in different forms. Many of these hardware elements provide identification and information storage, information collection, information processing, communication, control, and actuation, (ii) access gateway layer: It takes care of message routing, publishing, and subscribing and performs cross-platform communication if required, (iii) the middleware layer interfaces the access gateway layer and the application layer. It is responsible for functions and takes care of issues like data filtering, data aggregation, semantic analysis, access control, and information discovery, such as EPC (Electronic Product Code) information service and ONS (Object Naming Service), and (iv) application layer that is responsible for delivering various applications to different users in IoT. Figure 2. represents a simplified IoT-based enterprise information systems (EIS) architecture for SCM.

An EIS is to acquire and manages data and serves as a decision-making system within a business organization. Therefore, the characteristics of an EIS can be analyzed in the context of decision-making purposes. Figure 2 illustrates data generation sources (e.g., RFID scanner, sensor, security camera, intelligent machine) in a supply chain environment, divided into different layers (e.g., perception layer, network layer, processing layer, application layer). With the evolution of the supply chain information

Figure 2. A layered IoT architecture for supply chain operation

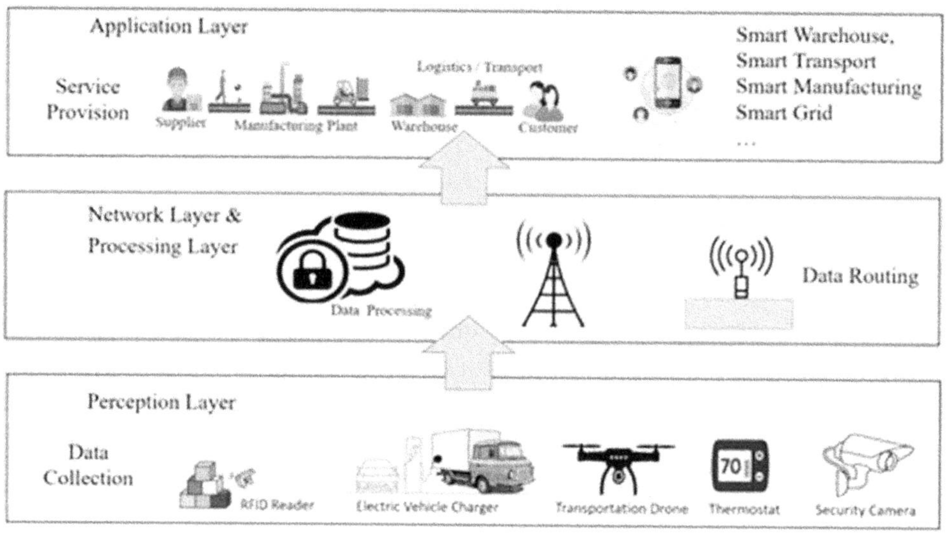

system, inputs, outputs, and system parameters can significantly change concerning time. For example, one can find that design variables have increased exponentially with the evolution of the supply chain EIS. In addition, the information systems for modern supply chains must accommodate the changes in the IT infrastructure (e.g., IoT, SOC) and the changes and uncertainties in the system environments.

Evolution of EIS Infrastructure

The primary functions of an EIS are (i) to acquire static and dynamic data from objects; (ii) to analyze data based on computer models; and (iii) to plan and control a system and optimize system performances using the processed data. Implementing a supply chain EIS paradigm relies heavily on available information technology (IT). As a result, IoT has been identified as a critical technology with a significant impact on the retail supply chain industry (Pal, 2021).

IoT becomes the foundation for connecting things, sensors, actuators, and other smart technologies. IoT is an extension of the Internet, and IoT technology gives immediate access to information about physical objects and leads to innovative services with high efficiency and productivity. The characteristics of IoT include (i) the pervasive sensing of objects; (ii) the hardware and software integration; and (iii) many nodes. In developing an IoT, objects must interact with each other, reacting autonomously to the changes in the operating environment (e.g., temperature, pressure).

Radio Frequency Identification (RFID) technology has received massive attention from the retail industry's daily operations as a critical component of the Internet of Things (IoT) world. In RFID-enabled retail supply chain automation, an EPC (Electronic Product Code) is allocated to an individual item of interest and is attached to an RFID tag for tracking and tracing purposes. RFID tag-attached items are transported from one business activity to another or moved within the trading partners. Individual partners interrogate RFID tags during transportation and add business-related contextual information into tags. In this way, involved business partners can check whether the items of interest have passed through the legitimate supply chain network. If any inappropriateness is traced, such items may be classified as counterfeit products and detained for further cross-checking.

Also, wireless sensor networks (WSNs) provide enterprises with cloud computing services. WSNs are the essential infrastructure for the implementation of IoT. Various hardware and software systems are available to WSNs: (i) Internet Protocol version 6 (IPv6) makes it possible to connect an unlimited number of devices, (ii) Wi-Fi and WiMAX provide high-speed and low-cost communication, (iii) Zigbee, Bluetooth, and RFID provide the communication in low-speed and local communication, and (iv) a mobile platform offers communications for anytime, anywhere and anything.

A simple IoT architecture composed of devices (e.g., machinery and equipment), networks, cloud-based storage, and information system applications is shown in Figure 2. This architecture consists of four layers: perception, network, processing, and application. The perception layer consists of electromechanical devices like sensors, RFID tag readers, security surveillance cameras, geographical positioning system (GPS) modules, and so on. These devices may be accompanied by other industrial appliances like conveyor systems, automated guided vehicles (AGVs), and different industrial robots for a manufacturing industry context. These devices' primary function is to capture sensory data, monitor environmental conditions and manufacturing assembly areas, and transport materials (e.g., semi-finished, finished products). These collected data need transportation to the processing layer. The processing layer consists of dedicated servers and data processing software that ultimately produce management information, and operational managers can act based on the produced information. In this way, the application layer produces user-specific decision information. A few critical IoT-based information system applications in industrial applications are smart factories, smart robotics, intelligent supply chains, and smart warehouse management. Besides, the importance of WSNs to industrial control systems has been discussed by researchers (Araujo et al., 2014). In the research field of WSNs, most ongoing work focuses on energy-efficient routing, aggregation, and data management algorithms; other challenges include the large-scale deployment and semantic integration of massive data (Aberer et al., 2014) and security (Gandino et al., 2014).

In industrial infrastructures, for the global industrial application dominated by physical systems, many processes address the needs of many t of data collected in real-time by many networked sensors that must be analyzed in real-time. Big data and real-time analytics applied to big data in cloud computing systems enable the implementation of these techniques to extract new information from the data. In addition, several industrial applications already use cloud computing architectures and services (Pal, 2020).

The trend toward virtualization of resources and critical aspects of real-world processes addresses the needs of many organizations for scalability and more efficient use of resource ownership. This way, cloud computing also plays a vital role in the modern manufacturing information system's automation purpose. Cloud computing is a large-scale, low-cost processing unit based on the IP connection for calculation and storage. The essential characteristics, such as on-demand self-service, are essential to support cloud computing applications for an enterprise in cost reduction, system flexibility, profit, and competitiveness.

However, a group of researchers has reported disadvantages of the centralized IoT information system architecture issues (Ali et al., 2019). A central point of failure could easily paralyze the whole data communication network. Besides, it is easy to misuse user-sensitive data in a centralized system; users have limited or no control over personal data. Centralized data can be tampered with or deleted by an intruder; therefore, the centralized system lacks guaranteed traceability and accountability.

The vast popularity of IoT-based information systems in the industry also demands the appropriate protection of security and privacy-related issues to stop system vulnerabilities and threats. Also, traditional security protections are not always problem-free. Hence, it is worth classifying different security problems relevant to IoT-based systems. This classification of security-related attacks would help industry-specific practitioners and researchers to understand which attacks are essential to their regular business operations.

Moreover, the security requirements of IoT-based information systems can encompass together the traditional networks with requirements appropriate to the unique constraints of WSNs. Therefore, the security requirements that should be investigated in the WSNs (Padmavathi & Shanmugapriya, 2009) (Bryan et al., 2005) can be classified into *major* and *minor requirements* (Padmavathi & Shanmugapriya, 2009), as described below.

Major Requirements

The primary requirements of IoT-based EIS are considered the standard security requirements: (i) *data confidentiality*, (ii) *source authentication*, (iii) *data integrity*, and (iv) *service availability*.

- **Data Confidentiality**: Data confidentiality requirements represent the ability to make sure that the privacy of transmitting important sensed data is never revealed to unauthorized hackers (or attackers) so that this data remains confidential. In other words, the gathered industrial operational data should not be exposed to unauthorized parties. Therefore, one of the protection methods is using data encryption with a secret key in the data-gathering process that the desired recipients and receivers only understand.
- **Source Authentication**: Data Authentication presents the capability of ensuring the reliability of the collected and transmitted data through the IoT networks by verifying its source and data origin. Cross-checking ensures the communication is genuine since the malicious node cannot be in the place of a trusted IoT node. Therefore, data source authentication is essential for the business action-related decision-making process.
- **Data Integrity**: Data integrity confirms that the collected and transmitted data within the IoT-based WSNs have never been corrupted, altered, or tampered with by adversaries, malicious intermediate nodes, or even by accident due to the harsh communication environment of WSNs.
- **Service Availability**: All IoT-based retail applications are the source of different business service categories. Service availability ensures that the desired WSNs are available for the communication services, and each node can use the data network resources even with the attendance of denial-of-service (DoS) attacks. Since the WSNs are collecting and transmitting the sensing data in charge of the communication services duty, the availability of WSNs is essential for the survivability of IoT services and applications.

Minor Requirements

The minor requirements are classified as (i) data freshness, (ii) self-organization, (iii) time synchronization, and (iv) secure localization.

- **Data Freshness**: The insurance of freshness in each transmitted message protects the data communication structures against replayed attacks. This is by ensuring that the old messages will not be replayed again, so the transmitted data will be recent, and it can be achieved by including a timer counter in the transmission packet.
- **Self-Organization:** According to the organizational nature of WSNs, it does not have a fixed infrastructure that makes each sensor node independent and flexible to be self-organized for different situations.
- **Time Synchronization:** It is required in most WSNs applications; for example, the sensor's radio could be turned off periodically to achieve a power-efficient mechanism.
- **Secure Localization:** WSNs' efficiency often relies on their capability of accurately and automatically locating all the network sensors. Nevertheless, attackers can respond to false signal strengths or replay signals to unsecured location data.

ANALYSIS OF POSSIBLE ATTACKS AND THREATS

A network attack is an effort to gain unauthorized access to sensitive information or compromise the network's confidentiality, authentication, integrity, or availability. Accordingly, the WSNs can be exposed to numerous types of attacks, which are in this chapter mainly classified into three categories in proposition to the important security requirements in (Padmavathi & Shanmugapriya, 2009) (Bryan et al., 2005) as shown in Table 1.

Table 1. Analysis of possible attacks and threats

Security Requirements	Possible Attacks		Description
Confidentiality and Authentication	Attacks on Privacy	Node replication attack Eavesdropping and passive monitoring attack Traffic analysis attack Camouflage attack	Replicate or copy a legitimate node identifier and add node copies into the existing WSN (Bryan et al., 2005); this will lead to the ability to communicate the entire network from the replicated node (Chan, 2003). When the WSN's communications have not been protected with an effective cryptographic mechanism, the adversary can listen to the communication data and quickly realize its contents (Walters et al., 2007). The attacker can detect some nodes with particular roles or activities which may provide important information about WSNs communications (Walters, 2007). The attacker adds malicious intermediate nodes to the WSNs (Jaydip, 2009). Later, these nodes can be used to masquerade as a regular node for advertising false routing information and attracting the communication packets into further forwarding in the intended WSNs.
Service Integrity	Stealthy Attacks		Adversaries can use stealthy attacks against the WSN's service integrity. The adversaries' goal in using stealthy attacks is to force the WSNs to accept false data values.

Table 1. continued

Security Requirements	Possible Attacks		Description
Availability	Physical Layer The Data Link Layer Network and Routing Layer Transport Layer	Jamming Attack Tampering Attack Collision Attack Exhaustion Attack Unfairness Attack Spoofed, Altered, or Replayed Routing Information Attack Selective Forwarding Attack Black Hole Attack Sinkhole Attack Sybil Attack Wormholes Attack Hello Flood Attacks Acknowledgment Spoofing Attack Flooding Attack De-synchronization Attack	Interfere with the authorized radio frequencies of the WSN's nodes (Bryan et al., 2005) (Mukherjee et al., 2014). It physically accesses the WSN's nodes and extracts data such as cryptographic keys and other sensitive information (Mukherjee et al., 2014). The collision arises when different node transmissions run concurrently with the same frequency range. Repeat the collision attack to consume all energy resources of the WSN's nodes until these nodes become dead to perform the resource exhaustion. (Sastry et el., 2013). Perform unfairness through irregularly using the mentioned link layer attacks against the WSNs. Disrupt the WSN's traffic by spoofing, altering, or replaying the routing information while exchanged among the sensor nodes. Use the selective forwarding attack by creating malicious nodes or compromising the network nodes. The attack can be adopted using these nodes to forward specific packets and drop others selectively. (Sastry et al., 2013). A specific form of selective forwarding attack wherein the malicious or compromised nodes drop all the received packets. Prepare a compromised node to look more attractive to its neighboring nodes by providing false routing information. One node submits several identities to the WSNs. This attack quickly affects algorithms and protocols such as distributed storage and fault-tolerant schemes. A link between two portions of the WSNs is characterized by low latency and allows attackers to replay the network messages (Sastry et al., 2013). The adversaries may use the Hello Flood attacks via high-powered transmitter nodes to deceive many nodes into believing they are neighbors within its range. Spoof the overheard acknowledgment messages between the attacking node and its neighbors to spread false information, such as wrong node status among the WSNs. Frequently creating new connection requests or ignoring legitimate requests while connection resources become exhausted or run to the maximum limit. (Sastry et al., 2013). This may be achieved, as an example, by frequently spoofing messages in the direction of to end host until it requests to retransmit the missed frames.

DISCUSSION ON IOT SECURITY ISSUES AND CHALLENGES

The IoT architecture is complex and assumed to deal with billions of sensors and objects interacting with each other and other entities, such as human beings or virtual entities (Rodrigo et al., 2013). Securing and protecting all these interactions is essential to preserving the highest system performance and limiting total incidents affecting the entire IoT. Multiple attack vectors are available to adversaries because of the critical features of IoT, such as global connectivity and accessibility (anyone can access it anyhow and anytime) (Han et al., 2016). Various heterogeneous objects presented in different contexts and communicating with each other fulfill the complexity of the IoT and then further complicate the deployment of security mechanisms. However, security services and solutions have become a significant challenge and are still in their initial stages. The current research on WSN security mainly provides solutions for subjective problems without considering the impact of IoT principles and features studied in this paper.

Confidentiality Challenges

In IoT security, the most challenging task is to keep communication data and information confidential. Several standard encryption functions can be used to achieve data secrecy among the communicating parties, such as shared secret keys and standard encryption algorithms, e.g., the AES block cipher, Blowfish, and Triple DES (Thakur & Nagesh, 2011). However, adopting data encryption alone as a security mechanism is not enough to protect data and information privacy. The attacker can execute a traffic analysis towards the eavesdropped cipher data, so sensitive information about this data can be released quickly. Moreover, node compromise complicates the confidentiality challenges when a malicious node is compromised as one communication endpoint, so sensitive data and information can be released. Furthermore, when utilizing a group-shared key, the malicious node can successfully compromise the radio frequency range of other sensor nodes and then eavesdrop and decrypt the sensitive data and information within the communication.

Source Authentication Challenges

The adversaries in ordinary sensor networks do not just alter the communication packets; their attacks can include additional injected false packets (Padmavathi & Shanmugapriya, 2009). Since WSNs are used in a shared wireless communication medium and applied in unattended environments, it is quite a challenging task to ensure data authentication. Source authentication can be attained by symmetric and asymmetric mechanisms, where the sending and receiving nodes share secret keys to verify the resource identity (Bryan et al., 2005), which is necessary to empower sensor nodes to distinguish between maliciously injected and spoofed packets or the original packets from the legitimate source. Practically, data authentication is required in most applications; for example, in military and safety-critical applications, the adversaries have obvious motivations to attack the sensor nodes by maliciously injecting data reports or false routing information. Correspondingly, civilian applications are expected as comparatively non-adversarial environments and are still exposed to risk without data authentication. Even if data authentication prevents the WSNs from maliciously injecting or spoofing packets by attackers, it is not solving the node compromise problem since the compromised node can authenticate itself into the network by getting the secret keys from the legitimate nodes. Nevertheless, intrusion detection techniques can be used to discover the compromised nodes around the network and rescind their secret cryptographic keys.

Data Integrity Challenges

Once the WSNs have a valid confidentiality measure, the adversaries cannot thieve the communication data. However, there is the possibility of WSNs being compromised by alterations. This is when false data is injected by a malicious node presented in the network or even when damage or loss of data is caused by unstable conditions of the wireless channel (Padmavathi & Shanmugapriya, 2009). For instance, some malicious nodes may inject false data or change the data inside the communication packets. At that time, these modified packets will be sent to the receiver (e.g., the base station of the WSNs). Nevertheless, the loss or damage of the sensed data may happen without the frivolity of a malicious node because of the harsh communication environment. Accordingly, data integrity is crucial to ensure that any transmitted data within the WSNs have not been transformed or destroyed in transit.

Availability Challenges

The WSNs can be attacked with jam communications through extravagant communications or computations that may attack the sensor nodes or any part of the WSNs and, as a result, affect the survivability of the network. Nevertheless, the failure of the base station availability ought to threaten the whole operation of WSNs. As an example of the monitoring application in the manufacturing process, losing availability can cause disappointment to sense the potential accidents and subsequent financial loss. WSNs can be available through the modicum presence of benign or compromised node failures (Elaine & Adrian, 2004). Adjusting standard encryption algorithms to appropriate WSN security requirements leads to extra costs. Many approaches are proposed in the literature; some adopt code modification and reuse as many codes. Other approaches used additional communications to attain the same goal. Also, more approaches impose strict limitations to data access or even suggest inadequate schemes (e.g., central point scheme) to shorten the algorithm. Therefore, the availability requirement is principal for preserving the operational services of WSNs and maintaining the whole network throughout its lifetime.

DEFENSE AGAINST VARIOUS ATTACKS

Defense against Passive Attacks

Defense against Passive Information Gathering The communications in WSNs are achieved through the air; therefore, we do not know whether the packets arrive to the intended people only or not. Hence detection of eavesdropping is almost impossible. Link layer encryption would prevent outsider attacks such as eavesdropping, and some of the solutions are provided in (Karlof & Wagner, 2003) (Perrig et al., 2002) (Deng et al., 2003) (Pietro et al., 2003) (Tubaishat et al., 2004). The bulk of the external attacks towards WSNs can be avoided by link-layer encryption and authentication using globally shared keys. For example, to provide link layer encryption, a group of researchers (Karlof et al., 2004) proposed TinySec for WSNs. SNEP (Secure Network Encryption Protocol), under the SPINS (Perrig et al., 2002) protocol set, is another famous encryption protocol devised for WSNs.

In (Slijepcevic et al., 2002), the authors proposed a SensorWare communication multicast model in which three levels of link-layer encryption are provided using the RC6 algorithm. They have chosen the RC6 algorithm because its selection of the number of rounds parameter directly affects the algorithm's security level. All sensors share an initial set of master keys in the network. At any time, one of the master keys in the list of master keys is active. The reason is to expose fewer data for known-ciphertext attacks, and more keys will be necessary as the network's lifetime extends. This critical selection is executed pseudo-randomly, and every node uses the same seed for randomizing function. Then, the random number is coupled to the list of the master keys to obtain the active master key.

Defense Against Active Attacks

Defense on Physical Layer is presented by (Muraleedharan & Osadciw, 2006); the authors propose a cross-layer security mechanism, namely "Swarm Intelligence", to detect Jamming-DoS attacks. They also provide countermeasures to mitigate this kind of attack. For example, JAM, a jammed area mapping service (Wood et al., 2003), is proposed for detecting jamming DoS attacks against WSNs. In addition, JAM provided a mapping protocol to detect a jammed region in a WSN. Besides, in terms of mitigation, JAM avoided the jammed part of the WSN by re-routing the packets, thus providing a remedy for the Jamming DoS attack.

In (Cagalj et al., 2007), the authors proposed a wormhole technique, customarily known to be an attack against WSNs, which could be effectively used to defer the Jamming DoS attack against WSNs. In order to defend WSN from node tampering attacks, nodes might be equipped with tamper-resistant hardware, in which any tampering attempt would wipe out the memory (and any other data storage) so that confidential information (such as the secret keys) would not be leaked. Although this is a wise and excellent solution, it comes with an additional cost of hardware which would increase the total cost of the WSN installation and cripple the most appealing feature of such networks: "low cost".

Other ways of fighting against node tampering would be disabling the JTAG interface of the sensors and using good password protection for the bootstrap loader of the sensor boards (Znaidi et al., 2008). Finally, a naive way of protecting the nodes against these attacks would be simply hiding the nodes by camouflaging them (Sharma & Ghose, 2010). Detection of the tampering attempts would require routine physical checking of the sensor nodes by eye or with special equipment such as magnifiers. This task might be tedious because sometimes nodes are deployed across dangerous and hard-to-reach places such as radioactive zones.

Defense on Application Layer

Defense against CoAP Exploit: As mentioned by (Rahman & Shah, 2016), the Transport Layer Security (TLS) variant for CoAP is Datagram Transport Layer Security (DTLS) – it is called CoAPs in this phase, which provides an additional protection layer. However, this comes with a high cost of additional computation and a large amount of handshake content in the message, which causes message fragmentation.

Defense against False Injection: Ye et al. (Ye et al., 2005) presented a "statistical en-route filtering (SEF)" technique for detecting false information (data) injected in the WSN. Besides, as a mitigation, a methodology is provided to filter those injected data and achieve a consensus on a measurement by introducing a collective secret.

Defense against Path-Based DoS: To defend against Path-based DoS (PDoS) attacks, Deng et al. presented a lightweight, efficient, and robust method that employed "one-way hash chains" that allowed intermediate sensor nodes to detect replayed and spurious packets (Deng et al., 2005). PDoS attack targets intermediary sensor nodes in a "multi-hop end-to-end data path" of sensor networks. In the proposed solution of Deng et al. (Deng et al., 2005), a "one-way hash chain" in each sensor node towards a communications path is configured, enabling each intermediary sensor node to detect PDoS attacks. Hence, intermediary sensor nodes block the dissipation of fabricated and/or replayed packets. Each packet destined from an endpoint includes an entirely new "one-way hash chain" number; thereby, replaying is prevented this way.

Defense on Data Link Layer

Defense against Collusion and Exhaustion: In order to defend WSNs against collusion and exhaustion attacks, the request rate of each node might be limited to some specific value (by decreasing the MAC admission control rate) so that the network can discard extra requests from the same node (attacker) (Znaidi et al., 2008). Another solution would be employing the time division multiplexing (TDM) technique which would provide dedicated time slots to each node to transmit their packets. It would allow each node a tiny period to access the channel. In this way, the channel usage of each node is limited, and attacks related to channel abuse are prevented. For example, if the corruption of the packets occurs partially (in bursts), employing error detection and error correction codes would be beneficial tools to fight against this kind of attack (Sharma & Ghose, 2010).

Defense against Denial of Sleep and Link Layer Flooding: Liu et al.'s anomaly detection-based IDS proposal works on ad hoc networks and fits well with the WSNs and IoT. In their proposal, each node participates in detecting abnormal nodes. Packet traffic at the MAC layer is analyzed and evaluated. Distributed and cooperative anomaly detection is achieved by creating feature vectors at each node and then fulfilling cross-feature analyses. It results in a local or global response (either from a single node or a collaborative response from multiple nodes) according to the seriousness of the attack situation. Finally, the proposed IDS is effective against MAC layer attacks, especially on denial of sleep and flooding attacks (Liu et al., 2005).

Defense against De-synchronization: Many applications require the IoT to have a low and deterministic delay, especially for IIoT applications with low delay tolerance. Having a deterministic network delay in a WSN is challenging in the best case when traditional MAC protocols are employed. To enable low power, high reliability, and deterministic WSNs, IETF recently proposed a 6TiSCH protocol that uses time-slotted channel hopping (TSCH) MAC with IPv6 addressing. This protocol dynamically assigns bandwidth resources to the nodes in the network according to the application requirements; hence it provides a communications stack for low-power and lossy networks such as IoT. In addition, the proposal includes secure communication of MAC layer frames so that any eavesdropping or packet capturing would have no benefit from these (Accettura & Piro, 2014).

Defense on Network Layer

Defense against Blackhole: Liu et al.'s anomaly detection-based IDS proposal works on each node and has also shown to be effective (but less compared to detecting attacks against the MAC layer) on the network layer, especially for the detection of a black hole and gray hole (packet dropping) attacks (Liu et al., 2005). In (Karakehayov, 2005), authors proposed a REWARD scheme to detect blackhole attacks against WSNs. Besides, this scheme provides a routing algorithm to avoid detected black holes; hence, the WSN resumes regular operation under blackhole attack. In (Krishnan & Srinivasan, 2016), the authors discussed the effects of network topology selection in WSNs on blackhole attacks. Their findings suggest that mesh topology is more resilient against blackhole attacks than star and tree topologies.

In (Prathapani et al., 2009)proposed using Honeypots, strolling software agents that create dummy Route-Request (RREQ) packets to attract and catch blackhole attack performers. The authors have illustrated the positive performance of the proposed detection approach through extensive simulation results using the ns-2 simulator. Watchdog-based intrusion detection systems proposed by (Tiwari et al., 2009) efficiently detect black holes and selective forwarding attacks. Sensor nodes in the clustered

WSN watch their neighbors and collaborate with the head of the cluster in order to be able to detect misbehavior. Although sensor nodes do not have a complete view of the network, they can still be effective in detecting intrusions with some definite probability and reporting it to the head of the cluster.

In (Medadian et al., 2009), Medadian et al. presented a method to cope with blackhole attacks, which introduces negotiating with neighboring nodes that claim to possess a route to the destination. If a node receives an RREP packet (corresponding answer to an RREQ packet), it forwards this packet to the source and starts an evaluation procedure about the replier. The evaluation procedure is based on the opinions of the nodes about the replier. Its neighbors save all activities of a node. Whenever the neighbors of a particular node are asked to send their opinions about it, the requester node gathers all opinions of the neighbors and concludes about the maliciousness of the replier node. The conclusion is based on several rules. First, the authors' simulation results show that the presented MAODV protocol provided better security and performed better in terms of packet delivery ratio than the legacy AODV protocol in the existence of black holes with minimum added delay and overhead.

In ActiveTrust (Liu et al., 2016), to detect blackhole attacks in WSNs, authors have created multi-detection routes in the areas with remaining energy, hence if an adversary does not know the detection routes (s)he will target those, and while executing the action (s)he will be disclosed. By this method, the location and behavior of an adversary can be determined by ActiveTrust to avoid black holes while creating the final data routes.

In (Wazid et al., 2013), authors presented a technique for detecting and preventing blackhole attacks in clustered-WSNs. In this methodology, a node called a coordinator is selected by all nodes dependent on the cluster-head selection criterion. The coordinator node is responsible for the authentication process, detection of intermediate node failures, and blackhole attacks. If a blackhole attacker is detected in the cluster, the coordinator removes it from the cluster; hence all the communications with this specific node are terminated.

FUTURE RESEARCH DIRECTIONS

The growth of IoT and its advancement in the industrial sector strain the computing resources needed to maintain the connectivity and data collection that IoT devices require (Chan, 2017). In this way, service-oriented computing comes into the picture by acting as the backbone of everything IoT offers. Cloud computing, setting up virtual servers, launching a database instance, and creating data pipelines to help run IoT solutions become easier (Chan, 2017). Moreover, data security is essential in such an environment where the cloud can improve security by providing proper authentication mechanisms, firmware, and software update procedures. Besides, the significant data attacks that are prevalent in the IoT world today: (i) data inconsistency, which helps an attack on data integrity, leading to data inconsistency in transit or data stored in a central database is referred to as Data Inconsistency (ii) unauthorized access control; and with unauthorized access, malicious users can gain data ownership or access sensitive data., and (iii) data breach or memory leakage refers to disclosing personal, sensitive, or confidential data in an unauthorized manner.

The data breach has severely threatened users' personal information in recent years. Researchers are highlighting different aspects of data breach-related issues. One such work (Gope & Sikdar, 2018) on preventing data breaches has proposed a lightweight privacy-preserving two-factor authentication scheme for securing communication between IoT devices. In the future, this research will review other research in IoT technology and data breach-related issues.

CONCLUSION

This chapter focused on security issues and potential solutions for IoT-based technologies that have created significant interest in the industrial world. For example, IoT technology has grown across various core supply chain applications, such as coordination, manufacturing, and other business process automation. However, each IoT-based business process automation has specific requirements; security vulnerability will always be a significant concern when deploying IoT applications. The chapter first analyzes the new security challenges presented by the features of IoT systems, mainly by resource-constrained IoT devices and the tight coupling of the cyber and physical worlds. Finally, the IoT-based information gathering and processing systems security design-related issues are summarized. In addition, a well-designed IoT deployment policy can reduce the risk of security attacks. Finally, this chapter summarizes common attacks, information system vulnerabilities, and potential countermeasures.

IoT is an evolving technological paradigm and is highly interconnected with applied research activities. For example, with the forthcoming advent of nanotechnology and the development of nanoscale devices, innovative solutions tackling channel modeling, information encoding, and communication protocols are also required to integrate these nanodevices into IoT-based retail solutions. In addition, the most attractive future research topics are related to integrating IoT with emerging technologies such as hybrid cloud platforms, fog, and cloudlet. Retail supply chain managers must be educated in safe, regular operations, which are important areas. Combing these technologies by enabling cross-domain integration with existing web technologies in a concept called the '*Web of Things*' (WoT) provides an even broader spectrum of new capabilities and functionalities. However, despite the enormous research efforts, many open issues and challenges keep future research frontiers attractive. Therefore, this chapter is valuable to the research community as it can be used as a starting point for future research and education training programs for retail supply chain managers.

REFERENCES

Accettura, N., & Piro, G. (2014). Optimal and secure protocols in the IETF 6tisch Communication Stack. *23rd International Symposium Industrial Electronics (ISIE),* (pp. 1469-1474). IEEE. 10.1109/ISIE.2014.6864831

Alfalla-Luque, R., Medina-Lopez, C., & Dey, P. K. (2013). Supply chain integration framework using literature review. *Production Planning and Control, 24*(8-9), 800–817. doi:10.1080/09537287.2012.666870

Atzori, L., Iera, A., & Morabito, G. (2010). The Internet of Things: A survey. *Computer Networks, 54*(15), 2787–2805. doi:10.1016/j.comnet.2010.05.010

Bryan, A., Perrig, V., & Gligor, P. (2005). Distributed detection of node replication attacks in sensor networks. *IEEE Symposium on Security and Privacy (S&P'05).* IEEE.

Butuan, I. (2013). *Prevention and detection of intrusions in wireless sensor networks.* [Ph.D. Dissertation, University of South Florida].

Butun, I., Morgera, S. D., & Sankar, R. (2014). A survey of intrusion detection systems in wireless sensor networks. *IEEE Communications Surveys and Tutorials, 16*(1), 266–282. doi:10.1109/SURV.2013.050113.00191

Cagalj, M., Capkun, S., & Hubaux, J. P. (2007). Wormhole-based antijamming techniques in sensor networks. *IEEE Transactions on Mobile Computing, 6*(1), 2007. doi:10.1109/TMC.2007.250674

Chan, H., Perrig, A., & Song, D. (2003). Security and privacy in sensor networks. *IEEE Computer Magazine, 36*(10), 103-105.

Christopher, M., & Towill, D. (2001). An integrated model for the design of agile supply chains. *International Journal of Physical Distribution & Logistics Management, 31*(4), 235–246. doi:10.1108/09600030110394914

Colema, L. (2006). Frequency of man-made disasters in the 20th century. *Journal of Contingencies and Crisis Management, 14*(1), 3–11. doi:10.1111/j.1468-5973.2006.00476.x

Deng, J., Han, R., & Mishra, S. (2003). A performance evaluation of intrusion-tolerant routing in wireless sensor networks. Information Processing in Sensor Networks. Springer.

Deng, J., Han, R., & Mishra, S. (2005). Defending against path-based dos attacks in wireless sensor networks, in *Proceedings of the 3rd ACM workshop on Security of ad hoc and sensor networks.* ACM. 10.1145/1102219.1102235

Elaine, E., & Adrian, P. (2004). Designing secure sensor networks. *IEEE Wireless Communications, 11*(6), 38–43. doi:10.1109/MWC.2004.1368895

Fleisch, E., & Tellkamp, C. (2005). Inventory inaccuracy and supply chain performance: A simulation study of a retail supply chain. *International Journal of Production Economics, 95*(3), 373–385. doi:10.1016/j.ijpe.2004.02.003

Han, G., Lei, S. S. C., & Jiankun, H. (2016). Security and privacy in Internet of things: Methods, architectures, and solutions. *Security and Communication Networks, 9*(15), 2641–2642. doi:10.1002ec.1497

Han, G., Lei, S. S. C., & Jiankun, H. (2016). Security and privacy in Internet of things: Methods, architectures, and solutions. *Security and Communication Networks, 9*(15), 2641–2642. doi:10.1002ec.1497

Jaydip, S. (2009). A Survey on Wireless Sensor Network Security. *International Journal of Communication Networks and Information Security, 1*(2), 55–78.

Kahlert, M., Constantinides, E., & de Vries, S. (2007*). The relevance of technological autonomy in the customer acceptance of IoT services in retail.* The second international conference on Internet of Things and Cloud Computing, Cambridge, United Kingdom.

Karakehayov, Z. (2005). Using reward to detect team black-hole attacks in wireless sensor networks. *Real-World Wireless Sensor Networks Workshop,* (pp. 20-21).

Karlof, C., & Wagner, D. (2003). Secure routing in wireless sensor networks: Attacks and countermeasures. *Ad Hoc Networks*, *1*(2), 293–315. doi:10.1016/S1570-8705(03)00008-8

Krishnan, S. N., & Srinivasan, P. (2016). A qos parameter based solution for black hole denial of service attack in wireless sensor networks. *Indian Journal of Science and Technology*, *9*(38), 2016.

Li, G., Yang, H., Sun, L., & Sohal, A. S. (2009). The impact of IT implementation on supply chain integration and performance. *International Journal of Production Economics*, *120*(1), 125–138. doi:10.1016/j.ijpe.2008.07.017

Liu, Y., Dong, M., Ota, K., & Liu, A. (2016). Activetrust: Secure and trustable routing in wireless sensor networks. *IEEE Transactions on Information Forensics and Security*, *11*(9), 2013–2017. doi:10.1109/TIFS.2016.2570740

Liu, Y., Li, Y., & Man, H. (2005). Mac layer anomaly detection in ad hoc networks. Information Assurance Workshop, IAW'05, (pp. 402-409). IEEE.

Medadian, M., Yektaie, M. H., & Rahmani, A. M. (2009). Combat with blackhole attack in aodv routing protocol in manet, in Internet, First Asian Himalayan International Conference on AH-ICI, IEEE, 1-5, 2009.

Mukherjee, A., Ali, A. F. S., Jing, H., & Lee, S. A. (2014). Principles of physical layer security in multiuser wireless networks: A survey. *IEEE Communications Surveys and Tutorials*, *16*(3), 1550–1573. doi:10.1109/SURV.2014.012314.00178

Muraleedharan, R., & Osadciw, L. A. (2006). Cross layer denial of service attacks in wireless sensor network using swarm intelligence, in Information Sciences and Systems. 40th Annual Conference, (pp. 1653–1658). IEEE.

Okorie, O., Turner, C., Charnley, F., Moreno, M., & Tiwari, A. (2017). *A review of data-driven approaches for circular economy in manufacturing*, 18th European Roundtable for Sustainable Consumption and Production, Skiathos Island, Greece.

Padmavathi, D., & Shanmugapriya, M. (2009). A Survey of Attacks, Security Mechanisms and Challenges in Wireless Sensor Networks. *International Journal of Computer Science and Information Security*, *4*(2), 1–9.

Pal, K. (2017). Building High Quality Big Data-Based Applications in Supply Chains. IGI Global Publication.

Pal, K. (2018). *Ontology-Based Web Service Architecture for Retail Supply Chain Management.* The 9th International Conference on Ambient Systems, Networks and Technologies, Porto, Portugal.

Pal, K. (2019). Algorithmic Solutions for RFID Tag Anti-Collision Problem in Supply Chain Management. *Procedia Computer Science*, *151*, 929–934. doi:10.1016/j.procs.2019.04.129

Pal, K. (2020). In I. Williams (Ed.), *Information sharing for manufacturing supply chain management based on blockchain technology, in cross-Industry Use of Blockchain Technology and Opportunities for the Future* (pp. 1–17). IGI Global.

Pal, K. (2021). Applications of Secured Blockchain Technology in Manufacturing Industry. In Subhendu Kumar Pani, Biju Patnaik, Sian Lun Lau, & Xingcheng Liu (eds.) Blockchain and AI Technology in the Industrial Internet of Things. IGI Global Publication.

Pal, K. (2023). Security Issues and Solutions for Resource-Constrained IoT Applications using Lightweight Cryptography. In Suhasini Verma, Vidhisha Vyas, Keshav Kaushik (eds.) Cybersecurity Issues, Challenges, and Solutions in Business World. IGI Global Publication.

Pal, K., & Yasar, A. (2020). Internet of Things and blockchain technology in apparel manufacturing supply chain data management. *Procedia Computer Science*, *170*, 450–457. doi:10.1016/j.procs.2020.03.088

Pal, K., & Yasar, A. (2023). *Internet of Things Impact on Supply Chain Management*. International Conference on Ambient Systems, Networks and Technology (ANT), Leuven, Belgium.

Perrig, A., Szewczyk, R., Tygar, J. D., Wen, V., & Culler, D. E. (2002). Spins: Security protocols for sensor networks. *Wireless Networks*, *8*(5), 521–534. doi:10.1023/A:1016598314198

Pietro, R. Di, Mancini, L. V., Law, Y. W., Etalle, S., & Havinga, P. (2003). Lkhw: A directed diffusion-based secure multicast scheme for wireless sensor networks, in Parallel Processing Workshops, 2003. Proceedings 2003 International Conference, (pp. 397– 406). IEEE.

Ping, L., Liu, Q., Zhou, Z., & Wang, H. (2011). Agile supply chain management over the Internet of Things. In *International Conference on the Management and Service Science (MASS)*. IEEE.

Prathapani, A., Santhanam, L., & Agrawal, D. P. (2009). Intelligent honeypot agent for blackhole attack detection in wireless mesh networks. In *IEEE 6th International Conference on Mobile Adhoc and Sensor Systems (MASS'09)*, (pp. 753-758). IEEE.

Qrunfleh, S., & Tarafdar, M. (2014). Supply chain information systems strategy: Impacts on supply chain performance and firm performance. *International Journal of Production Economics*, *147*(1), 340–350. doi:10.1016/j.ijpe.2012.09.018

Rahman, R. A., & Shah, B. (2016). Security analysis of IoT protocols: A focus in COAP, in Big Data and Smart City (ICBDSC). *3rd MEC International Conference*, (pp. 1-7). IEEE.

Rahman, R. A., & Shah, B. (2016). Security analysis of iot protocols: A focus in COAP, in Big Data and Smart City (ICBDSC). *2016 3rd MEC International Conference*, (pp. 1–7). IEEE.

Rai, A., Patnayakuni, R., & Seth, N. (2006). Firm performance impacts of digitally enabled supply chain integration capabilities. *Management Information Systems Quarterly*, *30*(2), 225–246. doi:10.2307/25148729

Rodrigo, R., Jianying, Z., & Javier, L. (2013). On the features and challenges of security and privacy in distributed internet of things, Computer Networks, Science Direct. *Elsevier B.*, *57*(10), 1–14.

Sastry, A. S., Shazia, S., & Vagdevi, S. (2013). Security threats in wireless sensor networks in each layer. *International Journal of Advanced Networking and Applications*, *4*(4), 1657.

Sharma, K. & Ghose, M. (2010). Wireless sensor networks: An overview on its security threats. *IJCA*, 42-45.

Sharma, K., & Ghose, M. (2010). Wireless sensor networks: An overview on its security threats [MANETs]. *IJCA, Special Issue on Mobile Ad-hoc Networks, 42–45*, 2010.

Slijepcevic, S., Potkonjak, M., Tsiatsis, V., Zimbeck, S., & Srivastava, M. B. (2002). On communication security in wireless ad-hoc sensor networks, in Enabling Technologies: Infrastructure for Collaborative Enterprises. Eleventh IEEE International Workshops (pp. 139–144). IEEE.

Slijepcevic, S., Potkonjak, M., Tsiatsis, V., Zimbeck, S., & Srivastava, M. B. (2002). On communication security in wireless ad-hoc sensor networks, in Proceedings of Eleventh IEEE International Workshops - Enabling Technologies: Infrastructure for Collaborative Enterprises, WET ICE 2002, 139-144.

Thakur, J., & Nagesh, K. (2011). DES, AES and Blowfish: Symmetric key cryptography algorithms simulation based performance analysis. *International Journal of Emerging Technology and Advanced Engineering*, *1*(2), 6–12.

Tiwari, M., Arya, K. V., Choudhari, R., & Choudhary, K. S. (2009). Designing intrusion detection to detect blackhole and selective forwarding attack in WSN based on local information. In *Computer Science and Convergence Information Technology, Fourth International Conference on ICCIT*, (pp. 824-828). IEEE.

Tubaishat, M., Yin, J., Panja, B., & Madria, S. (2004). A secure hierarchical model for sensor network. *SIGMOD Record*, *33*(1), 7–13. doi:10.1145/974121.974123

Vanpoucke, E., Vereecke, A., & Muylle, S. (2017). Leveraging the Impact of Supply Chain Integration Through Information Technology. *International Journal of Operations & Production Management*, *37*(4), 510–530. doi:10.1108/IJOPM-07-2015-0441

Walters, J. P., Zhengqiang, Z., Weisong S., & Vipin, C. (2007). Wireless sensor network security: A survey. *Security in distributed, grid, mobile, and pervasive computing*, (pp. 367-404).

Wazid, M., Katal, A., Sachan, R. S., Goudar, R., & Singh, D. (2013). Detection and prevention mechanism for blackhole attack in wireless sensor network. In *International Conference on Communication and Signal Processing (ICCSP)*, (pp. 576-581). IEEE. 10.1109/iccsp.2013.6577120

Whitmore, A., Agarwal, A., & Da Xu, L. (2014). The Internet of Things – A survey of topics and trends. *Information Systems Frontiers*, *17*(2), 261–274. doi:10.100710796-014-9489-2

Wood, D., Stankovic, J. A., & Son, S. H. (2003). Jam: A jammed area mapping service for sensor networks. In Real-Time Systems Symposium, (pp. 286–297). IEEE.

Ye, F., Luo, H., Lu, S., & Zhang, L. (2005). Statistical en-route filtering of injected false data in sensor networks. *IEEE Journal on Selected Areas in Communications*, *23*(4), 839–850. doi:10.1109/JSAC.2005.843561

Yong, W., Garhan, A., & Byrav, R. (2006). A survey of security issues in wireless sensor networks. *IEEE Communications Surveys and Tutorials*, *8*(2), 1–22.

Yu, J., Subramanian, N., Ning, K., & Edwards, D. (2015). Product delivery service provider selection and customer satisfaction in the era of internet of things: A Chinese e-retailers' perspective. *International Journal of Production Economics*, *159*(1), 104–116. doi:10.1016/j.ijpe.2014.09.031

Znaidi, W., Minier, M., & Babau, J. P. (2008). An ontology for attacks in wireless sensor networks, PhD dissertation, INRIA, 2008.

KEY TERMS AND DEFINITIONS

Cryptography: Blockchain's transactions achieve validity, trust, and finality based on cryptographic proofs and underlying mathematical computations between various trading partners.

Decentralized Computing Infrastructure: These computing infrastructures feature computing nodes that can make independent processing and computational decisions irrespective of what other peer computing nodes may decide.

Internet of Things (IoT): The Internet of Things (IoT), also called the Internet of Everything or the Industrial Internet, is now a technology paradigm envisioned as a global network of machines and devices capable of interacting with each other. The IoT is recognized as one of the most important areas of future technology and is gaining vast attention from a wide range of industries.

Supply Chain Management: A supply chain consists of a network of *key business processes* and facilities, involving end-users and suppliers that provide products, services, and information.

Warehouse: A warehouse can also be called a storage area, and it is a commercial building where raw materials or goods are stored by suppliers, exporters, manufacturers, or wholesalers, they are constructed and equipped with tools according to special standards depending on the purpose of their use.

Compilation of References

Abrazeh, S., Mohseni, S.-R., Zeitouni, M. J., Parvaresh, A., Fathollahi, A., Gheisarnejad, M., & Khooban, M.-H. (2023). Virtual hardware-in-the-loop FMU co-simulation based digital twins for heating, ventilation, and air-conditioning (HVAC) systems. *IEEE Transactions on Emerging Topics in Computational Intelligence*, *7*(1), 65–75. doi:10.1109/TETCI.2022.3168507

Accenture. (2020). *COVID-19: Consumers change how they shop, work and live.* Accenture. https://www.accenture.com/ie-en/insights/retail/coronavirus-consumer-behavior-research

Accenture. (2020). *Supply Chain Disruption & How to Respond.* Accenture. https://www.accenture.com/us-en/insights/consulting/coronavirus-supply-chain-disruption

Accettura, N., & Piro, G. (2014). Optimal and secure protocols in the IETF 6tisch Communication Stack. *23rd International Symposium Industrial Electronics (ISIE),* (pp. 1469-1474). IEEE. 10.1109/ISIE.2014.6864831

ACSM. (2022). *SCOR Digital Standard 2022.* SCOR Model.

Agrawal, P., & Narain, R. (2018). Digital supply chain management: An overview. *IOP Conference Series. Materials Science and Engineering*, *455*(1), 012074. doi:10.1088/1757-899X/455/1/012074

Aheleroff. (2020). *A Digital Twin Reference for Mass Personalization in Industry 4.0.* ScienceDirect.

Aheleroff. (2021). *Digital Twin as a Service (DTaaS) in Industry 4.0: An Architecture Reference Model.* ScienceDirect.

Akyuz, G., & Erkan, T. (2010). Supply chain performance measurement: A literature review. *International Journal of Production Research*, *48*(17), 5137–5155. doi:10.1080/00207540903089536

Albors-Garrigos, J. (2020). Barriers and enablers for innovation in the retail sector: Co-innovating with the customer. A case study in grocery retailing. *Journal of Retailing and Consumer Services*, *55*, 102077. doi:10.1016/j.jretconser.2020.102077

Alfalla-Luque, R., Medina-Lopez, C., & Dey, P. K. (2013). Supply chain integration framework using literature review. *Production Planning and Control*, *24*(8-9), 800–817. doi:10.1080/09537287.2012.666870

Aliahmadi, A., & Nozari, H. (2022, July). Evaluation of security metrics in AIoT and blockchain-based supply chain by Neutrosophic decision-making method. In *Supply Chain Forum: An International Journal* (pp. 1-12). Taylor & Francis.

Aliahmadi, A., Nozari, H., Ghahremani-Nahr, J., & Szmelter-Jarosz, A. (2022). *Evaluation of key impression of resilient supply chain based on artificial intelligence of things (AIoT).* arXiv:2207.13174.

Aliahmadi, A., Nozari, H., & Ghahremani-Nahr, J. (2022). Big Data IoT-based agile-lean logistic in pharmaceutical industries. *International Journal of Innovation in Management. Economics and Social Sciences*, *2*(3), 70–81.

Almujeem, N. S. (2021). GCC countries' geoeconomic significance to China's geopolitical ends. *Review of Economics and Political Science*. https://doi.org/ doi:10.1108/REPS-11-2019-0152

Amazon. (2020). *More than 100 million items delivered to healthcare and government organizations*. Amazon. https://www.aboutamazon.com/news/company-news/over-100-million-items-delivered-to-healthcare-and-government-organization
s

Analytics, J. (2009). White Paper: A Guide To Creating Dashboards People Love to Use. https://goo.gl/QGGHty.

Annarelli, B., Battistella, C., & Nonino, F. (2020). A framework to evaluate the effects of organizational resilience on service quality. *Sustainability (Basel)*, *12*(3), 958. doi:10.3390u12030958

APICS. (n.d.). *Rough-Cut capacity planning*. APICS. http://apicsforum.com/ebook/capacity_planning

Ascm. (2022, September 19). *ASCM releases new SCOR Digital Standard*. PR Newswire. https://www.prnewswire.com/news-releases/ascm-releases-new-scor-digital-standard-301626710.html

Atzori, L., Iera, A., & Morabito, G. (2010). The Internet of Things: A survey. *Computer Networks*, *54*(15), 2787–2805. doi:10.1016/j.comnet.2010.05.010

Automate Po Changes & enable supplier collaboration. (2022, April 14). SourceDay. https://sourceday.com/

Awan, S., Ahmed, S., Ullah, F., Nawaz, A., Khan, A., Uddin, M. I., Alharbi, A., Alosaimi, W., & Alyami, H. (2021). IoT with blockchain: A futuristic approach in agriculture and food supply chain. *Wireless Communications and Mobile Computing*, *2021*, 2021. doi:10.1155/2021/5580179

Bakken Center for Spirituality & Healing. (n.d.). *Understanding Complex Systems.*

Banker, S. (2022). Supply Chain Management is Broken. Can a Radical New Way Of Thinking Be The Solution? *Forbes.*

Barnett, J., & Clark, T. (2019). Reducing e-commerce returns through product presentation. *International Journal of Retail & Distribution Management*, *47*(9), 1008–1020.

Bell, C., Higgs, R., Vickers, S., Toncinich, S., & Haslett, T. (2003). Using System modelling to understand the dynamics of supply chains. Monash University. *Working Paper*, *70*(03).

Ben-Daya, M., Hassini, E., & Bahroun, Z. (2017). Internet of things and supply chain management: A literature review. *International Journal of Production Research*, *57*(15-16), 4719–4742. doi:10.1080/00207543.2017.1402140

Bernard, M. (2012). *Key Performance Indicators (KPIs): The 75 Measures Every Manager Needs To Know*. FT Press. https://goo.gl/v7r4hZ,

Bim, A. Ş. Y. İ. (2021). *Finansal ve Faaliyet Tabloları*. BIM. https://www.bim.com.tr/categories/105/yatirimci-iliskileri.aspx

Bin, S. (2020). *K-Means Stock Clustering Analysis Based on Historical Price Movements and Financial Ratios*. [Theses, Claremont McKenna College] https://scholarship.claremont.edu/cmc_theses/2435

Bizim Toptan Satış Mağazaları, A. Ş. Y. İ. (2021). Bizim Toptan Satış Mağazaları A.Ş. Yatırımcı İlişkileri Finansal ve Faaliyet Raporları. https://www.biziminvestorrelations.com/default.aspx

Blokdyk, G. (2020). *Supply Chain Visibility Initiatives A Complete Guide*. IBM.

Bloomberg. (2021). *Colonial Pipeline Cyber Attack: Hackers Used Compromised Password.* Bloomberg. https://www.bloomberg.com/news/articles/2021-06-04/hackers-breached-colonial-pipeline-using-compromised-password

Blue Yonder. (2020). *Supply Chain Visibility in a Time of Crisis: What the 2020 Visibility Report Tells Us.* Blue Yonder. https://blog.blueyonder.com/2020-visibility-report/

Bowman, R. J. (2013). *SKU Proliferation: Is There a Cure for the Disease?* SupplyChainBrain. https://www.supplychainbrain.com/blogs/1-think-tank/post/17575-sku-proliferation-is-there-a-cure-for-the-disease

Boyson, S., Corsi, T. M., & Paraskevas, J.-P. (2021). Defending digital supply chains: Evidence from a decade-long research program. *Technovation, 102380.* doi:10.1016/j.technovation.2021.102380

Bryan, A., Perrig, V., & Gligor, P. (2005). Distributed detection of node replication attacks in sensor networks. *IEEE Symposium on Security and Privacy (S&P'05).* IEEE.

Butcher, D. (2021, October 27). 5 ways digital technology will transform the supply chain. *MasterControl.* https://www.mastercontrol.com/gxp-lifeline/5-ways-digital-technology-will-transform-the-supply-chain/

Butuan, I. (2013). *Prevention and detection of intrusions in wireless sensor networks.* [Ph.D. Dissertation, University of South Florida].

Butun, I., Morgera, S. D., & Sankar, R. (2014). A survey of intrusion detection systems in wireless sensor networks. *IEEE Communications Surveys and Tutorials, 16*(1), 266–282. doi:10.1109/SURV.2013.050113.00191

Buyukkececi, Z. (2020). Cross-country differences in anxiety and behavioral response to the Covid-19 pandemic. *European Societies*, 1–31. doi:10.1080/14616696.2020.1828975

Cachon, G., & Terwiesch, C. (2008). *Matching supply with demand.* McGraw-Hill Publishing.

Cagalj, M., Capkun, S., & Hubaux, J. P. (2007). Wormhole-based antijamming techniques in sensor networks. *IEEE Transactions on Mobile Computing*, *6*(1), 2007. doi:10.1109/TMC.2007.250674

Camerinelli, E., & Cantu, A. (2006). Measuring the Value of the Supply Chain: A Framework. *Supply Chain Practice, 8*(2), 40–59.

Campuzano Bolarín, F., Lisec, A., & Esteban, F. (2008). Inventory cost consequences of variability demand process with a multi-echelon supply chain. *Logistics & Sustainable Transport.*, *1*(3), 1–12.

Carrefour, S. A. Y. İ. (2021). CarrefourSA Yatırımcı İlişkileri Finansal ve Faaliyet Raporları. https://yatirimciiliskileri.carrefoursa.com/tr-tr

Cecere, L. (2022). Insights from a Two-Year Journey to Define Outside-In Supply Chain Planning Processes. *Forbes.*

CFI. (2018). *Financial Ratios eBook.* CFI. corporatefinanceinstitute.com/resources/ebooks

Chae, B., Olson, D., & Sheu, C. (2014). The impact of supply chain analytics on operational performance: A resource-based view. *International Journal of Production Research, 52*(16), 4695–4710. doi:10.1080/00207543.2013.861616

Chain Store Age . (2022). *Home Page.* Chain Store Age. https://chainstoreage.com/kroger-launches-ambitious-ai-transformation-program

Chan, H., Perrig, A., & Song, D. (2003). Security and privacy in sensor networks. *IEEE Computer Magazine, 36*(10), 103-105.

Cheng, E. (2023). 5G Indoor Positioning. *Pointr Tech.* https://www.pointr.tech/blog/5g-indoor-positioning

Chen, K., Golhar, D. Y., & Banerjee, S. (2023). Blockchain applications and challenges for supply chain and Industry 4.0: A literature review. *International Journal of Applied Decision Sciences*, *16*(1), 1–41. doi:10.1504/IJADS.2023.127957

Chen, R., Xie, Y., & Liu, Y. (2021). Defining, conceptualizing, and measuring organizational resilience: A multiple case study. *Sustainability (Basel)*, *13*(5), 2517. doi:10.3390u13052517

Choi, T.-M. (2021). Fighting against COVID-19: What operations research can help and the sense-and-respond framework. *Annals of Operations Research*. doi:10.100710479-021-03973-w PMID:33688111

Chopra, S. (2021). *Supply chain management: Strategy, planning and operation* (7th ed.). Pearson Education.

Choudhury, A., Behl, A., Sheorey, P. A., & Pal, A. (2021). Digital supply chain to unlock new agility: A TISM approach. *Benchmarking*, *28*(6), 2075–2109. doi:10.1108/BIJ-08-2020-0461

Chowdhury, P., Paul, S. K., Kaisar, S., & Moktadir, M. (2021). COVID-19 pandemic related supply chain studies: A systematic review. *Transportation Research Part E, Logistics and Transportation Review*, *148*, 102271. doi:10.1016/j.tre.2021.102271 PMID:33613082

Christopher, M., Peck, H., & Towill, D. (2006). A Taxonomy for Selecting Global Supply Chain Strategies. *International Journal of Logistics Management*, *17*(2), 277–287. doi:10.1108/09574090610689998

Christopher, M., & Towill, D. (2001). An integrated model for the design of agile supply chains. *International Journal of Physical Distribution & Logistics Management*, *31*(4), 235–246. doi:10.1108/09600030110394914

Christopher, M., Towill, D., Aitken, J., & Childerhouse, P. (2009). Value Chain Classification. *Journal of Manufacturing Technology Management*, *20*(4), 460–474. doi:10.1108/17410380910953720

Chu, S., Leung, J., & Cheung, W. (2015). *On IoT Impact Of Supply Chain Visibility*. ICEB 2015 Proceedings, Hong Kong, SAR China.

CNN. (2011). *Toyota making drastic production cuts after Japan quake, tsunami*. CNN. http://www.cnn.com/2011/WORLD/asiapcf/04/20/japan.toyota/index.html

Colema, L. (2006). Frequency of man-made disasters in the 20th century. *Journal of Contingencies and Crisis Management*, *14*(1), 3–11. doi:10.1111/j.1468-5973.2006.00476.x

Conley, P. (2023, February 24). Online return rates dropped in 2022, according to NRF study. *Digital Commerce 360*. https://www.digitalcommerce360.com/2022/12/15/online-return-rates-dropped-in-2022-according-to-nrf-study/

Corazza, L., Zhang, J., Arachchilage, D. K., & Scagnelli, S. D. (2023). Blockchain and Sustainability Disclosure: A Scenario-Based Application for Supply Chains. *Sustainability (Basel)*, *15*(1), 571. doi:10.3390u15010571

Cynthia, B., & Keith, L. S. (2011, January–March). Organizational Change Management: A Test of the Effectiveness of a Communication Plan. *Communication Research Reports*, *28*(1), 62–73. doi:10.1080/08824096.2011.541364

Dadzie, K., Dadzie, C., Johnston, W. J., Winston, E., & Wang, H. (2022). The integration of logistics and marketing practice into baseline supply chain practices in the emerging markets. *Journal of Business and Industrial Marketing*, *38*(2), 367–383. doi:10.1108/JBIM-01-2022-0002

Davenport, T. (2006). Competing on Analytics. *Harvard Business Review*.

Davies, S. E., & Wenham, C. (2020). Why the COVID-19 response needs international relations. *International Affairs*, *96*(5), 1227–1251. doi:10.1093/ia/iiaa135 PMID:34191916

Davis, M. (2010). *Case Study for Supply Chain Leaders: Dell's Transformative Journey Through Supply Chain Segmentation.* Gartner. https://www.gartner.com/doc/1468717/case-study-supply-chain-leaders

Deepu, T. S., & Ravi, V. (2021). Supply chain digitalization: An integrated MCDM approach for inter-organizational information systems selection in an electronic supply chain. *International Journal of Information Management Data Insights*, *1*(2), 100038. doi:10.1016/j.jjimei.2021.100038

Deng, J., Han, R., & Mishra, S. (2003). A performance evaluation of intrusion-tolerant routing in wireless sensor networks. Information Processing in Sensor Networks. Springer.

Deng, J., Han, R., & Mishra, S. (2005). Defending against path-based dos attacks in wireless sensor networks, in *Proceedings of the 3rd ACM workshop on Security of ad hoc and sensor networks.* ACM. 10.1145/1102219.1102235

Deste, M., & Halifeoğlu, M. (2019). Perakende Ticaret Sektöründeki İşletmelerin Tedarik Zinciri Yönetimi Açısından Finansal Performans Kriterlerinin Belirlenmesi: BIST'de Bir Uygulama Perakende Ticaret Sektöründeki İşletmelerin Tedarik Zinciri Yönetimi. *Journal of Social Sciences Institute/Sosyal Bilimler Enstitüsü Dergisi, 9*(18).

Diageo. (2022). *Supporting supply chain visibility in volatile times.* Diageo. https://www.diageo.com/en/news-and-media/stories/2022/supporting-supply-chain-visibility-in-volatile-times

Dolan, S. (2022). Last Mile Shipping Delivery Explained. *Business Insider.* https://www.businessinsider.com/last-mile-delivery-shipping-explained?r=US&IR=T

DuBravac, S. (2021). *Connecting manufacturors with the future of how 5G is transforming the landscape.* Manufacturing Institute. https://www.themanufacturinginstitute.org/research/connecting-manufacturers-with-the-future-how-5g-is-transforming-the-manufacturing-landscape/

Duchek, S. (2019). Organizational resilience: A capability-based conceptualization. *Business Research*, *13*(1), 215–246. doi:10.100740685-019-0085-7

Duchek, S., Raetze, S., & Scheuch, I. (2019). The role of diversity in organizational resilience: A theoretical framework. *Business Research*, *13*(2), 387–423. doi:10.100740685-019-0084-8

Dundas. (n.d.). *Dashboards Demystified.* Dundas. https://goo.gl/OriOSu.

Dünya. (2021). 7 Yılda 15 Bin Yeni Market Açılması Bekleniyor. *Dünya.* https://www.dunya.com/ekonomi/7-yilda-15-bin-yeni-market-acilmasi-bekleniyor-haberi-612010

Dykes, B. (2011). Web Analytics Action Hero: Using Analysis to Gain Insight and Optimize Your Business. *Adobe Press.* https://goo.gl/OWZSKn.

Dyton, J. (2021). 5G can better communications. *Connected Remag.* https://connectedremag.com/das-in-building-wireless/5g/can-better-communications-and-5g-solve-some-of-the-supply-chain-problems/

Eckerson, W. (2009). Performance Management Strategies: How to Create and Deploy Effective Metrics. *TDWI Best Practices Report Q1 2009.*

Elaine, E., & Adrian, P. (2004). Designing secure sensor networks. *IEEE Wireless Communications*, *11*(6), 38–43. doi:10.1109/MWC.2004.1368895

Eljelly, A. M. (2019). Reverse logistics in the era of e-commerce: A review. *International Journal of Supply Chain Management*, *8*(1), 292–303.

Enterprise Management Associates. (2012). White Paper: Business Intelligence Platforms for Mid-size Organizations: Comparing Birst, MicroStrategy, Oracle and SAP BusinessObjects. EMA. https://goo.gl/lm2XRC.

Erdem, M., & Erkan, T. E. (2019). Elvaluation Of Supply Chain Performance Using An Integrated Two-Step Clustering And Interval Type-2 Fuzzy TOPSIS Method: A Case Study. *Pamukkale Üniversitesi Sosyal Bilimler Enstitüsü Dergisi*, (37), 141–160.

Erdoğan, N. K., Altınırmak, S., & Karamaşa, Ç. (2016). Comparison of multi criteria decision making (MCDM) methods with respect to performance of food firms listed in BIST. *Copernican Journal of Finance & Accounting*, *5*(1), 67–90. doi:10.12775/CJFA.2016.004

European Commission. (2019). *SME performance review*. EC. https://ec.europa.eu/growth/smes/business-friendly-environment/performance-review_en

Farrell, L. (2020). 4 Capacity Planning Challenges in L&D (And How to Overcome Them). *Cognota*. https://cognota.com/blog/4-capacity-planning-challenges-in-ld-and-how-to-overcome-them/

Federal Reserve Bank of New York. (2023). *Global Supply Chain Pressure Index*. New Yotrk Fed. https://newyorkfed.org/research/policy/gscpi

FencesT. (n.d.). Retrieved from http://apicsforum.com/ebook/time_fences

Fettke, P., Loos, P., & Zwicker, J. (2005). *Business Process Reference Models: Survey and Classification*. Third International Conference on Business Process Management (BPM), Nancy, France. https://goo.gl/TQILgk.

Fisher, M. L. (1997). What Is the Right Supply Chain for Your Product? *Harvard Business Review*, (March–April), 105–116.

Fleisch, E., & Tellkamp, C. (2005). Inventory inaccuracy and supply chain performance: A simulation study of a retail supply chain. *International Journal of Production Economics*, *95*(3), 373–385. doi:10.1016/j.ijpe.2004.02.003

Ford, M. W., & Greer, B. M. (2005). The Relationship between Management Control System Usage and Planned Change Achievement: An Exploratory Study. *Journal of Change Management*, *5*(1), 29–46. doi:10.1080/14697010500036031

Fortune. (2022). *Global 500*. Fortune. https://fortune.com/ranking/global500/

Gademann, N., van Helden, F., & Kuijsten, W. (n.d.). *S&OP a threefold approach to strategic planning*. ORTEC Counsiling. https://www.ortec-consulting.com/market-views/s-and-op-a-threefold-approach-to-strategic-planning/

Gai, K., Zhang, Y., Qiu, M., & Thuraisingham, B. (2022). Blockchain-enabled service optimizations in supply chain digital twin. *IEEE Transactions on Services Computing*, 1–12. doi:10.1109/TSC.2022.3192166

Gallup. (2013). Most Change Initiatives Fail -- But They Don't Have To. *Business Journal*. http://businessjournal.gallup.com

Ganesan, S., Venkatesan, S., & Karthikeyan, K. (2019). An empirical analysis of reverse logistics practices in e-commerce. *Journal of Cleaner Production*, *209*, 1539–1550.

Gartner and Supply Chain Digest. (2016). Highlights of the Gartner-SCDigest Supply Chain Study 2016. SC Digest. http://www.scdigest.com/firstthoughts/16-07-21.php?cid=10995

Gattorna, J. (2006). *Living Supply Chains*. Pearson.

Gautam, A. (2022, August 31). Transforming Reverse Logistics through the Digital Route. *Innoverdigital.* https://innoverdigital.com/transforming-reverse-logistics-through-the-digital-route/

Geethan, K. A. V., Jose, S., Koshy, A., & Samuel, A. B. (2011). Methodology for Study of Characteristics and Time Reduction in Reverse Supply Chain Using System Dynamics. *International Conference on Sociality and Economics Development, IPEDR Vol.10.* IGI Global.

GEODIS. (2017). *Supply chain worldwide survey.* GEODIS. https://geodis.com/sites/default/files/2019-03/170509_GEODIS_WHITE-PAPER.PDF

Ghahremani-Nahr, J., Aliahmadi, A., & Nozari, H. (2022). An IoT-based sustainable supply chain framework and blockchain. *International Journal of Innovation in Engineering, 2*(1), 12–21.

Giering, M. (2008). Retail sales prediction and item recommendations using customer demographics at store level. *SIGKDD Explorations, 10*(2), 84–89. doi:10.1145/1540276.1540301

Goić, M., Levenier, C., & Montoya, R. (2021). Drivers Of Customer Satisfaction In The Grocery Retail Industry: A Longitudinal Analysis Across Store Formats. *Journal of Retailing and Consumer Services, 60,* 102505. doi:10.1016/j.jretconser.2021.102505

Goldratt, E. M., & Cox, J. (2016). *The goal: a process of ongoing improvement.* Routledge. doi:10.4324/9781315270456

Greig, S. (2018). *Measuring Integration Complexity. IT's Complicated!* Medium.

GS1. (2018). *New report shows RFID delivers retail sales increase by up to 5.5%.* GS1. https://www.gs1.org/articles/new-report-shows-rfid-delivers-retail-sales-increase-by-55

Gül, A., & Erdem, M. (2022). Gıda Perakende Firmalarının Finansal Performanslarının Entropi-TOPSIS Yöntemiyle Analizi. *European Journal of Science and Technology.* doi:10.31590/ejosat.1029907

Gunasekaran, A., Papadopoulos, T., Dubey, R., Wamba, S. F., Childe, S. J., Hazen, B., & Akter, S. (2017). Big data and predictive analytics for supply chain and organizational performance. *Journal of Business Research, 70,* 308–317. doi:10.1016/j.jbusres.2016.08.004

Gupta, V. (2019). Procurement Strategies for Digital Supply Chains: Concepts and Best Practices [Chapter]. *Technology Optimization and Change Management for Successful Digital Supply Chains,* IGI Global. doi:10.4018/978-1-5225-7700-3.ch002

Gupta, V., & Chutani, A. (2020). Supply chain financing with advance selling under disruption. *International Transactions in Operational Research, 27*(5), 2449–2468. doi:10.1111/itor.12663

Gupta, V., He, B., & Sethi, S. P. (2015). Contingent sourcing under supply disruption and competition. *International Journal of Production Research, 53*(10), 3006–3027. doi:10.1080/00207543.2014.965351

Gupta, V., Ivanov, D., & Choi, T.-M. (2021). Competitive pricing of substitute products under supply disruption. *Omega, 101,* 102279. doi:10.1016/j.omega.2020.102279 PMID:32836689

GVR. (2020). *Food & Grocery Retail Market Size, Share & Trends Analysis Report By Product (Food Cupboard, Beverages), By Distribution Channel (Supermarkets & Hypermarkets, Online), By Region (APAC, Europe), And Segment Forecasts, 2022 - 2030.* Grand View Research. https://www.grandviewresearch.com/industry-analysis/food-grocery-retail-market

Han, G., Lei, S. S. C., & Jiankun, H. (2016). Security and privacy in Internet of things: Methods, architectures, and solutions. *Security and Communication Networks*, *9*(15), 2641–2642. doi:10.1002ec.1497

Harrison, J. M., & Van Mieghem, J. A. (1999). Multi-resource investment strategies: Operational hedging under demand uncertainty. *European Journal of Operational Research*, *113*(1), 17–29. doi:10.1016/S0377-2217(97)00425-6

Hepfer, M., & Lawrence, T. B. (2022). The heterogeneity of organizational resilience: Exploring functional, operational and strategic resilience. *Organization Theory*, *3*(1), 263178772210747. doi:10.1177/26317877221074701

Higgins-Dunn, N. (2022). *How China's strict Covid policies led to supply chain bottlenecks*. CNBC. https://www.cnbc.com/2022/08/19/how-chinas-covid-policies-lead-to-hampered-supply-chains-higher-inflation.html

Hillmann, J., & Guenther, E. (2020). Organizational resilience: A valuable construct for management research? *International Journal of Management Reviews, 23*(1). Wiley. https://doi.org/ doi:10.1111/ijmr.12239

Hou, B. (2016). Financial Distress Prediction of K-means Clustering Based on Genetic Algorithm and Rough Set Theory. *Chemical Engineering Transactions*, *51*. Advance online publication. doi:10.3303/CET1651085

i2 Technologies. (2007). *Supply Chain Leader Magazine*. i2 Technologies.

Iakovou, E., & White, C. (2020). *How to build more secure, resilient, next-gen U.S. supply chains*. Brookings. https://tiny.cc/hu13vz.

IBISWORLD. (2022). *Supermarkets & Grocery Stores in the US - Market Size 2002–2027*. Ibis World. https://www.ibisworld.com/industry-statistics/market-size/supermarkets-grocery-stores-united-states/

IBM. (2023). *Supply Chain Visibility Software and Solutions*. IBM. https://www.ibm.com/supply-chain/visibility

Icaro. (2020). Using a Digital Twin for Production Planning and Control in Industry 4.0. International Series in Operations Research & Management Science book series (Vol. 289). ISOR.

INCOSE. (n.d.). *Systems of Systems Primer*. INCOSE.

INFORMS. (n.d.). *What is Analytics?* Informs. https://goo.gl/odWhqS.

Inman, D. (n.d.). *2022 Retail Returns Rate Remains Flat at $816 Billion*. NRF. https://nrf.com/media-center/press-releases/2022-retail-returns-rate-remains-flat-816-billion#:~:text=As%20retail%20sales%20continue%20to,returned%20to%20retailers%20this%20year.%22

Ivanov, D. (2020). Viable supply chain model: Integrating agility, resilience and sustainability perspectives—lessons from and thinking beyond the COVID-19 pandemic. *Annals of Operations Research*. Springer. https://doi.org/ doi:10.1007/s10479-020-03640-6

Ivanov, D., & Dolgui, A. (2020). Viability of intertwined supply networks: Extending the supply chain resilience angles towards survivability. A position paper motivated by COVID-19 outbreak. *International Journal of Production Research*, *58*(10), 2904–2915. doi:10.1080/00207543.2020.1750727

Jaydip, S. (2009). A Survey on Wireless Sensor Network Security. *International Journal of Communication Networks and Information Security*, *1*(2), 55–78.

JD.com to launch unmanned robot delivery fleet in quarantined Wuhan. (2020, February 5). KrASIA. https://kr-asia.com/jd-com-to-launch-unmanned-robot-delivery-fleet-in-quarantined-wuhan

John, B. (2022). Reducing Supply Chain Disruptions in Life Science. *The Hartford.* https://www.thehartford.com/insights/covid-19/reduce-life-science-supply-chain-disruptions

Johnson, N. (2009). *Simply Complexity: A Clear Guide to Complexity Theory.* Oneworld Publications.

Johnston, D. (2012). The Shift to Reshoring. *Real Results Magazine.* http://www.jda.com/realresultsmagazine/view-article.cfm?did=2867

Jones, W. A. (2018). Artificial intelligence and leadership: A few thoughts, a few questions. *Journal of Leadership Studies, 12*(3), 60–62. doi:10.1002/jls.21597

Juneja, P. (n.d.). *Capacity Planning.* Management Study Guide. https://www.managementstudyguide.com/capacity-planning.htm

Kahlert, M., Constantinides, E., & de Vries, S. (2007*). The relevance of technological autonomy in the customer acceptance of IoT services in retail.* The second international conference on Internet of Things and Cloud Computing, Cambridge, United Kingdom.

KAP. (2021). *KAP Finansal Tablolar.* KAP. https://www.kap.org.tr/

Kaplan, R. S. (2010). Conceptual Foundations of the Balanced Scorecard. Harvard Business School Accounting & Management Unit. *Working Paper No. 10-074.* https://ssrn.com/abstract=1562586

Karakehayov, Z. (2005). Using reward to detect team black-hole attacks in wireless sensor networks. *Real-World Wireless Sensor Networks Workshop*, (pp. 20-21).

Karlof, C., & Wagner, D. (2003). Secure routing in wireless sensor networks: Attacks and countermeasures. *Ad Hoc Networks, 1*(2), 293–315. doi:10.1016/S1570-8705(03)00008-8

Karp, T. (2005). Unpacking the Mysteries of Change: Mental Modeling. *Journal of Change Management, 5*(1), 87–97. doi:10.1080/14697010500057573

Kartz, J. (2011). *Creating High-Value Supply Chains.* Industry Week. http://www.industryweek.com/companies-amp-executives/creating-high-value-supply-chains

Karumanchi, M. D., Sheeba, J. I., & Devaneyan, S. P. (2023). Nonlinear integrity algorithm for blockchain based supply chain databases. In *Pervasive Computing and Social Networking* (pp. 169–181). Springer. doi:10.1007/978-981-19-2840-6_13

Kaur, A., Singh, G., Kukreja, V., Sharma, S., Singh, S., & Yoon, B. (2022). Adaptation of IoT with Blockchain in Food Supply Chain Management: An Analysis-Based Review in Development, Benefits and Potential Applications. *Sensors (Basel), 22*(21), 8174. doi:10.339022218174 PMID:36365871

Kenett, R. S. (2020). *The digital twin in Industry 4.0: A wide-angle perspective.* AEAI.

Khan, N., Silva S., & Kandl, T. (2012). *A software based solution to facilitate end to end information supply chain visibility.* ICSSSM12, Shanghai, China. . doi:10.1109/ICSSSM.2012.6252359

Kiesmüller, G. P., Inderfurth, K., & Zsifkovits, H. (2017). Reverse logistics network design in the era of the internet of things. *International Journal of Production Economics, 183*, 487–501.

Kim, M., & Chai, S. (2017). The impact of supplier innovativeness, information sharing and strategic sourcing on improving supply chain agility: Global supply chain perspective. *International Journal of Production Economics, 187*(1), 42–52. doi:10.1016/j.ijpe.2017.02.007

Knut. (2020). *Resetting Supple Chains for the Next Normal.* McKinsey. https://www.mckinsey.com/capabilities/operations/our-insights/resetting-supply-chains-for-the-next-normal

Kochan, C., Nowicki, D. R., Sauser, B., & Randall, W. S. (2018). Impact of cloud-based information sharing on hospital supply chain performance: A system dynamics framework. *International Journal of Production Economics, 195*, 168–185. doi:10.1016/j.ijpe.2017.10.008

Kotter, J. P. (1996). *Leading Change.* Boston Harvard Business School Press.

Kou, G., Peng, Y., & Wang, G. (2014). Evaluation of clustering algorithms for financial risk analysis using MCDM methods. *Information Sciences, 275*, 1–12. doi:10.1016/j.ins.2014.02.137

KPMG. (2020). *Sektörel Bakış 2020 - Perakende.* KPMG. https://home.kpmg/tr/tr/home/gorusler/2020/01/sektorel-bakis-2020-perakende.html

Krishnan, S. N., & Srinivasan, P. (2016). A qos parameter based solution for black hole denial of service attack in wireless sensor networks. *Indian Journal of Science and Technology, 9*(38), 2016.

Lacity, M. C., & Van Hoek, R. (2021). How Walmart Canada used blockchain technology to reimagine freight invoice processing. *MIS Quarterly Executive*, 219–233. doi:10.17705/2msqe.00050

Lau, G. (2022). Mitigate Supply Chain Disruptions. *Shift 4 Shop.* https://blog.shift4shop.com/mitigate-supply-chain-disruption

Lau, H. S., & Hing-Ling Lau, A. (1995). The multi-product multi-constraint newsboy problem: Applications, formulation and solution. *Journal of Operations Management, 13*(2), 153–162. doi:10.1016/0272-6963(95)00019-O

Lazar, M.-J. (2022, March 30). 20 statistics on ecommerce returns you need to know in 2021. *ReadyCloud.* https://www.readycloud.com/info/20-statistics-on-ecommerce-returns

Lee, A. J. T., Lin, M.-C., Kao, R.-T., & Chen, K.-T. (2010). *An Effective Clustering Approach to Stock Market Prediction.* Paper presented at the PACIS.

Lee, H.L. & Tang, C.S. (2000). *A review of recent developments in supply chain management.* NIH.

Lee, H. L., Padmanabhan, V., & Whang, S. (1997). Information distortion in a supply chain: The bullwhip effect. *Management Science, 43*(4), 546–558. doi:10.1287/mnsc.43.4.546

Leonard, M. (2020). *MSC adds instant quotes to website.* Supply Chain Dive. https://www.supplychaindive.com/news/msc-instant-booking-quotes/580869/

Levy, M. (2022). *Value of Speed.* KPMG. https://advisory.kpmg.us/articles/2022/value-of-speed.html

Liao, B., Yano, C. A., & Esturi, S. (2017). Optimizing Site Qualification Across the Supply Network at Western Digital. *Interfaces*, *47*(4), 305–319. doi:10.1287/inte.2017.0898

Li, G., Yang, H., Sun, L., & Sohal, A. S. (2009). The impact of IT implementation on supply chain integration and performance. *International Journal of Production Economics*, *120*(1), 125–138. doi:10.1016/j.ijpe.2008.07.017

Linton, J. D., Klassen, R., & Jayaraman, V. (2016). Sustainable supply chains: An introduction. *Journal of Operations Management*, *41*, 1–8.

Little, J. D., & Graves, S. C. (2008). Little's law. In *Building intuition* (pp. 81–100). Springer. doi:10.1007/978-0-387-73699-0_5

Liu, Y., Li, Y., & Man, H. (2005). Mac layer anomaly detection in ad hoc networks. Information Assurance Workshop, IAW'05, (pp. 402-409). IEEE.

Liu, Y., Dong, M., Ota, K., & Liu, A. (2016). Activetrust: Secure and trustable routing in wireless sensor networks. *IEEE Transactions on Information Forensics and Security*, *11*(9), 2013–2017. doi:10.1109/TIFS.2016.2570740

Lixin, D., Ying, L., & Zhiguang, Z. (2008, 6-8 April 2008). *Selection of Logistics Service Provider Based on Analytic Network Process and VIKOR Algorithm.* Paper presented at the 2008 IEEE International Conference on Networking, Sensing and Control. IEEE. 10.1109/ICNSC.2008.4525400

Lovell, A., Saw, R., & Stimson, J. (2005). Product Value-Density: Managing Diversity Through Supply Chain Segmentation. *International Journal of Logistics Management*, *16*(1), 142–158. doi:10.1108/09574090510617394

Ludmila, V., & Renate, Z. (2019). The role of small business in the economy and methods of its government support using the example of the Republic of Latvia. *Economics and Culture*, *16*(2), 72–81. doi:10.2478/jec-2019-0023

Manary, M. P., & Willems, S. P. (2008). Setting safety-stock targets at Intel in the presence of forecast bias. *Interfaces*, *38*(2), 112–122. doi:10.1287/inte.1070.0339

Mao, H., & Gorg, H. (2020). Friends like this: The impact of the US – China trade war on global value chains. *World Economy*, *43*(7), 1776–1791. doi:10.1111/twec.12967

Martinez, W. L., Martinez, A. R., & Solka, J. L. (2017). *Exploratory Data Analysis with MATLAB*. Chapman and Hall/CRC.

Mason-Jones, R., Naylor, B., & Towill, D. (2000). Engineering the Leagile Supply Chain. *International Journal of Agile Management*, *2*(1), 54–61.

Mazman İtik, Ü. (2021). Mali Tablolar Analizi: Borsa İstanbul (BİST)'da Faaliyet Gösteren Bir Gıda İşletmesinde Uygulama (2015-2019). *Elektronik Sosyal Bilimler Dergisi*, *20*(80), 1641–1661.

McIntire, J. (2016). Supply Chain Visibility – From. *Theory into Practice.*

McKinsey. (2020). *Tracking the impact of coronavirus on US small businesses*. McKinsey. https://www.mckinsey.com/industries/financial-services/our-insights/tracking-us-small-and-medium-sized-business-sentiment-during-covid-19

McKinsey. (2021). *Beyond COVID-19: The new consumer behavior is sticking in the tissue industry.* McKinsey. https://www.mckinsey.com/industries/paper-forest-products-and-packaging/our-insights/beyond-covid-19-the-new-consumer-behavior-is-sticking-in-the-tissue-industry

Mckinsey. (2022). *State of Grocery Europe 2022: Navigating the market headwinds.* McKinsey. https://www.mckinsey.com/industries/retail/our-insights/state-of-grocery-europe-2022-navigating-the-market-headwinds

Medadian, M., Yektaie, M. H., & Rahmani, A. M. (2009). Combat with blackhole attack in aodv routing protocol in manet, in Internet, First Asian Himalayan International Conference on AH-ICI, IEEE, 1-5, 2009.

Melnyk, S. A., Calantone, R. J., Luft, J., Stewart, D. M., Zsidisin, G. A., Hanson, J., & Burns, L. (2005). An empirical investigation of metrics alignment process. *International Journal of Productivity and Performance Management, 54*(5/6), 312–324. doi:10.1108/17410400510604494

Melnyk, S., Stewart, D., & Swink, M. (2004). Metrics and performance measurement in operations management: Dealing with the metrics maze. *Journal of Operations Management, 22*(3), 209–217. doi:10.1016/j.jom.2004.01.004

Men, F., Yaqub, R. M. S., Yan, R., Irfan, M., & Fatima, M. e. (2022). Resource-based theory perspective in the textile industry: The impact of the digital supply chain on operational performance. *Frontiers in Environmental Science, 10*, 1017297. doi:10.3389/fenvs.2022.1017297

Michael, R. (2021). *How 5G connectivity can help your warehouse operations.* MMH. https://www.mmh.com/article/how_5g_connectivity_can_help_your_warehouse_operation

Migros Ticaret, A. Ş. Y. İ. (2021). Migros Ticaret A.Ş. Yatırımcı İlişkileri Finansal ve Faaliyet Raporları. *Migros kurumsal.* https://www.migroskurumsal.com/yatirimci-iliskileri/kurumsal

Miran, C. (2020). *5G's impact on transport and logistics: $280bn of benefits in 2030.* STL.

Morawski, A. (2022). Manufacturing 4.0: How 5G could revolutionize the supply chain. *Oracle Communications Blog.* https://blogs.oracle.com/oracle-communications/post/manufacturing-40-how-5g-could-revolutionize-the-supply-chain

Mukherjee, A., Ali, A. F. S., Jing, H., & Lee, S. A. (2014). Principles of physical layer security in multiuser wireless networks: A survey. *IEEE Communications Surveys and Tutorials, 16*(3), 1550–1573. doi:10.1109/SURV.2014.012314.00178

Mulcahy, R. (2010). Business Intelligence Definitions and Solutions. *CIO Magazine.* https://goo.gl/VA8Wzx.

Muraleedharan, R., & Osadciw, L. A. (2006). Cross layer denial of service attacks in wireless sensor network using swarm intelligence, in Information Sciences and Systems. 40th Annual Conference, (pp. 1653–1658). IEEE.

Murray, M. (2018). Master Scheduling Tracks Manufacturing Output. *The Balances MB.* https://www.thebalancesmb.com/master-scheduling-2221212

Mzugovic. (2022, June 30). History of reverse logistics is at the core of the stories of war, Retail, eCommerce, and automotive aftermarket. *GlobalTranz.* https://www.globaltranz.com/resource-hub/history-of-reverse-logistics/

Nadler, D. A., & Tushman, M. (1989). Organizational Frame Bending: Principles for Managing Reorientation. *The Academy of Management Executive*, *3*(3), 194–204.

Nahmias, S., & Cheng, Y. (2009). *Production and operations analysis* (Vol. 6). McGraw-hill.

Nahr, J. G., Nozari, H., & Sadeghi, M. E. (2021). Green supply chain based on artificial intelligence of things (AIoT). *International Journal of Innovation in Management. Economics and Social Sciences*, *1*(2), 56–63.

Najafi, S. E., Nozari, H., & Edalatpanah, S. A. (2022). Artificial Intelligence of Things (AIoT) and Industry 4.0–Based Supply Chain (FMCG Industry). *A Roadmap for Enabling Industry 4.0 by Artificial Intelligence*, 31-41.

Najmi, A. (2022, December 16). *What supply chains really are and why it matters*. The Network Effect. https://supplychainbeyond.com/what-is-a-supply-chain-and-why-it-matters/

Najmi, A., Gholamian, M., & Makui, A. (2013). Supply chain performance models: A literature review on approaches, techniques, and criteria. *Journal of Operations and Supply Chain Management*, *6*(2), 94–113. doi:10.12660/joscmv6n2p94-113

Naylor, J., Naim, M., & Berry, D. (1999). Leagility: Integrating the Lean and Agile Manufacturing Paradigms in the Total Supply Chain. *International Journal of Production Economics*, *62*(1–2), 107–118. doi:10.1016/S0925-5273(98)00223-0

Nelson, J. (2019). *Understanding the benefits of supply chain agility*. The Hackett Group. https://www.thehackettgroup.com/insights/understanding-the-benefits-of-supply-chain-agility/

Netland, T., & Alfnes, E. (2008). *A practical tool for supply chain improvement – experiences with the supply chain maturity assessment test (SCMAT)*. EurOMA/POMS/JOMSA Conference, Tokyo, Japan.

NetSuite.com. (2020, November 26). *Decoding the digital supply chain*. Oracle NetSuite. https://www.netsuite.com/portal/resource/articles/erp/digital-supply-chain.shtml

NewStream. (2022). *Five ways to minimize supply chain disruptions*. NewStream Enterprises. https://www.newstreaming.com/5-ways-to-minimize-supply-chain-disruptions/

Nguyen, H. A., Ha, H. H., & Doan, T. D. (2020). The impact of supply chain quality management on firm performance: Empirical evidence from Vietnam. *Uncertain Supply Chain Management*, 331–350. doi:10.5267/j.uscm.2019.11.005

Nitescu, D. C., Murgu, V., & Caprita, E. D. (2019). Impact of labor, FDI and R&D on business sustainability. *Amfiteatru Economic, 21*(Special Issue 13), 795-815. https://doi.org/ doi:10.24818/EA/2019/S13/795

Noreen, E., Smith, D., & Mackey, J. T. (1995). *Theory of Constraints and Its Implications for Management Accounting: A Report on the Actual Implementation of The Theory of Constraints*. North River Press, Incorporated.

Nozari, H., Fallah, M., & Szmelter-Jarosz, A. (2021). A conceptual framework of green smart IoT-based supply chain management. *International journal of research in industrial engineering, 10*(1), 22-34.

Nozari, H., & Aliahmadi, A. (2022). Lean supply chain based on IoT and blockchain: Quantitative analysis of critical success factors (CSF). *Journal of Industrial and Systems Engineering*, *14*(3), 149–167.

Nozari, H., Fallah, M., Kazemipoor, H., & Najafi, S. E. (2021). Big data analysis of IoT-based supply chain management considering FMCG industries. *Бизнес-информатика*, *15*(1, 1 (eng)), 78–96. doi:10.17323/2587-814X.2021.1.78.96

Nozari, H., & Szmelter, A. (Eds.). (2018). *Global supply chains in the pharmaceutical industry.* IGI Global.

Nozari, H., Szmelter-Jarosz, A., & Ghahremani-Nahr, J. (2022). Analysis of the Challenges of Artificial Intelligence of Things (AIoT) for the Smart Supply Chain (Case Study: FMCG Industries). *Sensors (Basel), 22*(8), 2931. doi:10.339022082931 PMID:35458916

NRF. (2021). *Retail Supply Chains and ESG.* NRF. https://nrf.com/topics/sustainability/esg-tool-kit/retail-supply-chains-and-esg

NRF. (2022). State of Retail. *NRF.* https://nrf.com/topics/economy/state-retail#:~:text=Retail%20sales%20grew%20on%20average,than%20%244.9%20trillion%20in%202022

O'Dwyer, J., & Renner, R. (2011). The promise of advanced supply chain analytics. *Supply Chain Management Review, 15*(1).

Okorie, O., Turner, C., Charnley, F., Moreno, M., & Tiwari, A. (2017). *A review of data-driven approaches for circular economy in manufacturing,* 18th European Roundtable for Sustainable Consumption and Production, Skiathos Island, Greece.

Otto, A., & Kotzab, H. (2003). Does supply chain management really pay? Six perspectives to measure the performance of managing a supply chain. *European Journal of Operational Research, 144*(2), 306–320. doi:10.1016/S0377-2217(02)00396-X

Oudani, M., Sebbar, A., Zkik, K., El Harraki, I., & Belhadi, A. (2023). Green Blockchain based IoT for secured supply chain of hazardous materials. *Computers & Industrial Engineering, 175*, 108814. doi:10.1016/j.cie.2022.108814

Özdamar, K. (2004). *Paket Programlar İle İstatistiksel Veri Analizi 2.* Kaan Kitabevi.

Padmavathi, D., & Shanmugapriya, M. (2009). A Survey of Attacks, Security Mechanisms and Challenges in Wireless Sensor Networks. *International Journal of Computer Science and Information Security, 4*(2), 1–9.

Pal, K. (2017). Building High Quality Big Data-Based Applications in Supply Chains. IGI Global Publication.

Pal, K. (2018). *Ontology-Based Web Service Architecture for Retail Supply Chain Management.* The 9th International Conference on Ambient Systems, Networks and Technologies, Porto, Portugal.

Pal, K. (2021). Applications of Secured Blockchain Technology in Manufacturing Industry. In Subhendu Kumar Pani, Biju Patnaik, Sian Lun Lau, & Xingcheng Liu (eds.) Blockchain and AI Technology in the Industrial Internet of Things. IGI Global Publication.

Pal, K. (2023). Security Issues and Solutions for Resource-Constrained IoT Applications using Lightweight Cryptography. In Suhasini Verma, Vidhisha Vyas, Keshav Kaushik (eds.) Cybersecurity Issues, Challenges, and Solutions in Business World. IGI Global Publication.

Pal, K., & Yasar, A. (2023). *Internet of Things Impact on Supply Chain Management.* International Conference on Ambient Systems, Networks and Technology (ANT), Leuven, Belgium.

Pal, K. (2019). Algorithmic Solutions for RFID Tag Anti-Collision Problem in Supply Chain Management. *Procedia Computer Science, 151*, 929–934. doi:10.1016/j.procs.2019.04.129

Pal, K. (2020). In I. Williams (Ed.), *Information sharing for manufacturing supply chain management based on blockchain technology, in cross-Industry Use of Blockchain Technology and Opportunities for the Future* (pp. 1–17). IGI Global.

Pal, K., & Yasar, A. (2020). Internet of Things and blockchain technology in apparel manufacturing supply chain data management. *Procedia Computer Science, 170*, 450–457. doi:10.1016/j.procs.2020.03.088

Pelaez, A. (2021). Supply Chain Management. *Ubidots.* https://ubidots.com/blog/iot-supply-chain-management/

Perrig, A., Szewczyk, R., Tygar, J. D., Wen, V., & Culler, D. E. (2002). Spins: Security protocols for sensor networks. *Wireless Networks*, *8*(5), 521–534. doi:10.1023/A:1016598314198

Petruzzi, N. C., & Dada, M. (1999). Pricing and the newsvendor problem: A review with extensions. *Operations Research, 47*(2), 183–194. doi:10.1287/opre.47.2.183

Phadnis, S., Sheffi, Y., and Caplice, C. (2022). *Strategic Planning for Dynamic Supply Chains.* Palgrave.

Phadnis, Caplice, C., Singh, M., & Sheffi, Y. (2014). Axiomatic foundation and a structured process for developing firm-specific Intuitive Logics scenarios. *Technological Forecasting and Social Change*, *88*(C), 122–139. doi:10.1016/j.techfore.2014.06.019

Pierce, F. (2012). The product life cycle is in decline. *Supply Chain Digital.* https://www.supplychaindigital.com/procurement/product-life-cycle-decline

Pietro, R. Di, Mancini, L. V., Law, Y. W., Etalle, S., & Havinga, P. (2003). Lkhw: A directed diffusion-based secure multicast scheme for wireless sensor networks, in Parallel Processing Workshops, 2003. Proceedings 2003 International Conference, (pp. 397– 406). IEEE.

Ping, L., Liu, Q., Zhou, Z., & Wang, H. (2011). Agile supply chain management over the Internet of Things. In *International Conference on the Management and Service Science (MASS).* IEEE.

Porter, M. (1996). What is Strategy. *Harvard Business Review.* PMID:10158475

Porter, M. E. (1996, November – December). What Is Strategy? *Harvard Business Review*, 4. PMID:10158475

Porteus, E. L. (1990). Stochastic inventory theory. DP Heyman, MJ Sobel, eds. Handbooks in operations research and management science, 2, 605-652.

Prathapani, A., Santhanam, L., & Agrawal, D. P. (2009). Intelligent honeypot agent for blackhole attack detection in wireless mesh networks. In *IEEE 6th International Conference on Mobile Adhoc and Sensor Systems (MASS'09),* (pp. 753-758). IEEE.

Pruyt, E. (2013). *Small System Dynamics Models for Big Issues: Triple Jump towards Real – World Complexity.* TU Delft Library. https://goo.gl/ge98Wt,

Pu, G., Qamruzzaman, M., Mehta, A. M., Naqvi, F. N., & Karim, S. (2021). Innovative finance, technological adaptation and SMEs sustainability: The mediating role of government support during COVID-19 Pandemic. *Sustainability (Basel), 13*(16), 9218. doi:10.3390u13169218

Qian, Y. (2006). K-means Algorithm And Its Application For Clustering Companies Listed. In *Zhejiang Province* (Vol. 37). WIT Transactions on Information and Communication Technologies.

Qrunfleh, S., & Tarafdar, M. (2014). Supply chain information systems strategy: Impacts on supply chain performance and firm performance. *International Journal of Production Economics*, *147*(1), 340–350. doi:10.1016/j.ijpe.2012.09.018

Rahman, R. A., & Shah, B. (2016). Security analysis of iot protocols: A focus in COAP, in Big Data and Smart City (ICBDSC). *2016 3rd MEC International Conference*, (pp. 1–7). IEEE.

Rahman, R. A., & Shah, B. (2016). Security analysis of IoT protocols: A focus in COAP, in Big Data and Smart City (ICBDSC). *3rd MEC International Conference*, (pp. 1-7). IEEE.

Rai, A., Patnayakuni, R., & Seth, N. (2006). Firm performance impacts of digitally enabled supply chain integration capabilities. *Management Information Systems Quarterly*, *30*(2), 225–246. doi:10.2307/25148729

Rai, S. S., Rai, S., & Singh, N. K. (2021). Organizational resilience and social-economic sustainability: COVID-19 perspective. *Environment, Development and Sustainability*, *23*(8), 12006–12023. doi:10.100710668-020-01154-6 PMID:33519297

Rasool, F., Greco, M., & Grimaldi, M. (2021). Digital supply chain performance metrics: A literature review. *Measuring Business Excellence*. doi:10.1108/MBE-11-2020-0147

Rodrigo, R., Jianying, Z., & Javier, L. (2013). On the features and challenges of security and privacy in distributed internet of things, Computer Networks, Science Direct. *Elsevier B.*, *57*(10), 1–14.

Rodrigues, F., & Ferreira, B. (2016). Product Recommendation based on Shared Customer's Behaviour. *Procedia Computer Science*, *100*, 136–146. doi:10.1016/j.procs.2016.09.133

Rogers, D. S., & Tibben-Lembke, R. S. (2001). Going backwards: reverse logistics trends and practices. *Reverse logistics: Quantitative models for closed-loop supply chains*, 1-27

Röglinger, M., Pöppelbuß, J., & Becker, J. (2012). Maturity Models in Business Process Management. *Business Process Management Journal*, *18*(2), 328–346. doi:10.1108/14637151211225225

Roscoe, S., & Baker, P. (2013). Supply chain segmentation in the sporting goods industry. *International Journal of Logistics*, *17*(2), 136–155. doi:10.1080/13675567.2013.837869

Rousseeuw, P. J. (1987). Silhouettes: A graphical aid to the interpretation and validation of cluster analysis. *Journal of Computational and Applied Mathematics*, *20*, 53–65. doi:10.1016/0377-0427(87)90125-7

Sabri, E. & Shaikh, S. (2010). *Lean & Agile Value Chain Management: A Guide to the Next Level of Improvement.* J. Ross Publishing.

Sabri, E. (2012). Enduring Transformation. *APICS Magazine.*

Sabri, E. (2012). Enduring Transformation: Performance measurement and governance make the difference. *APICS Magazine.* https://www.apics.org/apics-for-individuals/apics-magazine-home/magazine-detail-page/2012/10/04/enduring-transformation,

Sabri, E. (2013). Strategies for Supply Chain Transformation. *Supply & Demand Chain Executive Magazine.* http://www.sdcexec.com/article/11122122/companies-struggle-to-decide-when-and-where-to-begin-and-how-to-translate-their-vision-into-goals-goals-into-strategies-and-strategies-into-process-changes-and-projects

Sabri, E. (2019). *Optimization of Supply Chain Management in Contemporary Organizations: Mastering Change Management for Successful Digital Supply Chain Transformation*, 85-106. IGI Global.

Sabri, E. (2019). *Technology Optimization and Change Management for Successful Digital Supply Chains.* IGI Global. https://www.igi-global.com/gateway/book/209464

Sabri, E. (2019). Transformation Framework for Supply Chain Segmentation in Digital Business. In E. Sabri (Ed.), *Technology Optimization and Change Management for Successful Digital Supply Chains* (pp. 54–84). IGI Global. doi:10.4018/978-1-5225-7700-3.ch004

Sabri, E., Gupta, A., & Beitler, M. (2006). *Purchase Order Management in B2B Environment: Best Practice & Technologies J.* ROSS PUBLISHING.

Sabri, E., & Shaikh, S. (2010). *Lean & Agile Value Chain Management (LAVCM): A Guide to the Next Level of Improvement. J.* Ross Publishing.

Sahay, B. S., & Ranjan, J. (2008). Real time business intelligence in supply chain analytics. *Information Management & Computer Security, 16*(1), 28–48. doi:10.1108/09685220810862733

Sandia National Laboratories (n.d.). *System-of-Systems – Center for Systems Reliability.* SNL.

Sastry, A. S., Shazia, S., & Vagdevi, S. (2013). Security threats in wireless sensor networks in each layer. *International Journal of Advanced Networking and Applications, 4*(4), 1657.

Schuh, C. (2017). *The purchasing chessboard* (3rd ed.). Springer. doi:10.1007/978-1-4939-6764-3

SEBoK, (2022). *Systems of Systems (SoS).* Sebokwiki.

Sedky, A. (2021). *The relationship between transformational, transactional, and passive-avoidant leadership styles and small business sustainability.* [Dissertation, Walden University]. https://scholarworks.waldenu.edu/dissertations/11331

Shafi, M., Liu, J., & Ren, W. (2020). Impact of COVID-19 pandemic on micro, small, and medium-sized enterprises operating in Pakistan. *Research in Globalization, 2*(1), 100018. doi:10.1016/j.resglo.2020.100018

Sharma, K. & Ghose, M. (2010). Wireless sensor networks: An overview on its security threats. *IJCA*, 42-45.

Sharma, K., & Ghose, M. (2010). Wireless sensor networks: An overview on its security threats [MANETs]. *IJCA, Special Issue on Mobile Ad-hoc Networks, 42–45*, 2010.

Shen, K.-Y., Hu, S.-K., & Tzeng, G.-H. (2017). Financial modeling and improvement planning for the life insurance industry by using a rough knowledge based hybrid MCDM model. *Information Sciences, 375*, 296–313. doi:10.1016/j.ins.2016.09.055

Sherman, R. J. (2020, May 4). Why has CPFR failed to scale? *CSCMPs Supply Chain Quarterly RSS.* https://www.supplychainquarterly.com/articles/57-why-has-cpfr-failed-to-scale

Siderius, C., Conway, D., Yassine, M., Murken, L., Lostis, P.-L., & Dalin, C. (2020). Multi-scale analysis of the water-energy-food nexus in the Gulf region. *Environmental Research Letters, 15*(9), 094024. doi:10.1088/1748-9326/ab8a86

Simchi-Levi, D., Clayton, A., & Raven, B. (2012). When One Size Does Not Fit All. *Sloan Review.* https://sloanreview.mit.edu/article/when-one-size-does-not-fit-all/

Simchi-Levi, D., Kaminsky, P., Simchi-Levi, E., & Shankar, R. (2008). *Designing and managing the supply chain: concepts, strategies and case studies.* Tata McGraw-Hill Education.

Simchi-Levi, D. (2003). Three Scenarios to Guide Your Global Supply Chain Recovery. *MIT Sloan Management Review.*

Singh, A., & Gupta, H. (2021). Reverse logistics: Issues and challenges in the era of e-commerce. *International Journal of Logistics Management, 32*(2), 300–319.

Singh, S., Kumar, R., Panchal, R., & Tiwari, M. K. (2020). Impact of COVID-19 on logistics systems and disruptions in food supply chain. *International Journal of Production Research*, *59*(7), 1–16. doi:10.1080/00207543.2020.1792000

Slijepcevic, S., Potkonjak, M., Tsiatsis, V., Zimbeck, S., & Srivastava, M. B. (2002). On communication security in wireless ad-hoc sensor networks, in Enabling Technologies: Infrastructure for Collaborative Enterprises. Eleventh IEEE International Workshops (pp. 139–144). IEEE.

Slijepcevic, S., Potkonjak, M., Tsiatsis, V., Zimbeck, S., & Srivastava, M. B. (2002). On communication security in wireless ad-hoc sensor networks, in Proceedings of Eleventh IEEE International Workshops - Enabling Technologies: Infrastructure for Collaborative Enterprises, WET ICE 2002, 139-144.

Solventure, S. (n.d.). *Rough Cut Capacity Planning*. Solventure Group. https://www.solventuregroup.com/content/rough-cut-capacity-planning/

Suketu, H. B. R. (2022). *Leveraging New Tech to Boost Supple Chain Resilience*. HBR. https://hbr.org/2022/10/leveraging-new-tech-to-boost-supply-chain-resilience

Sun, H., Ren, Y., & Yeo, K. (2005). Capability Maturity Model for Supply Chain Management. *International Conference on Management Science and Applications*, Chengdu, China.

Svoboda, S. (2020, August 17). *Ways Supply Chain Visibility Can Help Mitigate Risk*. Hitachi Solutions. https://global.hitachi-solutions.com/blog/supply-chain-visibility/

Swift, C., Guide, V. D. R. Jr, & Muthulingam, S. (2019). Does supply chain visibility affect operating performance? Evidence from conflict minerals disclosures. *Journal of Operations Management*, *65*(5), 406–429. doi:10.1002/joom.1021

Takeda, A., & Kanamori, T. (2014). Using financial risk measures for analyzing generalization performance of machine learning models. *Neural Networks*, *57*, 29–38. doi:10.1016/j.neunet.2014.05.006 PMID:24914491

Tan, P.-N., Steinbach, M., & Kumar, V. (2018). *Introduction to Data Mining (2nd Edition)*: Pearson. technofunc. https://www.technofunc.com/index.php/domain-knowledge/retail-industry/item/importance-of-retail-industry#:~:text=the%20retail%20community.-,Consumers%20benefit%20from%20retailing%20as%20retailers%20perform%20marketing%20functions%20that,to%20enhance%20a%20product's%20image

Tan, K. H., Zhan, Y., Ji, G., Ye, F., & Chang, C. (2015). Harvesting big data to enhance supply chain innovation capabilities: An analytic infrastructure based on deduction graph. *International Journal of Production Economics*, *165*, 223–233. doi:10.1016/j.ijpe.2014.12.034

Tarafdar, M., & Qrunfleh, S. (2016). Agile supply chain strategy and supply chain performance: Complementary roles of supply chain practices and information systems capability for agility. *International Journal of Production Research*, *55*(4), 925–938. doi:10.1080/00207543.2016.1203079

Tavakkoli-Moghaddam, R., Ghahremani-Nahr, J., Samadi, P., Nozari, H., & Najafi, E. (2021). Applications of Internet of Things in the Food Supply Chain: A Literature Review. *J. Appl. Res. Ind. Eng*, *1*, 34–55.

Thakkar, J., Kanda, A., & Deshmukh, S. (2009). Supply chain performance measurement framework for small and medium scale enterprises. *Benchmarking*, *16*(5), 702–723. doi:10.1108/14635770910987878

Thakur, J., & Nagesh, K. (2011). DES, AES and Blowfish: Symmetric key cryptography algorithms simulation based performance analysis. *International Journal of Emerging Technology and Advanced Engineering*, *1*(2), 6–12.

The Kroger Co. (2017). The Kroger Co. https://www.thekrogerco.com/

Thomas, K. (2012). Supply chain segmentation: 10 steps to greater profits. *Supply Chain Quarterly*. https://www.supplychainquarterly.com/topics/Strategy/201201s egmentation

Thomson Reuters. (2022, January 31). *How procurement and supply chains drive corporate ESG objectives*. Thomson Reuters. https://tax.thomsonreuters.com/blog/procurement-supply-chain -environmental-social-governance-objectives/

Time Buckets. (2000). In P. M. Swamidass (Ed.), *Encyclopedia of Production and Manufacturing Management*. Springer.

Time. (2022). *China's Zero-Covid Is Here To Stay, Experts Say*. Time. https://time.com/6233563/china-zero-covid-end/

Timotius, E., & Octavius, G. S. (2021). Global Changing of Consumer Behavior to Retail Distribution due to Pandemic of COVID-19: A Systematic Review. *Journal of Distribution Science*, *19*(11), 69–80. doi:10.15722/JDS.19.11.202111.69

Tiwari, M., Arya, K. V., Choudhari, R., & Choudhary, K. S. (2009). Designing intrusion detection to detect blackhole and selective forwarding attack in WSN based on local information. In *Computer Science and Convergence Information Technology, Fourth International Conference on ICCIT*, (pp. 824-828). IEEE.

Tomlin, B. (2006). On the Value of Mitigation and Contingency Strategies for Managing Supply Chain Disruption Risks. *Management Science*, *52*(5), 639–657. doi:10.1287/mnsc.1060.0515

Tomlin, B. (2009). Disruption-management strategies for short life-cycle products. [NRL]. *Naval Research Logistics*, *56*(4), 318–347. doi:10.1002/nav.20344

Transform your direct materials sourcing. (n.d.). LevaData. https://www.levadata.com/

Trebilcock, B. (2021). *Transforming procurement at Nordstrom*. Supply Chain 24/7. https://www.supplychain247.com/article/transforming_procurem ent_at_nordstrom/Procurement

Trkman, P., McCormack, K., De Oliveira, M. P. V., & Ladeira, M. B. (2010). The impact of business analytics on supply chain performance. *Decision Support Systems*, *49*(3), 318–327. doi:10.1016/j.dss.2010.03.007

Tubaishat, M., Yin, J., Panja, B., & Madria, S. (2004). A secure hierarchical model for sensor network. *SIGMOD Record*, *33*(1), 7–13. doi:10.1145/974121.974123

Turner, S., & Endres, A. (2017). Strategies for enhancing small-business owners' success rates. *International Journal of Applied Management and Technology*, *16*(1), 34–49. doi:10.5590/IJAMT.2017.16.1.03

Tyagi, P., & Pabalkar, D. V. (2021). Impact of covid-19 over purchasing behaviour of the consumers. *European Journal of Molecular and Clinical Medicine*, *8*(2), 561–571. https://ejmcm.com/article_7383_de7ea8fc87741a4ea22042820803b 72d.pdf

Tyko, C. M. (2020). *Coronavirus rationing: Target, Walmart limit purchases of hand sanitizer, disinfecting wipes, toilet paper*. USA TODAY. https://www.usatoday.com/story/money/2020/03/11/coronavirus-preparation-walmart-target-ration-limiting-hand-sanitizer-di sinfecting-wipes/5020751002/

Ülker, Y., & Arslan, Ö. (2020). Türkiye'de Gıda Perakendeciliği Sektöründe Finansal Analiz Ve Bir Uygulama. *MANAS Sosyal Araştırmalar Dergisi*, *9*(4), 2531–2546. doi:10.33206/mjss.704398

UN. (2017). *Global Mobility Report*. UN. https://sustainabledevelopment.un.org/content/documents/2643Global_Mobility_Report_2017.pdf

USA Today. (2020). Target same-day services like Drive Up and Shipt delivery grew by 278% fueled by COVID-19. *USA Today*. https://www.usatoday.com/story/money/2020/05/20/target-earnings-2020-digital-sales-grow-coronavirus/5226791002/

USDA. (2022). New USDA Policy on Salmonella in Poultry Offers Hope for Progress on Foodborne Illness · Consumer Federation of America. *Consumer Federation of America*. https://consumerfed.org/press_release/new-usda-policy-on-sal monella-in-poultry-offers-hope-for-progress-on-foodborne-ill
ness/

van Looy, A. (2013a). *BPMM Sample (N=69)*. Amy Van Looy. https://goo.gl/dbiVkQ, Accessed March 2014.

van Looy, A. (2013b). Which Business Process Maturity Model Best Fits Your Organization? *BPTrends*. https://goo.gl/1yCkEA.

van Looy, A. (2014). *Business Process Maturity: A Comparative Study on a Sample of Business Process Maturity Models*. Springer. doi:10.1007/978-3-319-04202-2

Vanpoucke, E., Vereecke, A., & Muylle, S. (2017). Leveraging the Impact of Supply Chain Integration Through Information Technology. *International Journal of Operations & Production Management*, *37*(4), 510–530. doi:10.1108/IJOPM-07-2015-0441

Vanyi, N. (2012). Members of a supply chain and their relationships. *Apstract, Applied Studies in Agribusiness and Commerce*, *6*(5), 133–136. doi:10.19041/APSTRACT/2012/5/21

Vatansever, M. (2008). *Görsel Veri Madenciliği Tekniklerinin Kümeleme Analizlerinde Kullanımı Ve Uygulanması*. [Master thesis, Yıldız Teknik Üniversitesi].

Wakolbinger, T., & Cruz, J. M. (2011). Supply chain disruption risk management through strategic information acquisition and sharing and risk-sharing contracts. *International Journal of Production Research*, *49*(13), 4063–4084. doi:10.1080/00207543.2010.501550

Walmart. (2019). *Homepage*. Corporate Walmart. https://corporate.walmart.com

Walters, J. P., Zhengqiang, Z., Weisong S., & Vipin, C. (2007). Wireless sensor network security: A survey. *Security in distributed, grid, mobile, and pervasive computing*, (pp. 367-404).

Wamba, S. F., Gunasekaran, A., Akter, S., & Dubey, R. (2019). The performance effects of big data analytics and supply chain ambidexterity: The moderating effect of environmental dynamism. *International Journal of Production Economics*, *222*, 107498. Advance online publication. doi:10.1016/j.ijpe.2019.09.019

Wazid, M., Katal, A., Sachan, R. S., Goudar, R., & Singh, D. (2013). Detection and prevention mechanism for blackhole attack in wireless sensor network. In *International Conference on Communication and Signal Processing (ICCSP)*, (pp. 576-581). IEEE. 10.1109/iccsp.2013.6577120

Whitmore, A., Agarwal, A., & Da Xu, L. (2014). The Internet of Things – A survey of topics and trends. *Information Systems Frontiers*, *17*(2), 261–274. doi:10.100710796-014-9489-2

Wienberger, D. (2010). *The Problem with the Data–Information–Knowledge–Wisdom Hierarchy.* HBR Blog Network. https://goo.gl/tDtQQD.

Wilson, G. (2012). *Designing and Building Great Dashboards - 6 Golden Rules to Successful Dashboard Design.* Geckoboard Blog. https://goo.gl/cJLCLK

Wood, D., Stankovic, J. A., & Son, S. H. (2003). Jam: A jammed area mapping service for sensor networks. In Real-Time Systems Symposium, (pp. 286–297). IEEE.

World Health Organization. (2020). *Pneumonia of unknown cause – China.* WHO. https://www.who.int/emergencies/disease-outbreak-news/item/2020-DON229

Xiao, L., & Cao, H. (2017). Organizational resilience: The theoretical model and research implication. *ITM Web of Conferences, 12*, 04021. 10.1051/itmconf/20171204021

Yang, M., Fu, M., & Zhang, Z. (2021). The adoption of digital technologies in supply chains: Drivers, process and impact. *Technological Forecasting and Social Change*, *169*, 120795. doi:10.1016/j.techfore.2021.120795

Yazdani, M., Torkayesh, A. E., Chatterjee, P., Fallahpour, A., Montero-Simo, M. J., Araque-Padilla, R. A., & Wong, K. Y. (2022). A fuzzy group decision-making model to measure resiliency in a food supply chain: A case study in Spain. *Socio-Economic Planning Sciences*, *101257*, 101257. Advance online publication. doi:10.1016/j.seps.2022.101257

Ye, F., Liu, K., Li, L., Lai, K.-H., Zhan, Y., & Kumar, A. (2022). Digital supply chain management in the COVID-19 crisis: An asset orchestration perspective. *International Journal of Production Economics*, *245*, 108396. doi:10.1016/j.ijpe.2021.108396 PMID:34931109

Ye, F., Luo, H., Lu, S., & Zhang, L. (2005). Statistical en-route filtering of injected false data in sensor networks. *IEEE Journal on Selected Areas in Communications*, *23*(4), 839–850. doi:10.1109/JSAC.2005.843561

Yerpude, S., Sood, K., & Grima, S. (2022). Blockchain-augmented digital supply chain management: A way to sustainable business. *Journal of Risk and Financial Management*, *16*(1), 7. doi:10.3390/jrfm16010007

Yong, W., Garhan, A., & Byrav, R. (2006). A survey of security issues in wireless sensor networks. *IEEE Communications Surveys and Tutorials*, *8*(2), 1–22.

Youngsu, L. & Rim, S. (2016). Quantitative Model for Supply Chain Visibility: Process Capability Perspective. *Mathematical Problems in Engineering.* Hindawi. doi:10.1155/2016/4049174

Yuen, K. F., Wang, X., Ma, F., & Li, K. X. (2020). The Psychological Causes of Panic Buying Following a Health Crisis. *International Journal of Environmental Research and Public Health*, *17*(10), 10. doi:10.3390/ijerph17103513 PMID:32443427

Yu, J., Subramanian, N., Ning, K., & Edwards, D. (2015). Product delivery service provider selection and customer satisfaction in the era of internet of things: A Chinese e-retailers' perspective. *International Journal of Production Economics*, *159*(1), 104–116. doi:10.1016/j.ijpe.2014.09.031

Zekhnini, K., Cherrafi, A., Bouhaddou, I., Benghabrit, Y., & Garza-Reyes, J. A. (2020). Supply chain management 4.0: A literature review and research framework. *Benchmarking*, *28*(2), 465–501. doi:10.1108/BIJ-04-2020-0156

Zhang, N., & Li, B. (2020). Pricing and coordination of green closed-loop supply chain with fairness concerns. *IEEE Access : Practical Innovations, Open Solutions*, *8*, 224178–224189. doi:10.1109/ACCESS.2020.3045152

Zhao, J., & Li, Y. (2021). Supply chain security evaluation model and index system based on a 5G information system. *Neural Computing & Applications.* doi:10.100700521-021-06584-5 PMID:34728901

Zhu, Z., & Liu, N. (2021). Early Warning of Financial Risk Based on K-Means Clustering Algorithm. *Complexity, 5571683*, 1–12. doi:10.1155/2021/5571683

Znaidi, W., Minier, M., & Babau, J. P. (2008). An ontology for attacks in wireless sensor networks, PhD dissertation, INRIA, 2008.

Zouari, D., Ruel, S., & Viale, L. (2020). Does digitalising the supply chain contribute to its resilience? *International Journal of Physical Distribution & Logistics Management, 51*(2), 149–180. doi:10.1108/IJPDLM-01-2020-0038

Zuokas, D., Gul, E., & Lim, A. (2022). How did COVID-19 change what people buy: Evidence from a supermarket chain. *Journal of Retailing and Consumer Services, 68*, 103010. doi:10.1016/j.jretconser.2022.103010

About the Contributors

Ehap Sabri, Ph.D., is an industry leader, business professor, and author with 25+ years of industry experience sought after for his expertise in strategy development and supply chain management. Dr. Sabri played a variety of advisory roles and provided management consulting services for several companies across different industries to develop and implement best practice strategies and processes, thereby deriving value and significant cost reductions. In addition, Dr. Sabri is an adjunct professor at the University of Texas at Dallas for the MBA Programs. Dr. Ehap Sabri has a doctorate in Industrial Engineering from the University of Cincinnati in Ohio. He is also a Certified Fellow in Production and Inventory Management (CFPIM) by APICS and has Lean Six Sigma Master Black Belt in process improvement. Ehap has published 4 books in supply chain management. He also serves as the board chairman for non-profit public charter school. He resides in Irving, TX with his wife and two daughters.

* * *

Neale Cornejo is an associate professor at the Tecnológico de Monterey within the National School of Engineering and Sciences where he currently directs the Doctoral Program in Engineering Sciences. He holds an undergraduate degree in Industrial Engineering from the University of Arizona and M.S. and Ph.D degrees in Industrial Engineering from Georgia Tech. He has taught both undergraduate and graduate level courses in operations research, logistics and supply chain management. His research interests are in the areas of applied optimization and logistics, and he has advised 29 M.S. and eight PhD theses. He has over 50 peer reviewed publications and a Mexican patent. Before pursuing an academic career, he was a consultant and implemented logistics-related solutions for numerous companies.

Mehmet Erdem received his Ph.D, M.Sc. and B.Sc. degrees in industrial engineering from Marmara University, Gazi University and Başkent University, respectively. He is currently a faculty member in the Department of Industrial Engineering at Ondokuz Mayıs University. His primary research interests are in vehicle routing, scheduling, heuristics, and data mining.

Shiva Esturi is Vice President of Global Supply Chain Management at Micron Technology, a world leader in innovative semiconductor-based memory solutions that transform how the world uses information. Shiva brings more than two decades of diverse experience in high-tech supply chain. He graduated in Industrial Engineering and Operations Research from National Institute of Industrial Engineering and bachelor's in mechanical engineering from Bangalore University, He is certified fellow in supply chain professional and certified fellow in production inventory management from association of supply chain management.

Javid Ghahremani-Nahr is a faculty member of Academic Center for Education, Culture, and Research (ACECR). He has received his Bachelor of Science degree in Industrial Engineering from Payame Noor University of Tabriz and his master's degree in Industrial Engineering from Kharazmi University of Tehran in the subfield of logistics and Supply chain management. His research interests are in the areas of Supply chain network design and Uncertainty models. He has worked on Supply chain network design such as blood supply chain, pharmacy supply chain, cold chain network model, Green supply chain.

Amit Gupta is a Mechanical Engineer from NIT, Calicut, India, and has an MBA in Supply Chain Management from Arizona State University. Amit has 20 years of experience in industry and consultancy with large Fortune 500 companies. He executed several large, global supply chain transformation initiatives delivering topline and bottom-line improvements. He lives in Gilbert, Arizona, with his wife and two kids.

Varun Gupta, Ph.D., is an associate professor of logistics and analytics at the Mike Cottrell College of Business, the University of North Georgia where he currently directs the logistics lab and the logistics and supply chain curriculum. His research interests include supply chain risk management, inventory management, and revenue management. He continues to teach courses on logistics, operations management, and quantitative methods for business at both undergraduate and graduate levels. He has over 10 years of experience working on academic-industry partnership projects in the broad areas of analytics, logistics, and supply chain management. Dr. Gupta continues to publish several top-tier journal articles, book chapters, and discipline-specific international conferences. He served on the board of a non-profit for the Millcreek education foundation. Dr. Gupta has a doctorate in Operations Management from the University of Texas at Dallas (UTD). He also earned a master's in business administration and a master's in business administration from UTD. He is a member of the Georgia Logistics Association (professional organization), INFORMS, and POMS (academic societies).

Mark Levy is a supply chain expert with over 25 years of experience building technology-based companies, innovative solutions, and cross-functional & cross-enterprise supply chain processes. His experience includes leading dozens of supply chain transformations for large, global manufacturing companies as both a management consultant, interim executive, and SaaS supply chain executive. Mark earned degrees from Stanford, Wharton, Penn Engineering, and credentials from APICS, as well as passing all 3 CFA exams.

Bo Liao leads Operations Research Team at Micron Technology since 2020. She is responsible for developing advanced mathematical models and algorithms for supply chain optimization at Micron. She holds a BBM in Information Management and Information Systems from Tsinghua University, an MS in Industrial Engineering and Operations Research, an MS in Business Administration, and PhD in Operations Management from University of California, Berkeley. Bo is a recipient of "Young Professional Emerging Leader Award" by CSCMP (Council of Supply Chain Management Professionals), and a recognized technical leader by "Technical Leadership Program" at Micron. Prior to joining Micron, she had worked at SanDisk and Western Digital for 6 years.

Esmail Najafi is an Associate Professor of Industrial Engineering Department at the Islamic Azad University, Science and Research Branch in Tehran, Iran. He received his B.A. in Power and Water

University of Technology (PWUT), his M.S. in Islamic Azad University. and his Ph.D. in Industrial Engineering from Science and Research Branch in Tehran, Iran. His research interests decision making, Data Envelopment Analysis, Engineering management and strategic management . His published research articles appear in journal or intelligent and fuzzy system, Mathematical Problems in Engineering, international journal of data envelopment analysis.

Adeel Najmi is the Chief Product Officer at SourceDay, and is leading innovations to shape the future of direct materials procurement. Adeel is a serial entrepreneur with 30+ years leadership in product management, engineering, and data science previously at LevaData, Symphony RetailAI, One Network Enterprises and Blue Yonder (formerly i2 Technologies and JDA Software). He is a pioneer in supply chain management with over a dozen patents spanning algorithms, modeling and user experience design specifically related to supply chain applications. He has guided dozens of successful digital transformations for Fortune 500 companies. Adeel is a multiple Supply Chain & Demand Executive "Pro to Know" selectee. He holds a doctorate in Industrial Engineering & Operations Research from University of California at Berkeley.

Hamed Nozari is a research assistant in Industrial engineering at the Iran university of science and technology. He holds a Ph.D. in Industrial Engineering with a focus on Production Management and Planning and PostDoc in Industrial Engineering from the Iran University of Science and Technology. He has taught various courses in the field of Industrial Engineering and has published many books and papers as well. Now he is a researcher in the field of digital developments and smart systems and optimization.

Kamalendu Pal is with the Department of Computer Science, School of Science and Technology, City, University of London. Kamalendu received his BSc (Hons) degree in Physics from Calcutta University, India, Postgraduate Diploma in Computer Science from Pune, India, MSc degree in Software Systems Technology from the University of Sheffield, Postgraduate Diploma in Artificial Intelligence from Kingston University, MPhil degree in Computer Science from the University College London, and MBA degree from the University of Hull, United Kingdom. He has published over hundred international research articles (including book chapters) widely in the scientific community with research papers in the ACM SIGMIS Database, Expert Systems with Applications, Decision Support Systems, and conferences. His research interests include knowledge-based systems, decision support systems, teaching and learning practice, blockchain technology, software engineering, service-oriented computing, sensor network simulation, and supply chain management. He is on the editorial board of an international computer science journal and is a member of the British Computer Society, the Institution of Engineering and Technology, and the IEEE Computer Society.

Laxita Sabadra is an innovative and passionate Mechanical Engineer with an MBA in Business Management from India. She also holds an MS in Supply Chain Management from the University of Texas at Dallas where she served as the head of operations team for the ASCM organization. Her experience includes working in the automotive, EV and Solar industries with expertise in Process Improvement, Product development and Strategic management. She has worked at Tesla and is currently a Program Manager with Lucid Motors in Silicon Valley. Laxita has a passion for writing and her research interests are in Global challenges and Sustainable solutions.

Ahmed Sedky is a Doctor of Business affiliated with the School of Business and Technology at Walden University, USA. He also holds a Master's Degree in Management of Foreign Trade Logistics (Supply Chain-related) from the Arab Academy for Science, Technology, and Maritime Transport (AAST). He is also a certified International Supply Chain Manager by IPSCMI – The United States, certified in coaching and mentoring by ILM - UK, and a certified PROSCI Change Practitioner from the United States. Dr. Sedky's research and knowledge are extensive in Project and Portfolio Management, Organizational Leadership, Engineering, Business Sustainability, Supply Chain Management, Strategy Management, and more. His knowledge also extends to International Business and Foreign Trade Logistics. He is an expert in applying quantitative and qualitative methodologies to solve business problems, analyze market trends, manage special projects and strategic initiatives, and establish private-label products in many countries. His professional experience exceeds 25 years in senior leadership roles across The United States, UK, Egypt, Saudi Arabia, and the United Arab Emirates. He is also well-known for being a well-rounded transformational business leader and for his contribution to social change.

Salim Shaikh (CPIM, CSCP) is Vice President at Blue Yonder and leads the Global Industry Strategy. As part of his role, he is responsible for partnering with customers to help them with their strategic goals and business priorities so that they can derive significant value, deliver business outcomes through their digital transformation journey. He has 25+ years of experience in supply chain transformation consulting in the industrial, automotive, aerospace & defense, hi-tech. He is a thought leader, speaker and author of twenty + publications, including three books on the subject of supply chain digital transformations and was honored with "2016 Supply Chain Pros To Know". Salim holds a Master's degree in Industrial Engineering from Purdue University and Master of Business Administration degree from University of Texas at Dallas.

Satyam Sinha is a seasoned Supply Chain professional with a short entrepreneurial stint in the recruitment industry. He has over 17 years of SCM experience in consulting, solution implementation and enhancement for key SCM processes across different geographies and industries. He was involved in end-to-end implementation of Blue Yonder (JDA/i2) solution for global customers. He is experienced in leading Digital Transformation initiatives and setting up Supply Chain Capability centers in large organizations. He is also an advisor in emerging startups. He has published a book on the experience of his startup failure. The name of the book is *My First Attempt to Failure* and it is available on Amazon.

Likhit Verma is innovative, entrepreneurial leader with a track record of improving company profitability and productivity by driving business and technology transformation across supply chains and sales operations. He is currently working as Sales Director with Ericsson North America. He received his MS in Supply Chain Management and MS in Information Technology Management from The University of Texas at Dallas.

Rohan Vishwasrao received his MS in Operations Research from the University of Texas at Austin in 2007 and his M.Tech in Industrial Engineering from IIT Bombay in 2003. Rohan has over 15 years of experience advising automotive and manufacturing clients in various areas of supply chain management; ranging from business strategy design & implementation, strategic network design, operational planning & scheduling, warranty analysis and shop-floor management.

Index

E

F

G

H

I

J

K

L

M

N

O

P

R

S

T

V

W

www.ingramcontent.com/pod-product-compliance
Lightning Source LLC
LaVergne TN
LVHW062119300926
849161LV00010B/2492